An Integrated Approach to

COMPUTER NETWORKS

BHAVNEET SIDHU
Computer Instructor,
Pace Canada College,
Surrey, BC,Canada

Former Lecturer,
Computer Science Deptt.,
Guru Nanak Dev University,
Amritsar (Punjab)

KHANNA BOOK PUBLISHING CO. (P) LTD.
Publisher of Science, Technology and Engineering Books
4C/4344, Ansari Road, Darya Ganj, New Delhi-110002
Phone: 011-23244447-48 **Mobile:** +91-99109 09320
E-mail: contact@khannabooks.com
Website: www.khannabooks.com

Dear Readers,

To prevent the piracy, this book is secured with HIGH SECURITY HOLOGRAM on the front title cover. In case you don't find the hologram on the front cover title, please write us to at contact@khannabooks.com or whatsapp us at +91-99109 09320 and avail special gift voucher for yourself.

Specimen of Hologram on front Cover title:

Moreover, there is a SPECIAL DISCOUNT COUPON for you with EVERY HOLOGRAM.

How to avail this SPECIAL DISCOUNT:

Step 1: Scratch the hologram
Step 2: Under the scratch area, your "coupon code" is available
Step 3: Logon to www.khannabooks.com
Step 4: Use your "coupon code" in the shopping cart and get your copy at a special discount
Step 5: Enjoy your reading!

Thanks,
Khanna Publishing House

An Integrated Approach to Computer Networks
by **Bhavneet Sidhu**

ISBN: 978-81-87325-72-7

Edition: 2026

To view complete list of books, please scan the QR Code:

Published by:
Khanna Book Publishing Co. (P) Ltd.
CIN: U22110DL1998PTC095547

Visit us at: www.khannabooks.com
Write us at: contact@khannabooks.com

Printed in Bharat.

Dedicated to

My Father, Hardeep Singh Sidhu

Foreword

Computer Networking is fastest emerging area of computer science. It carries a lot of importance academically and commercially. A lot of research is being carried out in the various working aspects of Computer Networks. An aware and trained manpower is required to tap the full potential of this field.

I am really happy to note that an excellent effort has been made by Ms. Bhavneet Sidhu to present before the student community, the very basics of Computer Networks in this book. I have gone through all the chapters of this book and find this book very lucidly written. The reader of this book will find the concepts very easy to understand and use. I hope this book will go a long way fulfilling the needs of the students!

I congratulate Ms. Bhavneet Sidhu and having completed this venture and wish her all the success for her future endeavors.

Dr. Hardeep Singh
Head, Deptt. of Computer Science & Technology
Guru Nanak Dev University Amritsar

About the Book

Computer communications and networks have become essential part of modern computing. As a designer, developer, programmer or user, it is absolutely necessary to have a good understanding of the concepts and techniques involved in these modern networking technologies. It is an exciting field and continues many technologies. There is explosive growth in this field and its demand continues to grow. Networks are changing not only computer science but also all of the society. This book treats the network as a system composed of interrelated building blocks, giving students and professionals the best possible conceptual foundation which help in understand in the current networking technologies as well as the further technologic. It is the objective of this book to provide a comprehensive text that can be used in education, research and development in this combined field of computer networks. The aim is to cover both theory and practice in a style that is not only instructive but also highly readable. The book provides a comprehensive treatment of computer communication standards, presented with in the framework of OSI. It covers leading edge developments in a broad range of standards relating to data communications and telecommunications. Because of the rich variety of standards in this area, no single book can hope to adequately cover all these standards. This book has been designed to be as modular as possible. Each modular chapter provides a complete description of major computer network technologies.

Salient features of the book :

- A review of key networking concepts, covering the technological characteristics of LANs, MANs and WANs, OSI and TCP/IP reference models, detailed comparison 'and critiques of these models.
- Clear explanation of different kinds of topologies and transmission media along with the advantages and disadvantages of each category.
- Detailed coverage of concepts like modulation, switching and multiplexing "techniques.
- It emphasizes on network architectures and protocols from the physical layer through the data link, network, transport session and presentation layers to the application layer.
- Detailed coverage of modems, repeaters, bridges, classification of bridges, gateways, routers and various routing algorithms with emphasis on distance vector and link state routing.
- Explanation of various network protocols like TCP, UDP, IP IPv6, HDLC, PPP, SCTP, DCCP, RPC, FTP, HTTP, DNS, RTSP, SSL, SIP, SNMP, SMTP, POP, IMAP, MIME.
- Provides a vital introduction to network security and management. Clear and concise explanations of cryptography, data compression, digital signature, RSA, DES.
- Covers various standards like X.25, X.400, X.500.
- Detailed discussion on various IEEE 802 standard and their comparisons.

About the Author

Mrs. Bhavneet Sidhu is presently working as a Computer Instructor at Pace Canada College, Surrey, BC, Canada. She worked as a lecturer for about 5 years in the Department of Computer Science and Technology at Guru Nanak Dev University, Amritsar. She obtained her MCA degree from Guru Nanak Dev University, Amritsar in 2001. She possesses over 11 years of teaching experience at various educational institutes, teaching general computer concepts, programming languages, computer networks, Microcomputer Applications, Advanced MS Office and Internet applications. She taught Computer Networks for more than 5 years and during this time, she developed keen interest in networking and was inspired to write a book on this field. She has written this book keeping in view the interest and the needs of the students.

Acknowledgement

I have been able to bring this book in present shape only because of hearty co-operation of number of heads and hands. Thanks being a small word cannot express the immense sense of gratitude one dwells in the heart towards anyone. This book is an acknowledgement in itself to the intensity, drive and competence of many individuals who have contributed to it. I would like to say a few heartful words to all those who helped me to complete this book.

First to all I would like thank the reviewer of this book Dr. Hardeep Singh, Professor, Department of Computer Science and Technology, Guru Nanak Dev University, who had gone through all chapters of this book and provided valuable comments many of which have been incorporated into this text. I am extremely thankful to him for devoting his valuable time and imparting knowledge to me. I pay special thanks to Dr. K.S. Kahlon, Department of Computer Science and Technology, Guru Nanak Dev University, Amritsar, for his encouragement and valuable suggestions at every stage.

The credit of this work also goes to my family for their love, affection and constant encouragement. My sincere thanks to my father, Mr. Hardeep Singh Sidhu and my mother, Mrs. Narinder Sidhu for their encouragement, faith and support. I would also like to thank my husband, Raminder Pal Singh Gill who motivated me to write a book and without whose loving support and patience, this book would never have been materialized. My special thanks to my loving sister Shampy Gill who helped me a lot in preparing the manuscript of this book. I am also grateful to all my friends and other family members for inspiring me to write this book.

Finally, it is the publisher that pulls everything together and does whatever is required to deliver the final product to the readers. Working with the team of Khanna Book Publishing Co. (P) Ltd. is a pleasure. Their professionalism and attention to detail could be seen in the end result.

Last, but not least, my thanks to my son Aarnav Gill. There were the times when I had to ignore him to complete this book. His endearing smiles always enthused me to write this book.

All the trademarks used in this book are highly acknowledged. I welcome electronic mails from any of the readers with comments and suggestions.

BHAVNEET SIDHU

E-mail: sidhu.bhavneet@gmail.com

CONTENTS

Chapter 11 : Introduction to LAN And MAN Protocols 294–330

Chapter 12 : Network Layer 331–392

Chapter 16 : Application Layer 464–491

Chapter 17 : Network Security 492–523

1

Introduction To Computer Networks

1.1 Data Communications

Communication is the process of transferring messages from one point to another. When we communicate we are sharing information. The sharing can be local or remote. Local communication is between the two individuals and it usually occurs face to face while remote communication takes place over distance. The term telecommunication means communication at a distance and it is usually carried out with the help of telephones, television etc.

The term data refers to raw facts, letters or symbols that are processed into meaningful information. In the strictest sense, data consists of the raw numbers that computers organize to produce information. Data can be in the form of sequence of bits or sequence of voltage shifts or a signal suitable for transmission. The field of data communications links the computer and the telecommunications industries. Computers are digital in nature and transfer information via parallel connections.

Definition

> *Data communication is basically the transmission of signals in a reliable and efficient manner.*

Evolution of Data Communication Systems

Data communication system came into existence shortly after computer was widely used in organizations. In order to take the services of the computer, user simply walked to the room where the computer was located and submitted a request for the computer to perform a service. The computer accepts the user's job, performed it operation and returned the results on hard-copy printouts. This process was called a batch run.

As the use of computer grew, it became inefficient for all users to walk to the computer room, submit their job and return to get the results. Consequently, computer based terminals were built and placed in user workspaces within a building. These systems required that the terminal be connected to the computer through some type of communication media in order for the user to transmit and receive signal to and from the computer.

Typically, private communication lines were wired between the computer and the workstation to meet this requirement. This approach also allowed many users to share the computational power. This concept is known as time-sharing, i.e., multiple users can share the facilities of the machine.

As organization grew and the need for the computer grew, it becomes necessary to share the computer with other users in different buildings. The simple private line was not sufficient and received data through telephone system. This approach is known as remote time-sharing.

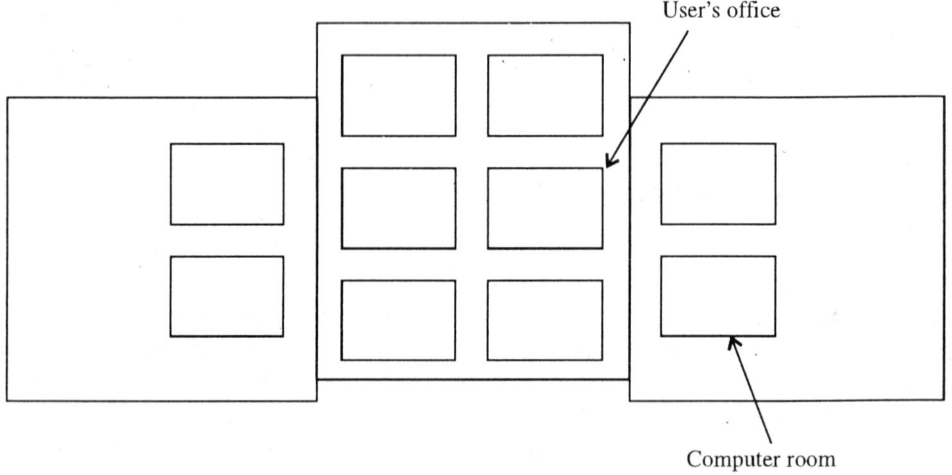

Fig. 1.1 (a)

a) User took jobs to the computer room and picked up the results (Batch runs).

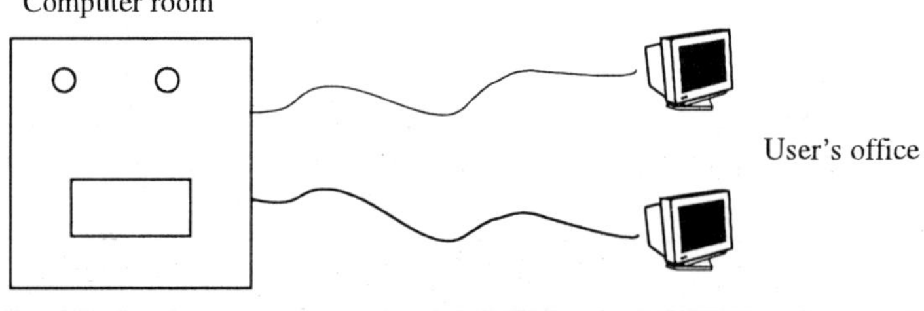

Fig. 1.1 (b)

b) The computer was then accessed by users with terminals (time sharing).

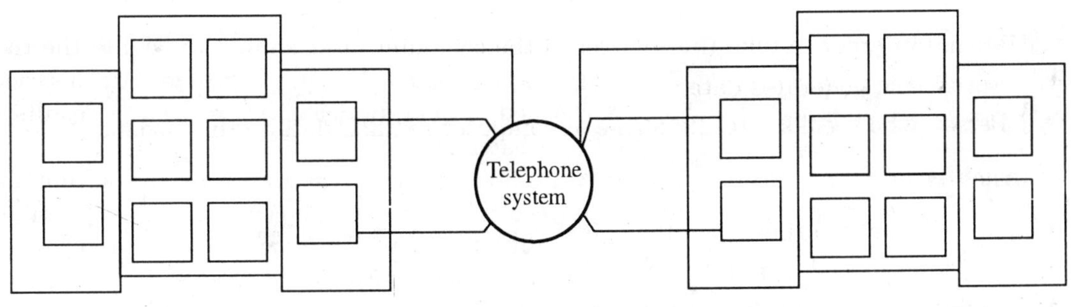

Fig. 1.1 (c)

c) The "Remote Users" eventually access the computer (remote time sharing).

1.2 A Communications Model

The purpose of a communication system is the exchange of data between two entities. The key elements of the model are as follows:

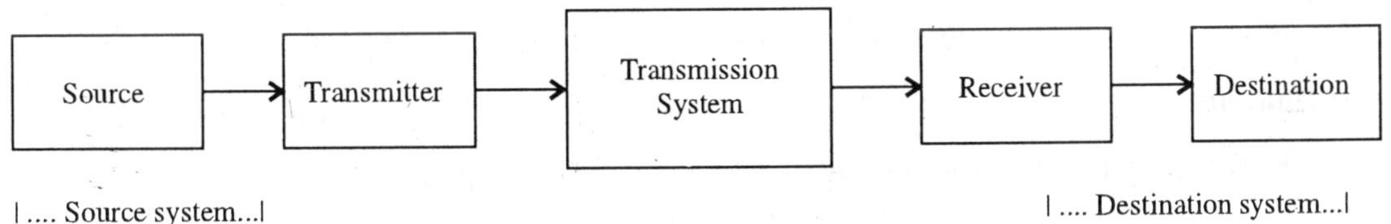

I .... Source system...I

I .... Destination system...I

E.g.,

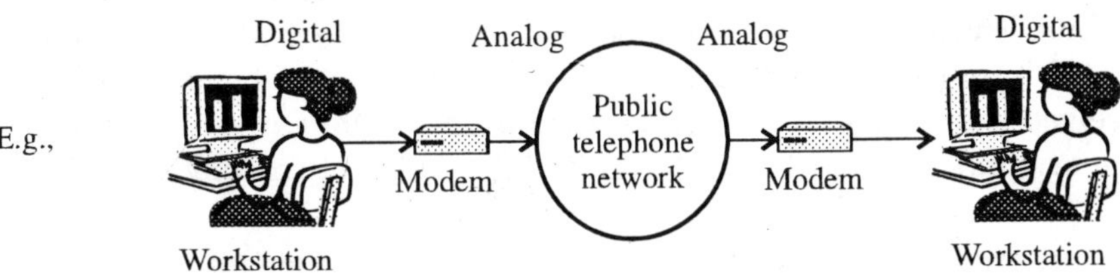

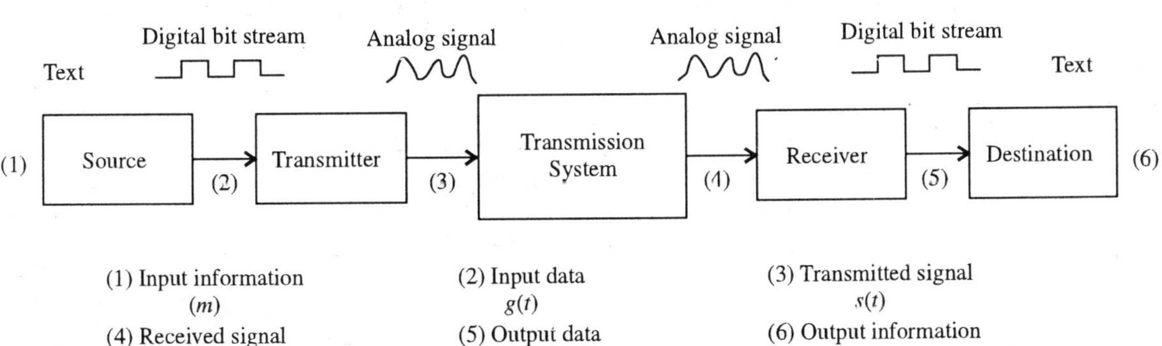

Fig. 1.2. Communication Model

1. Source

- Entity that generates data.
- Person who speaks into the phone or computer sending data to the modem.

2. Transmitter

- Device to transform/encode the signal generated by the source.
- The transformed signal is actually sent over the transmission system.
- Modem transforms digital data to analog signal that can be handled by telephone network.

3. Transmission System

- Medium that will allow transport of signal from one point to another.
- Telephone network for our computer/modem example.

4. Receiver

- Device to decode the received signal for handling by destination device.
- Modem converts the received analog data back to digital for use by the computer.

5. Destination

- Entity that finally uses the data.
- Computer on the other end of receiving mode.

In the figure1.2, the input data (m) are transferred to a transmitter as a sequence of voltage shift $[g(t)]$ representing bits. The transmitter is connected directly to the medium and converts the incoming stream $[g(t)]$ into a signal $[s(t)]$ has number of impairment before reaches the receivers. Thus the received signal $r(t)$ may differ to some degree from $s(t)$. The receiver will attempt to estimate the original $s(t)$ based on $r(t)$ and its knowledge of the medium, produce a sequence of bits $g(t)'$. The message m' is viewed by user.

Consider telephone conversion, the input to the telephone is a message (m) in the form of sound waves and these converted by the telephone into electrical signals of the same frequency. These signals are transmitted without modification over the telephone lines. Hence, the input signal $g(t)$ and the transmitted signal $s(t)$ are identical. The signal $s(t)$ will suffer some distortion over the medium, so that $r(t)$ will not be identical to $s(t)$.

Data transmission occurs between transmitter and receiver over some transmission medium. In both cases, communication is in the form of electromagnetic wave.

The term *direct link* is used to refer to the transmission path between two devices in which signals propagate directly from transmitter to receiver with intermediate devices. Or other than amplifier or repeater used to increase signal strength. This can be applying both guided and unguided media.

A guided transmission medium is point to point: It provides a direct link between two devices and only **two devices** are sharing the medium.

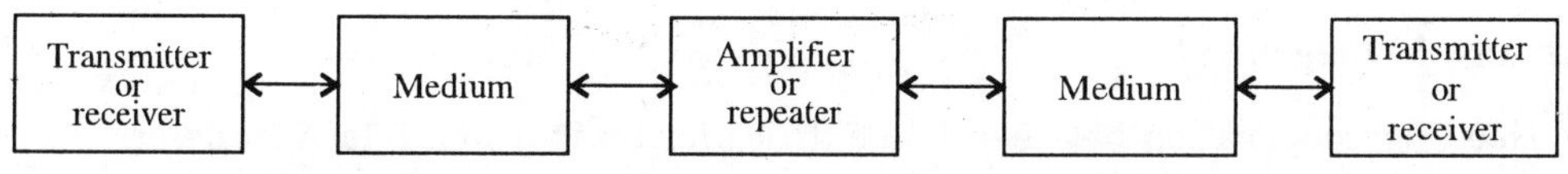

Fig. 1.3 (a) Point to Point

In a Multipoint guided configuration, more than two devices share the same medium.

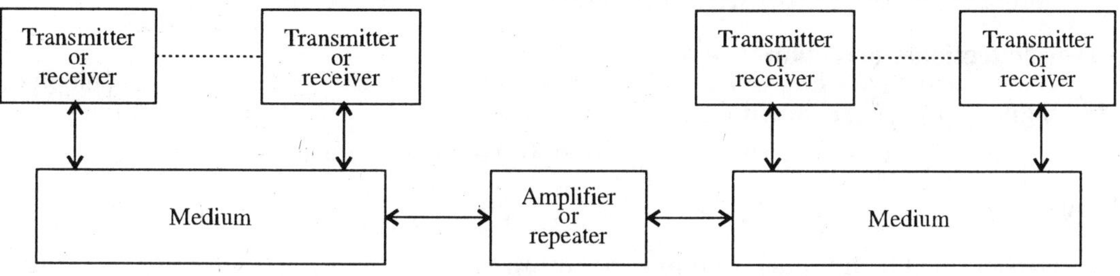

Fig. 1.3 (b) Multipoint

1.2.1 Tasks to be Accomplished in the Model

The purpose of a communication system is to transmit an information-bearing signal, from a source, located at one point, to a user or destination, located at another points some distance away.

1. Transmission System Utilization

- Efficient use of transmission network typically shared among a number of communicating devices.
- Multiplexing is used to share the total capacity of network among a number of consumers.
- Congestion control to ensure that the system does not get overwhelmed by excessive transmission network demand.

2. Interface

- Point of interaction or communication between two entities, such as a device and the transmission system.
- Communication is achieved through signal generation.
- Properties of signal
  - ☐ Possible to propagate through the transmission system.
  - ☐ Possible to interpret as data by the receiver.

3. Synchronization

- Operation of transmitter and receiver in unison.
- Receiver must be able to determine when a signal begins to arrive and when it ends.
- Receiver must also know the duration of each signal element.

4. Exchange Management

- Need for cooperation between two entities for bidirectional data transfer.
- Conventions or protocols to decide whether data is transferred simultaneously by more than one entity in a network connection or whether they take turns.
- Other things to worry about are the amount of data to be transferred, data format, and error detection/correction capabilities.

5. Error Detection/Correction

- Signal may get distorted during transmission.
- Cannot afford to alter the contents of data being transmitted.

6. Flow Control

- Collection of techniques used in serial communications to stop the sender sending data until the receiver can accept it.
- Receiver typically has a fixed size buffer into which received data is written as soon as it is received; when the amount of buffered data exceeds a "high water mark", the receiver will signal to the transmitter to stop transmitting until the process reading the data has read sufficient data from the buffer that it has reached its "low water mark", at which point the receiver signals to the transmitter to resume transmission.

7. Addressing/Routing

- Source must identify the identity of intended destination in a shared network.
- Transmission system must ensure that only the intended destination receives the data.
- The transmission system may choose any of the various available routes to deliver the data; it may even send data in parts with each part taking a different route.

8. Recovery

- In the event of transmission interruption, should the transmitter resend entire data, or send the remaining data only from the point of interruption.

9. Message Formatting

- Preestablished patterns of signals between transmitter and receiver.

10. Security

- Safe delivery of data to intended recipient only.
- Data should not get modified during transmission.
- Data must be authenticated to be from the sender only.

11. Network Management

- Configure the system.

- Monitor system status.
- React to failure and overload .
- Plan for future growth.

1.2.2 Classification of Communication

Communication is broadly divided into two categories:

1. Line Communication

The medium of transmission is a pair of conductors called transmission line. This is also called as line channel. This means that in line communication, the transmitter and the receiver are connected through a wire or line.

2. Wireless or Radio Communication

In wireless communication message is transmitted through open space by electromagnetic waves called as radio waves. Radio waves are radiated from the transmitter in open space through a device called antenna. A receiving antenna intercepts the radio waves at the receiver. All the radio, T.V. and satellite broadcasting are wireless or radio communication.

1.2.3 Example of Data Communications : E-Mail

Consider the figure 1.2 to study this example

1. Keyboard receives data and puts it in computer memory as a sequence of bits m.
2. Data goes from memory to modem over local communications bus of the computer, and is denoted by $g(t)$ during this transition phase.
3. It is picked up by modem (transmitter) and converted to sequence of voltage shifts (digital-to-analog conversion) which are sent over the network (communications medium); data are now denoted by $s(t)$.
4. Finally, the signal reaches the destination (receiver) as $r(t)$ because it may get modified during the transmission by addition of noise.
5. Receiver attempts to recover the signal $g(t)$ from $r(t)$ and produces a sequence of bits $g'(t)$.
6. The final message m' should generally be as close to m as possible, ideally an exact copy of m.

1.3 What Is A Network?

A network means an interconnected system of things or people. To understand the meanings of a network consider the following cases:

1. He owned a network of shops.
2. Retirement meant dropping out of a whole network of people who had been part of my life.

3. A communication system consisting of a group of broadcasting stations that all transmit the same programs.
4. A system of intersecting lines or channels like a railroad network or a network of canals.
5. An electronic network that means a system of interconnected components or circuits.

1.4 Computer Network

It is a set of computers that are connected and able to exchange data. It can be defined as a communications system that links two or more computers and peripheral devices and enables transfer of data between the components. It is a hardware mechanism that computers use to communicate. The computers in a network share information, software, peripheral devices and processing power.

Definition

> *A* ***computer network*** *is a connected set of autonomous computers. Normally each computer has its own operating system that is basically a network operating system. Then the user is aware of the network and the different computers in a network operating system. A user must explicitly connect to other computers in order to communicate with them.*

A **distributed system** is also a connected set of computers, but the system hides the existence of the network and the user is not aware of the different computers. A single system (operating system) runs on all computers and distributes work etc. without the user's knowledge or assistance.

1.4.1 How do Networks Fit into Computer Systems?

There are three primary ways in which networks are used by computers.

Distributed Operating Systems. User sees a single large virtual computer system. The system hides the details of the network and the existence of multiple machines from the user, providing the abstraction of a single virtual computer system. The presence of the network is integrated into the system, and the services can be accessed transparently, that is, without the user knowing that the service does not reside on the local machine. There are few true distributed operating systems in existence, and none are commercial products.

Autonomous System. Standalone machines run fine even disconnected from network. Users invoke special commands to use the network. That is, explicit commands are needed to access files on remote machines.

Network File System. Mostly autonomous machines share file systems located on remote file servers. The network is not totally integrated into the system (all processes run on the local machine, for instance), but remote files are accessed transparently. These are the most common systems today. Client-server paradigm means that clients receive services from server(s) on the network by sending requests of service to the server(s), the server(s) perform the requested work and send results back to the clients.

1.5 Goals Of Computer Networking

The main purpose of computer networking is to allow distributed programs to communicate. This is a sweeping definition, covering local and wide-area networks (LANs and WANs) and modems, the world-wide web and Internet telephony. It excludes older communications technologies such as traditional telephony and the broadcast media, which were never designed for computer-to-computer communication.

What separates computer communication from the other technologies is the need to exchange bytes and collections of bytes among programs. This imposes a number of requirements:

1. It must be possible for a program to indicate where the bytes must go, by specifying a destination address, which uniquely identifies the receiver.
2. It must be possible for a computer to send the bytes to at least another computer, which must be "closer" (by some definition of "closer") to the destination. Communicating with a directly connected computer is done at the data link layer. Forwarding the packet towards the destination is the job of the network layer.
3. In some applications, if bytes are not correctly received at the destination, the sender should send them, until the destination acknowledges their receipt. This is a job for the transport layer, which can also slow down the sender if the network or the receiver is overwhelmed. The transport layer may also decide which of many programs on a given destination machine needs to receive the bytes.

Some examples of what can happen when these requirements are not met:

- A user telnets to an address, but the address identified two different computers, so the user inadvertently types the password on a competitor's machine.
- If it is not possible to send bytes, the network is down. No web, email, chat, file transfers, stock quotes.
- If the bytes are not sent closer to the intended destination, they might wander around the net forever, taking up valuable resources.
- If the bytes are sent incorrectly, the web page might look funny, the file could be corrupted, the wrong command could be issued on the remote machine, or the email could be delivered to the wrong person.
- If the network or the receiver are given more data than they can handle, everything gets very, very slow.

Some of the uses of computer networks are listed below:

- Computer communications and networks have become essential part of modern computing.
- As a designer, developer, programmer or user, it is absolutely necessary to have a good

understanding of the concepts and techniques involved in these modern networking technologies.

- It is an exciting field and combines many technologies.
- There is explosive growth in this field and its demand continues to grow.
- It provides employment opportunities both in industrial and service sector.

1.5.1 Primary Functions of Computer Networks

The primary function of computer networks is to provide access to hardware and software resources that will allow users to perform one or more of the following activities:

- **File serving** : A large storage disk drive acts as a central storage repository.
- **Print serving :** Providing the authorization to access a particular printer, accept and queue print jobs, and providing a user access to the print queue to perform administrative duties.
- **Video transfers :** High speed LANs are capable of supporting video image and live video transfers.
- **Manufacturing support :** LANs can support manufacturing and industrial environments.
- **Academic support :** In classrooms, labs, and wireless.
- **E-mail support.**
- **Interconnection between multiple systems.**

1.5.2 Advantages of Computer Networks

Computer networks make a more cost-effective use of hardware and software. The various advantages of computer networks are listed below:

Resource Sharing. One printer (or other hardware) can be shared by many machines instead of requiring each machine to have its own printer. Other expensive resources include plotters, color laser printers, terminals, storage devices, special machine architectures, etc.

Information Sharing : Electronic mail, news groups, WWW.

Improved Reliability : Eliminate single points of failure through replication.

Reduced Cost : More processing power and storage capacity by buying many PCs and workstations than a single main frame machine.

Effect on Society : Networks are changing not only computer science but all of society. Typical uses of networks include:

- **E-mail :** Very quick turn-around, one can have an email conversation with someone else across the world in a matter of seconds, almost real-time.
- **Bulletin board :** Instead of having private message exchange, everyone can post to

bulletin board, making it a public forum. There are a few thousands specialized newsgroups.

- World Wide Web
- Storing files on a file server, giving users access to their files regardless of what machine they actually use.
- Anonymous FTP service : Users place files on a special account where anyone with network access can copy the files using FTP to their own machines.

1.5.3 Disadvantages of Computer Networks

- Equipment and support can be costly.
- Level of maintenance continues to grow.
- Private ownership possible.
- Some types of hardware may not interoperate.
- Just because a LAN can support two different kinds of packages does not mean their data can interchange easily.
- A LAN is only as strong as its weakest link, and there are many links.

1.6 Network Hardware And Transmission Technology

The medium through which a host computer transfers data to and from other computers is called the subnet. Usually, it is some kind of cable, but there are other kinds as well, e.g., radio (perhaps over a satellite), infrared light, etc.

There are two main types of subnets:

1. Point-to-Point Subnets

Data is sent on a path directly to the destination host. No other hosts are involved. This is common in cable-based WANs.

Key points about point-to-point networks

- Each communication line connects a pair of nodes.
- A packet (or message) is transmitted from one node to another.
- Intermediate nodes, in general, receive and store entire packet and then forward to the next node.
- Also called "store-and-forward" or "pack-switched" networks.
- Some topologies to represent such networks are: star, ring, tree.
- Routing algorithms are important for deciding a route in these networks.
- Typically used for large networks.

2. Shared Media subnets

These are also known as **Broadcasting subnets**. Each data packet is sent to all hosts, but is addressed in such a way that only the destination host listens. This is common in satellite-based WANs and in LANs.

Key points about broadcast networks

- Have a single communication media shared by all computers on the network.
- Some topologies to represent such networks: bus, satellite, radio.
- Short messages, or packets, are sent from one machine and received by all machines.
- Address held within the packet specifies intended destination.
- Packet not intended for a machine is ignored by that machine.
- Multicasting
  - Transmission is sent only to a subset of machines
  - Possible by reserving one bit in the address field to indicate the presence of multicasting, with remaining bit holding a group number
  - A machine can subscribe to one or more groups
  - Packet sent to a group is delivered to all machines in that group
- Typically used for smaller localized networks.

1.6.1 Data Communication Networking

It is impractical to connect every pair of communicating devices directly as point-to-point connection because:

- Any pair of devices may be very far apart, making it expensive to have multiple dedicated links.
- A set of devices may require a link to many other devices at different times, for example telephones in an organization.

The above problem can be solved by attaching each device to a communication network. Most networks can be categorized into one of the following classes: wide area networks, metropolitan area networks, local area networks and internetwork. Internetwork is a connection of two or more networks.

1.7 Network Classifications

The two most important characteristics of a network are size and shape. Both of these factors influence the transmission technologies and communication protocols that the network uses.

- Networks are classified according to the area over which they extend.
- The smallest networks consist of two nodes connected by a cable in the same room.
- The largest networks include millions of nodes around the world.
- The size and extension of a network depend on the number of nodes that need to communicate, and where these nodes are in relation to each other.

Types of Networks

I. **Server-based Networks :** Server-based networks are defined by the presence of servers on a network that provide security and administration of the network. Other computers are the clients of the network.

II. **Peer Networks :** Peer networks are defined by a lack of central control over the network. There are no servers in peer networks. Users simply share disk space and resources, such as printers and faxes.

III. **Hybrid Networks :** Hybrid networks have all three types of computers on them. This means that while most shared resources are located on servers, network users still have access to any resource being shared by peers in your workgroup.

Advantages of Server-Based Networks

- Strong central security.
- Central file storage, which allows all users to work from the same set of data and provides easy backup of critical data.
- Ability of servers to pool available hardware and software, lowering overall costs.
- Ability to share expensive equipment, such as laser printers.
- Optimized dedicated servers, which are faster than peers at sharing network resources.
- Less intrusive security.
- Freeing users from the task of managing the sharing of resources.
- Easy manageability of a large numbers of users.
- Central organization, which keeps data from getting lost among computers.

Disadvantages of Server-Based Networks

- Expensive dedicated hardware.
- Expensive network operating system software and client licenses.
- A dedicated network administrator is usually required.
- When server goes down, operations will cease across the network.

Advantages of Peer Networks

- No extra investment in server hardware or software is required.
- Easy setup.
- No network administrator required.
- Ability of users to control resources sharing.
- No reliance on other computers for their operation.
- Lower cost for small networks.

Disadvantages of Peer Networks

- Additional load on computers because of resource sharing.

- Inability of peers to handle as many network connections as servers.
- Lack of central organization.
- No central point of storage for file archiving.
- Requirement that users administer their own computers.
- Weak and intrusive security.
- Lack of central management, which makes large peer networks hard to work with.

Advantages and Disadvantages of Hybrid Networks

Share many advantages and disadvantages of server-based and peer computers.

How do you decide which type of network to use?

■ **Use Peer-to-peer if**

- There are fewer than 10 people in your organization.
- The people in your organization are sophisticated computer users.
- Security is not an issue or if users can be trusted to maintain good security.
- The cost of an additional computer just to serve files exceeds available funds.
- Users can be relied upon to back up their own data.
- Users are physically close together and there are no plans for expansion of the network.

■ **Use A Server-based Network if**

- There are more than 10 people in your organization.
- Many of the people are not sophisticated computer users.
- Your organization maintains information that must be centrally controlled.
- You have enough users that central file servers and applications are cost-effective.
- A central administrator will administer the network and set network policies.

1.8 Types Of Networks, By Size

Networks can be classified depending on how large area they cover.

1.8.1 Local Area Network (LAN)

Computers networked together in a self-contained group form a Local Area Network, or LAN. A LAN typically is contained within a single building or a group of neighbouring buildings. It is a communication network that interconnects a variety of data communicating devices within a small geographic area and broadcasts data at high data transfer rates with very low error rates. Two computers linked together at home are the simplest form of a LAN. Several hundred computers cabled together across several buildings at school form a more complex LAN. LANs are usually connected with coaxial or CAT5 cable.

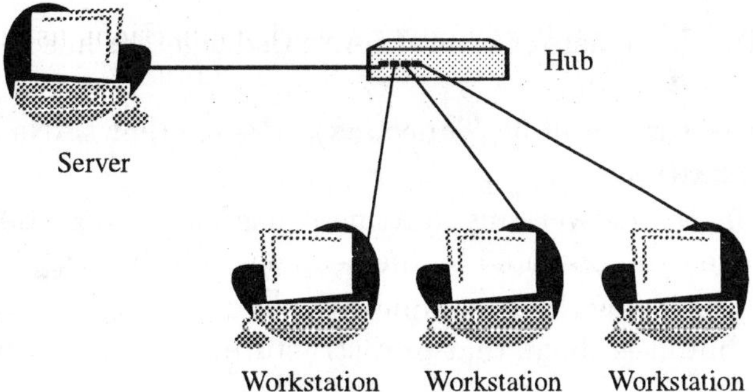

Fig. 1.4 Local Area Network

In a typical LAN configuration, one computer is designated as the file server. It stores all of the software that controls the network, as well as the software that can be shared by the computers attached to the network. Computers connected to the file server are called workstations. The workstations can be less powerful than the file server, and they may have additional software on their hard drives. On most LANs, cables are used to connect the network interface cards in each computer.

Characteristics of LANs

1. Smaller scope compared to WANs, typically a single building or campus. (10 m–1 km)
2. Usually owned by same organization as attached devices.
3. Distinguished from other networks by size, transmission technology, and topology.
4. Small size restriction binds the worst-case transmission time and simplifies network management.
5. Internal data rates on LANs are much greater than those of WANs.
6. Make use of a broadcast network approach rather than a switching approach :
   a. No intermediate switching nodes.
   b. Transmitter/receiver at each node communicates over a medium shared by other nodes.
   c. Transmission from any station is received by every other station.
   d. Data are transmitted in packets, allowing only one station to transmit at any given time.
7. Generally use a single cable for transmission to which all machines are attached.
8. Traditional speed is 10-100 Mbps, with low delay and with fewer errors.
9. LAN topologies are bus and ring. (Topologies to be discussed in next chapter)

1.8.2 Campus Networks

When computers are connected across multiple buildings, the entire collection of computers is often referred to as a campus network.

Characteristics of campus networks are:

- A campus network consists of several LANs tied together in some way to form a larger network.
- Campus networks are built by connecting LANs to other LANs with an organization's networking infrastructure.
- In other words, the networking equipment used to connect LANs to form a campus network is owned and operated by the people within the organization.
- When all of the networking equipment and transmission systems belong to the organization that uses them, that infrastructure is called private facilities.

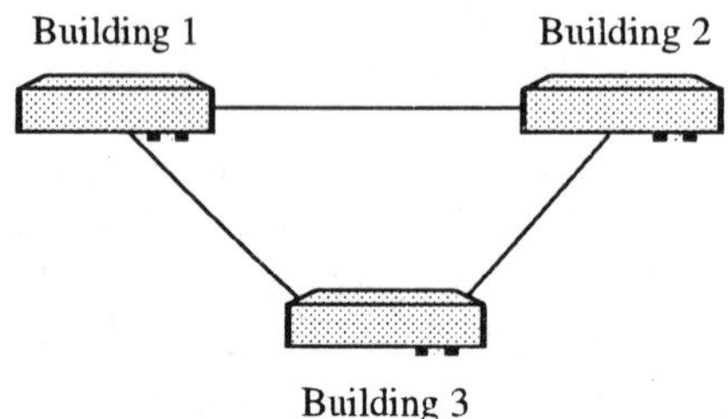

Fig. 1.5 Campus Networks

1.8.3 Wireless LANs

Not all networks are connected with cabling; some networks are wireless. Wireless LANs use high frequency radio signals, infrared light beams, or lasers to communicate between the workstations and the file server or hubs. Each workstation and file server on a wireless network has some sort of transceiver/antenna to send and receive the data. Information is relayed between transceivers as if they were physically connected. For longer distance, wireless communications can also take place through cellular telephone technology, microwave transmission, or by satellite.

A workstation in a wireless LAN can be anywhere as long as it is within transmitting distance to an access point.

Characteristics of wireless LANs are:

- Newer IEEE 802.11 and 802.11b standard defines various forms of wireless LAN connections.
- Speeds up to 11 Mbps with 802.11b standard.
- Workstations reside within a basic service set, while multiple basic service sets create an extended service set.
- Two basic components necessary : the client radio, usually a PC card with an integrated antenna, and the access point (AP), which is an Ethernet port plus a transceiver.
- The AP acts as a bridge between the wired and wireless networks and can perform basic routing functions.
- Workstations with client radio cards reside within a basic service set, while multiple basic service sets create an extended service set.

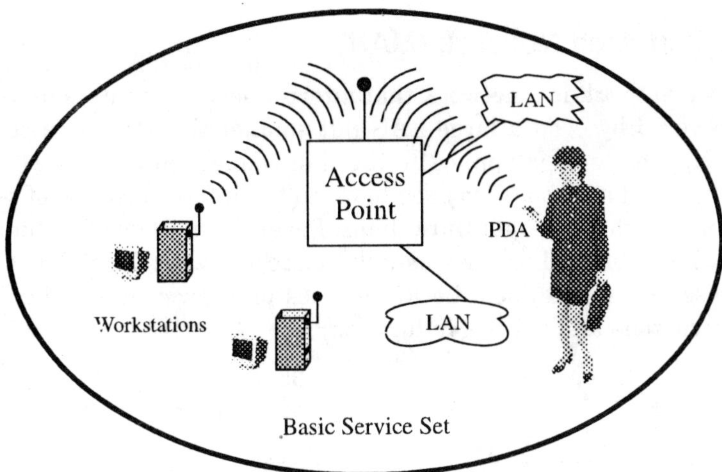

Fig. 1.6 A Wireless LAN Configuration

- With directional antennae designed for point-to-point transmission (rare), 802.11b can work for more than 10 miles.
- With an omni-directional antenna on a typical AP, range may drop to as little as 100 feet.
- Distance is inversely proportional to transmission speed — as speed goes up, distance goes down.
- In actual tests, 11 Mbps 802.11b devices managed 5.5 Mbps .
- To provide security, most systems use Wired Equivalent Privacy (WEP), which provides either 40- or 128-bit key protection.

Some Wireless Standards

- IEEE 802.11 (older 2 Mbps)
- IEEE 802.11b (11 Mbps, 2.4 GHz)
- IEEE 802.11a (54 Mbps, 5 GHz, in 2002)
- IEEE 802.11g (54 Mbps, 2.4 GHz, in 2002)
- HiperLAN/2 (European standard, 54 Mbps in 5 GHz band)

Peer-to-Peer LANs

Characteristics of peer-to-peer LANs :

- Not as common as server-based LANs.
- Less, if any, reliance on servers.
- Most peer-to-peer LANs still use one or more servers.
- Interesting collaborative-type applications.

1.8.4 Metropolitan Area Network (MAN)

A Metropolitan Area Network is a network that interconnects computers in a geographic area larger than that covered by even a large LAN but smaller than the area covered by a wide area network (WAN). The term is applied to the interconnection of networks in a city into a single larger network, and it also is also used to mean the interconnection of several local area networks by bridging them with **backbone** lines. Several branches of a chain store within a city might find a MAN useful. MANs are usually connected with fiber-optic cable, microwave transceivers or leased data landlines. Local libraries and government agencies often use a MAN to connect to citizens and private industries.

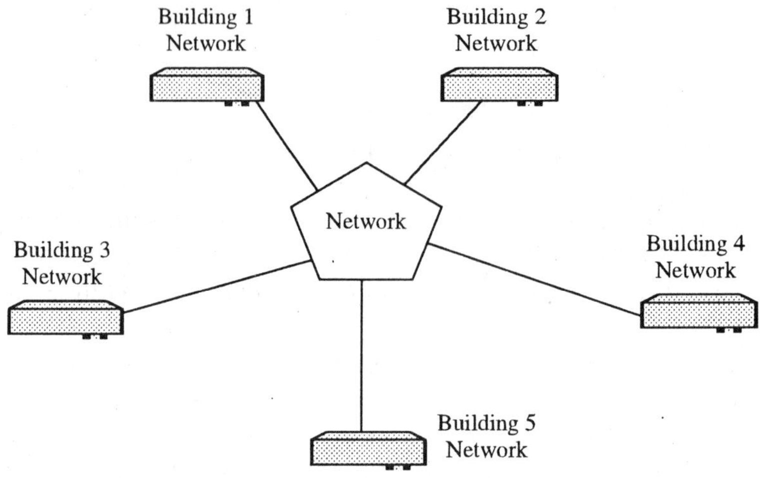

Fig. 1.7 A Metropolitan Area Network

Characteristics of MANs

1. A metropolitan area network (MAN) interconnects two or more LANs across a city-wide area and it can extend up to 50 km.
2. Fiber optics is a popular technology for MANs.
3. It may be private or public.
4. It may involve a number of organizations, e.g., cable TV networks (CATV), ATM networks, a business might interconnect several branch offices.
5. One of the primary differences between a MAN and campus network is that a campus network uses private facilities for interconnecting individual LANs, and a MAN uses public or shared facilities leased from a local telephone company.
6. These leased services include point-to-point lines such as T-carriers (fractional T1, T1, or T3), or switched services such as Integrated Services Digital Network (ISDN), frame relay, or Asynchronous Transfer Mode (ATM).

1.8.5 Wide Area Network (WAN)

A WAN is geographically large. It is often formed by joining together of LANs in distant places.

A national banking organization, for example, may use a WAN to connect all of its branches across the country. The difference between LANs and WANs is getting blurry as fiber optic cables have allowed LAN technologies to connect devices many kilometers apart. WANs are usually connected using the Internet, ISDN landlines or satellite. It might cover a large city a country, or the whole world. It is often a point-to-point system.

Within each city, we may have LAN, campus, and MAN connectivity. The WAN portions of the network are the connections that provide communication between cities. Information travels across the WAN portion of the network only when it is destined for another computer in another city.

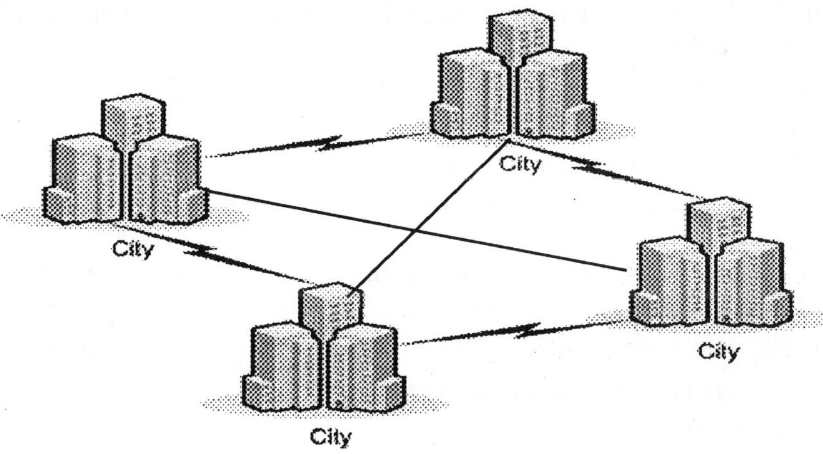

Fig. 1.8 A Wide Area Network

Characteristics of WANs

1. They generally spread over a large geographic area, from across the city to across the continent (100-1000 km).
2. Require crossing public area and may rely on circuits provided by a common carrier.
3. Typically is made up of a number of interconnected switching nodes.
4. Transmission from one device goes through internal nodes of the network to a specified destination device.
5. Nodes are not concerned with the contents of the message but just bounce the message to the next node towards the destination.
6. Implemented using circuit switching, packet switching, frame relay, or ATM.

(a) Circuit switching

- A dedicated communication path is established between source and destination through the network nodes.
- Path is a connected sequence of physical links between nodes.
- On each link, a logical channel is dedicated to the connection.
- Data from the source is transmitted through the dedicated link as fast as possible.
- No delay between reception and retransmission of data at each node.

- Best example is the telephone network.

(b) Packet switching

- No dedicated transmission capacity along a path.
- Data are sent in terms of packets.
- Packets travel through the network from node to node.
- At each node, packet is received and stored briefly before being transmitted to the next node.
- Commonly used for computer-to-computer communications.
- Considerable amount of overhead to compensate for errors.
- Additional bits to add redundancy and extra processing at each node for error detection and correction.
- Average data rate of about 64kbps.

(c) Frame relay

- Removes the disadvantage of extra overhead in packet switching.
- Takes advantage of high transmission speed and low error rates in modern networks.
- Uses variable length packets called frames.
- Most of the overhead is stripped with error control.
- Operates efficiently to about 2Mbps.

(d) Asynchronous transfer mode or ATM

- Also known as cell relay.
- Commercial state-of-the-art networks.
- Uses fixed length packets called cells to reduce the processing overhead.
- Provides little overhead for error control, depending on inherent reliability of transmission network and higher order logic at stations for error detection and recovery.
- Works in the order of 10–100 Mbps range and may even achieve Gbps range.
- Data rate on each channel in the system can be dynamically set on demand.

ATM vs. Circuit Switching

- Circuit switching allows only fixed-data-rate circuits for the end systems.
- ATM allows multiple virtual channels with data rates that are dynamically defined at the time of creation of virtual channel.
- ATM is efficient due to the use of small fixed-size cells allowing it to offer a constant data rate channel while using packet switching.

7. ISDN and Broadband ISDN

- Integrated services digital network.
- Designed to replace existing public telecom network while delivering a wide range of services.
- Multiple networks within national boundaries with a single, unified view dictated by user interface standards.
- First generation or narrowband ISDN

- Uses 64kbps channel with circuit switching and frame relay.

□ Second generation or broadband ISDN

- Supports high data rates at 100s of Mbps with packet switching and ATM.

1.8.6 Network Cloud

When an organization must connect more than a few sites over a metropolitan or wide area, a cloud network is usually more economical and flexible than a mesh of point-to-point links. The network cloud represents a public mesh network of switching devices, often owned by a telephone company.

Common types of cloud networks include the public telephone system, the Internet, or switched transmission services such as frame relay or ATM.

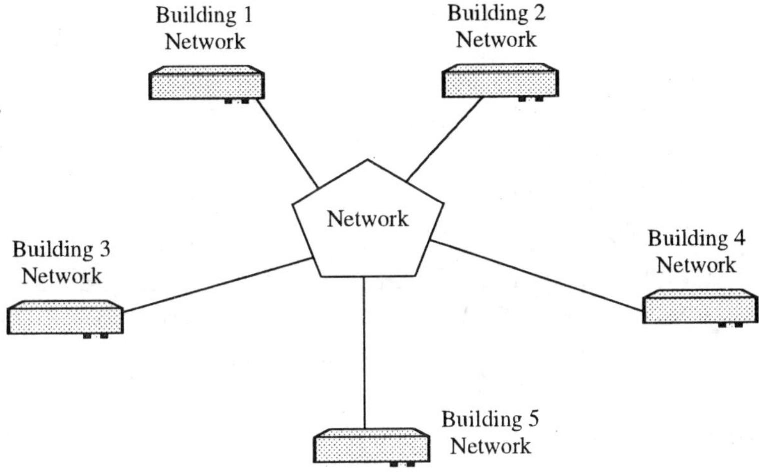

Fig. 1.9 A Network Cloud

To use the services of a cloud network, a company subscribes to the service, and then sets up a point-to-point connection between each location and a device at the edge of the cloud. The network provider is responsible for moving each message across the cloud to its destination.

1.8.7 The Internet

The Internet is a global network that came into being when the first WANs were interconnected. It allows any user on a LAN to communicate with any other user on any other LAN. The Internet is not regulated by any single body or government, and is defined at any particular moment by the users currently using it. The Internet is a form of mesh topology, because there are many possible routes data can travel between one user and another user. When you dial up your Internet Service Provider (ISP) at home, you are becoming part of a global network that has hundreds of millions of other users connected at the same time. The Internet relies on the global acceptance of protocol standards such as TCP/IP, HTTP, POP, IMAP and FTP.

Internet Growth

- The *Internet* has grown from a research prototype to a global communication system.
- During 1998, one computer per second was added to the Internet.
- The *Internet* has been doubling in size every nine to twelve months.
- The graph in Fig 1.10 shows the Logarithmic Growth of Internet:

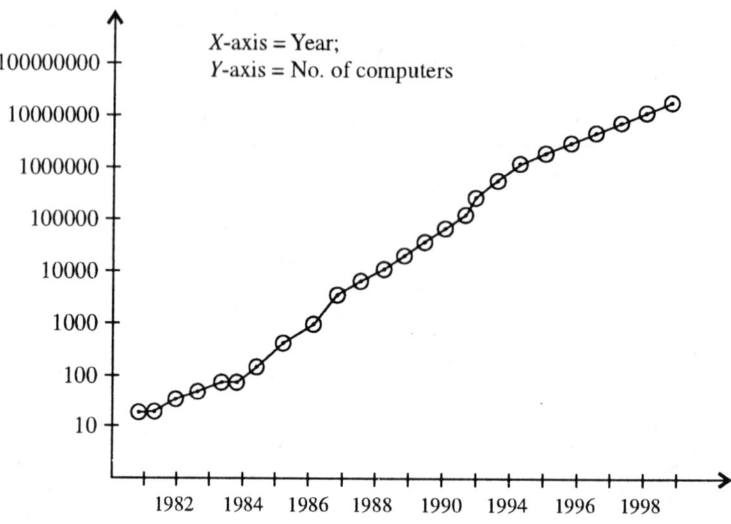

Fig. 1.10 Logarithmic growth of Internet

Probing the Internet

How does one obtain data on Internet growth?

- *Ping* : simple probing tool to determine if a specific computer is available and attached to a network.
    - ☐ Sends a message to a specified computer
    - ☐ Waits a short time for a response
    - ☐ If a reply arrives, ping reports the computer is alive, otherwise the computer does not respond.
- *Traceroute* : simple tool to determine the path from one computer to another computer on a network.
    - ☐ Uses a program like ping to determine if the computers en-route is available.
    - ☐ Keeps a list of all computers along the path.

1.9 Communication Between Processes

Computers and processes generally cooperate using three methods of communication:

- Master/slave
- Peer-to-peer
- Client/server

In a LAN, peer-to-peer and client/server communication are the most common.

1.9.1 Master/Slave Communication

Master/slave communication occurs when one node has much greater computing capacity than another. For example, a typical master/slave relationship occurs in mainframe environments where a powerful central computer runs all the applications, stores all the data, and does all the processing.

Key points of master/slave communication

- Simple "dumb" terminals function as slaves to this master, because they have no real processing or data storage capability.
- Individual terminals may not initiate an interaction, but must wait for the master mainframe to command it to send information.
- The slave merely displays text received from the master and sends information to the master in the form of the operator's keystrokes.

1.9.2 Peer-to-peer Communication

A 'peer' is a person who is on the same level of authority and power as you. In a Peer-to-Peer network, there is no computer with more control or authority than any other. There is no file server, little protection of one workstation against another, no hierarchy of "super users" and "standard users". Any computer can begin a network transaction with any other computer on the network.

Peer-to-Peer networks usually are used in the home or very small organizations with trusted users who want to share files, an Internet connection, or a printer. Without a server, costs are low and installation is simple, but users are vulnerable to each other.

Peer-to-Peer Computing (P2P) is an alternative to the traditional centralized (or client-server) computing model. A centralized model uses server-based sharing and requires an intermediary such as a Web, e-mail, or corporate server. P2P has two or more computers linked for the purpose of sharing information files (locally or remotely) with each taking an equal role in the data-transfer process without a central server. No server is needed to share information among systems; instead, each user's computer handles the serving. There are, however, flavours of P2P: some models do not use a central server, while others use central servers to hold directories and to direct traffic (but not to store data).

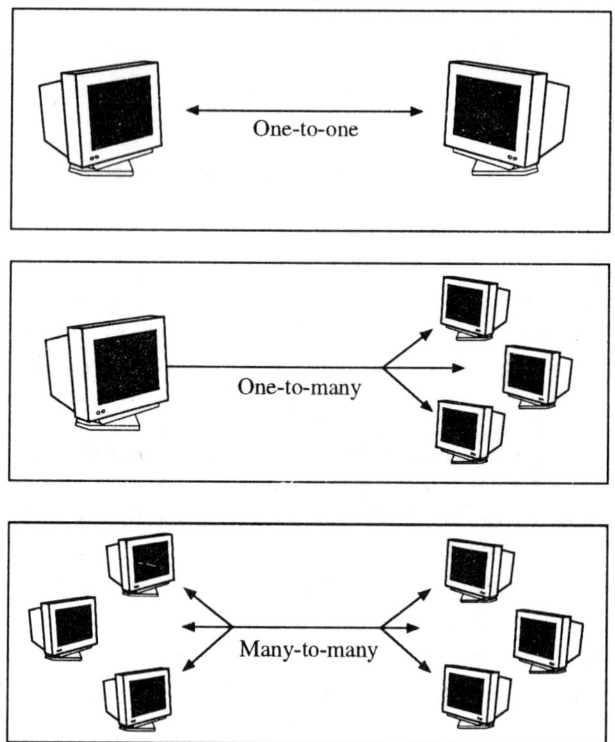

Fig. 1.11 Peer-to-Peer Networking

Key points of peer-to-peer communication

- When two processes have roughly the same power and can perform approximately the same services for each other, we call them "peer" processes.
- When processes use peer-to-peer communication, neither one controls the other.
- A peer-to-peer computer network allows various combinations of workers to share files, folders, applications, and printers.
- No single computer sets the rules for these interactions.
- However, each computer's user can decide what resources to make available to other peer users.
- Most popular desktop OSs, such as Windows 2000 or the Mac OS, has built-in software for creating peer-to-peer networks.

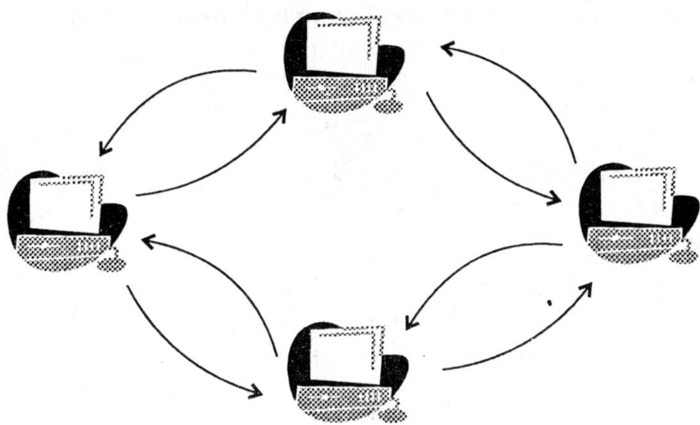

Fig. 1.12 Peer-to-Peer Communication

1.9.3 Client/Server Communication

In client-server networking one computer program (the 'client') asks another computer program (the 'server') to provide a service, such as looking up and providing data. It is similar to you (the client) asking your mum (the server) where your clean socks are. The main difference is that a real server does not respond, "Wherever you dropped them, you messy child."

In a network, the client/server model provides a convenient way to interconnect programs distributed across different locations. Computer transactions using the client/server model are very common. For example, to check your bank account from your computer, a client program in your computer forwards your request to a server program at the bank. That program may in turn forward the request to its own client program that sends a request to a database server at another bank computer to retrieve your account balance. The balance is returned back to the bank data client, which in turn serves it back to your computer, which displays the information for you. The client/server model has become one of the central ideas of network computing.

When using the Internet, your web browser is a client program that requests services (such as the sending of Web pages or files) from a web server in another computer somewhere on the Internet.

Typically, a client process is found on a lower capability, end-user node, such as a workstation or personal computer (PC). The server process runs on a node with larger capacity or greater power, such as a network file server. A client/server network is implemented with a specialized network operating system (NOS) such as Novell NetWare, Windows NT Server, or Windows 2000 Server. Unix and Linux also provide client/server features.

Both client and server processes are dedicated to their respective tasks, and those roles never reverse. However, the same computing machine can run multiple processes.

Some of those processes can be servers of some functions, and some can be clients of other servers. Thus it is important to remember that "server" refers to a process, not necessarily a particular machine.

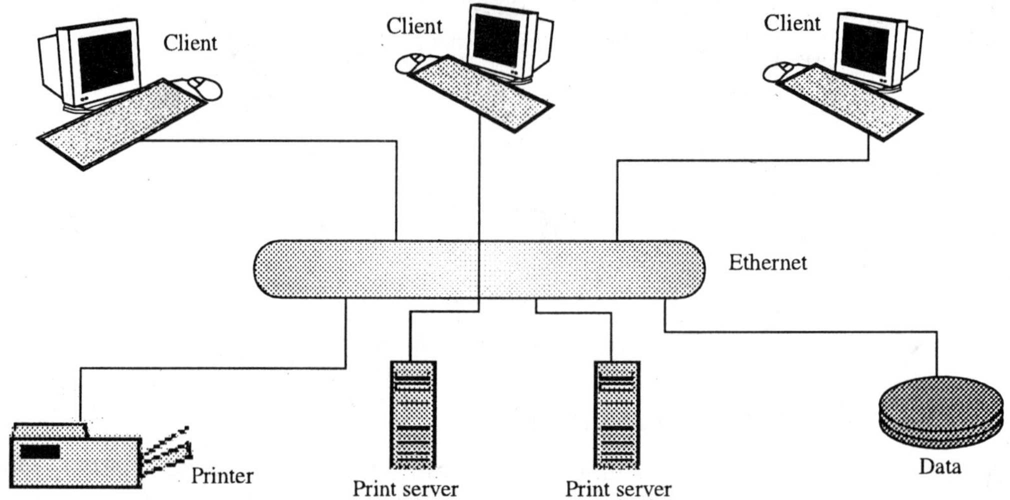

Fig. 1.13 Client/Server Communication

Client and server processes interact with each other by transmitting request/reply pairs. The client process initiates an interaction by issuing a request to the server. The server process responds with a reply satisfying the request. This request/reply communication essentially divides a task into two parts and executes each part on a different system on the network.

Also, peer-to-peer communication can still occur on a client/server network. If servers have been established for shared functions such as file sharing or printing, two computers may still exchange data as peers.

Client and server processes share a common protocol. However, the protocol defines entirely different conventions for communications originating from the client and those originating from the server. This is in contrast with peer-to-peer communication, in which the protocol is more or less the same in both directions.

Key points of client/server communication

- Another way that processes can communicate is for one process to assume the role of client and the other that of server.
- The client process makes requests for the server process to perform some task.
- Client/server communication is typically used to allow sharing of centralized resources, such as data, applications, peripheral devices, or storage space.

1.9.4 Comparing Communication Methods

Peer-to-Peer Advantages	Peer-to-Peer Disadvantages	Client/Server Advantages	Client/Server Disadvantages
Simplicity	Not practical in large networks	Access to common resources	Complexity
Low cost	Most OSs limit number of nodes connected	Scalable to very large environments	High cost for small networks
Easy to manage in small networks	No single point for backup and administration	Dedicated shared resources and administration points	Often requires trained personnel
Easy to trouble shoot			Harder to trouble-shoot

1.10 Types Of Servers

A server is a heavy-duty computer designed to be the core of a network. It does not have any special or exotic hardware in it, but it is designed to work continuously for long periods under heavy workloads to control the network and run the network operating system. The different types of servers are discussed below:

1.10.1 File Servers

When a network is based on a central file server, it allows networked computers to share resources such as printers, and users can store their files in a secure centralized location. The file server offers services to all users, but each workstation on the network does its own processing. For example, if a user wanted to use a spreadsheet she would run the spreadsheet on her own PC, but would be able to save her work in her home directory on the server, and use a shared network printer.

File servers typically have very large hard disks, lots of memory, and are stored under high security. In large networks, there is often more than one file server, to distribute the workload or to handle specialist tasks. (such as a proxy server, web server, email server, login server, print server, CD-ROM server etc.)

Since the file server is the heart of the network, if it fails it can severely affect network users, so it is usually treated like royalty. They are usually kept firmly under lock and key in air-conditioned rooms with uninterruptible power supplies (UPS) to protect against power blackouts, brownouts and voltage spikes.

1.10.2 Application Servers

While a file server (as its name suggests) serves out files to users, an application server actually runs programs on behalf of users. Similar to the earliest mainframe computers that ran programs for users and send the results of the calculations to the users, an application server actually runs application programs like Word, Excel, databases itself.

It allows **Thin Client Computing** (e.g. Citrix Metaframe and Windows Terminal Server): users' workstations need only be very cheap and low powered (really just a keyboard, screen, mouse) and enough IQ to send the user's typing and clicking to the application server. The application server is the real brain of the outfit. It runs the programs for the user and sends back screen images that appear on the user's screen.

The benefit for an organization is that they can use any old nasty, horrible, low powered computer as a workstation and it will *behave* as if it were a fire breathing, supercharged state-of-the-art PC. This is handy, for example, if the organization needs lots of workstations but does not have much cash; or if they need to put workstations in high-risk areas such as factories or on construction sites. If the PC is wrecked by dust or is stolen, it does not matter a lot because it was cheap and there is no valuable data stored on it: all data is stored securely and centrally on the application server.

Another benefit is that network managers do not have to configure hundreds of workstations: any change to software or operating system settings is done once, on the application server. It is far easier to install a new program once, on the application server, than it is to go around and install it on 200 workstations! Application servers typically have twin CPUs, a gigabyte of RAM, massive hard disks... **very expensive!**

1.10.3 Server Blades

A **server blade** is an entire server (processor, system memory, network connection, and associated electronics) on a single motherboard, which slides into an enclosure that can contain dozens of other blades. The enclosure supplies all of the blades with power, fans and cabling.

Unlike traditional servers in individual boxes, the use of server blades takes little physical room and allows thousands of blades to be deployed relatively cheaply. It is also quite easy to service the hardware, increase its power and manage the hardware resources. Installing, servicing, and removing blades is much easier than working with chassis-mounted servers. Shared power supply, cabling, fans and storage reduce the number of duplicated and failure-prone components in the environment. IT managers can easily monitor, configure, and troubleshoot systems. Organizations can also add to their systems in much smaller, more precise increments. Perhaps most important, blades offer the highest computing densities: they can't be beaten when measuring how much processing grunt you can get into a square meter of floor space.

1.10.4 Information Appliances

Information appliances are specialized servers dedicated to one task. They are extremely easy to install and add to infrastructure. Using specialized and proprietary components with embedded operating systems, they require little or no administration. Their abilities are preinstalled and preconfigured, and web browsers are used for configuration and administration. They are the classic "black box" devices where the user does not need to know *how* they work, just that they *do* work.

Information Appliances (also called network appliances) are a growing new class of dedicated devices that include: Internet (web) servers, Proxy/caching servers, Database servers, Email servers, and File servers.

Their Benefits Include

- Easy and quick installation
- Big cost saving for management and administration
- Easy remote configuration through a Web browser
- Operators do not have to be computer experts
- They need minimal user intervention
- They provide support for multiple versions of every leading operating system and are not tied to a specific OS
- Many are upgradeable via FTP or downloading code from the Internet
- They should not require any client software (programs on other computers in the organization)

A common information appliance is the multipurpose server appliance that provides, in one little box, some features as:

- Internet connectivity
- Website hosting
- A proxy server, to cache (store) downloads to avoid having to download them again soon afterwards
- Firewall servers
- Web access
- E-mail
- FTP
- Virtual Private Networking (VPN) facilities to connect employees, customers and e-business networks
- Print server functions (controlling printers on the network)
- File server operations
- Enterprise database management
- Transaction acceleration software
- Cluster administration (managing groups of servers)
- E-commerce hosting (e.g., website "shopping trolleys")

The product usually consists of an embedded OS with features like e-mail and Internet access managed through a browser, network-connected hardware, a hard disk, a processor, routing software, and a modem. Most appliances use a version of Linux running on an Intel processor.

Who uses information appliances rather than traditional servers? Those who want a job done, but don't want to be forever fiddling with settings and software installation. Dedicated information appliances often lack the sheer power of traditional servers, but score points for ease of use, flexible management, and reliability. Small organizations with little IT expertise would find such appliances attractive.

The drawback to such appliances is a result of their "sealed unit" nature : they are not usually designed to be expanded or seriously reconfigured. Like laptop computers, what you buy will be all you will have for the life of the product.

1.11 How Servers Are Different To Desktop Computers?

Servers tend to differ from the average computer in terms of:

Memory : Servers require large amounts of RAM to work efficiently. Application servers require huge amounts of RAM to run programs for remote users.

Storage : Servers need very large and fast hard disks. Many large servers use RAID (Redundant Array of Independent [or Inexpensive] Disks) arrays for maximum reliability and speed. RAID uses a group of hard disks that work as a unit and usually offer built-in backup of data. RAID disks are usually "Hot Swap" drives that can be removed and inserted without turning off the server or disrupting the network's operation.

Processing power : While processing power is not so important in a file server, application servers benefit greatly from having multiple CPUs.

Backup : Most servers have inbuilt high-capacity tape backup drives to protect against data loss. Tape drives usually use QIC (Quarter Inch Cartridge) tapes.

Connectivity : Servers often have two or more fast network cards to multiply the rate at which they can send and receive data to the rest of the network.

Robustness : Since servers run all day for years on end, the components used in them need to be of higher quality than those in the average desktop computer. As you may suspect a server will cost far more than a desktop PC - perhaps up to ten times as much.

Scalability : Servers are designed to be expandable as network demand grows. Scalability is the ability to increase the size and power of equipment and networks as required. Many servers let you add up to 8 hard disks, two power supplies, two NICs (Network Interface Cards), two CPUs etc. The design and engineering of this expandability is expensive.

The larger the network, the more work a server must perform. Bigger networks often use multiple servers to share the workload. Special load balancing software is used to distribute the workload efficiently between the servers.

Sometimes, networks use specialist servers that are dedicated to jobs such as:

- Login servers — which authenticate users
- Proxy servers — which cache recent downloads in case they're requested again
- DHCP servers — which allocate IP addresses to users as they log in
- Print servers — which manage the queues of print jobs
- CD towers and Virtual CD servers - which imitate large CD towers

- Web servers and FTP servers - which handle requests for web pages or files from the Internet
- Email servers - which receive, store and distribute e-mail.

On smaller networks, most of these services are performed by software in a single server. Overworked servers can be helped by using server blades. These slim units plug easily into a network and act as file servers. Network storage can be enhanced by plugging in NAS (Network Access Storage) units. With up to 960G of hard disk in a slim package, NAS devices greatly expand a network's storage capacity.

1.12 What Is Networking Hardware?

Networking hardware includes all computers, peripherals, interface cards and other equipment needed to perform data processing and communications within the network.

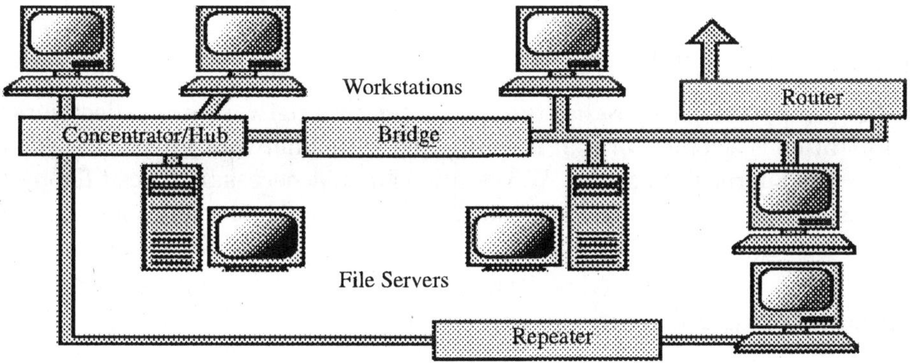

Fig. 1.14 Components of networking hardware.

It includes the following components:

1. File Servers
2. Workstations
3. Network Interface Cards
4. Concentrators/Hubs
5. Repeaters
6. Bridges
7. Routers

1. File Servers

A file server stands at the heart of most networks. It is a very fast computer with a large amount of RAM and storage space, along with a fast network interface card. The network operating system software resides on this computer, along with any software applications and data files that need to be shared.

The file server controls the communication of information between the nodes on a network. For example, it may be asked to send a word processor program to one workstation, receive a database file from another workstation, and store an e-mail message during the same time period. This requires a computer that can store a lot of information and share it very quickly. File servers should have at least the following characteristics:

- 166 megahertz or faster microprocessor (Pentium, PowerPC)
- A fast hard drive with at least nine gigabytes of storage
- A RAID (Redundant Array of Inexpensive Disks) to preserve data after a disk casualty
- A tape back-up unit (i.e. DAT, JAZ, Zip, or CD-RW drive)
- Numerous expansion slots
- Fast network interface card
- At least of 32 MB of RAM

2. Workstations

All of the computers connected to the file server on a network are called workstations. A typical workstation is a computer that is configured with a network interface card, networking software, and the appropriate cables. Workstations do not necessarily need floppy disk drives or hard drives because files can be saved on the file server. Almost any computer can serve as a network workstation.

3. Network Interface Cards

The network interface card (NIC) provides the physical connection between the network and the computer workstation. Most NICs are internal, with the card fitting into an expansion slot inside the computer. Some computers, such as Mac Classics, use external boxes, which are attached to a serial port or a SCSI port. Laptop computers can now be purchased with a network interface card built-in or with network cards that slip into a PCMCIA slot.

Network interface cards are a major factor in determining the speed and performance of a network. It is a good idea to use the fastest network card available for the type of workstation you are using.

The three most common network interface connections are Ethernet cards, LocalTalk connectors, and Token Ring cards. According to an International Data Corporation study, Ethernet is the most popular, followed by Token Ring and LocalTalk.

Ethernet Cards

Ethernet cards are usually purchased separately from a computer, although many computers (such as the Macintosh) now include an option for a pre-installed Ethernet card. Ethernet cards contain connections for either coaxial or twisted pair cables (or both). If it is designed for coaxial cable, the connection will be BNC. If it is designed for twisted pair, it will have a RJ-45 connection. Some Ethernet cards also contain an AUI connector. This can be used to attach coaxial, twisted pair, or fiber optics cable to an Ethernet card. When this method is used there is always an external transceiver attached to the workstation.

Local Talk Connectors

LocalTalk is Apple's built-in solution for networking Macintosh computers. It utilizes a special adapter box and a cable that plugs into the printer port of a Macintosh. A major disadvantage of LocalTalk is that it is slow in comparison to Ethernet. Most Ethernet connections operate at 10 Mbps (Megabits per second). In contrast, LocalTalk operates at only 230 Kbps (or .23 Mbps).

Ethernet Cards vs. LocalTalk Connections	
Ethernet	**LocalTalk**
Fast data transfer (10 to 100 Mbps)	Slow data transfer (.23 Mbps)
Expensive - purchased separately	Built into Macintosh computers
Requires computer slot	No computer slot necessary
Available for most computers	Works only on Macintosh computers

Token Ring Cards

Token Ring network cards look similar to Ethernet cards. One visible difference is the type of connector on the back end of the card. Token Ring cards generally have a nine pin DIN type connector to attach the card to the network cable.

4. Concentrators/Hubs

A concentrator is a device that provides a central connection point for cables from workstations, servers, and peripherals. In a star topology, twisted-pair wire is run from each workstation to a central concentrator. Hubs are multislot concentrators into which can be plugged a number of multi-port cards to provide additional access as the network grows in size. Some concentrators are passive that is they allow the signal to pass from one computer to another without any change. Most concentrators are active that is they electrically amplify the signal as it moves from one device to another. Active concentrators are used like repeaters to extend the length of a network. Concentrators are:

- Usually configured with 8, 12, or 24 RJ-45 ports
- Often used in a star or star-wired ring topology
- Sold with specialized software for port management
- Also called hubs
- Usually installed in a standardized metal rack that also may store net modems, bridges, or routers

5. Repeaters

Since a signal loses strength as it passes along a cable, it is often necessary to boost the signal with a device called a repeater. The repeater electrically amplifies the signal it receives and rebroadcasts it. Repeaters can be separate devices or they can be incorporated into a concentrator. They are used when the total length of your network cable exceeds the standards set for the type of cable being used.

A good example of the use of repeaters would be in a local area network using a star topology with unshielded twisted-pair cabling. The length limit for unshielded twisted-pair cable is 100 meters. The most common configuration is for each workstation to be connected by twisted-pair cable to a multi-port active concentrator. The concentrator amplifies all the signals that pass through it allowing for the total length of cable on the network to exceed the 100 meter limit.

6. Bridges

A bridge is a device that allows you to segment a large network into two smaller, more efficient networks. If you are adding to an older wiring scheme and want the new network to be up-to-date, a bridge can connect the two.

A bridge monitors the information traffic on both sides of the network so that it can pass packets of information to the correct location. Most bridges can "listen" to the network and automatically figure out the address of each computer on both sides of the bridge. The bridge can inspect each message and, if necessary, broadcast it on the other side of the network.

The bridge manages the traffic to maintain optimum performance on both sides of the network. You might say that the bridge is like a traffic cop at a busy intersection during rush hour. It keeps information flowing on both sides of the network, but it does not allow unnecessary traffic through. Bridges can be used to connect different types of cabling, or physical topologies. They must, however, be used between networks with the same protocol.

7. Routers

A router translates information from one network to another; it is similar to a super intelligent bridge. Routers select the best path to route a message, based on the destination address and origin. The router can direct traffic to prevent head-on collisions, and is smart enough to know when to direct traffic along back roads and shortcuts. While bridges know the addresses of all computers on each side of the network, routers know the addresses of computers, bridges, and other routers on the network. Routers can even "listen" to the entire network to determine which sections are busiest—they can then redirect data around those sections until they clear up.

If you have a school LAN that you want to connect to the Internet, you will need to purchase a router. In this case, the router serves as the translator between the information on your LAN and the Internet. It also determines the best route to send the data over the Internet. Routers can:

- Direct signal traffic efficiently

- Route messages between any two protocols
- Route messages between linear bus, star, and star-wired ring topologies
- Route messages across fiber optic, coaxial, and twisted-pair cabling

1.13 What Is A Network Operating System?

Unlike operating systems, such as DOS and Windows95 that are designed for single users to control one computer, network operating systems (NOS) coordinate the activities of multiple computers across a network. The network operating system acts as a director to keep the network running smoothly.

The two major types of network operating systems are:

- Peer-to-Peer
- Client/Server

Peer-to-Peer

Peer-to-peer network operating systems allow users to share resources and files located on their computers and to access shared resources found on other computers. However, they do not have a file server or a centralized management source (See fig. 1.15). In a peer-to-peer network, all computers are considered equal; they all have the same abilities to use the resources available on the network. Peer-to-peer networks are designed primarily for small to medium local area networks. AppleShare and Windows for Workgroups are examples of programs that can function as peer-to-peer network operating systems.

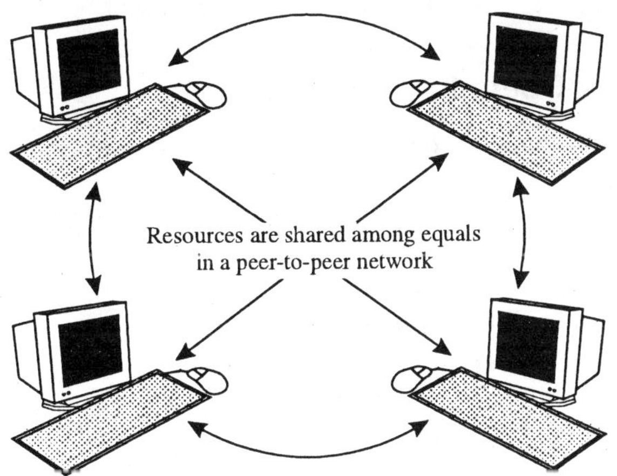

Fig. 1.15 Peer-to-Peer Network

Client/Server

Client/server network operating systems allow the network to centralize functions and applications in one or more dedicated file servers (See fig. 1.16). The file servers become the heart of the system, providing access to resources and providing security. Individual workstations (clients) have access to the resources available on the file servers. The network operating system provides the mechanism to integrate all the components of the network and allow multiple users to simultaneously share the same resources irrespective of physical location. Novell Netware and Windows NT Server are examples of client/server network operating systems.

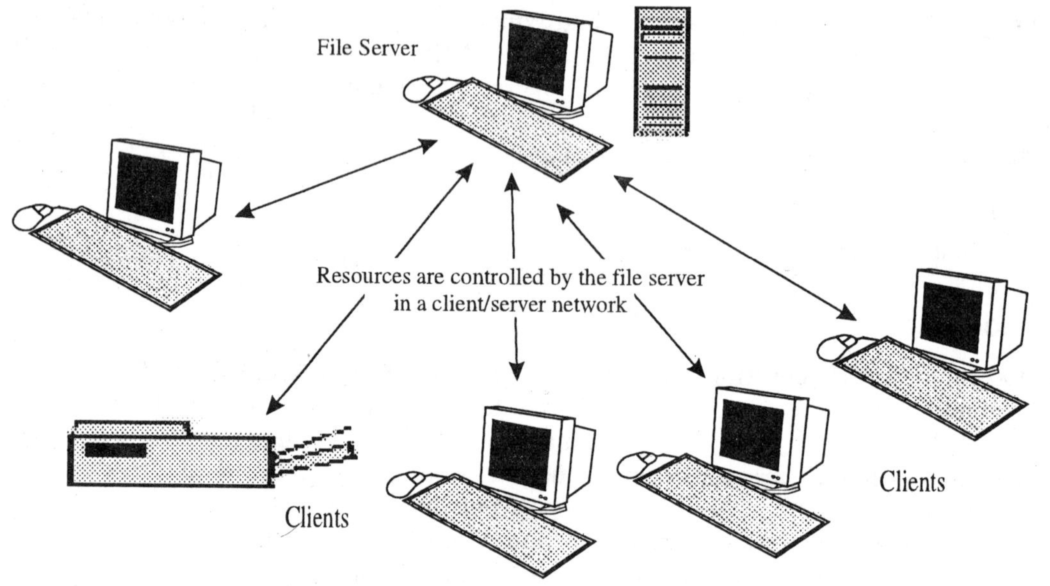

Fig. 1.16 Client/server network

Examples of Network Operating Systems

The following list includes some of the more popular peer-to-peer and client/server network operating systems.

- AppleShare
- LANtastic
- Microsoft Windows for Workgroups
- Microsoft Windows NT Server
- Novell Netware.

• • •

2

Network Topologies

2.1 What Is A Topology?

A topology is a generalized geometric configuration of some class of objects that join together. Topologies are the architectural "drawings" that show the overall physical configuration for a given communications system.

In networking, the term topology refers to the layout of connected devices on a network. It can be considered as the logical "shape" of the network wiring. This logical shape does not necessarily correspond to the actual *physical* layout of the devices on the network. For example, the computers on a home LAN may be arranged in a circle, but it would be highly unlikely to find an actual ring topology there.

'Logical' means how it looks as a pure design concept, rather than how it actually looks physically, e.g., the topology pictures you will see have nice straight lines between bits of the network, they don't try to show all the corners that need to be turned and holes that have to be drilled in a real cable installation.

A topology will indicate the access methods and will govern the rules that are used to design and implement the communication system. They represent the drawing of your network cable plant. It is important to make a distinction between a topology and architecture. A topology is concerned with the physical arrangement of the network components. In contrast, architecture addresses the components themselves and how a system is structured (cable access methods, lower level protocols, topology, etc.). An example of architecture is 10 base T Ethernet that typically uses the star topology.

Each topology has its advantages and disadvantages: usually related to cost, complexity, reliability and traffic "bottlenecks".

2.2 Basic Architectures

Prior to today's complicated computer network topologies, computer networks often consisted of either point-to-point or multipoint links.

(A) Point-to-Point

A point-to-point link is a direct connection between two devices (nodes). One example of this is a PC connected to a printer. A more common example is a mainframe terminal connected to a mainframe front-end processor.

(B) Multi Point

A multipoint link is a connection between three or more points on a link. Year's age, multipoint links were used to connect multiple terminals to a mainframe front-end processor.

In today's LAN environment, multipoint links are used to connect multiple devices in bus, tree or star topologies.

Addressing and Bandwidth

Point to point links are different than multipoint because it implies dedicated bandwidth. Because the bandwidth is dedicated in a point-to-point environment, no addressing (of nodes) is needed.

In a multipoint link the channel (the communication path) is shared which complicates communication and the efficiency of using the channel.

2.3 Types Of Topologies

The different types of topologies are discussed below:

2.3.1 Star Topology

In a Star Network, all the nodes (PCs, printers and other shared peripherals) are connected to the central server.

It has a central connection point - like a hub or switch. A star topology is designed with each node (file server, workstations, and peripherals) connected directly to a central network hub or concentrator (See fig. 2.1).

All traffic emanates from the hub of the star. Data on a star network passes through the hub or concentrator before continuing to its destination. The hub or concentrator manages and controls all functions of the network. It also acts as a repeater for the data flow. This configuration is common with twisted pair cable; however, it can also be used with coaxial cable or fiber optic cable. The hub offers a common connection for all stations on the network. Each station has its own direct cable connection to the hub.

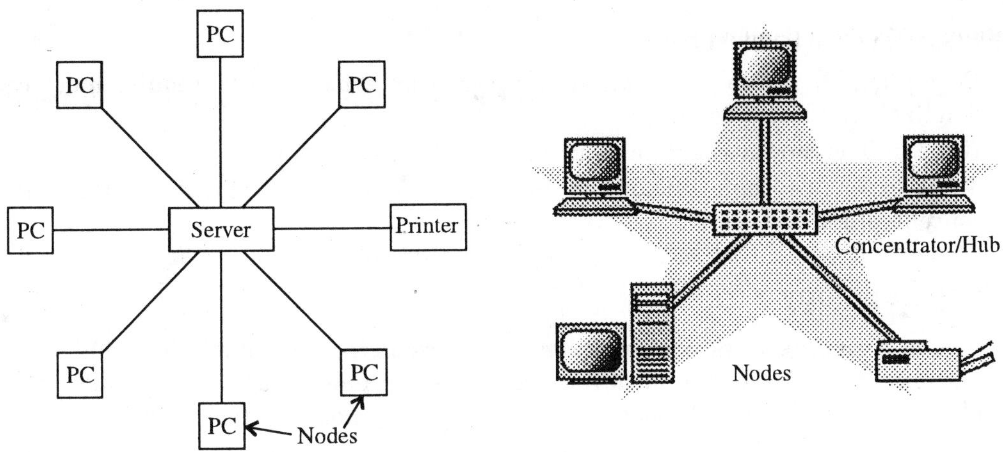

Fig. 2.1 Star Topology

Features of Star Network

- In a star network each node is connected by a point-to-point link to a central point.
- These central points are called hubs, concentrators or multipoint repeaters.
- These central points can be passive or active.
- If passive these hubs simply connect the points of the star.
- If active, these hubs regenerate (repeat) the electrical signals they receive.
- A hub-centered star topology is a broadcast network, because the hub copies each signal to all other computers attached to it.
- The hub may have extra features like LEDs that indicate activity and errors on each port, making it even easier to isolate problems.
- With the introduction of switches, you can dramatically increase network performance by replacing the hub with a switch.

Advantages of a Star Topology

1. Easy to install and wire.
2. Easy to add new stations as each station has its own direct cable connection to the hub. If a cable is cut, it only affects the computer that was attached to it.
3. It can accommodate different wiring. It can be installed using twisted pair, coaxial cable or fiber optic cable.
4. Since all information in a star topology goes through a central point star, topologies are easy to troubleshoot. A star can simplify troubleshooting because stations can be disconnected from the hub one at a time until the problem is isolated.
5. The main advantage is that one malfunctioning node does not affect the rest of the network.

Disadvantages of a Star Topology

1. Depending on where the hubs are located, star networks can require more cable length than a linear topology.
2. If the hub or concentrator fails, nodes attached are disabled.
3. More expensive than linear bus topologies because of the cost of the hub or concentrators.

2.3.2 Ring Topology

All the nodes in a ring network are connected in a closed circle of cable. Messages that are transmitted travel around the ring until they reach the computer that they are addressed to, the signal being refreshed by each node. There may or may not be a fileserver.

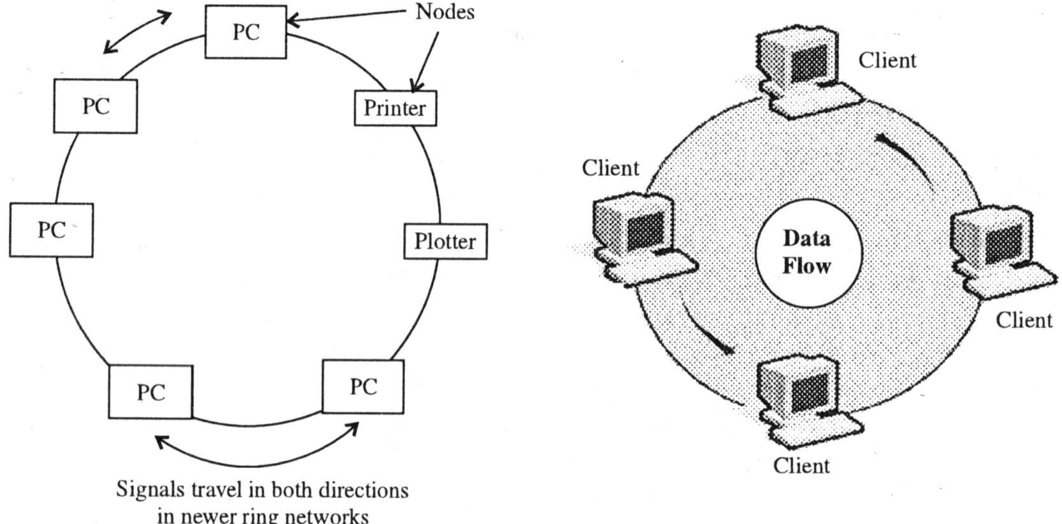

Fig. 2.2 Ring Topology

In a ring network, every device has exactly two neighbours for communication purposes. All messages travel through a ring in the same direction. There are no terminated ends to the cable; the signal travels around the circle in a clockwise direction.

Under the ring concept, a signal is transferred sequentially via a "token" from one station to the next. When a station wants to transmit, it "grabs" the token, attaches data and an address to it, and then sends it around the ring. The token travels along the ring until it reaches the destination address. The receiving computer acknowledges receipt with a return message to the sender. The sender then releases the token for use by another computer.

Each station on the ring has equal access but only one station can talk at a time. In contrast to the 'passive' topology of the bus, the ring employs an 'active' topology. Each station repeats or 'boosts' the signal before passing it on to the next station.

Rings are normally implemented using twisted pair or fiber-optic cable.

Features of Ring Network

- A "pure" ring topology is a collection of separate point-to-point links, arranged to make a ring.
- Each node's network interface card (NIC) has one input and one output connection, so each node is connected to two links.
- When a node receives a signal on its input connection, its repeater circuitry retransmits that signal, immediately and without buffering, to its output connection.
- Thus, in many rings, data flows only in one direction.
- To send a message, a node transmits new bits onto the ring.
- If a message is addressed to a node, that node copies bits off the ring as they go by.
- If a node receives a message that is not addressed to it, it repeats the message without copying it.

Advantages of Ring Topology

1. Growth of system has minimal impact on performance. The ring networks can be larger than bus or star because each node regenerates the signal.
2. Degrade nicely under high utilization. Everybody gets to talk...
3. Fault tolerance builds into the design (can bypass damaged nodes).
4. All stations have equal access.
5. Data packets travel at a greater speed.

Disadvantages of Ring Topology

1. Expensive topology.
2. Failure of one computer may impact others. A failure in any cable or device breaks the loop and will take down the entire segment.
3. It is complex to implement and to extend the network; you must break the ring (which brings the network down). If any device is added to or removed from the ring, the ring is broken and the segment fails.
4. Data clashes can also occur if two machines send messages at the same time. Tokens or electronic signals that travel around the ring were invented to solve this problem. In a Token Ring Network, a computer can only send a message when the token is with it at the time.

2.3.3 Mesh Topology

In the topologies shown above, there is only one possible path from one node to another node. If any cable in that path is broken, the nodes cannot communicate. In a mesh topology, every device has a dedicated point-to point link to every other device. Such a network is called *complete* because between any two devices there is a special link; one could not add any non-redundant additional links.

Mesh topology uses *lots* of cables to connect every node with every other node. It is very expensive to wire up, but if any cable fails, there are many other ways for two nodes to communicate. Some WANs, like the Internet, employ mesh routing. In fact the Internet was deliberately designed like this to allow sites to communicate even during a nuclear war.

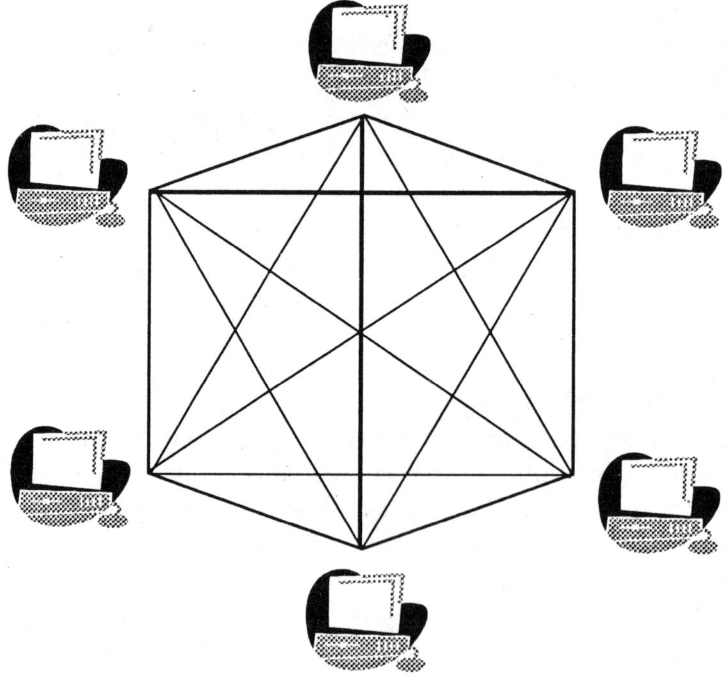

Fig. 2.3 Mesh Topology

Features of Mesh Network

- In a mesh topology, point-to-point links directly connect every site to every other site.

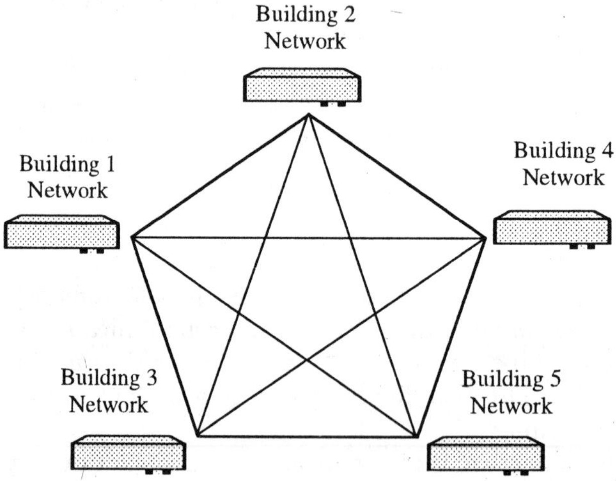

Fig. 2.4 Mesh Network

- Mesh networks are usually built over time as new sites are added to the overall network.
- A mesh topology is often used for MAN or WAN networks.
- The number of point-to-point links increases sharply with the number of locations. Thus, if a network must connect more than a few sites, a mesh topology is usually too expensive.

Advantages of Mesh Topology

1. Redundant links between devices.
2. *Good security*: If the line is not tapped only the intended recipient can see the data.
3. *Reliability*: Increasing network traffic does not affect the speed of other connections.
4. Easy fault identification and -isolation, an unusable link does not incapacitate the entire system

Disadvantages of Mesh Topology

1. Each node must have an interface for every other device.
2. Large amounts of cable for many devices to be connected in a mesh environment. A mesh topology for n devices needs $n \times \frac{(n-1)}{2}$ connections. It is therefore hard to install and expensive because of the extensive cabling.
3. Unless each station sends to every other station frequently, bandwidth is wasted. (Links that are not being used).
4. Another disadvantage is that there is only a limited amount of I/O-ports in a computer, but every connection uses one up.

2.3.4 Bus Topology

In a bus topology, all stations are attached to the same cable. In the Bus Network, messages are sent in both directions from a single point and are read by the node (computer or peripheral on the network) identified by the code with the message. Most Local Area Networks (LANs) are Bus Networks because the network will continue to function even if one computer is down.

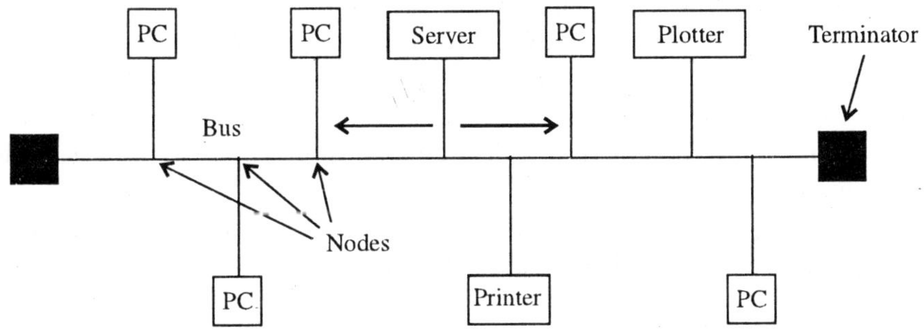

Fig. 2.5 Bus Topology

The purpose of the terminators (resistors) at either end of the network is to stop the signal being reflected back. If a bus network is not terminated, or if the terminator has the wrong level of resistance, each signal may travel across the bus several times instead of just once. This problem increases the number of signal collisions, degrading network performance.

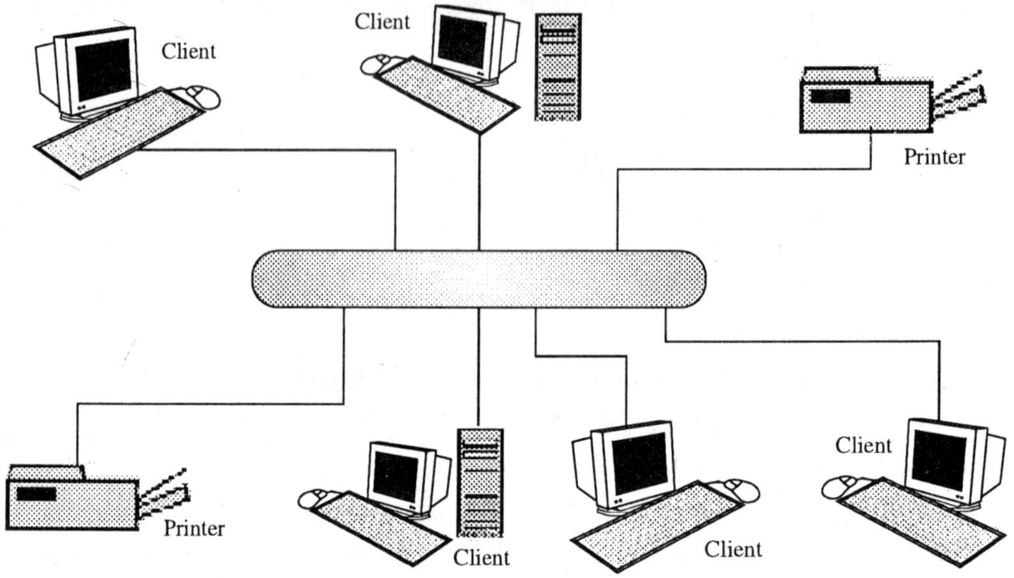

Fig. 2.6 Bus Topology

In a bus topology, signals are broadcast to all stations. Each computer checks the address on the signal (data frame) as it passes along the bus. If the signal's address matches that of the computer, the computer processes the signal. If the address doesn't match, the computer takes no action and the signal travels on down the bus.

Only one computer can 'talk' on a network at a time. A media access method called CSMA/CD is used to handle the collisions that occur when two signals are placed on the wire at the same time. The bus topology is passive. In other words, the computers on the bus simply 'listen' for a signal; they are not responsible for moving the signal along.

A bus topology is normally implemented with coaxial cable. Different types of bus topology are discussed below:

(a) **Regular Bus** : In a regular bus, each computer is attached to the cable segment (called a backbone) by means of a drop cable (a shorter cable connecting the computer to the backbone)

(b) **Local Bus** : In a local bus, each computer is attached directly to the backbone in a daisy-chain configuration by means of a T-connector. Peer-to-peer networks are often configured as a local bus.

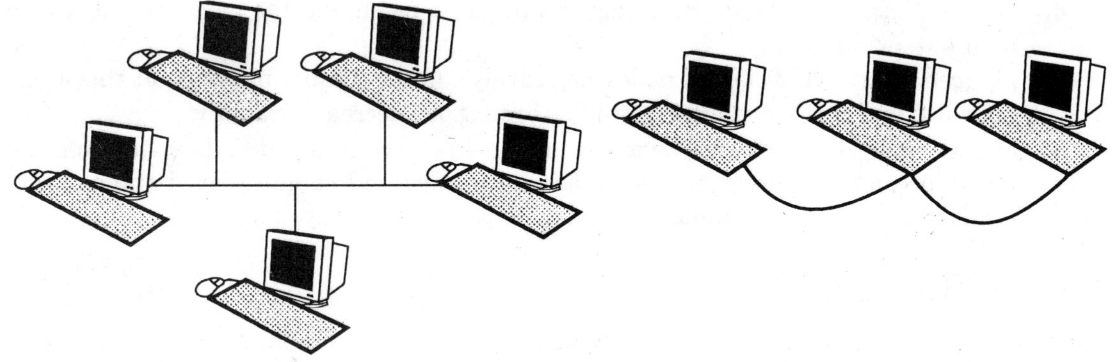

Fig. 2.7 Regular Bus

Fig. 2.8 Local Bus

Features of Bus Network

- A bus is a single electrical circuit to which all devices in the network are connected (although the bus might be made up of many individual pieces of wire).
- A bus topology is a broadcast network.
- When a node transmits data, the signal travels down the bus in both directions.
- Each node connected to the bus receives the signal as it passes that connection point.
- However, a node ignores any signal that is not specifically addressed to it.
- The cable is terminated at each end.
- The wiring is normally done point to point.
- A faulty cable will take the entire LAN down.

Advantages of Bus Topology

1. Bus topologies are relatively easy to install and don't require much cabling compared to other topologies.
2. Easy to connect a computer or peripheral to a linear bus.
3. Requires less cable length than a star topology, as you only need to chain the stations together.
4. There is no central point of failure on a bus because there is no hub.
5. Simple and easy to implement and extend.
6. Well suited for temporary networks that must be set up in hurry.
7. Failure of one station does not affect others.

Disadvantages of a Linear Bus Topology

1. Entire network shuts down if there is a break in the main cable.
2. Terminators are required at both ends of the backbone cable.
3. Difficult to identify the problem if the entire network shuts down.
4. Not meant to be used as a stand-alone solution in a large building.
5. Maintenance costs may be higher in the long run.

6. *More expensive cabling* : Because the line must be shared the cable has to have a high bandwidth.
7. *Not very fast* : Addition of nodes negatively affects the performance of the whole network, and if there is a lot of traffic throughput decreases rapidly.
8. *Higher error probability* : The more components work on a signal the more probable errors become. As the signal has to be multiplexed and demultiplexed and as every connected device is examining them errors can more easily occur.

2.3.5 Tree Topology

Also known as the 'Hierarchical topology', the tree topology is a combination of bus and star topologies. It consists of groups of star-configured workstations connected to a linear bus backbone cable. Tree topologies allow for the expansion of an existing network and enable schools to configure a network to meet their needs. They are very common in larger networks.

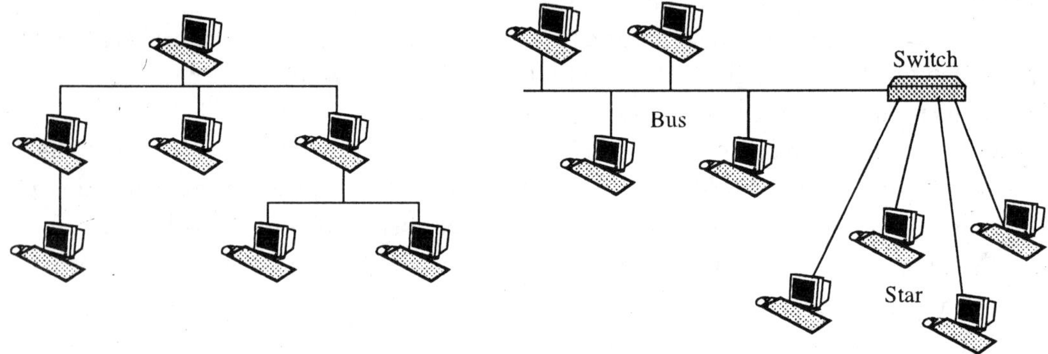

Fig. 2.9 Tree Topology

A typical scenario is : A file server is connected to a 24-port switch. A cable goes from the switch to a computer room where it connects to another switch. Many cables pass from this switch to the computers in the computer room. The node at the highest point in the hierarchy-usually a file server-controls the network.

Advantages of a Tree Topology

1. Point-to-point wiring for individual segments.
2. Supported by several hardware and software vendors.

Disadvantages of a Tree Topology

1. Overall length of each segment is limited by the type of cabling used.
2. If the backbone line breaks, the entire segment goes down.
3. More difficult to configure and wire than other topologies.

2.3.6 Hybrid Topology

Hybrid networks are simply networks that use multiple topologies. WANs usually use point-to-point links to connect remote rings or stars. The hybrid topology is popular in designing building, campus and enterprise networks.

There are many different ways the basic topologies can be combined. The World Wide Web itself is a giant hybrid topology.

- A hybrid star bus topology is a bus topology where at least one of the stations is replaced with the hub star topology network.
- A hybrid star ring topology looks like a star network except that the hub is wired as a logical ring. Such a hub is much easier to implement than a physical ring topology.
- A hybrid mesh topology is any hybrid topology where some of the key computers are connected in a mesh fashion. The WWW has its domain name servers as part of a hybrid mesh network.

A simple hybrid topology is shown in figure 2.10.

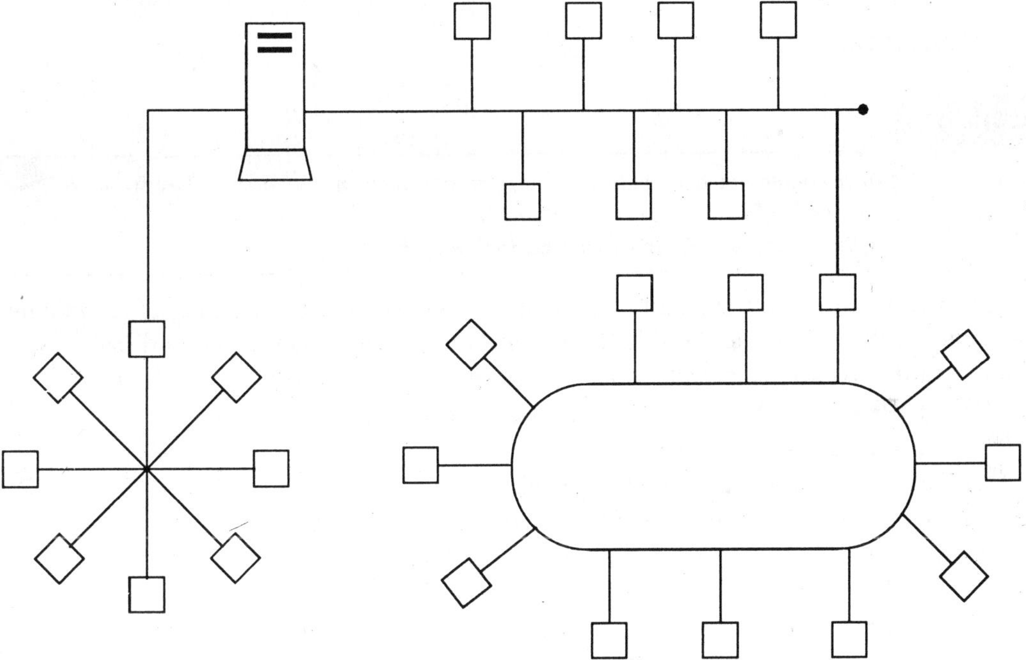

Fig. 2.10 Hybrid topology

2.3.7 Considerations When Choosing A Topology

- **Money :** A linear bus network may be the least expensive way to install a network; you do not have to purchase concentrators.

- **Length of cable needed :** The linear bus network uses shorter lengths of cable.
- **Future growth :** With a star topology, expanding a network is easily done by adding another concentrator.
- **Cable type :** The most common cable in schools is unshielded twisted pair, which is most often used with star topologies.

As a general rule, a bus topology is the cheapest to install, but may be more expensive to maintain because it does not provide for redundancy.

2.4 Access Methods

When several devices are connected to a single channel forming a multipoint connection, rules of communication need to be followed so that devices transmit and receive data without having their transmissions garbled. Access methods are the rules devices follow to access, transmit and release the communications channel.

2.4.1 Contention

Definition

In a contention access system, devices can transmit whenever they want to. No one mandates if or when a device can transmit. Stations transmit when they are ready without regard for what other stations may be doing.

Stations transmitting at the same moment in time cause a co-mingling of signals on the media. This is called a collision and both stations' messages are damaged and lost.

There are two popular methods to reduce large amount of collisions on the media:

(i) CSMA/CD Carrier Sense Multiple Access/Collision Detection

- Used by Ethernet and 802.3
- Listens to cable prior to transmission
- Detects collisions and retransmits at random interval

(ii) CSMA/CA Carrier Sense Multiple Access/Collision Avoidance

- Used by Localtalk
- Listen to cable prior to transmission
- Avoids collisions by transmission and reception of RTS (Request to Send) and CTS (Clear to Send) packets.

Advantages

- Simple
- Little overhead
- Throughput is high at light loads

Disadvantages

- As load increases throughput drops sometimes to unacceptable levels.
- There is no guarantee that a station will be able to transmit (in theory)

2.4.2 Polling

Definition

Polling designates one device as a Master Controller who is in charge of who can transmit. The master queries each other device called secondaries or slaves to see if they have information to transmit.

One of the most common polling topologies is a star where the points of the star are secondary or slave machines and the master is the hub. This is a popular method to connect terminals to a terminal or communications controller.

Advantages

- Central control of channel access
- Priorities can be set
- Deterministic access to the media

Disadvantages

- Polling uses up a lot of bandwidth sending requests, acknowledgements and listening for messages
- Practical Implementation
- Assembly line or Robotic operation.

2.4.3 Token Passing

Definition

A special frame called a token is passed in an orderly manner from node to node. When a device has the token it temporarily had control of the media and can transmit. Passing the token distributes access control to each of the nodes attached to the media.

Each device knows whom it receives the token from and who to pass the token to when finished. Each device on the network gets the opportunity to receive the token. Devices can only hold the token for a short amount of time before relinquishing it.

Several popular token passing topologies are in use. IEEE 802.5 Token Ring and IEEE 802.4 Token Bus. FDDI (Fiber Distributed Data Interface) also uses a token like access scheme.

Advantages

- Token passing is deterministic and is suitable for controlling automated equipment.
- Token passing schemes allow for setting priority.
- When the channel load is increased, throughput increases as well. High loads do not decrease data throughput.
- Token passing may offer the highest data throughput under high load conditions.

Disadvantages

- Token passing requires complicated software in all devices. This makes the hardware and software used to operate a token passing access scheme more expensive than a Collision based scheme.

• • •

3

Reference Models : OSI and TCP/IP

3.1 Network Architecture

This is the network's design. The term architecture can refer to either hardware or software, or to a combination of hardware and software.

Definition

Architecture—*principal subsystems that make up a system.*
Architectural model—*shows the principal subsystems that make up a pictorial representation of the system (i.e., with the use of a block diagram).*
Abstract machine model—*models the interfacing of subsystems (sometimes called a layered model); organizes a system into a series of layers each of which provides a set of services and each layer defines an abstract machine that provides services to the next level of the abstract machine.*
Reference model—*derived from the study of the application domain and represent an idealized architecture that includes all the features that systems might incorporate. It may be used as a basis for implementation.*

3.2 Programs, Processes, Protocols And Layers

In the previous chapter, the various ways that computers and networks can be physically connected was described. However, network communication relies on more than simple hardware connections. Several layers of software components are also necessary to exchange data between applications on different linked computers. Peer-to-peer and client/server are the most common methods of communicating in a LAN.

The terms "program" or "application" means a complete set of routines that provide a high-level function of some sort. For example, a word processing application performs the general task of creating documents. However, that broad task is composed of many sub processes, such as opening files, saving files, copying and pasting text, or deleting data.

Therefore, we use the term "process" instead of "program" to refer to some subset of functions (still possibly quite complex) that fits into a larger program or is part of a large system. This distinction is important because some processes within a program are designed to communicate and cooperate with other processes over a network. The term process is used especially when talking about a program when it is executing (in operating systems [OSs], an executing program is a process). Each program or process provides a service to the end user or to another program or process.

For example, a World Wide Web (Web) browser provides a service to the user by retrieving Web pages from a Web server, then displaying them on the user's monitor.

But many different protocols may need to cooperate to provide a single service to a user. For example, when a Web server sends data to a Web browser, it uses Hypertext Transfer Protocol (HTTP) in conjunction with Transmission Control Protocol (TCP) and Internet Protocol (IP). Each of these protocols is a separate entity with its own specific functions. They provide services to each other, not directly to the end user. IP provides a service to TCP, TCP provides a service to HTTP, and so forth.

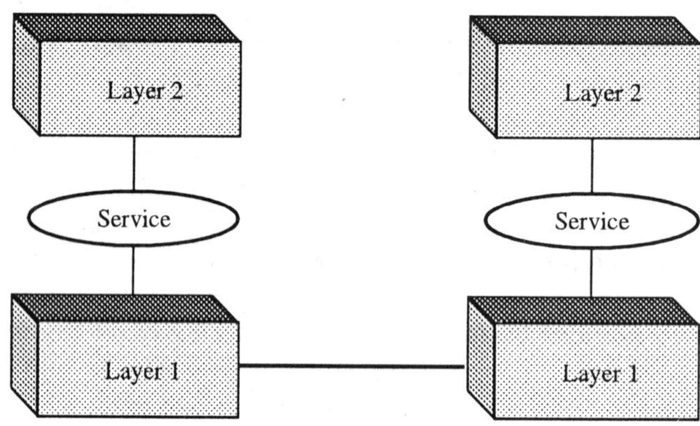

Fig. 3.1 Layered hierarchy

These interactions between processes and protocols form a layered hierarchy or protocol stack. In a protocol stack, each process uses the service of the process in the layer below it, and provides a service to a process in the layer above it.

3.3 Layer Structure And Protocol Hierarchies

In order to reduce the design complexity of network software and obtain the independence between software and hardware, we carry out a functional cutting of the whole communication process into **layers** or **abstraction levels**. A layer corresponds to a set of functions or processes coherent with each other and providing a given global function. Two adjacent layers have independent functions but they interconnect through what we call an **interface** : layers exchange data through interfaces. Let's take a concrete example : A washing machine! Let's consider the washing machine as a layer (its function is "to wash"). It is connected to two other layers—the electricity layer and the water layer. Interfaces are the socket and plug system and the water tube.

In computer networking terms, a layer is a process (or set of processes) that provides services to the next higher layer and uses the services of the next lower layer.

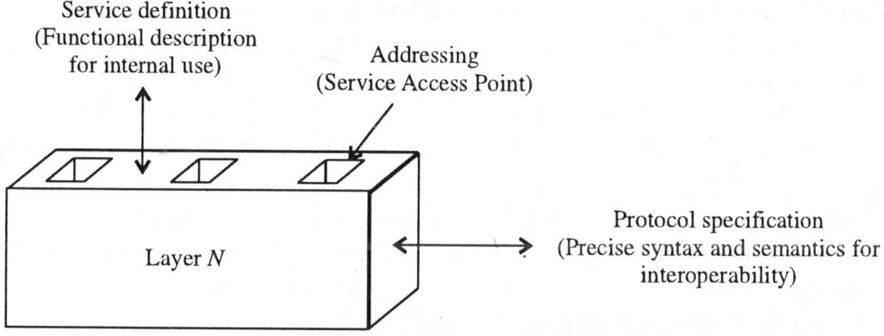

Fig. 3.2 Pictorial view of layer *N*

Protocols correspond to a given implementation of a layer. This model is actually based on the famous saying: "divide to reign". The set of layers and protocols is called **network architecture**. The set of protocols used by a system with one protocol per layer is called the **stack of protocols** (example of protocol stack : TCP/IP).

To work, each layer uses the previous one. Each layer must provide some services to the previous ones, without these latter to "know" the details of the implementation of these services. This guarantee that the whole system is modular and those implementations are independent with each other. In such a system, the layer *N* of a machine is in charge of the communication with the layer *N* of another machine using one or several protocols and underlying layers.

As we read earlier, two adjacent layers are connected together by an **interface**. This interface defines the services a lower layer provides to the upper layer. When designing a network architecture, and still in order to respect the independence of implementations, it is very important to define these interfaces. Layers must therefore carry out a very well defined set of functions. Later, we will see interfaces are developed around **primitives**.

3.3.1 Principles of Layer Design

As a machine may run several processes (or programs) that may use the network resources, and as a machine may communicate with many other processes, it is essential that every layer have a mechanism to identify senders (local processes) and receivers (remote processes).

There are few data transmission rules. A communication may indeed be carried out in many ways :

- **Simplex communication :** The data is carried only in one direction.
- **Semi-duplex communication :** The data can be carried in both directions, but not at the same time.
- **Duplex communication :** The data can be carried in both directions at the same time.

Then we must consider the quality of transmission: a layer must be able to detect errors due to physical communication circuits. There are a lot of error detection and correction systems, but both ends have to agree about the system to use. Besides, ends must have a system that allows them to send to the other an acknowledgment message to tell that the message has been correctly received. There is actually another quality issue: preserving of the order of messages. The sender must make possible for the receiver to reorder messages, for instance by numbering messages, but this does not explain how to order messages effectively.

Still another important issue: some processes are not able to handle message of any size. We must therefore provide reassembling, transmission and reassembling mechanisms. Such mechanisms may also be useful for the opposite problem : in order to improve the transmission rate, we may need to split a message into smaller parts. The receiving end must then be able to reassemble the small message into the big first one.

These issues are the most important we must consider when developing layer. We may however consider some others: receiving end congestion (this happens for instance when the sender is too fast), rational rule-based message routing, multiplexing problems (especially for the physical layer) when the underlying layer has a limited amount of transmission channels... .

The reasons for this division of network functions include the following:

- Layers divide the aspects of network operation into less complex elements.
- Layers define standard interfaces for plug-and-play compatibility.
- Layers enable engineers to specialize design and development efforts on modular functions.
- Layers promote symmetry in the different network modular functions so that they work together.
- Layers prevent changes in one area from affecting other areas, so each area can evolve more quickly.
- Layers divide the complexity of networking into separate, easy to learn operations.

3.3.2 Characteristics of Layers

- Multiple protocols and processes work together in a layered arrangement.
- Cooperating layers of protocols are called a "protocol stack" or a "protocol suite".
- In a protocol stack, the services offered by each layer progress from abstract, higher

level services in the top layers, to more concrete, transmission-oriented services in the bottom layers.

- Thus, a program that resides at the highest layer typically provides many sophisticated services to the user.
- However, most of these services are actually implemented, directly and indirectly, by the lower layers.
- Because a program provides services only to the layer above it and uses services only of the layer below it, a change to any given layer affects only the layer above it.
- Layering breaks a single large program into parts isolated from one another according to function, making the program easier to write and change.
- Layering does, however, extract a performance penalty.
- There is some overhead associated with moving data through multiple layers of protocols; however, the benefit is generally worth the performance price.
- Layering applies to protocols as well as services.
- In a system that has a layered architecture, each process communicates only with its peer process.
- Otherwise, as with services, a change to one process would affect many other processes.
- Each pair of peers communicates with a common protocol that is appropriate to the services they provide.
- Therefore, each layer of processes uses a corresponding layer of protocols. For example, in a Web interaction, TCP on the client communicates with TCP on the server. HTTP on the client communicates with HTTP on the server, and so forth.

When different layers of protocols work together, they use the following basic techniques:

Encapsulation—On the sending node, each protocol adds its own header to a message as it moves downward through the stack. Each header contains information that is useful to the receiving process. Thus, peer processes communicate through their respective protocol headers.

Segmentation—If a layer receives a message that is too long, it divides the message into manageable fragments.

Decapsulation—On the receiving node, each protocol removes its own protocol header before passing the encapsulated message up to the layer above.

Reassembly—If a message was segmented, one of the processes on the receiving end reassembles the segments into their correct order, then passes the restored message up to the layer above.

3.3.3 What Is A Protocol?

A protocol is an agreement on language, data formats, order, speed, etc, that layers on the same level use to communicate. It is basically a set of rules that governs the communications between computers on a network. These rules include guidelines that regulate the following characteristics of a network :

- Access method
- Allowed physical topologies
- Types of cabling
- Speed of data transfer.

Two devices or processes can exchange information when they both use the same protocol. Each type of process may use a different protocol, even when multiple processes are running on the same computing device. A communication protocol typically adds "administrative" data to the beginning of a message.

That non-message data is called a protocol header. A protocol header functions like an envelope or a packing label to describe the content of a message, its length, the identity of its sender or recipient, the time of day it was sent, and any other information that the communicating processes need to know about the message itself.

Simple example of protocol : an ordinary conversation between two friends. Actually, a given number of implicitly established rules regulate the conversation. For instance, these rules are: don't speak both at the same time and speak about the same subject. These rules form a protocol.

Key Elements of a Protocol

Syntax : Data formats and signal levels.
Semantics : Control information for coordination and error handling.
Timing : Speed matching and sequencing.

Protocol Architecture

It is layered structure of hardware and software to support exchange of data between systems/distributed applications. It states set of rules for transmission of data between systems. Usually there are one or more common protocols for every layer.

3.3.4 Characteristics of Protocols

1. Direct/indirect Communication

The direct communication includes point-to-point link and indirect communication includes switched communication network.

(a) Point-to-point link

- ☐ Two entities share a link, allowing direct communication.
- ☐ Entities may also connect through a number of intermediate hosts, bringing in the issue of access control, making the protocol more complex.

(b) Switched communications network

- ☐ Entities depend on other entities for data exchange.

- Entities may be connected over local network (Ethernet) or may belong to different networks. (Internet).

2. Monolithic/Structured Protocol

(a) Monolithic protocol

- All protocol logic (for every layer) is combined into one unit.
- Problem in changing any aspect of the protocol (such as virtual circuit request).

(b) Structured protocol

- Set of protocols with hierarchical/layered structure.
- Clearly shows the distinction between different layers of logic.

3. Symmetric/Asymmetric Protocol

(a) *Symmetric protocol* : It involves communication between peer entities.
(b) *Asymmetric protocol* : It involves client/server type of relationship.

4. Standard/nonstandard protoco

(a) *Standard protocols* : They are commonly accepted protocols that have been agreed on by a standards body.

(b) *Nonstandard protocol* : They are built for specific communications situation.

3.3.5 Functions of Protocols

1. Encapsulation

It states that data as well as control information are contained in each PDU (Protocol Data Unit). The specifics of the address are encapsulated into the message. The data from next higher layer and the control information is known as protocol data unit or PDU. Header in each transport PDU contains control information to be used by peer transport protocol at destination.

Examples of items in PDU :

Destination SAP (Service Access Point) : Address information for destination transport layer for data delivery.

Sequence Number : Allows assembly of messages from packets that arrive out of order.

Error-detection code : Extra information embedded by the transmitting transport entity to allow receiver to perform error detection and correction.

2. Segmentation and Reassembly

The segmentation implies to segment the data stream into small bounded size blocks or PDUs.

Reasons for Segmentation

- Communications network may accept data blocks only up to a certain size (53 octets for ATM, 1526 octets for Ethernet).

- Efficient error control with smaller PDU size; fewer bits retransmitted in the event of failure.
- Better access to shared transmission facilities, with shorter delay; nobody can monopolize the network.
- Smaller buffers at receiver stations.
- Can pause transfer for checkpoint and recovery.

Disadvantages with segmentation

- Larger overhead with smaller PDU size.
- More interrupts as PDUs announce their arrival.
- More time spent to process smaller PDUs.

The reassembly states that segmented data is reassembled into messages appropriate for application level.

3. Connection Control

There are two kinds of data transfer that are as follows:

(a) **Connectionless data transfer :** In such transfer each PDU is independent of other PDUs.

(b) **Connection-oriented data transfer :** It is used if stations are to be connected for long time or protocol details are to be worked out dynamically. It is also known as logical association, or virtual circuit, with three phases:

1. **Establish connection :** One station issues a connection request to the other, with or without involving a central authority. The receiver may accept or reject the connection. The request may include negotiating syntax, semantics, and timing of protocol. The protocol may have some options to be negotiated at connection time, such as PDU size.
2. **Transfer data :** Exchange data and control information (flow control, error control). Data flows in one direction while acknowledgements flow in the other.
3. **Terminate connection :** Either side may terminate connection by sending a request. The connection may be terminated by a central authority. The PDUs are sequentially numbered as they are sent. Each side keeps track of outgoing numbers (generated locally), and incoming numbers (generated by other host).

4. Ordered delivery

PDUs may not arrive in order in which they are sent. The connection-oriented protocols require the PDU order to be maintained. So the PDUs are numbered sequentially as they are generated. There is a problem if sequence numbers repeat after over flow.

5. Flow control

It is the function of receiving entity to limit the amount of data sent by transmitter. This is achieved by a technique known as stop-and-wait. In this each PDU must be acknowledged before next one can be sent. It is implemented in several protocols.

6. Error control

It guards against loss or damage of data and control information. It is implemented as error detection and retransmission. The detection of error by receiver makes him discard the PDU. No acknowledgement by the receiver makes the sender retransmit the PDU. Also with error correction code, the receiver may be able to correct the error at destination.

7. Addressing

Addressing Level : It is the level in the communications architecture at which an entity is named. The network-level address or IP address used to route a PDU through network (also called Network Service Access Point or NSAP). Upon arrival at destination, the PDU must be routed to port or Service Access Point (SAP) for the application.

Addressing scope :

Global address:

- **Global nonambiguity**—One system to one address but possible to have more than one address for the system.
- **Global applicability**—Any system can be identified from anywhere.

A port may not be unique in the network unless attached to a system (think of SMTP port on every system in a network)

Connection identifiers : Useful for connection-oriented data transfer (virtual circuit) but meaningless for connectionless data transfer (datagram). They are identified by a connection name during the data transfer phase.

Addressing mode

- Individual or unicast address {reference to a single system or port}
- Multicast or broadcast address

8. Multiplexing

It implies combining several signals for transmission on some shared medium. It is possible to have multiple virtual circuits terminating into a single end system. It can also be accomplished via port names. Different types of multiplexing are as follows:

Upward multiplexing : Multiple higher-level connections are multiplexed on a single lower-level connection. It includes connecting your PC to ISP for multiple applications, including web, email, telnet, ftp etc.

Downward multiplexing : Split a single higher-level connection over a number of lower-level connections. It is useful for reliability, performance, or efficiency.

9. Transmission services

It includes additional services, such as priority, quality of service, and security.

3.3.6 Different Types of Addresses Used by Protocols

Each protocol may use a different type of address to direct a message to the correct process on the intended destination device. These addresses fall into two general categories:

(1) Physical address
(2) Logical address

Physical Addresses

A physical address is a unique identifier hard-coded into the NIC (Network Interface Card) of each node. Its other common names are:

- Hardware address
- NIC (or adapter) address
- Medium Access Control (MAC) address
- Data Link address

The designers of the most popular MAC-layer protocols (Ethernet, Token Ring, and Fiber Distributed Data Interface [FDDI]) have allocated 48 bits for the hardware address. Each NIC comes with a hardware address preconfigured from the factory. NIC manufacturers register hardware addresses with a worldwide central authority to guarantee the numbers they assign do not conflict with those of any other manufacturer. This guarantees that each hardware address is globally unique. It would be natural to want to associate the term "physical address" with the Physical Layer.

However, the Physical Layer is only concerned with transmitting and receiving bits from the physical medium, and does not "see" bits as organized into meaningful patterns, such as an address. The physical address, or hardware address, is actually processed by OSI Layer 2, the Data Link Layer. (OSI model to be discussed in the next section) This hardware address is the address ultimately required for frames to be delivered to a destination network node.

Logical Addresses

Lgical addresses are symbolic identifiers. These are assigned by software and are used by processes operating at OSI Layer 3 and above. There are two primary types of logical addresses:

- Network addresses, such as an IP address. (e.g., 234.25.54.8)
- Port or process addresses, such as a port number. (e.g., Port 25)

Data often starts out (at the higher layers) addressed to some symbolic name, such as the host name in the command Telnet Serverhost. The name "serverhost" is the logical address of the destination the user is attempting to contact using the telnet (TCP/IP) application and protocol. But if the message is actually to be delivered to this host, the sending computer must somehow discover the destination's physical address. In this case, an intermediate logical address (the IP address) will first be derived from the symbolic name using some sort of a name service process, such as Domain Name System (DNS).

Then a protocol such as Address Resolution Protocol (ARP) can find the hardware address that corresponds to that IP address. When the sending node knows all of these addresses, it can finally transmit the data to its destination. The most important fact to remember about logical addresses is that a logical address will not get the information "into the box". Only a hardware address used by the Data Link Layer, whether a broadcast address, multicast (group) address, or unicast (individual) address, can physically deliver a frame to the destination device.

3.3.7 Layers of Addresses

Physical and logical addresses work together to transmit information from source to destination within a segment of a network. As an example, consider how a Web server returns data in response to a client request.

- The server responds by sending a frame of information across an Ethernet network to the client that made the request.
- The HTTP process running on the server creates an HTTP header that contains protocol information used to communicate with the peer HTTP process running on the client.
- HTTP on the server uses TCP to establish a connection with the client, and reliably transfer the HTTP response to the client software.
- Thus, the TCP process running on the Web server communicates with the TCP process running on the client.
- TCP on the server communicates with IP on the server to transmit the TCP message across the network, packet by packet.
- IP on the Web server indirectly communicates with its IP peer on the client.
- IP on the Web server also communicates with the Web server's Ethernet driver.
- The Ethernet driver is responsible for transmitting a frame of information, consisting of the packet and message, to the next node in the network across a physical link.
- It does this by relying on the services of the Ethernet NIC and the Physical Layer (the cables and connectors).
- In this scenario, three addresses are used by the sending and receiving computers to communicate between application processes.
- At the lowest level, the Ethernet processes, located on the NICs of the server and client, use Ethernet physical addresses to transmit a frame from NIC to NIC.
- Each frame contains an IP packet, or portion of a packet.
- IP addresses indicate which host on the network should get each packet located inside the Ethernet frame.
- Each packet contains a TCP message, or portion of a message.

- As the receiving IP process receives all packets that make up the TCP message, it passes the messages or fragments up to TCP.
- TCP reassembles the original message, and then passes it to the destination software process address (port).

3.4 Interfaces And Services

The goal of every layer is to provide services to the upper layer. In this case, we say the underlying layer is a service provider to the upper layer, which is a service user. Active elements of a layer are called entities. These entities can be software entities (a process for instance) or hardware entities (a chip for instance). Entities from the same layer N of two different machines are called peer entities.

Services of a layer N can be reach using service access points (SAP). Each SAP is uniquely identified by an address. Typically, SAPs of the phone network are phone sockets and addresses are simply phone numbers.

In order to make two adjacent layers to communicate, some rules must be set up for the interface. An entity from the layer $N + 1$ gives to an entity of the layer N an Interface Data Unit (IDU) through the SAP. The IDU is actually made up with 2 things: a Service Data Unit (SDU) and some Interface Control Information (ICI):

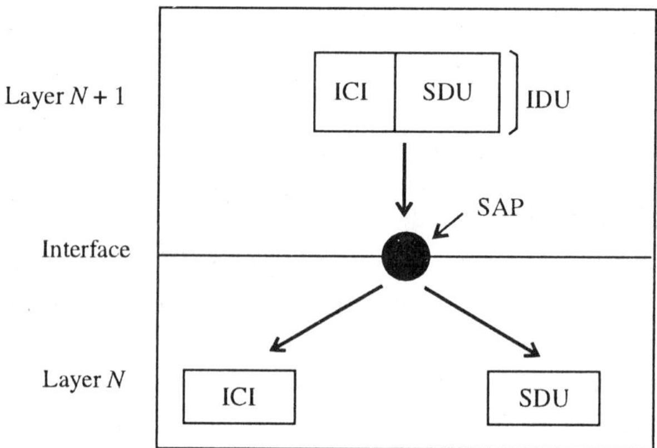

Fig. 3.3 Communication between layers is done through interface

The SDU is the data that 2-peer entities exchange, but it is also what the layer $N + 1$ of the sender gives to the layer N. The control information is used to help the lower layer. It is for example the number of bytes contained in the SDU (this can be used in the function that controls data integrity).

To send a SDU, a layer N might need to split it into several parts. When exchanging this data with its peer entity, every piece of data is fitted with a Protocol Control Information (PCI) contained in a header, and then sent as a Protocol Data Unit (PDU). Headers are used by peer entities to carry their peer protocol. This PDU then becomes the SDU for the layer N and is going to be sent to the layer $N - 1$ via the SAP. Here is how all this works:

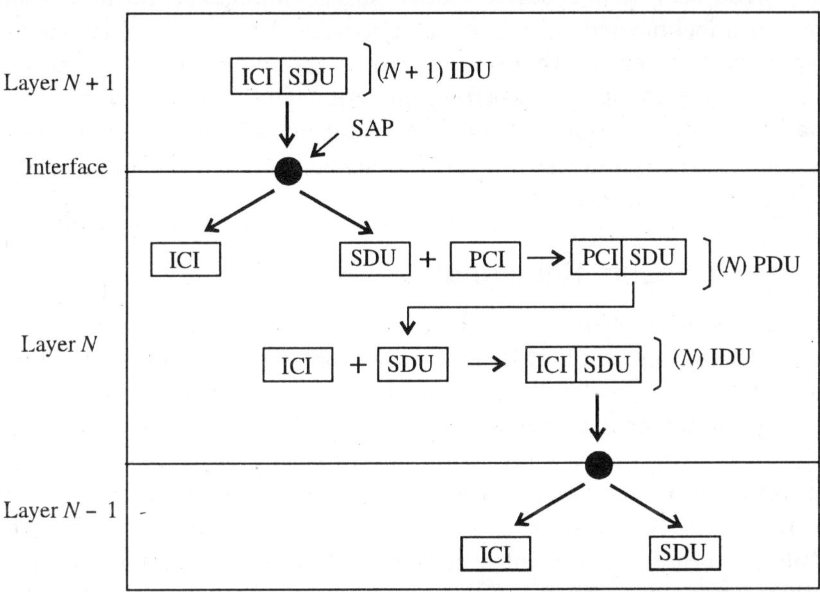

Fig. 3.4 Communication between layers

Finally, all messages fit together. This mechanism is often described as a wrapping mechanism.

3.4.1 Service Primitives

A service is formally a set of primitives or operations a user or other entities can invoke to access the service. That is what materializes an interface. We commonly classify service primitives into four classes:

Primitive	Meaning
Request	An entity is requesting a service (we are requesting a connection to a remote computer)
Indication	An entity is informed of an event (the receiver has just received a connection request)
Response	An entity is responding to an event (the receiver is sending the permission to connect)
Confirm	An entity acknowledges the response to its request (the sender acknowledge the permission to connect to the remote host)

Most primitives need parameters. For instance, parameters of a CONNECT. request (used to query a connection) are the machine you want to connect to, the service you want to use (FTP, telnet...) and the maximum size of exchanged packets.

An acknowledged service is a service that requires a request, an indication, a response and a confirm. An unacknowledged service is a service that requires only a request and an indication. Typically, the service that establishes a connection is an acknowledged service because the peer entity must agree to set the connection. On the other hand, data transmission may be an unacknowledged service, whether we want an acknowledgement or not.

On an implementation point of view, primitives correspond to functions we can use in a program to access a given service.

3.4.2 Services/Protocols Relations

When thinking about network protocols, it is important to distinguish between *service* and *protocols*. A *service* is a high level, abstract description of the functionality provided, while a *protocol* is the specific set of rules that specify the meaning of messages exchanged by peer entities. A protocol implements a service.

A service is a set of primitives a layer provides to the upper layer. The service defines the operations a layer may realize, but it does not tell how these operations are really realized. The most characteristic element of a service is the interface between two adjacent layers.

Conversely, a protocol is a set of rules that applies to the meaning and format of messages exchanged between two peer entities. Entities use protocols to implement service specifications. A service may therefore remain the same with two different protocols.

Protocols and services are different, but they are close to each other. We must not confuse. A service is rather an abstract notion, although the protocol corresponds to what really happens. This distinction actually answers to modern programming and implementation requirements. It is equivalent to making the distinction between an algorithm and its implementation.

3.4.3 Connection-Oriented Services and Connectionless Services

Layers may provide : Connection oriented service or **connectionless service** to the upper layers. The user is generally most concerned about which service that is given end-to-end, but the same alternatives may in principle be provided by any layers.

Connection Oriented Service : like e.g., the telephone. The various tasks performed in this are as follows:

1. Establish a connection (dial and get an answer).
2. Communicate over the connection (speak).
3. Delete the connection (hang up).

You get a "pipe" between the endpoints. You do not have to put an address on each piece of data, the address was provided at connection establishment. The pipe might transfer a sequence of messages (with recognizable boundaries) or a sequence of bits. Normally the transfer is reliable (no data lost or duplicated). Normally the order is maintained.

The connection-oriented service requires a connection to be set between two points. The receiver then expects the sender to transmit data. At the end of the transmission, the connection is stopped.

Connectionless Service : A complete address must be put on each message, e.g., like on letters (snail-mails). There is normally no guarantee that messages arrive in the same order they are sent. The service may be reliable or unreliable; the latter is called **datagram service**. Datagram service may offer acknowledgements to the sender when a message is delivered : "Acknowledged Datagram Service". Then you know what was delivered and what was lost. A reply might also be required : "Request-Reply".

The connectionless service is characterized by the independence of transmitted messages. Someone can receive a message without being aware of it. Messages can then follow different routes. The consequence is that we can receive messages in an inverted order. The typical example for this kind of service is the mail system: someone writes a letter and sends it without warning the addressee. This letter may then arrive after a second letter the same guy may have sent to the same addressee. Routes followed by these two letters may be different.

3.4.4 Interface

It is basically the way to access the service that each layer provides to above layers. It is typically a set of commands or procedures. **Interfaces** are an agreement between different layers in the same host. **Protocols** are an agreement between the same layers on different hosts.

In a network, all layers at a certain level must use the same protocol, but the interfaces between layers on different hosts might be different. In each layer there is normally a process that manages the communication. Processes on the same level (on different hosts) are called peer processes.

What type of service fits what application data?

Reliable message stream	:	Sequence of pages
Reliable byte stream	:	Remote login
Unreliable connection	:	Digitized voice
Unreliable datagram	:	Electronic junk mail
Acknowledged datagram	:	Registered mail
Request-reply	:	Database query

3.5 Reference Models

Now that we have discussed layered networks, it is time to look at some examples. In the next two sections we will discuss two important network architectures:

1. OSI reference model
2. TCP/IP reference model

3.6 Open Systems Interconnection—Reference Model (OSI-RM)

The complexity of modern computer networks has given rise to several conceptual models for explaining how networks work. One of the most common of these models is the International Standards Organization's Open Systems Interconnection (OSI) Reference Model, also referred to as the OSI seven-layer model. The model is called ISO OSI because it deals with connecting open systems i.e., systems that are open for communication with other systems. It is an abstract description of the digital communications between application processes running in distinct systems. The model employs a hierarchical structure of seven layers. Each layer performs value-added service at the request of the adjacent higher layer and, in turn, requests more basic services from the adjacent lower layer.

The OSI reference model illustrates the networking process as being divided into seven layers that are stated as follows:

Media Layers : Controls physical delivery of the message over the network.

1. Physical Layer
2. Data Link Layer
3. Network Layer

Host Layers : Provide accurate data delivery between computers.

4. Transport Layer
5. Session Layer
6. Presentation Layer
7. Application Layer

This theoretical construct makes it easier to learn and understand the concepts involved. At the top of the model is the application that requires access to a resource on the network, and at the bottom is the network medium itself. As data moves down through the layers of the model, the various protocols operating there prepare and package it for transmission over the network. Once the data arrives at its destination, it moves up through the layers on the receiving system, where the same protocols perform the same process in reverse.

Levels 1 through 3 are network-specific, and differ depending on what physical network you are using. Levels 4 through 7 comprise network-independent, higher-level functions. Each layer describes a particular function (instead of a specific protocol) that occurs in data communications.

The upper 5 layers are software only

Layer 2 is hardware and software

Layer 1 is hardware only

The seven layers function from lowest level (machine level) to highest level (the level at which most human interaction takes place), as follows:

Application	Comprise the applications that use the network.
Presentation	Ensures that data is presented to the applications in a consistent fashion.
Session	Manages the connections between applications.
Transport	Ensures error-free data transmission.
Network	Manages the connections to other machines on the network.
Data Link	Provides reliable delivery of data across the physical layer (which is usually inherently unreliable).
Physical	Describes the physical media of the network. For example, the fiber optic cable required for a Fiber Distributed Data Interface (FDDI) network is part of the physical layer.

3.6.1 Evolution of OSI

The International Standards Organization, based in Geneva, Switzerland, is a multinational body of representatives from the standards-setting agencies of about 30 countries. These agencies include the American National Standards Institute (ANSI) and British Standards Institute (BSI). Because of the multinational nature of Europe, and their critical need for intersystem communication, the market for OSI-based products is particularly strong there. As a result, the European Computer Manufacturers' Association (ECMA) has played a major role in developing the OSI standards. In fact, European networking vendors and users are generally further advanced in their OSI implementations than are their American counterparts, who rely principally on proprietary solutions such as IBM's Systems Network Architecture (SNA) or the Internet's transmission Control Protocol/Internet Protocol (TCP/IP).

Creating the OSI standards has been a long, drawn-out process : The ISO began work on OSI protocols in the late 1970s, finally releasing its seven-layer architecture in 1984. It wasn't until 1988 that the five-step standards-setting process finally resulted in stabilized protocols for the upper layers of the OSI reference model. As the OSI protocols continue to stabilize, the marketplace will encourage vendors to become more compliant. In turn, OSI will continue it's evolution-incorporating the technological advances that inevitably occur in the electronics marketplace.

3.6.2 A brief introduction to the OSI Reference Model

The Open System Interconnection (OSI) model is a set of protocols that attempt to define and standardize the data communications process. The OSI model is set by the International Standards Organization (ISO). The OSI model is a concept that describes how data communications should take place. It divides the process into seven groups, called layers. The OSI model is not a single definition of how data communications actually takes place in the real world. Numerous protocols may exist at each layer. The OSI model states how the process should be divided and what protocols should be used at each layer. If a network vendor implements one of the protocols at each layer, its network components should work with other vendors' offerings.

The OSI model is modular. Each successive layer of the OSI model works with the one above and below it. At least in theory, you may substitute one protocol for another at the same layer without affecting the operation of layers above or below. For example, Token Ring or Ethernet hardware should operate with multiple upper-layer services, including the transport protocols, network operating system, internetwork protocols, and applications interfaces. However, for this interoperability to work, vendors must create products to meet the OSI model's specifications.

Although each layer of the OSI model provides its own set of functions, it is possible to group the layers into two distinct categories.

The first four layers—physical, data link, network, and transport provide the end-to-end services necessary for the transfer of data between two systems. These layers provide the protocols associated with the communications network used to link two computers together.

The top three layers—the application, presentation, and session layers provide the application services required for the exchange of information. That is, they allow two applications, each running on a different node of the network, to interact with each other through the services provided by their respective operating systems.

Two important terms in this chapter are:

- International Standards Organization : **ISO**—*(A bunch of people)*.
- Open Standards Interconnect : **OSI**—*(A bunch of documents)*.

The International Standards Organization (ISO) developed a theoretical model of how networks should behave and how they are put together. The ISO's model is used through the industry today to describe various networking issues. It is also of use in a learning or training environment where a novice can use it as a point of reference to learn how various technologies interact, where they reside, what functions they perform and how each protocol communicates with other protocols. This model is called the Open Standards Interconnect (OSI) Model.

Most of the protocols in common use today pre-date the OSI model, so they don't conform exactly to the seven-layer structure. In most cases, single protocols combine the functions of two or more of the layers in the model, and the boundaries between protocols often don't exactly conform to the layer boundaries of the OSI model. However, the model remains an excellent tool for studying the networking process, and professionals frequently make reference to functions and protocols associated with specific layers.

The standards and protocols associated with the OSI reference model are the cornerstone of the open systems concept for linking the literally dozens of dissimilar computers found in offices throughout the world.

3.6.3 What is OSI and what is not ?

While discussing the OSI reference model it is important to understand what the model does not specify as well as what it actually spells out. The ISO created the OSI reference model solely to describe the external behavior of electronics systems, not their internal functions.

The reference model does not determine programming or operating system functions, nor does it specify an application-programming interface (API). Neither does it dictate the end-user interface-that is, the command-line and/or icon-based prompts a user uses to interact with a computer system. OSI merely describes what is placed on a network cable and when it will be placed there. It does not state how vendors must build their computers, only the kinds of behavior these systems may exhibit while performing certain communications operations.

The OSI standards can be grouped into pairs-one defines the services offered by a network component, while the second specifies the protocol used by that component to provide the defined service. This concept permits a vendor to develop network elements that are more or less ignorant of the other components on the network. They are said to be ignorant in that they may need to know that other network components exist, but not the specific details about their operating systems or interface buses. One of the primary benefits of this concept is that vendors can change the internal design of their network components without affecting their network functionality, as long as they maintain the OSI-prescribed external attributes.

Connection Types

The OSI model is inherently connection-oriented, but the services each OSI layer provides can either be connection-oriented, or connectionless. In the three-step connection-oriented mode operation (the steps are connection establishment, data transfer, and connection release), an explicit binding between two systems takes place. In connectionless operation, no such explicit link occurs. Data transfer takes place with no specified connection and disconnection function occurring between the two communicating systems. Connectionless communication is also known as datagram communication.

KEY POINTS ABOUT OSI MODEL

- A layered model used to implement a layered data communications system.
- Each layer performs a subset of the required communication functions.
- Each layer relies on the next lower layer to perform more primitive functions.
- Each layer provides services to the next higher layer.
- Changes in one layer should not require changes in other layers.
- OSI is not a product!
- May be used to implement a layered data communications system.
- Establish a common reference for standards development.
- May result in qualify “open” products with the use of these standards.

3.6.4 The OSI Environment

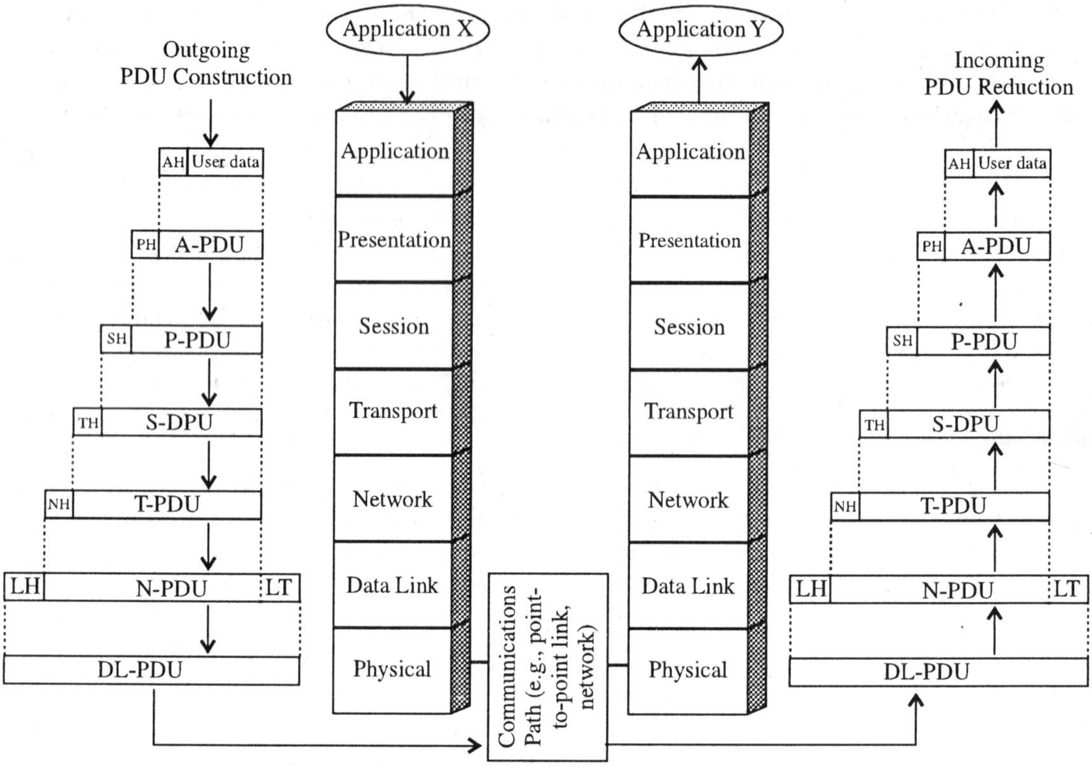

Outgoing
PDU Construction
AH User data
PH A-PDU
SH P-PDU
TH S-DPU
NH T-PDU
LH N-PDU LT
DL-PDU
Application X
Application
Presentation
Session
Transport
Network
Data Link
Physical
Communications
Path (e.g., point-
to-point link,
network)
Application Y
Application
Presentation
Session
Transport
Network
Data Link
Physical
Incoming
PDU Reduction
AH User data
PH A-PDU
SH P-PDU
TH S-DPU
NH T-PDU
LH N-PDU LT
DL-PDU

Fig. 3.5 Transmission in OSI Model

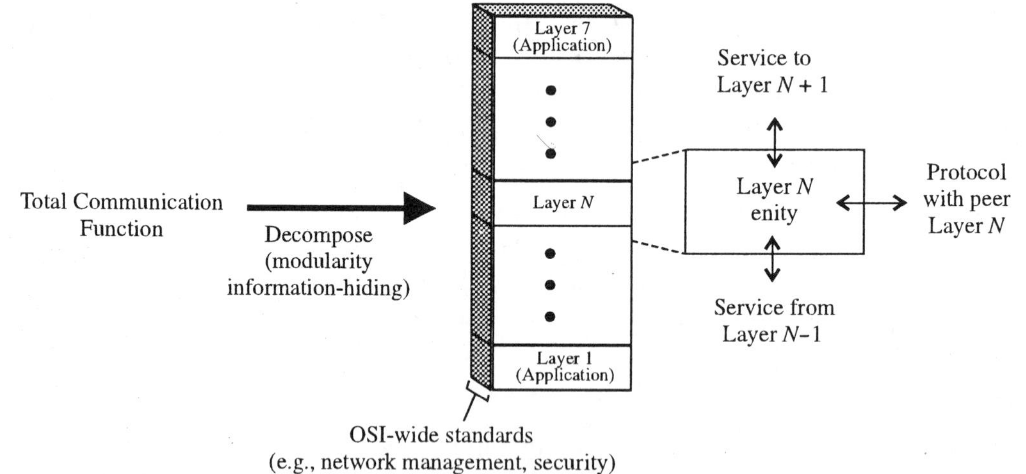

Fig. 3.6 Structure of layers

OSI as Framework for Standardization

The reasons for layering the functions include the following:

1. **Accelerates evolutions**—Improvements can be made on a modular level, without affecting other areas of the network.
2. **Ensures interoperable technology**—Changing or upgrading a service on one layer can be done without forcing change on another layer.
3. **Reduces complexity**—By breaking up network communication into smaller parts. When different level of abstraction is needed a layer should be created.
4. **Standardizes interfaces**—Creates an "open environment" so that multiple vendors' products can be incorporated into a network. The role of each layer should be preferred with an eye towards defining internationally standardized protocols.
5. **Facilitates learning**—By making the process easier to comprehend.

The OSI model itself is not network architecture because in each layer it does not define the exact services and protocols to be used. It just tells function of each layer. However, ISO has also created standard for all the layers, although these are not part of the reference model itself.

3.6.5 Functions of Layers

The functions of various layers are discussed below:

1. Physical Layer

The physical layer, at the bottom of the OSI model, is, as the name implies, the layer that defines the nature of the network's hardware elements, such as what medium the network uses, how the network is installed, and the nature of the signals used to transmit binary data over the network. So the Physical layer provides for physical connectivity between networked devices. Transmission and receipt of data from the physical medium is managed at this layer. It defines the electrical, mechanical, procedural, and functional specifications for activating, maintaining, and deactivating the physical link between end systems. The transmission of data is accomplished through the use of such things as wires, connectors, and voltages. Repeaters operate at the Physical layer.

The Physical layer receives data from the Data Link Layer, and transmits it to the wire. The Physical layer controls frequency, amplitude, phase modulation of the signal used for transmitting data, and performs demodulation and decoding upon receipt.

The physical layer is responsible for two jobs:

1. Communication with the Data link layer.
2. Transmission and receipt of data.

The physical layer also defines what kind of network interface adapter must be installed in each computer and what kind of hubs (if any) to use. Physical layer options include various types of copper or fiber optic cable, as well as many different wireless solutions. In the case of a LAN, the physical layer specifications are directly related to the data-link layer protocol used by the network. When you select a data-link layer protocol, you must use one of the physical layer specifications supported by that protocol.

The other communications element found at the physical layer is the particular type of signaling that is used to transmit data over the network medium. For copper-based cables, these signals are electrical charges. For fiber optic cables, the signals are pulses of light. Other types of network media can use radio frequencies, infrared pulses, and other types of signals. In addition to the physical nature of the signals, the physical layer dictates the signaling scheme that the computers use. The signaling scheme is the pattern of electrical charges or light pulses used to encode the binary data generated by the upper layers. Ethernet systems use a signaling scheme called Manchester encoding, and Token Ring systems use a scheme called Differential Manchester.

Summary of the major functions and services performed by the physical layer is as follows:

1. The Physical Layer provides the service of transmitting a signal, across a physical communication medium that represents binary bits. It is concerned with transmitting raw bits over a communication channel. It is concerned with ensuring that when one sends a "1" bit, the other side receives a "1" bit.
2. It defines
   - Electrical Properties
   - Transmission Media
   - Transmission Devices
   - Physical Topologies
   - Data signaling
   - Data synchronization
   - Data Bandwith
3. The transmission media can be a copper cable (coaxial or twisted pair), a fiber optic cable, or a radio channel.
4. The Physical Layer includes the following types of hardware devices that send and receive signals over each type of physical medium:
   (a) NICs
   (b) Fiber optic transceivers
   (c) Radio transceivers
   (d) Modms
5. Physical Layer processes are concerned only with the physical signals that represent data bits.
6. Thus, they are only "aware" of signals over the medium, and are not concerned with any device that may be at the other end of the wire or channel.
7. This also means that Layer 1 processes cannot detect errors in data transmission.
8. Most error detection, and all error correction, is the responsibility of higher layers.

9. Four important characteristics
   (a) **Mechanical :** Physical properties of the interface to transmission medium.
   (b) **Electrical :** Representation of bits in terms of voltage levels.
   (c) **Functional :** Functions of individual circuits of physical interface between a system and transmission medium.
   (d) **Procedural :** Sequence of events by which bit streams are exchanged.

2. Data Link Layer

Data link Layer is the second layer of the OSI model. The data link layer performs various functions depending upon the hardware protocol used, but has four primary functions:

1. Communication with the Network layer above.
2. Segmentation of upper layer datagram (also called packets) into frames in sizes that can be handled by the communications hardware.
3. Bit Ordering Organizing the pattern of data bits before transmission (packet formatting)
4. Communication with the Physical layer below:

This layer provides reliable transit of data across a physical link. The data link layer is concerned with physical addressing, network topology, physical link management, error notification, ordered delivery of frames, and flow control.

The IEEE has divided this layer into two sublayers:

1. The MAC sublayer
2. The LLC sublayer.

Bridges and Switches operate at the data link layer. The protocol at the data-link layer is the medium between the computer's networking hardware and its networking software. Network layer protocols pass their outgoing data down to the data-link layer protocol, which packages it for transmission over the network. When the other systems on the network receive the transmitted data, their data-link layer protocols process it and pass it up to the network layer.

When it comes to designing and building a LAN, the data-link layer protocol you choose is the single most important factor in determining what hardware you buy and how you install it. To implement a data-link layer protocol, you need the following hardware and software:

- Network interface adapters. (When an adapter is a discrete card plugged into a bus slot, it is referred to as a network interface card or NIC.)
- Network adapter drivers.
- Network cables (or other media) and ancillary connecting hardware.
- Network hubs. (in some cases)

By far the most popular data-link layer LAN protocol in use today (and throughout the history of the LAN) is Ethernet. Token Ring is a distant second, followed by other protocols such as the Fiber Distributed Data Interface (FDDI).

Data-link layer protocol specifications typically include the following three basic elements:

- A format for the frame. (that is, the header and footer applied to the network layer data before transmission)
- A mechanism for controlling access to the network medium.
- One or more physical layer specifications for use with the protocol.

Frame Format

The data-link layer protocol encapsulates the data it receives from the network layer protocol by adding a header and footer to it, forming what is called a frame (see Figure 3.7). Using the mail analogy given earlier, the header and footer are the equivalent of the envelope that you use to mail a letter. They contain the address of the system sending the packet and the address of its destination system. The addresses are referred to as hardware addresses or media access control (MAC) addresses, to distinguish them from addresses used at other layers of the OSI model.

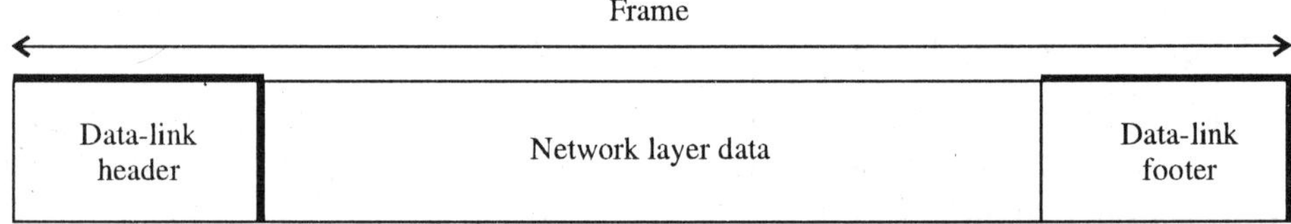

Fig. 3.7 A typical data-link layer protocol frame contains source and destination address fields, a network layer protocol identifier, and error detection information.

Media Access Control

One of the main functions of the data-link layer protocol is to provide a mechanism that regulates access to the network medium. This mechanism, called a *media access control (MAC) mechanism*, provides each computer with an equal opportunity to transmit its data while minimizing the occurrence of packet collisions.

The MAC mechanism is one of the primary defining characteristics of a data-link layer protocol. Ethernet uses a MAC mechanism called Carrier Sense Multiple Access with Collision Detection (CSMA/CD). Several other protocols, including Token Ring, use a scheme called token passing.

Physical Layer Specifications

The data-link layer protocols used on LANs often support more than one network medium, and the protocol standard includes one or more physical layer specifications.

Summary of the major functions and services performed by the data link layer is as follows:

1. It provides means of activating, maintaining and deactivating a reliable link.

2. It addresses groups of bits to a device located across a single physical transmission path, called a link.
3. Each group of bits that the Data Link Layer transmits is called a frame. A frame is a bit sequence that starts and finishes with a certain (unique) bit pattern.
4. To form a frame, the Data Link Layer encapsulates a Network Layer packet within a header and trailer.
5. The header contains the hardware address of the destination node.
6. The trailer contains a Frame Check Sequence (FCS) value that the receiving node uses for error detection.
7. The Data Link Layer is the only OSI layer that adds a trailer to the data it transmits.
8. Each frame carries a packet of data across a single physical link.
9. The encapsulated packet does not change, but a new frame is built around the packet for the trip across each link.
10. Thus, we often say that the Data Link Layer is concerned with transmitting data to the next node in the network.
11. It provides mechanisms for error detection and correction. If we wish error-free transfer at this level, there must be some resending scheme, but normally an error report to the receiver is sufficient. It guarantees that the delivered data is correct, but not that all data is delivered.
12. Popular Data Link protocols include :
    (a) High-Level Data Link Control (HDLC)
    (b) Synchronous Data Link Control (SDLC)
    (c) Link Access Procedure for *D*-channel (LAPD), used in ISDN
    (d) LAN protocols such as Ethernet, Token Ring, and FDDI
    (e) WAN protocols such as frame relay, ATM and ISDN

3. Network Layer

This layer provides connectivity and path selection between two end systems. The network layer is the layer at which routing occurs. Internet Protocol (IP), Internet Control Message Protocol (ICMP) and Internet Group Management Protocol (IGMP) all function at the Network layer. Outbound data is passed down from the Transport layer, is encapsulated in the Network layer's protocol and then sent to the Data link layer for segmentation and transmission.

Inbound data is de-fragmented in the correct order, the IP headers are removed and then the assembled datagram is passed to the Transport layer.

The Network layer is concerned with the following primary functions:

1. Communication with the Transport layer above.
2. Management of connectivity and routing between hosts or networks.
3. Communication with the Data link layer below.

At first glance, the network layer seems to duplicate some of the functions of the data-link layer. This is not so, however, because network layer protocols are responsible for end-to-end communications, while data-link layer protocols function only on the local LAN. To say that network layer protocols are responsible for end-to-end communications means that the network layer protocol is responsible for a packet's complete journey from the system that created it to its final destination. Depending on the nature of the network, the source and destination systems can be on the same LAN, on different LANs in the same building or on LANs separated by thousands of miles. When you connect to a server on the Internet, for example, the packets your computer creates may pass through dozens of different networks before reaching their destination. The data-link layer protocol may change many times to accommodate those dozens of networks, but the network layer protocol remains intact throughout the trip.

Like the data-link layer protocol, the network layer protocol applies a header to the data it receives from the layer above it, as shown in figure 3.8. The unit of data created by the network layer protocol, which consists of the transport layer data plus the network header, is called a *datagram*.

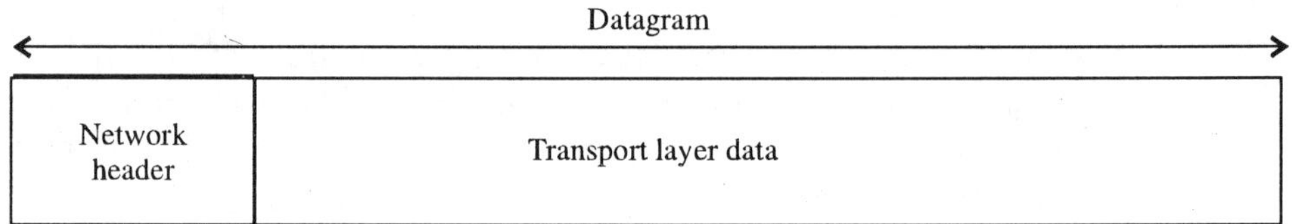

Fig. 3.8 The network layer protocol packages transport layer information into a datagram.

The functions associated with the network layer are discussed below:

(i) Addressing

The network layer protocol header contains source address and destination address fields, just as the data-link layer protocol does. However, in this case, the destination address is the packet's final destination, which may be different from the data-link layer protocol header's destination address. For example, when you type the address of a Web site in your browser, the packet your system generates contains the address of the Web server as its network layer destination, but the data-link layer destination is the address of the router on your LAN that provides you with Internet access.

IP has its own addressing system that is completely separate from the data-link layer addresses. Each computer on an IP network is assigned a 32-bit IP address by an administrator or an automated service.

(ii) Fragmenting

Network layer datagrams may have to pass through many different networks on the way to their destinations, and the data-link layer protocols that the datagrams encounter can have different properties and limitations. One of these limitations is the maximum packet size permitted by the protocol.

During the fragmentation process, the network layer protocol splits the datagram into as many pieces as necessary to make them small enough for transmission using the data-link layer protocol. Each fragment becomes a datagram in itself that continues the journey to the network layer destination. The fragments are not reassembled until all of the datagrams that make up the transmission reach the destination system. In some cases, datagrams may be fragmented, and their fragments may be fragmented again repeatedly before reaching their destination.

(iii) Routing

Routing is the process of directing a datagram from its source, through an inter-network, and to its ultimate destination using the most efficient path possible. On complex internetworks such as the Internet or a large corporate network, there are often many possible routes to a given destination. The designers of the network deliberately create redundant links so that in the event of a failure of one of the computers on the network, traffic can still find its way to its destination.

The individual LANs that make up an internetwork are connected by routers. The function of a router is to receive incoming traffic from one network and transmit it to a particular destination on another network. There are two types of systems involved in internetwork communications, *end systems and intermediate systems*. End systems are the source of individual packets and also their ultimate destination. Routers are the intermediate systems. The router then processes the packet and sends it back down through the stack to be transmitted to its next destination, as shown in Figure 3.9.

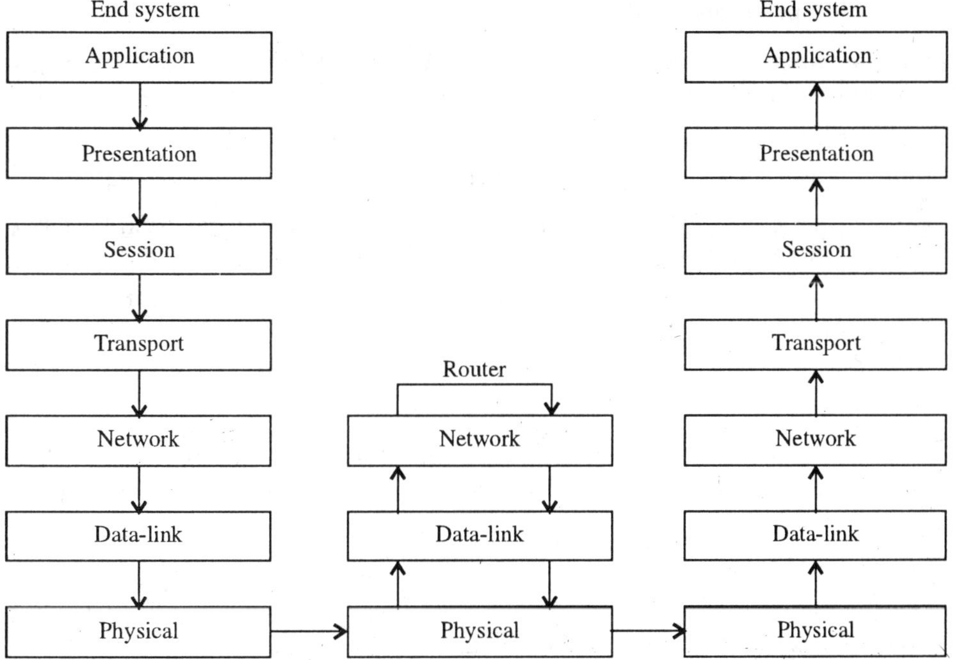

Fig. 3.9 The network layer protocol in a router is responsible for accepting incoming packets and transmitting them to the next stop on their journey.

(iv) Identifying the Transport Layer Protocol

Just as the data-link layer header specifies the network layer protocol that generates the data that it transports, the network layer header identifies the transport layer protocol from which it receives the data that it carries. With this information, the receiving system can pass the incoming datagrams to the correct transport layer protocol.

Summary of the major functions and services performed by the network layer is as follows:

1. The Network Layer is responsible for transmitting data packets between source and destination nodes that may not be connected by the same physical link.
2. The Network Layer addresses a data packet to the logical description of a computer that may be located several links away from the source.
3. If the source and destination nodes are not directly connected, then the Network Layer must use intermediate nodes, when necessary, to get a packet to its destination.
4. Unlike a Data Link address, which is globally unique, a Network Layer address is a logical identifier.
5. Each Network Layer address is only unique within a single network.
6. If a packet's source and destination are in different networks, the Network Layer may have to resolve different addressing conventions and duplicated node addresses used in different types and versions of networks.
7. The Network Layer also moves packets to and from node types that may use different Data Link protocols.

For example, when a router forwards a packet from an Ethernet LAN to a frame relay network, it removes the Ethernet header and trailer and builds a new frame formatted for the frame relay network.

8. Common Network Layer protocols include:
   (a) X.25—X.25 is an older packet switching protocol that has been largely replaced by faster protocols based on the same basic approach.
   (b) IP—IP is the primary Layer 3 protocol used across the Internet and in many LANs.
   (c) Internetwork Packet Exchange (IPX)—IPX is Novell NetWare's proprietary Network Layer protocol.
9. Worries about congestion—hosts sending data into the network faster than the network can handle.

4. Transport Layer

This is layer four of the OSI reference model. This layer is responsible for reliable network communication between end nodes. The transport layer provides mechanisms for the establishment, maintenance and termination of virtual circuits, transport fault detection and recover and information flow control.

It is the transport layer's responsibility to see to the detection of errors and retransmission of data to recover those errors or lost data. The Transport layer may use a variety of techniques such as a Cyclic Redundancy Check, windowing and acknowledgements. If data is lost or damaged it is the Transport layer's responsibility to recover from that error.

The primary functions of transport layer are:

1. Communicate with the Session layer above.
2. Detect errors and lost data, retransmit data, reassemble datagrams into data streams.
3. Communicate with the Network layer below:

The transport layer protocols provide services that complement those provided by the network layer. The transport and network layer protocols used to transmit data are often thought of as a matched pair. The difference between the protocols provided at the transport layer within a particular protocol suite is that some are connection oriented and some are connectionless.

A *connection-oriented* protocol is one in which the two communicating systems exchange messages to establish a connection before they transmit any application data. This ensures that the systems are both active and ready to exchange messages. When you use a Web browser to connect to an Internet server, the browser and the server first perform what is known as a three-way handshake to establish the connection. Only then does the browser transmit the address of the desired Web page to the server. When the data transmission is completed, the systems perform a similar handshake to break down the connection.

Connection-oriented protocols also provide additional services such as packet acknowledgment, data segmentation, flow control, and end-to-end error detection and correction. Systems generally use this type of protocol to transmit relatively large amounts of information that can't tolerate even a single bit error, such as data or program files, and these services ensure the correct transmission of the data. Because of these services, connection-oriented protocols are often said to be *reliable*. Reliable here is a technical term that refers to the fact that each packet transmitted using the protocol has been acknowledged by the recipient and verified as having been transmitted without error. The drawback of this type of protocol is that it greatly increases the amount of control data exchanged by the two systems. In addition to the extra messages needed to establish and terminate the connection, the header applied by a connection-oriented protocol is substantially larger than that of a connectionless one.

A *connectionless* protocol is one in which there is no preliminary communication between the two systems before the transmission of application data. The sender simply transmits its data to the destination without knowing if the system is ready to receive data, or even if the system exists.

Connection-oriented and connectionless protocols are not limited to the transport layer. Network layer protocols are usually connectionless, for example, because they leave the reliability functions to the transport layer. Transport layer protocols typically provide a path through the layers above, just as network and data-link layer protocols do.

Summary of the major functions and services performed by the transport layer is as follows:

1. It offers direct end-to-end communication, e.g., error free transfer between the source host and the destination host.
2. It takes the information to be sent and breaks it into individual packets that are sent and reassembled into a complete message by the Transport Layer at the receiving node.
3. Also provide a signaling service for the remote node so that the sending node is notified when its data is received successfully by the receiving node.
4. Data may have been reordered, doubled or lost on its way through the network. This layer fixes such errors. It ensures that data are delivered error free, in sequence and with no losses or duplication.
5. Transport Layer protocols include the capability to acknowledge the receipt of a packet. If no acknowledgement is received, the Transport Layer protocol can retransmit the packet or time-out the connection and signal an error.
6. Transport protocols can also mark packets with sequencing information so that the destination system can properly order the packets if they're received out-of-sequence.
7. In addition, Transport protocols provide facilities for insuring the integrity of packets and requesting retransmission should the packet become garbled when routed.
8. Transport protocols provide the capability for multiple application processes to access the network by using individual local addresses to determine the destination process for each data stream.
9. The Transport Layer or Layer 4, addresses data to a particular process running on a destination computer.
10. Peer software processes at either end of a connection use the Transport Layer to carry on a conversation. Processes in the Transport Layer act as if their nodes are adjacent.
11. They rely on lower layers to handle the details of passing data through intermediate nodes across the network. Thus, Layer 4 insulates the higher levels from all concerns about the transportation of data.
12. Basic services provided by the Transport Layer include :
    (a) Addressing
    (b) Connection management
    (c) Flow control and buffering
    (d) Multiplexing and parallelization
    (e) Reliable and sequenced delivery
    (f) Service quality managemet
13. The most common Transport Layer protocols are:
    (a) TCP—TCP works in conjunction with IP, in the widely used TCP/IP protocol stack.

(b) Sequenced Packet Exchange (SPX)—SPX is Novell NetWare's Transport Layer protocol. It works in conjunction with IPX.

5. Session Layer

This is layer five of the OSI reference model. This layer establishes, manages, and terminates sessions between applications and manages data exchange between presentation layer entities.

The session layer tracks connections, also called 'sessions'. The session layer should keep track of multiple file downloads requested by a particular FTP application or multiple telnet connections from a single terminal client or web page retrievals from a Web server.

The session performs the following functions:

1. Communication with the Presentation layer above.
2. Organize and manage one or more connections per application, between hosts.
3. Communication with the Transport layer below.

The session layer is the point at which the actual protocols used on networks begin to differ substantially from the OSI model. There are no separate session layer protocols as there are at the lower layers. Session layer functions are instead integrated into other protocols that also include presentation and application layer functions. The transport, network, data-link and physical layers are concerned with the proper transmission of data across the network, but the protocols at the session layer and above are not involved in that part of the communications process. The most important services of session layer are called **dialog control** and **dialog separation**.

The exchange of information between two systems on the network is called a dialog and **dialog control** is the selection of a mode that the systems will use to exchange messages. When the dialog is begun, the systems can choose one of two modes, two-way alternate (TWA) mode or two-way simultaneous (TWS) mode. In TWA mode, the two systems exchange a data token, and only the computer in possession of the token is permitted to transmit data. This eliminates problems caused by messages that cross in transit. TWS mode is more complex, because there is no token and both systems can transmit at any time, even simultaneously.

Dialog separation is the process of creating checkpoints in a data stream that enable communicating systems to synchronize their functions. The difficulty of the checkpointing process depends on whether the dialog is using TWA or TWS mode. Systems involved in a TWA dialog perform minor synchronizations, which require only a single exchange of checkpointing messages, while systems using a TWS dialog perform a major synchronization using a major/activity token.

Summary of the major functions and services performed by the session layer is as follows:

1. The Session Layer and the Presentation Layer above it, provides reusable services for the applications that reside in the Application Layer.
2. The Session Layer facilitates a step-by-step interaction between two entities. It establishes the session, manages the dialog to prevent simultaneous transmission,

and ends the session gracefully. A single session may continue across one or more connections. Similarly, a single connection may support one or more sessions.

3. Provides name recognition and the functions needed to communicate over the network.
4. Provides synchronization between user tasks by placing checkpoints in the data stream. It provides synchronization such as recovering from transport layer failure. For example, a file transfer may take two minutes, during which the network failed (power outage, for example). As long as the host is still running properly, the session layer should recover from this network failure without much intervention of the users. Similar case in a PC editing program such as Word, if a bad disk is encountered, one shouldn't have to start from scratch.
5. Provides dialog between the communicating processes to regulate who transmits and who receives.
6. Provides a cleaner interface to the transport layer. For example, one that is not operating system specific (e.g., sockets).

6. Presentation Layer

This is layer six of the OSI reference model. This layer ensures that information sent by the application layer of one system will be readable by the application layer of another. The presentation layer is also concerned with the data structures used by programs and therefore negotiates data transfer syntax for the application layer.

The Presentation layer handles the conversion of data formats so that machines can 'present' data created on other systems. The presentation layer would handle the conversion of data in JPG/JPEG format to Sun Raster format so that a Sun machine can display a JPG/JPEG image.

The Presentation layer performs the following functions:

1. Communication with the Application layer above.
2. Translation of standard data formats to formats understood by the local machine.
3. Communication with the Session layer below.

There is only one function found at the presentation layer, and that is the translation of syntax between different systems. In some cases, computers communicating over a network use different syntaxes, and the presentation layer enables them to negotiate a common syntax for the network communications. When the communicating systems establish a connection at the presentation layer, they exchange messages containing information about the syntaxes they have in common, and together they choose the syntax they will use during the session.

Both of the systems involved in the connection have an *abstract syntax*, which is their native form of communication. During the negotiation process, the systems choose transfer syntax. The transmitting system converts its abstract syntax to the transfer syntax and the receiving system converts the transfer syntax to its own abstract syntax. When called for, the systems can select a transfer syntax that provides additional services, such as data compression or encryption.

Summary of the major functions and services performed by the presentation layer is as follows:

1. The Presentation Layer deals with the format or representation, of computer information.
2. It resolves differences between different types of character encoding systems, such as Extended Binary Coded Decimal Interchange Code (EBCDIC) and the American Standard Code for Information Interchange (ASCII) character code.
3. It provides security by encrypting and decrypting data. It also compresses data before transmitting it, to use the communication channel more efficiently.
4. It determines the format used to exchange data among networked computers. So it is sometimes called the network's translator. It changes the format from an application layer format to an intermediate format that both computers recognize.

7. Application Layer

This is layer seven of the OSI reference model. This layer provides services to application processes (such as electronic mail, file transfer, and terminal emulation) that are outside of the OSI model. The application layer identifies and establishes the availability of intended communication partners (and the resources required to connect with them), synchronizes cooperating applications, and establishes agreement on procedures for error recovery and control of data integrity.

The application layer is the application in use by the user. This could be a web browser, an FTP, IRC or Telnet client. The Application layer provides the user interface and is responsible for displaying data and images to the user in a recognizable format. The application layers job is to organize and display data in a human compatible format, and to interface with the Presentation layer.

The application layer is the entrance point that programs use to access the OSI model and utilize network resources. Most application layer protocols provide services that programs use to access the network, such as the Simple Mail Transfer Protocol (SMTP), which most e-mail programs use to send e-mail messages. In some cases, such as the File Transfer Protocol (FTP), the application layer protocol is a program in itself.

Application layer protocols often include the session and presentation layer functions. As a result, a typical protocol stack consists of four separate protocols, which run at the application, transport, network and data-link layers.

Summary of the major functions and services performed by the application layer is as follows:

1. It refers to the user programs themselves.
2. The Application Layer contains programs that invoke the underlying services of the network. Some of these applications are written specifically for one network, while others are widely used standard applications.
3. When these applications need to communicate with peers over the network, they can use their own protocols, plus the services of the lower layers.

4. Application Layer programs include:
   (a) User applications, such as e-mail or file transfer, provide standard services directly to the user.
   (b) Each of these applications has its own standard protocol at the Application Layer level.
   (c) Application services, such as virtual filestores, provide services to other applications, but not directly to the user.
   (d) These facilities simplify application development by allowing programmers to use a common service rather than duplicating the same features in every application.
5. It offers direct access for Applications to use network resources.

3.6.6 Summary Of OSI Model

Layer	Layer Function	Unit of Information	Address Type
Application	User functionality	Program	
Presentation	Character representation, Data Compression, Security	Character and words	
Session	Establishing, conducting and ending sessions		
Transport	Transmitting messages from sending computer process to receiving computer process	Message	Process to process between applications
Network	Transmitting individual packet across a network	Packet	Packet address identifying receiver's network and host location
Data Link	Transmitting frames containing packets across a link through route to final destination	Frame	NIC (next node in network)
Physical	Transmitting bits in the form of signals across physical media	Bit	

3.6.7 The Data Transmission Through The OSI Model

The transmitting process gives the data to be sent to the receiving process to the application layer that adds to them an application header AH (AH may be empty). The result is then transmitted to the presentation layer.

The presentation layer then transforms this message and adds (or not) a new header (possibly empty). The presentation layer does not know and does not have to know the possible existence of AH; actually, for the presentation layer, AH is part of the user data. Once the data processing is finished, the presentation layer sends the new "message" to the session layer and the same process starts again.

The data then reach the physical layer that will indeed transmit the data to the recipient. Once received, the message will go up the layers and the headers are gradually removed until it reaches the receiving process.

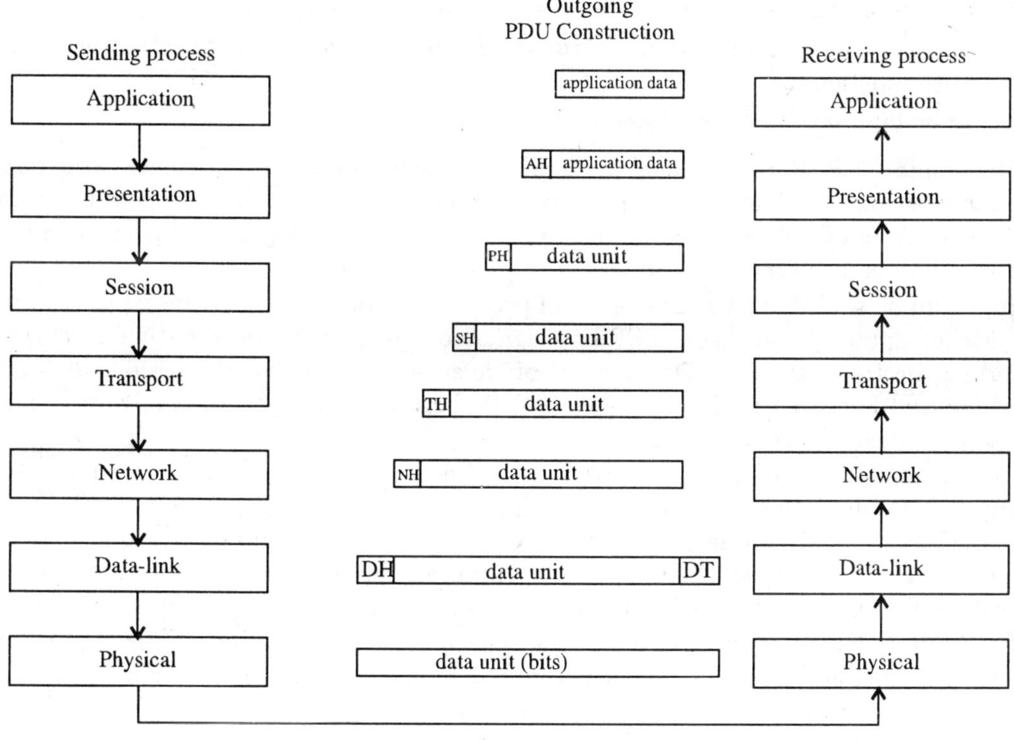

Fig. 3.10 Data transmission through the OSI model

The most important concept is as follows: it should be considered that each layer is programmed as if it were really horizontal, i.e., as if it dialogued directly with its receiving peer layer. When dialoguing with its peer layer, each layer adds a header and sends it to its peer layer.

3.7 TCP/IP Reference Model

The TCP/IP reference model is a specification for a networking stack on a computer. It exists to provide a common ground for network developers. This allows easier interconnection of the different vendor supplied networks, reducing the cost of installing completely new networks in order for one to work with another.

The TCP/IP reference model is the network model used in the current Internet architecture. It has its origins back in the 1960's with the grandfather of the Internet, the ARPANET. This was a research network sponsored by the Department of Defense in the United States. The following were seen as major design goals:

- Ability to connect multiple networks together seamlessly.
- Ability for connections to remain intact as long as the source and destination machines were functioning.
- To be built on flexible architecture.

The name TCP/IP refers to a suite of data communication protocols. The name is misleading because TCP and IP are only two of dozens of protocols that compose the suite. Its name comes from two of the more important protocols in the suite: the *Transmission Control Protocol* (TCP) and the *Internet Protocol* (IP).

So, it can be said that TCP/IP is a set of protocols that govern the transfer of information from one computer to another. TCP/IP originated out of the investigative research into networking protocols that the Department of Defense (DoD) initiated in 1969. In 1968, the DoD Advanced Research Projects Agency (ARPA) began researching the network technology that is now called *packet switching.*

The original focus of this research was to facilitate communication among the DoD community. However, the network that was initially constructed as a result of this research, then called ARPANET, gradually became known as the Internet. The TCP/IP protocols played an important role in the development of the Internet. Because of the history of the TCP/IP protocol suite, it is often referred to as the *DoD protocol suite* or the *Internet protocol* suite.

TCP/IP was developed in 1978 under the sponsorship of the United States Department of Defense to answer a need for a technology that will enable networks implementing proprietary and incompatible communication protocols to communicate with one another. It was first implemented in 1980 to link the educational and research institutions that comprised the DOD's Applied Research Projects Agency Network (ARPANET), the precursor to the present Internet. Soon, it was incorporated into the Unix operating system and became a standard in 1983.

It is not so much of a model, but a base set of protocols. Procotols came first, where in OSI reference model, the model came first. Model provides a nice basis to talk about networks. TCP/IP provides better protocols for using them.

OSI is not widely accepted, especially in the U.S. The major reason is that TCP/IP has been a fine working model and most of the companies have invested heavily into TCP/IP. There are some other criticisms about the OSI model.

- It would be nice if all layers were of roughly equal size and complexity—in practice, the session layer and presentation layer are absent from many existing architectures.
- Some functions—addressing, flow control, retransmission—are duplicated at each layer, resulting in degraded performance.
- The initial specification of the OSI model ignored the connectionless model, thus leaving much of the LANs behind.
- The OSI model has too many layers the data has to travel through, which will impact the performance.

TCP/IP is composed of several protocols that cooperatively implement the task of computer-to-computer communication. Computer professionals agree that computer communication protocols are best implemented using a layered approach where two or more protocols are grouped into a functional layer that are then placed atop each other in a layered stack.

In contrast to the OSI model that had seven layers, the TCP/IP protocol only had four. These are the application, transport, network and data link layers all of which have also been defined in the more complete OSI model.

We have said that TCP/IP is a layered set of protocols. In order to understand what this means, it is useful to look at an example. A typical situation is sending mail. First, there is a protocol for mail. This defines a set of commands which one machine sends to another, e.g., commands to specify who the sender of the message is, who it is being sent to, and then the text of the message. However this protocol assumes that there is a way to communicate reliably between the two computers. Mail, like other application protocols, simply defines a set of commands and messages to be sent. It is designed to be used together with TCP and IP.

TCP is responsible for making sure that the commands get through to the other end. It keeps track of what is sent, and retransmits anything that did not get through. If any message is too large for one datagram, e.g., the text of the mail, TCP will split it up into several datagrams, and make sure that they all arrive correctly. Since these functions are needed for many applications, they are put together into a separate protocol, rather than being part of the specifications for sending mail. You can think of TCP as forming a library of routines that applications can use when they need reliable network communications with another computer. Similarly, TCP calls on the services of IP. Although the services that TCP supplies are needed by many applications, there are still some kinds of applications that don't need them. However there are some services that every application needs. So these services are put together into IP. As with TCP, you can think of IP as a library of routines that TCP calls on, but which is also available to applications that don't use TCP. This strategy of building several levels of protocol is called "*layering*", forming a *stack*. We think of the applications programs such as mail, TCP, and IP, as being separate "layers", each of which calls on the services of the layer below it.

Generally, TCP/IP applications use 4 layers:

1. Application layer
2. Transport layer

3. Network layer
4. Host to Network layer

3.7.1 TCP/IP Features

The popularity of the TCP/IP protocols did not grow rapidly just because the protocols were there, or because connecting to the Internet mandated their use. They met an important need (worldwide data communication) at the right time, and they had several important features that allowed them to meet this need. These features are:

- Open protocol standards, freely available and developed independently from any specific computer hardware or operating system. Because it is so widely supported, TCP/IP is ideal for uniting different hardware and software, even if you don't communicate over the Internet.
- Independence from specific physical network hardware. This allows TCP/IP to integrate many different kinds of networks. TCP/IP can be run over an Ethernet, a token ring, a dial-up line, an FDDI net, and virtually any other kind of physical transmission medium.
- A common addressing scheme that allows any TCP/IP device to uniquely address any other device in the entire network, even if the network is as large as the worldwide Internet.
- Standardized high-level protocols for consistent, widely available user services.

3.7.2 Functions of Layers

The functions of different layers in TCP/IP are discussed below:

1. Application Layer

The top layer in the Internet reference model is the *application layer*. This layer provides functions for users or their programs, and it is highly specific to the application being performed. It provides the services that user applications use to communicate over the network, and it is the layer in which user-access network processes reside. These processes include all of those that users interact with directly, as well as other processes of which the users are not aware.

This layer includes all applications protocols that use the host-to-host transport protocols to deliver data. Other functions that process user data, such as data encryption and decryption and compression and decompression, can also reside at the application layer.

The application layer also manages the sessions (connections) between cooperating applications. In the TCP/IP protocol hierarchy, sessions are not identifiable as a separate layer, and these functions are performed by the host-to-host transport layer. Instead of using the term "session", TCP/IP uses the terms "socket" and "port" to describe the path (or virtual circuit) over which cooperating applications communicate. A *session* is a connection over a TCP or UDP port that is made between two computers. Most of the application protocols in this layer provide user services, and new user services are added often. For cooperating applications to be able to exchange data, they must agree about how data is represented. The application layer is responsible for standardizing the presentation of data.

TCP/IP's application layer specifies how user programs and processes interact with the lower layer protocols to provide data transfer services for the user. TCP/IP's application layer includes protocols for implementing common user services such as electronic mail, terminal emulation and file transfer. Most of these applications implement a client-server model wherein clients request services from servers waiting for services at some pre- defined memory locations.

The most widely known and implemented TCP/IP application layer protocols are listed below:

File Transfer Protocol (FTP)

It performs basic interactive file transfers between hosts. The file transfer protocol (FTP) allows a user on any computer to get files from another computer, or to send files to another computer. Security is handled by requiring the user to specify a user name and password for the other computer. Provisions are made for handling file transfer between machines with different character set, end of line conventions, etc. This is not quite the same thing as more recent NFS (*Network File System*) or Netbios protocols. Rather, FTP is a utility that you run any time you want to access a file on another system. You use it to copy the file to your own system. You then work with the local copy.

Telnet

It enables users to execute terminal sessions with remote hosts. The network terminal protocol (TELNET) allows a user to log in on any other computer on the network. You start a remote session by specifying a computer to connect to. From that time until you finish the session, anything you type is sent to the other computer. Note that you are really still talking to your own computer. But the telnet program effectively makes your computer invisible while it is running. Every character you type is sent directly to the other system. Generally, the connection to the remote computer behaves much like a dialup connection. That is, the remote system will ask you to log in and give a password, in whatever manner it would normally ask a user who had just dialed it up. When you log off of the other computer, the telnet program exits, and you will find yourself talking to your own computer.

Simple Mail Transfer Protocol (SMTP)

It supports basic message delivery services. This facility allows you to send messages to users on other computers. Originally, people tended to use only one or two specific computers. They would maintain "mail files" on those machines. The computer mail system is simply a way for you to add a message to another user's mail file. The SMTP protocol is used for the transmission of e-mails. SMTP takes care of sending your email to another computer. Normally your email is sent to an email server (SMTP server), and then to another server or servers, and finally to its destination.

HyperText Transfer Protocol (HTTP)

Supports the low-overhead transport of files consisting of a mixture of text and graphics. It uses a stateless, connection- and object-oriented protocol with simple commands that support selection and transport of objects between the client and the server.

Domain Name System (DNS)

Also called *name service*; this application maps IP addresses to the names assigned to network devices.

Routing Information Protocol (RIP)

Routing is central to the way TCP/IP works. RIP is used by network devices to exchange routing information. RIP works well in small environments but has serious limitations when used in larger internetworks. RIP determines the best path through an Internet by looking only at the number of hops between the two end nodes.

Simple Network Management Protocol (SNMP)

A protocol that is used to collect management information from network devices.

Network File System (NFS)

A system developed by Sun Microsystems that enables computers to mount drives on remote hosts and operate them as if they were local drives.

Some protocols, such as Telnet and FTP, can only be used if the user has some knowledge of the network. Other protocols, like RIP, run without the user even knowing that they exist.

2. Transport Layer

Its transport layer enables end-to-end data transfer by delivering data from an application to its remote peer. TCP/IP's transport protocols provide end-to-end data delivery service for the upper layer application protocols.

The two most important protocols employed at this layer are:

(i) Transmission Control Protocol (TCP)
(ii) User Datagram Protocol (UDP)

TCP provides reliable, full-duplex connections and reliable service by ensuring that data is resubmitted when transmission results in an error (end-to-end error detection and correction). Also, TCP enables hosts to maintain multiple, simultaneous connections.

Transmission Control Protocol

Transmission Control Protocol (TCP) is a connection-oriented protocol that implements a reliable transfer of information from one computer to another. It defines how to set up and tear down a connection between the two peer layers in communicating computers. It specifies how a sliding window mechanism can control the amount of data that flows from one computer to another so as not to flood the buffers of the receiving computer. It also provides ways of varying the amount of data sent when congestion occurs in the network medium.

Applications that require the transport protocol to provide reliable data delivery use TCP because it verifies that data is delivered across the network accurately and in the proper sequence. **TCP is a reliable, connection-oriented, byte-stream protocol**. Let's look at each of the terms—reliable, connection-oriented, and byte-stream—in more detail. TCP provides reliability with a mechanism called **Positive Acknowledgment with Re-transmission (PAR)**. Simply stated, a system using PAR sends the data again, unless it hears from the remote system that the data arrived okay.

TCP is connection-oriented. It establishes a logical end-to-end connection between the two communicating hosts. Control information, called a *handshake*, is exchanged between the two endpoints to establish a dialogue before data is transmitted.

The type of handshake used by TCP is called a *three-way handshake* because three segments are exchanged. Figure 3.11 shows the simplest form of the three-way handshake. Host A begins the connection by sending host B a segment with the "Synchronize sequence numbers" (SYN) bit set. This segment tells host B that A wishes to set up a connection, and it tells B what sequence number host A will use as a starting number for its segments. (Sequence numbers are used to keep data in the proper order.) Host B responds to A with a segment that has the "Acknowledgment" (ACK) and SYN bits set. B's segment acknowledges the receipt of A's segment, and informs A which Sequence Number host B will start with. Finally, host A sends a segment that acknowledges receipt of B's segment, and transfers the first actual data.

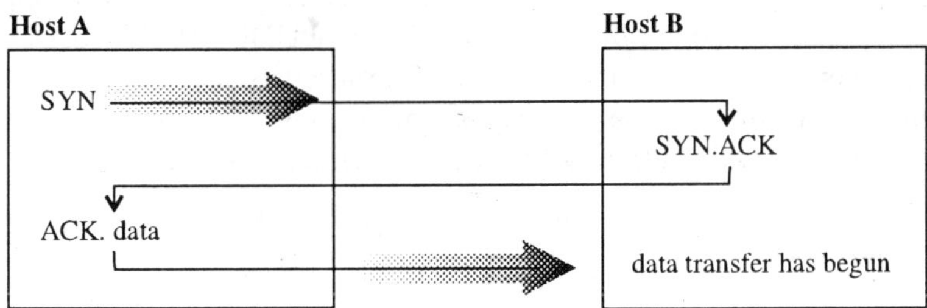

Fig. 3.11 Three-way handshake

After this exchange, host *A*'s TCP has positive evidence that the remote TCP is alive and ready to receive data. As soon as the connection is established, data can be transferred. When the cooperating modules have concluded the data transfers, they will exchange a three-way handshake with segments containing the "No more data from sender" bit (called the FIN bit) to close the connection. It is the end-to-end exchange of data that provides the logical connection between the two systems.

TCP views the data it sends as a continuous stream of bytes, not as independent packets. Therefore, TCP takes care to maintain the sequence in which bytes are sent and received. The Sequence Number and Acknowledgment Number fields in the TCP segment header keep track of the bytes.

User Datagram Protocol

When error correction is not required, UDP provides unreliable datagram service (connection-less) that enhances network throughput at the host-to-host transport layer. UDP is an unreliable, connectionless datagram protocol. "Unreliable" merely means that the protocol has no technique for verifying that the data reached the other end of the network correctly. Within your computer, UDP will deliver data correctly.

User Datagram Protocol (UDP) makes available a connection-less mechanism for sending data from one computer to another. It specifies an unreliable method of data delivery without regard to whether the receiving computer received the data or whether the data was received out of sequence. It leaves to the higher-level protocols the function of ensuring that the data are received completely. UDP offers an alternative to TCP for applications where loss of some data is acceptable.

Why do applications programmers choose UDP as a data transport service?

A number of good reasons exist. If the amount of data being transmitted is small, the overhead of creating connections and ensuring reliable delivery may be greater than the work of retransmitting the entire data set. In this case, UDP is the most efficient choice for a host-to-host transport layer protocol.

Applications that fit a "query-response" model are also excellent candidates for using UDP. The response can be used as a positive acknowledgment to the query. If a response is not received within a certain time period, the application just sends another query. Still other applications provide their own techniques for reliable data delivery and do not require that service from the transport layer protocol. Imposing another layer of acknowledgment on any of these types of applications is redundant.

Both TCP and UDP define the concept of ports which are storage locations where servers wait for connections. The transport protocol used (TCP or UDP), IP address and port address makes for a unique combination that may be used to identify a particular connection in one computer system. Programmers use a programming construct called sockets that are IP address and port number combinations to uniquely identify one message from another inside a computer system.

TCP vs. UDP

TCP	UDP
Connection Oriented	Connectionless
Sequenced Delivery	
End-to-end Acknowledgements	
Error Check	Optional Error Check
If time-out : Retransmit	

3. Internet Layer

TCP/IP's Internet layer provides the inter-network's virtual image, specifies network addressing and implements the routing function. TCP/IP's network protocols concern themselves with logical addressing of devices in the network and the routing of data within a networked environment.

Internet Protocol (IP) stands out as the most used protocol in the TCP/IP protocol suite. It defines the logical addressing of network devices and the mechanisms for segmenting and best-effort delivery of data from one computer system to another. IP requires that each network device be given an address in the form of four dotted decimal numbers that range from 1 to 255. The IP address is used in combination with a subnet mask to identify the subnetwork number, network number and host identification number of a particular network device.

IP also specifies how IP packets are routed in the internetwork. Routers are internetwork devices that link two or more networks. They can move packets from one network to another using a routing table that may be manually configured or dynamically maintained by a routing protocol. Routing Information Protocol (RIP) was among the first routing protocols to be deployed for intra-domain routing. However, its techniques left much to be desired particularly in metric measurement and speed of convergence. RIP was soon replaced by the Open Shortest Path First (OSPF) protocol that offered a more efficient distance metrics measurement and faster internetwork convergence.

IP depends on the Internet Control Message Protocol (ICMP) specifications for tracking down and reporting status and errors in packet transmission. It uses the Internet Group Management Protocol (IGMP) to implement data delivery for multicast applications that send packets to a selected group of network devices.

Dynamic Host Configuration Protocol (DHCP) defines the processes and data formats for implementing automatic distribution of IP configuration data in a network. A computer's TCP/IP stack need to be configured with valid IP configuration data for it to be able to actively exchange packets with other computers in the internetwork. DHCP specifies how system administrators can implement automatic IP host configuration for all devices in the network.

Internet Protocol

IP is a *connectionless protocol*, which means that IP does not exchange control information (called a *handshake*) to establish an end-to-end connection before transmitting data. In contrast, a *connection-oriented protocol* exchanges control information with the remote computer to verify that it is ready to receive data before sending it. When the handshaking is successful, the computers are said to have established a *connection*. IP relies on protocols in other layers to establish the connection if connection-oriented services are required.

IP also relies on protocols in another layer to provide error detection and error recovery. Because it contains no error detection or recovery code, IP is sometimes called an unreliable protocol. This is not to say that the protocol cannot be relied on - quite the contrary. IP can be relied upon to accurately deliver your data to the connected network, but it doesn't check whether that data was correctly received. Protocols in other layers of the TCP/IP architecture provide this checking when it is required.

The Internet Protocol is the building block of the Internet. Its functions include:

- Defining the datagram, which is the basic unit of transmission in the Internet.
- Defining the Internet addressing scheme.
- Moving data between the Network Access Layer and the Host-to-Host Transport Layer.
- Routing datagrams to remote hosts.
- Performing fragmentation and re-assembly of datagrams.

The functions performed at this layer are as follows:

- **Define the datagram, which is the basic unit of transmission in the Internet.** The TCP/IP protocols were built to transmit data over the ARPANET, which was a *packet switching network*. A packet is a block of data that carries with it the information necessary to deliver it—in a manner similar to a postal letter that has an address written on its envelope. A packet switching network uses the addressing information in the packets to switch packets from one physical network to another, moving them toward their final destination. Each packet travels the network independently of any other packet. The *datagram* is the packet format defined by IP.
- **Define the Internet addressing scheme.** IP delivers the datagram by checking the destination address in the header. If the destination address is the address of a host on the directly attached network, the packet is delivered directly to the destination. If the destination address is not on the local network, the packet is passed to a gateway for delivery. *Gateways* and *routers* are devices that switch packets between the different physical networks. Deciding which gateway to use is called routing. IP makes the routing decision for each individual packet.
- **Move data between the Network Access Layer and the Host-to-Host Transport Layer.** When IP receives a datagram that is addressed to the local host, it must pass the data portion of the datagram to the correct host-to-host transport layer protocol. This selection is done by using the *protocol number* in the datagram header. Each host-to-host transport layer protocol has a unique protocol number that identifies it to IP.
- **Route datagrams to remote hosts.** Internet gateways are commonly (and perhaps more accurately) referred to as IP routers because they use IP to route packets between networks. In traditional TCP/IP jargon, there are only two types of network devices: gateways and hosts. Gateways forward packets between networks and hosts do not. However, if a host is connected to more than one network (called a *multi-homed host*), it can forward packets between the networks. When a multi-homed host forwards packets, it acts like any other gateway and is considered to be a gateway.
- **Fragment and reassemble datagrams.** As a datagram is routed through different networks, it may be necessary for the IP module in a gateway to divide the datagram into smaller pieces. A datagram received from one network may be too large to be transmitted in a single packet on a different network. This condition only occurs when a gateway interconnects dissimilar physical networks.

Each type of network has a *maximum transmission unit* (MTU), which is the largest packet it can transfer. If the datagram received from one network is longer than the other network's MTU, it is necessary to divide the datagram into smaller fragments for transmission. This division process is called *fragmentation.*

4. Host to Network Layer

It is the lowest layer in the TCP/IP reference model. It is a pretty strange layer. Indeed, it seems to comprise both physical and data link layers of the OSI model. Actually, this layer has not been really specified; the only constraint of this layer is to allow a host to send IP packets of a network. The implementation of this layer is free. In more concrete terms, this implementation is typical of the technology used to build the local network (LAN). For example, LANs use Ethernet; Ethernet is an implementation of the host- network layer.

The design of TCP/IP hides the function of this layer from users—it is concerned with getting data across a specific type of physical network (such as Ethernet, Token Ring, etc.). This design reduces the need to rewrite higher levels of a TCP/IP stack when new physical network technologies are introduced (such as ATM and Frame Relay).

The functions performed at this level include encapsulating the IP datagrams into *frames* that are transmitted by the network. It also maps the IP addresses to the physical addresses used by the network. One of the strengths of TCP/IP is its addressing scheme, which uniquely identifies every computer on the network. This IP address must be converted into whatever address is appropriate for the physical network over which the datagram is transmitted.

Data to be transmitted is received from the internetwork layer. The network access layer is responsible for routing and must add its routing information to the data. The network access layer information is added in the form of a header, which is appended to the beginning of the data.

This layer contains the protocols that the computer uses to deliver data to the other computers and devices that are attached to the network. The protocols at this layer perform three distinct functions:

- They define how to use the network to transmit a frame, which is the data unit passed across the physical connection.
- They exchange data between the computer and the physical network.
- They deliver data between two devices on the same network. To deliver data on the local network, the network access layer protocols use the physical addresses of the nodes on the network. A physical address is stored in the network adapter card of a computer or other device, and it is a value that is "hardcoded" into the adapter card by the manufacturer.

Because of its robustness and flexibility, TCP/IP has become the de facto computer-to-computer communication standard in both the local and wide area networks. As an open standard, TCP/IP has a built-in capability to evolve and adapt as changes in the physical layer move at an astounding pace. Unless a more robust, efficient, and acceptable protocol suite is developed that can surpass its power and flexibility, we feel that TCP/IP will remain useful in the years to come.

3.8 Comparison And Contrast Between The OSI And TCP/IP Model

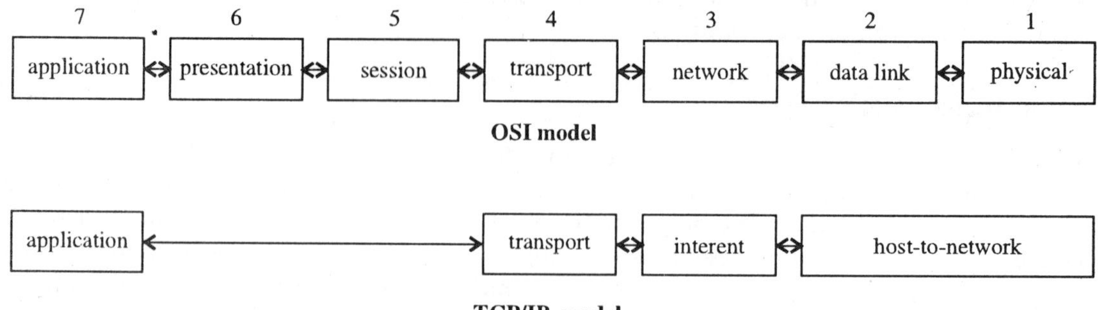

Fig. 3.12 Layer structure of OSI and TCP/IP

Main points of comparison are shown in the table below:

	OSI Model Reference	TCP/IP Model Reference
Service, interface and protocol	Service, interface and protocol are not clearly defined. For example, the only real services offered by the Internet layer are • Send IP Packet • Receive IP Packet	Protocols in the OSI model are better hidden and can be replaced relatively easily as the technology changes, which is one of the main objectives of layered protocols.
Functionalities	Because models were invented before protocols, functionalities put in each layer are not very optimized.	In this case, the protocols have been invented before models, so the functionalities are perfectly described.
Number of layers	Seven layers, Network (Internet), Transport and Application layers being similar to TCP/IP	Only four layers.
Connectionless/ Connection-oriented communication	Both connectionless and connection-oriented communications are supported in the network layer, but only connection-oriented communication in the transport layer.	Only one mode in the network layer (connectionless) but both modes in the transport layer are supported, giving the users a choice.

Also there are two main points to be discussed for the comparison of these two models:

I. Comparison of the protocol layers that correspond to each other.

II. General Comparison : It will include the following points:

(a) Focus of Reliability Control

(b) Roles of Host system

(c) De-jure vs. De-facto

3.8.1 The Comparison of Different Layers

The Upper Layers

OSI	TCP/IP
Application (Layer 7) Presentation (Layer 6) Session (Layer 5)	Application

The Session Layer

The Session layer permits two parties to hold on going communications called a session across a network.

- Not found in TCP/IP model.
- In TCP/IP, its characteristics are provided by the TCP protocol. (Transport Layer)

The Presentation Layer

The Presentation Layer handles data format information for networked communications. This is done by converting data into a generic format that could be understood by both sides.

- Not found in TCP/IP model.
- In TCP/IP, this function is provided by the Application Layer.
  e.g., External Data Representation Standard (XDR)
  Multipurpose Internet Mail Extensions (MIME)

The Application Layer

The Application Layer is the top layer of the reference model. It provides a set of interfaces for applications to obtain access to networked services as well as access to the kinds of network services that support applications directly.

- OSI : FTAM, VT, MHS, DS, CMIP
  TCP/IP : FTP, SMTP, TELNET, DNS, SNMP
- Although the notion of an application process is common to both, their approaches to constructing application entities are different.

Approaches used in constructing application entities

ISO Approach

- Sometime called Horizontal Approach.
- OSI asserts that distributed applications operate over a strict hierarchy of layers and are constructed from a common tool kit of standardized application service elements.
- In OSI, each distributed application service selects functions from a large common "toolbox" of application service element (ASEs) and complements these with application service elements that perform functions specific to given end- user service.

TCP/IP Approach

- Sometime called Vertical Approach.
- In TCP/IP, each application entity is composed of whatever set of function it needs beyond end to end transport to support a distributed communications service.
- Most of these application processes builds on what it needs and assumes only that an underlying transport mechanism (datagram or connection) will be provided.

Transport Layer

OSI	TCP/IP
Transport (Layer 4)	Transport (TCP/UDP)

- The functionality of the transport layer is to provide "transparent transfer of data from a source end open system to a destination end open system".
- Transport is responsible for creating and maintaining the basic end-to-end connection between communicating open systems, ensuring that the bits delivered to the receiver are the same as the bits transmitted by the sender; in the same order and without modification, loss or duplication

Comparing Transport for Both Models

- The features of UDP and TCP defined at TCP/IP Transport Layer correspond to many of the requirements of the OSI Transport Layer. There is a bit of bleed over for requirements in the session layer of OSI since sequence numbers, and port values can help to allow the Operating System to keep track of sessions, but most of the TCP and UDP functions and specifications map to the OSI Transport Layer.
- The TCP/IP and OSI architecture models both employ all connection and connectionless models at transport layer. However, the Internet architecture refers to the two models in TCP/IP as simply "connections" and datagrams. But the OSI reference model uses the connection-oriented mode only.

Network vs. Internet

- Like all the other OSI Layers, the network layer provides both connectionless and connection-oriented services. As for the TCP/IP architecture, the Internet layer is exclusively connectionless.

OSI	TCP/IP
Network (Layer 3)	Internet

- **X.25 Packet Level Protocol**—OSI's Connection-oriented Network Protocol.
  The CCITT standard for X.25 defines the DTE/DCE interface standard to provide access to a packet-switched network. It is the network level interface, which specifies a virtual circuit (VC) service. A source host must establish a connection (a VC) with the destination

host before data transfer can take place. The network attempts to deliver packets flowing over a VC in sequence.

- **Connectionless Network Service**—Both OSI and TCP/IP support a connectionless network service: OSI as an alternative to network connections and TCP/IP as the only way in use.
- **OSI Routing Architecture**—End systems (ESs) and intermediate systems (ISs) use routing protocols to distribute ("advertise") some or all of the information stored in their locally maintained routing information base. ESs and ISs send and receive these routing updates and use the information that they contain (and information that may be available from the local environment, such as information entered manually by an operator) to modify their routing information base.
- **TCP/IP Routing Architecture**—The TCP/IP routing architecture looks very much like the OSI routing architecture. Hosts use a discovery protocol to obtain the identification of gateways and other hosts attached to the same network (subnetwork). Gateways within autonomous systems (routing domains) operate an interior gateway protocol (intradomain IS-IS routing protocol), and between autonomous systems, they operate exterior or border gateway protocols (interdomain routing protocols). The details are different but the principles are the same.

Data Link/Physical vs. Subnet

OSI	TCP/IP
Data link layer (Layer 2) Physical (Layer 1)	Host to Network layer

Data Link Layer

The function of the *Data Link Layer* is "provides for the control of the physical layer, and detects and possibly corrects errors which may occur". In another words, the Data Link Layer transforms a stream of raw bits (0's and 1's) from the physical into a data frame and provides an error-free transfer from one node to another, allowing the layers above it to assume virtually error-free transmission.

Physical Layer

The function of the Physical Layer is to provide "mechanical, electrical, functional and procedural means to activate a physical connection for bit transmission". Basically, this means that the typical role of the physical layer is to transform bits in a computer system into electromagnetic (or equivalent) signals for a particular transmission medium (wire, fiber, ether, etc.)

Comparing to TCP/IP

These 2 layers of the OSI correspond *directly* to the host to network layer of the TCP/IP model.

- Majority of the time, the lower layers below the Interface or Network layer of the TCP/IP model are seldom or rarely discussed. The TCP/IP model does nothing but to high light the fact the host has to connect to the network using some protocol so it can send IP packets over it. Because the protocol used is not defined, it will vary from host to host and network to network.

- After much deliberation by organizations, it was decided that the Network Interface Layer in the TCP/IP model corresponds to a combination of the OSI Data Link Layer and network specific functions of the OSI network layer (e.g., IEEE 802.3).
- Since these two layers deal with functions that are so inherently specific to each individual networking technology, the layering principle of grouping them together related functions is largely irrelevant.

3.8.2 Summary of the Comparison of Layers in Both Models

OSI seven-layers Model		TCP-IP Reference Model	
It is the totality of all applications and their relating protocols that use networks and have not yet been represented by the lower layers.	Application	Application	Like OSI Model, it contains all the higher-level protocols.
Here are the standards necessary for unambiguously representing data and more generally, syntax of messages to be transmitted (simple text, executable code, pictures...).	Presentation	—	Because no need for them was perceived, Presentation and Session layers are not included in the TCP/IP Model
It establishes a connection with another node and manages the data flow from the higher layers to the lower ones by managing the timing of data transmission and the memory buffer managing, when several applications try to transmit data at the same time.	Session	—	—
It handles the transmission, reception and error checking of the data.	Transport	Transport	The same as OSI Model

It is concerned with the physical transmission of the data from computer to computer. There is one further level of software to be considered, the network level. It routes the packages across a particular network.	Network	Internet	It is the linchpin that holds the whole architecture together : it permits to send and receive packets, even if they are in random order.
It handles the transmission of a framed set of data (usually a sequence of bits) from one point in a network (node) to another one. This layer also represents the boundary between hardware (e.g., CRC) and software implementation (e.g., physical addressing).	Data Link	Host-to-network	The TCP/IP reference model does not really say much about what happens here, except to point out that the host has to connect to the network using some protocol so it can send IP packets over it. This protocol is not defined and varies from host to host and network to network.
The physical medium used to transmit the information. To specify this layer, it is necessary to define the physical properties of the connection, such as mechanical properties, electrical/optical properties, functional aspects of the data transmission (modulation/demodulation for example) and procedural aspects of data transmission (e.g., bit stuffing to ensure that special signals are un-equivocal).	Physical		

3.8.3 General Comparison

It includes the following topics

(a) Focus of Reliability Control
(b) Roles of Host System
(c) De-jure vs. De-facto

Focus of Reliability Control

- Implementation of the OSI model places emphasis on providing a reliable data transfer service, while the TCP/IP model treats reliability as an end-to-end problem.
- Each layer of the OSI model detects and handles errors, all data transmitted includes checksums. The transport layer of the OSI model checks source-to-destination reliability.
- In the TCP/IP model, reliability control is concentrated at the transport layer. The transport layer handles all error detection and recovery. The TCP/IP transport layer uses checksums, acknowledgments, and timeouts to control transmissions and provides end-to-end verification.

Roles of Host System

Hosts on OSI implementations do not handle network operations (simple terminal), but TCP/IP hosts participate in most network protocols. TCP/IP hosts carry out such functions as end-to-end verification, routing, and network control. The TCP/IP Internet can be viewed as a data stream delivery system involving intelligent hosts.

De-jure vs. De-facto (OSI)

OSI

- Standard legislated by official recognized body. (ISO)
- The OSI reference model was devised *before* the protocols were invented. This ordering means that the model was not biased toward one particular set of protocols, which made it quite general. The down side of this ordering is that the designers did not have much experience with the subject and did not have a good idea of which functionality to put in which layer.
- Being general, the protocols in the OSI model are better hidden than in the TCP/IP model and can be replaced relatively easily as the technology changes.
- Not so widespread as compared with TCP/IP. (Complex, costly)
- More commonly used as teaching aids.

De-jure vs. De-facto (TCP/IP)

TCP/IP

- Standards adopted due to widespread use. (Internet)
- The protocols came first, and the model was really just a description of the existing protocols. There was no problem with the protocols fitting the model, but it is hardly possible to be use to describe other models.
- "Get the job done" orientation.
  Over the years it has handled most challenges by growing to meet the needs.
- More popular standard for internetworking for several reasons:

- Relatively simple and robust compared to alternatives such as OSI.
- Available on virtually every hardware and operating system platform (often free).
- The protocol suite on which the Internet depends.

3.9 Criticism Of The Reference Models

We can find several elements showing that OSI and TCP/IP models and protocols are not perfect. These elements are discussed below:

3.9.1 Criticism of the OSI Model

The OSI Model is often criticized as being overly complex, offering too many choices. It is usually contrasted with the Internet or TCP/IP protocol suite by such critics. The concept of layers introduced in the OSI model has two motivations:

1. Primarily technically, but secondarily politically, it is a modularization technique, taken from software engineering and re-applied to the systems engineering of communications architectures (a term used instead of model).
2. Secondarily technically, but primarily politically, each layer (module) can be implemented by a different supplier, to a service specification and must only rely on the service specifications of other layers (modules).

By the Mid 1990's it was clear that the protocols inspired by the International Standards Organizations' Open Systems Interconnection Reference Model (OSIRM), in particular those promulgated by the CCITT and similar bodies had failed to gain any significant acceptance except at the lowest levels and there was widespread criticism of the OSIRM itself.

The failure of the protocols is related to a number of issues

- The protocols were slow to be finalized.
- The protocols were difficult to understand and implement.
- It was difficult to obtain copies of the standards documents.

In all respects the contrast with the protocols associated with the Internet is clear and stark. The Internet protocols are simple, described in plain English, freely available and had the advantage of being early in the field whereas the OSIRM/CCITT protocols are elaborate and abstruse. The Internet protocols were developed in response to a direct and immediate need. The Internet protocols were developed in the context of computer networking rather than the highly regulated world of the national telecommunication bodies that were heavily involved in the OSIRM protocol developments.

Even so it could be and has been suggested that the OSIRM based protocols could or would eventually replace the original Internet protocols as the OSIRM based protocols became better understood and the consequences of the informal design of the Internet protocols became clearer. It now seems most unlikely that this will happen. This is, of course, partly due to the complete market dominance of the Internet protocols and related products but there are also fundamental problems with the OSIRM.

The reference model further specifies seven levels (or layers). This seven-layer model has been reproduced in practically every text on communications, unfortunately the chosen levels bear little relation to the practicalities of communications protocol implementation and null layers and sub-layers are common.

The Internet protocols fit in a much less rigidly defined framework with no formally defined layers but hierarchical use of "lower" protocols by "higher" protocols being common. To those familiar with the formal framework of the OSIRM the Internet Protocols seem "adhoc" and pragmatic, as indeed they are. It is a matter of observation that the OSIRM community has not produced anything like the World Wide Web or the Usenet.

The OSIRM can be further criticized for inadequate support for the concept of interconnected networks and the various management functions such as name service. Interconnected networks imply that entities on two networks that are not directly connected can still communicate even though the networks may be quite different. This has always been fundamental for the Internet community. Such Internet protocols seem to fit between level 3 and level 4 of the OSIRM. They rely on network services to transport data from one part of a network to another (i.e. from one gateway to another) but they are used by end-to-end protocols such as TCP which belong at level 4 of the OSIRM.

Management services simply do not seem to fit very well into the hierarchical model. The simplest examples of management services are various name servers (such as DNS), connectivity tests (such as PING) and more general network management protocols (such as SNMP). Such things can be seen either as services in their own right or as facilities to be used by other services. The most striking issue concerning the OSI model is that it is perhaps the most studied and most unanimously accepted network structure and yet it is not the model that it is really implemented and used. **The specialists, who analyzed this failure, determined 4 main reasons that are stated below:**

1. It was not the right moment

David Clark from the MIT has developed the following theory regarding the manner to publish a standard at the right time. To him, in the cycle of life of a standard, there are 2 principal peaks of activity: the research carried out in the field covered by the standard, and the industrial investments for the implementation and deployment of the standard. These two peaks are separated by a off-peak of activity that actually appears to be the ideal moment for the publication of the standard : it is neither too early compared to research so that we control the technology, nor too late for the investments and manufacturers are ready to spend capital to implement it.

The OSI model was perfectly released regarding research, but alas, the TCP/IP model was already receiving huge investments (when the OSI model was released, the American universities were already successfully using TCP/IP) and the manufacturers did not feel like investing on it.

2. It was not the right technology

The OSI model is maybe to complete and too complex. The gap between the concrete use (implementation) and the model is sometimes significant. Indeed, few programs can use or wrongly use the 7 layers of the model: the session and presentation layers are hardly used and on contrary the data link and network layers are often split into several sub- layers, since they are pretty complex.

The OSI model is in fact too complex to be effectively and properly implemented. The committee that wrote the standard even had to leave aside some technical points, like security and coding, so much it was delicate to preserve a well-defined role to each layer completed with these extra technical points. This model is also redundant (the flow control and the error control appear in most layers). At the implementation level, TCP/IP is much more optimized and effective.

The most significant criticism that one can make against the OSI model is that it is not adapted at all to telecommunication applications on computer! Some choices are in disagreement with the way computers and software communicates. The standard actually uses "system interruptions" to report events, and with high level programming languages, that is not very realizable.

3. It was not the right implementation

This simply comes from the fact that the model is relatively complex, and therefore the first implementations were pretty heavy and slow. Conversely, the first implementation of TCP/IP in the Unix system of the Berkeley University (BSD) was free and relatively effective. Historically, people thus had a natural tendency to use TCP/IP.OSI Model was often synonym of "poor quality"

4. It was not the right policy

Actually, the OSI model suffered from its too strong standardization. The efforts of implementation of the model were above all "bureaucratic" and therefore people might have discredited the model.

3.9.2 The Future of the OSI Model

Regarding its use and implementation, and in spite of an update of the model in 1994, the OSI model has clearly lost the war against TCP/IP. Only few dominating manufacturers keep the model but it is likely to disappear, all the more quickly since the Internet (and thus TCP/IP) is developing.

However, the OSI model will still remain for a while in memories for several reasons. First, it is one of the first main efforts as regards standardization in the area of networks. Manufacturers now tend to do with TCP/IP, but also WAP, UMTS etc. what they were supposed to do with the OSI model, namely to propose standardizations from the beginning. The OSI model will also remain memories for another reason: even if TCP/IP is the model concretely used, people have tendency and use OSI like the current network model of reference. In fact, TCP/IP and OSI have very close structures, and it is especially the effort of standardization of OSI which imposed this general "confusion" between the 2 models. One commonly tends to consider TCP/IP as the real implementation of OSI.

From the above discussion we have concluded the following critiques of OSI Reference Model

- OSI protocols haven't been tested widely before having been standardized. They are not based on existing practice in large scale computer networking, like the Internet
- OSI standards are (compared to Internet standards) very expensive and difficult to obtain.
- The OSI reference model is too complex and has too many layers.
- Having to have to understand the very difficult documentation isn't very motivating.
- Promising new network technologies like ATM networks don't fit in the OSI reference model very well and many important techniques like LANs, RPC and stateless protocols became popular after the OSI reference model had been standardized.
- Having two completely incompatible alternative protocols (CLNP and X.25) at the network layer (and consequently many different transport layers that try to compensate for the differences) isn't what helps you in building up a fully interconnected easy to use and maintain global network.

3.9.3 Critiques of TCP/IP Model

- TCP/IP Model does not clearly distinguish the concepts of service, interface and protocol. So we can say that the TCP/IP model does not make the distinction between specifications and implementation : IP is a protocol that is an integral part of the specifications of the model.
- Consequently, the TCP/IP Model is not much of a guide for designing new networks using new technologies. This model is not general at all and efficient to describe other protocols.
- We can also speak about the host-network layer : Indeed, it is not a real abstraction layer, insofar as its specification is not accurate enough. The host-to-network layer is not really a layer at all in the normal sense that the term is used in the context of layered protocols. It is an interface between the network and data link layers. The TCP/IP Model does not include separate layers between Physical and Data Link layers: there is only a Host to Network Layer.

From the above criticisms we concluded two main points:

- OSI Model is very useful (except Session and Presentation layers) for discussing computer networks, but **OSI protocols are not very popular.**
- TCI/IP Model is almost non-existent, and on the contrary **TCP/IP protocols are very popular.**

Manufacturers are then obliged to propose solutions to fill in the lacks. Finally, we notice that the physical and data link layers are as important as the transport layer. From this fact, we may propose a hybrid model with 5 layers, which would gather the good points of every model:

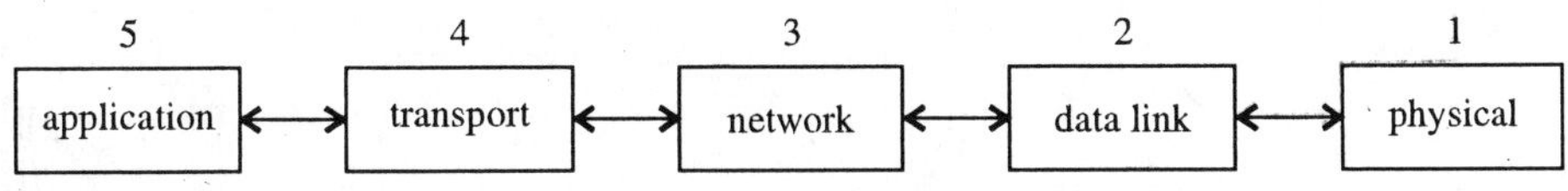

Fig. 3.13 Hybrid model of reference

Finally, this model is the real reference in the Internet world. We have kept most layers of the OSI model (all but the session and presentation layers) because they are well specified. On the other hand, OSI's protocols have no success and finally, we have kept those from the TCP/IP model.

• • •

4

Transmission Media

Introduction

Network media is the actual path over which an electrical signal travels as it moves from one component to another. Modern networks can utilize several types of network media. Most networks use some type of cable for the connection media. Air is sometimes used. Wireless technologies, such as infrared and satellite communications, will become increasingly important in the future. This chapter describes the common types of network media, including twisted-pair cable, coaxial cable, fiber-optic cable and wireless media.

A data communications network must have cabling to allow individual computers and other peripherals to talk to one another and share resources. And wouldn't it be easier if there were only one type available? There would be fewer hassles when it came time to figure out such things as line speeds, line capacities, variations in line distortion, and so on. However, there are a number of types, ranging in cost and capabilities.

4.1 Few Important Points about the Electrical Interface

- To transmit binary data over transmission channels, the binary digits making up each element to be transmitted must be converted into electrical signals.

Binary 1	+V volts
Binary 0	–V volts

- On receiving these signals, the receiver interprets +V volts as binary 1 and –V volts as binary 0.

- In practice transmitted electrical signals are attenuated and distorted by the transmission medium, so that the receiver is unable to discriminate between binary 1 and 0 signals.

The basic idea of data transmission is to encode data as energy and transmit energy and then decode energy at destination back into data. Energy can be electrical, light, radio; sound, ... Each form of energy has different properties and requirements for transmission.

4.1.1 Bit-Wise Data Transmission

Transmitted energy is carried through some sort of medium. Media can be copper, glass, air...

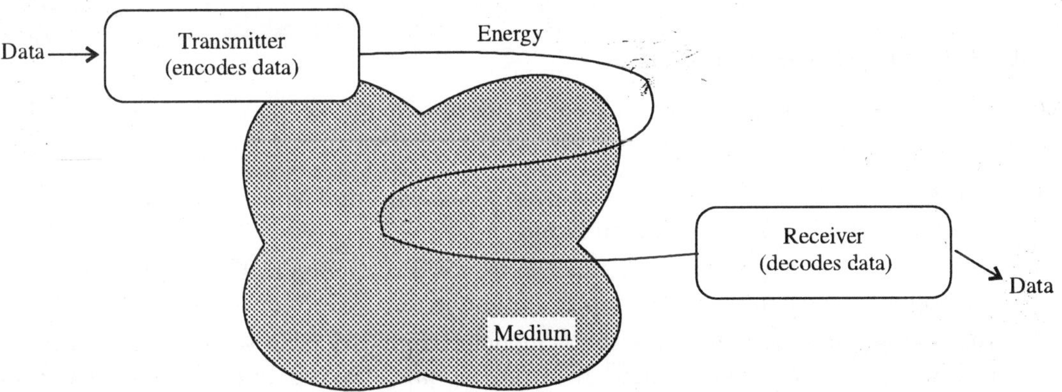

Fig. 4.1 Data transmission

So we can say that data transmission requires:

- *Encoding* bits as energy
- *Transmitting* energy through medium
- *Decoding* energy back into bits

Transmitter and receiver must agree on encoding scheme and transmission timing.

Measures of Transmission Rates

- *Baud* rate measures number of signal changes per second.
- *Bits* per second measures number of bits transmitted per second.
- In RS-232, each signal change represents one bit, so baud rate and bits per second are equal.
- If each signal change represents more than one bit, bits per second may be greater than baud rate.

4.2 Classification Of Transmission Media

There are two major classes of transmission media:

1. Conducted or Guided Media

Waves are guided along solid medium. Such media use a conductor such as a wire or a fiber optic cable to move the signal from sender to receiver.

Some basic categories in it are:

- **Twisted-pair wire**—Copper wire twisted into a spiral shape. Wires are twisted together to reduce noise and crosstalk.
- **Coaxial Cable**—Improved version of twisted pair. Consists of conductors insulated from each other enclosed in a polyethylene jacket.
- **Fiber-Optics**—Offers higher data rates, reduced noise, and larger bandwidth.

2. Wireless or Unguided Media

Such media use radio waves of different frequencies and do not need a wire or cable conductor to transmit signals. Some categories in it are:

- **Microwave**—Consists of a transmitter, receiver, and the atmosphere. It is also referred to as line of sight transmission.
- **Radio**—Unlike microwave transmission that is directional, radio transmission is omni directional. The signals need simpler antennas.
- **Infrared**—Infrared signals, with frequencies from 300 GHz to 400 THz can be used for short-range communication. Infrared signals, having high frequencies, cannot penetrate walls.
- **Satellites**—Satellites are transponders (units that receive on one frequency and retransmit on another) that are set in geostationary orbits directly over the equator.

4.2.1 Characteristics of A Medium

There are three important parameters for communication media:

Bandwidth: (Capacity) Number of bits per second. Greater bandwidth implies higher data rates

Delay: The time elapsed until data starts arriving at the other end.

Loss: Error rate.

Medium	Bandwidth	Delay	Loss
Truck with magnetic tapes or CDs	Very high	Very, very high	Low
Copper	Medium	Low	Varying, sensitive
Radio link • earth based • by satellite	 Quite high High	 Low High	 Medium Medium
Fiber optics	Very high	Low	Very high

Data transmissions depend on the characteristics of the signal and of the medium.

- For guided media, the medium is the dominant factor.
- For unguided media, the bandwidth of the signal is the dominant factor.

Now we will discuss each kind of transmission media in detail.

4.3 Magnetic Media

Data transmission between two machines takes place in the following way:

- The source machine writes data onto magnetic tapes or floppy disks.
- The tapes or disks are physically transported to the destination machine by a station wagon, truck, or airplane.
- The destination machine reads the data from the tapes or disks.

A simple calculation, suppose:

- A standard 8-mm video tape can hold 7 gigabytes.
- A box can hold 1000 tapes, for a total capacity of 7000 gigabytes.
- A box of tapes can be delivered anywhere in the US in 24 hours by Federal Express and other companies.

The effective bandwidth is 56-gigabits/86400 sec or 648 Mbps, which is slightly better than the high-speed version of ATM (622 Mbps). If the destination is only an hour away by road, the bandwidth is increased to over 15 Gbps. The cost is 10 cents per gigabyte - no network carrier on earth can compete with this!

Advantages : High bandwidth and cost effective.
Disadvantages : Off-line and poor delay characteristics.

4.4 Twisted Pair

Twisted pair is most widely used media for local data distribution. Twisted-pair cable is a type of cabling that is used for telephone communications and most modern Ethernet networks. A pair of wires forms a circuit that can transmit data. The pairs are twisted to provide protection against *crosstalk*, the noise generated by adjacent pairs. The twisting introduces an inductive component that opposes the capacitivity between the two threads. When electrical current flows through a wire, it creates a small, circular magnetic field around the wire. When two wires in an electrical circuit are placed close together, their magnetic fields are the exact opposite of each other. Thus, the two magnetic fields cancel each other out. They also cancel out any outside magnetic fields. Twisting the wires can enhance this *cancellation effect.* Using cancellation together with twisting the wires, cable designers can effectively provide self-shielding for wire pairs within the network media.

While twisted-pair cable is used by older telephone networks and is the least expensive type of local-area network (LAN) cable, most networks contain some twisted-pair cabling at some point along the network.

Since some telephone sets or desktop locations require multiple connections, twisted pair is sometimes installed in two or more pairs, all within a single cable. For some business locations, twisted pair is enclosed in a shield that functions as a ground. This is known as shielded twisted pair (STP). Ordinary wire to the home is unshielded twisted pair (UTP).

In shielded twisted pair cables, each pair has a metal sheath around it for better protection against interference. Unshielded twisted pair lacks the sheath, but has the advantage of being more flexible and thinner. Twisted pair cable is being replaced over time by coaxial cable and fiber-optic cable, which have greater signal capacity.

Twisted pair is now frequently installed with two pairs to the home, with the extra pair making it possible for you to add another line (perhaps for modem use) when you need it. Twisted pair comes with each pair uniquely color-coded when it is packaged in multiple pairs. Different uses such as analog, digital, and Ethernet require different pair multiples.

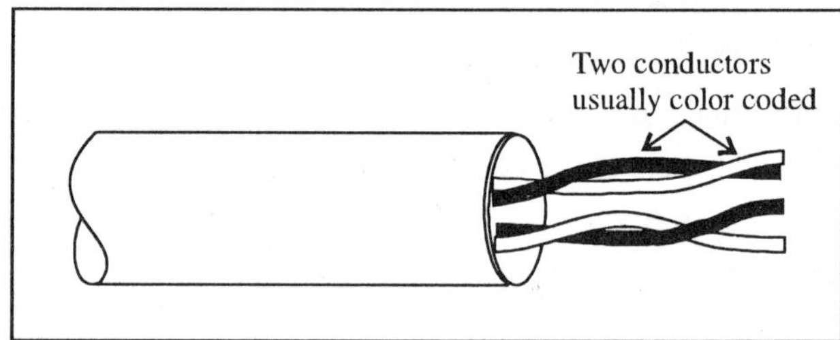

Fig. 4.2 Twisted-wire pairs (2 wire pairs shown)

Although twisted pair is often associated with home use, a higher grade of twisted pair is often used for horizontal wiring in LAN installations because it is less expensive than coaxial cable. The wire you buy at a local hardware store for extensions from your phone or computer modem to a wall jack is not twisted pair. It is a side-by-side wire known as silver satin. The wall jack can have as many five kinds of hole arrangements or pinouts, depending on the kinds of wire the installation expects will be plugged in (for example, digital, analog, or LAN).

The advantages of using telephone wires are their relative low cost and their availability. Their disadvantages include susceptibility to signal distortion errors and the relatively low transmission rates they provide over long distances. Twisted wire can handle a data flow of up to approximately one megabit per second (Mbps) over several hundred feet. For a small local-area network with a limited number of users, twisted-pair is an ideal choice because it is both inexpensive and easy to install. A phenomenon called **crosstalk exists** in twisted-wire pairs whenever transmission occurs at a high rate of speed. Crosstalk is taking place whenever you can hear someone else's conversation in the background; while you're trying to carry on a conversation with your party. With voice communications this really isn't a problem; however, crosstalk can inhibit the high-speed transmission required for data communications.

Twisted-wire pairs used in data communications are either private or public lines. **Private lines** are those provided by the user. **Public lines** are those provided by a common carrier such as American Telephone and Telegraph (AT&T). Generally, public lines are used whenever distances are great or the terrain or other environmental factors prohibit the use of private lines. Public lines may be either switched lines or leased lines.

Switched lines are used whenever the amount of data to be transmitted is short in duration or when many locations must be contacted for relatively short periods of time. There is a drawback. The telephone company cannot guarantee you exactly which path or switching equipment such a connection will use. Therefore, the speed and quality of the switched connection are questionable.

Leased lines come into play when the connection time between locations *A* and *B* is long enough to cover the cost of leasing, or if higher speeds than those available with switched lines must be attained. Leased lines can also be conditioned by the telephone company to lower the error rate and increase transmission speeds. Conditioned leased lines typically operate at speeds of up to 64,000 bits per second (bps). Very-high-speed connections are also available from the common carrier. These are designated *T*1, *T*2, *T*3 and *T*4 and offer transmission rates of 1.5, 6.3, 46, and 281 million bits per second (Mbps), respectively.

Two basic types of twisted-pair cable exist:

1. Unshielded twisted pair (UTP)
2. Shielded twisted pair (STP).

4.4.1 UTP Cable

Unshielded twisted pair is the most common kind of copper telephone wiring. UTP cable is a medium that is composed of pairs of wires. UTP cable is used in a variety of networks. Each of the eight individual copper wires in UTP cable is covered by an insulating material. In addition, the wires in each pair are twisted around each other.

UTP cable relies solely on the cancellation effect produced by the twisted wire pairs to limit signal degradation caused by electromagnetic interference (EMI) and radio frequency interference (RFI). To further reduce crosstalk between the pairs in UTP cable, the number of twists in the wire pairs varies. UTP cable must follow precise specifications governing how many twists or braids are permitted per meter (3.28 feet) of cable.

UTP cable offers many advantages.

1. **Size :** UTP is small and does not quickly fill up wiring ducts. Because UTP has an external diameter of approximately 0.43 cm (0.17 inches), its small size can be advantageous during installation. Because it has such a small external diameter, UTP does not fill up wiring ducts as rapidly as other types of cable. This can be an extremely important factor to consider, particularly when installing a network in an older building.
2. **Inexpensive :** UTP cable is less expensive than other types of networking media. In fact, UTP costs less per meter than any other type of LAN cabling.
3. **Easy installation :** It is thin, flexible and easy to string between walls.
4. As UTP can be used with most of the major networking architectures, it continues to grow in popularity.

UTP does have its disadvantages:

1. **Susceptibility to interference :** It is more susceptible to interference than most other types of cabling. The pair twisting does help, but it does not come close to making the cable impervious to electrical noise.
2. **Limited segment length :** It is limited to segments of 100 meters.

Although UTP was once considered to be slower at transmitting data than other types of cable, this is no longer true. In fact, UTP is considered the fastest copper-based medium today.

The following summarizes the features of UTP cable:

- Speed and throughput-10 to 1000 Mbps.
- Average cost per node-Least expensive.
- Media and connector size-Small.
- Maximum cable length-100 m (short).

Commonly used types of UTP cabling are as follows:

- **Category 1**—Used for telephone communications. Not suitable for transmitting data.
- **Category 2**—Capable of transmitting data at speeds up to 4 megabits per second (Mbps).
- **Category 3**—Used in 10BASE-T networks. Can transmit data at speeds up to 10 Mbps.
- **Category 4**—Used in Token Ring networks. Can transmit data at speeds up to 16 Mbps.
- **Category 5**—Can transmit data at speeds up to 100 Mbps.
- **Category 5e**—Used in networks running at speeds up to 1000 Mbps (1 gigabit per second [Gbps]).
- **Category 6**—Typically, Category 6 cable consists of four pairs of 24 American Wire Gauge (AWG) copper wires. Category 6 cable is currently the fastest standard for UTP.

4.4.2 STP Cable

STP is similar to UTP in that the wire pairs are twisted around each other. STP also has shielding around the cable to further protect it from external interference. The shielding further reduces the chance of crosstalk but the shielding increases the overall diameter and weight of the cable. The maximum segment length of STP cable is 100 meters.

Shielded twisted pair is a special kind of copper telephone wiring used in some business installations. An outer covering or shield is added to the ordinary twisted pair telephone wires; the shield functions as a ground.

Shielded twisted-pair (*STP*) cable combines the techniques of shielding, cancellation, and wire twisting. Each pair of wires is wrapped in a metallic foil. The four pairs of wires then are wrapped in an overall metallic braid or foil, usually 150-ohm cable. As specified for use in Ethernet network installations, STP reduces electrical noise both within the cable (pair-to-pair coupling, or crosstalk) and from outside the cable (EMI and RFI).

The **advantages of STP include:**

1. Greater protection from interference and crosstalk due to shielding.
2. Better electrical characteristics than unshielded cables.
3. Easily terminated with modular connector.

The **disadvantages to STP include:**

1. **Cost** : STP has a higher cost per foot
2. **Grounding** : The STP Shield must be grounded at both ends. If it is improperly grounded, the shield acts like an antenna and picks up unwanted signals.
3. **Difficulty in installation** : Heavier, less flexible, STP is more difficult to install.
4. **Thickness** : Because of its thickness it may not fit down narrow cable ducts.
5. No segment length advantage despite the heavier and thicker cable.
6. Can be tapped, breaching security.

The following summarizes the features of STP cable:

- Speed and throughput-10 to 100 Mbps.
- Average cost per node-Moderately expensive.
- Media and connector size-Medium to large.
- Maximum cable length-100 m (short).

When comparing UTP and STP, keep the following points in mind:

- The speed of both types of cable is usually satisfactory for local-area distances.
- These are the least-expensive media for data communication. UTP is less expensive than STP.
- Because most buildings are already wired with UTP, many transmission standards are adapted to use it, to avoid costly rewiring with an alternative cable type.

Use Twisted-Pair Cable

- If your LAN is under budget constraints.
- If you want a relatively easy installation where computer connections are simple.
- DO NOT USE IF you must be absolutely sure of data integrity transmitted over great distances at high speeds.

4.5 Coaxlal Cable

Coaxial Cable is high-capacity cable widely used for high-frequency transmission of telephone, television, and digital audio signals. The cable is very effective at carrying many analog signals at high frequencies.

Coaxial cable is often referred to as simply "coax". Not only is coax the most commonly used cable, but also the least expensive, most reliable, most convenient, and easily maintained way of transferring electronic images in a CCTV system. Coax is available from many manufacturers and comes in a variety of sizes, shapes, colors, specifications and capabilities. Coaxial cables have become an essential component of our information superhighway. They are found in a wide variety of residential, commercial and industrial installations. From broadcast, community antenna television (CATV), local area network (LAN), closed circuit television (CCTV) to many other applications, coax has laid the foundation for a simple, cost effective communications infrastructure.

Coaxial Cable is also widely used in the telecommunications industry, such as the telephone system where coax reaches the pole or drop nearest to the subscriber's house, and a twisted-pair cable comes into the house and to the telephone. Coaxial can also be a good solution for providing residences and small business with high-speed data access because it is generally wired in a bus topology, it requires less cable than other solutions and does not require a hub, cutting down on cost.

In contrast to twisted-pair wires, coaxial has the capacity to transmit information 80 times faster, has much higher bandwidth, offers greater protection from noise and interference and can support greater cable lengths between network devices. Coaxial cable also offers relatively high immunity to interference from noise sources, so it is often used in manufacturing environments.

Coaxial cable supports 10 to 100 Mbps and is relatively inexpensive, although it is more costly than UTP on a per-unit length. However, coaxial cable can be cheaper for a physical bus topology because less cable will be needed. Coaxial cable can be cabled over longer distances than twisted-pair cable. For example, Ethernet can run approximately 100 meters (328 feet) using twisted-pair cabling. Using coaxial cable increases this distance to 500m (1640.4 feet).

Coax Construction

Common "coax" cable RG59//U, RG6/U, and RG11/U is circular. Each has a center conductor surrounded by dielectric insulating material, which in turn is covered by a braid to shield against electromagnetic interference (EMI). The outer covering is the "jacket".

The coaxial cable's two conductors are separated by a nonconductive or dielectric material. The outer conductor (braid) acts as a shield and helps isolate the center conductor from spurious electromagnetic interference. The outer covering helps physically protect the conductors.

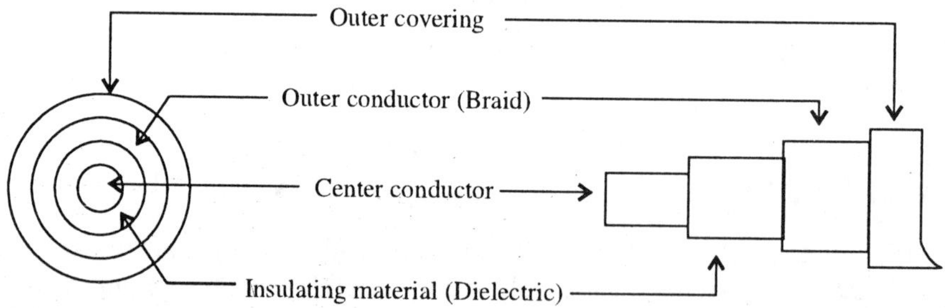

Fig. 4.3 Coaxial cable

Coaxial cable is called "coaxial" because it includes one physical channel that carries the signal surrounded (after a layer of insulation) by another concentric physical channel, both running along the same axis. Data is transmitted through the center channel, while the outer channel serves as a line to ground. These two conductors usually carry equal currents in opposite directions.

Description of Various Parts

Inner/Center Conductor

The center conductor is the primary means of carrying a video signal. The center conductor comes in varying diameters, usually ranging from 14 gauge to 22 gauge. The structure of the center conductor generally is solid copper or copper- clad steel, designated as bare copper weld or BCW. Variation in the size of the center conductor has an overall effect on the amount of DC resistance offered by cable. Cables that contain large diameter center conductors have lower resistances than cables with smaller diameters. This decreased resistance of large diameter cable enhances the ability of a cable to carry a video signal over a longer distance with better clarity, but it is also more expensive and harder to work with.

Dielectric Insulating Material

Surrounding the center conductor is an evenly made dielectric insulating material that is available in some form of either polyurethane or polyethylene. This dielectric insulator helps determine the operating characteristics of coax cable by maintaining uniform spacing between the center conductor and its outer elements over the entire length of the cable. Dielectrics made of cellular polyurethane or foam is less likely to weaken a video signal than those made with solid polyethylene. This lower attenuation is desirable when calculating the loss/length factor of any cable. Foam also gives a cable greater flexibility, which may make an installer's job easier. Although foam dielectric material offers the best performance, it can absorb moisture, which will change its electrical behavior.

Braid or Shield

Wrapped around the outside of the dielectric material is a woven copper braid (shield), which acts as a second conductor or ground connection between the camera and the monitor. It also acts as a shield against unwanted external signals commonly called electromagnetic interference or EMI, which may adversely affect a video signal. The amount of copper or wire strands in the braid determine how much EMI it keeps out. Commercial grade coax cables containing loosely woven copper braid have shielding coverages of approximately 80 percent. These cables are suitable for general-purpose use in applications where electrical interference is known to be low. They also work well when the cable is to be installed in metal conduit or pipe, which also aids in shielding.

Outer Jacket

The last component comprising a coax cable is the outer jacket. Although other materials are used, polyvinyl chloride or PVC, is commonly used in its construction. Available in many colors such as black, white, tan and gray, the jacket lends itself to both indoor and outdoor applications.

Coaxial cable offers several advantages

1. It can be run with fewer boosts from repeaters for longer distances between network nodes than either STP or UTP cable. Repeaters regenerate the signals in a network so that they can cover greater distances. Longer segment lengths than UTP or STP.
2. Coaxial cable is less expensive than fiber-optic cable, and the technology is well known; it has been used for many years for all types of data communication.
3. Familiar and fairly easy to install.
4. Better electrical characteristics (lower attenuation and great bandwidth) than shielded or unshielded cables.
5. Coaxial cable provides superior noise immunity over conventional twisted pairs. As with other media, its immunity to noise is subject to the impact of variables such as the application and the environment. Baseband systems usually provide immunity of 50 to 60 decibels (dB), while broadband systems operate with 85 to 100 dB.
6. Generally good data security.
7. Easy to connect.
8. *Built-in shielding* : The entire cable is surrounded by a non-conduction outer shield, usually made of rubber, Teflon or plastic.
9. More resistant to interference and attenuation than twisted-pair cabling. Attenuation is the loss of signal strength which begins to occur as the signal travels further along a copper cable.

Disadvantages of coaxial cable are :

1. Coaxial cable is not as easy to run as UTP, because it is not as flexible or thin.
2. *Expensive* : Coaxial cable is more expensive than UTP. High attenuation rate makes it expensive over long distance.
3. *Bulky* : Requires more room in wiring ducts than UTP.
4. May become obsolete due to technological advances.

Types of Coaxial Cable : Baseband and Broadband

There are many different forms of coaxial cable; however, they are usually divided into two classifications—those used for **baseband transmission**, and those used for **broadband transmission**. The primary distinction between the two cable types is the characteristic impedance. (Impedance is the measure of how much voltage must be applied to the cable to achieve a given signal strength. Measured in Ohms). Baseband cable has a characteristic impedance of 50 ohms and is used for digital transmission mainly in Ethernet networks, while broadband cable impedance is 75 ohms and is used for analog transmission like in cable television (CATV) and Cable Internet. Using the wrong cable will cause network problems.

4.5.1 Baseband Coaxial Cable

Baseband systems use digital encoding techniques to carry digital data over a digital transmission line. In baseband transmission, all of the available frequencies in the transmission medium are used by one signal. Base band is a 50 ohm cable, which is commonly used for digital transmission. The bandwidth possible depends on the length of the cables used. For example, with 1 km cables a data rate of 1 to 2 Gbps is feasible. Longer cables can also be used, but only at lower data rates or with periodic amplifiers.

The baseband coaxial cable is usually referred to as Ethernet cable, because it was originally used in the Ethernet Networks. In baseband systems there is no modulation of the signal. Transceivers are used to place digital signals directly onto the cable. These signals are encoded using some of the techniques such as Manchester or Differential Manchester phase encoding. The digital signal occupies the entire bandwidth of the cable; thus, baseband cables have only one channel in operation at any moment in time. Transmission is bidirectional. That is, a signal inserted at any point on the medium propagates in both directions to the ends.

Many baseband implementations operate in the range of 10 Mbps for standard Ethernet, although others, such as Token Ring at 16 Mbps, operate at higher rates.

Coax comes in several sizes. Standard Ethernet cable, called **Thick Coaxial** or Thick Ethernet, is about the diameter of a man's thumb and **Thin Coaxial** or Thin Ethernet, is about as thick as a woman's pinky finger. Thicker coax is more robust, harder to damage, and transmits data over longer distances. It's also more difficult to connect.

Baseband Summary

<table>
<tr><td rowspan="2">• Unmodulated digital signal.
• Single channel.
• Bidirectional propagation of signal.
• No need of modems—low cost installation.</td><td>Advantages—
1. Simplicity
2. Low cost
3. Ease of installation and maintenance</td></tr>
<tr><td>Disadvantages—
1. Limited distances
2. Data and voice only</td></tr>
</table>

4.5.2 Broadband Coaxial Cable

Broadband systems use modulation techniques to transmit digital data over analog carrier waves. Broadband transmission lines can be much longer than baseband lines. The word "Broadband" is a generic term. It refers to the wide bandwidth characteristics of a transmission medium and it's ability to carry numerous voice, video or data signals simultaneously. The medium could be coaxial cable, fiber-optic cable, UTP Media Twist or a wireless system.

Broadband is a 75 ohm cable that is commonly used for analog transmission. In broadband systems, analog signals are transmitted on the cable using both frequency and phase-modulation techniques. Broadband systems are divided up into multiple channels, frequently the 6Mhz channels used for television broadcasting. Each channel can also be used for CD-quality audio, or a digital bit stream that would be independent of the others. Television and data can also be mixed on one broadband cable.

Broadband and cable TV take advantage of coax's ability to transmit many signals at the same time. Each signal is called a channel. Each channel travels along at a different frequency, so it does not interfere with other channels. Signals are modulated into Radio Frequency (RF) channels that are 6 MHz or 7 MHz wide in bandwidth. By dividing services into separate channels, different types of signals can co-exist and travel in opposite directions "inbound and outbound" along the same coaxial cable.

Broadband systems offer significantly increased bandwidth capabilities due to the fact that there are multiple channels on each cable. Typical broadband implementations with highly saturated cables may yield aggregate bandwidths as high as 100 Mbps.

The broadband, and carrier band cables transmit analog signals, therefore modem converts the digital signal to analog signal prior to transmission of the data. A modem at the receiving end of the medium will convert the analog signal to a digital signal. The analog signal that carries digital data can travel longer distances and is more immune to electrical noise interferences, and signal degradation damage.

The carrier band cable that is sometimes called single channel broadband, covers only one analog frequency signal spectrum. Therefore, carrier band coaxial cables are less expensive than broadband coaxial cables, and the modems used in carrier band systems are less expensive than the modems used in broadband systems.

Coaxial cable can be used in both a point-to-point mode and a broadcast mode. In local network bus architectures, multiple devices are usually "dropped" from a single cable. Depending on the application and the required data rates, a broadband system may support thousands of connections. Amplifiers are usually placed at intervals of 0.5 to 1.5 km to regenerate the signals.

Broadband coaxial cables are divided into two types of systems:

1. Dual cable systems use two cables, one for each direction.
2. Mid-split systems use one cable, but the frequency is divided such that one portion of the frequency is used in one direction, the second is used for the other direction.

Broadband Summary

• Digital signal modulated onto RF carrier (analog). • Channel allocation based on FDM. • Head-End for bidirectional transmission. • Stations connected via RF modems.	**Advantages—** 1. Data, voice and video. 2. Greater distances. 3. Greater bandwidth.
	Disadvantages— 1. Cable design. 2. Alignment and maintenance. 3. High cost, requires modems. 4. Lack of well developed standards.

4.5.3 Uses of Coaxial Cable

Cable TV

Coaxial cable is used by cable TV companies to deliver service to user homes and businesses. Cable systems were originally designed to deliver broadcast television signals efficiently to subscribers' homes. To ensure that consumers could obtain cable service with the same TV sets they use to receive over-the-air broadcast TV signals, cable operators recreate a portion of the over-the-air radio frequency (RF) spectrum within a sealed coaxial cable line.

Circuits in coax network usually wired in bus topology, and need to have signal amplifiers installed at points along the network. The amplifiers can be one-way or two-way; the two-way amplifiers permit the provision of interactive services over the network, allowing consumers to select from a menu of services (for example, home shopping, videos on demand, or educational services).

Cable Internet

Cable Internet access is delivered through coaxial cable by a Cable Modem at the user's end. A Cable Modem sends and receives data to and from the Internet by using the existing coaxial cable TV network. Cable TV Networks are high band-with networks, i.e., 550 to 750 MHz by their very nature of design.

Digital data signals are transmitted over radio frequency (RF) carrier signals on a cable system. For two-way communication, there is one carrier signal that carries data in the "downstream" direction (from the cable network to the customer), and another that carries data in the "upstream" direction (from the customer to the cable network). Higher-frequency signals flow toward the subscriber and lower-frequency signals flow toward the broadcasting head-end. This upstream and downstream bandwidth is shared by the active data subscribers connected to a given cable network segment, typically 500 to 2,000 homes on a modern HFC network.

To deliver data services over a cable network, one television channel (in the 85–750 MHz range) is typically allocated for downstream traffic to homes and another channel (in the 5–65 MHz band) is used to carry upstream signals. Each downstream band can carry one analog video channel, up to 27 Mbps data stream. Typically, cable internet access provide has maximum of 1.5–6 Mbps of bandwidth on the system. However, due network sharing that bandwidth on the network segment performance can be much lower.

The cable modem access network operates at Layer 1 (physical) and Layer 2 (media access control/logical link control) of the Open System Interconnect (OSI) Reference Model. Thus, Layer 3 (network) protocols, such as IP traffic, can be seamlessly delivered over the cable modem platform to end-users.

A Cable Modem Termination System (CMTS) communicates through these channels with cable modems located in subscriber homes to create a virtual local area network (LAN) connection. All cable modems can receive from and send signals only to the CMTS, but not to other cable modems on the line. A typical CMTS consists of an Input interface, Router, Cable Modem card and a powerful Microprocessor. Most cable modems are external devices that connect to a personal computer (PC) through a standard Ethernet card or Universal Serial Bus (USB) connection.

4.6 Fiber Optics

Our current "age of technology" is the result of many brilliant inventions and discoveries, but it is our ability to transmit information and the media we use to do it, that is perhaps most responsible for its evolution. Progressing from the copper wire of a century ago to today's fiber optic cable, our increasing ability to transmit more information, more quickly and over longer distances has expanded the boundaries of our technological development in all areas.

Fiber-optic cable is a networking medium capable of conducting modulated light transmissions. It is the best choice if a secure network is needed. Because the cable transmits light, the transmissions are immune to interference caused by electrical or electronic devices. Also, if your network will run through an area of heavy industrial activity or a work place with strong radio frequency interference, fiber optic cable is the most appropriate choice.

Fiber optics is being used to transmit television, voice, and digital data signals by light waves over flexible hair like threads of glass and plastic. It has evolved into a system of great importance and use since the 1980's.

4.6.1 Fiber Optic Cable

It consists of thousands of clear glass fiber strands, each approximately the thickness of a human hair. If you look closely at a single optical fiber, you will see that it has the following parts:

- Core—Thin glass center of the fiber where the light travels.
- Cladding—Outer optical material surrounding the core that reflects the light back into the core.
- Buffer coating—Plastic coating that protects the fiber from damage and moisture.

Hundreds or thousands of these optical fibers are arranged in bundles in optical cables. The bundles are protected by the cable's outer covering, called a jacket.

Transmission is made possible by the transformation of digital data into modulated light beams, which are sent through the cable by a laser light-emitting diode (LED) type device at incredibly fast speeds. Transmission rates available (as of 1990) range up to approximately 1 billion (or giga) bits per second (Gbps), with speeds over 2 Gbps possible. When thinking in terms of frequencies, light frequencies are extremely high. They are approximately 600,000 times that of the highest television channel. In terms of data communications, the higher the frequency of the signal, the more information it can carry. Put simply, every hair like fiber within a fiber optic cable has the capacity to carry many hundreds of local-area network channels simultaneously.

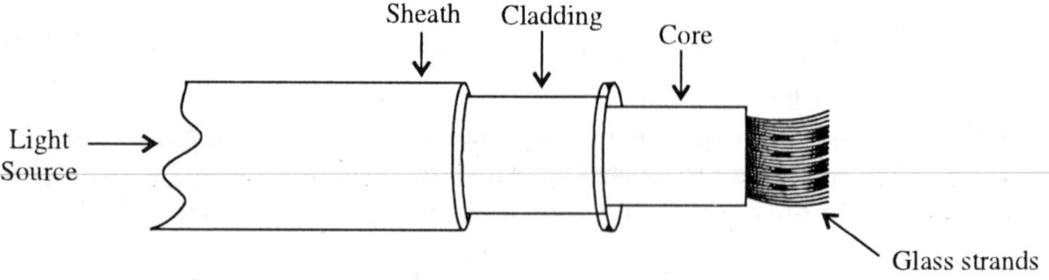

Fig. 4.4 Fibre optic cable

Fiber

Some 10 billion digital bits can be transmitted per second along an optical fiber link in a commercial network, enough to carry tens of thousands of telephone calls. Hair-thin fibers consist of two concentric layers of high-purity silica glass the core and the cladding, which are enclosed by a protective sheath. Light rays modulated into digital pulses with a laser or a light-emitting diode move along the core without penetrating the cladding.

The light stays confined to the core because the cladding has a lower refractive index-a measure of its ability to bend light. Refinements in optical fibers, along with the development of new lasers and diodes, may one day allow commercial fiber-optic networks to carry trillions of bits of data per second.

Construction

Today's low-loss glass fiber optic cable offers almost unlimited bandwidth and unique advantages over all previously developed transmission media. The basic point-to-point fiber optic transmission system consists of three basic elements: the optical transmitter, the fiber optic cable and the optical receiver.

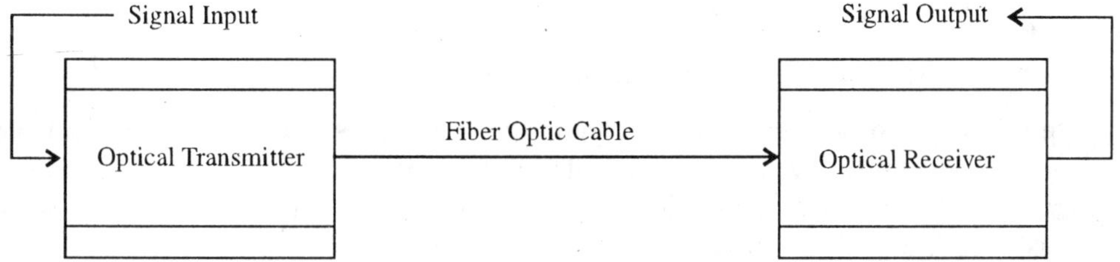

Fig. 4.5 Fiber optic transmission system

The Optical Transmitter : The transmitter converts an electrical analog or digital signal into a corresponding optical signal. The source of the optical signal can be either a light emitting diode, or a solid-state laser diode. The most popular wavelengths of operation for optical transmitters are 850, 1300, or 1550 nanometers.

The Fiber Optic Cable : The cable consists of one or more glass fibers, which act as wave-guides for the optical signal. Fiber optic cable is similar to electrical cable in its construction, but provides special protection for the optical fiber within. For systems requiring transmission over distances of many kilometers or where two or more fiber optic cables must be joined together, an optical splice is commonly used.

The Optical Receiver : The receiver converts the optical signal back into a replica of the original electrical signal. The detector of the optical signal is either a PIN-type photodiode or avalanche-type photodiode.

Composition of Optical Fiber :

- Silica based glass or plastic filaments are spun and packed into bundles of several hundreds or thousands. Bundles may be put together as rods or ribbons and sheets.

- These bundles are flexible and can be twisted and contorted to conduct light and images around corners.
- The thin glass center of the fiber where the light travels is called the "core".
- The outer optical material surrounding the core that reflects the light back into the core is called the "cladding".
- In order to protect the optical surface from moisture and damage, it is coated with a layer of buffer coating.

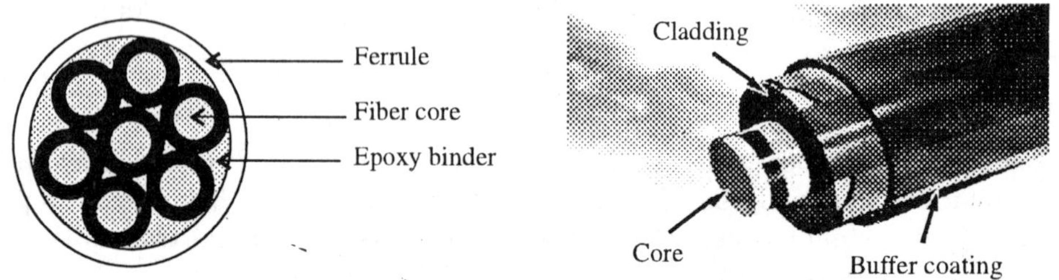

Fig. 4.6 Structure of fiber optic cable

How Does an Optical Fiber Transmit Light?

Suppose you want to shine a flashlight beam down a long, straight hallway. Just point the beam straight down the hallway—light travels in straight lines, so it is no problem. What if the hallway has a bend in it? You could place a mirror at the bend to reflect the light beam around the corner. What if the hallway is very winding with multiple bends? You might line the walls with mirrors and angle the beam so that it bounces from side-to-side all along the hallway. This is exactly what happens in an optical fiber.

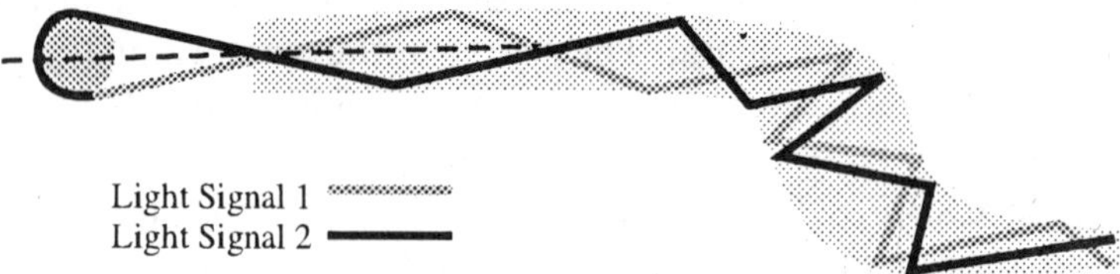

Fig. 4.7. Diagram of total internal reflection in an optical fiber.

The light in a fiber-optic cable travels through the core (hallway) by constantly bouncing from the cladding (mirror-lined walls), a principle called total internal reflection. Because the cladding does not absorb any light from the core, the light wave can travel great distances. However, some of the light signal degrades within the fiber, mostly due to impurities in the glass. The extent that the signal degrades depends on the purity of the glass and the wavelength of the transmitted light (for example, 850 nm = 60 to 75 percent/km; 1,300 nm = 50 to 60 percent/km; 1,550 nm is greater than 50 percent/km). Some premium optical fibers show much less signal degradation—less than 10 percent/km at 1,550 nm.

Types of Fiber Optic Cable

There are two types of fiber optic cable commonly used:

1. Single mode optical fiber.
2. Multimode optical fiber.

4.6.2 Single Mode Cable

It is a single stand of glass fiber with a diameter of 8.3 to 10 microns that has one mode of transmission. Single Mode fiber with a relatively narrow diameter, through which only one mode will propagate carries higher bandwidth than multimode fiber, but requires a light source with a narrow spectral width. Synonyms are mono-mode optical fiber, single-mode fiber, single-mode optical waveguide, and uni-mode fiber.

Single-mode fiber gives you a higher transmission rate and up to 50 times more distance than multimode, but it also costs more. Single-mode fiber has a much smaller core than multimode. The small core and single light-wave virtually eliminate any distortion that could result from overlapping light pulses, providing the least signal attenuation and the highest transmission speeds of any fiber cable type.

Single-mode optical fiber is an optical fiber in which only the lowest order bound mode can propagate at the wavelength of interest typically 1300 to 1320 nm.

``Single mode fibre"
single path through the fiber

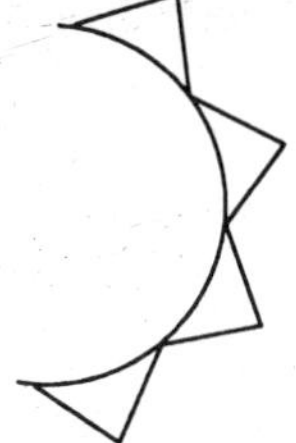

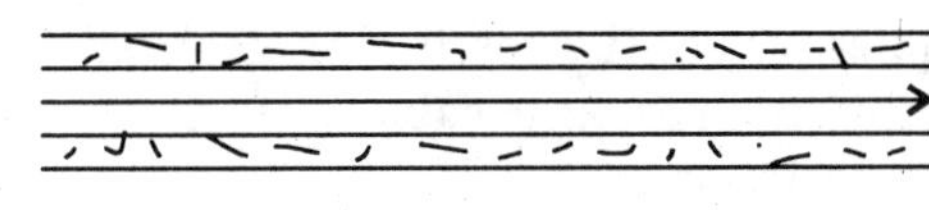

Fig. 4.8 Single mode cable

4.6.3 Multimode Cable

Multimode cable is made of glass fibers, with a common diameter in the 50-to-100 micron range for the light carry component (the most common size is 62.5). POF is a newer plastic-based cable that promises performance similar to glass cable on very short runs, but at a lower cost.

Multimode fiber gives you high bandwidth at high speeds over medium distances. Light waves are dispersed into numerous paths, or modes, as they travel through the cable's core typically 850 or 1300 nm. Typical multimode fiber core diameters are 50, 62.5, and 100 micrometers. However, in long cable runs (greater than 3000 feet [914.4 mL]), multiple paths of light can cause signal distortion at the receiving end, resulting in an unclear and incomplete data transmission.

``Multi mode fibre''
multiple paths through the fiber

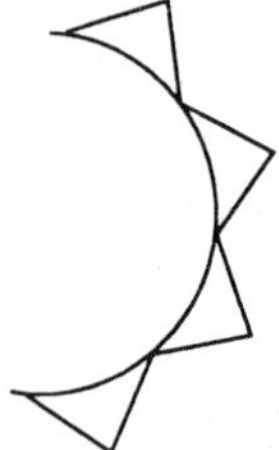

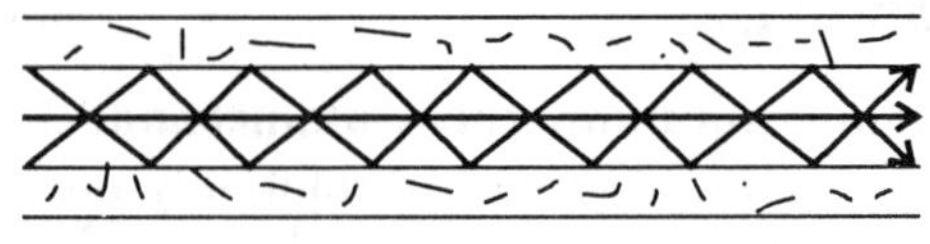

Fig. 4.9 Multimode cable

4.6.4 Advantages and Disadvantages of Fiber Optics over Copper Wire

The advantages of fiber optics over copper wire are discussed below:

1. **Ease Of Installation**—Increasing transmission capacity of wire cables generally makes them thicker and more rigid. Such thick cables can be difficult to install in existing buildings where they must go through walls and cable ducts. Fiber cables are easier to install since they are smaller and more flexible. One way to simplify installation in existing buildings is to run cables through ventilation ducts. However, fire codes require that such plenum cables be made of costly fire retardant materials that emit little smoke. The advantage of fiber types is that they are smaller and hence require less of the costly fire retardant materials. The small size, lightweight and flexibility of fiber optic cables also make them easier to be used in temporary or portable installations.
2. **Less expensive**—Several miles of optical cable can be made cheaper than equivalent lengths of copper wire. This saves your provider (cable TV, Internet) and you money.
3. **Thinner**—Optical fibers can be drawn to smaller diameters than copper wire. A 3/8-inch (12 pair) fiber/cable operating at 140 Mb/s can handle as many voice channels as a 3-inch diameter copper (900) twisted-pair cable.
4. **High Bandwidth Over Long Distances**—Fiber optics have a large capacity to carry high speed signals over longer distances without repeaters than other types of cables. The information carrying capacity increases with frequency. This however, doesn't mean that optical fiber has infinite bandwidth, but it's certainly greater than coaxial cables. Generally, coaxial cables have a bandwidth parameter of a few MHz/km, where else the fiber optic cable has a bandwidth of 400MHz/km. (These figures are just approximations and do vary from cable to cable!) This is an important factor that leads to the choice of fiber for data communications.
5. **Low Loss**—Current single-mode fibers have losses as low as 0.2 dB per km. Multimode losses are down to 1 dB (at 850 or 1300 nm). This creates opportunities for longer distances without costly repeaters.

6. **Immunity to Electromagnetic Interference**—Electromagnetic Interference is a common type of noise that originates with one of the basic properties of electromagnetism. Magnetic field lines generate an electrical current as they cut across conductors. The flow of electrons in a conductor generates a magnetic field that changes with the current flow. Electromagnetic Interference does occur in coaxial cables, since current does cut across the conductor. Fiber optics is immune to this EMI since signals are transmitted as light instead of current. Thus, they can carry signals through places where EMI would block transmission.
7. **Higher carrying capacity**—Because optical fibers are thinner than copper wires, more fibers can be bundled into a given-diameter cable than copper wires. This allows more phone lines to go over the same cable or more channels to come through the cable into your cable TV box.
8. **Light signals**—Unlike electrical signals in copper wires, light signals from one fiber do not interfere with those of other fibers in the same cable. This means clearer phone conversations or TV reception.
9. **Low power**—Because signals in optical fibers degrade less, lower-power transmitters can be used instead of the high-voltage electrical transmitters needed for copper wires. Again, this saves your provider and you money.
10. **Digital signals**—Optical fibers are ideally suited for carrying digital information, which is especially useful in computer networks.
11. **Non-flammable**—In some cases, transmitting signals electrically can be extremely dangerous. Most electric potentials create small sparks. The sparks ordinarily pose no danger, but can be really bad in a chemical plant or oil refinery where the air is contaminated with potentially explosive vapours. One tiny spark can create a big explosion. Potential spark hazards seriously hinder data and communication in such facilities. Fiber optic cables do not produce sparks since they do not carry current. Since the only carrier in the fiber is light, there is no possibility of a spark from a broken fiber. Even in the most explosive of atmospheres, there is no fire hazard, and no danger of electrical shock to personnel repairing broken fibers.
12. **Lightweight**—An optical cable weighs less than a comparable copper wire cable. Fiber-optic cables take up less space in the ground. The same fiber-optic cable weighs approximately 132 lbs per kilometer. The twisted pair cable weighs approximately 16,000 lbs.
13. **Non-conductivity**—This allows for installation in areas with high electromagnetic interference such as utility lines, railroad tracks and power-carrying lines or even areas with a high lightening-strike incidence. Fiber optic cables are virtually unaffected by outdoor atmospheric conditions, allowing them to be lashed directly to telephone poles or existing electrical cables without concern for extraneous signal pickup. A serious concern with outdoor cables in certain computer networks is that they can be hit by lightning, causing destruction to wires and other cables that are involved in the network. Certain computer companies are aware of this problem and trying to solve it by having protective devices for wire circuits to block current and voltage surges. Any conductive cables can carry power surges or ground loops. Fiber optic cables can be made non-conductive by avoiding metal in their design.

14. **Security**—Magnetic fields and current induction work in two ways. They don't just generate noise in signal carrying conductors; they also let the information on the conductor to be leaked out. Fluctuations in the induced magnetic field outside a conductor carry the same information as the current passing through the conductor. Shielding the wire, as in coaxial cables can reduce the problem, but sometimes shielding can allow enough signal leaks to allow tapping, which is exactly what we wouldn't want. There are no radiated magnetic fields around optical fibers; the electromagnetic fields are confined within the fiber. That makes it impossible to tap the signal being transmitted through a fiber without cutting into the fiber. Since fiber optics do not radiate electromagnetic energy, emissions cannot be intercepted and physically tapping the fiber takes great skill to do undetected. Thus, the fiber is the most secure medium available for carrying sensitive data.
15. **Wide Temperature Range**—Fibers and cables can be manufactured to meet temperatures from -40°F to +200°F. Resistance to temperatures of 1,000°F has been recorded.
16. **Fewer Repeaters**—Few repeaters, if any, are required because of increased performance of light sources and continuing increases in fiber performance.
17. **Stable Performance**—Fiber optics is affected less by moisture that means less corrosion and degradation. Therefore, no scheduled maintenance is required. Fiber also has greater temperature stability than copper systems.
18. **Topology Compatibility**—Fiber is suitable to meet the changing topologies and configurations necessary to meet operation growth and expansions. Technologies such as wavelength division multiplexing (WDM), optical multiplexing, and drop and insert technologies are available to upgrade and recon-figure system designs.
19. **Material Availability**—Material (silica glass) required for the production of fiber is readily available in a virtually unending supply.

Despite the many advantages of fiber-optic systems, there are some disadvantages:

1. **Overload**—Unlike electrical cables where only one signal is allowed, optical cables have the ability for multiple light signals to simultaneously move through the cable; sometimes so many signals are moving through the cable that it becomes jammed and information slows down.
2. **Different signals**—Most devices work of electrical signals so to use an optical cable, the signal must be converted to light, sent through the wire, and then converted back to an electrical signal; in a copper wire, the signal always stays electrical.
3. **Fear of New Technologies**—Because the technology is considered to be new, people are reluctant to change and use these methods. The use of metric and physics is still an unfamiliar area to many established users. Many industries are just more comfortable with the use of standard electrical systems and do not like new systems.
4. **Economic Evaluation**—The major practical problem with fiber optics is that it usually costs more than ordinary wires. All costs elements involved in economic evaluation can be grouped into two main classes; which are investment costs and

operation costs. The investment costs usually includes expenditures related to acquiring and owning properties and plants, in this case changing wires to fiber optic cables. All investment costs should be considered, such as those incurred for equipment and materials (also including storage and handling costs), engineering costs and miscellaneous costs. Operation costs include the usage of fiber optics and the wear and tear of it. The higher cost of fiber is often not by itself. Fiber optic cables are much cheaper than coaxial cables. The main difference comes when all the other components of fiber optics add up, such as transmitters, receivers, couplers and connectors. Fiber systems require separate transmitters and receivers because they cannot directly use the electrical output of computer devices; that signal must be converted into optical form and then converted back into electrical form. Fiber optic connectors and couplers are more expensive than any other electrical components. These costs are the ones that add up and form the major disadvantage of fiber optics.

5. **System Reconfiguration**—One of the drawbacks in fiber optics is system reconfiguration. Converting existing hardware and software for the use of fiber optics does take a lot of time and money that also reduces the turnover for any profit-making firm in the market. Sometimes it may be more convenient to transmit high-speed computer data serially (one bit after another) than sending several bits at a time in parallel over separate wires. This changeover requires modification in both hardware and software. Minor differences can cause old programs to crash and make data in old files unreadable. Even though the need for such modifications can be reduced by designing fiber optic systems with interfaces that look just like electric ones, it would not make most efficient use of fiber transmission capacity and would increase costs.
6. **Limitations in Local Area Networks**—In Local Area Networks, fiber optics are not used as widely as one would expect. One reason is the implementation requires great deal of changes in current networks and systems. This requires a lot of time and effort that the management is not willing to sacrifice. People are comfortable with what they have and don't want to change. Although most problems regarding program changing can be solved, the solutions to it will take much longer than expected. Thus, any new program has to be a big improvement over the old one to justify a significant change (although the great improvement usually means that the old program does not work).

Another fundamental problem in fiber optic LANs is the change in technology. The hardware and software to make LAN run efficiently add up to an expensive package. If many terminals in a building must be in constant touch with each other and a variety of other hardware, such as printers and storage devices, LAN will be cost efficient. However, if the real need is to keep the terminals in touch with a mainframe computer, it would be cheaper to run cables between them and the mainframe. If the terminals need to talk to each other, ordinary telephone lines could very well be used, as telephone lines are much cheaper than fiber optics.

Fiber-Optic Considerations

■ **USE IF :**

- Need to transmit @ very HIGH speeds over LONG distances in a very secure media.

■ **DON'T USE IF :**

- Are under a tight budget.
- Do not have the expertise available to properly install it and connect devices to it.

Fiber-Optic Cable Characteristics

- Can accommodate data transfer much faster than coaxial or twisted pair cable.
- Data sent as pulses of light over threads of glass at gigabits-per second.
- TWO small glass strands : one send and one receives (together know as the "core").
- Lines are free of electromagnetic interference.
- Difficult to tap.
- Data can travel for miles without a signal degradation.
- Laser transmitters send the modulated light pulses and optical receivers receive them.
- Two major types of fiber optic cable exist : Single-mode and multimode.

Single Mode	Multimode
Often used for inter-city telephone trunks and video applications	Usually specified for LANs and WANs

4.7 Cabling Summary

Now that we've examined the major bounded media, let's take a quick look at how they compare.

Twisted Pair Cable			
	Advantages		Disadvantages
1.	Inexpensive	1.	Susceptible to RFI and EMI
2.	Often available in existing phone system	2.	Not as durable as coax
3.	Well tested and easy to get	3.	Doesn't support as high a speed as other media

Coaxial Cable			
	Advantages		**Disadvantages**
1.	Fairly resistant to RFI and EMI.	1.	Can be effected by strong interference.
2.	Supports faster data rates than twisted pair.	2.	More costly than TP.
3.	More durable than TP.	3.	Bulkier and more rigid than TP.

Fiber Optic Cable			
	Advantages		**Disadvantages**
1.	Highly secure.	1.	Extremely costly in product and service.
2.	Not affected by RFI and EMI.	2.	Sophisticated tools and methods for installation.
3.	Highest bandwidth available.		
4.	Very durable.	3.	Complex to layout and design.

Point-to-point transmission			
	Data rate	**Bandwidth**	**Repeater distance**
Twisted pair	4 Mbps	3 MHz	2-10 km
Coaxial cable	500 Mbps	350 MHz	1-10 km
Optical fiber	2 Gbps	2 GHz	10-100 km

4.8 Wireless Transmission

The above discussed technologies require physical connections in order to transmit signals. Wireless transmission means sending and receiving signals without wires. Examples include radio, microwave, and satelite. Today we use all of these forms to transmit data. The dream of being able to communicate data in networks without having deal with the constraints of physical cabling is very much realized today. Wide area networks obviously make use of wireless technology to transmit data around our globe. The acceptance of wireless networks on the local level has been significantly hindered, however, for a number of reasons.

The transmissions and receptions in wireless media are achieved by means of an antenna and can be

- **Directional :** Point-to-point focused beams employing high frequencies.

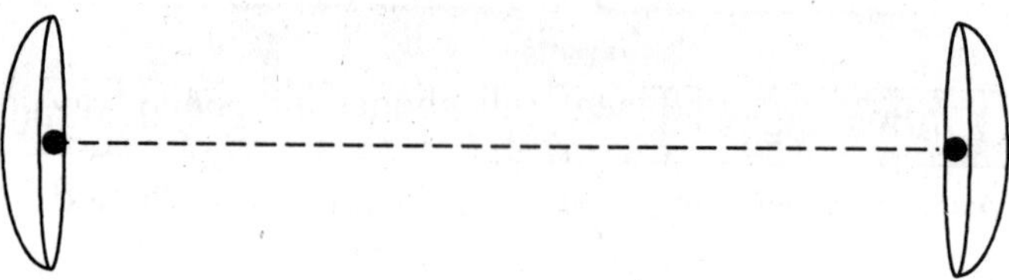

Fig. 4.10. Directional

- **Omni directional :** Waves propagating in all directions using signals of lower frequencies.

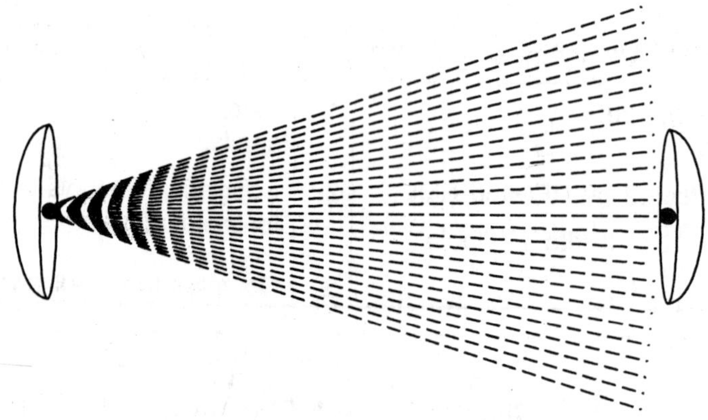

Fig. 4.11. Omni directional

Meaning of Wireless

"Wireless" means transmitting signals over invisible radio waves instead of wires. Garage door openers and television remote controls were the first wireless devices to become a part of everyday life. Now the cordless keyboard and mouse, PDAs and digital and cellular phones are commonplace.

Working of Wireless Networks

Wireless data is predominately transferred over two kinds of networks : wide area networks (WANs) and local area networks (LANs). These networks are similar to their wired counterparts-they just use radio-waves instead of copper or fiber.

WANs can cover areas as large as several countries. Wireless LANs, already popular in airports and hotels, are often used to replace or enhance wired LANs. They can cover a range of 500 feet indoors and up to 1,000 feet outdoors. They may service a smaller area than their WANs, but LANs can transfer data much faster, at speeds up to 11 Mbps. Wireless LANs are used primarily for data; they do not usually support voice traffic.

Technologies Involved

First a word about how wireless technologies are referred to. You'll read a lot about "generations" of wireless, which correspond to the rate and quality of data and voice transmission. The first generation was analog voice (the earliest cell phones). The second generation is digital (such as more efficient cell phones with voice and data at rates of 9.6 Kbps to 14.4 Kbps). Currently carriers are working on what they call 2.5 generation or 2.5 G, transmission rates, which will carry data up to 114Kbps. The future is 3 G, which will include multimedia and data transmission rates of up to 2 Mbps to 5 Mbps, advanced roaming capabilities, as well as the sought after (by some) “always-on” potential.

When it comes to WANs, there are so many technologies used to send data through the air. One of the most used and talked about is wireless application protocol (WAP). WAP-enabled devices offer a limited version of the Web designed to work on the small black-and-white screens of phones and PDAs. When WAP service first came out during the summer of 2000, market hype depicted it as the Internet on a phone. But how could the Net fit on such a little screen? Even though WAP failed in the consumer marketplace, it is still among the most common ways to send data to phones and PDAs.

Within the current digital world of wireless, there are four primary technologies: code-division multiple access (CDMA), global system for mobile communication (GSM), integrated dispatch enhanced network (iDEN), which is used by Nextel, and time division multiple access (TDMA). Bluetooth, a LAN technology, enables devices rather than a network to communicate. With an operating range of only 30 feet, Bluetooth can be used in a headset to wirelessly listen to audio on a computer and send photographs from a digital camera to the computer.

Difference between Wireless and Mobile

A laptop is a mobile device. The Lotus Notes application on that laptop is mobile because it resides on the laptop but needs to connect through a wired modem connection before it can be used. A cell phone is a wireless device. The Lotus Notes application on that cell phone is wireless because it can receive data wirelessly-that is, without being plugged into a wired connection.

The Evolution of Wireless

Wireless technology is not new and has been widely used in many industries for years. Manufacturing, courier services, and retail are just some of the industries successfully using wireless for inventory control, package tracking, and pricing applications to increase productivity and streamline procedures. In the past, wireless technology was used for dedicated applications, but this is rapidly changing with the advent of wireless LAN standards and 802.11 technologies.

The popularity of wireless networking is growing and users have recognized the many benefits of using mobile technology.

Some of the benefits of wireless technology are stated below:

- True mobility—the means to conduct business without physical cable attachment to the network.
- Increased productivity.
- Lower cabling costs—can eliminate the need for new cable plants or extensions of existing cabling.

- New network access—provides network access where it was previously difficult to deploy traditional wired LANs (e.g., manufacturing, warehousing, temporary office space, leased buildings, etc.).
- Broad OS support—Windows, Macintosh, Palm OS, etc.
- Easy installation.
- Rapid deployment.
- Lower long term costs.

Limitations of wireless technology

Despite the many benefits of wireless technology, enterprise users are only beginning to adopt wireless LANs. Unlike wired networks, wireless networks transmit their data over open-air waves—through walls, ceilings, and floors—giving possible access to anyone within range of the radio waves. The lack of strong security in early implementations of 802.11b technology using Wired Equivalent Privacy (WEP) security showed the danger and ease of how wireless LANs could be compromised—giving enterprises no confidence in deploying immature wireless LAN technology.

1. First and foremost, you need to realize that wireless communications will never be perfect. The experience will never mimic what you're used to seeing on your PC.
2. When it comes to WANs, bandwidth and spectrum are major limitations. The networks are slow. When transmitting data, you're forced to send smaller bits of data just so the information moves as quickly as possible. The size of the device that's accessing the information is also an issue.
3. Phones and PDAs have small screens-often only a couple of inches in diameter-and it is not easy to see large documents on them. Think of a contractor trying to read an architect's blueprints on a job site.
4. When it comes to voice transmission, you need to remember that wireless is a radio-based technology, which calls for transmission towers and receivers that are positioned to dodge interference

Wireless Networking

The traditional approach to networking computers involves a physical connection between systems on the network. Wireless networking is based on transmission that is not propagated over physical media. Of special interest is application of the wireless technology to urban networking—a Metropolitan Area Network (MAN).

Under the broadest definition of the term, existing wireless communications systems include radio, infrared and cellular technologies—that is, radio and TV broadcasting, cellular telephony, specialized mobile radio, wireless data, microwave and satellite services. As with other communication technologies, wireless systems are converting to digital. At this point in time, wireless technologies have not evolved sufficiently to serve as replacements to traditional wire-based technologies, but do provide promising solutions in certain niches or gaps not well served by wire.

Wireless networking is a collective term for solutions for two quite different problems:

- In some cases, it can be difficult or impossible to install a conventional wired network infrastructure; this is one place where wireless technologies are used.
- The other area of activity is solving the problem of the mobile or portable network device.

4.8.1 The Electromagnetic Spectrum

In this section we shall consider the physical properties of free-space electromagnetic waves, and how the atmosphere influences the propagation of electromagnetic waves. In the following sections, we shall describe how these properties have determined the selection of frequencies for communication.

The electromagnetic spectrum is divided up into a number of bands, as shown in table below:

Table 4.1 The frequencies of the electro-magnetic spectrum

Description	Frequency	Wavelength
High frequency	3—30 MHz	100—10 m
VHF	50—100 MHz	6—3 m
UHF	400—1000 MHz	75—30 cm
Microwaves	3×10^9—10^{11} Hz	10 cm—3 mm
Milimetre waves	10^{11}—10^{12} Hz	3 mm—0.3 mm
Infrared	10^{12}—6×10^{14} Hz	0.3 mm—0.5 μm
Light	6×10^{14}—8×10^{14} Hz	0.5 μm—0.4 μm
Ultra-voilet	8×10^{14}—10^{17} Hz	0.4 μm—10^{-9} m
X-rays	10^{17}—10^{19} Hz	10^{-9} m—10^{-13} m
Gamma rays	$> 10^{19}$ Hz	$< 10^{-13}$ m

Propagation of waves in free-space is different from that in cable or waveguides. With respect to signal propagation, these latter are one-dimensional systems and a wave does not lose energy as it travels, except that due to absorption or scattering. In three-dimensions waves radiate spherically. When waves traveling in free-space are obstructed, new waves result from the interaction. There are four types of interaction:

1. **Reflection :** This occurs when a wave meets a plane object. The wave is reflected back without distortion.
2. **Refraction :** This occurs when a wave encounters a medium with a different wave speed. The direction and speed of the wave is altered.
3. **Diffraction :** This occurs when the wave encounters an edge. The wave has the ability to turn the corner of the edge. This ability of waves to turn corners is called diffraction. It is markedly dependent on frequency—the higher the frequency, the

less diffraction. Very high frequencies (light) hardly diffract at all; "light travels in straight lines".

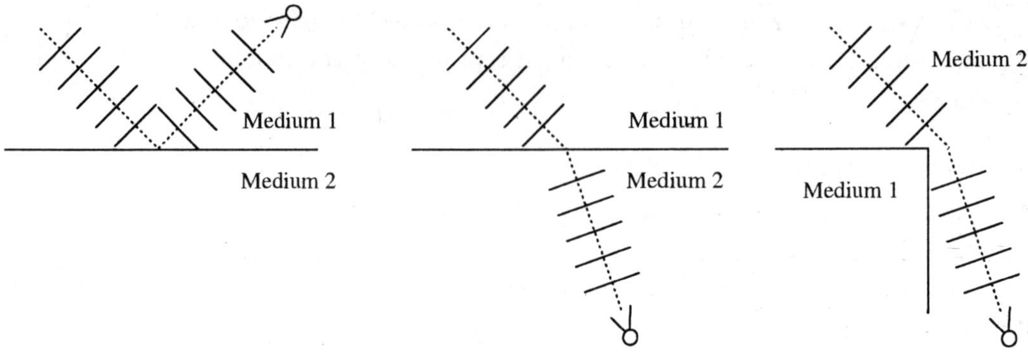

Fig. 4.12 Reflection, refraction and diffraction of an electromagnetic wave

4. **Scattering :** Catch-all description of wave interactions that are too complex to be described as reflection, refraction or diffraction. Typically the result of scattering is to remove radiation of the wave and re-radiate it over a wide range of directions. Scattering too is strongly frequency dependent. Usually it will increase with frequency.

4.8.2 Different Types of Unguided Media

Unguided transmission media is data signals that flow through the air. They are not guided or bound to a channel to follow. They are classified by the type of wave propagation.

RF Propagation

There are three types of RF (radio frequency) propagation:

- Ground Wave
- Ionospheric
- Line of Sight (LOS)

Ground wave propagation follows the curvature of the Earth. Ground waves have carrier frequencies up to 2 MHz. AM radio is an example of ground wave propagation.

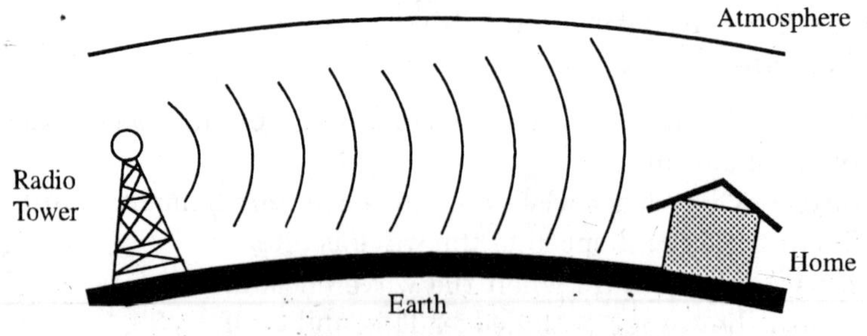

Fig. 4.13 Ground wave propagation

Ionospheric propagation bounces off of the Earth's ionospheric layer in the upper atmosphere. It is sometimes called double hop propagation. It operates in the frequency range of 30–85 MHz. Because it depends on the Earth's ionosphere, it changes with the weather and time of day. The signal bounces off of the ionosphere and back to earth. Ham radios operate in this range.

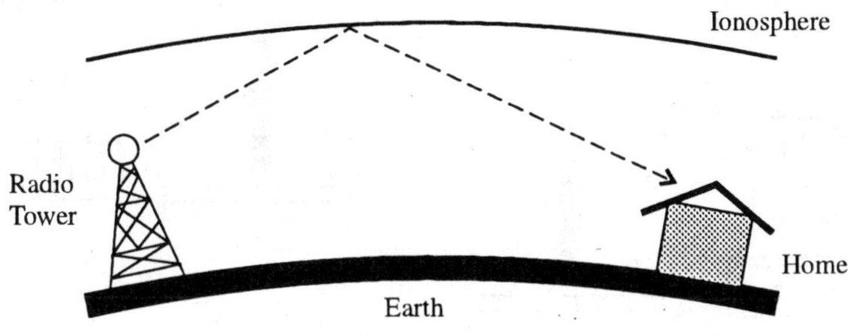

Fig. 4.14 Ionospheric propagation

Line of sight propagation transmits exactly in the line of sight. The receive station must be in the view of the transmit station. It is sometimes called space waves or tropospheric propagation. It is limited by the curvature of the Earth for ground-based stations (100 km, from horizon to horizon). Reflected waves can cause problems. Examples of line of sight propagation are: FM radio, microwave and satellite.

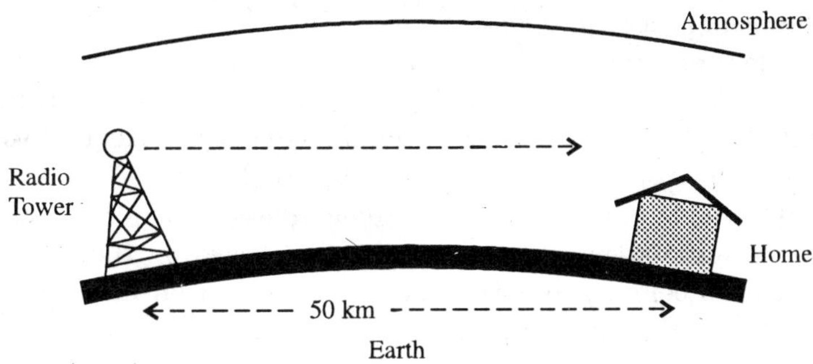

Fig. 4.15 Line of sight propagation

Unguided media can travel from source to destination in several ways, ground propagation, sky propagation and line of sight propagation. Various types of unguided media are explained below.

4.9 Radio Waves

Electromagnetic waves in the frequency range between 3 kHz and 1 GHz are radio waves and waves ranging between 1 and 300 GHz are called microwaves. Radio transmitters are omni directional and can easily penetrate walls, floors, ceiling and the like. Electrically speaking, the waves that are classified as radio waves have certain frequencies that are grouped together for certain uses. Some are available for data transmission, but the bandwidth necessary to perform high-speed data transfers is not found at any given slot on the radio spectrum. Many vendors are now employing spread-spectrum technology where the available slots in the radio spectrum are all used together. Using this technology, speeds at upto 2 Mbps have been achieved.

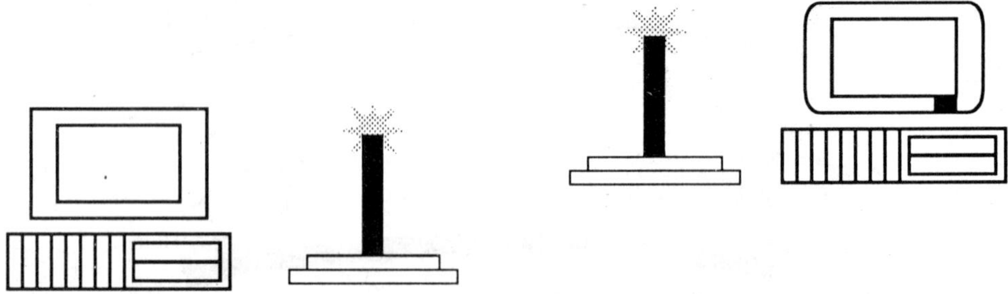

Fig. 4.16 Radio-based LANs use portable transmitters and receivers at each LAN device

Radio-based LANs do have to contend with the interference that occurs daily in the workplace. That interference can come from a number of different electrical sources and can be quite impacting on LAN performance. For radio systems using only a small portion of the radio spectrum (narrowband systems), this could mean that problem might be insurmountable. The vendors of spread-spectrum products claim that their products can isolate interference problems and avoid using those frequencies.

Though radio offers portability to any node within range, its unbounded nature makes it somewhat less secure. A "non-friendly" could, in theory, listen in to your radio broadcasts. The eavesdropper would have to, of course, know what frequency or frequencies you were using. Once that hurdle was overcome, your LAN would be laid bare.

Radio, though limited by its speed, may be the wireless transmission method of choice for many desktops because of its low cost and capabilities. However, the delay of regulation has cost radio a few months before standardization. This has given infrared vendors at least a little time to create competing products.

Radio	
Advantages	**Disadvantages**
1. Transmission not line of sight.	1. Limited bandwidth means less data throughput.
2. Inexpensive products. 3. Direct point-to-point linking to receiving station.	2. Some frequencies subject to FCC regulation.
4. Ideal for portable devices.	3. Highly susceptible to interference.

4.10 Microwave Link Communication

Electromagnetic waves in the frequency range 1 to 300 GHz are called microwaves. Microwave transmission is line of sight transmission. The transmit station must be in visible contact with the receive station. This sets a limit on the distance between stations depending on the local geography. Typically the line of sight due to the Earth's curvature is only 50 km to the horizon! Repeater stations must be placed so the data signal can hop, skip and jump across the country.

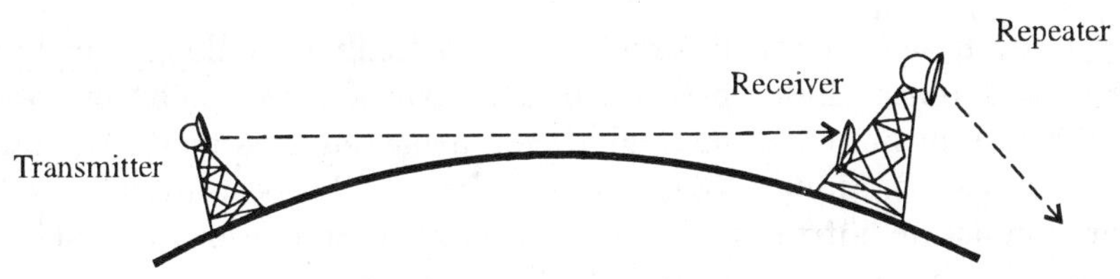

Fig. 4.17 Line of sight transmission

Microwaves are omni directional and the transmitting antenna can narrowly focus the wave. Microwaves need omnidirectional antennas that send out signals in one direction. Due to their unidirectional properties, microwaves are very useful for unicast communication between a sender and a receiver. They are used in cellular telephones, satellite networks and wireless LANS.

The maturity of radio frequency (RF) technology has permitted the use of microwave links as the major trunk channel for long distance communication. The use of microwave links has major **advantages** over cabling systems :

- **Freedom from land acquisition rights**—The acquisition of rights to lay cabling, repair cabling, and have permanent access to repeater stations is a major cost in the provision of cable communications. The use of radio links, that require only the acquisition of the transmitter/receiver station, removes this requirement. It also simplifies the maintenance and repair of the link.
- **Ease of communication over difficult terrain**—Some terrains make cable laying extremely difficult and expensive, even if the land acquisition cost is negligible.

The use of microwave links has a number of **disadvantages** that mainly arise from the use of free-space communication:

- **Bandwidth allocation is extremely limited**—The competition for RF bandwidth from various competing users leads to very strict allocations of bandwidth. Unlike cabling systems, that can increase bandwidth by laying more cables, the radio frequency (RF) bandwidth allocation is finite and limited. In practice, bandwidth allocations of 50MHz in the carrier range 300 MHz to 1 GHz are typical.
- **Atmospheric effects**—The use of free-space communication results in susceptibility to weather effects, particularly rain.
- **Transmission path needs to be clear**—Microwave communication requires line-of-sight, point-to-point communication. The frequency of repeater stations is determined

by the terrain. Care must be taken in the system design to ensure freedom from obstacles. In addition, links must be kept free of future constructions that could obstruct the link.

- **Interference**—The microwave system is open to RF interference.
- **Restrictive Costs**—The cost of design, implementation and maintenance of microwave links is high. Many countries are not well equipped with good technical resources to provide efficient and continuous operation.

The modern urban environment presents a particular challenge, in that bandwidth allocation, RF interference, link obstruction and atmospheric pollution place maximum constraints on the system simultaneously. However, urban environments also have the highest land acquisition values too. Many modern cities have found it cost effective to build a single, very high tower to house an entire city's trunk communication microwave dishes. These towers are now a common feature of the modern urban landscape.

As the demand for bandwidth increases, microwave links will become increasingly unable to deliver. The use of increased carrier frequencies in the millimetre wave region would be advantageous. However, for technical reasons, no efficient method of producing large quantities of millimetre power have been found. This is a necessity, given the increase in atmospheric attenuation at millimetre wave frequencies.

4.11 Satellite Communication

A communication satellite:

- Is used for link ground stations.

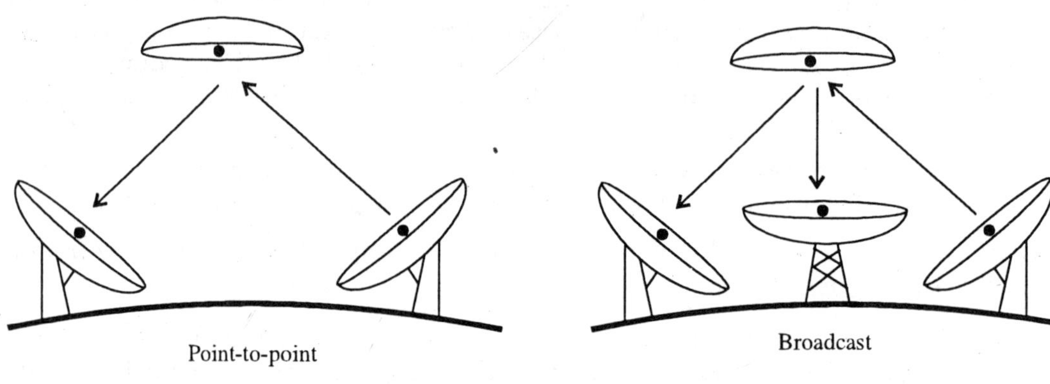

(a) Point-to-point transmission (b) Broadcast transmission

Fig. 4.18

- Operates on a number of frequency bands, called transponder channels.
- Receives transmissions on one frequency band (uplink), and transmits on another frequency (downlink).
- Satellite period of rotation equals the earth's period of rotation at height of 34,784 km.
- Used for TV distribution, long-distance telephone, and business networks.

Satellites are transponders (units that receive on one frequency and retransmit on another) that are set in geostationary orbits directly over the equator. These geostationary orbits are 36,000 km from the Earth's surface. At this point, the gravitational pull of the Earth and the centrifugal force of Earth's rotation are balanced and cancel each other out. Centrifugal force is the rotational force placed on the satellite that wants to fling it out into space.

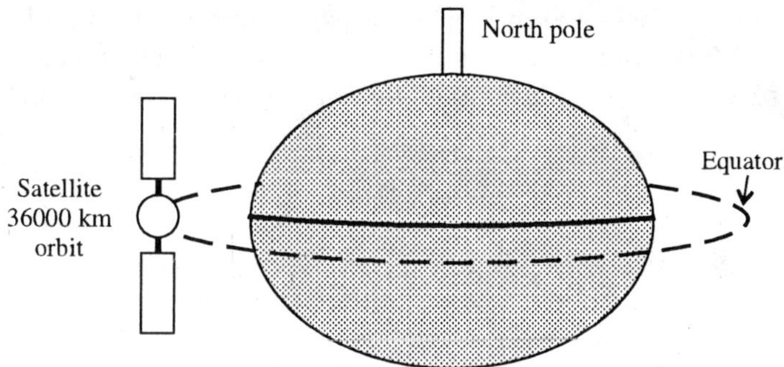

Fig. 4.19 (a) Geostationary satellite

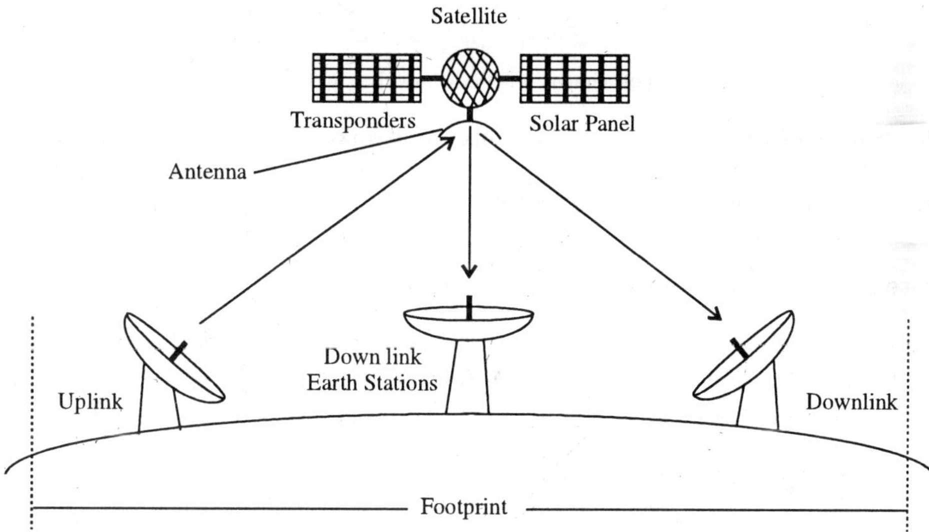

Fig. 4.19 (b) Satellite communication

The uplink is the transmitter of data to the satellite. The downlink is the receiver of data. Uplinks and downlinks are also called Earth stations because they are located on the Earth. The footprint is the "shadow" that the satellite can transmit to, the shadow being the area that can receive the satellite's transmitted signal. (As shown in figure 4.19 (b))

Satellite communication became a possibility when it was realised that a satellite orbiting at a distance of 36000 Km from the Earth would be geostationary, i.e. would have an angular orbital velocity equal to the Earth's own orbital velocity. It would thus appear to remain stationary relative to the Earth if placed in an equatorial orbit. This is a consequence of Kepler's law that the period of rotation T of a satellite around the Earth was given by:

$$T = \frac{2\pi r^{3/2}}{\sqrt{(gsR^2)}}$$

where r is the orbit radius, R is the Earth's radius and $gs = 9.81\ \text{ms}^{-2}$ is the acceleration due to gravity at the Earth's surface. As the orbit increases in radius, the angular velocity reduces, until it is coincident with the Earth's at a radius of 36000 Km. In principle, three geostationary satellites correctly placed can provide complete coverage of the Earth's surface (Fig. 4.20).

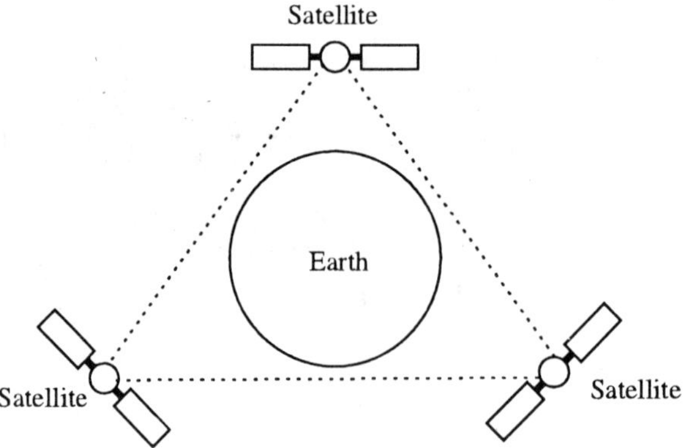

Fig. 4.20 Geostationary satellites providing global coverage

For intercontinental communication, satellite radio links become a commercially attractive proposition. Space communication showed phenomenal growth in the 1970s, and will continue to grow for some years to come. The growth has been so rapid that there is now danger of overcrowding the geostationary orbit.

Satellite communication has a number of advantages:

- The laying and maintenance of intercontinental cable is difficult and expensive.
- The heavy usage of intercontinental traffic makes the satellite commercially attractive.
- Satellites can cover large areas of the Earth. This is particularly useful for sparsely populated areas.

Satellite communication has some disadvantages also:

- Technological limitations preventing the deployment of large, high gain antennas on the satellite platform.
- Over-crowding of available bandwidths due to low antenna gains.
- The high investment cost and insurance cost associated with significant probability of failure.
- High atmospheric losses above 30 GHz limit carrier frequencies.

Satellite systems are extremely expensive. As an example, the break down for a particular British satellite is as shown in Table 4.2.

Table 4.2 Example costs for a satellite system

Item	Cost ($ Million)
Satellite construction	300
Investment finance	300
Insurance	300
Launch	100
	1000

Recently there has been interest in **low-earth orbiting (LEO)** satellites. Here, a satellite placed in a **1000 Km** orbit has an orbital time of 1 hour. These satellites can be operated in a **store-and-forward** mode, picking up data at one part of the globe and physically transferring it to another. Because the data-rates and orbit radius are greatly reduced, small, low-cost satellites and ground stations are possible. However, such satellites have yet to demonstrate any commercial success.

4.12 Infrared Waves

Infrared signals, with frequencies from 300 GHz to 400 THz can be used for short-range communication. Infrared signals, having high frequencies, cannot penetrate walls. This can be advantageous since it prevents interference between one system in one room and another system in another room. However this characteristic make infra-red signals useless for long distance communications.

Infrared technology uses the invisible portion of the light spectrum with wavelengths just a little less than those of red light. These frequencies are very high offering nice data transfer rates. Modern infrared LANs can achieve throughput at 16 Mbps with potential for better. We are used to seeing infrared technology utilized for our television or VCR remotes.

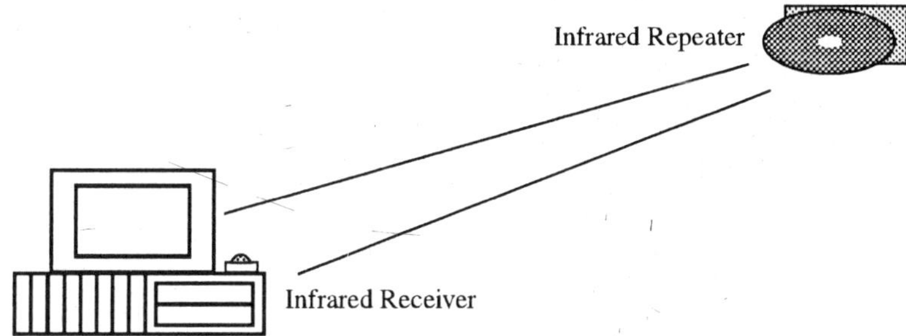

Fig. 4.21 Infrared transmissions offer potential for high-speed data transfer but are limited by inability to penetrate walls and floors.

Infrared technology involves the use of an infrared transmitter like a LED along with a receiver, typically a photodiode. These components operate in a line-of-sight fashion. That is, nothing can obstruct the pathway between them. Fortunately these signals can be bounced off walls and ceilings providing transmission around obstacles. Line-of-sight means, however, that these signals cannot be broadcast through walls, severely limiting infrared LANs.

Modern infrared systems use a repeater device simply to retransmit a signal from one room into another. This device is generally mounted on the ceiling or high in a corner to alleviate as many obstacles as possible. These systems also use a process called "diffusion" to send the signal in a wide path across a room thus reducing the chance of signals not getting past a single obstacle.

The good news about infrared technology is that it may not be very costly to implement. Since infrared items have been around a while, significant resources exist to mass produce infrared products. Advances in the technology will probably lead to faster products without as many limitations. Infrared transmissions now are limited to a relatively short distance, and used outdoors, are extremely susceptible to atmospheric conditions.

Infrared	
Advantages	**Disadvantages**
1. Higher bandwidth means superior throughput to radio.	1. Limited in distance.
2. Inexpensive to produce.	2. Cannot penetrate physical barriers like walls, ceilings, floors, etc.
3. No longer limited to tight interroom line-of-sight restrictions.	

• • •

5

Electromagnetic Signals And Modulation

5.1 Electromagnetic Waves

All energy in the universe travels in waves and those waves radiate outwards from a source, just as waves ripple outwards from a stone tossed in a pond. Without actually going into the physics of particle or wave theory, nearly all signals are part of the electromagnetic spectrum and those that are not are based on kinetic energy (such as sound).

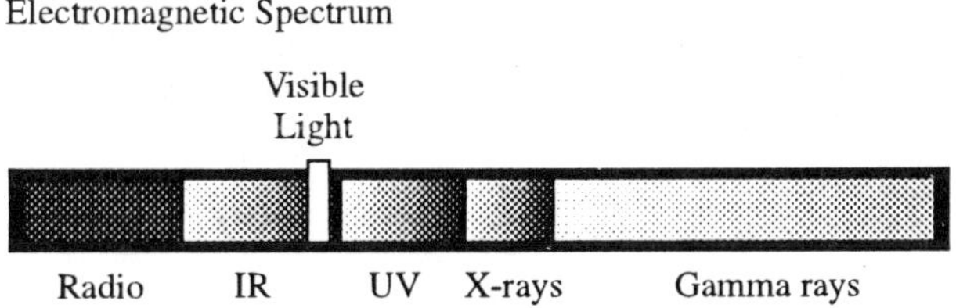

All radiation is said to have *wavelength*, *amplitude*, *frequency*, *phase* and power. Everything from gamma rays all the way down through the visible light spectrum to radio waves are all electromagnetic energy and differ primarily in frequency.

The wavelength of electromagnetic energy is measured in distance (meters), its frequency is measured in time (cycles per second) as is its phase (what value the wave has at any single instant in time), and amplitude is measured in power (electron volts).

Electromagnetic waves are frequently represented mathematically using a sine wave on a cartesian graph. A sine wave begins with a high value at the origin (where the X and sin X cross in the graph below), rises, falls and then returns the X-axis. This single sine cycle is said to pass through 360 *degrees of phase*. When represented on a polar-rectal graph, you get a circle (360 degrees). In polar rectal coordinates, the values are a distance from the origin plus an angle from 0 degrees.

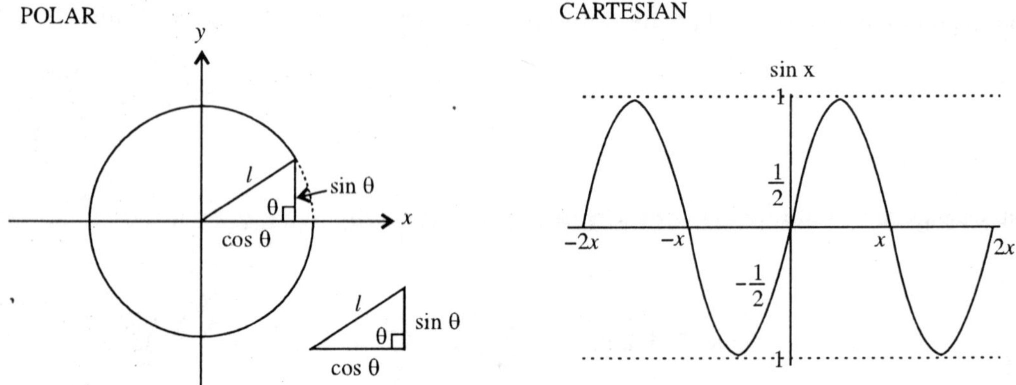

Fig. 5.1 Representation of electromagnetic waves

Below is a graph that illustrates a specific frequency at 1 hertz. It shows it's **amplitude**, its **frequency** (1 *hertz per second*) and its **phase** value at several points in time between zero seconds and 1 second.

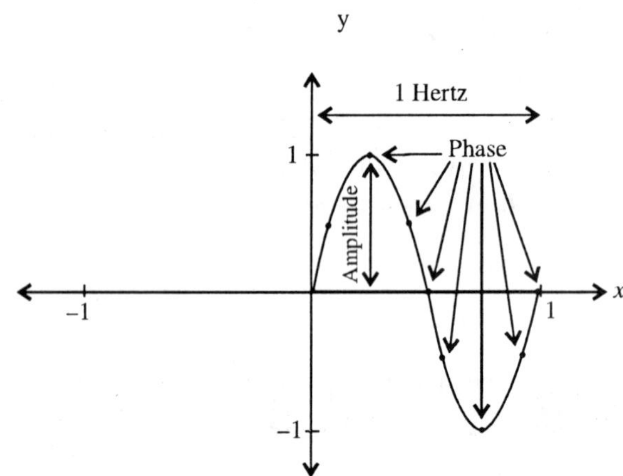

Fig. 5.2 Graph representing amplitude frequency and phase of an electromagnetic wave

Frequency

Frequency is how fast you shake the string with your hand. The faster you shake your hand, the more 'waves' you make. The number of 'waves' that happen in one second is the 'frequency' of a signal. The high points of the moving string are the maximums, and the lowest points are the minimums. The distance between one minimum and the next maximum is referred to as a 'wave'. The distance between the minimum of the first wave and the minimum of the next wave is called the 'period'.

Amplitude

If you keep moving your hand at the same speed, but change the distance you raise your hand, you are changing the amplitude. Big movements create larger waves, small movements create smaller waves. How 'high' (or 'low') the wave goes is referred to as 'amplitude'.

Output Power and Signal Strength

If you crack the string like a whip, it hits the door with force. The harder you 'crack' the string, the harder it hits the door. This is 'output power'. You can move your hand the same distance, but do it with more force and the string reacts with more force.

Signalling

Once a system of computing devices and cabling has been built, a method of getting the information onto the transmission media must exist. This is called the signalling technique. Electromagnetic signal can be either *continuous* or *discrete*. A **continuous signal** is one in which the signal intensity varies in a smooth fashion over time, i.e., no break or no discontinuous in the signal.

A **discrete signal** is one in which the signal intensity maintain a constant level for same period of time and then changes to another constant level.

The movement of the signal over its transmission path is referred to as *signal propagation*.

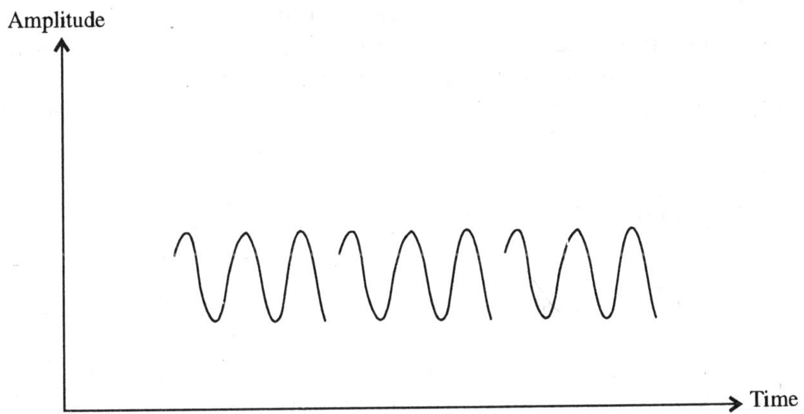

Fig. 5.3 Continuous Signal

The sine wave is the fundamental continuous signal.

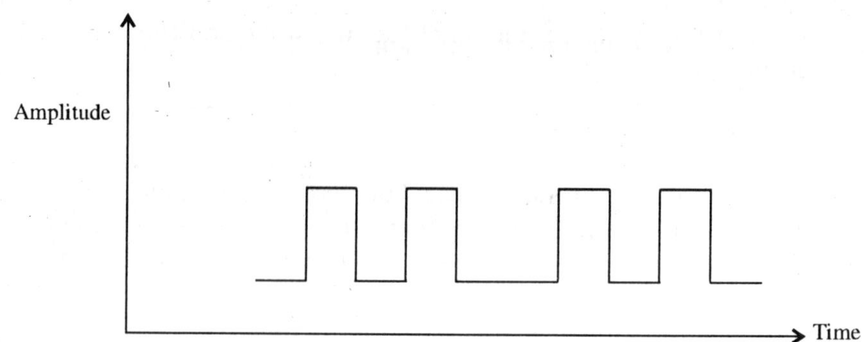

Fig. 5.4 Discrete Signal

5.2 Analog communications

In the analog communications, information is represented as a continuous electromagnetic wave form. Analog is best explained by examining the transmission of a natural form of information, such as sound or human speech, over an electrified copper wire. Information which is analog in its native form (voice and image) can vary continuously in terms of intensity (volume or brightness) and frequency (tone or color). Those variations in the native information stream are translated in an analog electrical network into variations in the amplitude and frequency of the carrier signal. In other words, the carrier signal is modulated (varied) in order to create an analog of the original information stream.

Bandwidth, in the analog world, is measured in hertz (Hz).

A string tied to a doorknob would be an 'analog' system. Analog systems are also known as wave systems. They have a value that changes steadily over time and can have any one of an infinite set of values in a range. If you put a measuring stick or ruler at a specific point along the string, you can measure the string's value every so many seconds at that point. When you watch it move, you will see it moves constantly. It doesn't instantly jump up and down the ruler.

5.2.1 Analog Signals

Analog data takes continuous values at some interval. For e.g., voice and video is continuously varying patterns of intensity. Most data collected by sensors such as temp, pressure are continuous-valued.

An *analog signal* is continuously varying electromagnetic wave that may be propagated over a variety of media depending on spectrum, e.g., wire media, twisted pair, co-axial cable, fiber optic cable etc. Analog signals are used to represent analog data. Generally, analog data are a function of time and occupy frequency spectrum, such data can be represented by an electromagnetic signal occupying the same spectrum. When the signalling technique in a local area network implementation is analog, the network is known as a **BROADBAND** network. Broadband networks require the presence of a carrier signal.

Broadband = Analog

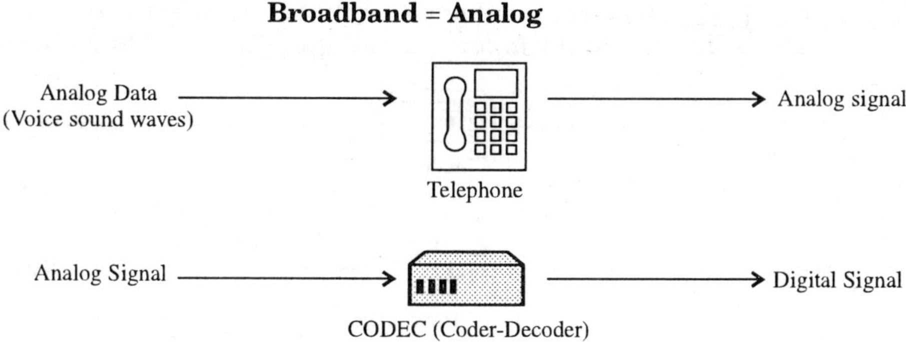

5.3 Digital Communications

Digital communications represents information in binary form (1's and 0's) through a series of discrete blips or pulses. While the natural world is analog in nature, computers (which are decidedly unnatural beings) are digital in nature. Computers process, store, and communicate information in *binary* form. That is to say that a unique combination of 1's and 0's has a specific meaning in a computer language. A bit (*binary digit*) is an individual 1 or 0. Multiple bits travel across a network in a *digital bit stream*.

5.3.1 Digital Signals

Digital signaling, in an electrical network, involves a signal that varies in voltage to represent one of two discrete and well-defined states : such as a positive (+) voltage and a null, or zero (0) voltage (unipolar); or a positive (+) or a negative (–) voltage (bipolar). The receiver monitors the signal, at a specific frequency and for a specific duration (*bit time*) to determine the state of the signal. Various data transmission protocols employ different physical states of the signal, such as voltage level or voltage transition. Because of the discrete nature of each bit transmitted, the bit form is often referred to as a *square wave*.

Digital signaling in an optical network can involve either the pulsing on and off of a light stream or a variation in the intensity of the light signal. Digital transmission over radio systems (e.g., microwave, cellular or satellite) can be accomplished by varying the amplitude of the signal. In the digital world, bandwidth is measured in *bits per second* (*bps*). The amount of bandwidth required depends on the amount of raw data to be sent, the desired speed of transmission of that set of data, and issues of transmission cost.

When the signalling technique in a local area network implementation is digital, the network is known as a **BASEBAND** network.

Baseband = Digital

Our string example is *not* a digital system. A digital system would be to flick the light switch on and off. There's no 'in between' values, unlike our string. If the switch you are using is not a dimmer switch, then the light is either on, or off. In this case, the transmitter is the light bulb, the media is the air, and the receiver is your eye. This would be a *digital* system.

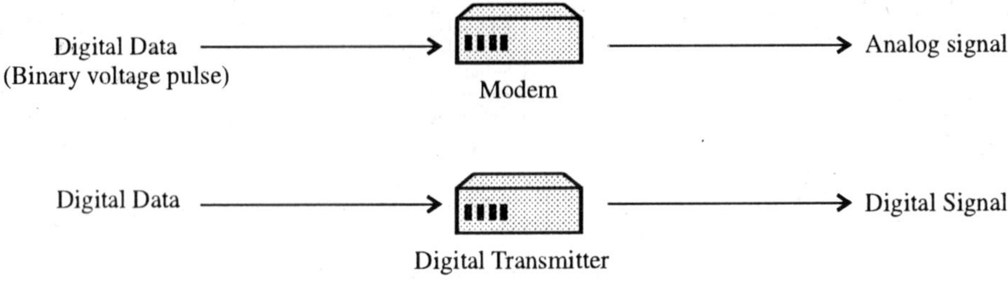

5.4 Media And Propagation Of Signals

The actual process of carrying a signal from point to point is called *propagation.* Copper, aluminum, tin or nickel wire is used to *propagate* electricity. Erbium-doped glass fibers, or plastic strands are used to *propagate* light. The air itself is used to propagate laser beams, radio waves or microwave.

The copper, aluminum, nickel, tin, glass fibers, plastic and the air are all referred to as *media* (or *the medium of transmission*). Our string *propagates* the movement of our hand to the doorknob. The time it takes to *propagate* a signal through a device or piece of media is called *propagation delay* or *latency*.

5.4.1 Transmitters, Receivers and Transmission Media

When you shake the string, you create a wave that radiates outwards from your hand down the string to the doorknob. This string is what we are using to transmit our signal. The string is the *transmission media*, our hand and arm is the *transmitter* and the doorknob is the receiver.

A device that can both transmit *and* receive is called a *transceiver*. Media is the stuff used to connect all the devices together. That can be the air, a cable or radio waves.

5.4.2 Carrier Signal

The process of data transmission requires some sort of signal to carry information across a medium. For copper medium, a signal can be the electrical voltage on the line. On optical cabling, it is the light. Through the atmosphere, it can be a radio, microwave or infrared signal. The carrier signal (sometimes called a carrier wave) provides the base signal into which data is inserted using some type of modulation technique. (Discussed later) Many systems have error detectors that signal a problem when the carrier signal disappears (no voltage on the copper wire, no light in the optical cable, etc.).

5.4.3 Analog Versus Digital Transmission: Which Is Better?

Although analog voice and video can be converted to digital, and digital data can be converted to analog, each format has its own advantages.

Analog : Advantages

Analog transmission offers advantages in the transmission of analog information. Additionally, it is more bandwidth-conservative and is widely available.

Analog Data : Analog has an advantage with respect to the transmission of information that is analog in its native form, such as voice, image and video. The process of transmission of such information is relatively straightforward in an analog format, whereas conversion to a digital bit stream requires conversion equipment. Such equipment adds cost, contributes additional points of failure, and can negatively affect the quality of the signal through the conversion process, itself.

Bandwidth : A raw information stream consumes less bandwidth in analog form than in digital form. This is particularly evident in CATV transmission, where 50 or more analog channels routinely are provided over a single coaxial cable system. Without the application of compression techniques on the same cable system, only a few digital channels could be supported.

Digital : Advantages

Digital transmission offers advantage in the transmission of digital information. Additionally, such data can be compressed effectively and relatively easily. Security of the data can be more readily ensured and the error performances of digital networks are much improved over their analog counterparts.

Finally, the cost-effectiveness of such networks is improved by virtue of the greater bandwidth they provide, especially since they can be more easily upgraded and more effectively managed.

Digital Data : Just as it is better to transmit analog information in an analog format, it is better to transmit digital information in a digital format. Digital transmission certainly has the advantage where binary computer data is being transmitted. The equipment required to convert digital data to an analog format and send the digital bit streams over an analog network can be expensive, susceptible to failure, and can create errors in the information.

Compression : Digital data can be compressed relatively easily, thereby increasing the efficiency of transmission. As a result, substantial volumes of voice, data, video and image information can be transmitted using relatively little raw bandwidth.

Security : Digital systems offer better security. While analog systems offer some measure of security through the *scrambling* or intertwining/mixing of several frequencies, scrambling is fairly simple to defeat. Digital information, on the other hand, can be *encrypted* to create the appearance of a single, pseudo-random bit stream. Thereby, the true meaning of individual bits, sets of bits or the total bit stream cannot be determined without having the key to unlock the encryption algorithm employed.

Quality : Digital transmission offers improved error performance (quality) as compared to analog. This is due to the devices that boost the signal at periodic intervals in the transmission system in order to overcome the effects of *attenuation*. Additionally, digital networks deal more effectively with noise, which always is present in transmission networks.

Summary of comparison of Analog and Digital Transmissions

	Analog	Digital
Data	Continuous (e.g., voice)	Discrete (e.g., text)
Signal	Continuous electromagnetic waves Used mainly for transmitting data across a network.	Sequence of voltage pulses Used mainly internally within computers.
Trans-mission	Transmission of analog signals without regards to their content (the data may be analog or binary). The signals become weaker (attenuated) with the distance. Amplifiers may be used to strengthen the signals, but as side effect they also boost the noise. This might not be a problem for analog data, such as voice, but is a problem for digital data.	Transmission that is concerned with the content of the signal. Repeaters are used to overcome attenuation. A repeater recovers the digital pattern from the signal it gets, and resubmits a new signal.

5.4.4 Need of Amplifiers and Repeaters

To understand the need of amplifiers and repeaters first we will discuss two important terms attenuation and noise.

Attenuation

Electromagnetic signals tend to weaken or *attenuate*, over a distance; this is particularly true of electrical signals carried over twisted pair copper wire, due to the level of resistance in the wire. It is also particularly true of microwave radio and other terrestrial radio systems, due to matter in the air. Attenuation is sensitive to carrier frequency, with higher frequency signals attenuating more than lower frequency signals.

Noise

Signals also tend to pick up noise as they transverse the network. Again, this is particularly true of twisted pair, copper wire systems. Such wires tend to act as antennae and, therefore, absorb noise from outside sources of Electromagnetic Interference (EMI). Thus, the quality of the signal degenerates as it is distorted by the noise.

Amplifiers Versus Repeaters

As we have noted, electromagnetic energy attenuates over a distance through either a wire or the air. Therefore, it is necessary to place some sort of device at regular intervals in a network to overcome this phenomenon. These boosting units read a weak incoming signal and create a stronger outgoing signal until the signal reaches another boosting unit, and so on. Analog networks make use of devices known as *amplifiers*, while *repeaters* are employed in digital networks.

Amplifiers (Analog)

The boosting devices in an analog network are known as *amplifiers*. Amplifiers boost, or amplify the weak incoming signal, much like an amplifier in a radio or TV. As it traverses the network the signal accumulates noise. Through every step of the transmission and through each amplifier, the noise is amplified along with the signal, creating the potential for significant accumulated noise at the receiving end of the transmission. The resulting *signal-to-noise* ratio can be unacceptable. Amplifiers typically are spaced every 18,000 feet or so in an analog network.

The impact of amplification on voice communications generally is tolerable, as humans are relatively intelligent receivers who can filter out the noise or, at least adjust to it. In the event of a truly garbled transmission, the human-to-human error detection and correction process simply involves a request for re-transmission. Should the quality of the connection be totally unacceptable, the connection can be terminated and re-established. Computer systems, however, are not so forgiving, and garbled data is of decidedly negative value.

Repeaters (Digital)

In a digital system, periodic amplifiers are replaced by *regenerative repeaters*, which regenerate the signal, rather than simply amplifying it. The repeater guesses the binary value (1 or 0) of the weak incoming signal based on its relative voltage level and regenerates a strong signal of the same value, without the noise. This process immensely enhances the signal quality. Repeaters are spaced at approximately the same intervals as amplifiers, although spacing is sensitive to the carrier frequency, which affects both transmission speed, or bandwidth provided, and the level of attenuation experienced.

The performance advantage of digital networks can be illustrated by comparing the error rate of amplifiers and regenerative repeaters. For example, a twisted-pair, analog network can be expected to yield an error rate on the order of 10^{-5}. In other words, digital data sent across an analog network will suffer 1 errored bit for every 100,000 bits transmitted. The very same twisted-pair network, if digitized and equipped with repeaters, will yield an expected error rate of 10^{-7} or 1 errored bit in every 10,000,000. This is an improvement of two orders of magnitude. Digital fiber optic systems, currently considered to be the ultimate, yield error rates in the range of 10^{-11} to 10^{-14} or an error rate as low as 1 bit for every 100,000,000,000,000 transmitted-virtually perfect !

5.4.5 The Conversion Process: Digital to Analog (D To A) and Analog to Digital (A To D)

Digital to Analog : Modems

As local loops generally are analog, computer communications across such circuits is not possible without the assistance of a device to accomplish the digital-to-analog conversion. Of course, one might gain access to a more expensive digital circuit, by so specifying, if it is available. The device that accomplishes this is known as modem. (Discussed later)

Analog to Digital : Codecs

The reverse conversion process is necessary to send analog information across a digital circuit. This is often the case in the carrier networks, where huge volumes of analog voice are digitized and sent across high capacity, digital circuits. This requirement also exists where high capacity digital circuits connect premise-based, PBX voice systems to central office exchanges or to other PBXs, assuming that the PBXs or COs have not already performed the conversion. As video also is analog in its native form, a similar process must be employed to send video across a digital circuit.

The device that accomplishes the A-to-D conversion is known as a *codec*. Codecs code an analog input into a digital (data) format on the transmit side of the connection, reversing the process or decoding the information, on the receive side, in order to reconstitute the analog signal.

Encoding is the process of converting an analog information stream (e.g., voice or video) into a digital data stream. The voice or video signal is sampled at frequent intervals with each sample of amplitude then being expressed in terms of a binary (computer) value, which is usually a 4-bit or 8-bit byte. The reverse process of *decoding* takes place on the receiving end, resulting in recomposition of the information in its original form or at least a reasonable approximation thereof.

5.5 Modulation

The point to modulation is to take a **message-bearing signal** and superimpose it upon a **carrier signal** for transmission. For ease of transmission carrier signals are generally high frequency for several reasons:

1. For easy (low loss, low dispersion) propagation as electromagnetic waves.
2. So that they may be simultaneously transmitted without interference from other signals.
3. So as to enable the construction of small antennas (a fraction, usually a quarter of the wavelength).
4. So as to be able to multiplex that is to combine multiple signals for transmission at the same time.

In communications, modulation is a process in which some characteristic of a wave (the carrier wave) is made to vary in accordance with an information-bearing signal wave (the modulating wave). Modulation is described as being performed at the physical layer of the OSI Model. The carrier signal can be an electrical current, a radio or microwave frequency or light. The original, unmodulated wave may be of any kind, such as sound or, most often, electromagnetic radiation, including optical waves. In modulation, it is processed in such a way that its amplitude, frequency, or some other property varies.

The process of modulation of the data also requires *demodulation* at the receiving end. Demodulation is the process by which the original signal is recovered from the wave produced by modulation.

Carrier Signal

In information technology, a carrier (or carrier signal) is a transmitted electromagnetic pulse or wave at a steady base frequency of alternation on which information can be imposed by increasing signal strength, varying the base frequency, varying the wave phase, or other means. This variation is called modulation. With the advent of laser transmission over optical fiber media, a carrier can also be a laser-generated light beam on which information is imposed.

Carrier detect (see modem lights) is a control signal between a modem and a computer that indicates that the modem detects a "live" carrier that can be used for sending and receiving information.

Signal modulation can be done in either of two main ways:

1. Analog modulation
2. Digital modulation

In telecommunications, an analog signal is one in which a base carrier's alternating current frequency is modified in some way, such as by amplifying the strength of the signal or varying the frequency, in order to add information to the signal. Broadcast and telephone transmission have conventionally used analog technology.

Types of analog modulation of a carrier include :

- **Amplitude modulation (AM) :** In which the voltage applied to the carrier is varied over time.
- **Frequency modulation (FM) :** In which the frequency of the carrier waveform is varied in small but meaningful amounts.
- **Phase modulation (PM) :** In which the natural flow of the alternating current waveform is delayed temporarily.

In recent years, digital modulation has been getting more common, while analog modulation methods have been used less and less. There are still plenty of analog signals around, however, and they will probably never become totally extinct.

Types of digital modulation include :

- Pulse Modulation Schemes
- Keying Schemes

5.6 Analog Modulation Schemes

The basic idea here is to superimpose the message signal in analog form on a carrier that is a sinusoid of the form

$$A \cos(\omega_c t + \phi)$$

There are three quantities that can be varied in proportion to the modulating signal: the **amplitude**, the **phase** and **frequency**. The first scheme is called Amplitude Modulation and the second two are called **Angle Modulation** schemes.

5.6.1 Amplitude Modulation

It is a method by which radio waves are altered for the transmission of broadcasting signals. AM waves are constant in frequency, but the amplitude of the transmitting wave varies in accordance with the signal being broadcast.

Amplitude

In physics, amplitude is the maximum displacement of an oscillation from the equilibrium position. For a transverse wave motion, as in electromagnetic waves, it is the height of a crest (or the depth of a trough). For a longitudinal wave, such as a sound wave, amplitude is the maximum distance a particle is pushed (due to compression) or pulled (due to rarefaction) from its resting position. A quiet sound has lower amplitude and a loud sound has higher amplitude. For a louder sound, more sound energy enters the ear every second. Amplitude is generally denoted by a.

AM (amplitude modulation) radio broadcasting is a method of transmitting audio-frequency signals that would otherwise travel not very far in space on their own and would have to be transmitted one at a time. The amplitude of the low-frequency audio signal is made to modulate (vary slightly) the amplitude of a continuously transmitted radio **carrier wave** of a higher frequency. In this way the **modulating signal** is imprinted on the carrier wave.

Amplitude modulation (AM) is the modulation method used in the AM radio broadcast band. In this system the intensity, or amplitude, of the carrier wave varies in accordance with the modulating signal. When the carrier is thus modulated, a fraction of the power is converted to sidebands extending above and below the carrier frequency by an amount equal to the highest modulating frequency. If the modulated carrier is rectified and the carrier frequency filtered out, the modulating signal can be recovered. This form of modulation is not a very efficient way to send information; the power required is relatively large because the carrier, which contains no information, is sent along with the information.

In a variant of amplitude modulation, called single sideband modulation (SSB), the modulated signal contains only one sideband and no carrier. The information can be demodulated only if the carrier is used as a reference. This is normally accomplished by generating a wave in the receiver at the carrier frequency. SSB modulation is used for long-distance telephony (such as in the amateur radio bands) and telegraphy over land and submarine cables.

In AM, the carrier itself does not fluctuate in amplitude. Instead, the modulating data appears in the form of signal components at frequencies slightly higher and lower than that of the carrier. These components are called *sidebands*. The lower sideband (LSB) appears at frequencies below the carrier frequency; the upper sideband (USB) appears at frequencies above the carrier frequency. The LSB and USB are essentially "mirror images" of each other in a graph of signal amplitude versus frequency, as shown in the figure 5.5. The sideband power accounts for the variations in the overall amplitude of the signal.

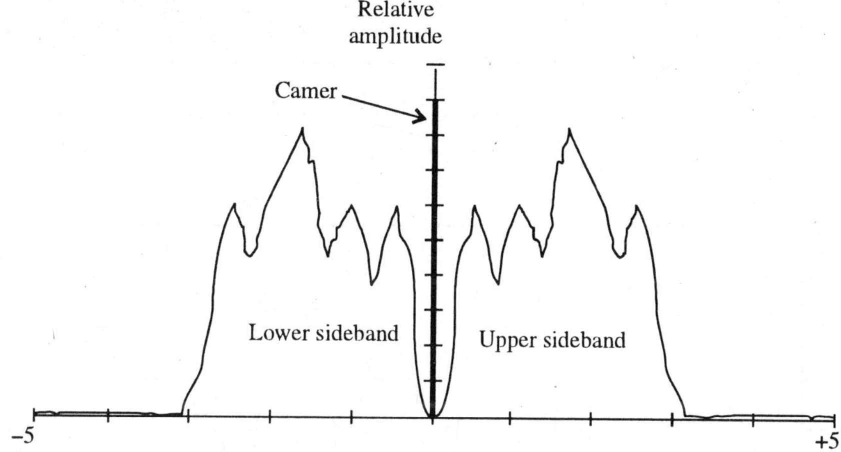

Fig. 5.5 Representation of sidebands

When a carrier is amplitude-modulated with a pure sine wave, up to 1/3 (33 percent) of the overall signal power is contained in the sidebands. The other 2/3 of the signal power is contained in the carrier, which does not contribute to the transfer of data. With a complex modulating signal such as voice, video or music, the sidebands generally contain 20 to 25 percent of the overall signal power; thus the carrier consumes 75 to 80 percent of the power. This makes AM an inefficient mode. If an attempt is made to increase the modulating data input amplitude beyond these limits, the signal will become distorted and will occupy a much greater bandwidth than it should. This is called *overmodulation* and can result in interference to signals on nearby frequencies.

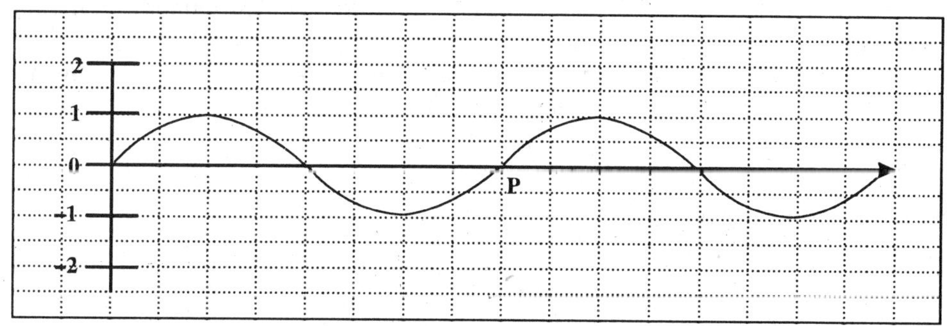

Fig. 5.6 (a) Data carrying signal

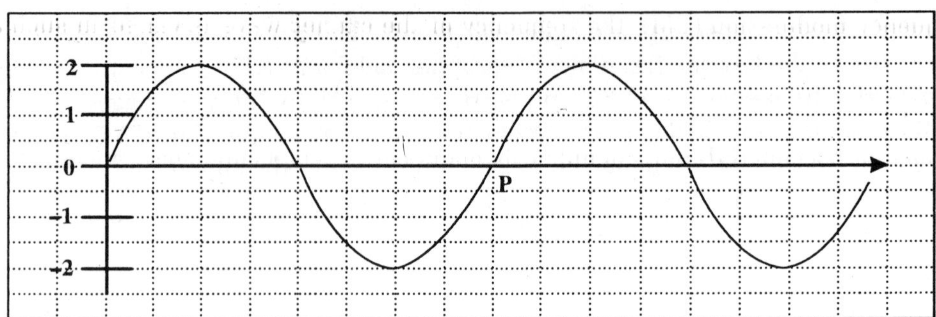

Fig. 5.6 (b) Carrier signal

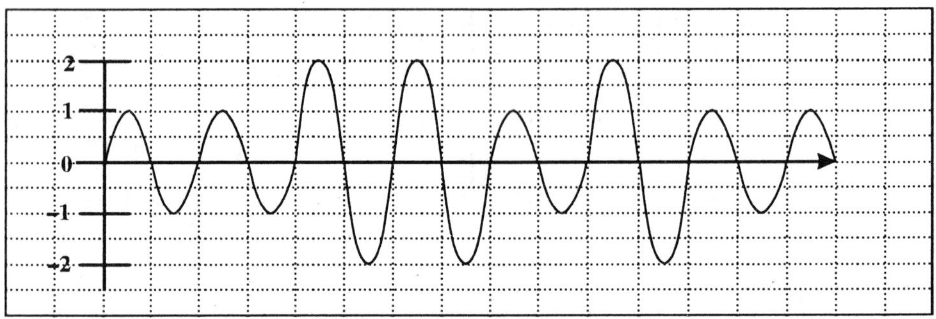

Fig. 5.6 (c) Amplitude modulated wave

The modulated wave is said to consist of three parts :

- The *carrier*, $A_0 \cos\{2\pi f_c t\}$, which is unaffected by the modulation.
- The *Upper Sideband Components*, $(f_c + f_m)$, which are an 'up converted' copy of the original modulation spectrum.
- The *Lower Sideband Components*, $(f_c - f_m)$, which are a 'mirror image' of the upper sideband spectrum.

AM also suffers from being prone to *interference* effects. The AM demodulator essentially measures the power or amplitude of the signals presented to it. Any other power, e.g., pulses radiated by electric drills, Tornado radars, etc. can also be detected. This is why AM radio tends to suffer from buzzes, crackles, whistles, etc. Other forms of modulation can avoid this sensitivity and are less prone to unwanted interference.

5.6.2 Frequency Modulation

In FM radio transmission, the frequency of the carrier wave is modulated, rather than its amplitude (as in AM broadcasts). The FM system is not affected by the many types of interference that change the amplitude of the carrier wave, and so provides better quality reception than AM broadcasts.

In frequency modulation (FM), the frequency of the carrier wave is varied in such a way that the change in frequency at any instant is proportional to another signal that varies with time. Its principal application is also in radio, where it offers increased noise immunity and decreased distortion over the AM transmissions at the expense of greatly increased bandwidth. The FM band has become the choice of music listeners because of its low-noise, wide-bandwidth qualities; it is also used for the audio portion of a television broadcast.

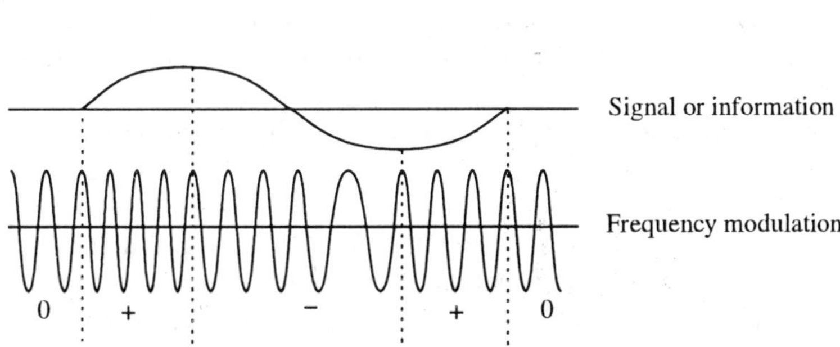

Fig. 5.7 Frequency modulation

This scheme can be used with analog or digital data. In analog FM, the frequency of the AC signal wave, also called the *carrier*, varies in a continuous manner. Thus, there are infinitely many possible carrier frequencies. In **narrowband FM**, commonly used in two-way wireless communications, the instantaneous carrier frequency varies by up to 5 kilohertz (kHz, where 1 kHz = 1000 hertz or alternating cycles per second) above and below the frequency of the carrier with no modulation. In **wideband FM**, used in wireless broadcasting, the instantaneous frequency varies by up to several megahertz (MHz, where 1 MHz = 1,000,000 Hz). When the instantaneous input wave has positive polarity, the carrier frequency shifts in one direction; when the instantaneous input wave has negative polarity, the carrier frequency shifts in the opposite direction. At every instant in time, the extent of carrier-frequency shift (the *deviation*) is directly proportional to the extent to which the signal amplitude is positive or negative.

In digital FM, the carrier frequency shifts abruptly, rather than varying continuously. The number of possible carrier frequency states is usually a power of 2. If there are only two possible frequency states, the mode is called frequency-shift keying (FSK). In more complex modes, there can be four, eight or more different frequency states. Each specific carrier frequency represents a specific digital input data state.

FM is a so-called angle modulation scheme; it was inspired by phase modulation but has proved to be more useful partly for its ease of generation and decoding.

The main advantages of FM over AM are:

1. Improved signal to noise ratio (about 25dB) with respect to man made interference.
2. Smaller geographical interference between neighboring stations.
3. Less radiated power.
4. Well-defined service areas for given transmitter power.

Disadvantages of FM:

1. Much more Bandwidth (as much as 20 times as much).
2. More complicated receiver and transmitter.

5.6.3 Phase Modulation

Phase modulation, like frequency modulation, is a form of angle modulation (so called because the angle of the sine wave carrier is changed by the modulating wave). The two methods are very similar in the sense that any attempt to shift the frequency or phase is accomplished by a change in the other.

Before discussing phase modulation let us understand the term phase.

Phase

In electronic signaling, phase is a definition of the position of a point in time (instant) on a **waveform** cycle. A complete cycle is defined as 360 degrees of phase as shown in upper wave of figure 5.8. Phase can also be an expression of relative displacement between or among waves having the same **frequency.**

Phase difference, also called *phase angle*, in degrees is conventionally defined as a number greater than −180, and less than or equal to +180. *Leading phase* refers to a wave that occurs "ahead" of another wave of the same frequency. *Leading phase* refers to a wave that occurs "behind" another wave of the same frequency. When two signals differ in phase by -90 or +90 degrees, they are said to be in *phase quadrature*. When two waves differ in phase by 180 degrees (−180 is technically the same as +180), the waves are said to be in *phase opposition*. Lower wave in figure 5.8 shows two waves that are in phase quadrature. The wave depicted by the dashed line leads the wave represented by the solid line by 90 degrees.

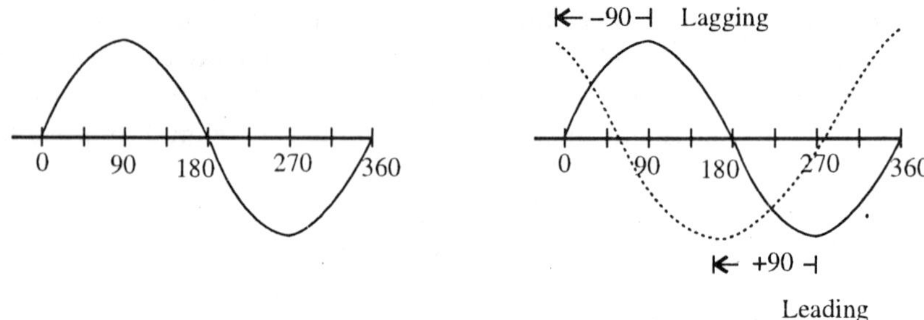

Fig. 5.8 Representation of phase quadrature

Phase is sometimes expressed in radians rather than in degrees. One radian of phase corresponds to approximately 57.3 degrees. Engineers and technicians generally use degrees; physicists more often use radians. The time interval for one degree of phase is inversely proportional to the frequency. If the frequency of a signal (in **hertz**) is given by f, then the time t_{deg} (in seconds) corresponding to one degree of phase is:

$$t_{deg} = \frac{1}{(360f)}$$

The time t_{rad} (in seconds) corresponding to one radian of phase is approximately:

$$t_{rad} = \frac{1}{(6.28f)}$$

Now let us discuss what is phase modulation? Phase modulation (PM) is a method of impressing data onto an alternating-current (AC) waveform by varying the instantaneous phase of the wave. This scheme can be used with analog or digital data.

In analog PM, the phase of the AC signal wave, also called the *carrier*, varies in a continuous manner. Thus, there are infinitely many possible carrier phase states. When the instantaneous data input waveform has positive polarity, the carrier phase shifts in one direction; when the instantaneous data input waveform has negative polarity, the carrier phase shifts in the opposite direction. At every instant in time, the extent of carrier-phase shift (the *phase angle*) is directly proportional to the extent to which the signal amplitude is positive or negative.

In digital PM, the carrier phase shifts abruptly, rather than continuously back and forth. The number of possible carrier phase states is usually a power of 2. If there are only two possible phase states, the mode is called biphase modulation. In more complex modes, there can be four, eight or more different phase states. Each phase angle (that is, each shift from one phase state to another) represents a specific digital input data state.

Phase modulation is similar in practice to frequency modulation (FM). When the instantaneous phase of a carrier is varied, the instantaneous frequency changes as well. The converse also holds: When the instantaneous frequency is varied, the instantaneous phase changes. But PM and FM are not exactly equivalent, especially in analog applications. When an FM receiver is used to demodulate a PM signal, or when an FM signal is intercepted by a receiver designed for PM, the audio is distorted. This is because the relationship between phase and frequency variations is not linear; that is, phase and frequency do not vary in direct proportion.

5.7 Digital Modulation Schemes

In these schemes one is interested in preparing a digital signal of 1's and 0's for transmission. This signal arises from several sources, for example:

1. Encoding type written characters (ASCII).
2. Sampling and quantizing speech.
3. Sampling and quantizing a video signal.

The simplest digital modulation scheme is called On Off Keying (OOK): here a signal is turned on in response to a 1 and off in response to a 0.

The main types of digital modulation schemes include:

- Pulse Modulation Schemes
- Keying Schemes

5.7.1 Pulse Modulation Schemes

Pulse modulation involves modulating a carrier that is a train of regularly recurrent pulses. The modulation might vary the amplitude (PAM or pulse amplitude modulation), the duration (PDM or pulse duration modulation) or the presence of the pulses (PCM or pulse code modulation). PCM can be used to send digital data; audio signals on a compact disc use pulse code modulation. Developed in 1939 by the English inventor Alec H. Reeves, pulse code modulation is the most important form of pulse modulation because it can be used to transmit information over long distances with hardly any interference or distortion; for this reason it has become increasingly important in the transmission of data in the space program and between computers. Although PCM transmits digital instead of analog signals, the modulating wave is continuous.

Pulse modulation techniques include:

- Pulse-code modulation (PCM).
- Pulse-width modulation (PWM).
- Pulse-amplitude modulation (PAM).
- Pulse-position modulation (PPM).

Pulse-code Modulation (PCM)

Pulse-code modulation (PCM) is a modulation technique. It is a digital representation of an analog signal where the magnitude of the signal is sampled regularly at uniform intervals of duration. Every sample is quantized to a series of symbols in a digital code, which is usually a binary code. PCM is used in digital telephone systems and for digital audio recording on compact discs. Morse code is a very simple example of pulse-code modulation.

In telephony, several PCM streams may be multiplexed into a larger aggregate data stream. The signals in PCM are binary; that is, there are only two possible states, represented by logic 1 (high) and logic 0 (low). This is true no matter how complex the analog waveform happens to be.

To obtain PCM from an analog waveform at the source (transmitter end) of a communications circuit, the analog signal amplitude is sampled (measured) at regular time intervals. The sampling rate, or number of samples per second, is several times the maximum frequency of the analog waveform in cycles per second or hertz. The instantaneous amplitude of the analog signal at each sampling is rounded off to the nearest of several specific, predetermined levels. This process is called quantization. The number of levels is always a power of 2, for example, 8, 16, 32 or 64. These numbers can be represented by three, four, five or six binary digits (bits) respectively. The output of a pulse code modulator is thus a series of binary numbers, each represented by some power of at the destination (receiver end) of the communications circuit, a pulse code demodulator converts the binary numbers back into pulses having the same quantum levels as those in the modulator. These pulses are further processed to restore the original analog waveform.

Pulse-code modulation can be either return-to-zero (RZ) or non-return-to-zero (NRZ). For a NRZ system to be synchronized using in-band information, there must not be long sequences of identical symbols, such as ones or zeroes. For binary PCM systems, the density of 1-symbols is called 'ones-density'.

Sampling Theorem

A signal can be reconstructed from a sample taken at

- Regular time intervals.
- A rate higher than twice the highest significant frequency.

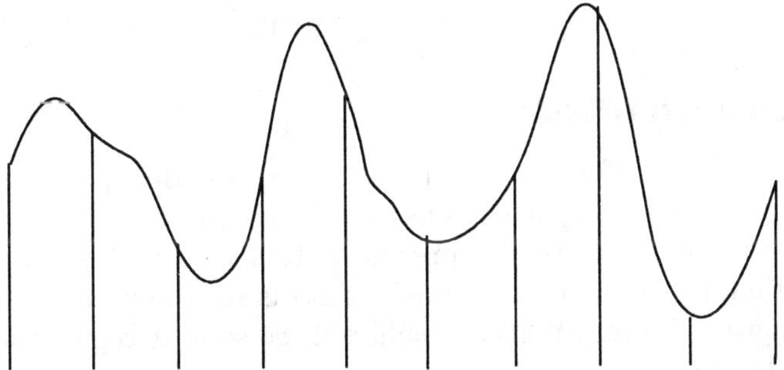

Fig. 5.9 A sample wave

The conversion has three stages :

Sampling of amplitude signals (PAM pulses).
Digitizing of the amplitude signals (PCM pulses).
Encoding of the stream of bits.

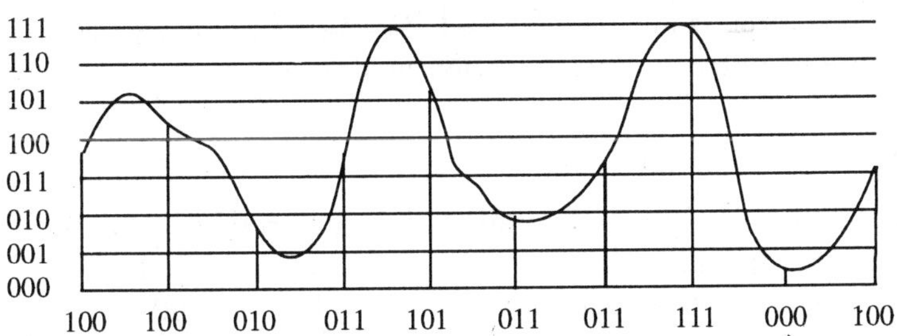

Fig. 5.10 Encoding of the stream of bits

- The quantization of the PAM pulse introduces **quantization error**, not allowing the recovery of the original pulse.
- A reduction in the signal distortion can be obtained by adding bits. The quantizing noise satisfies S/N = 6n + 1.8 dB.

- A reduction in the signal distortion can be obtained by nonuniform quantization which is finer at low amplitudes.

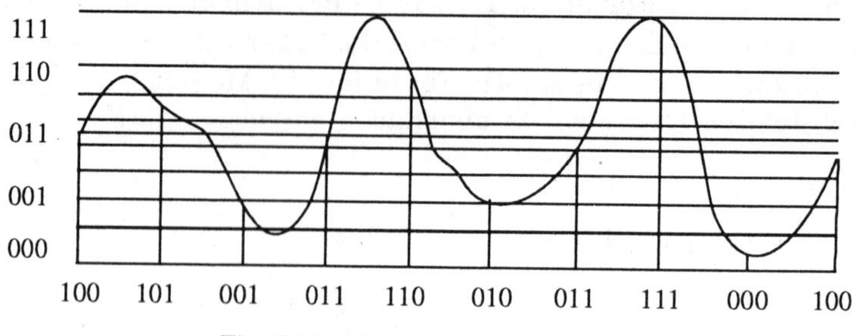

Fig. 5.11 Nonuniform quantization

- For voice signals, nonlinear encoding improved the PCM S/N ratio by 24-30 dB.

Pulse-width Modulation (PWM)

This form of modulation is often used in control applications, as the average value is proportional to the pulse width. It is also easy to demodulate.

Pulse-width modulation is a way to represent data over a communications channel. With pulse-width modulation, the value of a sample of data is represented by the length of a pulse. Pulses of various lengths (the information itself) will be sent at regular intervals (the carrier frequency of the modulation).

PWM is also used to vary the total amount of power delivered to a load without resistive waste. An RC filter can be used to smooth the pulse train into a steady analog voltage. This method is commonly used in DC motor speed control.

Pulse-amplitude Modulation (PAM)

Pulse-amplitude modulation is encoded in the amplitude of a series of signal pulses. Pulse-amplitude modulation is now rarely used, having been largely superseded by pulse-code modulation and more recently by pulse-position modulation.

Pulse-position Modulation (PPM)

Pulse-position modulation is a form of signal modulation in which the message information is encoded in the temporal spacings between a sequence of signal pulses.

This method is not used very frequently, because other methods are usually more suitable for typical data transmission, however one common use of PPM is for the radio control of model aircraft. Here the position of each pulse represents the angular position of an analogue control on the transmitter. The number of pulses per frame gives the number of controllable channels available. The advantage of using PPM for this type of application is that the electronics required to decode the signal is extremely simple, which leads to small, low weight receiver/decoder units, essential in model aircraft where every weight saving is necessary. Servos made for model radio control include some of the electronics required to convert the pulse to the motor position—the receiver is merely required to demultiplex the separate channels and feed the pulses to each servo.

5.7.2 Keying Schemes

In these schemes either the frequency or phase of a carrier signal is keyed in response to patterns of 1's and 0's. Of course one could also key the amplitude, but this is what we already called PAM. Frequency Shift Keying (FSK) stands for the process of keying between two different frequencies.

Frequency-shift Keying (FSK)

Frequency-shift keying (FSK) is a method of transmitting digital signals. The two binary states, logic 0 (low) and 1 (high), are each represented by an analog waveform. Logic 0 is represented by a wave at a specific frequency, and logic 1 is represented by a wave at a different frequency. A modem converts the binary data from a computer to FSK for transmission over telephone lines, cables, optical fiber, or wireless media. The modem also converts incoming FSK signals to digital low and high states, which the computer can "understand".

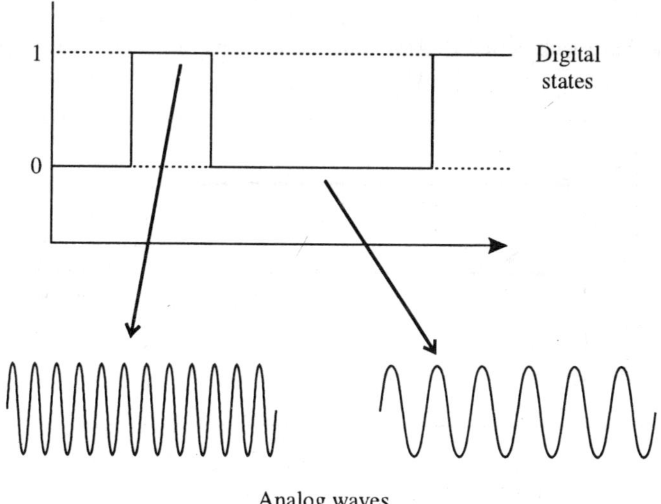

Fig. 5.12 Representation of analog waves corresponding to digital states

The FSK mode was introduced for use with mechanical teleprinters in the mid-1900s. The standard speed of those machines was 45 baud, equivalent to about 45 bits per second. When personal computers became common and networks came into being, this signaling speed was tedious. Transmission of large text documents and programs took hours; image transfer was unknown. During the 1970s, engineers began to develop modems that ran at faster speeds, and the quest for even-greater bandwidth has continued ever since. Today, a standard telephone modem operates at thousands of bits per second. Cable and wireless modems work at more than 1,000,000 bps (one megabit per second or 1 Mbps), and optical fiber modems function at many Mbps. But the basic principle of FSK has not changed in more than half a century.

Phase Shift Keying (PSK)

Phase-shift keying (PSK) is a method of transmitting and receiving digital signals in which the phase of a transmitted signal is varied to convey information.

So it is a technique that shifts the period of a wave.

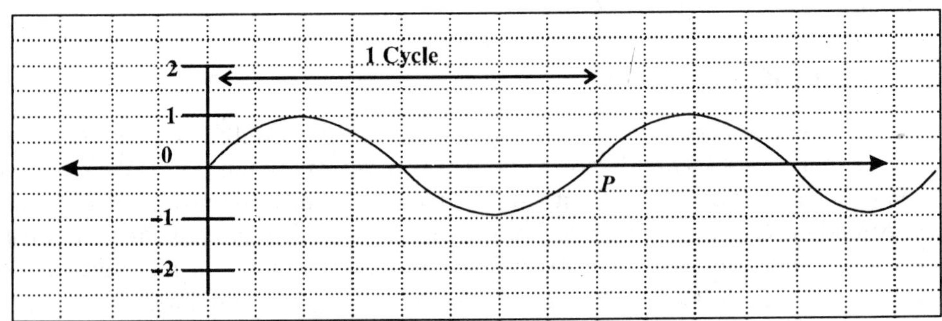

Fig. 5.13
The wave with period *P*. Also notice that the start of wave's period is at 0

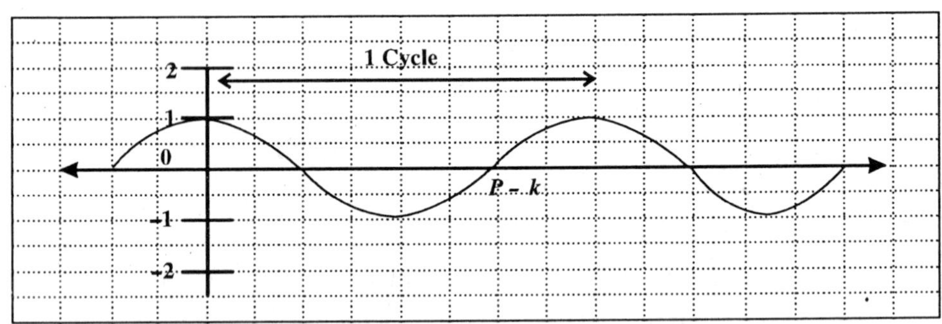

Fig. 5.14
This is the same wave as the first, but its phase has been shifted. Notice that the period starts at the wave's highest point (1).

So what's the point? It just so happens that we have shifted this wave by **one quarter** of the wave's full period. We can shift it another quarter, if we wanted to, so the original wave would be shifted by **half** its period. And we could do it one more time, so that it would be shifted three **quarters** of its original period.

This means we have 4 separate waves. So why not let each wave stand for some binary value? Since there are 4, we can let each wave signify 2 bits (00, 01, 10, 11):

Bit value	Amount of shift
00	None
01	1/4
10	1/2
11	3/4

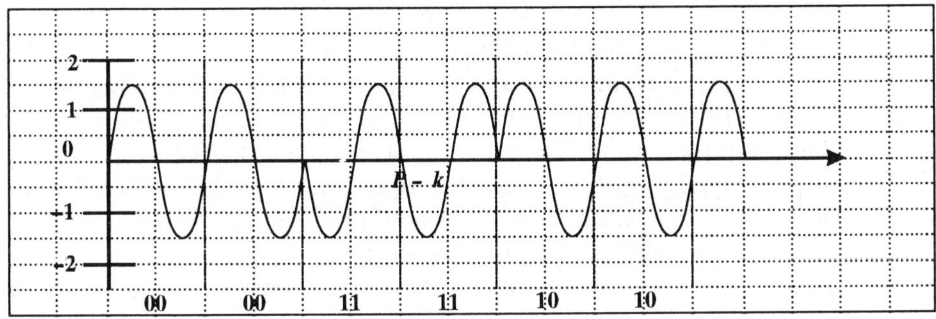

Fig. 5.15 Phase shift keying

This technique of letting each shift of a wave represent some bit value is **phase shift keying**.

It is a technique for switching phases in response to the signal. As before we have quadrature versions of PSK which are referred to as either QPSK or 4-PSK, 8-PSK, etc. The 1200 Baud full duplex, 2400 Baud full duplex and 4800-baud full duplex modems use 4-PSK or 8-PSK.

In channels where there is rapid fading such as mobile radio (wireless) channels it is useful to use PSK modulation, since the decoder does not need to keep track of the intensity of the received signal. For greater noise immunity in these applications, one uses a so-called differential modulation scheme, where one encodes the changes in the group of bits being encoded. Thus, for example digital cellular radio in North America uses a so-called differential PSK-4 scheme.

There are several schemes that can be used to accomplish PSK. The simplest method uses only two signal phases: 0 degrees and 180 degrees. The digital signal is broken up time wise into individual bits (binary digits). The state of each bit is determined according to the state of the preceding bit. If the phase of the wave does not change, then the signal state stays the same (low or high). If the phase of the wave changes by 180 degrees—that is, if the phase reverses—then the signal state changes (from low to high, or from high to low). Because there are two possible wave phases, this form of PSK is sometimes called biphase modulation.

More complex forms of PSK employ four or eight wave phases. This allows binary data to be transmitted at a faster rate per phase change than is possible with biphase modulation. In four-phase modulation, the possible phase angles are 0, +90, -90, and 180 degrees; each phase shift can represent two signal elements. In eight-phase modulation, the possible phase angles are 0, +45, −45, +90, −90, +135, −135, and 180 degrees; each phase shift can represent four signal elements.

5.8 Introduction To Modems

The need to communicate between distant computers led to the use of the existing phone network for data transmission. Most phone lines were designed to transmit analog information-voices, while the computers and their devices work in digital form-pulses.

You can't simply transmit bits directly across telephone lines. It first needs to be converted into sound waves. If you've ever picked up your telephone while you were using your modem, you've no doubt heard a constant loud, screeching noise. This noise is the sound of digital information after it's been converted to analog sound waves.

In order to use an analog medium, a converter between the two systems is needed. This converter is the MODEM that performs MODulation and DEModulation of transmitted data. It accepts serial binary pulses from a device, modulates some property (amplitude, frequency, or phase) of an analog signal in order to send the signal in an analog medium, and performs the opposite process, enabling the analog information to arrive as digital pulses at the computer or device on the other side of connection. So a modem's purpose is to convert digital information to analog signals (modulation), and to convert analog signals back into useful digital information (demodulation).

Modems, in the beginning, were used mainly to communicate between data terminals and a host computer. Later, the use of modems was extended to communicate between end computers. This required more speed and the data rates increased from 300 bps in early days to 28.8 Kbps today. Today, transmission involves data compression techniques that increase the rates, error detection and error correction for more reliability.

Today's modems are used for different functions. They act as textual and voice mail systems, facsimiles, and are connected or integrated into cellular phones and in notebook computers enabling sending data from anywhere. The future might lead to new applications. Modem speeds are not expected to be increased much over today's 28.8 kbps. Further dramatic speed increases will require digital phone technology such as ISDN and fiber optic lines.

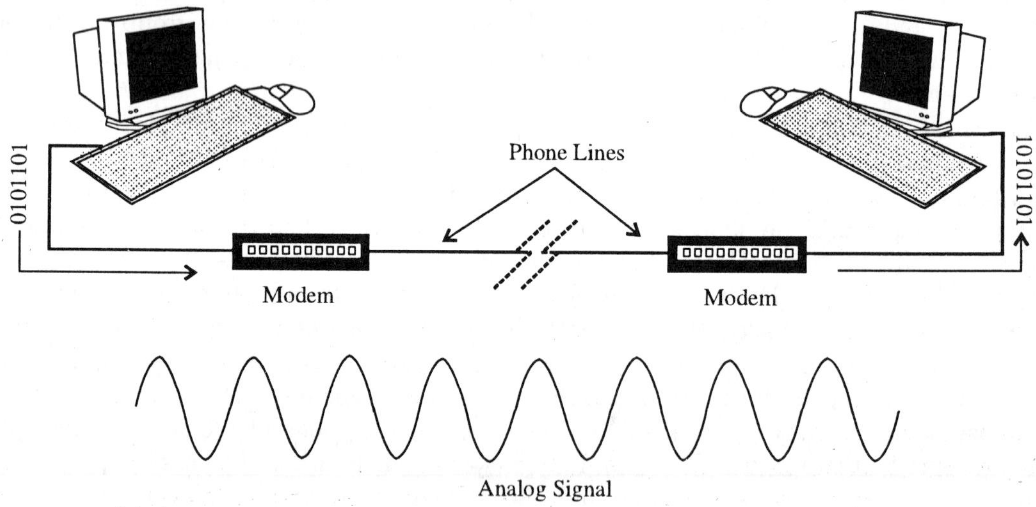

Fig. 5.16 Transmission of data using modems

There are many different types of modems in use operating at different speeds and conforming to different standards. To function, the modems on both sides of the connection must agree to use the same standard. When modems connect, they must negotiate:

- Quality of the line.
- Speed.
- Options such as encoding and compression.
- Disable echo suppression.

This negotiation takes about 10 seconds for a V.34 modem and is usually heard as a series of squeals from your modem. Some systems may use a modem to connect to distant computers over a dedicated or leased line. This line is always connected between the two points. No dialing or hang-up is required. Frequently these modems can operate without the initial parameter negotiation since they can be configured during installation to be compatible.

Aside from the transmission protocols that they support, the following characteristics distinguish one modem from another.

5.8.1 Characteristics of Modems

1. Speed : The speed at which the modem can send data is measured in bps (bits per second). Typical modem speeds are: 300, 600, 1200, 2400, 4800, 9600, 14.4K, 19.2K, 28.8K bps.

bps : It measures how fast the modem can transmit and receive data. At slow rates, modems are measured in terms of baud rates. The carrier signal is characterized by the number of signal intervals, or pulses, that are transmitted per second. Each pulse is called a **baud**.

The slowest rate is 300 baud (about 25 cps). At higher speeds, modems are measured in terms of bits per second (bps).

Bps stands for **b**its **p**er **s**econd. Bps is a measure of how many bits can be transmitted during one pulse (one baud). So,

$$\textbf{bps} = \textbf{baud} \times \textbf{number of bits per baud}$$

The fastest modems run at 57,600 bps, although they can achieve even higher data transfer rates by compressing the data. Obviously, the faster the transmission rate, the faster you can send and receive data. Note, however, that you cannot receive data any faster than it is being sent. If, for example, the device sending data to your computer is sending it at 2,400 bps, you must receive it at 2,400 bps. It does not always pay, therefore, to have a very fast modem. In addition, some telephone lines are unable to transmit data reliably at very high rates.

A modem operating at 9600 bps is *still* only transmitting at 1200 baud. But it is "packing" 8 bits into each baud:

$$\textbf{9600 bps} = \textbf{1200 baud} \times \textbf{8 bits per baud}$$

2. Voice/data : Many modems support a switch to change between voice and data modes. In data mode, the modem acts like a regular modem. In voice mode, the modem acts like a regular telephone. Modems that support a voice/data switch have a built-in loudspeaker and microphone for voice communication.

3. Auto-answer : An auto-answer modem enables your computer to receive calls in your absence. This is only necessary if you are offering some type of computer service that people can call in to use.

4. Data compression : Some modems perform data compression, which enables them to send data at faster rates. However, the modem at the receiving end must be able to decompress the data using the same compression technique.

5. Flash memory : Some modems come with *flash memory* rather than conventional ROM, which means that the communications protocols can be easily updated if necessary.

6. Fax capability : Most modern modems are fax modems, which means that they can send and receive faxes.

7. Self Testing : Newer modems have self-testing features. They can test the digital connection to the terminal/computer and the analog connection to a remote modem. They can also check the modem's internal electronics.

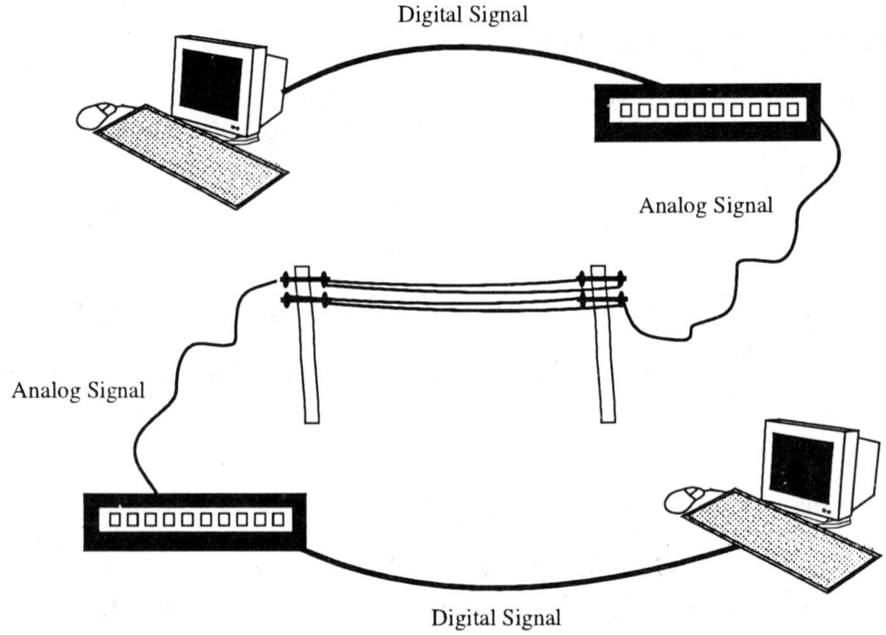

Fig. 5.17 Transmission of signals

Buying and using a modem used to be relatively easy. Not too long ago, almost all modems transferred data at a rate of 2400 Bps (bits per second). Today, modems not only run faster, they are also loaded with features like error control and data compression. In addition, modems also act like traffic cops, monitoring and regulating the flow of information. That way one computer doesn't send information until the receiving computer is ready for it. Each of these features—modulation, error control, and data compression—requires a separate kind of protocol. That's what some of the terms you see like **V.32**, **V.32** bis, **V.42** bis and **MNP5** refer to.

5.8.2 Standards and Protocols

Communication between two devices might work only when the interface is defined and agreed. In order to enable modems of various types and different manufacture to communicate, interface standards were developed by some standard organizations. For modems, the standards define techniques used for modulation, for error correction, for data compression, and other attributes. There are some standard organizations for the development of interface standards: The ITU—International Telecommunications Union an agency of the United Nations (Geneva, Switzerland), ISO—International Standards Organization, and CCITT—International Telegraph and Telephone Consultative Committee a group of ITU.

While the modem interfaces are standardized, a number of different protocols for formatting data to be transmitted over telephone lines exist. Some, like CCITT V.34, are official standards, while others have been developed by private companies. Most modems have built-in support for the more common protocols—at slow data transmission speeds at least, most modems can communicate with each other. At high transmission speeds, however, the protocols are less standardized.

5.8.3 Types of Modems

There are two types of modems : **internal modem** and **external modem**.

Internal modem

A modem that resides on an expansion board that plugs into a computer. An internal modem is a plug-in circuit board that sits inside the computer. It incorporates the serial port on-board. They are less expensive than external modems because they do not require a case, power supply and serial cable. They appear to the communication programs as if they were an external modem for all practical purposes.

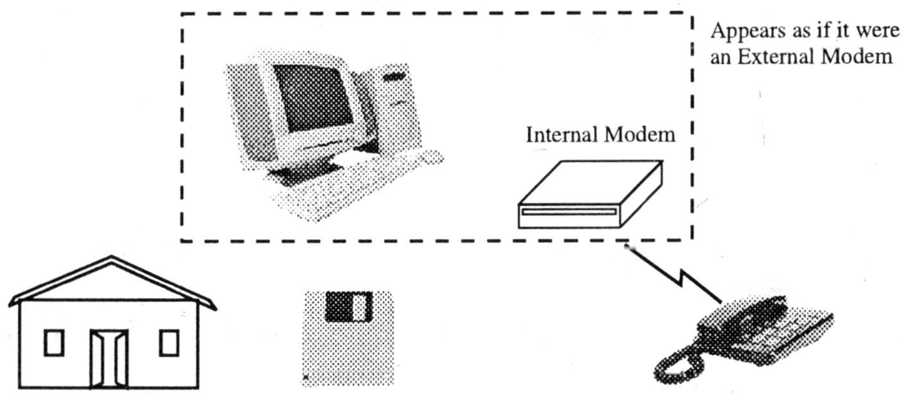

Fig. 5.18 Internal modem

External modem

External modems are separate boxes, and you have to have a cable to connect to the serial port that is on the back of your computer (most, but not all computers have a serial port available).

It is a modem that resides in a self-contained box outside the computer system. Contrast with an internal modem, which resides on a printed circuit board inserted into the computer.

External modems tend to be slightly more expensive than internal modems. Many experts consider them superior because they contain lights that indicate how the modem is functioning. In addition, they can easily be moved from one computer to another. However, they do use up one COM port.

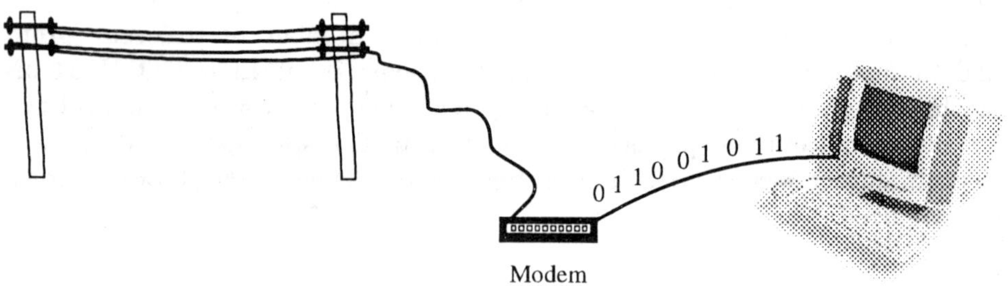

Fig. 5.19 Transmission of data using external modem

Fortunately, there is one standard interface for connecting external modems to computers called *RS*-232. Consequently, any external modem can be attached to any computer that has an RS-232 port, which almost all personal computers have.

External modems sit next to the computer and connect to the serial port using a straight-through serial cable.

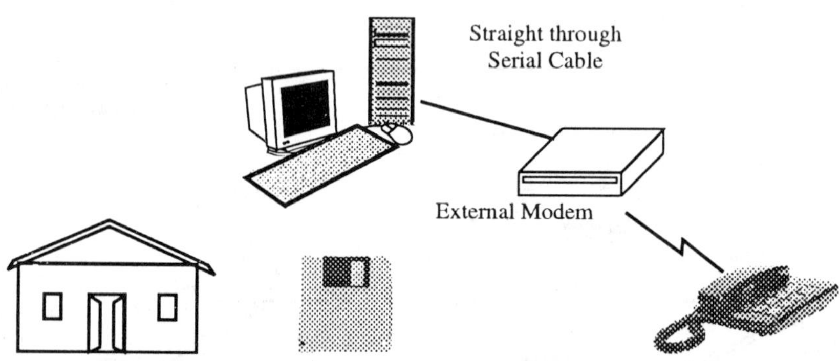

Fig. 5.20 External modem

5.8.4 Classification of Modems

The modems can be classified according to their characteristics:

- Range
  - Short Haul
  - Voice Grade (VG)
  - Wideband
- Line Type
  - Dial-up
  - Leased
  - Private
- Operation Mode
  - Half Duplex
  - Full Duplex
  - Simplex
- Synchronization
  - Asynchronous
  - Synchronous
- Modulation
  - AM
  - FM/FSK
  - PM
  - TCM

Classifying Modems According to Range

Short Haul

Short haul modems are cheap solutions to systems of short ranges (up to 15 km), which use private lines and are not part of a public system. Short haul modems can also be used, even if the end-to-end length of the direct connection is longer than 15 km, when both ends of the line are served by the same central office in the telephone system. These lines are called "local loops". Short haul modems are distance-sensitive, because signal attenuation occurs as the signal travels through the line. The transmission rate must be lowered to ensure consistent and error-free transmission on longer distances.

Short haul modems tend to be cheaper than other modems for two reasons:

(1) No circuitry is included in them to correct for differences between the carrier frequency of the demodulator and the frequency of the modulator.

(2) Generally no circuitry is included to reduce/correct for noise rejection, which is less of a problem over short distances than over long distances.

Voice Grade (VG)

Voice-grade modems are used for unlimited destination, using a moderate to high data rate. These modems are expensive and their maintenance and tuning are sophisticated. Communication channels are leased lines and dial-up.

Voice-band telephone network is used for data transmission. A user-to-user connection may be either dedicated or dialed. The links in the connection are the same in the two cases, and the only difference for the user is that for some impairments (particularly attenuation and delay distortion), a dedicated (*private* or *leased*) line is guaranteed to meet certain specifications, whereas a dialed connection can only be described statistically.

Wideband

Wideband modems are used in large-volume telephone-line multiplexing, dedicated computer-to-computer links. These modems exceed high data rates.

Classifying Modems According To—Line Type

Leased, Private

Leased, private or dedicated lines (usually 4-wire) are for the exclusive use of "leased-line" modems—either pair (in a simple point-to-point connection) or several (on a multidrop network for a polling or a contention system). If the medium is the telephone network, their transmission characteristics are usually guaranteed to meet certain specifications, but if the link includes any radio transmission, the quality of it may be as variable as that of a switched (i.e. nondedicated) line.

Dial up

Dial-up modems can establish point-to-point connections on the PSTN by any combination of manual or automatic dialing or answering. The quality of the circuit is not guaranteed, but all phone companies establish objectives. The links established are almost always 2-wire because 4-wire dialing is tedious and expensive.

* Two and Four-Wires Lines

A four-wire (4W) line is a pair of two-wire (2W) lines, one for transmitting and one for receiving, in which the signals in the two directions are to be kept totally separate. Perfect separation can be maintained only if the four-wire configuration is sustained from transmitter to receiver. The lines may be combined in a 4W/2W network (often called a *hybrid* or a *hybrid transformer*) at any point in the signal path. In this case impedance mismatches will cause reflections and interference between the two signals.

Classifying Modems According To—Operation Mode

Half Duplex

Half duplex means that signals can be passed in either direction, but not in both simultaneously. A telephone channel often includes an echo-suppressor, allowing transmission in only one direction, this renders the channel half-duplex. Echo suppressors are slowly being replaced by echo cancellers, which are theoretically full-duplex devices.

When a modem is connected to a two-wire line, its output impedance cannot be matched exactly to the input impedance of the line, and some part of its transmitted signal (usually badly distorted) will always be reflected back. For this reason half-duplex receivers are disabled (received data is clamped) when their local transmitter is operative. Half-duplex modems can work in full-duplex mode.

Full Duplex

Full duplex means that signals can be passed in either direction, simultaneously. Full duplex operation on a two-wire line requires the ability to separate a receive signal from the reflection of the transmitted signal. This is accomplished by either FDM (frequency division multiplexing) in which the signals in the two directions occupy different frequency bands and are separated by filtering, or by Echo Canceling (EC).

The implication of the term full duplex is usually that the modem can transmit and receive simultaneously at full speed. Modems that provide a low-speed reverse channel are sometimes called split-speed or asymmetric modems. Full duplex modems will not work on half-duplex channels.

Simplex

Simplex means that signals can be passed in one direction only. A remote modem for a telemetering system might be simplex and a 2-wire line with a common unidirectional amplifier is simplex.

Classifying Modems According To—Synchronization

Asynchronous Modems

Most of the modems that operate in slow and moderate rates, up to 1800 bps, are asynchronous (using asynchronous data). Asynchronous modems operate in FSK modulation and use two frequencies for transmission and another two for receiving. Asynchronous modems can be connected in different options to the communication media:

- Using 2-wire or 4-wire interface.
- Using switched lines or leased lines.
- Using interface to call unit/automatic answer, when dialing-up.

Asynchronous data

Asynchronous data is not accompanied by any clock, and the transmitting and receiving modems know only the nominal data rate. To prevent slipping of the data relative to the modems' clocks, this data is always grouped in very short blocks (characters) with framing bits (start and stop bits). The most common code used for this is the seven-bit ASCII code with even parity.

Synchronous Modems

Synchronous modems operate in the audio domain, at rates up to 28800 bps in audio lines, used in telephones systems (using synchronous data). The usual modulation methods are the phase modulation and integrated phase and amplitude (at higher rates than 4800 bps).

In synchronous modems, equalizers are used, in order to offset the misfit of the telephone lines. These equalizers are inserted in addition to the equalizers that sometimes already exist in the telephone lines.

These equalizers can be classified into three main groups:

1. *Fixed/statistical equalizer*—these equalizers offset the signal according to the average of the known attenuation in each frequency. Tuning the equalizer is sometimes done in the factory and stays fixed; usually they are used to operate at low rates in a dial up line.
2. *Manually adjusted equalizer*—these equalizers can be tuned to optimal performance to a given line. These equalizers should be re-tuned when the line is replaced and periodically. Specially, it should be tuned frequently when the line is of a low quality and its parameters are changed frequently. Tuning is done using a button inside the modem (or on the external board).
3. *Automatic equalizer*—these equalizers are tuned automatically when the connection is established. Depending on the line quality in a specific moment, in a process of about 15ms to 25ms, after the first tuning, the equalizer samples the line continually and adjusts itself to the changed conditions, so the modem operates at each moment under optimal conditions. The fitness process operates, in some modems, at rates of 2400 times in a second.

Synchronous modems operate in the same manner as asynchronous modems. However, synchronous modems operate at higher rates and since the requirements to transmit at these rates is increasing, most of the innovations are implemented for synchronous modems.

In synchronous modems the channel can be split for several consumers at various speeds. Modems who have this ability are called SSM - Split System Modem. These modems can use a simple split or a split using multipoint connection.

Synchronous data is accompanied by a clock signal. Synchronous data is almost always grouped in blocks, and it is the responsibility of the data source to assemble those blocks with framing codes and any extra bits needed for error detecting and/or correcting according to one of many different protocols (BISYNC, SDLC, HDLC, etc.). The data source and destination expect the modem to be transparent to this type of data, conversely, the modem can ignore the blocking of the data.

Classifying Modems According To—Modulation

Communication channels like telephone lines are usually analog media. Analog media is a bandwidth-limited channel. In the case of telephone lines the usable bandwidth frequencies is in the range of 300 Hz to 3300 Hz.

Data communication means moving digital information from one place to another through communication channels. These digital information signals have the shape of square waves and the meaning of "0" and "1".

If such digital signals were transmitted on analog media the square waves of the digital signals would be distorted by the analog media. The receiver that receives these distorted signals will be unable to interpret accurately the incoming signals. These digital signals must be converted into analog signals so that the communication channels can carry the information from one place to another. The technique that enables this conversion is called modulation.

Modulation is a technique of modifying some basic analog signal in a known way in order to encode information in that basic signal. Any measurable property of an analog signal can be used to transmit information by changing this property in some known manner and then detecting those changes at the receiver end. The signal that is modulated is called the carrier signal because it carries the digital information from one end of the communication channel to the other end. The device that changes the signal at the transmitting end of the communication channel is called the modulator. The device at the receiving end of the channel, which detects the digital information from the modulated signal, is called the demodulator. There are three modulation techniques; (Discussed before) each of them changes one of the properties of the basic analog signal.

5.8.5 A Look At The Future

So what's in the future for today's modems? Not much, unfortunately. The available bandwidth in today's phone lines has reached its limit; the only way modem companies are going to be able to compete is to develop better and faster compression algorithms.

But all hope is not lost! Cable modems may be the "next big thing"!

5.8.6 Cable Modems

The term "Cable Modem" is quite new and refers to a modem that operates over the ordinary cable TV network cables. Basically you just connect the Cable Modem to the TV outlet for your cable TV, and the cable TV operator connects a Cable Modem Termination System (CMTS) in his end (the Head-End).Actually the term "Cable Modem" is a bit misleading, as a Cable Modem works more like a Local Area Network (LAN) interface than as a modem.

Cable modems don't connect to your phone line; they connect to the same coaxial cable that you connect your television to. The idea behind cable modems to allow faster direct access to the Internet via your cable company, which, because of recent legislation, may enter the telecommunications market.

With speeds of up to 36 Mbps, cable modems download data in seconds that might take fifty times longer with a dial-up connection. Best of all, it's always on, so there is no need to connect and no more busy signals! This service is now available in parts of the United States, Europe and Asia.

5.9 Codec

Codec is basically "**co**der/**dec**oder", which describes a device or program capable of performing transformations on a data stream or signal. Codecs can both put the stream or signal into an encoded form (often for transmission, storage or encryption) and retrieve, or decode that form for viewing or manipulation in a format more appropriate for these operations. Codecs are often used in videoconferencing and streaming media solutions.

For instance, many multimedia data streams need to contain both audio and video data, and often some form of metadata that permits synchronization of the audio and video. Each of these three pieces of data may be handled by different programs, processes or hardware; but for the multimedia data stream to be useful in stored or transmitted form, they must be encapsulated together. The raw encoded form of audio and video data is often called essence, to distinguish it from the metadata information that together make up the information content of the stream and any "wrapper" data that is then added to aid access to or improve the robustness of the stream. File formats like ".ogg", ".mpg", ".avi", ".mov", etc. are used to store information encoded by a codec.

• • •

6

Switching Principles

Introduction

Telecommunication Networks can be mainly classified into two groups based on the criteria of who has made the decision of which nodes are not going to receive the transmitted information. When the network takes the responsibility of this decision, we have a switching network. When this decision is left to the end-nodes, we have a broadcast network that can be divided in packet radio networks, satellite networks and local area networks.

Communication Units

The two important communication units are discussed below:

Message

The unit of communication from the programmer's perspective. Its size is limited only by the user memory space.

Packet

Fixed-size smallest unit of communication containing *routing information* (e.g., a destination address) and **sequencing** information in its **header**. Its size is of order hundreds or thousands of bytes or words.

6.1 Switching Mechanism

It determines how network resources are allocated for data transmission, i.e., **how** and **when** the input channel is connected to the output channel selected by the routing algorithm. It is the actual mechanism that removes data from input channels and places them on output channels.

Switching is concerned with connecting any communicating end-points in a network without the need of having direct, dedicated connections between all the possible end-points in the network. Its purpose is to efficiently determine the transmission links that are used in transporting information between two end-points. It is essentially a Physical Layer (Layer 1) and Data-Link Layer (Layer 2) function, and although its description will involve some description of routing type problems, it should not be confused with Network level (Layer 3) routing functions.

Switching Principles

Historically, most communications systems have started with point-to-point links which directly connect together the users wishing to communicate using a dedicated communications circuit. As the distance between users increases beyond the length of the cable (e.g., the length of a telegraph wire), the connection between the users was formed by a number of sections that were connected end-to-end in series to form the circuit. The connection between the users (*A* and *D*) in the figure below (i.e., *A* and *D*) is represented by a series of links (*AB*, *BC* and *CD*) each link connects two entities known as nodes. For a point-to-point circuit, (also known as a permanent circuit) the nodes are patch panels that provide a simple connection between the two links (i.e., the two transmission circuits).

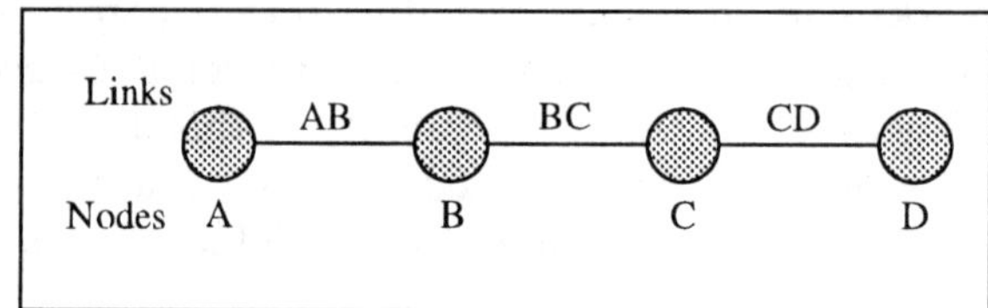

Fig. 6.1 A connection between two systems *A* and *D* formed from 3 links

As the number of connected users increased, it has become infeasible to provide a circuit that connects every user to every other user, and some sharing of the transmission circuits (known as "switching") has become necessary. To accomplish this goal, the data communications network has evolved. A network is a set of nodes that are interconnected to permit the exchange of information.

In this section, we will begin to discuss how various types of "switching" work. Three switching techniques have been proposed for building networks:

- Circuit switching.
- Message switching.
- Packet switching (both virtual circuit and datagram).

Each allows sharing communication facilities among multiple users (end systems) and each uses equipment located at the nodes (intermediate systems) to replace the patch-panels used in a point-to-point connection. Packet switching is most often used for data communication. Most networks consist of many links (see the figure 6.2) that allow more than one path through the network between nodes. A data communications network must be able to select an appropriate path for each required connection.

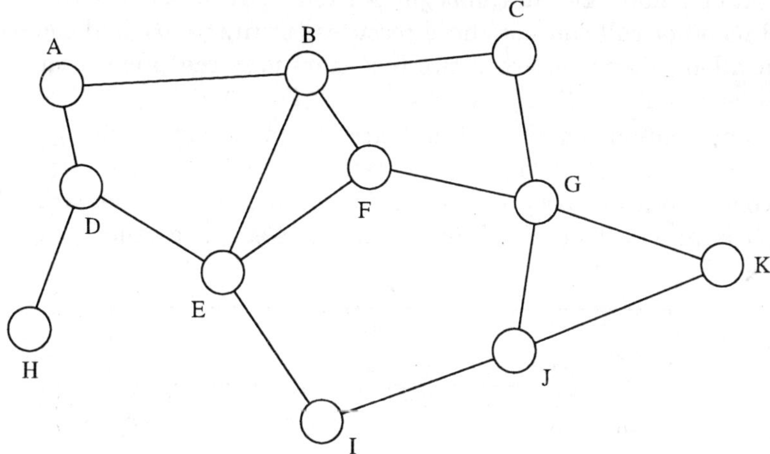

Fig. 6.2 A mesh of network nodes (*A—K*) connected by links

Any of the three approaches (circuit switching, message switching, and packet switching) could yield minimum delay in a particular situation, though situations where message switching yields minimum delay are rare. The relative performance of circuit switching and packet switching depends strongly on the speed and "cost" of establishing a connection.

6.2 Circuit Switching

In a network like the phone system, communication requires the establishment of a dedicated path between the communicating parties.

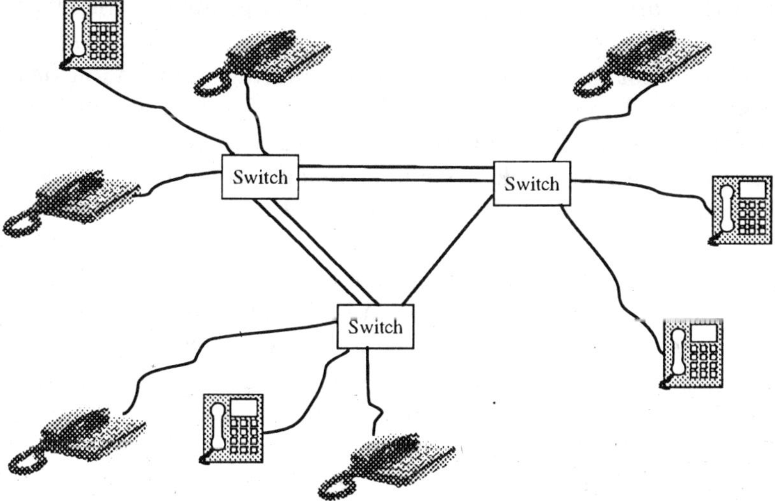

Fig. 6.3 Circuit switcing

Circuit switching is the most familiar technique used to build a communications network. It is used for ordinary telephone calls. Phone networks use circuit switching: an end-to-end circuit must be set up before the call can begin. A fixed share of network resources is reserved for the call, and no other call can use those resources until the original connection is closed. This means that a long silence between two teenagers uses the same resources as an active negotiation between two fast-talking lawyers.

It allows communications equipment and circuits, to be shared among users. Each user has sole access to a circuit (functionally equivalent to a pair of copper wires) during network use. Consider communication between two points *A* and *D* in a network. The connection between *A* and *D* is provided using (shared) links between two other pieces of equipment, *B* and *C*.

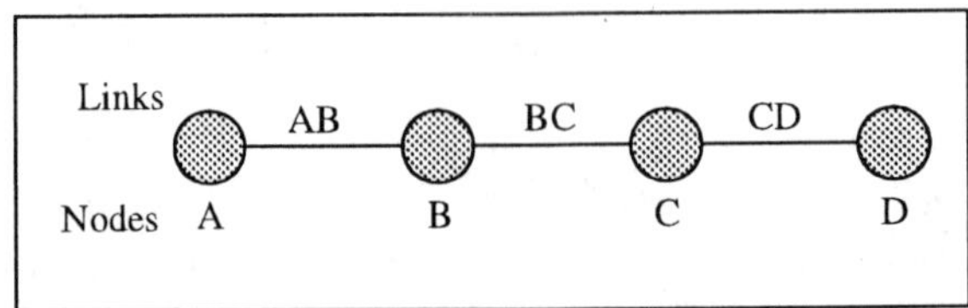

In a circuit-switched network, a dedicated circuit must first be connected. Once the circuit has been "nailed up", transmission can begin. When the transmission is complete, the circuit is released for the next transmission.

Let us look at a simple telephone call. When you remove the receiver from the telephone and dial a telephone number, the telephone company searches its database to determine which circuit should be used to deliver the telephone call. If it is a long distance call, the switch knows it must connect to another telephone company office, where a switch called a tandem is located. The tandem switch will then use a circuit that connects it to another office, the toll office switch.

This process continues until there are circuits connected from the originator to the destination. These circuits cannot be used for any other telephone call; they are dedicated to this one call until the call is complete. Once the call is complete, the circuits can then be released and used for another call.

Circuit switching is not an efficient method for routing any kind of data, whether it is digital voice or user data. The circuit is wasted much of the time because no transmission is using the bandwidth of the circuit 100 percent of the time. Any time there are idle period on the circuit, the circuit is being wasted. It would be much more efficient to have a transmission facility capable of transmitting many different conversations over the same circuit at the same time.

This was achieved (sort of) through multiplexing. A circuit can be divided into channels, with each channel used for a transmission. Digital telephone circuits are multiplexed and are capable of transmitting several different conversations at the same time on the same circuit.

There is one catch; each channel then becomes dedicated to the conversation until the caller disconnects. Then the channel can be released for another transmission. So, in the case where there are 24 channels (the common denominator in today's digital facilities), there can be 24 different conversations going on at once over the same facility.

This is better than wasting the circuit for one transmission, but it could still be better. Imagine having no channels. Transmissions are sent over the same circuit as needed, but there are no limits to the number of conversations that can be sent over the same facility at the same time.

Network use is initiated by a connection phase, during which a circuit is set up between source and destination, and terminated by a disconnect phase. These phases, with associated timings, are illustrated in the figure below.

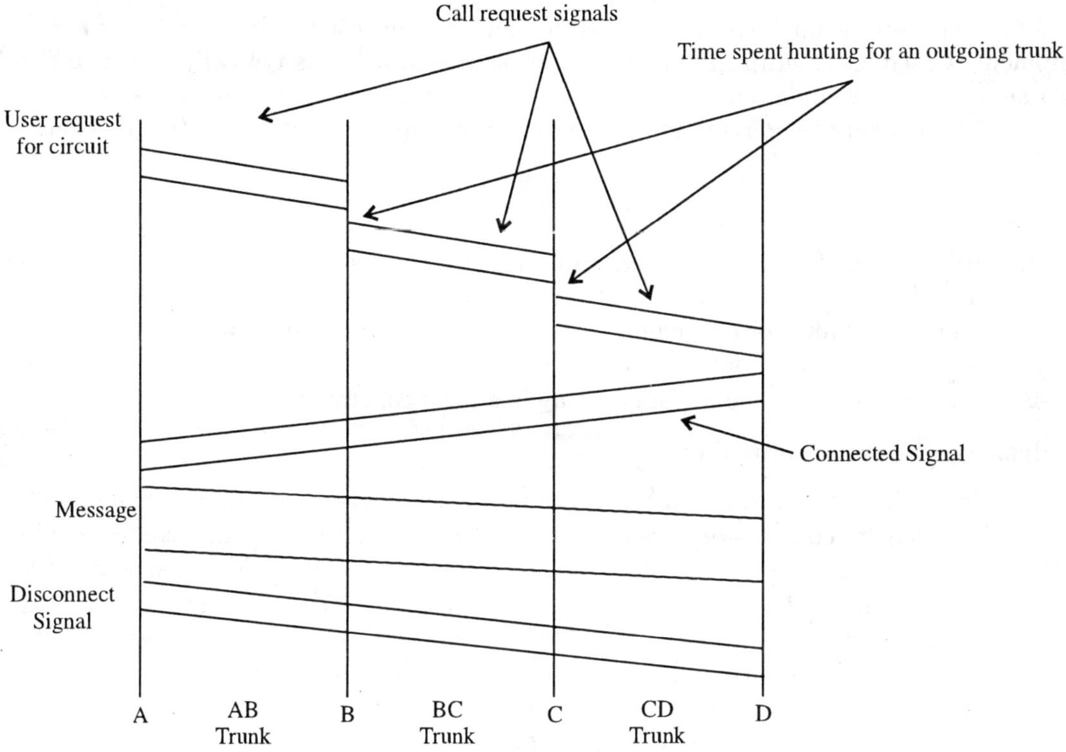

Fig. 6.4 Circuit switched connection between *A* and *D*

In figure 6.4, the most important events in the life of a connection in a four-node circuit-switching network are shown. When a connection is established, the origin-node identifies the first intermediate node (node *A*) in the path to the end-node and sends it a communication request signal. After a user requests a circuit, the desired destination address must be communicated to the local switching node (*B*). In a telephony network, this is achieved by dialing the number.

Node *B* receives the connection request and identifies a path to the destination (*D*) via an intermediate node (*C*). This is followed by a circuit connection phase handled by the switching nodes and initiated by allocating a free circuit to *C* (link *BC*), followed by transmission of a call request signal from node *B* to node *C*. In turn, node C allocates a link (*CD*) and the request is then passed to node *D* after a similar delay.

The circuit is then established and may be used. While it is available for use, resources (i.e., in the intermediate equipment at *B* and *C*) and capacity on the links between the equipment are dedicated to the use of the circuit.

After completion of the connection, a signal confirming circuit establishment (a connect signal in the diagram) is returned; this flows directly back to node *A* with no search delays since the circuit has been established. Transfer of the data in the message then begins. After data transfer, the circuit is disconnected; a simple disconnect phase is included after the end of the data transmission.

Delays for setting up a circuit connection can be high, especially if ordinary telephone equipment is used. Call setup time with conventional equipment is typically on the order of 5 to 25 seconds after completion of dialing. New fast circuit switching techniques can reduce delays. Trade-offs between circuit switching and other types of switching depend strongly on switching times.

Advantages of circuit switching

1. Fixed bandwidth, guaranteed capacity (no congestion). It enables performance guarantees such as guaranteed maximum delay, which is essential for real-time applications like voice conversations. It is also much easier to do detailed accounting for circuit-switched network usage.
2. Low varience end-to-end delay (delay is almost constant).

Disadvantages of circuit switching

1. Connection set-up and tear-down introduces extra overhead (thus initial delay).
2. User pay for circuit, even when not sending data. Circuit switching can be inefficient since total channel capacity dedicated to the connection even if channel is not utilized.
3. Other users can't use the circuit even if it is free of traffic (statistics show that during a typical phone conversation, 64-73% of the time one speaker talking, 3-7% of the time both speakers talking, 20-33% of the time both speakers silent).
4. Cannot do any data rate conversion or encoding or decoding.
5. It is used for short duration communication.

6.3 Message Switching

Sometimes there is no need for a circuit to be established all the way from the source to the destination. In a computer network, computer's themselves can act as switches.

In a computer network, it is reasonable to imitate the telegraph system rather than the phone company. All of the digital data is sent from the source to the destination as a unit. When there are intermediate nodes between the source and destination, each intermediate node must receive the entire message before sending it on to the next intermediate or final destination. This is called "store and forward" transmission. The intermediate nodes may have to make a decision as to which route the message will be sent. A header is attached to the beginning of the message to identify the destination.

Consider a connection between the users (*A* and *D*) in the figure below (i.e., *A* and *D*) is represented by a series of links (*AB*, *BC* and *CD*).

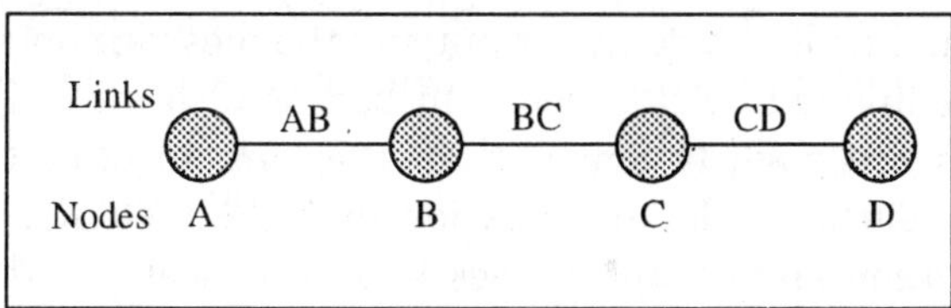

For instance, when a telex (or email) message is sent from *A* to *D*, it first passes over a local connection (*AB*). It is then passed at some later time to *C* (via link *BC*), and from there to the destination (via link *CD*). At each message switch, the received message is stored, and a connection is subsequently made to deliver the message to the neighboring message switch. Message switching is also known as store-and-forward switching since the messages are stored at intermediate nodes through their route to their destinations.

Figure 6.5 shows life connection events for a message-switching network. When a connection is established, the origin-node identifies the first intermediate node in the path to the end-node and sends it the whole message. After receiving and storing this message, the first intermediate node (node A) identifies the second one (node B) and, when the transmission line is not busy, the former sends the whole message (store-and-forward philosophy). This process is repeated up to the end-node. As can be seen in figure 6.5 no communication release or establishment is needed.

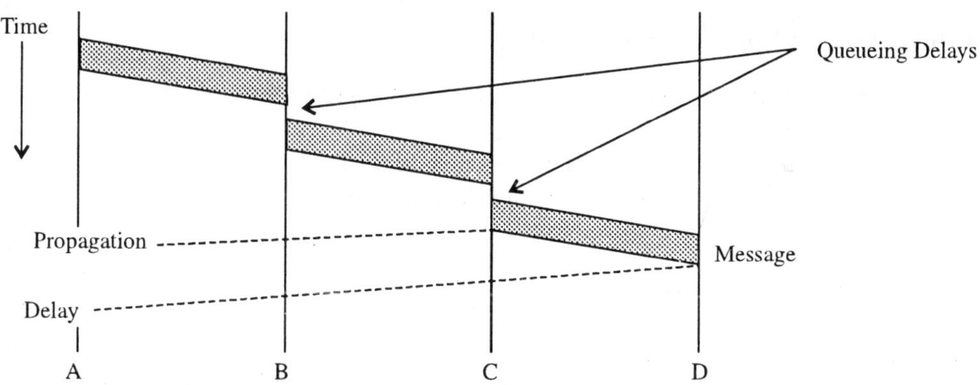

Fig. 6.5 The use of message switching to communicate between *A* and *D*

The figure illustrates message switching; transmission of only one message is illustrated for simplicity. As the figure indicates, a complete message is sent from node *A* to node *B* when the link interconnecting them becomes available. Since the message may be competing with other messages for access to facilities, a queuing delay may be incurred while waiting for the link to become available. The message is stored at *B* until the next link becomes available, with another queuing delay before it can be forwarded. It repeats this process until it reaches its destination.

Circuit setup delays are replaced by queuing delays. Considerable extra delay may result from storage at individual nodes. A delay for putting the message on the communications link (message length in bits divided by link speed in bps) is also incurred at each node through route. Message lengths are slightly longer than they are in circuit switching, after establishment of the circuit, since header information must be included with each message; the header includes information identifying the destination as well as other types of information.

Although message switching is still used for electronic mail and telex transmission, it has largely been replaced by packet switching (in fact, most electronic mail is carried using message switching with the links between message switches provided by packet or circuit-switched networks).

Advantages of Message Switching

1. Data channels are shared among communication devices improving the use of bandwidth.
2. Messages can be stored temporarily at message switches, when network congestion becomes a problem.
3. Priorities may be used to manage network traffic.
4. Broadcast addressing uses bandwidth more efficiently because messages are delivered to multiple destinations.

Disadvantages of Message Switching

1. Variable and indeterminate delays. Occasional long message on a link blocks it for other, shorter messages.
2. Totally unsuitable for conversational voice services.
3. Too slow for interactive computer services that require response times of ~ 1's.

6.4 Packet Switching

In packet switching there are no dedicated circuits. Each circuit in a packet-switching network carries many different transmissions at the same time. The only rule is that every data unit sent through a packet-switching network must have enough information in the header that the nodes in the network can determine how to route the data unit. This tends to add overhead to the data unit, but the trade-off is well invested.

Message switching becomes packet switching if "logical" messages are broken up into smaller units. Any message exceeding a network-defined maximum length is broken up into shorter units, known as packets, for transmission; the packets, each with an associated header, are then transmitted individually through the network.

Definition

> *"In packet-switching networks, a transmission unit of fixed maximum size that consists of binary digits representing both data and a header containing an identification number, source and destination addresses, and sometimes error-control data."*

The packets can be variable sized or (more often) fixed sized. The size of a packet is usually much smaller than the total data size. Packet sizes range from 48 bytes for ATM to 1500 bytes for Ethernet to 8K bytes for frame relay. Intermediate nodes must receive an entire packet before sending on towards the destination, but they do not have to receive the entire message. Each packet needs a header to identify its destination.

Another advantage of packet switching is the ability to route data units over any route, rather than a fixed route. For example, if I have a lot of data to send, the data will have to be divided into many different data units. These data units do not have to follow the same route in a packet-switching network.

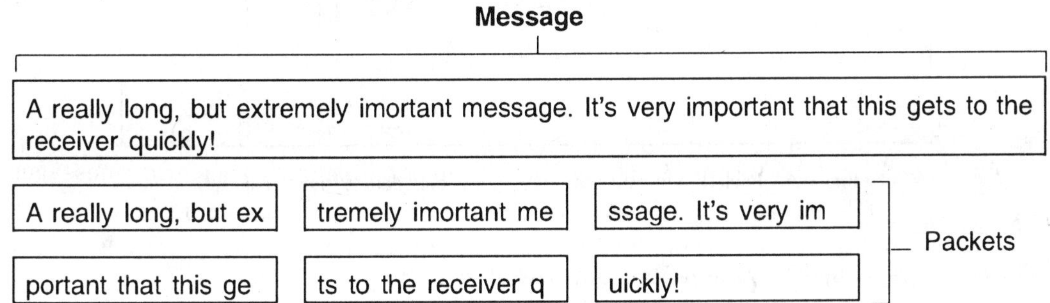

The trick is being able to place the data units in the proper order when they are received. If data units are routed over different paths, it is highly likely that the first data unit may be received after subsequent data units, which means the order of transmission is now mixed up. The protocols used in packet-switching networks have the ability to reassemble the data units into their proper order.

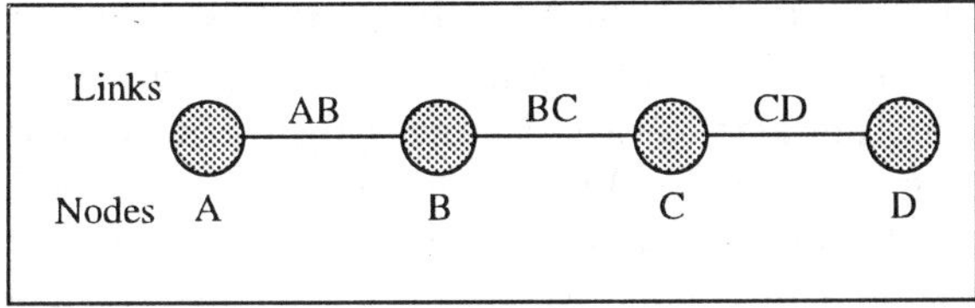

The fundamental difference in packet communication is that the data is formed into packets with a pre-defined header format (i.e., PCI), and well known "idle" patterns that are used to occupy the link when there is no data to be communicated.

A packet network equipment discards the "idle" patterns between packets and processes the entire packet as one piece of data. The equipment examines the packet header information (PCI) and then either removes the header (in an end system) or forwards the packet to another system. If the out-going link is not available, then the packet is placed in a queue until the link becomes free. A packet network is formed by links that connect packet network equipment.

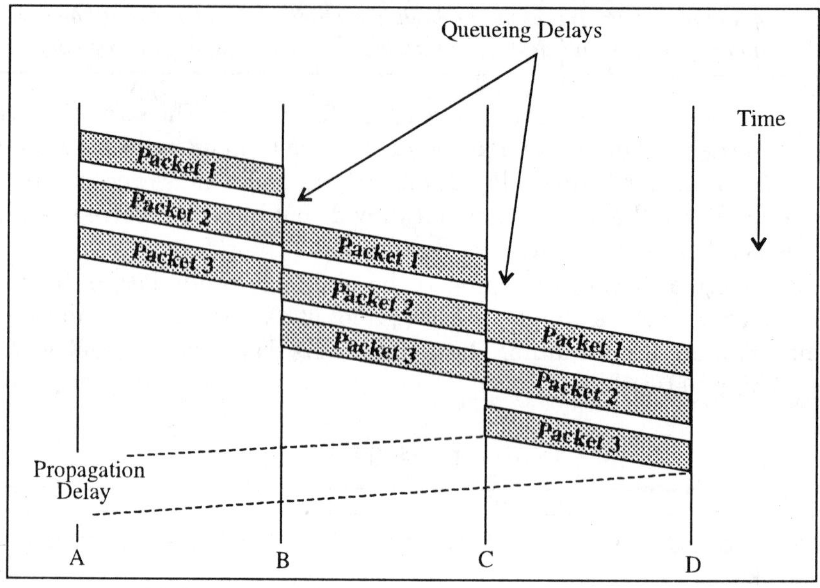

Fig. 6.6 Packet-switched communication between systems *A* and *D*. (The message in this case has been broken into three parts labeled 1–3)

There are two important benefits from packet switching.

1. The first and most important benefit is that since packets are short, the communication links between the nodes are only allocated to transferring a single message for a short period of time while transmitting each packet. Longer messages require a series of packets to be sent, but do not require the link to be dedicated between the transmission of each packet. The implication is that packets belonging to other messages may be sent between the packets of the message being sent from *A* to *D*. This provides a much fairer sharing of the resources of each of the links.
2. Another benefit of packet switching is known as "pipelining". Pipelining is visible in the figure 6.6. At the time packet 1 is sent from *B* to C, packet 2 is sent from *A* to *B*; packet 1 is sent from *C* to *D* while packet 2 is sent from *B* to C, and packet 3 is sent from *A* to *B*, and so forth. This simultaneous use of communications links represents a gain in efficiency, the total delay for transmission across a packet network may be considerably less than for message switching, despite the inclusion of a header in each packet rather than in each message.

Types of packet switched network

Two basic approaches to packet switching are common which are as follows:

1. Datagram Packet Networks.
2. Virtual Circuit Packet Networks.

6.4.1 Datagram Packet Networks

The most common is datagram switching (also known as a "best-effort network" or a network supporting the connection-less network service). This is what is used in the network layer of the Internet.

Datagram transmission uses a different scheme to determine the route through the network of links. Using datagram transmission, each packet is treated as a separate entity and contains a header with the full information about the intended recipient. The intermediate nodes examine the header of a packet and select an appropriate link to an intermediate node that is nearer the destination. In this system, the packets do not follow a pre-established route, and the intermediate nodes (usually known as "routers") do not require prior knowledge of the routes that will be used.

A datagram network is analogous to sending a message as a series of postcards through the postal system. Each card is independently sent to the final destination (using the postal system). To receive the whole message, the receiver must collect all the postcards and sort them into the original order. Not all postcards need be delivered by the postal system, and not all take the same length of time to arrive.

Packet switching based on datagram

The most important events in the life of a communication in a datagram switching network are shown in figure 6.7. The origin-node identifies the first intermediate node in the path and begins to send packets. Each packet carries an origin-node and end-node identifier. The first intermediate node (node A) begins to send packets, without storing the whole message, to the following intermediate node. This process is repeated up to the end-node. As there is neither connection establishment nor connection release, the path follow for each packet from the origin-node to the end-node can be different and therefore, as a consequence of different propagation delays, they can arrive disordered.

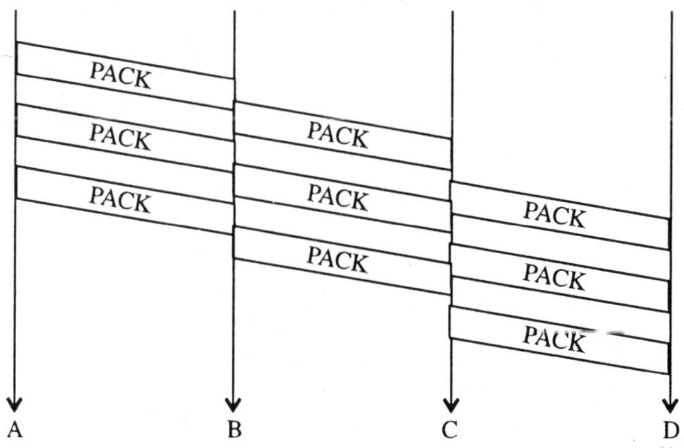

Fig. 6.7
The use of datagram switching to communicate between A and D

In a datagram network delivery is not guaranteed (although they are usually reliably sent). Enhancements, if required, to the basic service (e.g., reliable delivery) must be provided by the end systems (i.e., user's computers) using additional software. The most common datagram network is the Internet, which uses the IP network protocol. Applications that do not require more than a best effort service can be supported by direct use of packets in a datagram network (using the User Datagram Protocol (UDP) transport protocol). Such applications include Internet Video, Voice Communication, messages notifying a user that she/he has received new email, etc. Most Internet applications need additional functions to provide reliable communication (such as end-to-end error and sequence control). Examples include sending email, browsing a web site, or sending a file using the file transfer protocol (FTP). This reliability ensures all the data is received in the correct order with no duplication or omissions. It is provided by additional layers of software algorithms implemented in the End Systems (*A*, *D*). Two examples of this are the Transmission Control Protocol (TCP), and the Trivial File Transfer Protocol (TFTP) that uses UDP.

One merit of the datagram approach is that not all packets need to follow the same path (route) through the network (although frequently packets do follow the same route). This removes the need to set-up and tear-down the path, reducing the processing overhead, and a need for Intermediate Systems to execute an additional protocol.

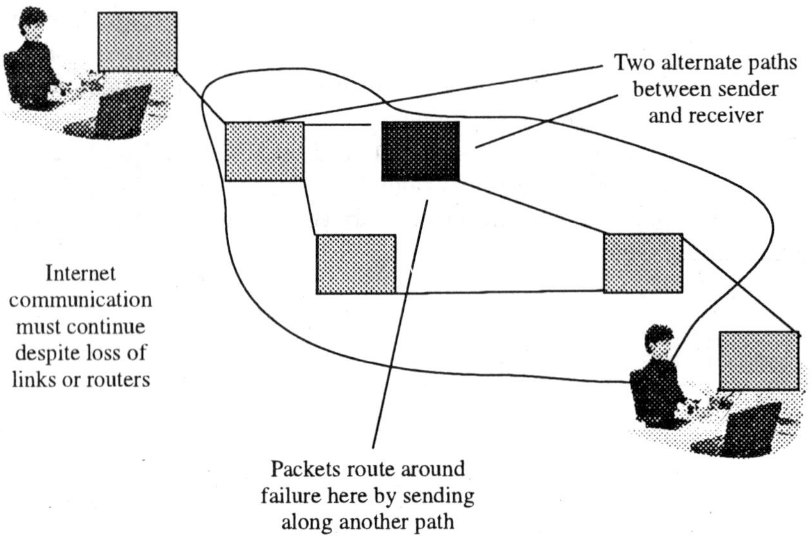

Fig. 6.8 Communication in a datagram network

Packets may also be routed around busy parts of the network when alternate paths exist. This is useful when a particular intermediate system becomes busy or overloaded with excessive volumes of packets to send. It can also provide a high degree of fault tolerance, when an individual intermediate system or communication circuit fails. As long as a route exists through the network between two end systems, they are able to communicate. Only if there is no possible way to send the packets, will the packets be discarded and not delivered. The fate (success/failure) of an application therefore depends only on existence of an actual path between the two End Systems. This is known as “fate sharing”—since the application shares the “fate” of the network.

6.4.2 Virtual Circuit Packet Networks

In virtual circuit packet switching, an initial setup phase is used to set up a fixed route between the intermediate nodes for all packets, which are exchanged during a session between the end nodes (analogous to the circuit-switched telephony network). At each intermediate node, an entry is made in a table to indicate the route for the connection that has been set up. Packets can then use short headers, since only identification of the virtual circuit rather than complete destination address is needed. The intermediate nodes (B, C) process each packet according to the information that was stored in the node when the connection was established.

Packet switching based on virtual circuit

Figure 6.9 shows the events for a virtual circuit (packet) switching network. When a connection is established, the origin-node identifies the first intermediate node (node A) in the path to the end-node and sends it a communication request packet. This process is repeated as many times as needed to reach. Then, the end-node sends a communication acknowledge packet to the origin-node through the intermediate nodes (A, B, C and D) that have been traversed in

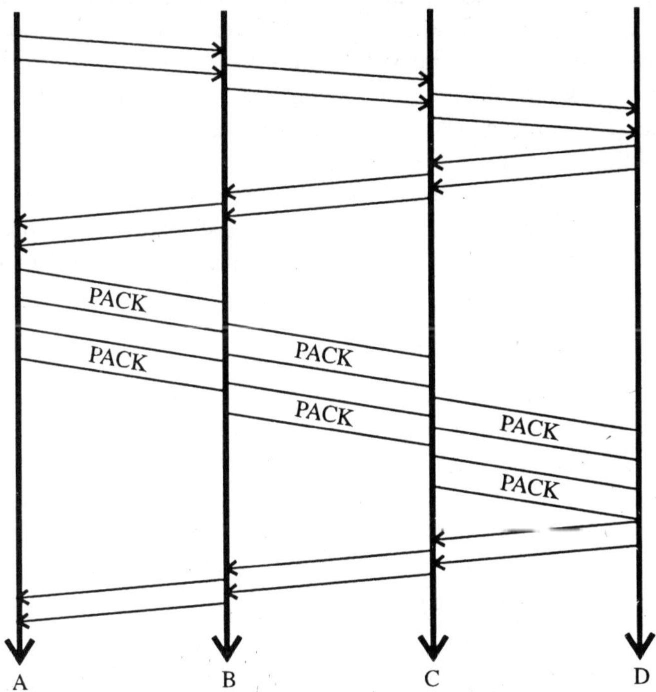

Fig. 6.9 Events for virtual circuit switching network

the communication request. The virtual circuit established on this way will be kept for the whole communication. Once a virtual circuit has been established, the origin-node begins to send packets (each of them has a virtual circuit identifier) to the first intermediate node. Then, the first intermediate node (node A) begins to send packets to the following node in the virtual circuit without waiting to store all message packets received from the origin-node. This process is repeated until all message packets arrive to the end-node. In the communication release, when the origin-node sends to the end-node a communication end packet, the latter answers with an acknowledge packet. There are two possibilities to release a connection:

- No trace of the virtual circuit information is left, so every communication is set-up as if it were the first one.
- The virtual circuit information is kept for future connections.

Enhancements to provide reliability may also be provided. Delivery of packets in proper sequence and with essentially no errors is guaranteed, and congestion control to minimize queuing is common. Delays are more variable than they are with a dedicated circuit, however, since several virtual circuits may compete for the same resources. An initial connection setup phase and a disconnect phase at the end of data transfer are required (as in the circuit-switched network). The most common form of virtual circuit network was ATM and X.25, which for a while were commonly used for public packet data networks.

Differences between datagram and virtual circuit networks

There are a number of important differences between virtual circuit and datagram networks. The choice strongly impacts complexity of the different types of node. Use of datagrams between intermediate nodes allows relatively simple protocols at this level, but at the expense of making the end (user) nodes more complex when end-to-end virtual circuit service is desired.

The Internet transmits datagrams between intermediate nodes using IP. Most Internet users need additional functions such as end-to-end error and sequence control to give a reliable service (equivalent to that provided by virtual circuits). This reliability may be provided by the Transmission Control Protocol (TCP), which is used end-to-end across the Internet, or by applications such as the trivial file transfer protocol (TFTP) running on top of the User Datagram Protocol (UDP).

When would you use datagram or virtual-circuit?

This choice depends on total number of packets, duration of the communication, traffic load, and also desired flexibility in case of heavy load or node or link failure.

If the communication is extended (either more packets, or communication over a longer period of time) then there is an advantage to establishing a virtual-circuit.

If the number of packets is small or the time of the connection needed is small, use datagram and avoid the overhead of establishing the virtual-circuit.

If you use datagram with multiple packets then the routing decision needs to be made for each packet independently. With virtual-circuit once the virtual-circuit is established the only delay is a queueing delay due to other users of that link. However, datagram is more flexible in that when there is congestion, a different route may be selected and so the overall throughput may be higher under heavy traffic load. The same applies in the case of a link or node failure—if the virtual-circuit was used the effect is more pronounced than if datagram were used. Also with virtual-circuit there is a possibility of providing end-to-end sequence and error control if needed at the network layer rather than at the transport layer.

Advantages of Packet Switching

1. Bandwidth optimized by enabling many devices to use the same communication channel.
2. Routes may be changed on the fly, achieving the best efficiency possible.
3. Entire messages not stored at switches reducing delays.
4. Line efficiency is greater since link is shared by packets from multiple connections.
5. Data rate conversion between hybrid links possible; in contrast circuit switching would revert to lowest common data rate.
6. Less hard drive space needed but more actual memory needed.
7. It is more flexible (i.e. doesn't care too much what's been sent, as long as it can be packetized).

Disadvantages of Packet Switching

1. More processing power required due to complex routing protocols. (Like recognizing when a packet has been lost).
2. No guarantee in delay.
3. Algorithms are more complicated.

6.5 Comparison Of Various Techniques

Circuit Switching vs. Packet Switching

Packet switching is favored over circuit switching for many different reasons. It is more reliable than circuit switching because if a particular circuit in the network should fail, the routers in the network simply route data units over different circuits, taking a different route altogether. In a circuit-switched network, this is not possible. If a circuit fails in the middle of a transmission, the entire connection must be released and a new one established, which means the conversation must start over again (think of being disconnected from a telephone call; the whole process of connecting must be repeated).

In principle, circuit switching and packet switching both are used in high-capacity networks. In circuit-switched networks, network resources are static, set in "copper" if you will, from the sender to receiver before the start of the transfer, thus creating a "circuit". The resources remain dedicated to the circuit during the entire transfer and the entire message follows the same path. In packet-switched networks, the message is broken into packets, each of which can take a different route to the destination where the packets are recompiled into the original message.

All the above can be handled by a router or a switch but much of IT today is going toward flat-switched networks. So when we're talking about circuit switching or packet switching, we are more and more talking about doing it on a switch.

Circuit-switched circuits are transparent to the user but there is no data rate matching/ any form of encoding or decoding, with dissimilar links. So this may be a disadvantage. The advantage is no delays at intermediate nodes.

Packet switching could have variable delays. Packets could arrive out of sequence. Packets must be digitized. Will work with mismatched links and will perform the data rate conversion.

Circuit switching

- Used in the telephone system: Network resources in the telephone system are reserved from your phone to the phone you call when you place the call; they're released when you hang up.

Packet switching

- Internet is packet switched: Data you wish to send is put into packets, which are then sent through the network. Network resources are only used during the time it takes to transmit each packet.

Feature	Circuit Switching	Packet Switching
Data sent as packets?	No	Yes
Packets follow same route?	N/A	May or may not (may for VC)
Resources reserved in network?	Yes	May or may not (not for DG)
Data send can experience variable latency	No	Yes
Connection establishment done?	Yes	VC:yes DG: no
State information stored at network nodes	?	VC: yes (tables to route virtual circuits) DG: no
Good for connection-less service	No	VC: yes DG: no
Impact of node/switch crash	All circuits through switch fail	VC: all virtual circuits through node fail DG: only packets at node are lost
Addressing info needed?	Only when call is set up	Every packet needs... VC: virtual circuit number DG: full source, destination address
Congestion control	Unnecescary	VC: easy if sufficient buffers allocated DG: hard

6.6 Cell Relay

Cell Relay is a newer approach to data networks. The cell is the data unit. In order to support voice, the data units must be small so that they can be processed quickly and sent through the network with minimal delay. This is not true with data, which favors large data units. Voice requires small data units, and data favors large data units.

In a cell relay network, the facility is used when needed. Whenever there is information to be transmitted, the switch simply sends the data units. There is no need to negotiate for a connection (as is the case in circuit switching), there is no need for a channel to be allocated (there are no channels in ATM), and as long as there is enough bandwidth to support it, there can be unlimited transmissions over the same facility.

6.7 Applications Of Switching Techniques

There's much talk about the coming mobile Internet, about how people will have a wireless, always on connection to the web. How will that come about? In two words, packet switching, a fundamental, elemental change between how wireless was delivered in the past and how it will be presented in the future.

Conventional cellular radio and landline telephony use circuit switching. A service like Cellular Digital Packet Data or CDPD, by contrast, employs packet switching. Wireless services now developing such as General Packet Radio Service or GPRS, Bluetooth, and 3G, will use packet switching as well.

Circuit switching dominates the public switched telephone network or PSTN. Network resources set up calls over the most efficient route, even if that means a call to New York from San Francisco goes through switching centers in San Diego, Chicago, and Saint Louis But no matter how convoluted the route, that path or circuit stays the same throughout the call. It's like having a dedicated railroad track with only one train, your call, permitted on the track at a time.

Packet switching dominates data networks like the Internet. A data call or communication from San Francisco to New York is handled much differently than with circuit switching. With circuit, all packets go directly to the receiver in an orderly fashion, one after another on a single track, like the train, hauling one boxcar after another. With packet switching routers determine a path for each packet or boxcar on the fly, dynamically, ordering them about to use any railroad track available to get to the destination. Other packets from other calls race upon these circuits as well, making the most use of each track or path, quite unlike the circuit switched calls that occupy a single path to the exclusion of all others.

Upon getting to their destination, the individual packets get put back into order by a packet assembler. That's because the different routes practically ensures that packets will arrive at different times. This approach is acceptable when calling up a web page or downloading a file, since a tiny delay is hardly noticed. But one notices even the tiniest delay with voice. This point is really important. Circuit switching guarantees the best sounding call because all packets go in order and there is no delay. Delays in packet switching for voice cause voice quality to fall apart, as anyone who has talked over the Internet can tell you.

As technology gets better with time, voice over packet switched networks will get better. Packet switched networks exist for the data communication needs of education, business, and government. These networks rely on telephone lines, of course, but the circuits are so arranged that they retain a permanent connection with their customers. The Public Data Network or Packet Switched Network stands as the data counterpart to the Public Switched Telephone Network. Unlike circuit switching, no one call takes up an entire channel for an entire session. Bits get sent only when traffic goes on, when people actually speak. During pauses in a conversation a channel gets filled with pieces of other conversations. Because your call doesn't hog an entire circuit the telephone system can permit an always-on connection. You might pay a flat monthly charge or by the bandwidth or bits you actually use. Whether wireless operators can afford to do so is difficult to decide. Too many customers' means building many more expensive cell sites. Even if technology permits we may stay with a per minute charge.

If packet switching is so efficient, why hasn't the landline public switched telephone network converted to it? The answer is time and money. Replacing circuit switched switches with packet switches across the country would be a monumental task, requiring billions of dollars over years and years. The legacy of circuit switching will be around for quite a long time, following us far into the new century. Still, traffic engineers must think about changing, with lengthy dial up calls to the internet placing huge demands on switches that were never planned for, circuits now tied up longer than ever imagined. But change has to come at some point, and the Internet's traffic now motivates engineers to move toward a unified switching method in the PSTN.

DSL and ASDL and cable modem connections will either speed or retard this transition; a local telephone company directs this broadband traffic to a packet switch, bypassing the existing local, circuit-based switch. As broadband users increase call holding times should decrease, as dial up modems are taken out of service. The local switch should not be as overwhelmed as many currently are. A Telco may then decide to delay a transition to packet switching.

● ● ●

7

Multiplexing Techniques

7.1 Telecommunication Fundamentals

Figure 7.1 shows a switching network. Lines are the media links. Ovals are called network nodes. Media links simply carry data from one point to other. Nodes take the incoming data and route them to an output port.

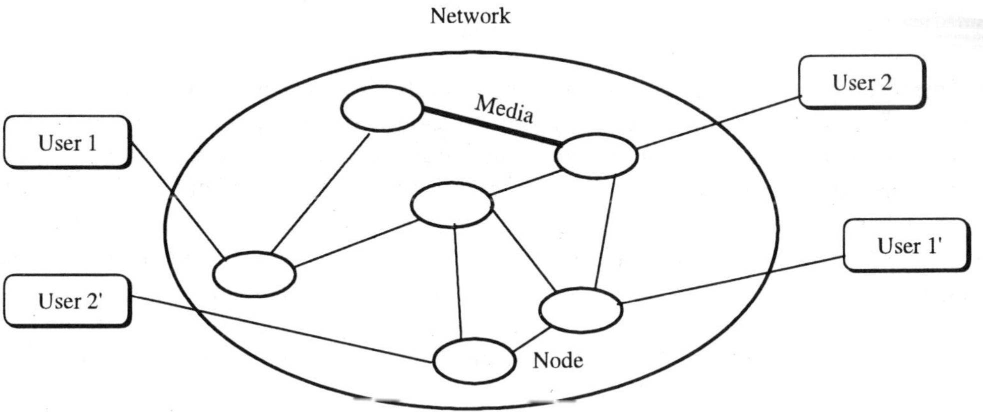

Fig. 7.1 Switching network

If two different communication paths intersect through this network they have to share some resources. Two paths can share a media link or a network node. Next sections describe these sharing techniques.

Media Sharing Techniques

Media sharing occurs when two communication channels use the same media.

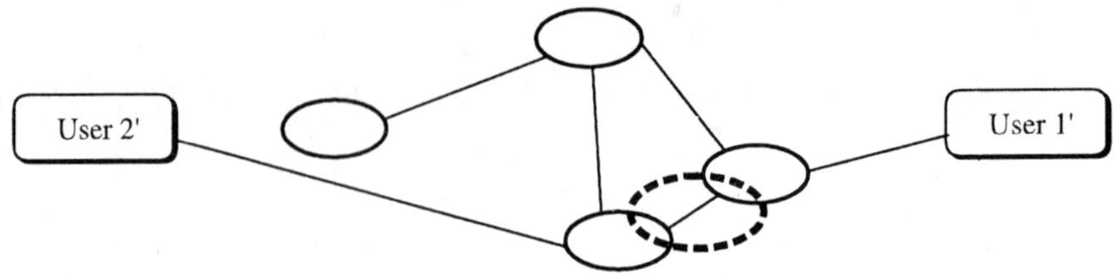

Fig. 7.2 Media sharing

This section presents how some communication channels can use the same media link without architecture considerations.

7.2 Information On Multiplexing

Sometimes, multiple users want to communicate using just one wire/fiber.

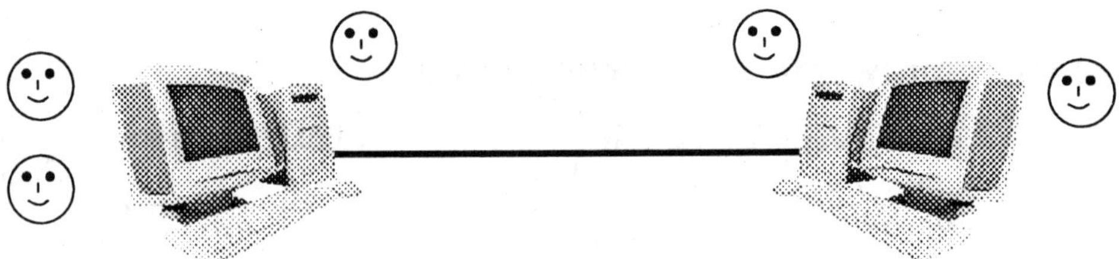

Fig. 7.3 Multiple users communicating using single wire

A communication system needs to convey multiple messages simultaneously from a number of information sources in one location to a number of users at another. Multiplexing schemes economically meet this need by combining the messages from several information sources to be transmitted as a complete group over a single transmission facility with provision at the receiver(s) for separation (demultiplexing) back to the individual messages.

Multiplexing is the set of techniques that allows the simultaneous transmission of multiple signals across a single data link. Whenever the transmission capacity of a medium linking two devices is greater than the transmission needs of the devices, the link can be shared in order to maximize the utilization of the link, much as one cable can carry a hundred channels of TV.

More information can be conveyed in a given amount of time by dividing the bandwidth of a signal carrier so that more than one modulated signal is sent on the same carrier. The carrier is sometimes referred to as a channel and each separate signal carried on it is called a subchannel. (In some usages, each subchannel is known as a channel.) The device that puts the separate signals on the carrier and takes them off of received transmissions is a multiplexer.

Definition

> *In telecommunications, multiplexing (MUXing) is the combining of two or more information channels onto a common transmission medium using multiplexer or (MUX). A demultiplexer performs the opposite function to a multiplexer in which a multiplexed channel is broken out into its constituent individual channels.*

Types of Multiplexing

In electrical communications, the two basic forms of multiplexing are time-division multiplexing (TDM) and frequency-division multiplexing (FDM). In optical communications, the analog of FDM is referred to as wavelength division multiplexing (WDM).

FDM is usually used for analog communication and TDM is used for digital communication.

The following are several examples of different multiplexing methods:

- **Time Division Multiplexing (TDM)** : A type of multiplexing that combines data streams by assigning each stream a different time slot in a set. TDM repeatedly transmits a fixed sequence of time slots over a single transmission channel.
- **Frequency Division Multiplexing (FDM)** : A multiplexing technique that uses different frequencies to combine multiple streams of data for transmission over a communications medium. FDM assigns a discrete carrier frequency to each data stream and then combines many modulated carrier frequencies for transmission. For example, television transmitters use FDM to broadcast several channels at once.
- **Statistical Time Division Multiplexing (STDM)** : Time slots are assigned to signals dynamically to make better use of bandwidth
- **Wavelength Division Multiplexing (WDM)** : Each signal is assigned a particular wavelength; a type of multiplexing developed for use on optical fiber. WDM modulates each of several data streams onto a different part of the light spectrum. WDM is the optical equivalent of FDM.

7.3 Time Division Multiplexing (TDM)

A type of multiplexing where two or more channels of information are transmitted over the same link by allocating a different time interval ("slot" or "slice") for the transmission of each channel, i.e., the channels take turns to use the link. Some kind of periodic synchronizing signal or distinguishing identifier is usually required so that the receiver can tell which channel is which.

Time-division multiplexing (TDM) is a method of putting multiple data streams in a single signal by separating the signal into many segments, each having a very short duration. Each individual data stream is reassembled at the receiving end based on the timing.

The circuit that combines signals at the source (transmitting) end of a communications link is known as a multiplexer. It accepts the input from each individual end user, breaks each signal into segments, and assigns the segments to the composite signal in a rotating, repeating sequence. The composite signal thus contains data from multiple senders. At the other end of the long-distance cable, the individual signals are separated out by means of a circuit called a demultiplexer, and routed to the proper end users. A two-way communications circuit requires a multiplexer/demultiplexer at each end of the long-distance, high-bandwidth cable.

If many signals must be sent along a single long-distance line, careful engineering is required to ensure that the system will perform properly. An asset of TDM is its flexibility. The scheme allows for variation in the number of signals being sent along the line, and constantly adjusts the time intervals to make optimum use of the available bandwidth. The Internet is a classic example of a communications network in which the volume of traffic can change drastically from hour to hour.

TDM becomes inefficient when traffic is intermittent because the time slot is still allocated even when the channel has no data to transmit. Statistical time division multiplexing was developed to overcome this problem.

7.3.1 Theory of Time Division Multiplexing

Time Division Multiplexing operates by dividing the network bandwidth into fixed bandwidth segments. Each segment or channel is assigned to a user and is given its own time slot for using the network. First, information from channel *A* is transmitted, then information from channel *B*, and so on in a regular sequence, cycling back to channel *A* and continuing. Bandwidth allocation is static, that is, each channel has a fixed predetermined bandwidth. Because of this multiplexing technique, TDM is protocol insensitive and is capable of combining various protocols onto a single high speed transmission link.

Conventional TDM systems usually employ either Bit-Interleaved or Byte-Interleaved multiplexing schemes. Each time slot accommodates either a bit (1 or 0) or a byte (usually 8 bits long to represent a character, number, or symbol).

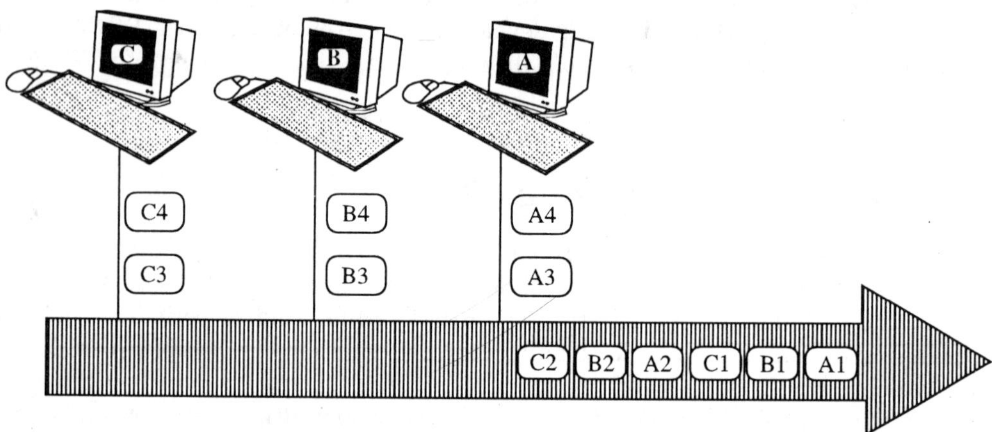

Fig. 7.4 High-bit-rate channel divided into series of time slots

It's often practical to combine a set of low-bit-rate streams, each with a fixed and pre-defined bit rate, into a single high-speed bit stream that can be transmitted over a single channel. This technique is called time division multiplexing (TDM) and has many applications, including wireline telephone systems and some cellular telephone systems. The main reason to use TDM is to take advantage of existing transmission lines. It would be very expensive if each low-bit-rate stream were assigned a costly physical channel (say, an entire fiber optic line) that extended over a long distance.

Consider, for instance, a channel capable of transmitting 192 kbit/sec from Chicago to New York. Suppose that three sources, all located in Chicago, each have 64 kbit/sec of data that they want to transmit to individual users in New York. As shown in figure 7.5 the high-bit-rate channel can be divided into a series of time slots, and the time slots can be alternately used by the three sources. The three sources are thus capable of transmitting all of their data across the single, shared channel. Clearly, at the other end of the channel (in this case, in New York), the process must be reversed (i.e., the system must divide the 192 kbit/sec multiplexed data stream back into the original three 64 kbit/sec data streams, which are then provided to three

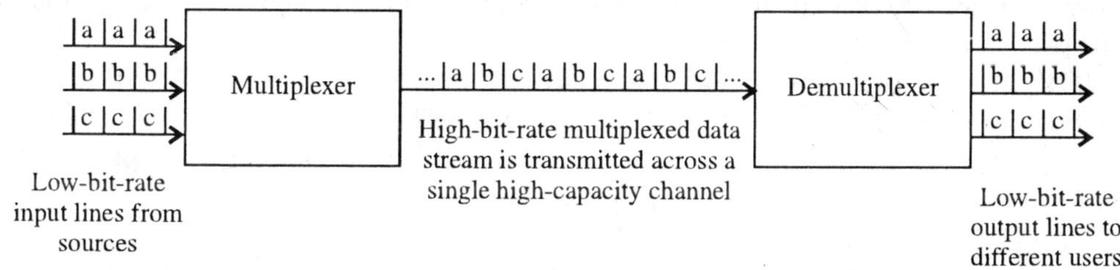

Fig. 7.5 Time division multiplexing

different users). This reverse process is called demultiplexing.

Choosing the proper size for the time slots involves a trade-off between efficiency and delay. If the time slots are too small (say, one bit long) then the multiplexer must be fast enough and powerful enough to be constantly switching between sources (and the demultiplexer must be fast enough and powerful enough to be constantly switching between users). If the time slots are larger than one bit, data from each source must be stored (buffered) while other sources are using the channel. This storage will produce delay. If the time slots are too large, then a significant delay will be introduced between each source and its user. Some applications, such as teleconferencing and videoconferencing, cannot tolerate long delays.

So far we have considered a form of TDM that is based on fixed slot assignments to each of the low-bit-rate data streams. In other words, each stream has predefined slot positions in the combined stream, and the receiver must be aware which slots belong to which input stream. Both transmission ends, the transmitter and the receiver, must be perfectly synchronized to the slot period. For this reason, the technique is usually called synchronous TDM.

There is another important version of TDM, usually referred to as **statistical TDM**. Statistical TDM is useful for applications in which the low-bit-rate streams have speeds that vary in time. For example, a low-bit-rate stream to a single terminal in a computer network may fluctuate between 2 kbit/sec and 50 kbit/sec during an active connection session (we've all seen variable speeds during Internet connections, for instance). If we assign the stream enough slots for its peak rate (that is, for 50 kbit/sec), then we will be wasting slots when the rate drops well below the peak value. This waste can be especially significant if the system has many variable-speed low-bit-rate streams.

7.3.2 Some examples of TDM based services

Public telephone networks

T1 : The T-carrier system is entirely digital, using pulse code modulation and time division multiplexing.

E1 : (or E-1) is a European digital transmission format and is the equivalent of the North American T-1 format.

Narrow-band ISDN (Integrated Services Digital Network)—is a set of standards for digital transmission over ordinary telephone copper wire as well as over other media. Home and business users who install ISDN adapters (in place of their modems) can download at up to 128 Kbps.

SONET (Synchronous Optical Network)—SONET is the U.S. (ANSI) standard for synchronous data transmission on optical media. SONET provides standards for a number of line rates up to the maximum line rate of 9.953 gigabits per second (Gbps). SONET is considered to be the foundation for the physical layer of the broad band ISDN.

7.3.3 Benefits and Shortcomings of TDM

The relative simplicity and low cost of TDM hardware devices makes it possible to build cost-effective networks of widely varying node count, geographic extent, capacity, and speed.

However, TDM is best utilized if everyone always has something to send, otherwise, it wastes time. Time Division Multiplexing operates with low network efficiency. For example, if one of the voice channels on our connection is inactive, the bandwidth dedicated to the channel is unavailable to the other users; therefore, the allotted time slot remains idle.

Another deficiency is TDM's inability to transport a dynamically varying combination of voice, fax, and LAN traffic. Because the bandwidth is statically allocated, the momentarily high bandwidth requirements of one channel on a network cannot be met. There is no way for one TDM channel to grab all of the network bandwidth, even for a short time, to expedite the transfer of a large amount of data.

7.3.4 Statistical Time Division Multiplexing

(STDM, StatMUX) A system developed to overcome some inefficiencies of standard time division multiplexing, where time slices are still allocated to channels, even if they have no information to transmit.

STDM uses a variable time slot length and by allowing channels to compete for any free slot space. It employs a buffer memory that temporarily stores the data during periods of peak traffic. This scheme allows STDM to waste no high-speed line time with inactive channels. STDM requires each transmission to carry identification information (i.e., a channel identifier). To reduce the cost of this overhead, a number of characters for each channel are grouped together for transmission.

Statistical TDM works by calculating the average transmission rates of the streams to be combined, and then uses a high-speed multiplexing link with a transmission rate that is equal to (or slightly greater than) the statistical average of the combined streams. Since the transmission rates from each source are variable, we no longer assign a fixed number of time slots to each data stream. Rather, we dynamically assign the appropriate number of slots to accommodate the current transmission rates from each stream. Because the combined rate of all the streams will also fluctuate in time between two extreme values, we need to buffer the output of the low-bit-rate streams when the combined rate exceeds the transmission rate of the high-speed link.

With statistical TDM, we are no longer relying on synchronized time slots with fixed assignments for each input stream, as we did with synchronous TDM. So how does the demultiplexer in statistical TDM know which of the received bits belongs to which data stream? Prior to transmission, we divide each stream of bits coming from a source into fixed-size blocks. We then add a small group of bits called a header to each block, with the header containing the addresses of the source and intended user for that block. The block and the header are then transmitted together across the channel. Combined, the block and header are called a packet.

Actually, the header may contain other information besides the source and user addresses, such as extra bits for error control or additional bits for link control (used, for example, to indicate the position of a particular block in a sequence of blocks coming from the same user, or to indicate priority level for a particular message). Extra bits can also be added to the beginning and end of a block for synchronization; a particular pattern of bits, called a start flag, can be used in the header to mark the start of a block, and another particular pattern of bits, called an end flag, can be used to conclude the block. Each block transmitted across the channel thus contains a group of information bits that the user wants, plus additional bits needed by the system to ensure proper transmission. These additional bits, while necessary to system operation, reduce the effective transmission rate on the channel. Figures 7.6 and 7.7 present the statistical TDM technique and the structure of a typical packet.

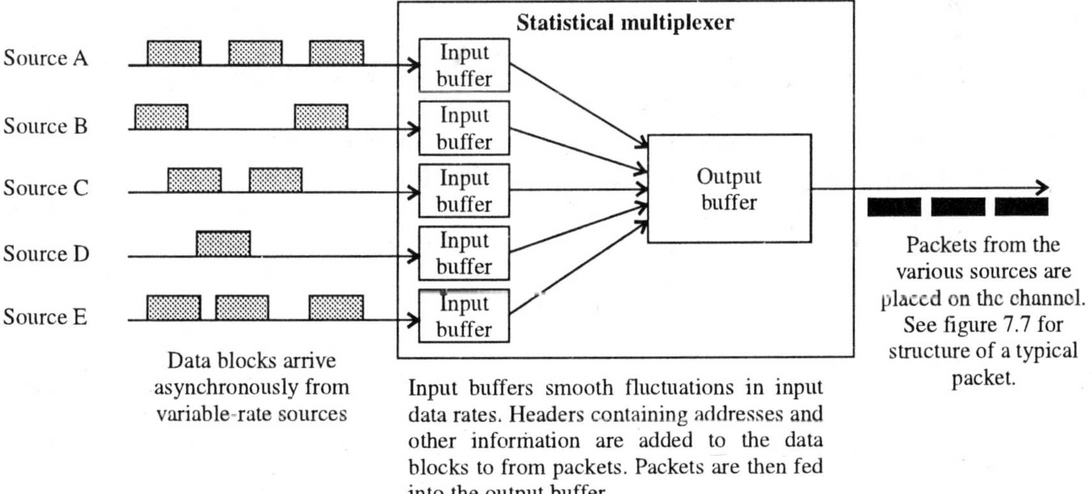

Fig. 7.6 Statistical TDM

Start flag	Address field	Control field	Information bits	Error control	End flag

Fig. 7.7 Structure of a typical statistical TDM packet

7.4 Frequency Division Multiplexing (FDM)

Frequency-division multiplexing (FDM) is a scheme in which numerous signals are combined for transmission on a single communications line or channel. Each signal is assigned a different frequency (subchannel) within the main channel.

FDM means that the total bandwidth available to the system is divided into a series of non-overlapping frequency sub-bands that are then assigned to each communicating source and user pair. Figure 7.8 show how this division is accomplished for a case of three sources at one end of a system that are communicating with three separate users at the other end. Note that each transmitter modulates its source's information into a signal that lies in a different frequency sub-band (Transmitter 1 generates a signal in the frequency sub-band between 92.0 MHz and 92.2 MHz, Transmitter 2 generates a signal in the sub-band between 92.2 MHz and 92.4 MHz, and Transmitter 3 generates a signal in the sub-band between 92.4 MHz and 92.6 MHz). The signals are then transmitted across a common channel.

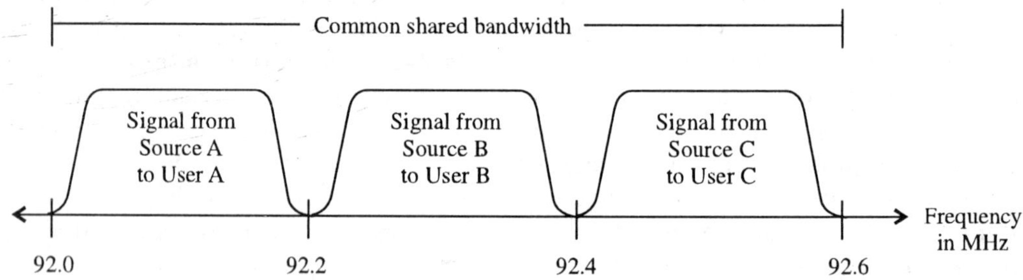

Fig. 7.8 Spectral occupancy of signals in an FDM system

At the receiving end of the system, bandpass filters are used to pass the desired signal (the signal lying in the appropriate frequency sub-band) to the appropriate user and to block all the unwanted signals. To ensure that the transmitted signals do not stray outside their assigned sub-bands, it is also common to place appropriate passband filters at the output stage of each transmitter. It is also appropriate to design an FDM system so that the bandwidth allocated to each sub-band is slightly larger than the bandwidth needed by each source. This extra bandwidth, called a guardband, allows systems to use less expensive filters (i.e., filters with fewer poles and therefore less steep rolloffs).

A typical analog Internet connection via a twisted pair telephone line requires approximately three kilohertz (3 kHz) of bandwidth for accurate and reliable data transfer. Twisted-pair lines are common in households and small businesses. But major telephone cables, operating between large businesses, government agencies, and municipalities, are capable of much larger bandwidths.

Suppose a long-distance cable is available with a bandwidth allotment of three megahertz (3 MHz). This is 3,000 kHz, so in theory, it is possible to place 1,000 signals, each 3 kHz wide, into the long-distance channel. The circuit that does this is known as a multiplexer. It accepts the input from each individual end user, and generates a signal on a different frequency for each of the inputs. This results in a high-bandwidth, complex signal containing data from all the end users. At the other end of the long-distance cable, the individual signals are separated out by means of a circuit called a demultiplexer, and routed to the proper end users. A two-way communications circuit requires a multiplexer/demultiplexer at each end of the long-distance, high-bandwidth cable.

When FDM is used in a communications network, each input signal is sent and received at maximum speed at all times. This is its chief asset. However, if many signals must be sent along a single long-distance line, the necessary bandwidth is large, and careful engineering is required to ensure that the system will perform properly. In some systems, a different scheme, known as time-division multiplexing, is used instead.

Where frequency division multiplexing is used as to allow multiple users to share a physical communications channel, it is called frequency-division multiple access (**FDMA**).

FDMA is the traditional way of separating radio signals from different transmitters.

7.4.1 Theory of Frequency Division Multiplexing

In many communication systems, a single, large frequency band is assigned to the system and is shared among a group of users. Examples of this type of system include:

Examples of this type of system include:

1.	A microwave transmission line connecting two sites over a long distance. Each site has a number of sources generating independent data streams that are transmitted simultaneously over the microwave link.
2.	AM or FM radio broadcast bands, which are divided among many channels or stations. The stations are selected with the radio dial by tuning a variable-frequency filter.
3.	A satellite system providing communication between a large numbers of ground stations that are separated geographically but that need to communicate at the same time. The total bandwidth assigned to the satellite system must be divided among the ground stations.
4.	A cellular radio system that operates in full-duplex mode over a given frequency band. The earlier cellular telephone system used analog communication methods. The bandwidth for these systems was divided into a large number of channels. Each pair of channels was assigned to two communicating end-users for full-duplex communications.

The figure 7.9 illustrates the FDM multiplexing process. The first PC terminal is sending "1010" whereas the second terminal is sending "0110". The multiplexing process starts by applying amplitude modulation into each signal by using different carrier frequencies as f_1 and f_2. Then both signals are combined and sent.

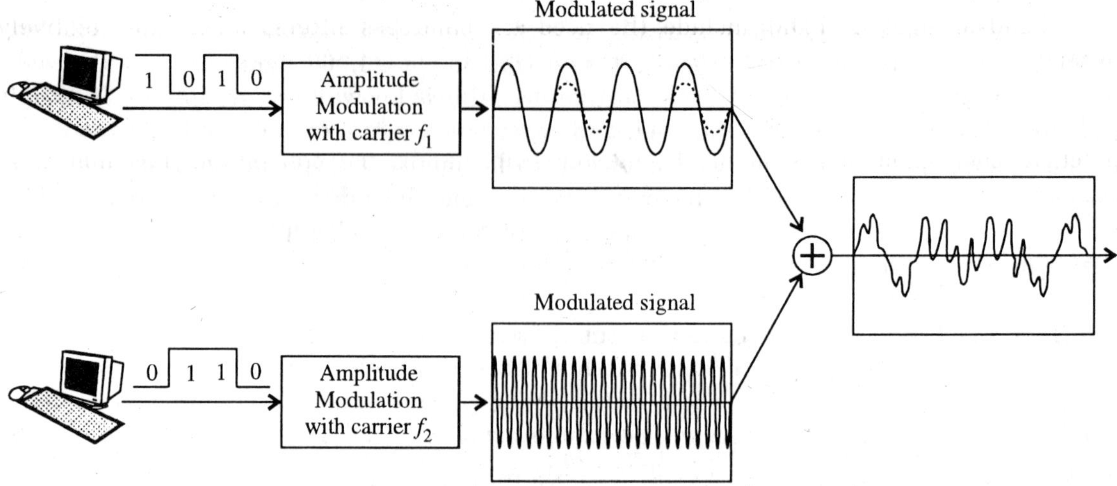

Fig. 7.9 FDM multiplexing process

In demultiplexing process, we use filters to decompose the multiplexed signal into its constituent component signals. Then each signal is passed to an amplitude demodulation process to separate the carrier signal from the message signal. Then, the message signal is sent to the waiting receiver.

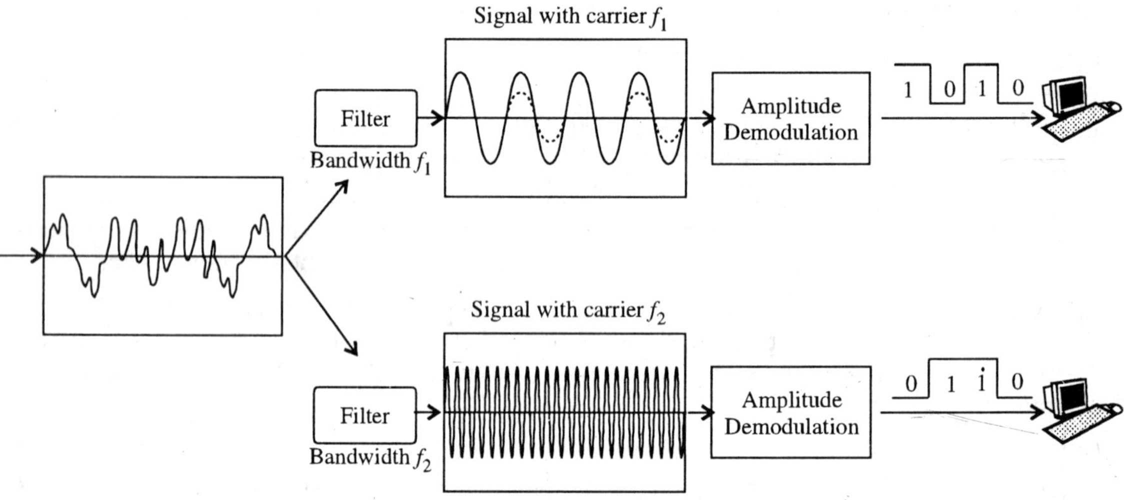

Fig. 7.10 FDM demultiplexing process

7.4.2 Advantages and Disadvantages of FDM relative to TDM

The main advantage is that unlike TDM, FDM is not sensitive to propagation delays. Channel equalization techniques needed for FDM systems are therefore not as complex as those for TDM systems.

Disadvantages of FDM include the need for bandpass filters, which are relatively expensive and complicated to construct and design (remember that these filters are usually used in the transmitters as well as the receivers). TDM, on the other hand, uses relatively simple and less costly digital logic circuits. Another disadvantage of FDM is that in many practical communication systems, the power amplifier in the transmitter has nonlinear characteristics (linear amplifiers are more complex to build), and nonlinear amplification leads to the creation of out-of-band spectral components that may interfere with other FDM channels. Thus, it is necessary to use more complex linear amplifiers in FDM systems.

7.4.3 OFDM (Orthogonal Frequency Division Multiplexing)

OFDM is a technique for increasing the amount of information that can be carried over a wireless network.

In frequency-division multiplexing, multiple signals, or carriers, are sent simultaneously over different frequencies between two points. However, FDM has an inherent problem: Wireless signals can travel multiple paths from transmitter to receiver (by bouncing off buildings, mountains and even passing airplanes); receivers can have trouble sorting all the resulting data out.

Orthogonal FDM deals with this multipath problem by splitting carriers into smaller subcarriers, and then broadcasting those simultaneously. Orthogonal FDM's (OFDM) spread spectrum technique distributes the data over a large number of carriers that are spaced apart at precise frequencies. This spacing provides the "orthogonality" in this technique, which prevents the demodulators from seeing frequencies other than their own. The benefits of OFDM are high spectral efficiency, resiliency to RF interference, and lower multi-path distortion. This is useful because in a typical terrestrial broadcasting scenario there are multipath-channels (i.e., the transmitted signal arrives at the receiver using various paths of different length). Since multiple versions of the signal interfere with each other (inter symbol interference (ISI)) it becomes very hard to extract the original information.

OFDM is sometimes called multi-carrier or discrete multi-tone modulation. It is the modulation technique used for digital TV in Europe, Japan and Australia.

Uses

DAB—OFDM forms the basis for the Digital Audio Broadcasting (DAB) standard in the European market.

ADSL—OFDM forms the basis for the global ADSL (asymmetric digital subscriber line) standard.

Wireless Local Area Networks—Development is ongoing for wireless point-to-point and point-to-multipoint configurations using OFDM technology.

In a supplement to the IEEE 802.11 standard, the IEEE 802.11 working group published IEEE 802.11a, which outlines the use of OFDM in the 5.8-GHz band.

7.5 Wavelength Division Multiplexing (WDM)

The analog of frequency division multiplexing in the optical domain is known as wavelength division multiplexing. In telecommunications wavelength division multiplexing (WDM) is a technology which multiplexes several optical carrier signals on a single optical fibre by using different wavelengths (colours) of laser light to carry different signals.

Note that this term applies to an optical carrier (which is typically described by its wavelength), whereas frequency division multiplexing typically applies to a radio carrier (which is more often described by frequency). However, since wavelength and frequency are inversely proportional, and since radio and light are both forms of electromagnetic radiation, the distinction is somewhat arbitrary.

The technique relies on the fact that a laser can be designed to emit monochromatic light. Each signal to be transmitted is attached to a laser that emits a different color light beam, all the light beams are sent at the same time and a receiving device splits the colors into the original signals again. The device that joins the signals together is known as a multiplexer, and the one that splits them apart is a demultiplexer. With the right type of fibre you can have a device that does both at once, and can function as an optical add-drop multiplexer and that ought to be called a modem but isn't.

7.5.1 WDM in Practice

In practice, WDM systems are built by combining signals from multiple different single-wavelength end devices onto a single fibre.The first WDM systems combined two signals and appeared around 1985. Modern systems can handle up to 160 signals and can expand a basic 10 Gbit/s fibre system to a theoretical total capacity of over 1.6 Tbit/s over a single fiber pair.

WDM systems are popular with telecommunications companies because they allow them to expand the capacity of their fibre networks without digging up roads again more than necessary which is extremely costly. By using WDM and optical amplifiers, they can accommodate several generations of technology development in their optical infrastructure without having to overhaul the backbone network. All they have to do is to upgrade the multiplexers and demultiplexers at each end.

This is often done by using optical-to-electrical-to-optical translation at the very edge of the transport network, thus permitting interoperation with existing equipment with optical interfaces.

Under WDM, the optical transmission spectrum is carved up into a number of non-overlapping wavelength (or frequency) bands, with each wavelength supporting a single communication channel operating at whatever rate one desires, e.g., peak electronic speed. Thus, by allowing multiple WDM channels to coexist on a single fiber, one can tap into the huge fiber bandwidth, with the corresponding challenges being the design and development of appropriate network architectures, protocols, and algorithms. Also, WDM devices are easier to implement since, generally, all components in a WDM device need to operate only at electronic speed; as a result, several WDM devices are available in the marketplace today, and more are emerging.

Current development activities indicate that this sort of WDM network will be deployed mainly as a backbone network for large regions, e.g., for nationwide or global coverage. End-users—to whom the architecture and operation of the backbone will be transparent except for significantly improved response times—will attach to the network through a wavelength-sensitive switching/routing node. An end-user in this context need not necessarily be terminal equipment, but the aggregate activity from a collection of terminals—including those that may possibly be feeding in from other regional and/or local subnetworks—so that the end-user's aggregate activity on any of its transmitters is close to the peak electronic transmission rate.

Dense and Coarse WDM

Early WDM systems were expensive and complicated to run. However, recent standardization and better understanding of the dynamics of WDM systems have made WDM much cheaper to deploy. The market has segmented into two parts, "dense" and "coarse" WDM.

Dense WDM (DWDM) is generally held to be WDM with more than 8 active wavelengths per fibre and with systems with fewer active wavelengths being classified as coarse WDM (CWDM).

7.5.2 Basic Operation

As explained before, WDM enables the utilization of a significant portion of the available fiber bandwidth by allowing many independent signals to be transmitted simultaneously on one fiber, with each signal located at a different wavelength. Routing and detection of these signals can be accomplished independently, with the wavelength determining the communication path by acting as the signature address of the origin, destination or routing. Components are therefore required that are wavelength selective, allowing for the transmission, recovery, or routing of specific wavelengths.

In a simple WDM system (Figure 7.11), each laser must emit light at a different wavelength, with all the lasers' light multiplexed together onto a single optical fiber. After

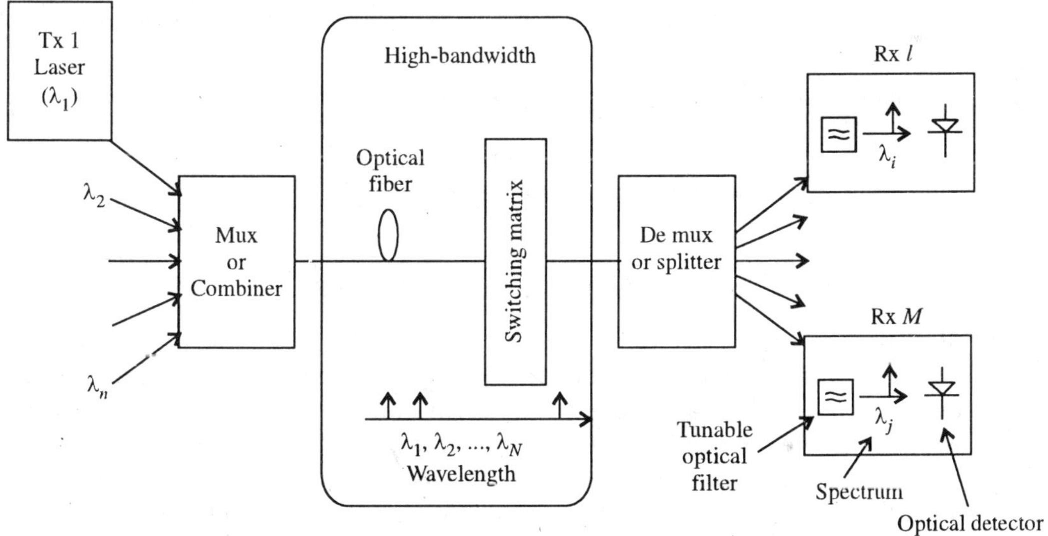

Fig. 7.11 A simple WDM system

being transmitted through a high-bandwidth optical fiber, the combined optical signals must be demultiplexed at the receiving end by distributing the total optical power to each output port and then requiring that each receiver selectively recover only one wavelength by using a tunable optical filter. Each laser is modulated at a given speed, and the total aggregate capacity being transmitted along the high-bandwidth fiber is the sum total of the bit rates of the individual lasers. An example of the system capacity enhancement is the situation in which ten 2.5-Gbps signals can be transmitted on one fiber, producing a system capacity of 25 Gbps. This wavelength-parallelism circumvents the problem of typical optoelectronic devices, which do not have bandwidths exceeding a few gigahertz unless they are exotic and expensive. The speed requirements for the individual optoelectronic components are, therefore, relaxed, even though a significant amount of total fiber bandwidth is still being utilized.

The concept of wavelength demultiplexing using an optical filter is illustrated in Figure 7.12. In the figure, four channels are input to an optical filter that has a nonideal transmission filtering function. The filter transmission peak is centered over the desired channel, in this case thereby transmitting that channel and blocking all other channels. Because of the nonideal filter transmission function, some optical energy of the neighboring channels leaks through the filter, causing interchannel, interwavelength cross-talk. This cross-talk has the effect of reducing the selected signal's contrast ratio and can be minimized by increasing the spectral separation between channels. Although there is no set definition, a nonstandardized convention exists for defining optical WDM as encompassing a system for which the channel spacing is approximately 10 nm.

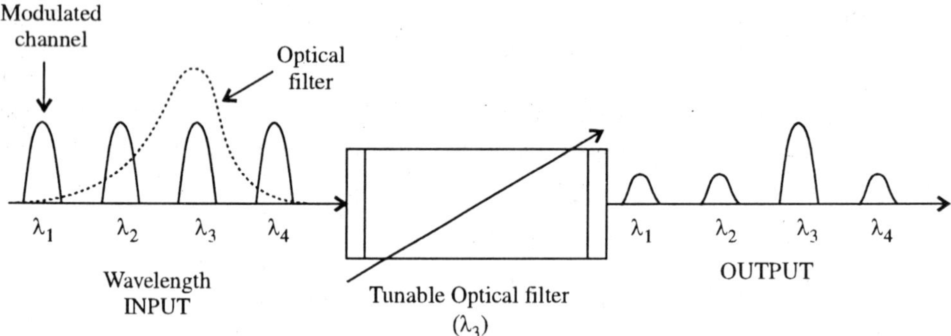

Fig. 7.12 Optical WDM channels being demultiplexed by an optical filter

7.6 Comparison Of Multiplexing Techniques

These are all methods that can be used for data communications and transmissions.

(a) **Time division multiplexing (TDM)** gives each host or signals a certain amount of transmission time. The available transmission time is divided into quanta. Each flow has access to the data link in a round-robin fashion.

The limitation of this technique is that hosts that don't have anything to transmit (which is usually the case) will tie up the link for nothing and block their share that could instead be used by other hosts. Therefore TDM is usually very inefficient.

(b) **Frequency division multiplexing (FDM)** works in a slightly different way. Each flow of data is sent simultaneously over the link at different frequencies (analog TV and radio are examples of FDM). The signals are modulated at the transmission end and demodulated at the receiving end.

The disadvantage is that the number of flows is fixed. Resizing quanta or adding frequencies is not practical.

(c) **Wave division multiplexing (WDM) or wavelength division multiplexing** multiplexes several optical carrier signals onto a single optical fiber. Each signal is transmitted at different wavelengths by using laser light. A multiplexer combines the signal together to be transmitted over the cable, and a demultiplexer separates them once then reaches the other side.

The great advantage that WDM has over the other two technologies is that the bandwidth can be increased without changing the transmission medium or cable. By upgrading the multiplexer and demultiplexer, bandwidth can be increased.

The disadvantage of this system is that the hardware is expensive.

To sum up, TDM is simple but inefficient. FDM allows maximum transmission link usage but cannot evolve easily. WDM is fast and evolutive but is expensive.

• • •

8

Telephone System And ISDN Services

Introduction To PSTN

The Public Switched Telephone Network (PSTN) has been evolving ever since Alexander Graham Bell made the first voice transmission over wire in 1876. This chapter discusses the beginnings of the PSTN and explains why the PSTN exists in its current state.

The oldest and largest telecommunications network in existence is the public switched telephone network (PSTN) that has in excess of 700 million subscribers.

For a long time, the PSTN was the only bearer network available for telephony. Today, many people choose the mobile telephone for their calls. Other bearer networks for voice transmission include integrated service digital network (ISDN), asynchronous transfer mode (ATM), frame relay and the Internet.

The PSTN's primary characteristics are listed below:

- Analog access, 300-3,400 Hz.
- Circuit-switched duplex connection.
- Switched bandwidth, 64 kbit/s, or 300-3,400 Hz for analog exchanges.
- Immobility or, at best, very limited mobility.
- Many functions in common with another bearer network : N-ISDN.

In the course of its long history, which started in 1876, the PSTN has undergone complete technical changes. Even factors such as network structure and network utilization have changed radically. The truly revolutionary changes have come about from the 1960s onwards—innovations such as data communication, telefax, and processor control technique, digital voice transmission, satellite communication, digital switching, optoelectronics, network intelligence structures and the Internet.

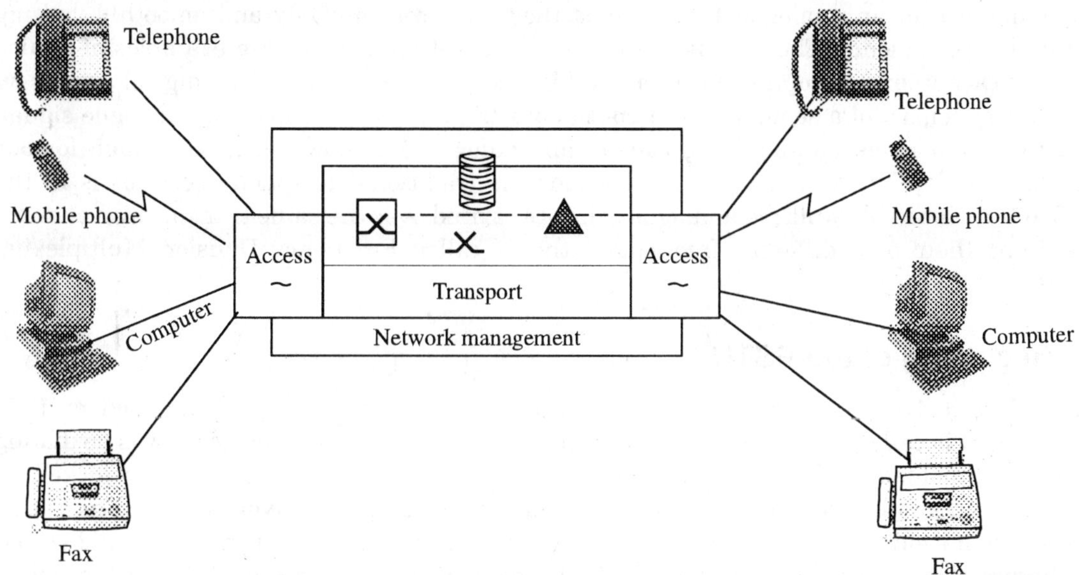

Fig. 8.1 PSTN reference model

To facilitate your understanding of the PSTN and the culture that formed today's telecommunications, we will briefly digress and step back in time to the early 1960s.

The telephone or phone (Greek: tele = far away and phone = voice) is a telecommunications device that transmits sound at great distances. Most telephones operate by means of electric signals. Most modern telephones operate as one part of a complex public switched telephone network of equipment which allows almost any phone user to speak to almost any other. Radiotelephony or wireless telephony transmits messages using radio. Until recently, the word telephone taken alone generally refered to a wired instrument attached to the telephone network. Recently cordless telephones and cell phones have become sufficiently common that no presumption can be made. Wired instruments, or cordless phones attached to wired bases generally provide Plain old telephone service (POTS). Recently Voice over IP has begun to displace POTS in areas where it is offered by Cable Television vendors.

The public switched telephone network (PSTN) is the concatenation of the world's public circuit-switched telephone networks, in much the same way that the Internet is the concatenation of the world's public IP-based packet-switched networks. Originally a network of fixed-line analog telephone systems, the PSTN is now almost entirely digital, and now includes mobile as well as fixed telephones.

The Public Switched Telephone Network (PSTN) is the oldest and largest telecommunications network in existence. PSTN is the telephone network that by default most of the world population is connected to if they have a telephone. In most of the cases a connection to another telephone network, e.g., is done on user request.

The PSTN network is sometimes called an analogue network -- in contrast for example to ISDN and GSM, which are digital networks. The reason is that the signals carried over the copper line are in an analogue form that is they have continuously and smoothly varying amplitude or frequency. The human voice and a musical instrument are examples of analog signals - both produce complex variations in frequency and amplitude. The digital signals on the contrary consist of a sequence of discontinuous fragments of the original analogue signal. A digital signal is only a simplified copy of an analogue one, however good enough for our imperfect senses. The frequency band used for the traditional telephony services is in the 300-3,400 Hz interval. Multiple analogue calls are carried over the same transmission channel by sending them over different frequency - this is called Frequency Division Multiplexing (FDM).

The Beginning of the PSTN

The first voice transmission, sent by Alexander Graham Bell, was accomplished in 1876 through what is called a ring-down circuit. A ring-down circuit means that there was no dialing of numbers; instead, a physical wire connected two devices. Basically, one person picked up the phone and another person was on the other end (no ringing was involved). Over time, this simple design evolved from a one-way voice transmission, by which only one user could speak, to a bi-directional voice transmission, whereby both users could speak. Moving the voices across the wire required a carbon microphone, a battery, an electromagnet, and an iron diaphragm.

It also required a physical cable between each location that the user wanted to call. The concept of dialing a number to reach a destination, however, did not exist at this time. To further illustrate the beginnings of the PSTN, see the basic four-telephone network shown in Figure 8.2. As you can see, a physical cable exists between each location.

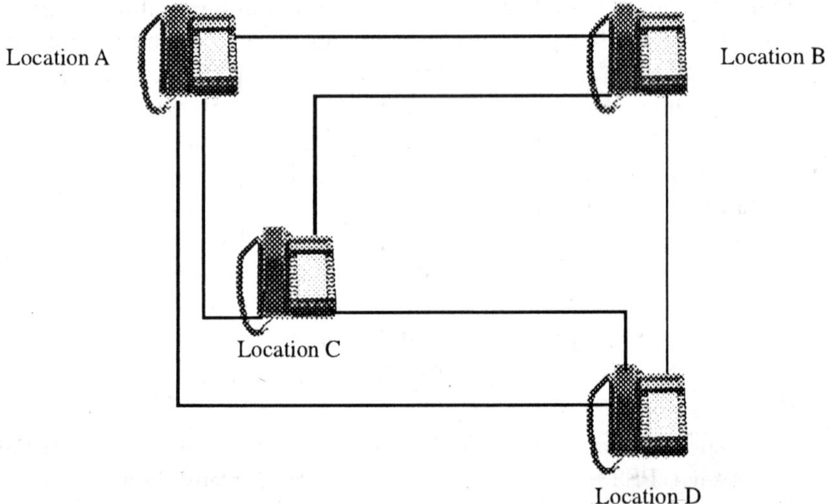

Fig. 8.2 Basic four-phone network

Place a physical cable between every household requiring access to a telephone, however, and you'll see that such a setup is neither cost-effective nor feasible (see Figure 8.3). To determine how many lines you need to your house, think about everyone you call as a value of N and use the following equation: $N \times (N - 1)/2$. As such, if you want to call 10 people, you need 45 pairs of lines running into your house.

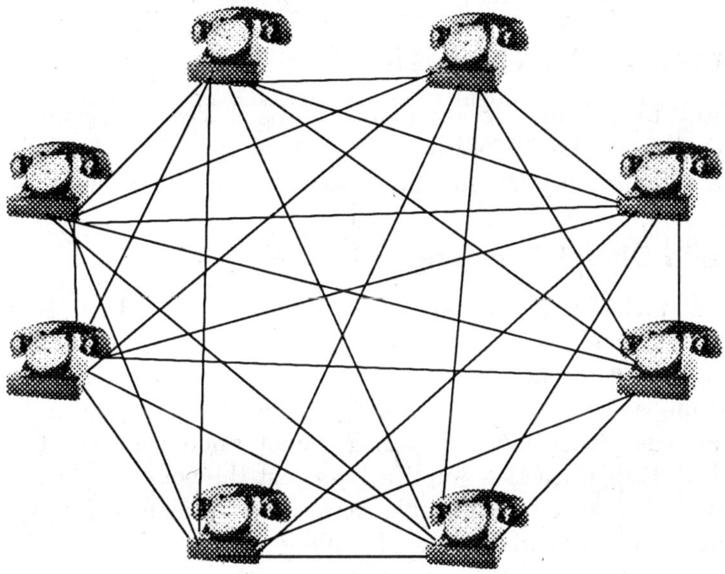

Fig. 8.3 Physical cable between all telephone users

Due to the cost concerns and the impossibility of running a physical cable between everyone on Earth who wanted access to a telephone, another mechanism was developed that could map any phone to another phone. With this device, called a **switch**, the telephone users needed only one cable to the centralized switch office, instead of seven. At first, a telephone

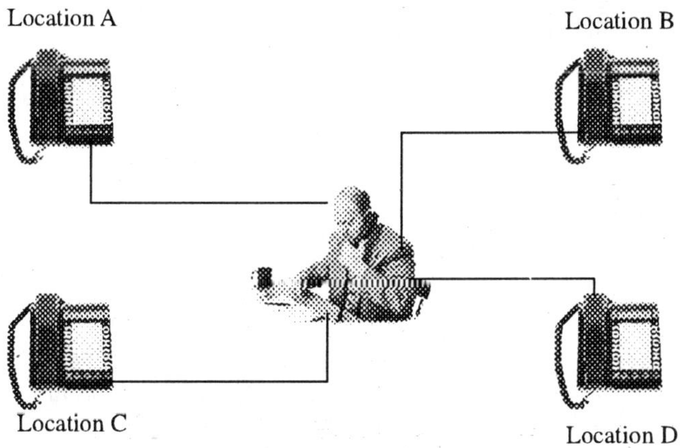

Fig. 8.4 Centralized operator : The human switch

operator acted as the switch. This operator asked callers where they wanted to dial and then manually connected the two voice paths. Figure 8.4 shows how the four-phone network example would look today with a centralized operator to switch the calls.

Now, skip ahead 100 years or so and the human switch is replaced by electronic switches. At this point, you can learn how the modern PSTN network is built.

8.1 Understanding PSTN Basics

Although it is difficult to explain every component of the PSTN, this section explains the most important pieces that make the PSTN work. The following sections discuss how your voice is transmitted across a digital network and basic circuit-switching concepts.

8.1.1 Analog and Digital Signaling

Everything you hear, including human speech, is in analog form. Until several decades ago, the telephony network was based on an analog infrastructure as well. Although analog communication is ideal for human interaction, it is neither robust nor efficient at recovering from line noise. (Line noise is normally caused by the introduction of static into a voice network.) In the early telephony network, analog transmission was passed through amplifiers to boost the signal. But, this practice amplified not just the voice, but the line noise as well. This line noise resulted in an often-unusable connection. Analog communication is a mix of time and amplitude. Figure 8.5, which takes a high-level view of an analog waveform, shows what your voice looks like through an oscilloscope.

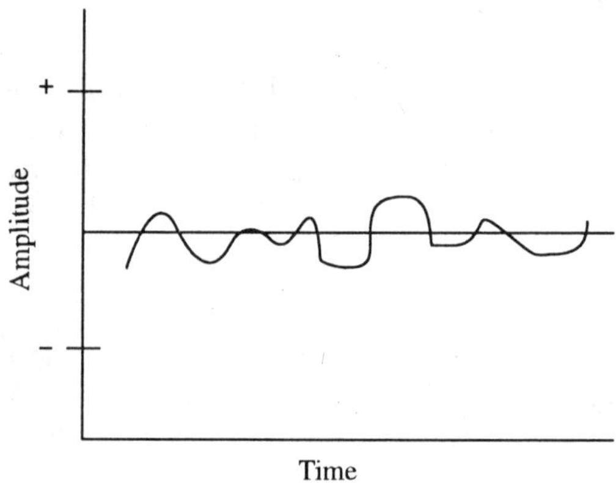

Fig. 8.5 Analog waveform

If you were far away from the *end office switch* (which provides the physical cable to your home), an amplifier might be required to boost the analog transmission (your voice).

Analog signals that receive line noise can distort the analog waveform and cause garbled reception. This is more obvious to the listener if many amplifiers are located between your home and the end office switch. Figure 8.6 show that an amplifier does not clean the signal as it amplifies, but simply amplifies the distorted signal. This process of going through several amplifiers with one voice signal is called accumulated noise.

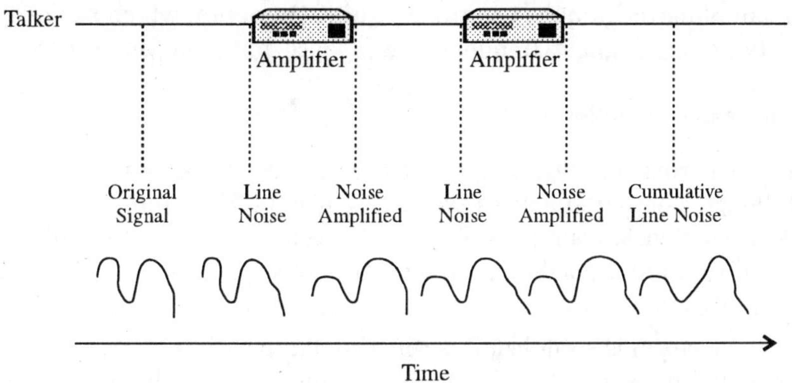

Fig. 8.6 Analog line distortion

In digital networks, line noise is less of an issue because repeaters not only amplify the signal, but also clean it to its original condition. This is possible with digital communication because such communication is based on 1's and 0's. So, as shown in Figure 8.7, the repeater (a digital amplifier) only has to decide whether to regenerate a 1 or a 0.

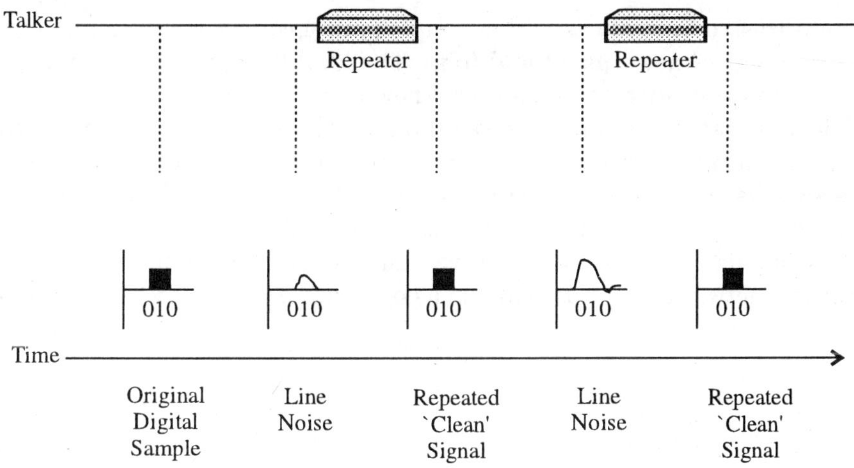

Fig. 8.7 Digital line distortion

Therefore, when signals are repeated, a clean sound is maintained. When the benefits of this digital representation became evident, the telephony network migrated to **Pulse Code Modulation (PCM)**.

Digital Voice Signals

PCM is the most common method of encoding an analog voice signal into a digital stream of 1's and 0's. All sampling techniques use the **Nyquist theorem**, which basically states that if you sample at twice the highest frequency on a voice line, you achieve good-quality voice transmission.

The PCM process is as follows:

- Analog waveforms are put through a voice frequency filter to filter out anything greater than 4000 Hz. These frequencies are filtered to 4000 Hz to limit the amount of crosstalk in the voice network. Using the Nyquist theorem, you need to sample at 8000 samples per second to achieve good-quality voice transmission.
- The filtered analog signal is then sampled at a rate of 8000 times per second.
- After the waveform is sampled, it is converted into a discrete digital form. This sample is represented by a code that indicates the amplitude of the waveform at the instant the sample was taken. The telephony form of PCM uses eight bits for the code and a logarithm compression method assigns more bits to lower-amplitude signals.

If you multiply the eight-bit words by 8000 times per second, you get 64,000 bits per second (bps). The basis for the telephone infrastructure is 64,000 bps (or 64 kbps).

8.1.2 Local Loops, Trunks, and Interswitch Communication

The telephone infrastructure starts with a simple pair of copper wires running to your home. This physical cabling is known as a **local loop**. The local loop physically connects your home telephone to the **central office switch** (also known as a *Class* 5 *switch* or *end office switch*). The communication path between the central office switch and your home is known as the **phone line**, and it normally runs over the local loop. The communication path between several central office switches is known as a **trunk**. Just as it is not cost-effective to place a physical wire between your house and every other house you want to call, it is also not cost-effective to place a physical wire between every central office switch. You can see in Figure 8.8 that a meshed telephone network is not as scalable as one with a hierarchy of switches.

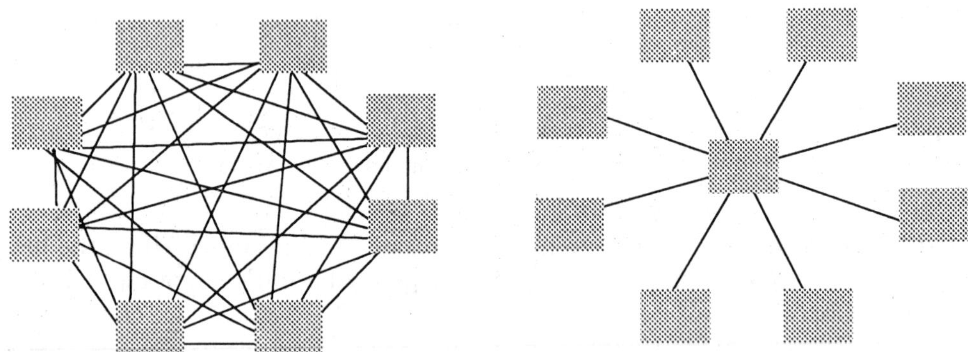

Fig. 8.8 Meshed network versus hierarchical network

Switches are currently deployed in hierarchies. End office switches (or central office switches) interconnect through trunks to **tandem switches** (also referred to as Class 4 switches). Higher layer tandem switches connect local tandem switches. Figure 8.9 shows a typical model of switching hierarchy.

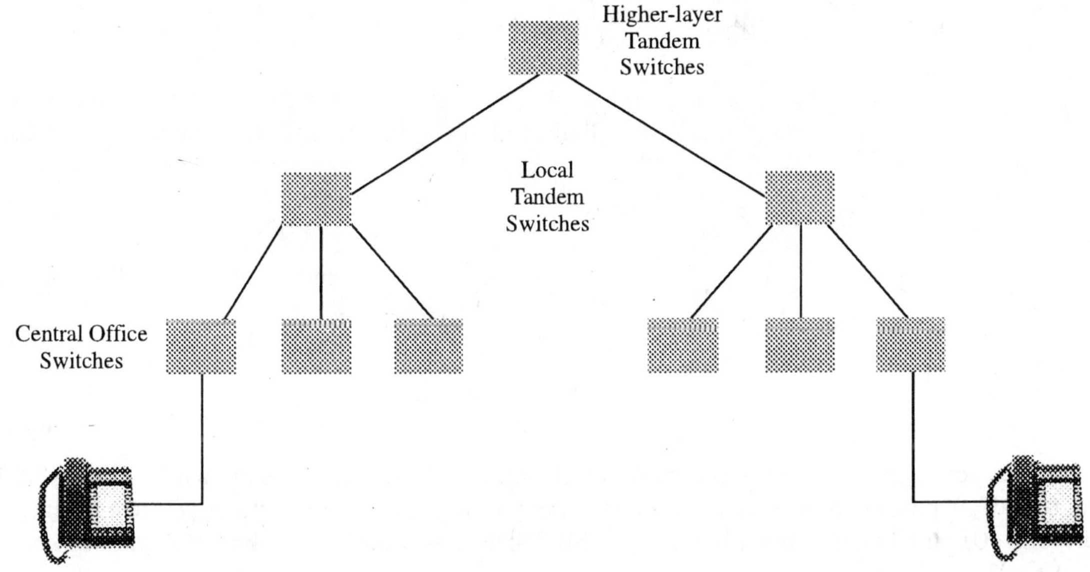

Fig. 8.9 Circuit-switching hierarchy

Central office switches often directly connect to each other. The direct connections that occur between central office switches depends to a great extent on call patterns. If enough traffic occurs between two central office switches, a dedicated circuit is placed between the two switches to offload those calls from the local tandem switches. Some portions of the PSTN use as many as five levels of switching hierarchy.

8.1.3 PSTN Signaling

Generally, two types of signaling methods run over various transmission media. The signaling methods are broken into the following groups:

- **User-to-network signaling** : This is how an end user communicates with the PSTN.
- **Network-to-network signaling** : This is generally how the switches in the PSTN intercommunicate.

User-to-Network Signaling

Generally, when using twisted copper pair as the transport, a user connects to the PSTN through analog, Integrated Services Digital Network (ISDN), or through a T1 carrier. The most common signaling method for user-to-network analog communication is **Dual Tone Multi-**

Frequency (DTMF). DTMF is known as in-band signaling because the tones are carried through the voice path. Figure 8.10 shows how DTMF tones are derived.

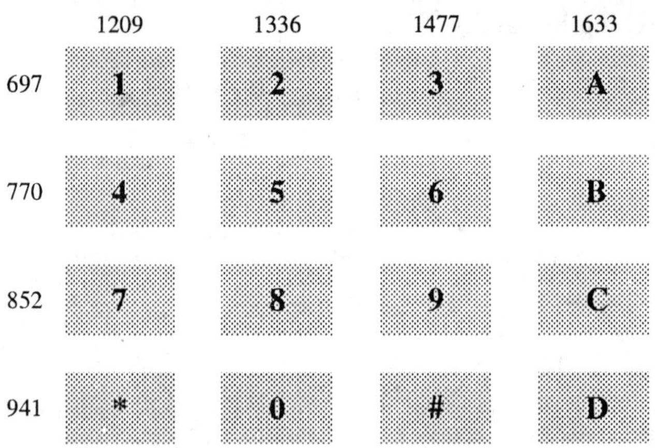

Fig. 8.10 Dual tone multi-frequency

When you pick up your telephone handset and press the digits (as shown in Figure 8.10), the tone that passes from your phone to the central office switch to which you are connected tells the switch what number you want to call. ISDN uses another method of signaling known as out-of-band. With this method, the signaling is transported on a channel separate from the voice. The channel on which the voice is carried is called a bearer (or B channel) and is 64 kbps. The channel on which the signal is carried is called a data channel (D channel) and is 16 kbps.

Out-of-band signaling offers many benefits, including the following:

- Signaling is multiplexed (consolidated) into a common channel.
- Glare is reduced (glare occurs when two people on the same circuit seize opposite ends of that circuit at the same time).
- A lower post dialing delay.
- Additional features, such as higher bandwidth, are realized.
- Because setup messages are not subject to the same line noise as DTMF tones, call completion is greatly increased.

In-band signaling suffers from a few problems, the largest of which is the possibility for lost tones. This occurs when signaling is carried across the voice path and it is a common reason why you can sometimes experience problems remotely accessing your voice mail.

Network-to-Network Signaling

Network-to-network communication is normally carried across the following transmission media:

- T1/E1 carrier over twisted pair.

- T3/E3, T4 carrier over coaxial cable.
- T3, T4 carrier over a microwave link.
- Synchronous Optical Network (SONET) across fiber media.

Network-to-network signaling types include in-band signaling methods such as Multi-Frequency (MF) and Robbed Bit Signaling (RBS). These signaling types can also be used to network signaling methods.

Digital carrier systems (T1, T3) use A and B bits to indicate on/off hook supervision. The A/B bits are set to emulate Single Frequency (SF) tones (SF typically uses the presence or absence of a signal-to-signal A/B bit transitions). These bits might be robbed from the information channel or multiplexed in a common channel (the latter occurs mainly in Europe).

MF is similar to DTMF, but it utilizes a different set of frequencies. As with DTMF, MF tones are sent in-band. But, instead of signaling from a home to an end office switch, MF signals from switch to switch.

Network-to-network signaling also uses an out-of-band signaling method known as Signaling System 7 (SS7) (or C7 in European countries). SS7 is beneficial because it is an out-of-band signaling method and it interconnects to the Intelligent Network (IN). Connection to the IN enables the PSTN to offer Custom Local Area Signaling Services (CLASS) services. SS7 is a method of sending messages between switches for basic call control and for CLASS. These CLASS services still rely on the end-office switches and the SS7 network. SS7 is also used to connect switches and databases for network-based services.

8.1.4 PSTN Services

The two basic services supported over PSTN are Voice and Data. They have different requirements from the point of view of the quality of service that is qualified as "acceptable". For example in the case of voice, some degradation of quality is allowed to level when the speech could be still understood and some noise is tolerable; at the same time delay is not tolerable, we do not want to get the words one by one with variable intervals. The case with data is to the contrary-delay is tolerable—for example, we do not mind if we see the Web site we are viewing coming in portions and during a variable interval of time (as far as we do not get bored), however "noise" is not acceptable because even little noise during data transmission would mean a strange looking web site (if we could understand that this is indeed a web site at all). This special requirement and the nature of the PSTN network itself have made the PSTN very slow when delivering data. The only way to overcome this is to introduce compression techniques that make the data smaller before it is sent over the PSTN.

The introduction of computer-controlled telephone exchanges during the 70s allowed for operators to create new, completely different subscriber services in the network. Today it is much easier for an operator to create a distinctive image for himself and to increase revenue. Some services are charged for, others are free. Many of the free services help to increase the number of successful calls, which in turn generates revenue. These services are normally known under the name Supplementary Services and Value added services.

Different PSTN operators in different countries have chosen to implement different PSTN services which means that not all possible PSTN services could be find in different countries and even within one and the same country depending on the PSTN operator's choice. The following list shows just few of the services that you may have on offer from your operator:

- **Calling line identification presentation (CLIP) :** Also called "caller ID", this service allows a called party to see the telephone number of an incoming call on a display connected to the telephone line. There are two commonly accepted ways of transmitting the CLIP information-via DTMF or Phase-Shift Key (PSK) signalling.
- **Call forwarding :** This service re-routes incoming calls to another number.
- **Call-back (completion of call to a busy subscriber) :** If the called subscriber is busy, the caller can order the call-back service, which means that he is queued for connection to the busy number and when that subscriber gets free the network will connect and notify the caller.
- **Call waiting :** A special signal is generated during a call in progress to indicate that a third party is trying to reach you.

To access and control those services via the telephone, service codes are used (for example the service code 21 is assigned to "call forwarding unconditional"). The subscriber usually activates these services by lifting the handset and then pressing a "star-digits-hash" combination. Also, the register button (R) is used, for example, when alternating between calls and for three-party calls. The system usually confirms the execution of a service by sending a tone or a recorded message.

In addition to offering you a pure voice service, a telephone can be an extremely efficient tool for a subscriber who wishes to send a message, make a financial transaction, or just send a short message (SMS) to another telephone. The PSTN treats such services as any other telephone connection: It sets up the connection to a proper destination after the subscriber has dialled the number of the service. When the call is answered, direct contact with the destination, e.g. a computer or a message gateway is established. The keypad telephone's DTMF signalling is then the tool mostly used for transferring information from the subscriber over the established connection.

DTMF, however, is not capable to provide in all cases all the means needed - for example, if a SMS message is to be sent/received it would require a full set of numbers and letters to be available which DTMF does not provide - instead the already mentioned Phase-Shift Key (PSK) signalling is used.

Of course when using a DECT (Digital Enhanced Cordless Telecommunications) phone and some corded PSTN phones all these may be well hidden from you behind a user friendly menu provided to you by the handset. On the handset display you may see the name of the service and what you may need is pressing a single key to activate it—the telephone itself then will identify the "star-digits-hash" combination needed and will send it to the network.

Connecting Digital devices to PSTN DECT phones, Faxes and Modems are some examples of digital user terminals that can be connected to a PSTN network. In order such devices to operate the digital signal needs to be converted to an analogue signal or as it is normally called "to be modulated". This is needed as well on the Transport network if it is a digital one, e.g., ISDN, ATM, IP. Different modulation techniques may be used. For many decades, A/D conversion of voice has been performed employing the so-called PCM coding. This is pure amplitude coding that results in a bi-directional connection having a bit rate of 64 kbit/s.

8.1.5 Drawbacks to the PSTN

Although the PSTN is effective and does a good job at what it was built to do (that is, switch voice calls), many business drivers are striving to change it to a new network, whereby voice is an application on top of a data network. This is happening for several reasons:

- Data has overtaken voice as the primary traffic on many networks built for voice. Data is now running on top of networks that were built to carry voice efficiently. Data has different characteristics, however, such as a variable use of bandwidth and a need for higher bandwidth. Soon, voice networks will run on top of networks built with a data-centric approach. Traffic will then be differentiated based upon application instead of physical circuits. New technologies (such as Fast Ethernet, Gigabit Ethernet, and Optical Networking) will be used to deploy the high-speed networks that needed to carry all this additional data.
- The PSTN cannot create and deploy features quickly enough. With increased competition due to deregulation in many telecommunications markets, LECs are looking for ways to keep their existing customers. The primary method of keeping customers is by enticing them through new services and applications. The PSTN is built on an infrastructure whereby only the vendors of the equipment develop the applications for that equipment. This means you have one-stop shopping for all your needs. It is very difficult for one company to meet all the needs of a customer. A more open infrastructure, by which many vendors can provide applications, enables more creative solutions and applications to be developed. It is also not possible with the current architecture to enable many vendors to write new applications for the PSTN. Imagine where the world would be today if vendors, such as Microsoft, did not want other vendors to write applications for its software.
- Data/Voice/Video (D/V/V) cannot converge on the PSTN as currently built. With only an analog line to most homes, you cannot have data access (Internet access), phone access, and video access across one 56-kbps modem. High-speed broadband access, such as digital subscriber line (DSL), cable, or wireless, is needed to enable this convergence. After the last bandwidth issues are resolved, the convergence can happen to the home. In the backbone of the PSTN, the convergence has already started.
- The architecture built for voice is not flexible enough to carry data. Because the bearer channels (B channels and T1 circuits), call-control (SS7), and service logic (applications) are tightly bound in one closed platform, it is not possible to make minor changes that might improve audio quality.

It is also important to note that circuit-switched calls require a permanent 64-kbps dedicated circuit between the two telephones. Whether the caller or the person called is talking, the 64-kbps connection cannot be used by any other party. This means that the telephone company cannot use this bandwidth for any other purpose and must bill the parties for consuming its resources. Data networking, on the other hand, has the capability to use bandwidth only when it is required. This difference, although seemingly small, is a major benefit of packet-based voice networking.

8.2 Introduction To ISDN

ISDN (Integrated Services Digital Network) is an all-digital communications network designed to bring the power of the digital network directly to the desktop. It is the ideal communications technology for the information age-perfect for students, cyberspacers, travelers, telecommuters, parents, business people, and corporate executives.

ISDN is often referred as the successor of the existing public networks like the telephone network, data and text networks (Telegraphy). The telephone network was first an analog network. In the early days telephony switching was made by the telephone operator, by plugging both ends of a wire in the right holes of a connection board. In those times the phones had no dialing mechanism. The user had to pick up the phone and tell the operator which connection he desires. After the invention of the dialing disk, switching could be automated, but fast connection set up was possible only after a partially digitization of the telephone net. Today the biggest part of the Telephone system is digital. Only the line from the user to the local exchange is analog. For the connection between two exchange points, digital lines are used (IDN—Integrated Digital Network). A continuation of this development leads to an overall digital network. ISDN is such a network, providing moreover services available in the past—only in other networks and/or with other interfaces, e.g. Teletex, Telefax. ISDN is built on top of IDN. It allows communication, not only with older equipment, for instance an analog telephone connected analog to the local exchange, but also with other networks, e.g., PSPDN (Public Switched Packet Data Network). Thus ISDN can be seen as an evolution rather than a revolution.

In simple terms, ISDN is a replacement for plain old telephone service, which was never designed to meet the needs of the information age. ISDN uses the same wiring that currently serves homes and businesses. You get ISDN service from the same companies who provide telephone service, and you use it to connect telephones, computers, and fax machines. The difference is that you get much faster, much more dependable connections for voice, data, fax, and even video—all through a single line. There is no other technology that comes close to delivering such communications benefits today.

Standard telephone service requires a separate phone line for each device to be used simultaneously. Not only can multiple lines be expensive, but also the amount of information that can be transmitted is limited with analog service; current technology allows 56 kilobits per second (Kbps). ISDN, however, provides multiple channels to operate concurrently on the same pair of wires, and each channel is capable of transmitting at 64 Kbps. Additionally, digital transmissions allow for reduced noise and interference on the carrier channels.

ISDN provides services and capabilities not available through standard telephone service. ISDN furnishes these services through a digital package when a call is initiated. The digital packet includes information regarding : (1) who is calling, (2) the type of call (data/voice/etc...), and (3) the number dialed, if more than one number is used for a single ISDN line. With the information provided, ISDN equipment can determine how to handle a call, based on user-defined preferences. Calls can be accepted, rejected or even rerouted. Data calls can even be routed to an Internet Protocol (IP) address.

Meaning of "ISDN"

"Integrated Services" refers to ISDN's ability to deliver two simultaneous connections, in any combination of data, voice, video, and fax, over a single line. Multiple devices can be attached to the line, and used as needed. That means an ISDN line can take care of most people's complete communications needs, without forcing the purchase of multiple analog phone lines at a much higher transmission rate.

The "Digital" in ISDN refers to its purely digital transmission, as opposed to the analog transmission of plain old telephone service. If you're using a modem for Internet access at this moment, your Internet service provider's modem has converted this site's digital content to analog signals before sending it to you, and your modem converts those signals back to digital when receiving (the same thing happens with every keystroke and mouse click you transmit). When you connect with ISDN, there is no analog conversion. ISDN transmits data digitally, resulting in a very clear transmission quality. There is none of the static and noise of analog transmissions that can slow transmission speed.

"Network" refers to the fact that ISDN is not simply a point-to-point solution like a leased line. ISDN networks extend from the local telephone exchange to the remote user and include all of the telecommunications and switching equipment in between.

Main characteristics

The probably most important keywords concerning ISDN are:

- End to end digital connection.
- Integration of multiple services (voice-, data-, video-, multimedia transmission).
- Standard terminal interface.

Access to ISDN

Two types of ISDN have been specified:

- **Narrowband-ISDN (NISDN).**
- **Broadband-ISDN (BISDN).**

The main difference between NISDN and BISDN is the transmission capacity and the used transfer mode. NISDN can serve with a capacity of up to 2Mbps, while for BISDN exist specifications for 150Mbps and 600Mbps. The term ISDN will basically refer to NISDN. BISDN will be discussed later on.

8.2.1 The Basics of ISDN

ISDN is based on a number of fundamental building blocks.

Channels

A channel is a connection between two users over the network, with a defined capacity of bps. A certain number of channels have been designed for the use of ISDN. There are two types of ISDN "channels" or communication paths:

- **B-channel**
  The Bearer ("B") channel is a 64 kbps channel that can be used for voice, video, data, or multimedia calls. B-channels can be aggregated together for even higher bandwidth applications.
- **D-channel**
  The Delta ("D") channel can be either a 16 kbps or 64 kbps channel used primarily for communications (or signaling) between switching equipment in the ISDN network and the ISDN equipment at your site.

The B channels are primarily for voice and data transmissions, while the D channel is used for signaling and packet transmissions. These ISDN channels are delivered to the user in one of two pre-defined configurations:

- **Basic Rate Interface (BRI)**
  BRI is the ISDN service most people use to connect to the Internet. An ISDN BRI connection supports two 64 kbps B-channels and one 16 kbps D-channel over a standard phone line. BRI is often called **"$2B + D$"** referring to its two B-channels and one D-channel.
- **Primary Rate Interface (PRI)**
  ISDN PRI service is used primarily by large organizations with intensive communications needs. An ISDN PRI connection supports 23 64 kbps B-channels and one 64 kbps D-channel (or **$23B + D$**) over a high speed DS1 (or $T - 1$) circuit. The European PRI configuration is slightly different, supporting $30B + D$.

BRI is the most common ISDN service for Internet access. A single BRI line can support up to three calls at the same time because it is comprised of three channels ($2B + D$). Two voice, fax or data conversations, and one packet switched data conversation can take place at the same time. Multiple channels or even multiple BRI lines can be combined into a single faster connection depending on the ISDN equipment you have. Channels can be combined as needed for a specific application (a large multimedia file transfer, for example), then broken down and reassembled into individual channels for different applications (normal voice or data transmissions).

BRI Applications

- ☐ Voice Transmissions
- ☐ Interactive Data Exchange
- ☐ LAN-to-LAN connections

- Bulk data transfer
- Interactive Video Conferencing
- Telecommuting
- Application shared devices and imagingElectronic Funds Transfer
- Electronic mail
- Facsimile
- Graphics
- Printing
- Retrieving or sending information from multiple databases

8.2.2 Use of ISDN

ISDN offers the speed and quality that previously was only available to people who bought expensive, point-to-point digital leased lines. Combined with its flexibility as a dial-up service, ISDN has become the service of choice for many communications applications. Popular ISDN applications include:

- Internet access.
- Telecommuting/remote access to corporate computing.
- Video conferencing.
- Small and home office data networking.

Why Should I Use ISDN to Access the Internet ?

More and more people are discovering that ISDN is the right Internet answer. As the Internet becomes more and more information-intensive with graphics, sound, video and multimedia, your ability to take advantage of these new resources depends on the speed of your Internet connection. With ISDN, your Internet access is:

- **Even faster** : By combining your two B-channels you have access to up to 128 kbps —more than four times as fast as a 28.8 kbps modem on a standard phone line. And ISDN's digital technology assures you the cleanest connection to the Internet so you won't be slowed down by re-transmissions because of old analog technology.
- **More efficient and economical** : ISDN brings increased capabilities, reduced costs and improved productivity to organizations both large and small. When you're looking for something on the Internet, you can get there faster. You can be more productive because you aren't waiting as long to get to that next website or download that large file.

ISDN Services

Two different groups of services are supported by ISDN: The bearer services and the teleservices. (See figure 8.11).

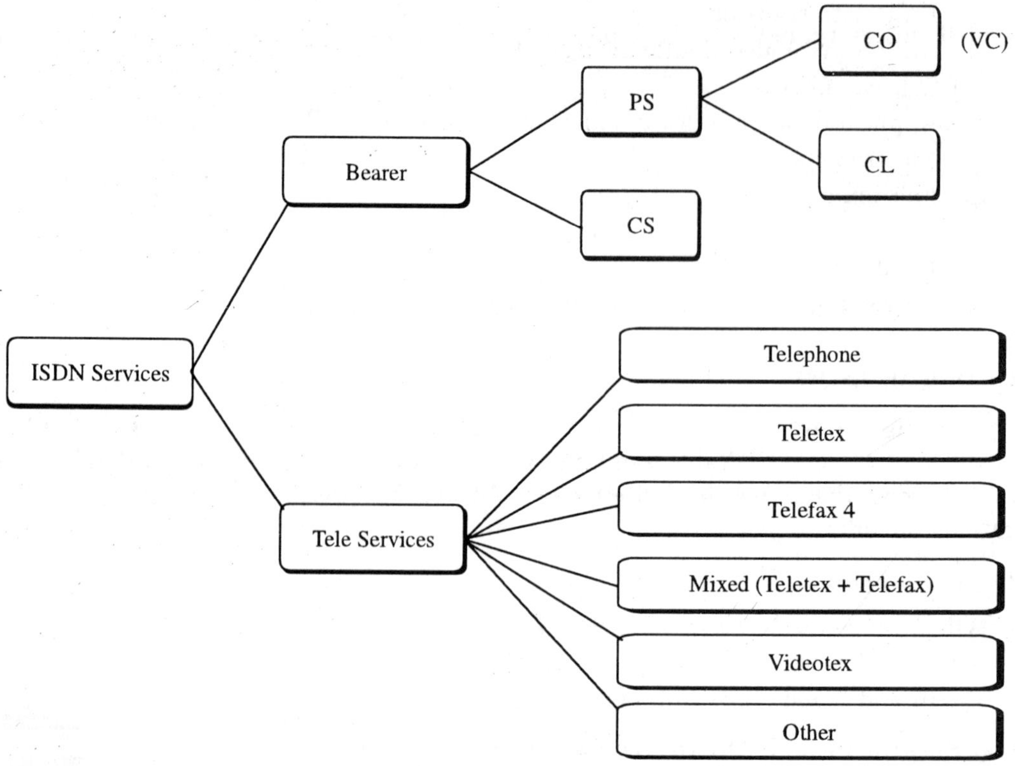

Fig. 8.11 Services of ISDN

Bearer Services

With ISDNs bearer services it is possible to transfer data between two subscribers. The network is acting in this case as a bit pipe. The bearer service can be divided into packet switching (PS), with both connection orientated (CO) and connectionless (CL) modes, and circuit switched connections.

ISDN Teleservices

- **Telephony** : This service enables subscribers to make phone calls using the ISDN. It is a considerable improvement to the (partially) analog telephone-system, as it offers a better signal-noise ratio and the attenuation is unaffected by distance.
- **Teletex** : Text transmission over ISDN is faster than the conventional teletex service over public data networks. It is possible to transmit a page (legal size or OSI A4) in less than 1 second. The connection with tele text terminals in other networks is supported. This includes circuit-switched as well as packet-switched networks.
- **Telefax (telefax 4)** : ISDN supports the pixel-orientated transmission of documents. CCITT has made recommendations for telefax4 and group 4 facsimile machines with a resolution of 300dpi and optionally 400dpi or 1200dpi. One page of legal size (or OSI A4) paper can be transmitted in 15 seconds when using the 400dpi resolution.

- **Still image transfer** : This service offers the possibility of transmitting TV freeze frames over ISDN. A still image sequence can be compressed and send with an update rate between 1 and 10 seconds, depending on the contents of the image.
- **Videophony** : Videophony is used to transmit moving pictures from person to person or person to group. Because of the relatively low transmission rate (64kbps or 2x64kbps) the quality of the video frames are inferior to TV frames (480x240 Pixel) and must be transmitted at a very high compression.
- **Alarm Services** : It is possible to make emergency calls over ISDN, even if the power supply on the user side breaks down and the *B*-channels cannot be used any more. An emergency call is made over the *D*-channel, which is then feeded by the provider.
- **Messaging** : This service provides a mailbox function for the user. Text and voice mail can be deposited in the mailbox, if the user is not available or both of his *B*-channels are busy. The recipient is sent a message from his mailbox over the *D*-Channel. He receives the notification even if his *B*-channels are used at that time.
- **Videotex** : Videotex is a retrieval service that enables the subscriber to view text and graphics based images.
- **Other services** : Some other services are: Telewriting for placing short messages (written with an electronic pen on note pad) in a mailbox. Teleaction is used for controlling installations like heating, gas, and water. Distribution services allow data transmission in a unidirectional way-but this service is much more interesting with the higher transmission rates of BISDN (video and TV transmission).

Benefits of ISDN

While ISDN accommodates telephones and fax machines, its most popular advantage is in computer applications. You can plug an ISDN adapter into a phone jack, like you would an analog modem, and get a much faster connection with no "line noise".

The most common ISDN service, Basic Rate Interface (BRI), provides two 64 Kbps channels per line. When the two channels are bonded in a single connection, you get a speed of 128 Kbps, which is about four times the actual top speed of the fastest analog modems. Compression can increase throughput to around 250 Kbps. ISDN affords many benefits to service providers and customers. The increasing popularity of ISDN allows pricing that continues to fall and compete with standard analog service. Some of the many benefits are:

Internet access is a great application for ISDN. Compared with even the fastest modem access, ISDN makes Web graphics appear almost immediately, and can reduce download times by over 75%. In many markets, it's actually cheaper than an isolated analog business line. Simultaneous audio, video, and data services over a single pair of copper wires reduces infrastructure and maintenance costs for service and subscribers.

ISDN BRI service can use data compression that boosts the 128 Kbps transmission rate to between 256 Kbps and 632 Kbps, depending upon the compression ratio used.

Digital transmissions produce clearer and quieter voice telephone service and more reliable and accurate connectivity than analog technology. Remote computer users benefit from high performance ISDN connections at home or on the road.

The various advantages of ISDN are discussed below:

1. Speed

The modem was a big breakthrough in computer communications. It allowed computers to communicate by converting their digital information into an analog signal to travel through the public phone network. There is an upper limit to the amount of information that an analog telephone line can hold. Currently, it is about 56 kb/s bidirectional. Commonly available modems have a maximum speed of 56 kb/s, but are limited by the quality of the analog connection and routinely go about 45–50 kb/s. Some phone lines do not support 56 kb/s connections at all.

ISDN allows multiple digital channels to be operated simultaneously through the same regular phone wiring used for analog lines. The change comes about when the telephone company's switches can support digital connections. Therefore, the same physical wiring can be used, but a digital signal, instead of an analog signal, is transmitted across the line. This scheme permits a much higher data transfer rate than analog lines. BRI ISDN supports an uncompressed data transfer speed of 128 kb/s, plus bandwidth for overhead and signaling. In addition, the latency, or the amount of time it takes for a communication to begin, on an ISDN line is typically about half that of an analog line. This improves response for interactive applications, such as games.

2. Multiple Devices

Previously, it was necessary to have a separate phone line for each device you wished to use simultaneously. For example, one line each was required for a telephone, fax, computer, bridge/router, and live video conference system. Transferring a file to someone while talking on the phone or seeing their live picture on a video screen would require several potentially expensive phone lines.

ISDN allows multiple devices to share a single line. It is possible to combine many different digital data sources and have the information routed to the proper destination. Since the line is digital, it is easier to keep the noise and interference out while combining these signals. ISDN technically refers to a specific set of digital services provided through a single, standard interface. Without ISDN, distinct interfaces are required instead.

3. Signaling

Instead of the phone company sending a ring voltage signal to ring the bell in your phone ("In-Band signal"), it sends a digital packet on a separate channel ("Out-of-Band signal"). The Out-of-Band signal does not disturb established connections, no bandwidth is taken from the data channels, and call setup time is very fast. For example, a V.90 or V.92 modem typically takes 30–60 seconds to establish a connection; an ISDN call setup usually takes less than 2 seconds.

The signaling also indicates who is calling, what type of call it is (data/voice), and what number was dialed. Available ISDN phone equipment is then capable of making intelligent decisions on how to direct the call.

Applications Of ISDN

ISDN in Business

For business users and even residential subscribers, videoconferencing is the biggest communication advancement that ISDN has to offer. With the simultaneous high-speed transfer of voice and video, ISDN can provide real time video communication on a PC that once was only capable on sophisticated systems costing upwards of $100,000.

A shared electronic chalkboard is another tool available through ISDN. Ideas and illustrations can be distributed in real time to remote locations so people in other cities or other countries can participate in meetings.

Telecommuting is becoming a rule more than an exception; more and more people are working from home. ISDN provides the facilities for users to tap into central network resources from the privacy of their own homes and do so with the functionality of a network node. Node connections are possible with Serial Line Interface Protocol (SLIP) and Point-to-Point Protocol (PPP).

ISDN in Education

Students will also reap the benefits of videoconferencing by relating with other students worldwide. Using the video capabilities of ISDN allows students to see the surroundings of other countries or speak with pen-pals. The value of videoconferencing in educational settings is unlimited.

Computers have become important learning tools for students. Children are introduced to computers and networking at an early age, and ISDN allows the high-speed connections to vast amounts of information and resources.

8.2.3 The Future of ISDN

There is and for years has been a global push to become a digital world. The main evidence of the digital age is the internetworking of computers, providing access to a wealth of resources and information.

ISDN technology, although plagued by political issues, is a cost-effective means to connect communication equipment of all types. As more of the compatibility issues are resolved, ISDN services will increasingly become the service of choice for businesses and residential customers. The rise in popularity should drive down equipment costs and make connection devices readily available off-the-shelf.

Although other digital services are competitive, most require expensive dedicated lines or possess inherent shortcomings like slow speed. ISDN technology is standardized and provides dynamic high-speed end-to-end digital connectivity over the existing worldwide telephone network.

ISDN continues to evolve with broadband ISDN availability in the near future. With ATM-based technology providing B-ISDN transmission speeds up to 600 Mbps or more, one would be hard-pressed to find a viable affordable alternative.

8.3 Broadband ISDN

The original specifications for the integrated services digital network (ISDN) were based around voice and non-voice telephone-type services: telephony, data, telex, facsimile, as it was hoped that the ISDN would evolve from the (then) emerging digital telephone networks. Indeed, this is one of the reasons that the fundamental element of an ISDN link is the 64Kb/s B-Channel. However, the planning for ISDN was started around 1976, and as technology evolved, so did the requirements of the users that wanted to use this technology. In 1988, the CCITT released a document that described a new set of **Broadband ISDN (B-ISDN)** services. To distinguish this new concept from the original ISDN service, we refer to the latter as **Narrowband ISDN (N-ISDN).**

Since then the CCITT has become the ITU. The B-ISDN work is far from complete, and some of the factors influencing the emergence of the B-ISDN from ITU are:

- **Demand** : Users (both commercial and residential) are showing interest in receiving high speed, reliable services.
- **Technology** : This has been one of the biggest factors. Advances in technology have increased demand, as well as the ability to supply it. As data processing technologies available to the user have become more sophisticated so has his/her demands, while high-speed transmission (based on the use of optical fibre), high speed switching and increased processing power make the realization of these demands possible.
- **Service integration** : There is a need to integrate both circuit switched and packet switched services into one network that can provide interactive and distribution services.
- **Flexibility** : The resulting network must be able to satisfy the needs of the users as well as the network operators in terms of its functionality and usability.

Broadband ISDN services

The need for a Broadband ISDN service sprung from the growing needs of the customers. The planned Broadband ISDN services can broadly be categorized as follows:

- **Interactive services** : These are services allowing information flow between two end users of the network, or between the user and the service provider. Such services can be subdivided:
    - **Conversational services** : These are basically end-to-end, real-time communications, between users or between a user and a service provider, e.g. telephone-like services. Indeed, B-ISDN will support N-ISDN type services. (Note also that the user-to-user signaling, user-to-network signaling, and inter-exchange signaling are also provided) Also the additional bandwidth offered will allow such services as video telephony, video conferencing and high volume, high-speed data transfer.
    - **Messaging services** : This differs from conversational services in that it is

mainly a store-and-forward type of service. Applications could include voice and video mail, as well as multi-media mail and traditional electronic mail.

- ☐ **Retrieval services :** This service provides access to (public) information stores, and information is sent to the user on demand only. This includes things like tele shopping, videotex services, still and moving pictures, tele software and entertainment.

- **Distribution services :** These are mainly broadcast services and are intended for mainly one way interaction from a service provider to a user:
  - ☐ **No user control of presentation :** This would be for instance, a TV broadcast, where the user can choose simply either to view or not. It is expected that cable TV companies will become interested in Broadband ISDN as a carrier for the high definition TV (HDTV) services that are foreseen for the future.
  - ☐ **User controlled presentation :** This would apply to broadcast information that the user can partially control, in that the user can decide which part of it he/she accesses, e.g., teletext and news retrieval services.

So we can say that the **B-ISDN needs to provide:**

- Broadband services.
- Narrowband services (for backwards compatibility).
- User-to-network signaling, to allow the B-ISDN user to initiate and control communication.
- Inter-exchange signaling within the network, to allow the network to provide and control resources as requested by the B-ISDN user or by another network exchange.
- User-to-user signaling, to allow B-ISDN users to send control, operation and maintenance information to each other.
- Management facilities for controlling and operating the network.

8.4 Asynchronous Transfer Mode (ATM)

To provide the new B-ISDN services, use of a technology called asynchronous transfer mode (ATM) is specified by ITU. Asynchronous Transfer Mode (ATM) has been accepted universally as the transfer mode of choice for Broadband Integrated Services Digital Networks (BISDN). ATM can handle any kind of information i.e. voice, data, image, text and video in an integrated manner. ATM provides good bandwidth flexibility and can be used efficiently from desktop computers to local area and wide area networks. ATM is a connection-oriented packet switching technique in which all packets are of fixed length i.e. 53 bytes (5 bytes for header and 48 bytes for information). No processing like error control is done on the information field of ATM cells inside the network and it is carried transparently in the network.

ATM meets the following objectives for BISDN networks:

1. Supports all existing services as well as emerging services in the future.
2. Utilizes network resources very efficiently.

3. Minimizes the switching complexity.
4. Minimizes the processing time at the intermediate nodes and supports very high transmission speeds.
5. Minimizes the number of buffers required at the intermediate nodes to bound the delay and the complexity of buffer management.
6. Guarantees performance requirements of existing and emerging applications.

8.4.1 Overview of ATM

Changes in the structure of the telecommunications industry and market conditions have brought new opportunities and challenges for network operators and public service providers. Networks that have been primarily focused on providing better voice services are evolving to meet new multimedia communications challenges and competitive pressures. Services based on asynchronous transfer mode (ATM) and synchronous digital hierarchy (SDH)/synchronous optical network (SONET) architectures provide the flexible infrastructure essential for success in this evolving market.

ATM, which was once envisioned as the technology of future public networks, is now a reality, with service providers around the world introducing and rolling out ATM and ATM-based services. The ability to exploit the benefits of ATM technology within the public network successfully will provide strategic competitive advantage to carriers and enterprises alike.

Definition

Asynchronous transfer mode (ATM) is a high-performance, cell-oriented switching and multiplexing technology that utilizes fixed-length packets to carry different types of traffic. ATM is a technology that will enable carriers to capitalize on a number of revenue opportunities through multiple ATM classes of services; high-speed local-area network (LAN) interconnection; voice, video, and future multimedia applications in business markets in the short term; and in community and residential markets in the longer term.

Asynchronous transfer mode (ATM) is a technology that has its history in the development of broadband ISDN in the 1970s and 1980s. Technically, it can be viewed as an evolution of packet switching. Like packet switching for data (e.g., X.25, frame relay), ATM integrates the multiplexing and switching functions, which is well suited for bursty traffic (in contrast to circuit switching), and allows communications between devices that operate at different speeds. Unlike packet switching, ATM is designed for high-performance multimedia networking. ATM technology has been implemented in a very broad range of networking devices:

- PC, workstation, and server network interface cards
- Switched-Ethernet and token-ring workgroup hubs
- Workgroup and campus ATM switches

- ATM enterprise network switches
- ATM multiplexers
- ATM—edge switches
- ATM—backbone switches

The term **asynchronous transfer mode** needs some explanation. The words **transfer mode** say that this technology is specific way of transmitting and switching through the network. The term **asynchronous** refers to the fact that the packets are transmitted using asynchronous techniques, and the two end-points need not have synchronized clocks. Also, the use and allocation of cells and their subsequent multiplexing and transmission through the network is determined in an asynchronous fashion, e.g. on demand, and is independent of the user. ATM will support both circuit switched and packet switched (sometimes referred to as **circuit mode** and **packet mode**, respectively) services.

ATM is also a capability that can be offered as an end-user service by service providers (as a basis for tariffed services) or as a networking infrastructure for these and other services. The most basic service building block is the ATM virtual circuit, which is an end-to-end connection that has defined end points and routes but does not have bandwidth dedicated to it. Bandwidth is allocated on demand by the network as users have traffic to transmit. ATM also defines various classes of service to meet a broad range of application needs.

8.4.2 ATM Technology

In ATM networks, all information is formatted into fixed-length cells consisting of 48 bytes (8 bits per byte) of payload and 5 bytes of cell header.

Header	Payload
5 bytes	48 bytes

Fig. 8.12 An ATM cell

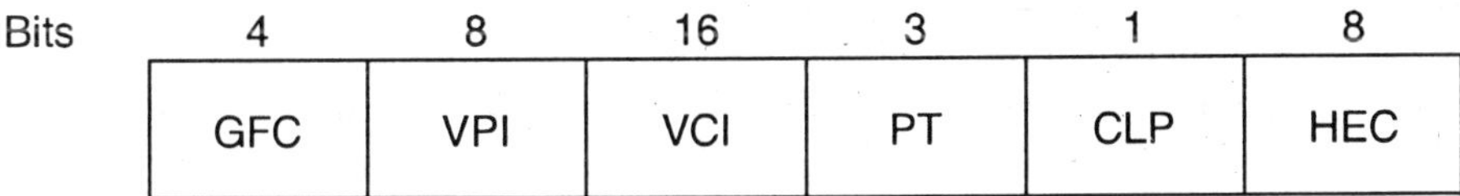

User-Network Interface (UNI)

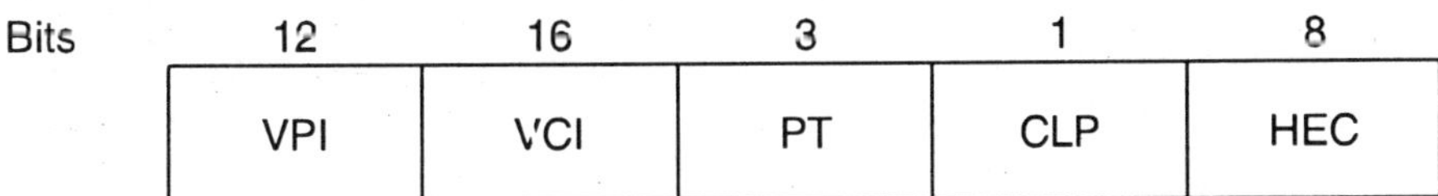

Network-Node Interface (NNI)

Fig. 8.13 Cell Header

The various fields of ATM Cell Header are discussed below:

- **GFC (Generic Flow Control)** : It permits transmissions of several terminals to be multiplexed on the same user interface—user to network traffic.
- **VPI/VCI (Virtual Path/Circuit Identifiers)** : This field contains 24/28 bits UNI/NNI. VPI field of 8 to 12 bits allows 256 to 4096 virtual paths each of 64,000 VCIs.
- **PT (Payload Type)** : It identifies payload type for OAM (Operations, Administration and Maintenance). Also reserved bits for explicit congestion control.
- **CLP (Cell Loss Priority)** : It is used for buffer management
    - If set (1) then the cell may be discarded according to network conditions - congestion control.
    - If not set (0) cell cannot be discarded.
- **HEC (Header Error Control)** : It is used to detect and correct errors in the header
    - Single bit error—correction is attempted
    - Multiple bit errors—cell discarded
    - Calculated using the polynomial $x^8 + x^2 + x + 1$

VPI / VCI

- ATM is connection oriented.
- Connections are identified by the Virtual Channel Identifier.
- A virtual channel is established at connection time and torn down at termination time.
- Multiple VCIs may be used for a multi-component service e.g. sound and video over separate VCIs in video-telephony.
- ATM switches perform switching on a per VCI basis.

The fixed cell size ensures that time-critical information such as voice or video is not adversely affected by long data frames or packets. The header is organized for efficient switching in high-speed hardware implementations and carries payload-type information, virtual-circuit identifiers, and header error check.

ATM is connection oriented. Organizing different streams of traffic in separate calls allows the user to specify the resources required and allows the network to allocate resources based on these needs. Multiplexing multiple streams of traffic on each physical facility (between the end user and the network or between network switches)—combined with the ability to send the streams to many different destinations—enables cost savings through a reduction in the number of interfaces and facilities required to construct a network.

ATM standards defined two types of ATM connections: virtual path connections (VPCs), which contain virtual channel connections (VCCs). **A virtual channel connection** (or virtual circuit) is the basic unit, which carries a single stream of cells, in order, from user to user. A collection of virtual circuits can be bundled together into a virtual path connection. **A virtual path connection** can be created from end-to-end across an ATM network. In this case, the ATM network does not route cells belonging to a particular virtual circuit. All cells belonging to a particular virtual path are routed the same way through the ATM network, thus resulting in faster recovery in case of major failures.

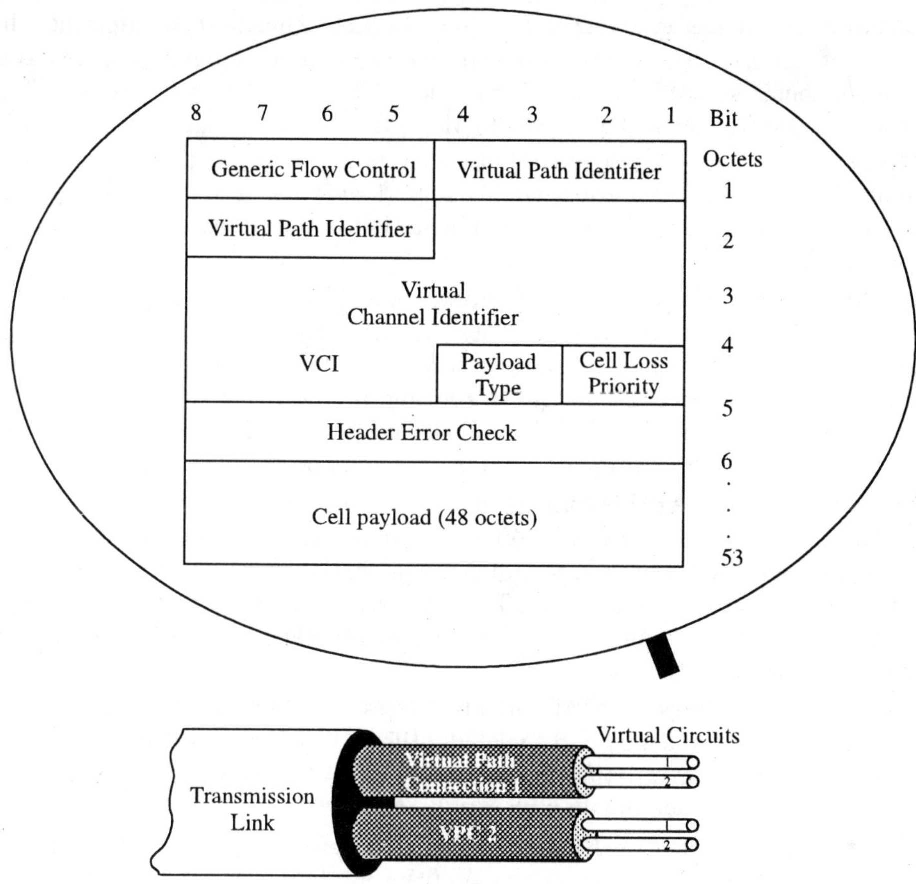

Fig. 8.14 Fixed-length cells

An ATM network also uses virtual paths internally for the purpose of bundling virtual circuits together between switches. Two ATM switches may have many different virtual channel connections between them, belonging to different users. These can be bundled by the two ATM switches into a virtual path connection. This can serve the purpose of a virtual trunk between the two switches. This virtual trunk can then be handled as a single entity by, perhaps, multiple intermediate virtual path cross connects between the two virtual circuit switches.

Virtual circuits can be statically configured as **permanent virtual circuits (PVCs)** or dynamically controlled via signaling as **switched virtual circuits (SVCs)**. They can also be point-to-point or point-to-multipoint, thus providing a rich set of service capabilities. SVCs are the preferred mode of operation because they can be dynamically established, thus minimizing reconfiguration complexity.

8.4.3 Basic Concepts in ATM

The basic concepts in ATM are discussed below:

- **Information Transfer :** ATM is a fast packet oriented transfer mode based on asynchronous time division multiplexing and it uses fixed length (53 bytes) cells. Each ATM cell consists of 48 bytes for information field and 5 bytes for header. The header is used to identify cells belonging to the same virtual channel and thus used in appropriate routing. Cell sequence integrity is preserved per virtual channel. ATM Adaptation layers (AAL) are used to support various services and provide service specific functions. This AAL specific information is contained in the information field of the ATM cell.
- **Routing :** ATM is a connection-oriented mode. The header values (i.e. VCI and VPI etc.) are assigned during the connection set up phase and translated when switched from one section to other. Signalling information is carried on a separate virtual channel than the user information. In routing, there are two types of connections i.e., Virtual channel connection (VCC) and Virtual path connection (VPC). A VPC is an aggregate of VCCs. Switching on cells is first done on the VPC and then on the VCC.
- **ATM Resources :** ATM is connection-oriented and the establishment of the connections includes the allocation of a VCI i.e. virtual channel identifier and/or VPI i.e. virtual path identifier and also includes the allocation of the required resources on the user access and inside the network. These resources, expressed in terms of throughput and quality of service, can be negotiated between user and network either before the call-set up or during the call.
- **ATM Cell Identifiers :** ATM cell identifiers, i.e. Virtual Path Identifier, Virtual Channel Identifier and Payload Type Identifier (PTI) are used to recognize an ATM cell on a physical transmission medium. VPI and VCI are same for cells belonging to the same virtual connection on a shared transmission medium.
- **Throughput :** Peak Cell Rate (PCR) can be defined as a Throughput parameter, which in turn is defined as the inverse of the minimum interarrival time. T between two consecutive basic events and T is the peak emission interval of the ATM connection. PCR applies to both constant bit rate (CBR) and variable bit rate (VBR) services for ATM connections. It is an upper bound of the cell rate of an ATM connection and there is another parameter sustainable cell rate (SCR) allows the ATM network to allocate resources more efficiently.
- **Quality Of Service :** Quality of Service (QoS) parameters includes cell loss, the delay and the delay variation incurred by the cells belonging to the connection in an ATM network. QoS parameters can be either specified explicitly by the user or implicitly associated with specific service requests. A limited number of specific QoS classes will be standardized in practice.
- **Usage Parameter Control :** In ATM, excessive reservation of resources by one user affects traffic for other users. So the throughput must be policed at the user-network interface by a Usage Parameter Control function in the network to ensure that the negotiated connection parameters per VCC or VPC between network and subscriber

is maintained by each other user. Traffic parameters describe the desired throughput and QoS in the contract. The traffic parameters are to be monitored in real time at the arrival of each cell. CCITT recommends a check of the peak cell rate (PCR) of the high priority cell flow (CLP = 0) and a check of the aggregate cell flow (CLP = 0 + 1), per virtual connection.

- **Flow Control :** In order to control the flow of traffic on ATM connections from a terminal to the network, a Generic Flow Control (GFC) mechanism is proposed by CCITT at the User to Network Interface (UNI). This function is supported by GFC field in the ATM cell header. Two sets of procedures are associated with the GFC field i.e., Uncontrolled Transmission which is for use in point-to-point configurations and Controlled Transmission which can be used in both point-to-point and shared medium configurations.

8.4.4 ATM Switching

ATM Switching is also known as fast packet switching. ATM switching node transports cells from the incoming links to outgoing links using the routing information contained in the cell header and information stored at each switching node using connection set-up procedure. Two functions at each switching node are performed by a connection set up procedure.

1. A unique connection identifier at the incoming link and the link identifier and a unique connection identifier at the outgoing link are defined for each connection.
2. Routing tables at each switching node are set up to provide an association between the incoming and outgoing links for each connection. VPI and VCI are the two connection identifiers used in ATM cells.

Thus the basic functions of an ATM switch can be stated as follows:

- Routing (space switching) that indicates how the information is internally routed from the inlet to outlet.
- Queueing that is used in solving contention problems if 2 or more logical channels contend for the same output.
- And final function is header translation that all cells, which have a header equal to some value *j* on incoming link, are switched to outlet and their header is translated to a value *k*. There are various switching networks existing and available from various manufacturers and research institutes for ATM switch architecture.

Performance Issues

There are 5 parameters that characterize the performance of **ATM** switching systems. They are discussed below:

1. **Throughput :** This can be defined as the rate at which the cells depart the switch measured in the number of cell departures per unit time. It mainly depends on the technology and dimensioning of the ATM switch. By choosing a proper topology of the switch, the throughput can be increased.

2. **Connection Blocking Probability** : Since ATM is connection oriented, there will be a logical connection between the logical inlet and outlet during the connection set up phase. Now the connection blocking probability is defined as the probability that there are not enough resources between inlet and outlet of the switch to assure the quality of all existing as well as new connection.
3. **Cell Loss Probability** : In ATM switches, when more cells than a queue in the switch can handle will compete for this queue, cells will be lost. This cell loss probability has to be kept within limits to ensure high reliability of the switch. In Internally Non-Blocking switches, cells can only be lost at their inlets/outlets. There is also possibility that ATM cells may be internally misrouted and they reach erroneously on another logical channel. This is called Cell Insertion Probability.
4. **Switching Delay** : This is the time to switch an ATM cell through the switch. The typical values of switching delay range between 10 and 1000Micro secs. This delay has two parts. 1.Fixed Switching Delay and it is because of internal cell transfer through the hardware. 2.Queueing delay and this is because of the cells queued up in the buffer of the switch to avoid the cell loss.
5. **Jitter on the Delay** : This is also called as Cell Delay Variation (CDV) and this is denoted as the probability that the delay of the switch will exceed a certain value. This is called a quantile.

8.4.5 Benefits of ATM

The high-level benefits delivered through ATM services deployed on ATM technology using international ATM standards can be summarized as follows:

- High performance via hardware switching with terabit switches on the horizon.
- Dynamic bandwidth for bursty traffic meeting application needs and delivering high utilization of networking resources; most applications are or can be viewed as inherently bursty; data applications are LAN-based and are very bursty, voice is bursty, as both parties are neither speaking at once nor all the time; video is bursty, as the amount of motion and required resolution varies over time.
- Class-of-service support for multimedia traffic allowing applications with varying throughput and latency requirements to be met on a single network.
- Scalability in speed and network size supporting link speeds of T1/E1 to OC-12 (622 Mbps) today and into the multi-Gbps range before the end of the decade; networks that scale to the size of the telephone network (i.e., as required for residential applications) are visualized.
- Common LAN/WAN architecture allowing ATM to be used consistently from one desktop to another; traditionally, LAN and WAN technologies have been very different, with implications for performance and interoperability.
- Opportunities for simplification via switched VC architecture; this is particularly for LAN-based traffic that today is connectionless in nature; the simplification possible through ATM VCs could be in areas such as billing, traffic management, security, and configuration management.

- International standards compliance in central-office and customer-premises environments allowing for multivendor operation.

ATM Applications

There are several practical applications using ATM Technology. ATM is going to be the Backbone Network for many broadband applications including Information SuperHighway. Some of the key applications can be mentioned as follows :

- Video Conferencing
- Desktop Conferencing
- Multimedia Communications
- ATM Over Satellite Communications
- Mobile Computing over ATM for Wire-less Networks

ATM technologies, standards, and services are being applied in a wide range of networking environments, as described briefly below (see Figure 8.15).

- **ATM services :** Service providers globally are introducing or already offering ATM services to their business users.
- **ATM workgroup and campus networks :** Enterprise users are deploying ATM campus networks based on the ATM LANE standards. Workgroup ATM is more of a niche market with the wide acceptance of switched-Ethernet desktop technologies.
- **ATM enterprise network consolidation :** A new class of product has evolved as an ATM multimedia network-consolidation vehicle. It is called an ATM enterprise network switch. A full-featured ATM ENS offers a broad range of in-building (e.g., voice, video, LAN, and ATM) and wide-area interfaces (e.g., leased line, circuit

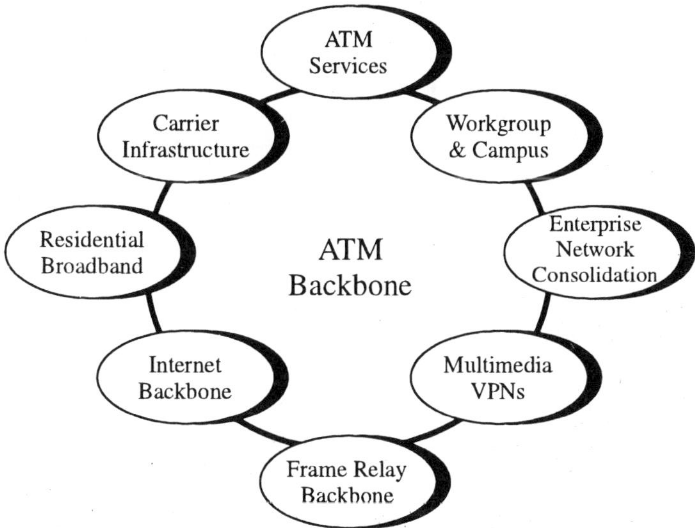

Fig. 8.15 ATM technologies standards and services

switched, frame relay, and ATM at narrowband and broadband speeds) and supports ATM switching, voice networking, frame-relay SVCs, and integrated multiprotocol routing.

- **Multimedia virtual private networks and managed services :** Service providers are building on their ATM networks to offer a broad range of services. Examples include managed ATM, LAN, voice and video services (these being provided on a per-application basis, typically including customer-located equipment and offered on an end-to-end basis), and full-service virtual private-networking capabilities (these including integrated multimedia access and network management).
- **Frame-relay backbones :** Frame-relay service providers are deploying ATM backbones to meet the rapid growth of their frame-relay services to use as a networking infrastructure for a range of data services and to enable frame relay to ATM service interworking services.
- **Internet backbones :** Internet service providers are likewise deploying ATM backbones to meet the rapid growth of their frame-relay services, to use as a networking infrastructure for a range of data services, and to enable Internet class-of-service offerings and virtual private intranet services.
- **Residential broadband networks :** ATM is the networking infrastructure of choice for carriers establishing residential broadband services, driven by the need for highly scalable solutions.
- **Carrier infrastructures for the telephone and private-line networks :** Some carriers have identified opportunities to make more-effective use of their SONET/SDH fiber infrastructures by building an ATM infrastructure to carry their telephony and private-line traffic.

• • •

9

Data Link Layer

Introduction

In this chapter we will study the design of layer 2, the data link layer (also known as the physical link control layer). The purpose of the data link layer is to transfer blocks of data without error between two adjacent devices. Adjacent devices are physically connected by a communication channel such as telephone lines, coaxial cables, optical fibres, or satellites. The implication of such a physical link is that the data bits are delivered in exactly the same order in which they are sent. The physical link has no inherent storage capacity; therefore the delay involved is the propagation delay over the link.

Transmission of data over the link would be very simple indeed if no error ever occurred. Unfortunately, this is not so in a real physical link for a number of reasons:

- Natural phenomena such as noises and interference are introduced into the link causing errors in detecting the data.
- There is a propagation delay in the link.
- There is a finite data processing time required by the transmitting and receiving stations.

A data link protocol thus has to be designed to ensure an error-free transmission and also to achieve an efficiency of the data transfer as high as possible. In this chapter we will discuss the services the datalink layer of the networking stack is required to have and the various existing layer 2 protocols, which cater to these requirements in different ways. The job of the datalink layer is to transfer the bits to the destination machine, which then can be handed over to the network layer for processing.

The datalink layer doesn't worry about getting bits on and off the medium. The design issues at this layer are the low-level concerns of communication: what about errors? What if the sender outstrips the receiver? How do we distinguish packets within a bit stream? How can we make the best use of the channel? What isn't considered at this layer is anything more than a single-hop away, i.e., no networking issues. All communication issues are point-to-point at this layer and the stream of bits is sequential.

One potential point of confusion when studying concepts like error and flow control: these issues arise in multiple layers, depending on the application, the medium, the design of the stack, etc.

Logical-Link

A Logical-link assumes that the sender is directly connected to the receiver.

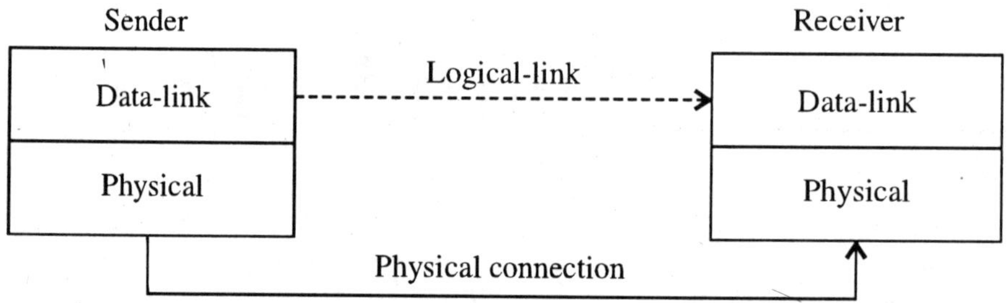

Fig. 9.1 Logical-link shown as dotted lines between sender and receiver

Actually the physical connection may go via any number of intermediate devices, including hubs and bridges.

9.1 Purpose of Data Link Layer

The goal of the data link layer is to provide reliable, efficient communication between adjacent machines connected by a single communication channel. Specifically:

1. Group the physical layer bit stream into units called frames. Note that frames are nothing more than "packets" or "messages". By convention, we'll use the term "frames" when discussing DLL packets.
2. Sender checksums the frame and sends checksum together with data. The checksum allows the receiver to determine when a frame has been damaged in transit.
3. Receiver recomputes the checksum and compares it with the received value. If they differ, an error has occurred and the frame is discarded.
4. Perhaps return a positive or negative acknowledgment to the sender. A positive acknowledgment indicate the frame was received without errors, while a negative acknowledgment indicates the opposite.
5. Flow control—Prevent a fast sender from overwhelming a slower receiver. For example, a supercomputer can easily generate data faster than a PC can consume it.
6. In general, provide service to the network layer. The network layer wants to be able

to send packets to its neighbors without worrying about the details of getting it there in one piece.

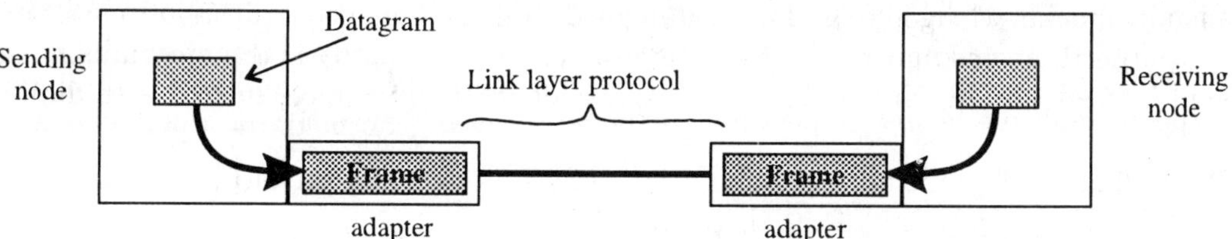

Fig. 9.2 Transmission of frames between sending receiving nodes

9.2 Design Issues

The datalink layer is designed to offer the following functionalities:

1. Services Provided to the Network Layer.
2. Framing.
3. Error Control.
4. Flow Control.

1. Services Provided to the Network Layer

Reliable delivery

Frames are delivered to the receiver reliably and in the same order as generated by the sender.

- The data link layer actually computes and verifies the checksum
- It maintain connection state which keeps track of frame orders and which frames require re-transmission.

Best effort

The receiver may not return acknowledgments to the sender, so the sender has no way of knowing if a frame has been successfully delivered. When would such a service be appropriate?

- When the error rate is very low and higher layer may be able to recover the errors by themselves, the data link layer doesn't have to provide the error recovery service.
- In some real-time applications requiring "better never than later" semantics. Old data may be worse than no data. For example, when a real-time speech is delivered over the network, later arrived speech clips are worse than simply dropping off a few of them.

Acknowledged Delivery

The receiver returns an acknowledgment frame to the sender indicating that a data frame was properly received. The sender keeps connection state, but may not necessarily retransmit unacknowledged frames. The receiver may receive frames out of order. The datalink layer in this case just hands the received frames to the higher layer and let the higher layer decide what to do.

Typically, each frame is assigned a unique sequence number, which the receiver returns in an acknowledgment frame to indicate which frame the ACK refers to. The sender must retransmit unacknowledged (e.g., lost or damaged) frames. One good question to ask here is : How does the receiver know that a frame is lost? (time-out usually is the mechanism used; if time-out is used, and buffers when the transfer is done, then we have to deal with duplicated frames)

Depending on the efficiency and error rate of the underlying physical layer, the datalink layer can be designed in any of the three ways:

(a) **Unacknowledged connectionless service**—This consists of the source host sending independent frames to the destination host without any sort of feedback/acknowledgment mechanism. Frame recovery due to line noise is left to the network layer. This kind of service is appropriate for high speed, low error communication channels such as an optical fiber network.

(b) **Acknowledged connectionless service**—Communication channels that are more error prone and hence require more reliable communication implement a feedback mechanism for each frame sent between two hosts. This enables the sender to know if the frame has arrived correctly or not. This ack sending mechanism is not a requirement but an optimization, because the transport layer can always send a message and wait for it to be acknowledged. However a message, (a unit of data in the transport layer), consists of several frames, (unit of data in the datalink layer), so the re-transmission of each faulty received message would bear a lot of overhead. Such a mechanism is useful on wireless channels that are inherently unreliable.

(c) **Acknowledged connection-oriented service**—This is the most sophisticated service the datalink layer can provide to the network layer. In this service the source and destination hosts establish a connection before any transfer of data takes place. Each frame is received in the same order it is sent in. The service also guarantees that each frame is received only once. Communication between two hosts takes place in three phases. First phase is connection setup, during which each side initializes counters and variables to keep track of frames. Second phase consists of actual frame transmission and the third phase consists of connection release, freeing up the resources

2. Framing

The physical layer deals with bit streams. Everything the datalink layer does is in the context of frames. Frames can be either bit or character oriented. The datalink layer receives a raw bit stream from the underlying physical layer. This bit stream is not guaranteed to be error free. On a noisy communication channel the received number of bits maybe less/more and/or different than the ones transmitted. In order to provide a reliable transfer to the network layer the data link layer breaks the bit stream into frames and computes the checksum for each frame. This checksum is also transmitted along with the frame. The destination host on receiving a frame computes another checksum from its data and compares it to the one transmitted. This enables the datalink layer of the destination host to detect and possibly correct frames, depending upon the method the checksum is computed in.

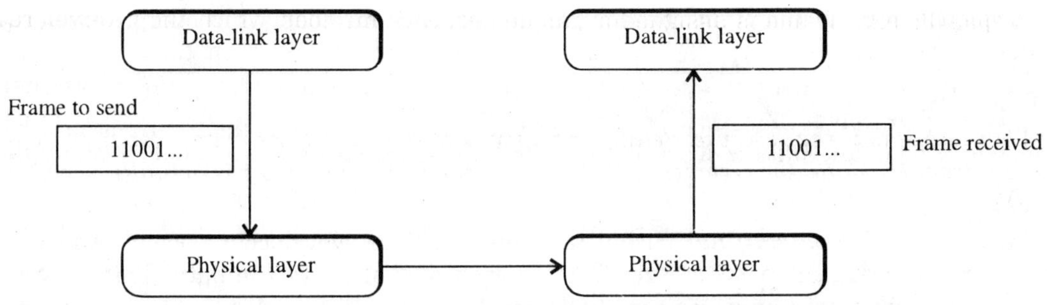

Fig. 9.3 Framing done at data link layer

A big question for the receiving datalink layer is how does it convert the stream of bits from the physical layer into a sequence of frames or packets? How can the receiver detect frame boundaries? That is, how can the receiver recognize the start and end of a frame? This issue is more complicated than it might seem. Some possible approaches are as follows:

(a) Length Count

Make the first field in the frame's header be the length of the frame. That way the receiver knows how big the current frame is and can determine where the next frame begins. Example:

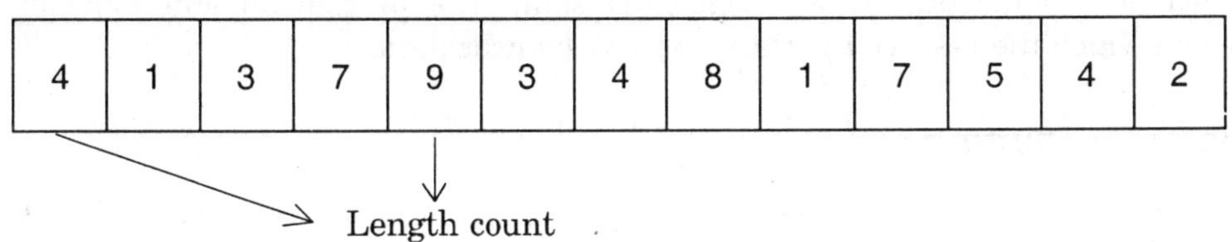

Disadvantage : Receiver loses synchronization when bits become garbled. If the bits in the count become corrupted during transmission, the receiver will think that the frame contains fewer (or more) bits than it actually does. Although checksum will detect the incorrect frames, the receiver will have difficulty resynchronizing to the start of a new frame. The above example is repeated with an error in length count.

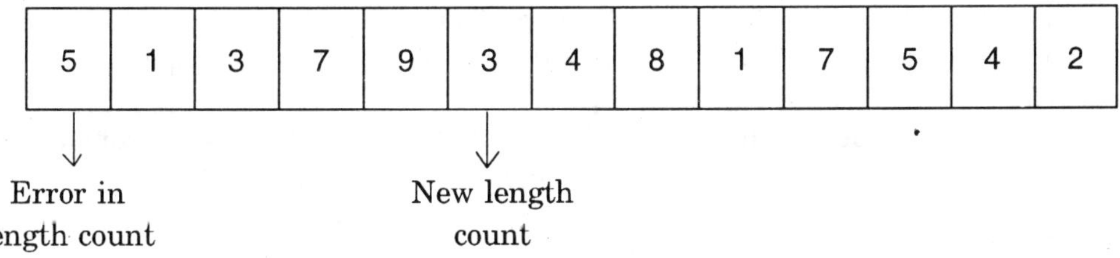

This technique is not used anymore, since better techniques are available.

(b) Bit Stuffing

It uses reserved bit patterns to indicate the start and end of a frame. For instance, use the

4-bit sequence of 0111 to delimit consecutive frames. A frame consists of everything between two delimiters.

■ Problem.

What happens if the reserved delimiter happens to appear in the frame itself? If we don't remove it from the data, the receiver will think that the incoming frame is actually two smaller frames!

Solution : Use bit *stuffing*. Within the frame, replace every occurrence of two consecutive 1's with 110. E.g., append a zero bit after each pair of 1's in the data. This prevents 3 consecutive 1's from ever appearing in the frame.

Likewise, the receiver converts two consecutive 1's followed by a 0 into two 1's, but recognizes the 0111 sequence as the end of the frame.

Example : The frame "1011101" would be transmitted over the physical layer as "0111101101010111".

Note : When using bit stuffing, locating the start/end of a frame is easy, even when frames are damaged. The receiver simply scans arriving data for the reserved patterns. Moreover, the receiver will resynchronize quickly with the sender as to where frames begin and end, even when bits in the frame get garbled.

The main **disadvantage** with bit stuffing is the insertion of additional bits into the data stream, wasting bandwidth. How much expansion? The precise amount depends on the frequency in which the reserved patterns appear as user data.

(c) Character Stuffing

It is based on the same idea as bit-stuffing, but operates on bytes instead of bits. It uses reserved characters to indicate the start and end of a frame. For instance, use the two-character sequence DLE STX (Data-Link Escape, Start of TeXt) to signal the beginning of a frame, and the sequence DLE ETX (End of TeXt) to flag the frame's end.

■ Problem.

What happens if the two-character sequence DLE ETX happens to appear in the frame itself?

Solution : Use character stuffing; within the frame, replace every occurrence of DLE with the two-character sequence DLE DLE. The receiver reverses the processes, replacing every occurrence of DLE DLE with a single DLE.

Example : If the frame contained "A B DLE D E DLE", the characters transmitted over the channel would be "DLE STX A B DLE DLE D E DLE DLE DLE ETX".

Disadvantage : Character is the smallest unit that can be operated on; not all architectures are byte oriented.

(d) Signal violations

The last technique is to use a signal for the start/stop frames that is normally not used to transmit data. This only works if there are such "illegal" signals in the coding scheme. For example, a Manchester code works like this:

The transition represents the data. Low-to-high is a 1, high-to-low a 0.

An illegal signal would then be a bit period where no transition takes place (i.e., high-high, or low-low)

The advantage of encoding violations is that no extra bandwidth is required as in bit-stuffing. Synchronization is another big advantage (as there is a always a transition)

The IEEE 802.4 standard uses this approach.

Finally, some systems use a combination of these techniques. IEEE 802.3, for instance, has both a length field and special frame start and frame end patterns.

3. Error Control

A bad communication channel can cause a variety of strange events during communication, like flipping of bits, losing bits from a frame, new bits in the frame, frames completely disappearing, either host going down.

Error control is concerned with ensuring that all frames are eventually delivered (possibly in order) to a destination. **Three items are required for it:**

Acknowledgements

The basic idea for error control is to provide a feedback channel from the receiver to the sender. This sort of feedback is known as acknowledgments, or ACKs.

Typically, reliable delivery is achieved using the "acknowledgments with retransmission" paradigm, whereby the receiver returns a special acknowledgment (ACK) frame to the sender indicating the correct receipt of a frame. In some systems, the receiver also returns a negative acknowledgment (NACK) for incorrectly-received frames. This is nothing more than a hint to the sender so that it can retransmit a frame right away without waiting for a timer to expire.

Timers

One problem that simple ACK/NACK schemes fail to address is recovering from a frame that is lost, and as a result, fails to solicit an ACK or NACK. What happens if an ACK or NACK becomes lost?

Retransmission timers are used to resend frames that don't produce an ACK. When sending a frame, schedule a timer to expire at some time after the ACK should have been returned. If the timer goes off, retransmit the frame.

Sequence Numbers

Retransmissions introduce the possibility of duplicate frames. To suppress duplicates, add sequence numbers to each frame, so that a receiver can distinguish between new frames and old copies.

This whole managing of timers and frame sequencing is an integral part of data link layer design.

4. Flow Control

It basically controls the rate of data transmission between two hosts. This is another of the important issues in the design of the data link layer, how to coordinate the rate of transmission between two hosts. What if the sender is sending data at a much faster rate than the receiver can process/accept, causing dropping of packets at the receiver end which further causes the sender to timeout on the ACK packets it is expecting, causing retransmission, leading to a less efficient network. The sender in such a case is usually throttled by using a feedback mechanism. There are various ways in which the receiver communicates to the sender using control frames about the number/rate of packets it can accept comfortably.

Usually, this is a dynamic process, as the receiving speed depends on such changing factors as the load, and availability of buffer space. One solution is to have the receiver extend credits to the sender. For each *credit*, the sender may send one frame. Thus, the receiver controls the transmission rate by handing out credits.

9.3 Error Detection And Correction

In data communication, line noise is a fact of life (e.g., signal attenuation, natural phenomenon such as lightning, and the telephone repairman). Moreover, noise usually occurs as bursts rather than independent, single bit errors. Data processing and transmission systems use a variety of techniques to detect and correct errors that occur, usually for any of the following reasons:

- Electrostatic interference from nearby machines or circuits.
- Attenuation of the signal caused by a resistance to current in a cable.
- Distortion due to inductance and capacitance.
- Loss in transmission due to leakages.

It has been estimated that an error occurs for every 1 in 200,000 bits. While most LAN technologies and optical cable networks reduce errors considerably, wireless networks and WAN links can have high error rates.

Types of errors

- **Bit errors** are errors that corrupt single bits of a transmission, turning a 1 into a 0, and vice versa. These errors are caused by power surges and other interferences.
- **Packet errors** occur when packets are lost or corrupted. Packet loss can occur during times of network congestion when buffers become full and network devices start discarding packets. Errors and packet loss also occur during network link failures.

Here we consider how to determine whether a logical unit of data has been received correctly (after either data transmission or storage), and if it is determined to be incorrect, how to attempt to correct it. Detecting and correcting errors requires **redundancy**—sending additional information along with the data. There are two types of attacks against errors:

- **Error correction strategy** : Send enough additional information to correct problems at the destination. This is called *FEC (forward error correction)*. The receiver is responsible for fixing errors, if possible.

- **Error detection strategy :** Send only enough extra information to detect an error, and then request a retransmission from the source. This is called *ARQ (automatic repeat request)*. In this case, both the sender and receiver may take part in retransmitting lost information. It uses ACKs and retransmissions to recover from the errors.

First we develop some terminology and mathematics needed to describe errors and then we give several methods of error detection and correction.

(a) **Hamming distance**—$H(a, b)$ = Number of bit positions in which 'a' differs from 'b', i.e., the number of 1's in a XOR b.

(b) **Forward error correction**—Enough redundancy is transmitted in the code that errors can be corrected by the receiver without retransmission (used when retransmission is impractical, as in distant space probes, simplex lines, broadcast media where many stations may have to listen to unnecessary retransmission).

(c) **Backward error correction**—Errors are detected and retransmission requested. (Most common, generally more efficient, but has the flaw that a single error, repeated in every retransmission, will mean that the message is never delivered).

9.3.1 Error Detection

Three possibilities in communication are:

- Frame is ok.
- Frame is bad and undetected.
- Frame is bad and detected.

Here the middle possibility should concern us.

Error Detection simply means that the receiver detects the fact that **some** errors exist in a received block.

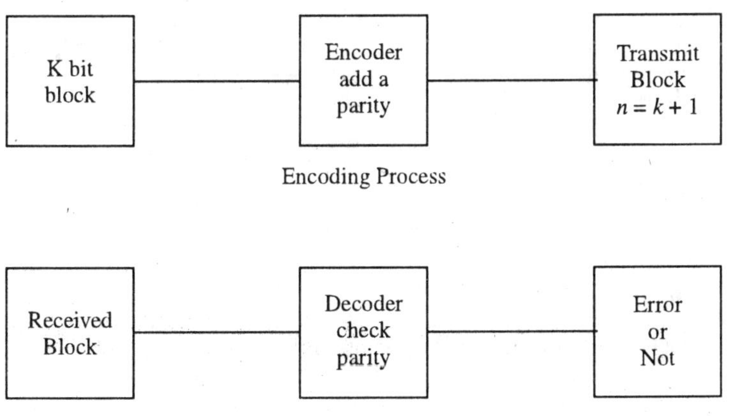

Fig. 9.4 Simple error detection scheme

This is typically achieved by adding redundant bits in each frame during its transmission. Based on all the bits in the frame (data + error check bits), the receiver may be able to detect errors in the frame. Then the sender retransmits that frame.

Principle of Error Detection

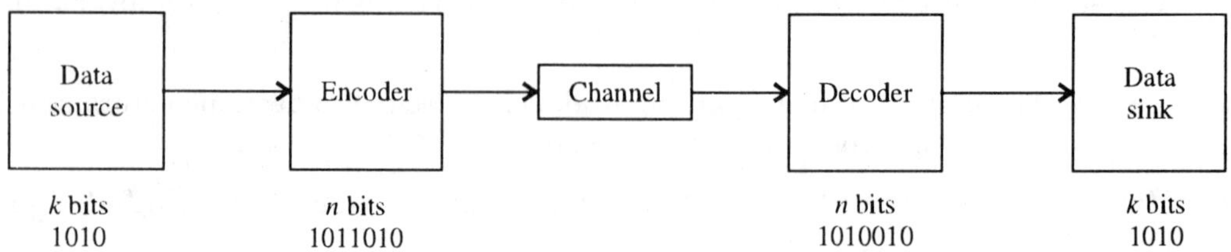

Fig. 9.5 Principle of error detection

- **Message (or Data) Source :** Source for information in bits (k-bits).
- **Encoding Process :** Process of converting a block of k-bit information to n-bit codeword, $n = k$.
- **Channel :** Medium in which n-bit codewords pass through.
- **Decoding Process :** Process of converting n bit received block to a k-bit message.
- **Message sink :** Destination for k-bit information in bits.

This principle is implemented in the following figure :

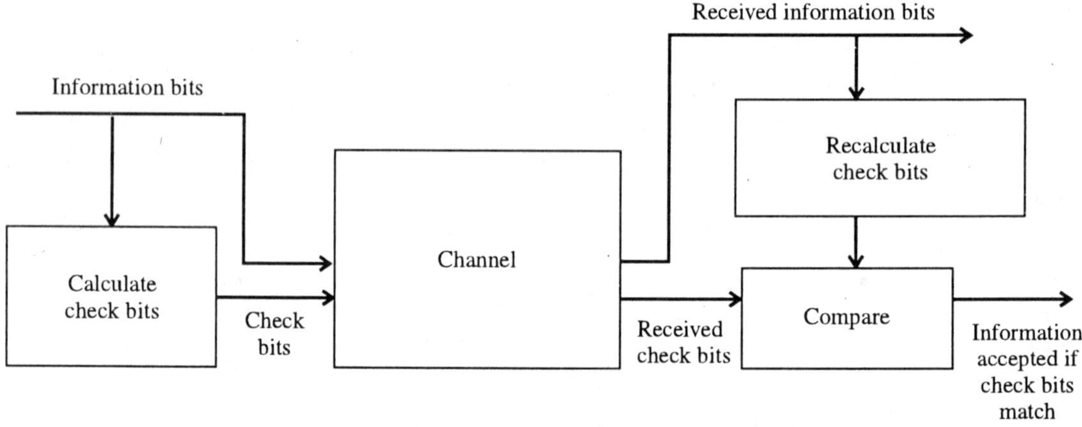

Fig. 9.6 Error detection scheme

Methods of Error Detection

The various error detection schemes available are listed below:

- Parity Check or Vertical Redundancy Check (VRC).
- Longitudinal Redundancy Check (LRC).

- Cyclical Redundancy Check (CRC).
- Checksum.

In this chapter we will discuss just the first two techniques.

1. Parity Check

This is the simplest error-detection mechanism. A parity bit (Redundant bit) is appended to a block of data, normally at the end of a 7-bit ASCII (American Standard Code for Information Interchange) character. Two techniques-even parity or odd parity-are available, and which method is used is up to the user. In **even parity**, a parity bit is selected so that the character has an even number of 1's. In odd parity, the parity bit is selected so that the character has an odd number of 1's.

For example, if even parity is selected and a computer receives a character with an odd number of 1's, it assumes an error and asks for a retransmission. Consider the following case:

Data to be sent : 1 1 0 1 1 0 1 1

Assume even parity generator : As the data contains even number of 1's so the parity bit is 0.

Block transmitted : Data bits 1 1 0 1 1 0 1 1 + Parity bit 0 → 1 1 0 1 1 0 1 1 0
Data received by the receiver : 1 1 0 0 1 0 1 1 0

The receiver counts the 1's and comes with odd number of 1s but there should be even number of 1,s so the receiver detects the corrupted data and asks for retransmission.

For small, non-critical data transmissions, this method is a reasonable tradeoff between reliability and efficiency. But it presents problems in cases where highly reliable data must be transmitted.

Limitation : The primary problem with using a single parity bit is that it cannot detect the presence of more than one transmission error. If two bits are incorrect, the parity can still be even and no error can be detected. So this method easily breaks down.

2. LRC

Longitudinal Redundancy Check scheme uses not only one parity bit per word (or row of the frame, considered now as a matrix), but also a "parity check character", comprising the entire last row of the matrix, with each bit in the row checking the parity of the corresponding column. The column parity bits form the last row and are called the LRC or the parity check character.

Consider the following example:

- There is a block of 16-bits to be transmitted.

  Data bits : 1 0 1 1 0 1 0 0 1 1 0 1 1 1 1 0

- Organize it in a table of two rows and eight columns:

  1 0 1 1 0 1 0 0
  1 1 0 1 1 1 1 0

- Calculate the parity bit for each column and create a new row of 8-bits that are the redundant or parity bits to be transmitted along with data.

```
          10110100
          11011110
          --------
LRC →     01101010    (Even Parity considered)
```

- Therefore, the data to be transmitted is Data bits + LRC

  1 0 1 1 0 1 0 0   1 1 0 1 1 1 1 0 + 01101010

- When the receiver receives the data it checks the LRC again and if some of the bits do not follow the even parity rule then the whole block is discarded.

Limitation : LRC will fail to detect errors that occur in an "even rectangular form", and other forms harder to describe as long as there are an even number of errors in each column and each row.

9.3.2 Error Correction

In the previous section we discussed error-detecting schemes. However, that kind of redundancy doesn't allow for the **correction** of the error. Error-correcting codes do exactly this: they add redundancy to the original message in such a way that it is possible for the receiver to detect the error and correct it, recovering the original message. This is crucial for certain applications where the re-sending of the message is not possible (for example, for interplanetary communications and storage of data). The crucial problem to be resolved then is how to add this redundancy in order to detect and correct errors in the most efficient way.

Error-correcting codes are particularly suited when the transmission channel is noisy. This is the case of wireless communication. Nowadays, all digital wireless communications use error-correcting codes.

Error correction is most useful in three contexts:

1. Simplex links (e.g., those that provide only one-way communication).
2. Long delay paths, where retransmitting data leads to long delays (e.g., satellites).
3. Links with very high error rates, where there is often one or two errors in each frame. Without forward error correction, most frames would be damaged, and retransmitting them would result in the frames becoming garbled again.

Rather than transmitting digital data in a raw bit for bit form, the data is encoded with extra bits at the source. The longer "code word" is then transmitted, and the receiver can decode it to retrieve the desired information. An error occurs when the receiver reads 1 as 0 or 0 as 1. To correct the error the receiver simply reverses the altered bit. So we are mainly to determine the position of bit where error has occurred. The hamming code discussed next, explains how to correct a single-bit error.

Hamming Code

In 1950, Richard Hamming developed an innovative way of adding bits to a number in such a way that transmission errors involving no more than a single bit could be detected and corrected.

The number of parity bits to be sent along with the data depends on the number of data bits. Some possible values are shown in table 9.1.

Data Bits :	4	8	16	32	64	128
Parity Bits :	3	4	5	6	7	8
Codeword :	7	12	21	38	71	136

Table 9.1

We can say that for N data bits, $(\log_2 N) + 1$ parity bits are required. In other words, for a data of size 2^n bits, $n + 1$ parity bits are embedded to form the codeword. It's interesting to note that doubling the number of data bits results in the addition of only 1 more data bit. Of course, the longer the codeword, and the greater the chance that more than error might occur.

Placing the Parity Bits

(From this point onward we will number the bits from left to right, beginning with 1. In other words, bit 1 is the most significant bit.)

The parity bit positions are powers of 2: {1, 2, 4, 8, 16, 32, ...}. All remaining positions hold data bits. Here is a table representing a 21-bit code word:

1	2	3	4	5	6	7	8	9	10	11	12	13	14	15	16	17	18	19	20	21
P	P		P				P								P					

The 16-bit data value 1000111100110101 would be stored as follows: (For 16-bit data there will 5 parity bits, so total bits in this codeword will be 21.)

1	2	3	4	5	6	7	8	9	10	11	12	13	14	15	16	17	18	19	20	21
P	P	1	P	0	0	0	P	1	1	1	1	0	0	1	P	1	0	1	0	1

Calculating Parity

For any data bit located in position N in the code word, the bit is checked by parity bits in different positions. The following table shows exactly which data bits are checked by each parity bit in a 21-bit code word:

Parity Bit	Checks the following Data Bits	Hint*
1	1, 3, 5, 7, 9, 11, 13, 15, 17, 19, 21	Use 1, skip 1, use 1, skip 1, ...
2	2, 3, 6, 7, 10, 11, 14, 15, 18, 19	Use 2, skip 2, use 2, skip 2, ...
4	4, 5, 6, 7, 12, 13, 14, 15, 20, 21	Use 4, skip 4, use 4, ...
8	8, 9, 10, 11, 12, 13, 14, 15	Use 8, skip 8, use 8, ...
16	16, 17, 18, 19, 20, 21	Use 16, skip 16, ...

Table 9.2

To see the logic behind building this table, look at the binary representation of each bit position. The p1 bit is calculated using all bit positions whose binary representation includes 1 in the right most position. This is explained below:

Binary representation of 1 is 0001. Then we will check for all values from 1 to 21 whose binary representations include 1 in right most position. You can verify that binary representations of all data bits in row 1 of table 9.2 include 1 in right most position.(3–0011, 5–0101, 7 -0111 and so on)

Similarly, the *p*2 bit calculated using bit positions with a 1 in second position and p4 bit calculated using bit positions with a 1 in third position and so on.

It is useful to view each row in this table as a bit group. As we will see later, error-correcting using the Hamming encoding method is based on the intersections between these groups, or sets, of bits.

Encoding a Data Value

Now it's time to put all of this information together and create a code word. We will use even parity for each bit group, which is an arbitrary decision. We might just as easily have decided to use odd parity.

For the first example, let's use the 8-bit data value 1 1 1 0 1 0 0 1, which will produce a 12-bit code word. Let's start by filling in the data bits:

1	2	3	4	5	6	7	8	9	10	11	12
P	P	1	P	1	1	0	P	1	0	0	1

Next, we begin calculating and inserting each of the parity bits.

P1 : To calculate the parity bit in position 1, we sum the bits in positions 3, 5, 7, 9 and 11 : $(1 + 1 + 0 + 1 + 0 = 3)$. This sum is odd (we are considering even parity), so parity bit should be assigned a value of 1. By doing this, we allow the parity to remain even:

1	2	3	4	5	6	7	8	9	10	11	12
1	P	1	P	1	1	0	P	1	0	0	1

P2 : To generate the parity bit in position 2, we sum the bits in positions 3, 6, 7, 10 and 11 : $(1 + 1 + 0 + 0 + 0 = 2)$. The sum is even, so we assign a value of 0 to parity bit 2. This produces even parity for the combined group of bits 2, 3, 6, 7, 10, and 11:

1	2	3	4	5	6	7	8	9	10	11	12
1	0	1	P	1	1	0	P	1	0	0	1

P4 : To generate the parity bit in position 4, we sum the bits in positions 5, 6, 7 and 12 : $(1 + 1 + 0 + 1 = 3)$. The sum is odd, so we set parity bit 4 to 1, making the parity even:

1	2	3	4	5	6	7	8	9	10	11	12
1	**0**	1	**1**	1	1	0	**P**	1	0	0	1

P8 : To generate the parity bit in position 8, we sum the bits in positions 9, 10, 11 and 12 : (1 + 0 + 0 + 1 = 2). This results in even parity, so we set parity bit 8 to zero, leaving the parity even:

1	2	3	4	5	6	7	8	9	10	11	12
1	**0**	1	**1**	1	1	0	**0**	1	0	0	1

All parity bits have been created, and the resulting code word is :

1 0 1 1 1 1 0 0 1 0 0 1

Detecting a Single Error

When a code word is received, the receiver must verify the correctness of the data. This is accomplished by counting the 1 bits in each bit group (mentioned earlier) and verifying that each has even parity. Recall that we arbitrarily decided to use even parity when creating code words. Here are the bit groups for a 12-bit code value:

Parity Bit	Bit Group
1	1, 3, 5, 7, 9, 11
2	2, 3, 6, 7, 10, 11
4	4, 5, 6, 7, 12
8	8, 9, 10, 11, 12

If one of these groups produces an odd number of bits, the receiver knows that a transmission error occurred. As long as only a single bit was altered, it can be corrected. The method can be best shown using concrete examples.

Example 1 : Suppose that the bit in position 4 was reversed, producing 101011001001. The receiver would detect an odd parity in the bit group associated with parity bit 4. After eliminating all bits from this group that also appear in other groups, the only remaining bit is bit 4. The receiver would toggle this bit, thus correcting the transmission error.

Example 2 : Suppose that bit 7 was reversed, producing 101111101001. The bit groups based on parity bits 1, 2, and 4 would have odd parity. The only bit that is shared by all three groups (the intersection of the three sets of bits) is bit 7, so again the error bit is identified:

Parity Bit	Bit Group
1	1, 3, 5, **7**, 9, 11
2	2, 3, 6, **7**, 10, 11
4	4, 5, 6, **7**, 12
8	8, 9, 10, 11, 12

Example 3 : Suppose that bit 6 was reversed, producing 101110001001. The groups based on parity bits 2 and 4 would have odd parity. Notice that two bits are shared by these two groups (their intersection): 6 and 7:

Parity Bit	Bit Group
1	1, 3, 5, 7, 9, 11
2	2, 3, **6**, **7**
4	4, 5, **6**, **7**, 12
8	8, 9, 10, 11, 12

But then, but 7 occurs in group 1, which has even parity. This leaves bit 6 as the only choice as the incorrect bit.

Alternate way of locating an error in a bit

The receiver takes the transmission and recalculates new values for $p1, p2, p4$ and $p8$ using the same sets of bits used by the sender plus the relevant parity (p) bit for each set. Then it assembles the new parity values into a binary number in order of p position:

$$(\mathbf{p8, p4, p2, p1})$$

Now consider the example 2 in which bit 7 is altered during transmission. Consider that the following data was transmitted with error in bit 7 .

1	2	3	4	5	6	**7**	8	9	10	11	12
1	0	1	1	1	1	**1**	0	1	0	0	1

Now using this data we will compute new values for $p1, p2, p4$ and $p8$.

p1 : 1 (Check bits 1, 3, 5, 7, 9, 11 and if odd take value as 1 else 0)
p2 : 1 (Check bits 2, 3, 6, 7, 10, 11 and if odd take value as 1 else 0)
p4 : 1 (Check bits 4, 5, 6, 7, 12 and if odd take value as 1 else 0)
p8 : 0 (Check bits 8, 9, 10, 11, 12 and if odd take value as 1 else 0)

Arranging this in order $(\mathbf{p8, p4, p2, p1})$ comes out to be 0111, which is binary representation for 7, and hence it gives the location of error. Once this bit is located, the receiver can reverse its value and correct the error.

Limitations of this scheme

- Can't correct multiple errors:

If two errors occur then this scheme could detect the presence of an error, but it would not be possible to correct the error. Consider, for example, that both bits 5 and 7 were incorrect. The bit groups based on parity bit 2 would have odd parity. Groups 1 and 4, on the other hand, would have even parity because bits 5 and 7 would counteract each other:

Parity Bit	Bit Group
1	1, 3, 5, 7
2	2, 3, 6, 7
4	4, 5, 6, 7

This would incorrectly lead us to the conclusion that bit 2 is the culprit, as it is the only bit that does not occur in groups 1 and 4. But toggling bit 2 would not fix the error—it would simply make it worse.

- Error correction is relatively expensive (computationally and in bandwidth). For example, 10 redundancy bits are required to correct 1 single-bit error in a 1000-bit message. Detection? In contrast, detecting a single bit error requires only a single-bit, no matter how large the message.

9.3.3 Burst Errors

Most of the techniques described do not handle burst errors well. LRC/VRC does reasonably well, since a burst no longer than word length will be detected by the LRC. In order to improve the performance of parity or Hamming codes in the presence of burst errors, we can buffer a frame of words, each with its own redundant bits, and then send out the bits of the frame column by column rather than by rows. If a burst is shorter than the number of rows in the frame, then each row will have one or fewer errors, and they will all be detected (or corrected). This is *interleaving* and may be done on the bit, byte, word or block level. Burst errors are distributed over the interleaved (time-division multiplexed) channels, so that if K channels are interleaved (i.e., an interleaving depth of K is used), then each channel suffers an error of length roughly $1/K$ of the original burst error. In this way, the LRC/VRC can detect bursts that are no longer than the number of rows in a column. LRC/VRC is a form of *concatenated coding*, another effective way to increase the power of error correction methods and resistance to burst errors.

9.4 Elementary Data Link Protocols

Before discussing elementary data link protocols we will have a brief introduction with the variables and procedures used in the implementation of data link protocols:

- **DLL Interaction with the Physical Layer**

- to_physical_layer to transmit frame.
- from_physical_layer to receive frame.

- **DLL Interaction with the Network Layer**
  - to_network_layer to pass packet upwards.
  - from_network_layer to get packet from network layer.

- **Wait-for-event (and event) :**
  This procedure only returns when something has happened, for example a frame arrives. Event says what happened (e.g., event = cksum_err).

- **Frame contents - kind, seq_no, ack, info**
  - First 3 contain control info and the last contains actual data.
  - Kind lets us know if frame contains only control information or if it contains control info. + data.
  - seq_no is used to number frames to differentiate them.
  - ack is used for acknowledgements.
  - info field of data frame contains a single packet. For a control frame info field is not used.

- **Packet and Frame:**
  - Network layer constructs a packet by taking a message from the transport layer and adds the network layer header to it.
  - Packet is then passed to DLL and put into the info field of the outgoing frame.
  - The destination DLL extracts the packet from the frame and sends packet to network layer (above it).

- Some more Procedures:
  - wait_for_event waits in a loop for events to occur. For example when a frame is sent by DLL, it starts a timer (in order to account for lost frames/replies). wait_for_event returns event = timeout.
  - to_network_layer, from_network_layer used to pass packets between network layer and DLL.
  - to_physical_layer, from_physical_layer used to pass frames between DLL and physical layer.
  - Frame number is counted from 0 - MAX_SEQ.

9.4.1 An Unrestricted Simplex Protocol/Utopia

In order to appreciate the step-by-step development of efficient and complex protocols such as SDLC, HDLC etc., we will begin with a simple but unrealistic protocol.

This is a simple data link protocol which makes certain assumptions that are far from true in the real world, but its sole purpose is to explain the working of the data link layer and then incrementally taking the assumptions off.

Assumption 1 : Data is transmitted in only one direction.
Assumption 2 : At both ends the network layers are always ready.
Assumption 3 : Infinite buffer size of the sender, receiver.
Assumption 4 : There is no error on the communication channel.
Assumption 5 : Processing time can be ignored.

It is also known as utopia because network layer processes incoming data infinitely quickly and there is an infinite amount of buffer space. The following two procedures are implemented in this protocol:

- **Sender** (runs in DLL of the source machine):
  - ☐ Go get something to send (buffer)
  - ☐ Copy it into info. field for transmission
  - ☐ Send information—do forever (in infinite loop)
- **Receiver** (runs in the DLL of the destination machine)
  - ☐ Frame arrival
  - ☐ Get the inbound frame
  - ☐ Pass data to host—do forever (in infinite loop)

Receiver processes frames as they are sent. There are no control fields. The channel is also assumed to be perfect.

Using state diagrams to represent protocols

The Utopia protocol can be represented using a state diagram for the sender and receiver.

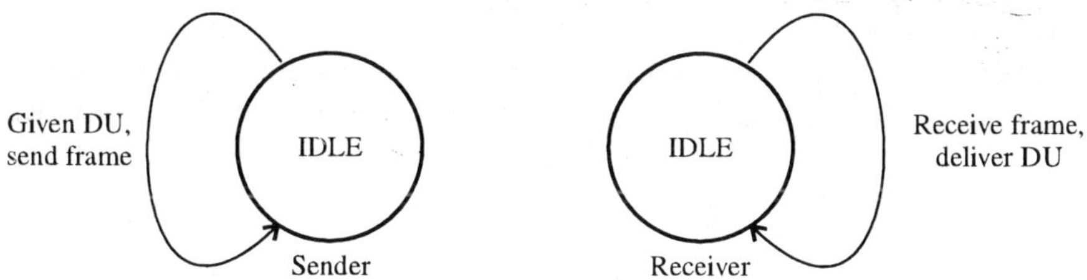

Fig. 9.7 State diagram for utopia protocol

About finite state machine diagrams

Finite state machines (FSM's) consist of states and arcs. The machine begins at a designated state. Arcs are directed arrows, each from a single state to another state (possibly the same one). Each arc has associated with it a list of conditions and actions. An arc is traversed, i.e., the machine may change state, if the conditions on the arc are met. When the arc is traversed the machine must perform the actions on the arc. It may not be feasible to use FSM's for all of the protocols that we describe.

The Utopia protocol provides a so-called best-effort service because it does the least amount of work to actually send the DU's (Data Units). In less than ideal circumstances Utopia may still be practical, e.g., when the probability of error is very small.

The summary of utopia is provided in the following table:

The Protocol:
• Sender collects message from network layer. • Prepares a frame buffer • Transfers to physical layer. • Receiver keeps waiting for frame arrival event. • On Event it collects frame from physical layer. • Transfers message to network Layer.
Analysis:
• Flow management is absent. • Works on a perfect channel only. • Unrealistic, thus little practical use.

9.4.2 Simplex Stop-and-Wait Protocol

Drop assumption that receiver can process incoming data infinitely fast. Stop-and-wait protocols are that where the sender sends one frame and then waits for acknowledgement. In this protocol, the contents of the acknowledgement frame are unimportant. Data transmission is one directional, but must have bidirectional line. It could have a half-duplex (one direction at a time) physical channel.

Consider sending frames from a fast machine to a slow machine. What happens if the slow machine is reading the data at half of the rate that the fast machine is sending it? Eventually

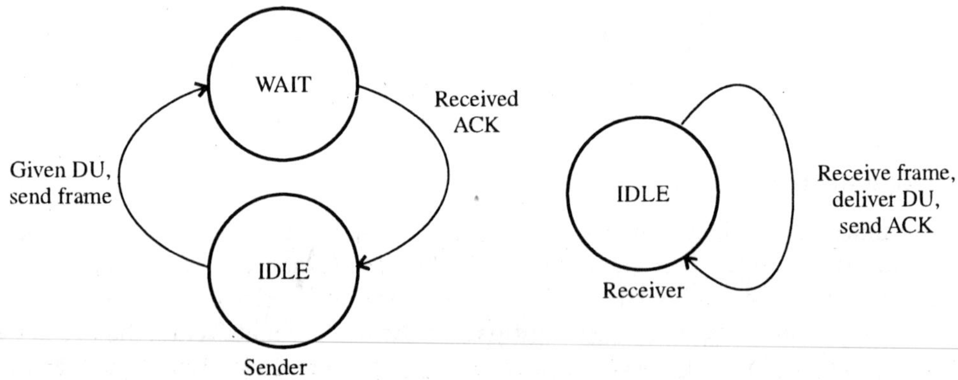

Fig. 9.8 State diagram for simplex stop-and-wait protocol

the sent data will be lost and never to be received. For this reason it is important to provide some kind of flow control.

The Stop-and-Wait protocol requires the receiver to send an acknowledgment PDU in return for every frame received. Such a PDU is often called an ACK. The sender will wait for the ACK before sending the next frame.

Time-lines

Time-lines are often used to demonstrate the operation of a protocol, e.g. the Stop-and-Wait protocol could be demonstrated as follows:

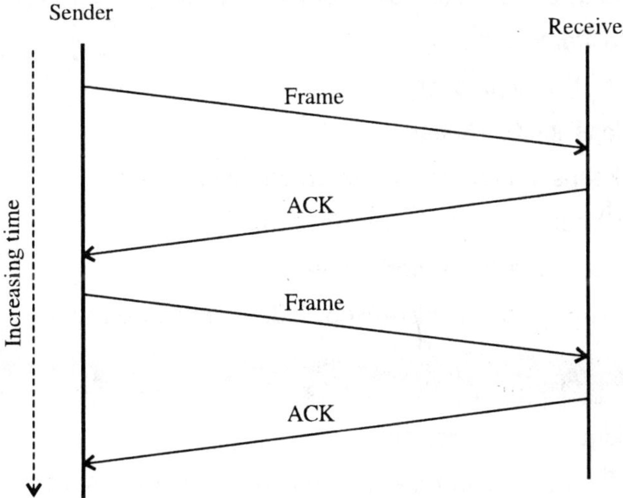

Fig. 9-9 Time-lines demonstrating stop-and-wait protocol

Properties of Stop-and-wait flow control

- Simplest form of flow control.
- Source entity transmits a frame.
- Destination entity sends back a signal to acknowledge receipt and to indicate that it can receive another frame.
- Source waits for acknowledgement before sending another frame.
- Destination can stop flow of data by withholding acknowledgement.
- Works well for sending a few large blocks.
- Preferable to send smaller blocks
  - ☐ Buffer size of receiver may be limited.
  - ☐ Shorter transmission time; damaged frame can be retransmitted in short time.
  - ☐ One station does not monopolize shared transmission medium (LAN) for extended time.
- Stop-and-wait not very good for multiple frames for a single message.

- Only one frame at a time can be in transit.
- If bit length of link is greater than frame length, we can have serious line deficiencies.
- Bit length is the number of bits on the link when stream of bits fully occupies the link.

The summary of Stop-and-Wait protocol is provided in the following table:

The Protocol:
• Sender Collects Message from Network layer. • Prepares a frame buffer. • Transfers to Physical layer. • Sender Waits for Go-Ahead. • Receiver keeps waiting for frame arrival event. • On Event it collects frame from physical layer. • Transfers message to network Layer. • Receiver Sends Go-Ahead (Acknowledgement) to Sender.
Analysis:
• Flow Management is possible. • Loss of ACK frame can repeat frame earlier sent by sender. • Receiver cannot detect repeated frame. • Channel on Other Side is required for returning the control frame. • Half-Duplex Physical channel can suffice as traffic at a time is only in one direction.

9.4.3 A Simplex Protocol for a Noisy Channel

Consider assumption 4 is no longer true; frames can be lost or damaged. But the receiver can detect damaged frames. This protocol suffer from a number of flaws—frames submitted out of order, duplication of frames, if an ack frame is lost the sender is kept waiting. Protocols in which the sender waits for an acknowledgment before sending the next frame are called **ARQ (Automatic Repeat Request) or PAR (Positive Ack with Retransmission).**

The protocols have a timeout for retransmission to deal with lost frames. This still does not solve the problem of duplication that requires for the frames to have sequence numbers.

Scenario of what could happen:

- A transmits frame one.
- B receives A1.
- B generates ACK.

- ACK is lost.
- A times out, retransmits.
- B gets duplicate copy (sending on to network layer).

To avoid duplicate frames, this protocol uses a sequence number. How many bits? 1-bit is sufficient because only concerned about two successive frames.

How long should the timer be? What if too long? (inefficient) What if too short? A problem because the ACK does not contain the sequence number of the frame which is being ACK'ed.

Scenario:

- A sends frame zero
- timeout of A
- resend frame A0
- B receives A0, ACKS
- B receives A0 again, ACKS again (does not accept)
- A gets A0 ACK, sends frame A1
- A1 gets lost
- A gets second A0 ACK, sends A2
- B gets A2 (rejects, not correct seq. number)
- will lose two packets before getting back on track (with A3,1)

This protocol differs from the previous two protocols in the respect that both sender and receiver have a variable whose value is remembered while the DLL is in the wait state.

Properties of Stop-and-Wait ARQ

- Very simple process.
- Based on stop-and-wait flow control technique.
- Source sends a frame and waits for ack.
- No other data frames are sent till receiver's ack is received.
- Error possibilities:
  1. *Frame damaged in transit*

     - ☐ Receiver detects damaged frame using error-detection techniques, and discards the frame.
     - ☐ No ack is sent to sender.
     - ☐ Sender retransmits after timeout expiration.
     - ☐ Sender must maintain a copy of what was sent till an ack is received.

  2. *Damaged ack*

     - ☐ Frame correctly received by receiver but ack damaged in transit.
     - ☐ Ack not recognized by sender who sends a second copy of same frame.
     - ☐ Receiver ends up with two copies of same frame.
     - ☐ Problem solved by labeling frames with 0 or 1.

The summary of ARQ is provided in the following table:

The Protocol:
• Sender Collects Message from Network layer. • Prepares a frame buffer with Info and Frame Sequence no. • Transfers to Physical layer. • Start a timer to time-out if ACK is not received. • Sender Waits for Next-Frame Event. • Receiver keeps waiting for frame arrival event. • On Event it collects frame from physical layer. • Check whether Frame Sequence is as expected. • Transfers message to network Layer. • Receiver Sends Go-Ahead (Acknowledgement) to Sender.
Analysis:
• Only Positive ACK is sent and timer controls retransmission. (PAR—positive ack with retransmission, ARQ—Automatic Repeat Request) • For a One to One ACK model 1 bit Frame Sequence number is sufficient. • May not be very efficient, as acknowledgement timer has to reset on every frame transaction. • Still a Half-Duplex Model.

9.5 Sliding Window Protocols

All the previously discussed protocols could possibly be used for a unidirectional data transfer; in the real world we need a bidirectional communication channel. One-way of doing this would be to have two separate channels, one for the data (forward) channel and one for its acknowledgments (reverse), but the reverse channel would almost be entirely wasted. A big improvement over this is using the same channel for transmitting data and control frames.

How do we achieve full duplex data transmission?

- **Possible solution**—Have two separate communication channels and use each one for simplex data traffic. **Disadvantage**—Bandwidth is almost entirely wasted.
- **Better solution**—Use the same circuit for data in both directions. By looking at the *kind* field in the header of an incoming frame, the receiver can tell whether the frame is data or ack.
- **Best solution—Piggybacking**—It is a technique of temporarily delaying outgoing acks so that they can be hooked onto the next outgoing data frame. **Advantage**—Better use of available channel bandwidth. Piggybacking introduces new problem. How long should the DLL wait for a packet onto which to piggyback the ack? Possible solution—If new packet arrives quickly, ack is piggybacked onto it. If no new packet has arrived by the end of a time period, DLL just sends separate ack frame.

Sliding Window Protocols assumes two-way communication (full duplex). It uses two types of frames:

1. Data.
2. Ack (sequence number of last correctly received frame).

To guarantee lossless delivery, a unique (increasing) sequence number (ID) is attached to every message. The combination of the message's sender address and its ID identifies every message uniquely. To overcome message loss, sender and receiver agree on some start ID. Now the IDs of messages received from a sender S always have to monotonically increase: if message 42 was received from S, the next message has to be 43. If a gap is detected, the receiver sends a retransmission request to the sender of the message. Upon receiving a retransmission request, the sender resends the message with the requested ID. Being able to resend old messages requires the senders to store recently sent messages for some time, usually until it is known that the receiver(s) has/have received all messages below a certain ID. In this case the messages below this ID may be deleted. When a receiver only sends retransmission requests when a gap is detected, the mechanism is called negative acknowledgment NAK. NAK is used in systems where message loss is infrequent, so NAKs would only rarely have to be used to retransmit lost messages.

When communication links are noisy and loss rate high, ACK schemes are preferred: a sender has to receive an acknowledgment from each receiver of a message. If ACKs are not received, the message is resent until an ACK has been received.

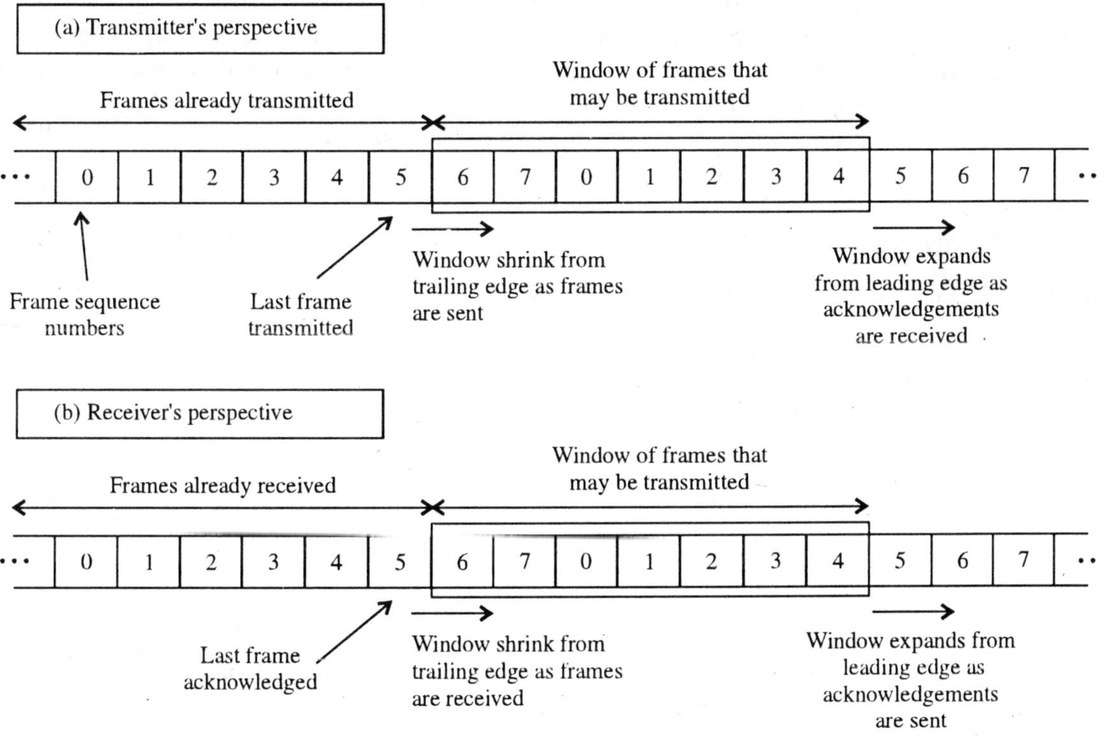

Fig. 9-10 Sliding windows

The idea of sliding windows is to keep track of the acknowledgements for each ID. However, a scheme in which a sender send a single message (e.g., to multiple receivers in a group) and then waits for all ACKs is too slow: a sender should be able to send a number of messages and a separate thread should receive ACKs, and resend messages with ACKs missing.

The senders and receivers each maintain a window of messages for which no ACKs have been received : **a window** is essentially a sequence of message IDs, starting with a low water mark and bounded by a high water mark. The sender keeps the value of expected acknowledgement; while the receiver keeps the value of expected receiving frame. Whenever an ACK is received, the low and high water marks are advanced by 1; this allows 1 more ACK to be received, therefore sliding the window 1 to the right. When the window is full, an ACK is either discarded, or some kind of flow control is used to throttle the sender until there is more space available. When the receiver receives the expected frame, it advances the window.

Sliding windows usually start out with a given size, however, more sophisticated protocols will dynamically adapt the window size, trying to find an agreed-upon size between sender and receiver.

The characteristics of sliding windows used at the sender and receiver usually involve:

(*a*) Error correction (by retransmission),

(*b*) Flow control

(*c*) Message ordering by sender (FIFO).

The latter property can easily be incorporated in a sliding window protocol, but sometimes, it is preferred to be implemented as a separate protocol for easier maintenance / replaceability.

Sliding window is used by most connection oriented network protocol, among others, the Point-to-Point protocol (PPP) which many people use to establish their home PC as temporary Internet node via a phone-line connection to an existing node. In fact, TCP also uses sliding window.

9.5.1 Parameters for a Sliding Window

Each sliding window uses three parameters:

1. The size of the window K,
2. The lower window edge LWE and
3. The upper window edge UWE.

Normally, K remains as a constant while LWE and UWE vary as frames are transmitted and acknowledged. Both the sender and receiver have their own set of parameters and their own interpretation.

Sender Window

- Sender maintains a list of consecutive sequence numbers corresponding to frames it is permitted to send. This list, termed the sending window, represents frames sent but not yet ack'd.

- When an ack arrives, the lower edge of the window is advanced to the corresponding sequence number, thereby allowing the sender to transmit new frames.

Note : When receiver sends an ack for frame 's', this is understood to mean that all frames up to and including 's' have been received.)

General example window for sender

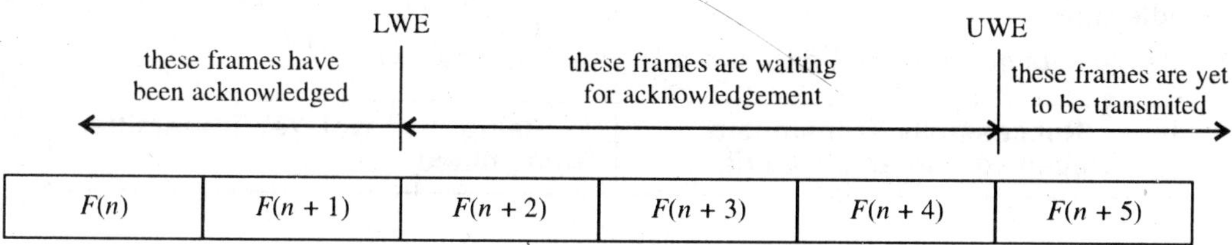

The **LWE** and **UWE** are initialized to 0. A frame can be transmitted by the sender if **UWE—LWE < K**. When a frame is transmitted **UWE** is incremented by 1. The **LWE** is incremented as ACK'S 's are received. In this way, there can be no more than **K** frames in the send buffer.

Receiver Window

- The receiver also maintains a receiving window, corresponding to the number of out-of-order frames it can accept. Frames falling outside the window are discarded without ack.

General example window for receiver

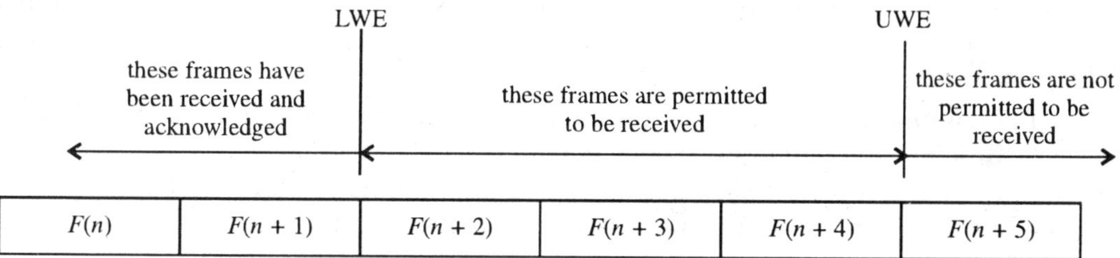

For the receiver, the semantics are slightly different. Frames within the window are those frames that are permitted to be received. Any other frames will be discarded. **LWE** can move forward any number of consecutive frames that have been acknowledged. Always **UWE = LWE + K**.

Properties of sliding window protocols:

- Used in TCP to make the transmission stream efficient
- Keep track of many acknowledged and un-acknowledged packets, instead of one at a time.
- Use network bandwidth better because they allow the sender to transmit multiple packets before waiting on each ACK.

- Transmit all packets in the window and slide it forward for each ACK received.
- Unacknowledged packets are constrained by the windows size (limited to a small fixed number).
- Sliding window performance depends upon the window size and speed in which the destination processes the packets.
- Well-tuned sliding window protocols keep the network saturated with packets (zero idle time).
- Three sets of sequenced packets in the sliding window:

Successfully Transmitted (Received and acknowledged)	Being Transmitted	Not Yet Transmitted

9.5.2 Stop-and-Wait—One Bit Sliding Window Protocol

One bit sliding window protocol is also called Stop-And-Wait protocol. In this protocol, the sender sends out one frame, waits for acknowledgment before sending next frame, thus the name Stop-And-Wait. This protocol requires little buffer space but provides poor line utilization.

Problem with Stop-And-Wait protocol is that it is very inefficient. At any one moment, only one frame is in transition. The sender will have to wait at least one round trip time before sending next. The waiting can be long for a slow network such as satellite link.

How to fix it?

1. We can use large frames;
2. Or we can use *pipelining* : allow multiple frames to be in transition simultaneously.

Pipelining

The idea of pipelining is to send frames continuously until some point in time, then the sender waits for ACK before sending more frames.

How many frames to send before waiting? The ideal situation is to fill in the "pipe" between the sender and the receiver, then the sender can continues receiving the ACKs from the receiver. This technology is called pipelining.

How to deal with the problem of errors? Two possible solutions exist.

1. Go Back n.
2. Selective Repeat.

9.5.3 Go-Back-n

What to do when a frame in the middle of a long stream is bad? Large number of succeeding frames may come to receiver before sender is told of error. On discovering error, a solution is go back n. Here receiver discards all subsequent frames (upto n) and sends no ack for the discarded frames. Eventually sender will retransmit all frames including lost/damaged one.

If there is one frame k missing, the receiver simply discards all subsequent frames $k + 1$,

$k + 2$, ..., sending no acknowledgments. So the sender will retransmit frames from k onwards. This can waste a lot of bandwidth if there is a high error rate.

The receiver detects receipt of an out-of-sequence frame and requests sender to retransmit all outstanding unACKd frames from the last correctly received frame. Or, the receiver sends a NAK to the primary when it first detects an out-of-sequence data frame. Thereafter the receiver discards all data frames until it receives the missing frame.

If an ACK is corrupted (say N and $N + 1$), then the sender will infer from receipt of the ACK for $N + 2$ that both N and $N + 1$ were received correctly, and will take the $N + 2$ ACK as sufficient for all three frames.

Since the receiver doesn't have to store frames out-of-sequence, it doesn't require much buffer space. Remember that it throws away the out-of-sequence frames it receives. Go-Back-N handles duplicate (lost ACKs) frames easily by simply discarding them. Selective-Retransmission can only know to discard a duplicate by maintaining a history list of received frames.

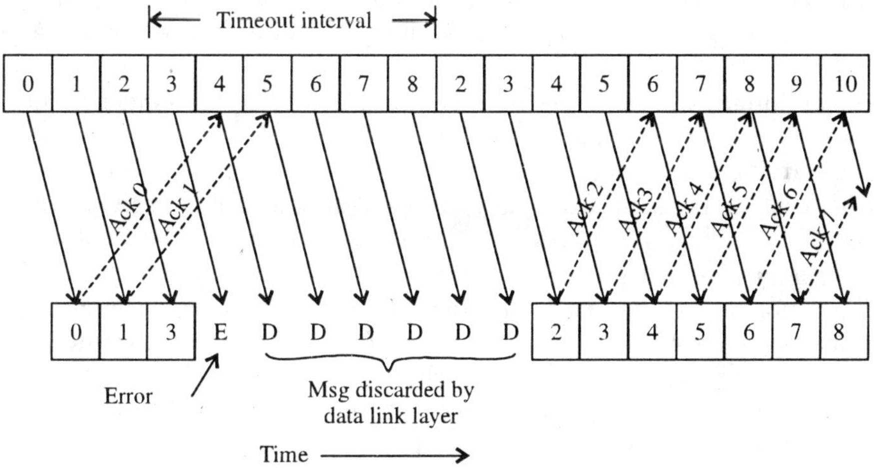

Fig. 9.11 Time line diagram for go back N

Most data communications is full duplex, i.e., you have as much bandwidth in one direction as you do in another. If you only use the reverse channel to send ACK/NAKs, then you will be wasting the bandwidth of the reverse channel (low utilization). One idea is to piggyback ACK/NAK traffic on the information frames that are flowing on the reverse channel.

Disadvantage of Go Back N

The error handling is not as efficient for Go Back N, since valid received frames are discarded.

Example : Look at an example with sender and receiver window size each equal to 4.

Now if 4 frames transmitted (seq nr 0–3), and sequence number 1 has an error. Subsequent frames 2–3 will also be discarded by receiver side. When Frame 1 times out, sender retransmits frame 1 as well as frames 2, 3. Upon reception, now the receiver can pass frames 1, 2 and 3 up to the network layer and update its receiver window.

9.5.4 Selective Repeat

Another strategy is to re-send only the ones that are actually lost or damaged. This protocol employs **the selective reject technique**. The protocol does not discard good frames because an earlier frame was damaged or lost provided that these good frames fall within the receiving window. Associated with each outstanding frame is a timer. When the timer goes off, (or when the transmitter is notified of any error), only that one frame is retransmitted, not all the outstanding frames, as in protocol go back *n*.

In this protocol, the receiver's window size is fixed, the maximum of which is (MaxSeq+1)/2. The maximum number is thus chosen to ensure that there will not be an overlapping between the new window and the previous window. The overlapping of windows means that the receiver would not be able to differentiate between a new frame and a retransmitted frame.

The receiver has a buffer reserved for each sequence number within its window. Whenever a frame arrives, its sequence number is checked to see if it falls within the receiver's window. If so, and if it has not already been received, it is accepted and stored regardless of whether or not it is the next frame expected by the host. Frames passed to the host must always be in order.

The receiver buffers all the frames after the lost one. When the sender finally noticed the problem (e.g., no ack for the lost frame is received within time-out limit), the sender retransmits the frame in question.

Example : Look at the same example as above with sender and receiver window size each equal to 4.

Now if 4 frames transmitted (seq nr 0-3), and sequence number 1 has an error. Frames 2-3 will *not* be ignored at receiver side, but they can be buffered. What happens when Frame 1 times out and is retransmitted? Upon reception, the receiver can pass frames 1, 2 and 3 up to the network layer and update its receiver window.

It can require large amounts of DLL memory if window is large. It works well if errors are rare, but if line is poor, wastes a lot of bandwidth on retransmitted frames.

Selective Repeat is more efficient than Go Back *n* in that

Selective repeat employs an auxiliary timer to prevent delay in piggybacking. If no reverse traffic has presented itself before the timer goes off, a separate acknowledgement is sent.

Whenever the receiver has reason to suspect that an error has occurred it sends a negative acknowledgement (NAK) frame back to the sender. Such a frame is a request for retransmission of the frame specified in the NAK.

9.6 Examples Of DLL Protocols

9.6.1 HDLC: High Level Data Link Control

Introduction

In this section we describe the International Standards Organization data link protocol HDLC (High-level Data Link Control). The HDLC protocol, an ISO data link layer protocol based on the IBM SDLC (Synchronous Data Link Control), is to ensure that data passed up to the next layer has been received exactly as transmitted (i.e., error free, without loss and in the correct order). Another important function of HDLC is flow control, which ensures that data is transmitted only as fast as the receiver can receive it). HDLC is a discipline for the management of information transfer over a data communication channel.

There are two distinct HDLC implementations: HDLC NRM (also known as SDLC) and HDLC Link Access Procedure Balanced (LAPB), the later is a more popular implementation. HDLC is usually used by X.25.

LAPB is a bit-oriented synchronous protocol that provides complete data transparency in a full-duplex point-to-point operation. It supports a peer-to-peer link in that neither end of the link plays the role of the permanent master station. HDLC NRM, on the other hand, has a permanent primary station with one or more secondary stations.

HDLC LAPB is a very efficient protocol, which requires a minimum of overhead to ensure flow control, error detection and recovery. If data is flowing in both directions (full duplex), the data frames themselves carry all the information required to ensure data integrity.

The concept of a frame window is used to send multiple frames before receiving confirmation that the first frame has been correctly received. This means that data can continue to flow in situations where there may be long "turn-around" time lags without stopping to wait for an acknowledgement. This kind of situation occurs, for instance in satellite communication.

Structure of HDLC

HDLC has a basic structure that governs the function and the use of control procedures. **The basic structure includes:**

- The definitions of primary and secondary station responsibilities.
- The design of information grouping for control and checking.
- The design of the format for transfer of information and control data.

Primary and secondary stations

A data link involves two or more participating stations. For control purposes one station on the link is designated a primary station, the others are secondary stations. The primary station is responsible for the organization of data flow and for the link level error recovery procedures.

A frame sent from a primary station is referred to as a command frame. A frame from a secondary to a primary is referred to as a response frame. Normally when a command is sent, a response or a string of responses is expected in reply.

On a point-to-point link either station could be the primary. On multidrop links and where polling is employed, the station that polls the other is the primary.

Frame structure

In HDLC the input data string to be transmitted over the link is broken up into data frames that are then transmitted sequentially. The input data string could be command, response or information.

1 byte	1-2 bytes	1 byte	variable	2 byte	1 byte
Flag	Address field	Control field	Information	FCS	Flag

Fig. 9.12 Frame format of HDLC

The header

Flag (01111110) : A frame is identified by this beginning flag F and contains only non-F bit patterns. HDLC uses bit-stuffing to achieve data transparency.

Address : Defines the address of the secondary station that is sending the frame or the destination of the frame sent by the primary station. It contains Service Access Point (6-bits), a Command/Response bit to indicate whether the frame relates to information frames (I-frames) being sent from the node or received by the node, and an address extension bit which is usually set to true to indicate that the address is of length one byte. When set to false it indicates an additional byte follows:

Extended address—HDLC provides another type of extension to the basic format. The address field may be extended to more than one byte by agreement between the involved parties.

Control Field : The control field contains information for controlling the link. It serves to identify the type of the frame. In addition, it includes sequence numbers, control features and error tracking according to the frame type. There are 3 types of frames:

I-frame

Information frame. This type of frame carries user's data.

S-frame

Supervisory frame : This is used for supervisory control functions such as acknowledgements, requesting transmission and requesting a temporary suspension of transmission.

U-frame

Unnumbered frame or Unsequenced frame: This is used to provide additional link control functions like:

- Have a variety of purposes, but most often used for establishing the link setup and disconnect.
- Sets up the data transfer mode, sequence number size. Also used to reset the link and other miscellaneous stuff

The Trailer

Frame Check Sequence : The FCS field contains a 16-bit Cyclic Redundancy Check

(CRC) error detecting code. The Frame Check Sequence (FCS) enables a high level of physical error control by allowing the integrity of the transmitted frame data to be checked.

Flag : This flag indicates the end of the frame. When this flag is detected the receiver examines the preceding two bytes and executes its error detection algorithm.

A flag may be followed by a frame, by another flag, or by an idle condition.

Data link channel states

Active channel state

A channel is in an ACTIVE state when the primary or a secondary is actively transmitting a frame, a single abort sequence or interframe time fill. In this state the right to continue transmission is reserved.

Abort : A station can abort a frame by transmitting at least seven contiguous ones. The receiving station will ignore the frame.

Interframe time fill : In this state continuous flag bytes are sent between frames.

Idle channel state : A channel is defined to be in an IDLE state when the transmission of 15 or more contiguous one bits is detected. In this state a primary must repoll a secondary before transmitting an I-frame to it.

9.6.2 Data Link Layer in the Internet

Two protocols used:

- SLIP—Serial Line IP
- PPP—Point-to-Point Protocol

9.6.2.1 SLIP- Serial Line IP

SLIP stands for Serial Line IP. While we will discuss IP in the network layer (because IP involves in routing), SLIP is used at datalink layer for serial line connection to the Internet. SLIP assembles frames by adding flag byte (character stuffing) to a raw IP packet. Some SLIP protocls just add the flag at the end; while others add at both front and rear.

The protocol was devised by Rick Adams in 1984. Some problems with SLIP:

- SLIP does not do any error detection or correction. It is upto the higher layers (transport layer) to accomplish this.
- SLIP supports only IP, so it won't talk to Novell and other protocols.
- In earlier version of SLIP, each side must know the other's IP address in advance. This limits the use of it.
- SLIP does not provide any form of authentication, neither party knows whom it is really talking to.
- Not an approved standard, many versions exist.

9.6.2.2 PPP—Point-to-Point Protocol

To overcome the problems in SLIP, the Internet Engineering Task Force (IETF) set up a group to develop PPP. PPP is a multiprotocol framing mechanism.

- It is suitable for use over modems, HDLC bit-serial lines, SONET and other physical layers.
- It supports error detection, option negotiation, header compression, and optionally reliable transmission using HDLC framing.

The datalink layer for the TCP/IP protocol stack is part of the ill-defined bottom "host to network" layer that also includes the physical layer. The current Internet standard for a data link protocol is PPP (Point-to-Point Protocol).

PPP consists of LCP (link control protocol) for bringing lines up and down, negotiating features like compression, etc. and NCP (network control protocol) which allows for different sorts of network layers (and thus makes PPP capable of being used for more than just IP).

PPP also supports authentication and the dynamic assignment of a network layer address, as well as the option to provide reliable service via sequence numbering of frames. PPP uses character stuffing to avoid problems with the flag showing up in the data field.

It can be used for dial-up and leased router-router lines. It provides:

1. Framing method to delineate frames. Also handles error detection.
2. Link Control Protocol (LCP) for bringing lines up, negotiation of options, bringing them down. These are distinct PPP packets.
3. Network Control Protocol (NCP) for negotiating network layer options.

Dial-up scenario

1. PC user initiates connection to ISP router, modems synchronize and negotiate, channel is established.
2. LCP packets are sent via PPP frames to router and negotiation of link parameters is done.
3. NCP packets are sent; dynamically assigned IP address is returned from router.
4. PC now a part of Internet, higher-level Internet protocols will work (FTP, HTTP, TELNET, etc).
5. User is done with connection.
6. NCP tears down the network connection, freeing the assigned IP address for re-use.
7. LCP tears down the data link connection.
8. Modem is told to hang-up.

PPP frame format

The PPP frame is character oriented (8-bytes per character).

Flag	Address	Control	Protocol	Payload	Checksum	Flag
1 byte	1	1	1 or 2	Variable	2 or 4	1
01111110	11111111	00000011				0 1111110
Identifies the start of the frame; character stuffing used for this value in payload	There are no addresses, always all 1s; assumed point-to-point	This value indicates an unnumbered frame; sequence number could be used over noisy medium	Tells what the payload contains (LCP, NCP, IP, IPX, Appletalk, etc)	Negotiated max by LCP, usually 1500 bytes	Size is negotiated	Marks end of frame

Fig. 9.13 Frame format of PPP

LCP includes the ability to negotiate away some of the fields (like address and control) which aren't used in most cases. Authentication takes place and must be successful before the NCP even begins.

The strength of PPP is that it supports multiple network protocols, and can be used harmoniously with various physical mediums, including PSTN/modems and SONET.

• • •

10

Multiple Access Protocols

Introduction

In the IEEE 802 protocols for shared multi-access LANs, the data link layer is divided into two sublayers:

1. LLC (Logical Link Control) layer
2. MAC (Media Access Control) layer

The upper LLC layer provides a way to address a station on LAN and exchange information with it. The lower MAC layer provides the interface between the LLC and the particular network medium that is in use (Ethernet, token ring, and so on).

In general, the **Media Access Control** topics are about **sharing** and **connecting** to a

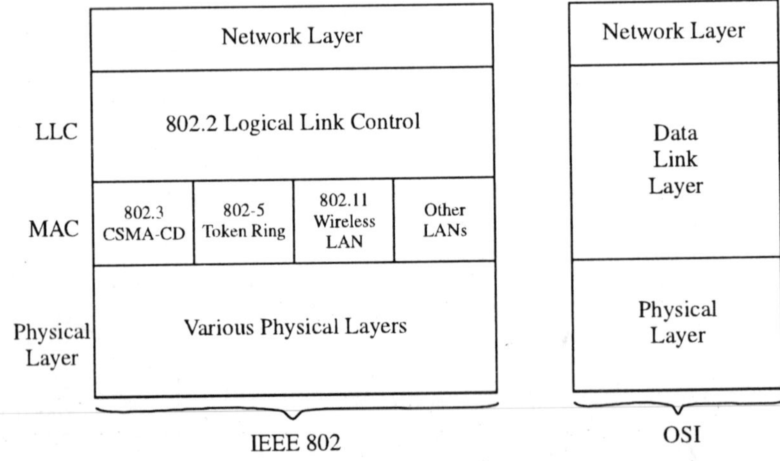

Fig. 10.1 IEEE standards mapped to the OSI model

medium. The **Logical Link Control** topics are about **setting up** and **maintaining** the connections for transmitting frames. (Already discussed in chapter 9). The MAC sublayer regulates the access to the channel shared by the nodes on a LAN. The LLC sublayer supervises the packet links between nodes, and presents a uniform interface to the network layer.

MAC involves controlling, which workstations can talk when. Easy part of layer – MAC is when a single wire directly connects two computers. More interesting part is when a number of workstations on a LAN share a single common wire or channel for communication; only one can use it at a time

"Garble" results when two workstations try to transmit at the same time. The goal of this layer is to maximize use of the channel & minimize waiting time for a workstation that wants to send.

FDM may work for wireless LANs or on some cables; TDM can be used in some cases; generally, they don't work well because computer communications are inherently bursty. The result is often that lots of channel capacity is wasted.

The MAC layer frames data for transmission over the network, and then passes the frame to the physical layer interface where it is transmitted as a stream of bits. Framing packages information into distinct units that are transmitted one at a time on the network. If a frame is corrupted during transmission, only it needs to be resent-not the entire transmission.

Individual LAN addresses are defined in the MAC layer. The MAC sublayer carries the physical address of each device on the network. This address is more commonly called a device's MAC address. The MAC address is a 48-bit address that's encoded on each network device by its manufacturer. It's the MAC address that the Physical layer uses to move data between nodes of the network. Workstations on the same LAN use the MAC address to forward packets to one another. When LANs are connected in an internetwork, higher-level addressing schemes such as IP (Internet Protocol) identify networks and nodes across the internetwork.

Assumptions about the LAN Environment

1. Network consists of N independent workstations, each generating FRAMES (sometimes called PACKETS) for transmission. For ease of analysis, we assume that all frames are the same size. (They don't have to be in real life, but it makes the analysis easier.)
2. There is only a single channel available for communication. All workstations can transmit on it, and all workstations can listen to it for frames addressed to them.
3. If two frames are transmitted simultaneously, they overlap and resulting signal is garbled. No errors on the communications channel other than from collisions between two or more frames.
4. There is an agreed-upon time rule for frame transmission. Either everybody is using continuous time (you can start whenever you are ready), or everybody is using slotted time (you can start transmitting only at the beginning of a predefined "slot").
5. There is an agreed-upon rule for carrier sense. Either all workstations are listing to the channel to see if it is in use, or nobody is.

The two entities of interest are as follows:

- **"Delay under light loading conditions"**—How long do I have to wait to transmit if I am ready and nobody else is?
- **"Channel utilization under heavy loading"**—When all work stations want to transmit data, how much of the time is the channel using to transmit data, and how much of the time is wasted for one reason or another?

10.1 Channel Allocation

The allocation of the channel can be done statically or dynamically. Static allocation is used in the telephone industry where the needs for the different stations (in this case telephone sets) are always the same. Thus it makes sense to split the available bandwidth and assign a fixed portion to each user. This strategy doesn't work for computer networks where the traffic is very busy. Thus in computer networks the channel allocation is done dynamically to adapt to the rapidly changing traffic.

Access Methods

Local area networks (LANs) are typically shared by a number of attached systems, and only one system at a time may use the network cable to transmit data. An access method defines how a system gains access to a shared network in a cooperative way so its transmissions do not interfere with the transmissions of other systems. Simultaneous access to the cable is either prevented by using a token-passing method or controlled with a carrier sensing and collision detection method.

Media Access is accomplished in three general ways:

- Contention—all devices send when they wish.
- Token-passing—devices send when it is their turn.
- Polling—devices are asked if they have anything to send.

Contention systems work by letting each device try to send a message on the net as needed, contending or competing with all the other devices for the bandwidth. Contention based access controls can work well for bursty traffic. They are asynchronous, distributed, random-access control techniques, simple to implement, and are generally efficient unless the network load is very high. The basic idea is to allow any node that wishes to do so, at any time, to transmit a frame. If it is successful in getting its frame through without interference from another node's transmission during its frame duration, then everything is fine. Otherwise, there is a mechanism for re-transmitting frames. The protocols that support such systems are known also as **Random Access Protocols.**

Two examples of protocols that support such systems are:

- **CSMA/CD** (Carrier Sense, Multiple Access, with Collision Detection)
- **CSMA/CA** (Carrier Sense, Multiple Access, with Collision Avoidance)

A **collision** occurs when two signal collide on the medium, causing signal loss. These are bursty protocols, best supporting intermittent transmissions. Only about 60 to 70 users can be supported on a segment. Time sensitivity is good, as users do not often have to wait for media access.

- **CSMA/CD (Carrier Sense Multiple Access/Collision Detection) :** Carrier sensing implies that network nodes listen for a carrier tone on the cable and send information when other devices are not transmitting. Multiple access means that many devices share the same cable. If two or more devices sense that the network is idle, they will attempt to access it simultaneously (contention), causing collisions. Each station must then back off and wait a certain amount of time before attempting to retransmit. Contention may be reduced by dividing networks with bridges or using switches. This is used by Ethernet.
- **CSMA/CA (Carrier Sense Multiple Access/Collision Avoidance) :** This access method is a variation on the CSMA/CD method. Nodes estimate when a collision might occur and avoid transmission during that period. This method is cheaper to implement, since collision detection circuitry is not required; however, it imposes more delay and can slow network throughput. In a CSMA/CA system, devices can be assigned time slices or can be required to ask permission to send, avoiding collisions. Apple LocalTalk is as an example of this.

Token Passing involves passing a token, a small data frame, from station to station. When a station has the token, it is that station's turn to access the medium. Examples of this method are:

- Token ring.
- FDDI.
- Token bus.

This type of media access is predictable and consistent, allowing large or small transmissions. It is not the best for time sensitive data since waits are built in, but it will support more devices than contention. Contention is best when the load is light and token passing is better with heavier loads and that both schemes crash under too much load.

Carrier sensing methods tend to be faster than token-passing methods, but collisions can bog down the network if it is heavily populated with devices. Token ring does not suffer from collision problems, but the current throughput rates on token ring networks are restrictive when compared to new high-speed Ethernet networks.

Polling is too slow and controlled to give the users the speed they expect from other network methods.

10.2 The ALOHA Random Access Protocol

The ALOHA protocol is an interesting example of a MAC protocol of the contention-type. It is the precursor of Ethernet and its subsequent standardization as IEEE 802.3 (CSMA-CD). To control which NICs are allowed to transmit at any given time, a protocol is required. This simplest protocol is known as ALOHA (this is actually an Hawaiian word, meaning "hello"). ALOHA allows any NIC to transmit at any time, but states that each NIC must add a checksum/CRC at the end of its transmission to allow the receiver(s) to identify whether the frame was correctly received.

The concept of the ALOHA system is applicable with modifications in other situations, such as a LAN of nodes attached to a common coaxial cable bus (the Ethernet concept). The actual implementations may be different, but the underlying concepts are the same for all ALOHA systems. The basic **characteristics of ALOHA** are the following:

- Fixed length frames, shared channel or medium.
- Frames carry address of destination node.
- Nodes transmit on common channel and listen to common channel for transmissions from other nodes.
- A node starts a frame transmission whenever it is ready to send, regardless of the state of the channel.
- A node can tell if its frame arrived at the destination node without collision, or if a collision occurred with another frame in an overlapping time interval thus corrupting both frames. (An ACK may be used, or the node listens to the downlink broadcast channel in the original ALOHA system for its own frame).

ALOHA is therefore a best effort service, and does not guarantee that the frame of data will actually reach the remote recipient without corruption. It therefore relies on ARQ protocols to retransmit any data, which is corrupted. An ALOHA network only works well when the medium has a low utilization, since this leads to a low probability of the transmission colliding with that of another computer, and hence a reasonable chance that the data is not corrupted. There are two categories of aloha:

1. Pure Aloha
2. Slotted Aloha

In pure ALOHA a node can start transmission at any time. In slotted ALOHA, all nodes have synchronized clocks marking frame boundary times (the clock period is the time for one frame transmission) and a node wishing to transmit does so at the start of the next frame slot. In both cases, a node transmits without checking the state of the channel. (In ALOHA, a node cannot necessarily "listen" to the uplink transmissions of another node, because these transmissions are directed by the transmitting antennae to the satellite station and not to the other nodes.)

10.2.1 Pure (Unslotted) ALOHA - 1

In this protocol a station transmits a frame whenever it has data to send. When the frame collides with other frame(s), retransmit it by waiting a random amount of time.

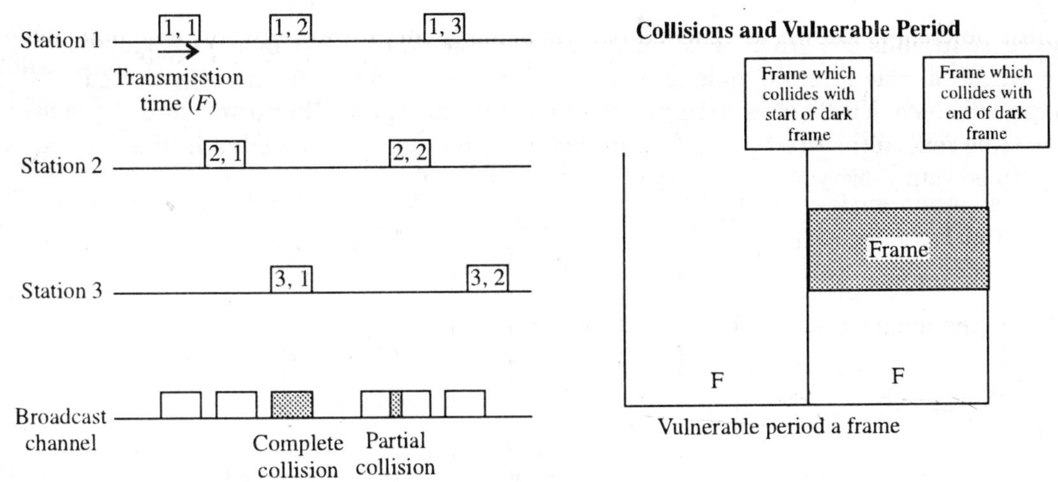

Fig. 10.2 Collisions in pure ALOHA

A frame (dark frame) collides whenever another transmission begins in the vulnerable period of the frame. Vulnerable period has length of 2 frame times.

Salient features of Pure ALOHA

- Simpler, no synchronization.
- Station sends data immediately.
- If a collision occurs, the data is resent after a random amount of time (to reduce probability of another collision).
- Contention—the channel is shared in a way that can lead to conflicts.
- No carrier sensing.
- Vulnerability—based on the time it takes to transmit a frame.
- Send packets without waiting for beginning of slot. As a result collision probability increases: packet sent at t0 collide with other packets sent in $[t_0 - 1, t_0 + 1]$.

10.2.2 An improvement : "Slotted ALOHA"

Rather than continuous time, use slotted time. Define a slot to be the time it takes to transmit one frame. (This is where assuming all frames are the same size simplifies things). Everybody is kept synchronized on slot times by signal from main campus. You can only start at the beginning of a slot. If you become ready to transmit after a slot has begun, you have to wait until the beginning of the next slot.

e.g., slot is 30 seconds, if you're ready 5 seconds in; you have to wait 25 seconds, even if nobody else is transmitting.

"Delay under light loading" goes up to one-half * slot time, on average, under "slotted ALOHA".

"Utilization under heavy loading" goes to 36.8% - double than pure ALOHA. The reason is decrease in collisions. In pure ALOHA, any frame could be in a collision with another frame start within a time interval 2t long (where t = time to transmit frame). In slotted ALOHA, you can only be in a collision starting at the same time as yours. That frame must have become ready to be sent in the previous t. (In other words, you can't collide with a frame that becomes ready to be sent after you've already started.)

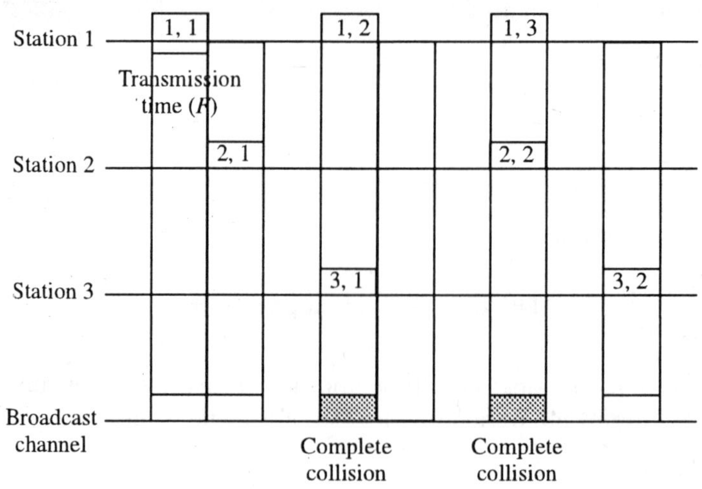

Fig. 10.3 Collisions in slotted ALOHA

Salient features of Slotted ALOHA

- Time is discrete. It is divided into equal size slots (= pkt trans. time).
- Timing required (cannot transmit frame until the beginning of the next time slot). A node with new arriving packet transmits at beginning of next slot.
- Increases throughput because of the way time is handled.
- Load dependent (increases in the load reduces performance).
- If collision occurs it retransmits packet in future slots with probability *p*, until successful.

Protocols can be improved by adding "carrier sense". In ALOHA, stations did not listen to the channel to see if anybody else was using it - they just transmitted.

10.3 Carrier Sense Multiple-Access (CSMA) Protocols

The fundamental reason for low channel utilization of Aloha protocol is that senders don't defer to each other even when another transmission is in progress. CSMA rectifies this problem by carrier sensing.

CSMA protocols are widely used in local area networks (LAN's) to control access to a shared communications channel such as a coaxial cable or radio frequency band. CSMA protocols are designed to exploit the property that the signal propagation time across the LAN is much smaller than the packet transmission time. Consequently, their performance depends on the exact timing of a sequence of asynchronous events originating at different points in the network.

In some shorter distance networks, it is possible to listen to the channel before transmitting. In radio networks, this is called "sensing the carrier". The CSMA protocol works just like Aloha except : If the channel is sensed busy, then the user waits to transmit its packet and a collision is avoided. This really improves the performance in short distance networks!

"Persistent" and "Non-Persistent" CSMA

Persistent CSMA (Most greedy) : A station listens to the carrier when it is ready to send; if it senses "empty", it transmits. If it senses "busy", it continues to listen until it senses "empty" and then immediately tries to transmit. (Called "1-persistent CSMA", because station transmits with probability 1 when it senses the carrier being empty)

Algorithm of 1-persistent CSMA

1. Station has data to send.
2. Listen to carrier.
3. If carrier is busy, wait until idle.
4. Transmit data.
5. If there is a collision, wait a random amount of time.
6. Goto 2.

1-persistent transmits as soon as the carrier becomes idle with a probability of 1. Because of propagation delay, a channel may send at the same time of another.

Two problems:

- **Obvious case :** Two workstations listening to carrier; will both sense "empty" at approximately the same time and will collide.
- **Less obvious :** All real transmission media have a finite propagation delay—it takes some time before a signal sent by one workstation is sensed by all other workstations on the wire. So a station listens to wire; senses it empty and begins transmission, only to find that somebody else had already been transmitting but signal hadn't made it that far yet. ***Result*** : collision.

Non-persistent CSMA (Least greedy) : A station listens to carrier; senses it busy; quits listening and waits a random time before starting to listen again. Each waiting station generates its own random wait time; chance of two stations being ready to transmit again at same time is small.

Algorithm of Non-persistent CSMA

1. Station has data to send.
2. Listen to carrier.
3. If available, send; else wait a random amount of time and goto 2.

Non-persistent does not wait constantly for an idle channel.

Advantage of non-persistent CSMA : Lower probability of collisions.

Disadvantage of non-persistent CSMA : Higher delay under light loading; you may be waiting for no reason (nobody else is going to transmit anyway).

Middle ground : p-persistent CSMA (Adjustable greedy) : Station listens to carrier; if it senses "empty" generates a random number and transmits with probability = p. With probability

$q = 1 - p$, station does not transmit, figuring the carrier is really busy, but the signal just hasn't reached this station yet.

Algorithm of *p*-persistent CSMA

1. Station has data to send.
2. Listen to carrier.
3. If idle, transmit with probability p; else wait until next time slot and goto 2.

All three of these strategies have higher utilization under heavy load than even slotted ALOHA but all except 1-persistent CSMA also have higher delay under light load.

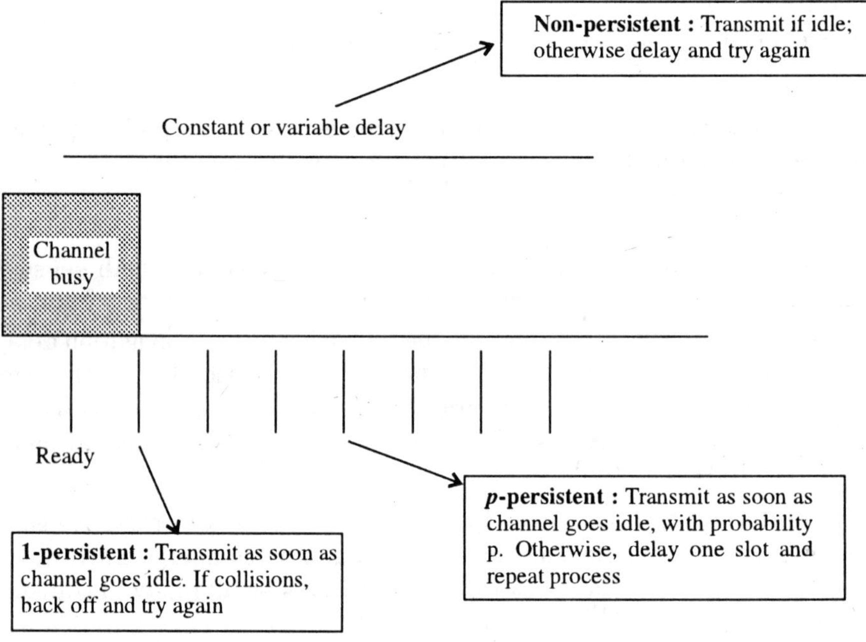

Fig. 10.4 Comparison of CSMA strategies

10.4 Carrier Sense Multiple Access/Collision Detection (CSMA/CD)

CSMA has inefficiency that if a collision occurred, the channel is unstable until colliding packets have been fully transmitted. CSMA/CD overcomes this as follows :

While transmitting, the sender is listening to medium for collision. Sender stops if collision has occurred. So we can say that :

CSMA : Listen Before Talking.
CSMA/CD : Listen While Talking.

CSMA/CD is the method used in Ethernet networks for controlling access to the physical media by network nodes. CSMA is a network access method used on shared network topologies such as Ethernet to control access to the network. Devices attached to the network cable listen (carrier sense) before transmitting. If the channel is in use, devices wait before transmitting. MA (multiple access) indicates that many devices can connect to and share the same network. All devices have equal access to use the network when it is clear. Even though devices attempt to sense whether the network is in use, there is a good chance that two stations will attempt to access it at the same time. On large networks, the transmission time between one end of the cable and another is enough that one station may access the cable even though another has already just accessed it. There are two methods for avoiding these so-called collisions, listed here :

- **CSMA/CD (Carrier Sense Multiple Access/Collision Detection) :** CD (collision detection) defines what happens when two devices sense a clear channel, and then attempt to transmit at the same time. A collision occurs, and both devices stop transmission, wait for a random amount of time, and then retransmit. This is the technique used to access the 802.3 Ethernet network channel. This method handles collisions as they occur, but if the bus is constantly busy, collisions can occur so often that performance drops drastically. It is estimated that network traffic must be less than 40 percent of the bus capacity for the network to operate efficiently. If distances are long, time lags occur that may result in inappropriate carrier sensing, and hence collisions.
- **CSMA/CA (Carrier Sense Multiple Access/Collision Avoidance) :** In CA (collision avoidance), collisions are avoided because each node signals its intent to transmit before actually doing so. This method is not popular because it requires excessive overhead that reduces performance.

Collision Detection (CD)—It can be used to modify CSMA. Listen to the carrier, even as you're transmitting. When you detect a collision, stop transmitting (it's a waste of time to send the rest of the frame; it will be thrown away anyway). It saves wasted time, thus increasing utilization under heavy load.

Collision strategy—Collisions can occur because 2 or more stations try to transmit simultaneously, or because one is already transmitting but its signal has not yet reached another station. When there is data waiting to be sent, each transmitting NIC also monitors its own transmission. If it observes a collision, it stops transmission immediately and instead transmits a 32-bit jam sequence. The purpose of this sequence is to ensure that any other node, which may currently be receiving this frame, will receive the jam signal in place of the correct 32-bit MAC CRC; this causes the other receivers to discard the frame due to a CRC error.

To ensure that all NICs start to receive a frame before the transmitting NIC has finished sending it, Ethernet defines a minimum frame size (i.e. no frame may have less than 46 bytes of payload). The minimum frame size is related to the distance, which the network spans, the type of media being used and the number of repeaters that the signal may have to pass through to reach the furthest part of the LAN. Together these define a value known as the Ethernet Slot Time, corresponding to 512 bit times at 10 Mbps.

When two or more transmitting NICs each detect a corruption of their own data (i.e. a collision), each responds in the same way by transmitting the jam sequence. The following sequence depicts a collision :

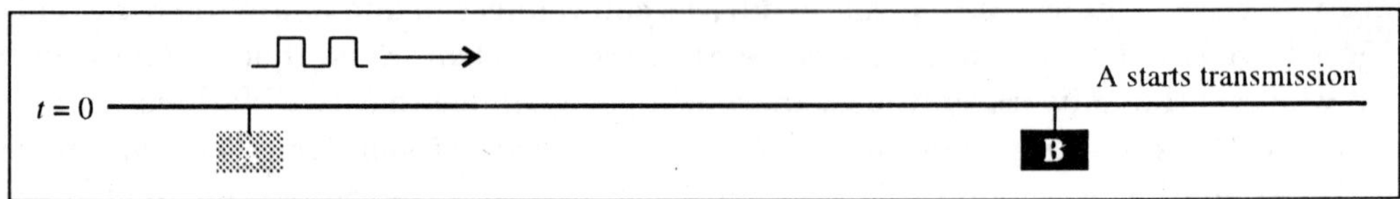

At time t=0, a frame is sent on the idle medium by NIC A.

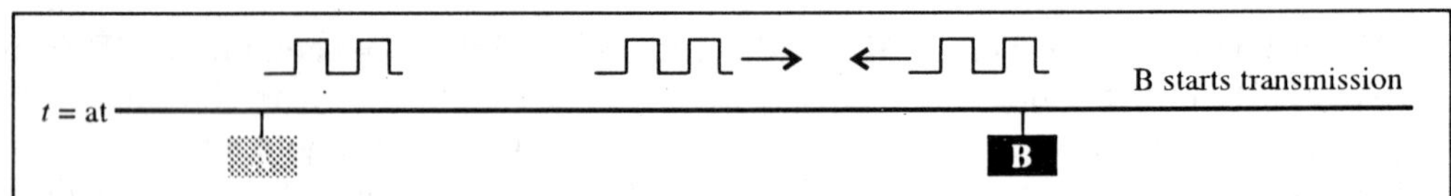

A short time later, NIC B also transmits. (In this case, the medium, as observed by the NIC at B happens to be idle too).

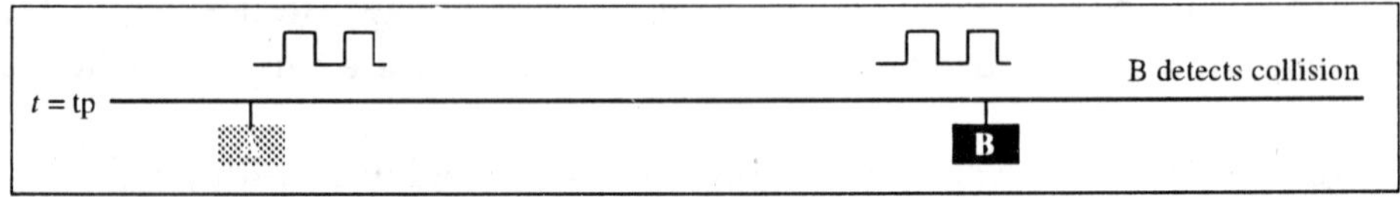

After a period, equal to the propagation delay of the network, the NIC at B detects the other transmission from A, and is aware of a collision, but NIC A has not yet observed that NIC B was also transmitting. B continues to transmit, sending the Ethernet Jam sequence (32 bits).

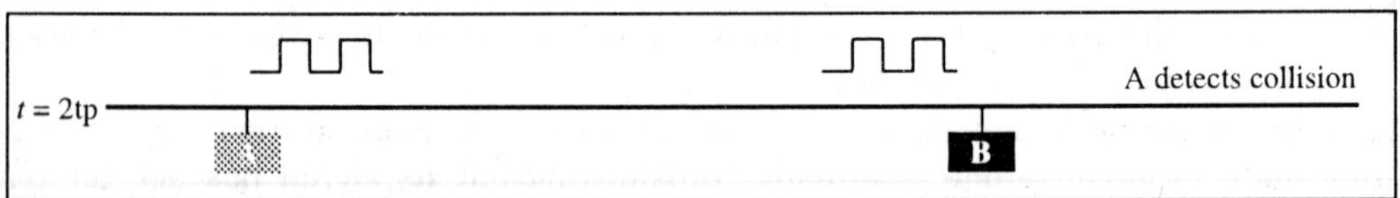

After one complete round trip propagation time (twice the one way propagation delay), both NICs are aware of the collision. B will shortly cease transmission of the Jam Sequence, however A will continue to transmit a complete Jam Sequence. Finally the cable becomes idle.

Performance of CSMA / CD

It is simple to calculate the performance of a CSMA/CD network where only one node attempts to transmit at any time. In this case, the NIC may saturate the medium and near 100% utilization of the link may be achieved, providing almost 10 Mbps of throughput on a 10 Mbps LAN.

However, when two or more NICs attempt to transmit at the same time, the performance of Ethernet is less predictable. The fall in utilization and throughput occurs because some bandwidth is wasted by collisions and back-off delays. In practice, a busy shared 10 Mbps Ethernet network will typically supply 2-4 Mbps of throughput to the NICs connected to it.

As the level of utilization of the network increases, particularly if there are many NICs competing to share the bandwidth, an overload condition may occur. In this case, the throughput of Ethernet LANs reduces very considerably, and much of the capacity is wasted by the CSMA/CD algorithm, and very little is available for sending useful data. This is the reason why a shared Ethernet LAN should not connect more than 1024 computers. Many engineers use a threshold of 40% Utilization to determine if a LAN is overloaded. A LAN with a higher utilization will observe a high collision rate, and likely a very variable transmission time (due to back off). Separating the LAN in to two or more collision domains using bridges or switches would likely provide a significant benefit (assuming appropriate positioning of the bridges or switches).

Salient features of CSMA with Collision Detection

- When 2 stations transmit and the collision is detected, the stations stop immediately.
- This saves bandwidth and time.
- Used in 802.3 and Ethernet.

10.5 Collision Free Protocols

While collisions do not occur with CSMA when a station is controlling the channel, they do occur during the contention period between one station releasing the channel and the next claiming it. These collisions affect system performance, especially when the cable is long and the frames are short. Collision free protocols aim to resolve the contention issues for the channel, and so result in no collisions at all.

Collision-free protocols divide the users into disjoint groups, such that a collision is impossible. An example of a collision-free protocol is the TDM protocol in which each user has a dedicated time slot. Collision-free protocols have high delay at low load, but the channel efficiency at high load is much better than that of contention protocols. The simplest collision-free methods are TDM and FDM. These allocation schemes are efficient when the number of users is small, and the traffic is continuous. Under conditions of bursty traffic, or when the number of users is large and variable, collision-free protocols are poor choices.

"Contention slots"—the time intervals spent deciding which station gets to transmit next.

There are two types of collision free protocols that are:

1. A Bit-Map Protocol
2. Binary Countdown

10.5.1 A Bit-Map Protocol

It is a Linear Search Approach as the channel is divided into reservation period and data transfer period. Each contention period consist of exactly N slots. If station X has a frame to send, it transmits a 1 bit during the Xth slot. The stations are only allowed to transmit during their allocated slot. Regardless of what station X does, station $X + 1$ gets the opportunity to transmit a 1 during slot $X + 1$, and so on (But it should only do so if it has some data queued, ready to be sent). An algorithm is then used to decide which station (out of those requesting the channel) is given access to it, and the data is then sent.

Simplest strategy : When one station finishes sending, each station on the network (in some pre-defined numerical order) broadcasts a "1" if it wants to transmit and a "0" otherwise. When everybody has done this, the stations transmit one at a time in numerical order. When everybody who wanted to send has done so, you start over.

Example :

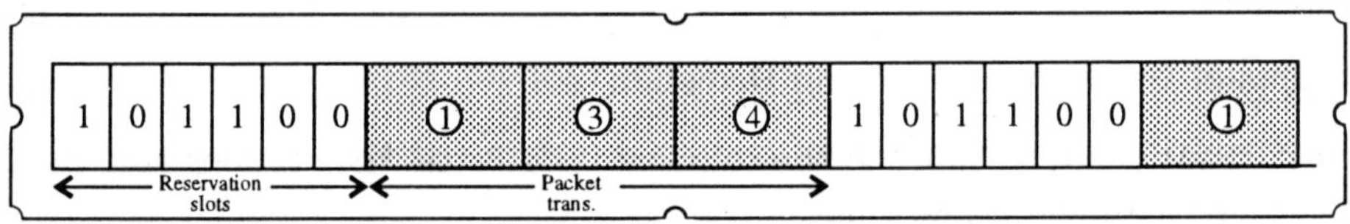

Fig. 10.5 Bit-map protocol

Here we have 6 users. Each user has a designated reservation slots. It favors the high numbered stations.

10.5.2 Binary Countdown

The problem with the basic bitmap protocol is that the overhead is 1 bit per station, so it does not scale well to networks with thousands of stations. Binary station addresses address this. A station wanting to use the channel broadcasts its address as a binary bit string, starting with the high-order bit. All addresses are assumed to be the same length. The bits in each position from different stations are 'ORed' together. As soon as a station attempting to transmit detects a bit which it did not send, it stops attempting to claim the channel; thus the station with the highest number is granted access to the channel. The following figure explains this protocol:

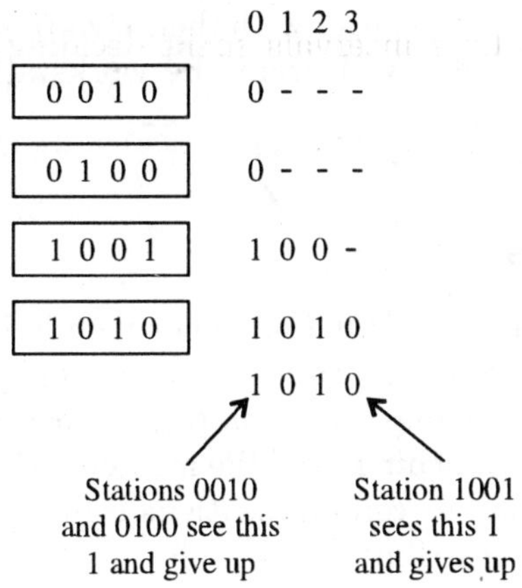

Fig. 10.6 Binary Countdown

Different, more complex algorithms include:

BRAP (Broadcast Recognition with Alternating Priorities)—As soon as a station inserts its "1" indicating it wants to talk, it starts sending-start the cycle of 1 and 0 with the next station, rather than the first each time.

MLMA (Multi-level Multi-Access)—Stations wanting to transmit contend using the "digits" in their station number, going from most-significant to least-significant-improves delay under light loading from the BRAP results

Adaptive Tree Walk protocol—Basically, a binary search over the set of stations. Organize the stations in a binary tree, and do a depth-first search to determine who gets to talk first.

10.6 Token and Token-Passing Access Methods

A token is a special control frame on token ring, token bus, and FDDI (Fiber Distributed Data Interface) networks that determines which stations can transmit data on a shared network. The node that has the token can transmit. Unlike contention-based networks, such as Ethernet, workstations on token-based networks do not compete for access to the network. Only the station that obtains the token can transmit. Other stations wait for the token rather than trying to access the network on their own. On Ethernet networks, "collisions" occur when two or more workstations attempt to access the network at the same time. They must back off and try again later, which reduces performance-especially as the number of workstations attached to a network segment increases.

In token ring networks, a station takes possession of a token and changes one bit, converting the token to a SFS (start-of-frame sequence). A field exists in the token in which workstations can indicate the type of priority required for the transmission. The priority setting is basically a request to other stations for future use of the token. The other stations compare a workstation's request for priority with their own priority levels. If the workstation's priority is higher, the other stations will grant the workstation access to the token for an extended period.

10.7 Polling Systems

Polling designates one device as a Master Controller who is in charge of who can transmit. The master queries each other device called secondaries or slaves to see if they have information to transmit. One of the most common polling topologies is a star where the points of the star are secondary or slave machines and the master is the hub. This is a popular method to connect terminals to a terminal or communications controller. There are two categories of polling systems: Centralized or Distributed

Centralized polling systems : A central controller transmits polling messages to stations in a certain order.

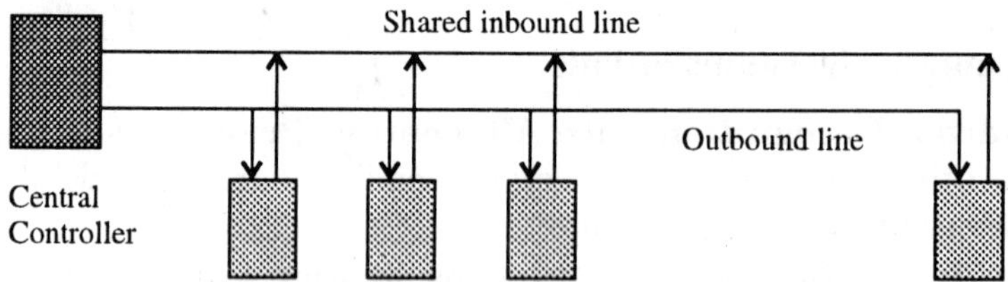

Fig. 10.7 Centralized polling systems

Distributed reservation systems : The permit for packet transmission is passed from a station to another in a certain order.

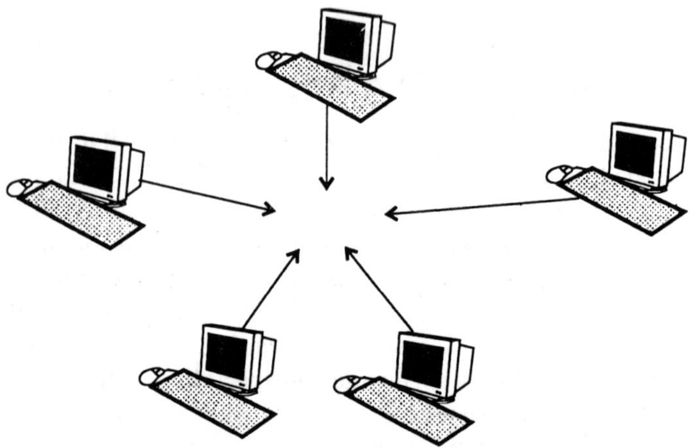

Fig. 10.8 Distributed reservation systems

Efficiency of general polling systems

Unlike the case of random access or reservation systems, the efficiency of a polling system can be arbitrarily close to 1.

Assumption : No bound for the number of packets that can be transmitted over a polling period.

What happens? The portion of walk times in a polling cycle becomes negligible when the system is heavily loaded and the polling cycle becomes extremely long as a result.

In practice, as the system load approaches 1, the length of polling cycles increases very fast, which in turn increase delays. The number of packets that a station can transmit over a single polling cycle is limited.

• • •

11

Introduction To LAN And MAN Protocols

Introduction

This chapter introduces the various LAN protocols and media-access methods used in a local-area network (LAN). Topics addressed focus on the methods and devices used in Ethernet/IEEE 802.3, Token Bus/IEEE 802.4, Token Ring/IEEE 802.5, CSMA/CA medium access protocol (IEEE 802.11), a wireless LAN protocol and Fiber Distributed Data Interface (FDDI). Also in this chapter we will discuss DQDB, a protocol designed to be used in MANs.

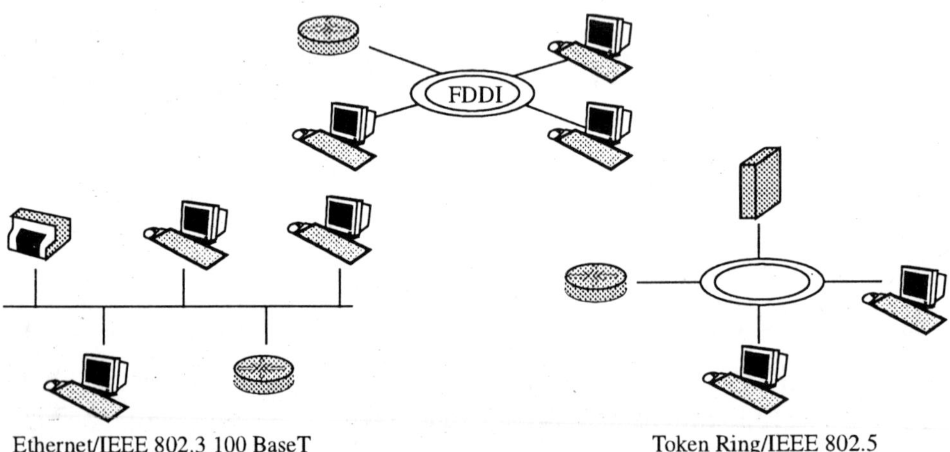

Fig. 11.1 Three LAN implementations used most commonly

What is a LAN?

A LAN is a high-speed data network that covers a relatively small geographic area. It typically connects workstations, personal computers, printers, servers, and other devices. LANs offer computer users many advantages, including shared access to devices and applications, file exchange between connected users, and communication between users via electronic mail and other applications.

Definition

A local area network (LAN) is:
- *A data communications medium.*
- *Characterized by having all sites on the same link.*
- *Confined to a small area, does not cross public right of way.*
- *Characterized by relatively high data rates.*

11.1 IEEE 802 Standards

The IEEE (Institute of Electrical and Electronic Engineers) is a technical association of industry professionals with a common interest in advancing all communications technologies. The IEEE or Institute of Electrical and Electronics Engineers define industry-wide standards that promote the use and implementation of technology. These committees are named for the standards they publish. The IEEE 802 committee sets the standards for networking. However, this committee is split into several smaller sub-committees such as IEEE 802.3 and IEEE 802.5. In general, IEEE 802 standards define physical network interfaces such as network interface cards, bridges, routers, connectors, cables, and all the signaling and access methods associated with physical network connections.

The 802 standards describe the three lowest layers of the network architecture:

- **Physical layer (layer 1)**—Describes the transmission medium, type of electrical signals used and how nodes are attached to the network (cables and connectors).
- **Medium Access Control (MAC) sublayer (layer 2)**—Implements methods that control a node's access to the shared transmission medium.
- **Data link layer (layer 3)**—Provides for reliable transmission (including error checking), delineates beginning and ending of frames (headers and trailers).

These standard LANs differ in their physical layer and their MAC sublayer but are compatible at their data link layer.

A set of network standards developed by the IEEE include:

- 802.1 Higher Layer LAN Protocols Working Group.
- 802.2 Logical Link Control Working Group.
- 802.3 Ethernet Working Group.

- 802.4 Token Bus Working Group.
- 802.5 Token Ring Working Group.
- 802.6 Metropolitan Area Network Working Group.
- 802.7 Broadband TAG.
- 802.8 Fiber Optic TAG.
- 802.9 Isochronous LAN Working Group.
- 802.10 Security Working Group.
- 802.11 Wireless LAN Working Group.
- 802.12 Demand Priority Working Group.
- 802.14 Cable Modem Working Group.
- 802.15 Wireless Personal Area Network (WPAN) Working Group.
- 802.16 Broadband Wireless Access Working Group.
- 802.17 Resilient Packet Ring Working Group.

Following are the some standards that we will discuss in this chapter:

IEEE 802.1 : Standards related to network management. Defines routing, bridging, and internetwork communications

IEEE 802.2 : General standard for the data link layer in the OSI Reference Model. Allows Network layer protocols to link to Physical layer and MAC sublayer protocols

IEEE 802.3 : Defines the MAC layer for bus networks that use CSMA/CD. This is the basis of the Ethernet standard.

IEEE 802.4 : Defines the MAC layer for bus networks that use a token-passing mechanism (token bus networks).

IEEE 802.5 : Defines the MAC layer for token-ring networks.

IEEE 802.6 : Standard for Metropolitan Area Networks (MANs).

LAN Protocols and the OSI Reference Model

LAN protocols function at the lowest two layers of the OSI reference model, between the

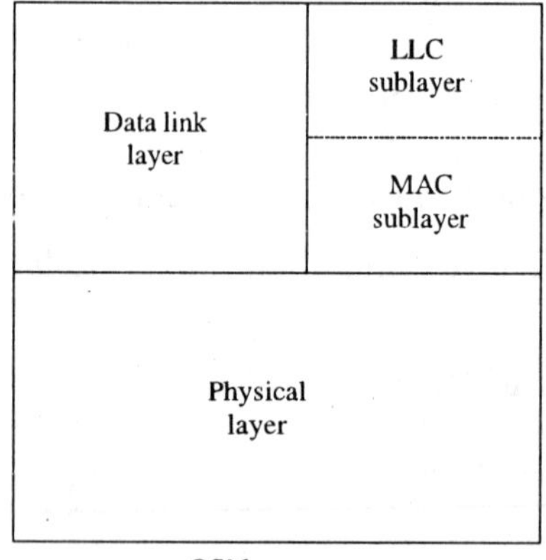

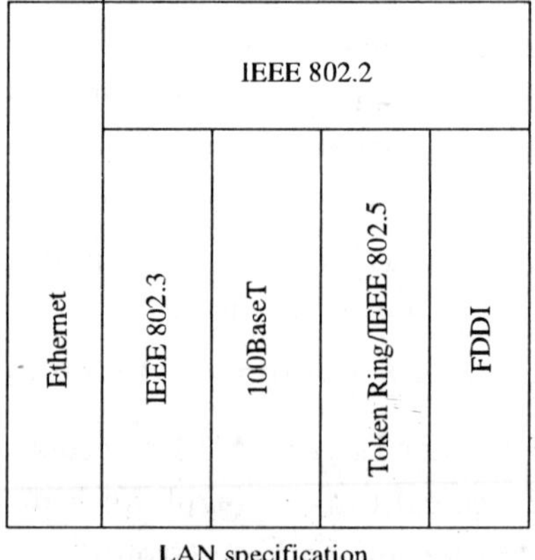

Fig. 11.2 Popular LAN protocols mapped to the OSI reference model

physical layer and the data link layer. Figure 11.2 illustrates how several popular LAN protocols map to the OSI reference model.

LAN Transmission Methods

LAN data transmissions fall into three classifications:

- Unicast.
- Multicast.
- Broadcast.

In each type of transmission, a single packet is sent to one or more nodes.

In a **unicast transmission**, a single packet is sent from the source to a destination on a network. First, the source node addresses the packet by using the address of the destination node. The package is then sent onto the network and finally, the network passes the packet to its destination.

A **multicast transmission** consists of a single data packet that is copied and sent to a specific subset of nodes on the network. First, the source node addresses the packet by using a multicast address. The packet is then sent into the network, which makes copies of the packet and sends a copy to each node that is part of the multicast address.

A **broadcast transmission** consists of a single data packet that is copied and sent to all nodes on the network. In these types of transmissions, the source node addresses the packet by using the broadcast address. The packet is then sent on to the network, which makes copies of the packet and sends a copy to every node on the network.

11.2 Higher Layer LAN Protocols (IEEE 802.1)

The IEEE 802.1 Working Group is chartered to concern itself with and develop standards and recommended practices in the following areas: 802 LAN/MAN architecture, internetworking among 802 LANs, MANs and other wide area networks, 802 Link Security, 802 overall network management, and protocol layers above the MAC & LLC layers.

The 802.1 working group has two active task groups : Internetworking and Link Security.

11.3 LLC : Logic Link Control (IEEE 802.2)

Logic Link Control (LLC) is the IEEE 802.2 LAN protocol that specifies an implementation of the LLC sublayer of the data link layer. IEEE 802.2 LLC is used in IEEE 802.3 (Ethernet) and IEEE 802.5 (Token Ring) LANs to perform these functions:

(a) Managing the data-link communication
(b) Link Addressing
(c) Defining Service Access Points (SAPs)
(d) Sequencing

LLC was originated from the High-Level Data-Link Control (HDLC) and it uses a subclass of the HDLC specification. LLC defines three types of operation for data communication:

Type 1 : Connectionless—The connectionless operation is basically sending but no guarantee of receiving.

Type 2 : Connection Oriented—The connection-oriented operation for the LLC layer provides these 4 services: Connection establishment; Confirmation and acknowledgement that data has been received; Error recovery by requesting received bad data to be resent; Sliding Windows, which is a method of increasing the rate of data transfer.

Type 3 : Acknowledgement with connectionless service.

The Type 1 connectionless service of LLC specifies a static-frame format and allows network protocols to run on it. Network protocols that fully implement a transport layer will generally use Type 1 service. The Type 2 connection-oriented service of LLC provides reliable data transfer. It is used in LAN environment that do not invoke network and transport layer protocols.

Protocol Structure—LLC : Logic Link Control (IEEE 802.2)

Recall from the OSI Model module that all packets deal with:

- What is being sent.
- Where is it being sent.

We will describe all packet structures in terms of these two parameters. In the case of the LLC PDU (Protocol Data Unit) the data field is what is being sent, and the source and destination access points (SSAP and DSAP) describe where it is being sent in terms of the multiplexing peer protocol.

Logic Link Control Layer (LLC) Header

8	16	24 or 32bits	Variable
DSAP	SSAP	Control	Data or LLC information

Fig. 11.3 LCC header

The various fields of LLC header are stated below:

- **Destination Service Access Point (DSAP)**—The DSAP is a seven-bit address with an eighth bit to indicate if it is a specific address (0) or a group (broadcast) address (1). The DSAP is not a station or device address; rather it designates the service control point where the message should be routed.
- **Source Service Access Point (SSAP)**—The SSAP is also a seven-bit address, but in this case the eighth bit is used to indicate if the message is a command (0) or a response (1). Like the DSAP, the SSAP designates a control point and not a station address. In the case of the SSAP, this is the control point from which the message originated.
- **Control**—The control field is either 8 or 16 bits long, with the length indicated by the

first two bits. The 16-bit fields are used to exchange sequence numbers, while the 8-bit variation is used for unsequenced information.

- **LLC information**—LLC data or higher layer protocols.

Features of IEEE Standard 802.2 : Logical Link Control

- Runs on top of 802.3-802.5 and provides error control and flow control.
- Hides differences among the 802 protocols and presents a single interface to the network layer.
- Three service options :
  - □ Unreliable datagram service.
  - □ Acknowledged datagram service.
  - □ Reliable connection-oriented service.

Below the 802.2 LLC are the MACs for the various physical LAN implementations. These standards are known as 802.3 for CSMA/CD, 802.4 for token passing bus, and 802.5 for token passing ring.

11.4 Ethernet (IEEE 802.3)

Ethernet is a networking technology defined by the Institute for Electrical and Electronic Engineers (IEEE) as IEEE standard of 802.3. This Physical Layer technology is the most popular Data Link Layer protocol because of its speed, lower cost, and worldwide acceptance. Ethernet can support nearly every protocol in use today, and can operate with any networking equipment that adheres to the IEEE standard. This openness, combined with the ease of use, has made Ethernet dominant in the local area network arena.

In the Ethernet standard, there are two modes of operation: half-duplex and full-duplex modes. In the half duplex mode, data are transmitted using the popular Carrier-Sense Multiple Access/Collision Detection (CSMA/CD) protocol on a shared medium. The main disadvantages of the half-duplex are the efficiency and distance limitation, in which the link distance is limited by the minimum MAC frame size. This restriction reduces the efficiency drastically for high-rate transmission. Therefore, the carrier extension technique is used to ensure the minimum frame size of 512 bytes in Gigabit Ethernet to achieve a reasonable link distance.

The Ethernet system consists of three basic elements:

1. The physical medium used to carry Ethernet signals between computers.
2. A set of medium access control rules embedded in each Ethernet interface that allow multiple computers to fairly arbitrate access to the shared Ethernet channel.
3. An Ethernet frame that consists of a standardized set of bits used to carry data over the system.

11.4.1 General Ethernet Features

There are a number of adaptations to the IEEE 802.3 Ethernet standard, including adaptations with data rates of 10 Mbits/sec; 100 Mbits/sec (Fast Ethernet); 1,000 Mbits/sec (Gigabit Ethernet); and, most recently, 10 Gigabit/sec Ethernet. The original forms of Ethernet used coaxial cable, but today most Ethernet networks are connected with Category 5 twisted-pair cable. Gigabit Ethernet and 10 Gigabit Ethernet run on fiber optic cables and are being deployed in metropolitan area networks as "metro Ethernets".

- **Shared media :** All nodes attached to the network take turns using the media. If the network is not busy, a shared scheme is very efficient; but if the network gets busy, nodes must wait to transmit or, worse, collisions occur that reduce performance.
- **Broadcast domains :** Just like a TV broadcast, transmitted frames are "heard" by all, but nodes receive only the frames that are addressed to them. Special broadcast frames are addressed to all nodes. These are used for multicasting and network maintenance.
- **CSMA/CD (Carrier Sense Multiple Access/Collision Detection) access method:** On a shared media, some method is required to prevent two or more nodes from transmitting at the same time, and to detect "collisions" that occur if two stations begin transmitting at the same time.
- **Collision domains :** A collision domain consists of a set of networked nodes that share the same medium and that contend for access to the cable. In other words, their transmissions can collide. Suppose you have a busy 50-node network, and the number of collisions is reducing performance. You divide the network with a bridge to create two 25-node networks. Now you have two separate collision domains and one broadcast domain (the bridge will propagate broadcasts and appropriate traffic from one segment to the other).
- **Framing method :** Several framing methods were specified early on, but most systems now conform to IEEE 802.3 framing. More recently, the framing method was changed to support higher data rates (Gigabit Ethernet). The 802.3 frame is discussed later.
- **Full-duplex mode :** The twisted-pair Ethernet adaptations support full-duplex mode, in which signals are transmitted on one wire and received on another. Coaxial cable does not support full-duplex mode. Since both end stations are transmitting on separate wires, there is no contention (in a switched environment). This greatly improves transmission speeds.
- **Cable types :** The earliest Ethernet adaptations support coaxial cable in a bus topology configuration (the cable runs from one node to the next). Later versions supported twisted-pair cable in a star configuration (each node is individually wired to a hub). Combinations of cabling schemes are possible.
- **Cable length :** There are cable-length limitations, depending on the media type. Overextended networks are subject to signal propagation delays that can cause a failure in the collision detection mechanism. When a cable is too long, nodes at far ends may not detect that another has begun transmission. Collisions will go undetected, and there will be continuous network errors until the cable is shortened and the end stations are able to detect one another's transmissions.

- **MAC addresses :** All Ethernet NICs (network interface cards) come with a preassigned 48-bit network address. This address is made up of a 24-bit number that identifies the vendor of the card and a 24-bit number assigned by the vendor to identify the card. The address is globally unique and is called the MAC address because it defines a node on the network at the MAC (Media Access Control) layer.

11.4.2 Ethernet Network Elements

Ethernet LANs consist of network nodes and interconnecting media. The network nodes fall into two major classes:

- **Data terminal equipment (DTE)**—Devices that are either the source or the destination of data frames. DTEs are typically devices such as PCs, workstations, file servers, or print servers that, as a group, are all often referred to as end stations.
- **Data communication equipment (DCE)**—Intermediate network devices that receive and forward frames across the network. DCEs may be either standalone devices such as repeaters, network switches, and routers, or communications interface units such as interface cards and modems.

The current Ethernet media options include two general types of copper cable : unshielded twisted-pair (UTP) and shielded twisted-pair (STP), plus several types of optical fiber cable.

11.4.3 The Basic Ethernet Frame Format

The IEEE 802.3 standard defines a basic data frame format that is required for all MAC implementations, plus several additional optional formats that are used to extend the protocol's basic capability. The basic data frame format contains the seven fields shown in Figure 11.4.

7	1	6	6	2	46-1500 bytes	4
Pre	SFD	DA	SA	Length Type	Data unit + pad	FCS

Fig. 11.4 The basic IEEE 802.3 Ethernet MAC Data Frame for 10/100Mbps Ethernet

- **Preamble (PRE)**—Consists of 7 bytes. The PRE is an alternating pattern of ones and zeros that tells receiving stations that a frame is coming, and that provides a means to synchronize the frame-reception portions of receiving physical layers with the incoming bit stream.
- **Start-of-frame delimiter (SFD)**—Consists of 1 byte. The SFD is an alternating pattern of ones and zeros, ending with two consecutive 1-bits indicating that the next bit is the left-most bit in the left-most byte of the destination address.
- **Destination address (DA)**—Consists of 6 bytes. The DA field identifies which station(s) should receive the frame. The left-most bit in the DA field indicates whether the address is an individual address (indicated by a 0) or a group address (indicated by a 1). The second bit from the left indicates whether the DA is globally administered

(indicated by a 0) or locally administered (indicated by a 1). The remaining 46 bits are a uniquely assigned value that identifies a single station, a defined group of stations, or all stations on the network.

- **Source addresses (SA)**—Consists of 6 bytes. The SA field identifies the sending station. The SA is always an individual address and the left-most bit in the SA field is always 0.
- **Length/Type**—Consists of 4 bytes. This field indicates either the number of MAC-client data bytes that are contained in the data field of the frame, or the frame type ID if the frame is assembled using an optional format. If the Length/Type field value is less than or equal to 1500, the number of LLC bytes in the Data field is equal to the Length/Type field value. If the Length/Type field value is greater than 1536, the frame is an optional type frame, and the Length/Type field value identifies the particular type of frame being sent or received.
- **Data**—Is a sequence of n bytes of any value, where n is less than or equal to 1500. If the length of the Data field is less than 46, the Data field must be extended by adding a filler (a pad) sufficient to bring the Data field length to 46 bytes.
- **Frame check sequence (FCS)**—Consists of 4 bytes. This sequence contains a 32-bit cyclic redundancy check (CRC) value, which is created by the sending MAC and is recalculated by the receiving MAC to check for damaged frames. The FCS is generated over the DA, SA, Length/Type, and Data fields.

11.4.4 Frame Transmission

Whenever an end station MAC receives a transmit-frame request with the accompanying address and data information from the LLC sublayer, the MAC begins the transmission sequence by transferring the LLC information into the MAC frame buffer.

- The preamble and start-of-frame delimiter are inserted in the PRE and SFD fields.
- The destination and source addresses are inserted into the address fields.
- The LLC data bytes are counted, and the number of bytes is inserted into the Length/Type field.
- The LLC data bytes are inserted into the Data field. If the number of LLC data bytes is less than 46, a pad is added to bring the Data field length up to 46.
- The FCS value is generated over the DA, SA, Length/Type, and Data fields and is appended to the end of the Data field.

After the frame is assembled, actual frame transmission will depend on whether the MAC is operating in half-duplex or full-duplex mode.

The IEEE 802.3 standard currently requires that all Ethernet MACs support half-duplex operation, in which the MAC can be either transmitting or receiving a frame, but it cannot be doing both simultaneously. Full-duplex operation is an optional MAC capability that allows the MAC to transmit and receive frames simultaneously.

Half-Duplex Transmission—The CSMA/CD Access Method

The CSMA/CD protocol was originally developed as a means by which two or more stations could share a common media in a switch-less environment when the protocol does not require central arbitration, access tokens, or assigned time slots to indicate when a station will be allowed to transmit. Each Ethernet MAC determines for itself when it will be allowed to send a frame.

The CSMA/CD access rules are summarized by the protocol's acronym:

- **Carrier sense**—Each station continuously listens for traffic on the medium to determine when gaps between frame transmissions occur.
- **Multiple access**—Stations may begin transmitting any time they detect that the network is quiet (there is no traffic).
- **Collision detect**—If two or more stations in the same CSMA/CD network (collision domain) begin transmitting at approximately the same time, the bit streams from the transmitting stations will interfere (collide) with each other, and both transmissions will be unreadable. If that happens, each transmitting station must be capable of detecting that a collision has occurred before it has finished sending its frame.

Each must stop transmitting as soon as it has detected the collision and then must wait a quasirandom length of time (determined by a back-off algorithm) before attempting to retransmit the frame.

Binary Exponential Backoff Algorithm

When there is a collision, the stations involved in the collision will execute the binary exponential backoff algorithm to reduce the possibility of futher collisions.

1. When a collision is detected, the sender generates a noise burst to insure that all stations recognize the condition and aborts the transmission.
2. Wait 0 or 1 contention period (2 τ, i.e., 2 end-to-end propagation time) before attempting transmission again.
3. If another collision is detected, wait 0, 1, 2 or 3 contention period. And repeat the protocol.
4. In general, wait between 0 and $2^r - 1$ contention periods, where r is the number of collisions encountered.
5. Finally, freeze interval at 1023 contention periods after 10 attempts and give up (report failure) after 16 attempts.

11.4.5 Objective

An Ethernet network consisting of 4 computers is illustrated below. The objective is to send a data packet from Computer 1 to Computer 2 in accordance with the Ethernet's CSMA/CD protocol.

The CSMA/CD protocol is described in the flow chart below. The first step in sending a packet is to check to see if any other computer is in the process of sending a packet (Other

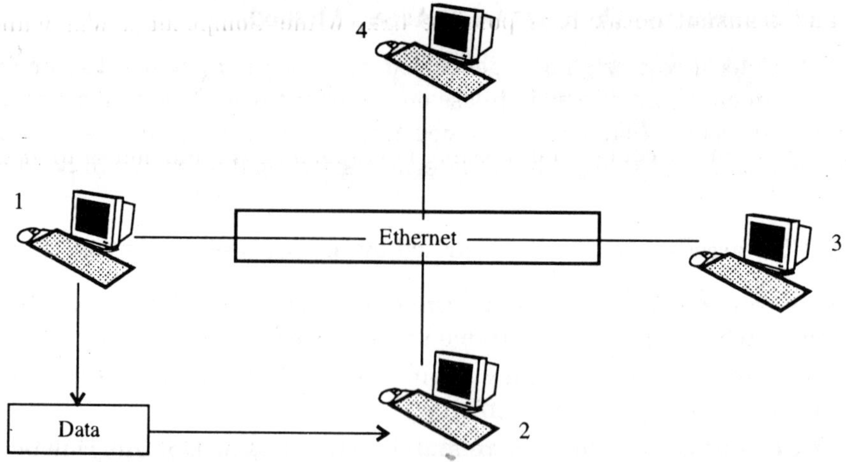

Fig. 11.5 Transmission of data from computer 1 to computer 2

carrier present?). If another computer is sending, then Computer 1 will wait until the network is available. If the network is available, then Computer 1 will start transmitting it's packet

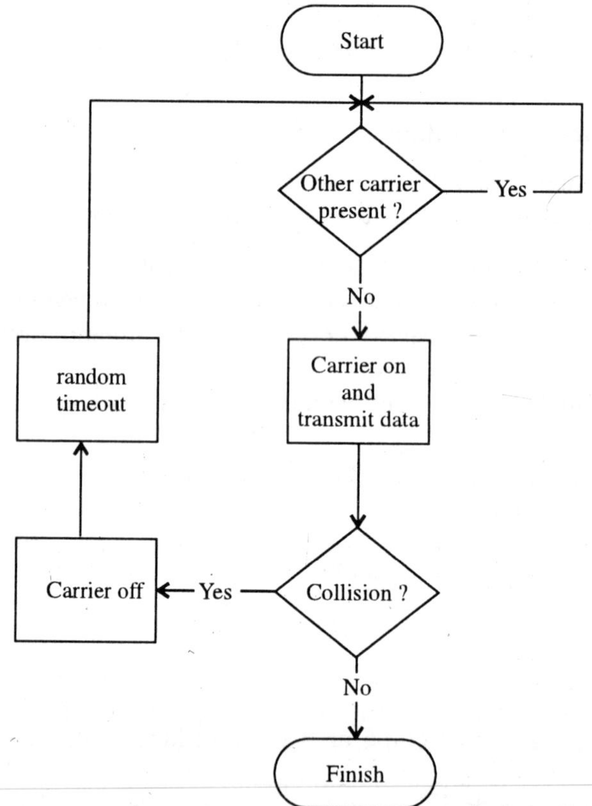

Fig. 11.6 Flowchart illustrating CSMA/CD protocol

(Carrier on and transmit data). It is possible that while Computer 1 was waiting for the network to become available, another computer was doing the same thing. In this event the other computer, which is following the same protocol as Computer 1, will start transmitting at the same time as Computer 1. This event is called a collision, and each computer is able to detect a collision when it occurs. The CSMA/CD response to a collision is to shut down the transmitter immediately, and then wait for a random period of time before trying again. This is analogous to two people accidentally starting to talk at the same time and their reaction to that "collision".

11.4.6 Specifications of Ethernet

Ethernet has evolved over the years to include a number of popular specifications. These specifications are due in part to the media variety, which they employ, such as coaxial, twisted-pair, and fiber-optic cabling. The original Ethernet supports a data rate of 10 megabits per second (Mbps) and specifies these possible physical media:

- 10BASE-2 (Thinwire coaxial cable with a maximum segment length of 185 meters).
- 10BASE-5 (Thickwire coaxial cable with a maximum segment length of 500 meters).
- 10BASE-F (Optical fiber cable).
- 10BASE-T (Ordinary telephone twisted pair wire).
- 10BASE-36 (Broadband multi-channel coaxial cable with a maximum segment length of 3,600 meters).

This designation is an IEEE shorthand identifier. The "10" in the media type designation refers to the transmission speed of 10 Mbps. The "BASE" refers to baseband signalling, which means that only Ethernet signals are carried on the medium (or, with 10BASE-36, on a single channel). The "*T*" represents twisted-pair; the "*F*" represents fiber optic cable; and the "2", "5", and "36" refer to the coaxial cable segment length (the 185 meter length has been rounded up to "2" for 200).

There are a number of new Ethernet standards that define the 100 Mbps Fast Ethernet system. These operate over twisted-pair and fiber-optic media.

The following table summarizes ethernet specifications:

Name	Cable	Max. segment	Nodes/ Seg.	Advantages
10Base5	Thick coax	500 m	100	Good for local area backbone
10Base2	Thin coax	200 m	30	Inexpensive
10Base-T	Twisted pair	100 m	1024	Easy maintenance
10Base-F	Fiber optics	2000 m	1024	Inter-building connection

10Base-T is now the most popular cabling scheme used for local area network. It is :

- easy to maintain.

- reduce the logical distance between stations (all connected at the hup), thus reducing the value of τ.

Fast Ethernet

The original Ethernet was based on a bus topology. Each station connects to the bus anywhere needed with a minimum physical distance one meter apart. Later a better technology is used called 10Base-T for 10 M bps unshielded twisted pair wire with a hub or router in the communications room (essentially Star topology).

Now the new Fast Ehternet took this one step futher, making it 100 M bps network with virtually no change in protocols and wirings. The Fast Ethernet protocol specification was completed by IEEE in 1995.

11.5 Token Ring (IEEE 802.5)

Token Ring is a LAN protocol defined in the IEEE 802.5 where all stations are connected in a ring and each station can directly hear transmissions only from its immediate neighbor. The Token Ring protocol is the second most widely used protocol on local area networks after Ethernet. The protocol deals with the problem of collision, which is defined, as a state where two stations transmit at the same time. In order to avoid the situation of collision there was a need to control the access to the network. This kind of control is possible by the use of a control (permission) called token. The token is passed from one station to another according to a set of rules. The ring consists of ring stations and transmission medium. Data travels sequentially from station to station. Only the station in possession of the token is allowed to transmit data. Each station repeats the data, checks for errors, and copies the data if appropriate. When the data is returned to the sending station, it removes it from the ring. The token Ring protocol supports priorities in transmission. It is implemented setting the priority bits in the Token Ring Frame.

Token Ring is a first and second layer protocol in the OSI seven layer model. The First release of Token Ring version was capable of 4Mbs data transmission rate; the transmission rate was improved later to 16Mbs. Token Ring can be operated on the following media's:

- Unshielded Twisted Pair (UTP).
- Shielded Twisted Pair (STP): Allowing a Max. of 260 stations at 16Mps rings.
- Coaxial cable (Thin\Thick\Broadband).
- Fiber Optics.

What is a Token?

Each token frame is three bytes long:

1. A 1-byte delimiter signals the start of a frame.
2. A 1-byte access control field contains priority information.
3. A 1-byte frame control field distinguishes data frames from control frames.

Note that token frames differ from regular frames by only 1 bit in the frame control field. Thus seizing the token consists of flipping a single bit during the copy operation. After seizing the token, a station may transmit data for no longer than the token holding time, typically 10 ms.

11.5.1 Features of Token Ring

The term "Token Ring" does not necessarily mean that the network is based on the ring topology. Most Token Ring networks use a star topology with central access points called multistation access units (MSAU). Two types of network cable, unshielded twisted-pair (UTP) and shielded twisted-pair (STP) determine the distance and number of workstations on the network. STP provides the greatest flexibility, but costs more. Each computer has a maximum distance of 100 meters (328 feet) from the MSAU when shielded wire is used and 45 meters (148 feet) when unshielded wire is used. Every MSAU can support up to 260 workstations using shielded wire, or up to 72 workstations using unshielded wire. Each ring can also support up to 33 MSAUs.

Token Ring networks can operate at 4 Mbps or 16 Mbps. Most hardware today supports 16 Mbps and can be configured to operate at any speed. With networks of heavy traffic, token passing is the most efficient network architecture. This is due to the fact that the token-passing technology eliminates network collisions because stations are not allowed to simultaneously transmit on the network. However, Ethernet is more effective on networks with light to moderate amounts of traffic.

Ring Benefits

- High reliability, the Ring can continue normal operation despite any single fault.
- Bypassing inactive stations.
- Effective use, 95% in Token Ring only whilst 30-40% in Ethernet.
- Excellent traffic handling (17.8 kb in TR, only 15kb in Ethernet.).
- Large maximum frame length.
- High bandwidth efficiency. 70% in Token Ring, 30% in Ethernet.
- Many media choices: UTP, STP, coax, fiber.
- Supports transmission priority.

11.5.2 Frame Format of Token Ring

Token Ring and IEEE 802.5 support two basic frame types : tokens and data/command frames. Tokens are 3-bytes in length and consist of a start delimiter, an access control byte, and an end delimiter. Data/command frames vary in size, depending on the size of the Information field. Data frames carry information for upper-layer protocols, while command frames contain control information and have no data for upper-layer protocols. Both formats are shown in Figure 11.7.

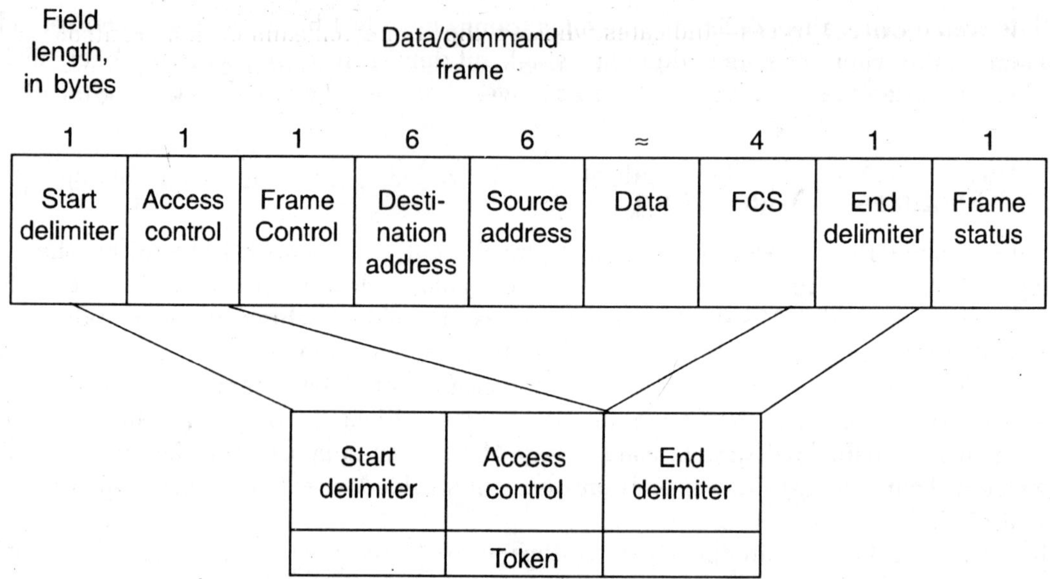

Fig. 11.7 IEEE 802.5 tokens and data/command frames

Token Frame Fields

The three token frame fields illustrated in Figure 11.7 are explained below:

- **Start delimiter**—Alerts each station of the arrival of a token (or data/command frame). This field includes signals that distinguish the byte from the rest of the frame by violating the encoding scheme used elsewhere in the frame.
- **Access-control byte**—Contains the Priority field (the most significant 3-bits) and the Reservation field (the least significant 3-bits), as well as a token bit (used to differentiate a token from a data/command frame) and a monitor bit (used by the active monitor to determine whether a frame is circling the ring endlessly).
- **End delimiter**—Signals the end of the token or data/command frame. This field also contains bits to indicate a damaged frame and identify the frame that is the last in a logical sequence.

Data/Command Frame Fields

Data/command frames have the same three fields as Token Frames, plus several others.

The Data/command frame fields illustrated in Figure 11.7 are explained below:

- **Start delimiter**—Alerts each station of the arrival of a token (or data/command frame). This field includes signals that distinguish the byte from the rest of the frame by violating the encoding scheme used elsewhere in the frame.
- **Access-control byte**—Contains the Priority field (the most significant 3-bits) and the Reservation field (the least significant 3-bits), as well as a token bit (used to differentiate a token from a data/command frame) and a monitor bit (used by the active monitor to determine whether a frame is circling the ring endlessly).

- **Frame-control bytes**—Indicates whether the frame contains data or control information. In control frames, this byte specifies the type of control information.
- **Destination and source addresses**—Consists of two 6-byte address fields that identify the destination and source station addresses.
- **Data**—Indicates that the length of field is limited by the ring token holding time, which defines the maximum time a station can hold the token.
- **Frame-check sequence (FCS)**—Is filled by the source station with a calculated value dependent on the frame contents. The destination station recalculates the value to determine whether the frame was damaged in transit. If so, the frame is discarded.
- **End Delimiter**—Signals the end of the token or data/command frame. The end delimiter also contains bits to indicate a damaged frame and identify the frame that is the last in a logical sequence.
- **Frame Status**—Is a 1-byte field terminating a command/data frame. The Frame Status field includes the address-recognized indicator and frame-copied indicator.

11.5.3 Ring Management

The mechanism of the network operation is consider being the mechanism in the steady state, but before this can take place the ring must be set up. Also if a new station wishes to join an operational ring it must first go through an initialization procedure to ensure that it does not interfere with the correct functioning of the current active ring. Also, during normal operation it is necessary for each active station on the ring to monitor its correct operation and if something is not working well it must take some action to try reestablish a correctly functioning ring. Those functions and others which meant to preserve the correct ring operation are called ring management.

There are two types of stations in the ring :

- Active Monitor (AM) station
- Standby Monitor (SBM) stations

There is only one Active Monitor station per ring. The Active Monitor is the ring manager. All other stations on the ring are Standby Monitor stations. Any station on the ring can be Active Monitor. The Active Monitor is chosen during a process called "Claim Token Process" and after the Active Monitor is chosen all other stations become "Standby Monitors" (SBM).

Active Monitor Duties

- One function of the active monitor is the removal of continuously circulating frames (orphan frames), from the ring. When a sending device fails, its frame may continue to circulate the ring. This can prevent other stations from transmitting their own frames and result in the network locking up. The active monitor can detect these frames, remove them from the ring and generate a new token.
- If a corrupted frame appears on the ring the active monitor can detect it, as it will have an invalid frame format, or an invalid checksum. In this type of case the active monitor drains the token and issues a new one.

- As there are 24-bits in a token the ring must be big enough to hold all of them. On each pass through the stations the token is delayed by one bit. If this one bit delay plus the delay due to the cable length adds up to less than 24-bits, the active monitor inserts extra delay bits so that the token can circulate correctly.

Standby Monitor Duties:

- Check for the presence of an active monitor at regular intervals.
- Go through a token-claiming process to determine a new active monitor if, for any reason the active monitor fails.

Priority System

Token passing is often called deterministic, because you can calculate the maximum time before a workstation can grab the token and begin to transmit. However, you can assign priorities to certain devices that will use the network more frequently. The token itself has a priority value that can be changed. The token is captured by a workstation and an information frame is sent out on the network in place of the token. A workstation with a priority equal to or higher than the priority value in the information frame can then seize the token. When the original token is put back on the network after the workstation is through transmitting, the priority value must be set back to the original value.

Fault Management

A Token Ring network is much more reliable for a number of reasons:

- **Active monitoring** : The active monitor is most likely the first station to be brought up on the Token Ring network. The active monitor performs maintenance functions, such as removing continuously circulated rings and generating new tokens.
- **Beaconing** : *Beaconing* refers to a frame that is sent around the network when a serious network problem occurs. This frame is sent to the nearest active upstream neighbor (NAUN) until the frame stops. When the frame stops, beaconing determines that the next upstream neighbor has a problem. If the station that initiated the beacon receives its own original beacon, it assumes the link failure has been fixed, and then regenerates the token. This is a more effective troubleshooting method compared to the difficulty of determining problems on a bus topology backbone, which gives no clear indication of which station has malfunctioned. However, beaconing is similar to the bus topology in that one break in the link can cause the entire network to stop.
- **Selective removal of stations** : More advanced Token Ring hardware can be used to isolate the failed port and automatically remove it from the ring. This ensures that a faulty station does not affect the rest of the network.

11.5.4 Objective

The objective is to send a data packet from Computer 2 to Computer 4. There are two types of packet: Free Tokens and Busy Tokens. Free tokens contain no data. Busy tokens contain data to be conveyed by the network. When there is no other activity in the network a free token is passed from computer to computer around the ring.

Step 1 : Computer 1

Let us begin our description with computer 1. It has no data to send so when it receives the free token from computer 4, it passes it to computer 2.

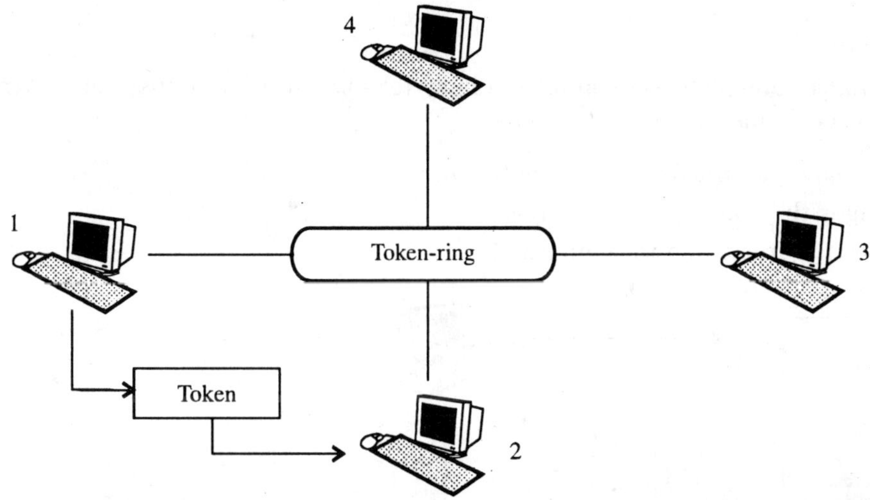

Fig. 11.8 Free token passed from computer 1 to computer 2

Step 2 : Computer 2

Computer 2 does have data to send. It performs the following steps:

- Changes the token status to busy.

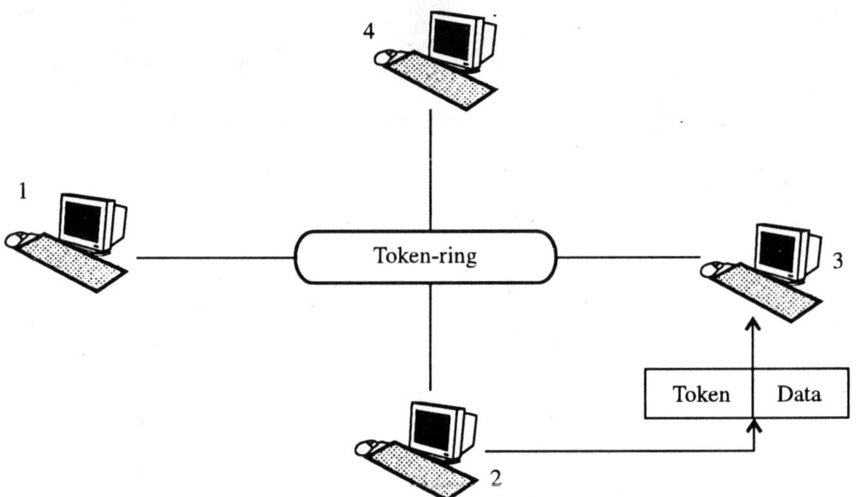

Fig. 11.9 Busy token and data passed from computer 2 to computer 3

- Attaches the data unit to the busy token.
- Passes the busy token and data to computer 3.

Step 3 : Computer 3

Computer 3 has no data of its own to send so when it receives the busy token from computer 4 it passes it to computer 4.

Step 4 : Computer 4

Computer 4 is the intended recipient of the busy token so when the busy token arrives from computer 3, it performs the following steps:

- Removes data unit from the busy token.
- Changes the token's status to free.
- Passes the free token to computer 1.

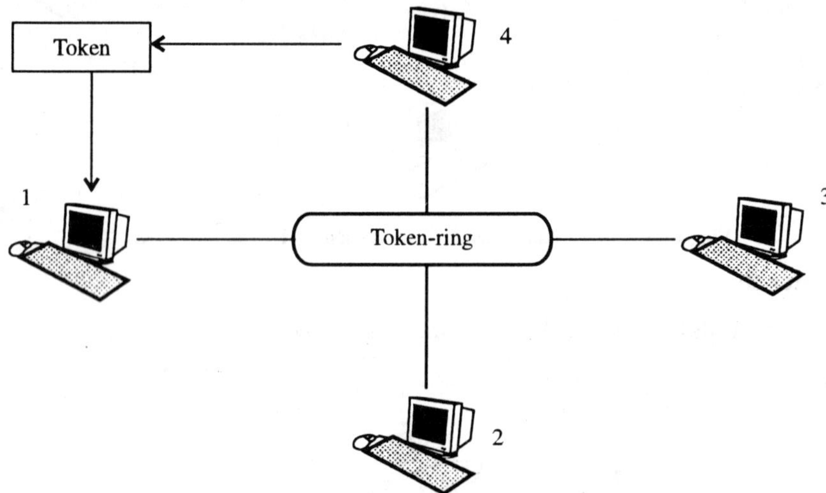

Fig. 11.10 Free token passed from computer 4 to computer 1

And the process continues.

The following flowchart illustrates token access method in a ring network.

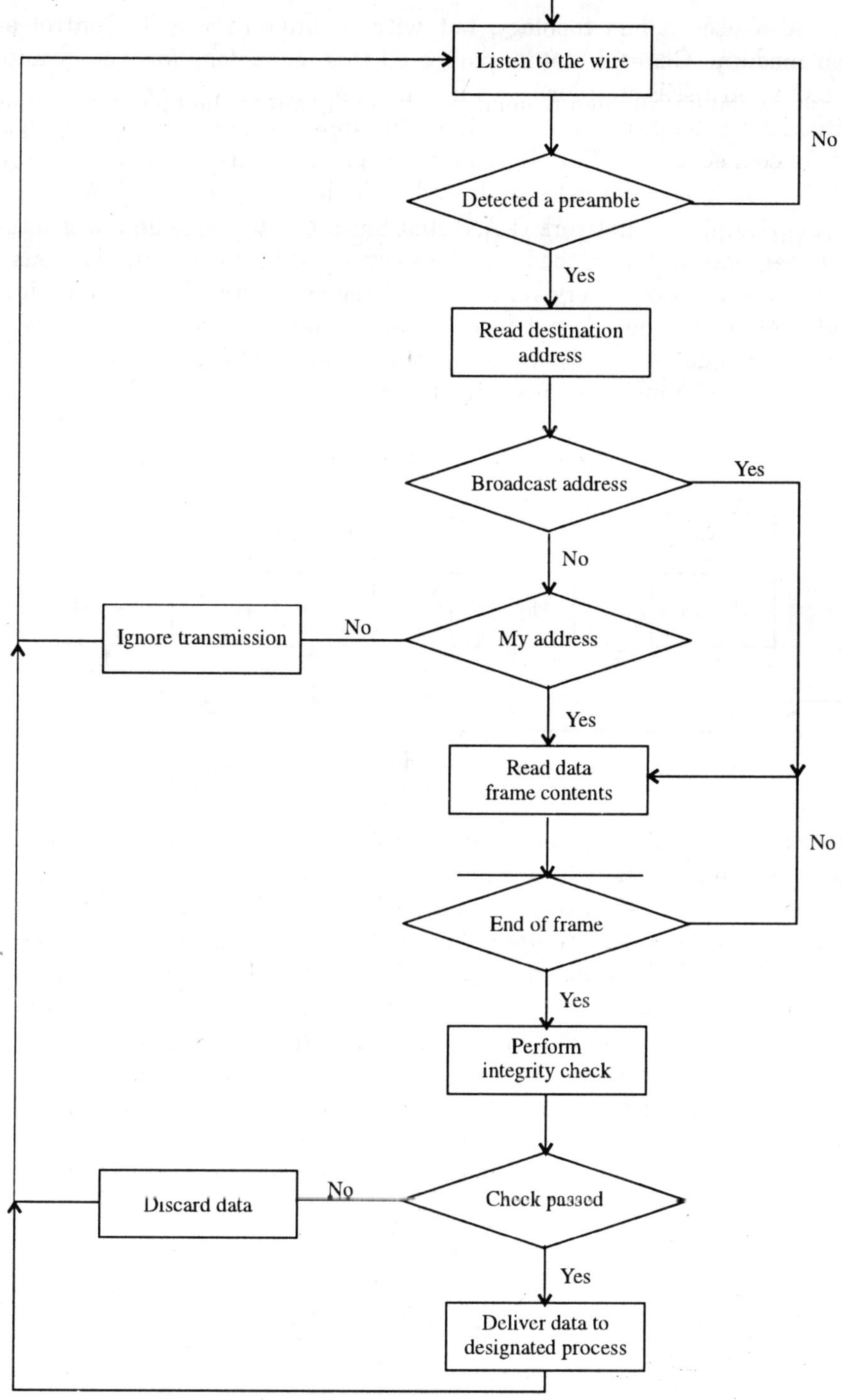

Fig. 11.11 Flowchart illustrating token access method in ring network

11.6 Token Bus (IEEE 802.4)

This version also uses a bus topology, but with a different way to control access to the transmission medium. General Motors pioneered this technology for factory automation and it was adopted as an IEEE standard, but it is not used much any more.

Token Bus LANs could transmit at 1, 5, or 10 Mbps speeds and were only approved to use coaxial cable to connect nodes. The physical layer specifications included several very complex ways of encoding data as electrical signals and make it totally incompatible with 802.3 LANs.

It is a type of local-area network (LAN) that has a bus topology and uses a token -passing mechanism to regulate traffic on the bus. So we can say that it is physically a bus and logically a ring. A token bus network is very similar to a token ring network, the main difference being that the endpoints of the bus do not meet to form a physical ring. Token bus networks are defined by the IEEE 802.4 standard. This protocol like the 802.5 Token ring network, use a token to allocate the channel to competing stations.

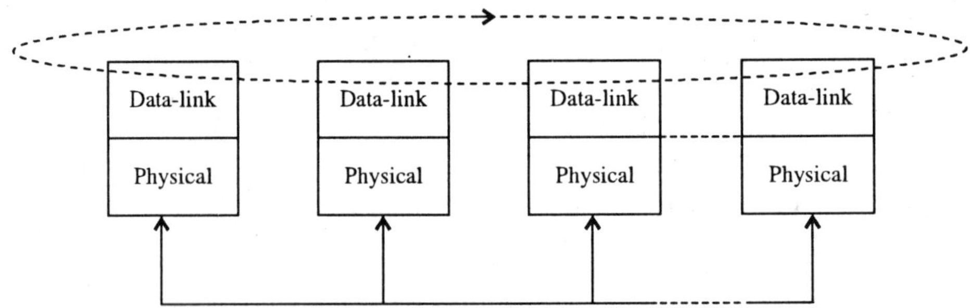

Fig. 11.12 A token passed from device to device around a logical ring

This bus network was developed mainly for factories, to overcome the problem of delays in Ethernet: we have seen that these delays can grow without limit if the network is loaded. This characteristic is not very attractive for real time and control applications. The factory automation people in the 802 committee liked the idea of a ring, but did not like its weakness: if the ring is interrupted, the whole network is down. Thus they proposed a new standard that has the robustness of Ethernet and the known worst-case of a ring network.

Logical Token Bus is a contention-less protocol. With this protocol the MAC sub-layers pass around a *token* and only the MAC sub-layer with the token can use the channel. When a particular MAC sub-layer has finished sending a frame, it sends the token to the next MAC sub-layer, and so on. If a MAC sub-layer has no frame to transmit then it simply passes the token to the next MAC sub-layer. Clearly the protocol can be applied for both half duplex and full duplex channels.

11.6.1 Token Bus Frame Format

Field	Preamble	Start of frame delimiter	Frame control	Destination address	Source address	Data	Check-sum bits	End delimiter
Size (bytes)	1	1	1	6	6	0–8174	4	1

Fig. 11.13 Token bus frame format

Token Bus fields and their uses:

- **Preamble**—A special bit pattern that marks the beginning of a frame.
- **Start of frame delimiter**—A special bit pattern that marks the start of the frame itself.
- **Frame control**—A 1-byte field used to indicate if the frame contains actual data or if it is a control message.
  - ◻ For data frames, it carries the frame's priority, indicator requiring the destination to acknowledge the receipt of the frame.
  - ◻ For control frames, the filed is used to specify the frame type, including token passing, letting new station enter the ring, allowing station to leave, and other maintenance functions.
- **Destination Address**—An address specifying a specific destination station, a group of stations, or all stations in the LAN. This address can be 16 bits or 48 bits in length, but all stations in the LAN must adhere to one format or the other.
- **Source Address**—The address of the originating station. This address has the same length requirements as the destination address.
- **Length of data**—Indicates exactly how much data is in the frame (since it can vary).
- **Data**—The data to be delivered by the frame, it can range from 0 to 8174 bytes. Note that the 802.4 data section can be much longer than the 802.3 data section. The data field can be upto 8182 bytes long when 2-byte address is used; it can be upto 8174 bytes long when 6-byte address is used.
- **Checksum**—32-bit CRC error detection information for finding errors in the frame.
- **End of frame delimiter**—A special bit pattern that marks the end of the frame. The last two bits of this field signal if the frame is the last frame to be transmitted and whether any station has detected an error in the frame.

11.6.2 Token Bus Operation

- There is a special frame called the token that contains a unique bit pattern. This token is passed from node to node in a predetermined way along the bus.
- Only the node that has the token is allowed to transmit a frame and all other nodes must wait for their turn. Once a node receives the token, it can transmit a frame if it

needs to. If a node has several small frames to send, it can send them all at one time, so long as it does not take longer than a preset time limit.

- If there are no frames to be transmitted, the token is immediately passed to the next node.
- Since only one node can transmit at a time, collisions are impossible.
- The physical topology is arranged as a bus, but the logical topology is a ring. Each node on the bus knows its "successor" node in the logical ring, and passes the token to that successor node. Data frames are passed along the bus in the same way. This allows a token bus LAN to be connected in a simpler way than a physical ring, but still act like one.
- Nodes on a token bus LAN can assign different priorities to frames and they will deliver all high priority frames before they send any of the lower priority frames. This allows nodes to guarantee that they can send real-time data every time that they get the token and, if they have any time left, send other data as well.

Stations are added to an 802.4 bus by an approach called response windows:

- While holding the token, a node issues a solicit-successor frame. The address in the frame is between it and the next successor station.
- Token holder waits one window time (slot time, equal to twice the end-to-end propagation delay).
- If no response, the token is transferred to the successor node.
- If response, a requesting node sends a set-successor frame and token holder changes its successor node address. Requested node receives token, sets its addresses, and proceeds.

A node can drop out of the transmission sequence. Upon receiving a token, it sends a *set-successor* frame to the predecessor, which orders the next node to give the token hereafter to its successor.

Priority Scheme

When the ring is initialized, stations are inserted into it in order of station address, from highest to lowest. The token bus defines four priority classes, 0, 2, 4, 6 for traffic, with 0 the lowest and 6 the highest. Conceptually, each station internally being divided into four substations, one at each priority level. As input comes into the MAC sublayer from above, data are checked for priority and routed to one of the four substations. Thus each substation maintains its own queue. When the token comes into the station over the cable, it is passed internally to the priority 6 substation, which may begin transmitting frames, if it has any. When it is done (or when its timer expires), the token is passed internally to the priority 4 substation. Setting the timer properly we can ensure that a guaranteed fraction of the total token holding time can be allocated to priority 6 traffic. The lower priorities will have to live with what is left over. Priority 6 traffic is guaranteed a known fraction of the network bandwidth and can be used to implement real-time traffic.

Overall Performance of Token Based Protocols

Token based protocols (token ring and token bus) are essentially contention-free protocols. They rely on coordination among stations.

- Under light load, few stations want to transmit. But they still have to wait for token to pass around. Token based protocols perform poorer than contention based protocol such as Ethernet at light load.
- Under heavy load, all stations want to transmit, thus coordination can avoid collision. Token based protocols perform better than contention based protocol such as Ethernet.

This is analog to waiting lines in a restaurant. When few people are around, the extra zig-zag lines are anoying. When many people want to eat, these lines help organize the crowd and people can get through fast.

11.7 Comparison Of Various IEEE Standards

11.7.1 Token Ring IEEE 802.5 Vs Ethernet IEEE 802.3

- Token Ring networks are deterministic in nature-nodes may only transmit at certain well defined times. Result is high bandwidth efficiency. Up to 90% in Token Ring, 40% in Ethernet.
- Token Ring performance does not deteriorate to the same extent as Ethernet when network traffic increases. This means that at high loads, the presence of collisions of data frames on Ethernet networks becomes a major problem and can seriously affect the throughput.
- By its nature Token Ring has a higher reliability, the ring can continue normal operation in most cases despite any single fault.
- Ethernet has an advantage over Token Ring in that the cost of network equipment is lower for Ethernet. Token Ring networks tend to be more expensive to set up and maintain than Ethernet, although hardware costs for Token Ring are decreasing.
- Advances in Ethernet technology have tended to be much more rapid than Token Ring. Gigabit Ethernet being an example of this. Token Ring technologies are being developed however to allow data transfer rates of 100Mbps using technologies such as Token Ring Switching.

11.7.2 Token Ring—IEEE 802.5 Vs Token Bus—IEEE 802.4

- These standards although similar in some respects were developed with different applications in mind. Token Bus (IEEE 802.4), networks use a Bus technology and do not have a centralized active monitor. Token Bus was designed with large factories in mind where machines and equipment would be moving around under computer control. Network failures could have serious consequences and so had to be avoided at all costs. On the other hand the Token Ring network standard was designed with office automation in mind, where a failure once in a rare while could be tolerated as the price for simpler system.

- Token Bus is not as deterministic as Token Ring but like Token Ring it has excellent throughput and efficiency at high load.
- Token Bus uses broadband transmission and cabling which obviously gives it a bandwidth advantage over Token Ring but the downside is the equipment costs (modems, wideband amplifiers, etc). The IEEE 802.4 protocol is also extremely complex compared to IEEE 802.5 and it has a substantial delay at low loads.

11.7.3 Comparison of 802.3, 802.4, and 802.5

Advantages of 802.3

- Low maintenance (low management complexity)
- Easy installation (in comparison with 802.4 and 802.5)
- Widely used (cheap components and a large amount of trained personnel)
- Low latency under low loads—get quick access when not many stations are transmitting—have to wait for a token with the other protocols

Disadvantages of 802.3

- Non-deterministic
- Utilization falls under a heavy load
- Lack of priorities
- Lack of acknowledgements
- Minimum frame length
- Efficiency drops as speed increases

Advantages of 802.4

- Uses cable TV equipment (no creation of new equipment)
- Deterministic
- Has priorities
- No minimum packet size (if you only have 1-bit to send, only send 1-bit)
- High utilization under a heavy load
- Efficiency doesn't drop with increased speed

Disadvantages of 802.4

- High management complexity
- Large analog component (since uses cable TV equipment)
- Not widely used
- Low efficiency under low loads
- Not suited for fiber optics

Advantages of 802.5

- Can use fiber
- Deterministic
- Has priorities
- Utilization high under loads
- No frame size restrictions

Disadvantages of 802.5

- High management complexity
- Breaks in the ring
- Installation (wire centers improve this my preventing you from having to break the ring to install a new station)
- High latency under low loads (must wait for the token to propagate around)

11.8 Distributed Queue Dual Bus—DQDB (IEEE 802.6)

Distributed Queue Dual Bus (DQDB), specified in the IEEE 802.6 standard, is a data-link layer communication protocol for Metropolitan Area Networks (MANs). DQDB is designed for data as well as voice and video transmission based on cell switching technology. DQDB, which permits multiple systems to interconnect using two unidirectional logical buses, is an open standard that is designed for compatibility with carrier transmission standards.

For a MAN to be effective it requires a system that can function across long, city-wide distances of several miles, have a low susceptibility to error, adapt to the number of nodes attached and have variable bandwidth distribution. Using DQDB, networks can be thirty miles long and function in the range of 34 Mbps to 155 Mbps. The data rate fluctuates due to many hosts sharing a dual bus as well as the location of a single host in relation to the frame generator, but there are schemes to compensate for this problem making DQDB function reliably and fairly for all hosts.

The **distributed queue dual bus (DQDB)** network uses a different kind of MAC method based on the use of a distributed queuing algorithm called **queued-packet distributed-switch (QPSX)** and a slotted ring arrangement. It uses two unconnected unidirectional buses, which are normally implemented as a series of point-to-point segments. DQDB also expects the use of optical fibre links.

11.8.1 Architecture of DQDB

The DQDB is composed of a two bus lines with stations attached to both and a frame generator at the end of each bus. The connections are normally point-to-point, but are often depicted in the tapped-bus type configuration as shown in Figure 11.14. The buses run in parallel in such a fashion as to allow the frames generated to travel across the stations in opposite directions. Both these buses always have a constant number of slots circulating on them. A slot on one bus is copied to the other.

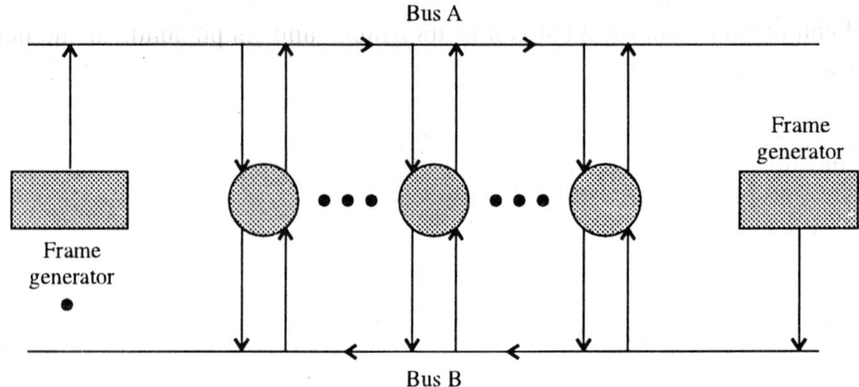

Fig. 11.14 Architecture of DQDB

The two buses in a DQDB network transmit cells in opposite directions and each node is connected to both buses.

The DQDB LAN or MAN transports data in fixed size **cells**, which happen to look very much like ATM cells (discussed in chapter 8). However, as DQDB offers a MAC service, the MAC frame may need to be segmented into several cells before transmission. The cell structure for DQDB is almost identical to that of an ATM cell. This similarity between the cell structure has been made so that the DQDB will be compatible with B-ISDN.

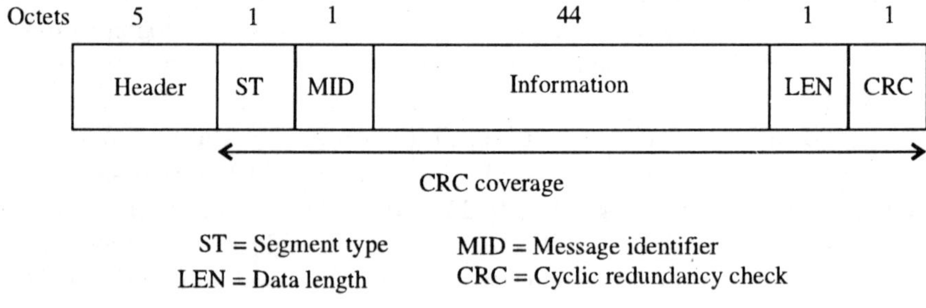

Fig. 11.15 A DQDB cell

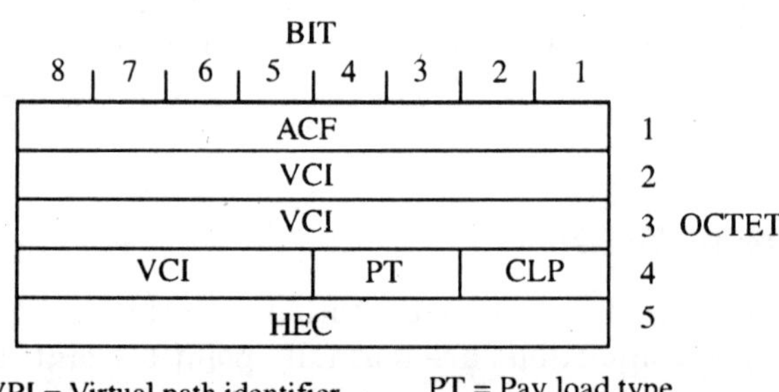

Fig. 11.16 A DQDB cell header

A DQDB cell differs from an ATM cell in its header and its payload. In the header of the DQDB cell there is no virtual path identifier (VPI) and the virtual channel identifier (VCI) has an additional 4-bits. The first 8 bits of the DQDB header form an access control field (ACF) (in ATM this is the first 8-bits of the VPI). Also, the next 4-bits (the final 4-bits of the VPI in ATM) form the first 4-bits of the VCI.

Also, the **CELL PAYLOAD** is structured as discussed below:

- **Segment type (ST)** : Identifies the cell as one of the following:
  - □ **Single segment** : Only this segment (no MAC fragmentation was required).
  - □ **First segment** : The first cell of a segmented MAC frame.
  - □ **Intermediate segment** : The intermediate cells in a fragmented MAC frame.
  - □ **Last segment** : The final cell of a segmented MAC frame.
- **Message identifier (MID)** : The MID is the same for all DQDB cells from the same MAC frame. This allows the identification of intermediate segments.
- **Information** : (part of) The MAC frame contents.
- **Length (LEN)** : The length of the information field.
- **CRC** : Covering everything the whole cell payload.

The **CELL HEADER** contains the following information:

- **Access control field (ACF)** : This contains the BUSY and REQUEST bits that are used in the operation of the QPSX mechanism. The BUSY bit indicates the slot is in use. The REQUEST bit is set in a slot by a node that is waiting to transmit.
- **Virtual channel identifier (VCI)** : This is not used in a DQDB MAN as there are no logical connections which require multiplexing—the ST and MID fields in the payload are used instead. In a DQDB LAN, there is the possibility for applications to make use of this field.
- **Payload type (PT)** : (same as ATM) It identifies payload type for OAM (Operations, Administration and Maintenance). Also reserved bits for explicit congestion control.
- **Cell loss priority (CLP)** : (same as ATM) It is used for buffer management.
  - □ If set (1) then the cell may be discarded according to network conditions—congestion control.
  - □ If not set (0) cell cannot be discarded.
- **Header error control (HEC)** : CRC for the header. It is used to detect and correct errors in the header.

11.9 CSMA/CA Medium Access Protocol (IEEE 802.11)

Introduction

The IEEE 802.11 standard defines the physical layer and media access control (MAC) layer for a wireless local area network. This standard is increasingly being deployed in wireless LAN communication.

Shared broadcast channels are often used in local area networks (LANs). Both wired 802.3 Ethernet network and wireless 802.11 LAN network must co-ordinate transmissions onto the shared communication channel. In case of 802.3 Ethernet, the shared channel is the shared wire whereas in case of wireless 802.11 LAN the shared channel is the radio frequency. The media access control (MAC) protocol co-ordinates the transmission. Although the IEEE 802.11 standard belongs to the same standard family as wired 802.3 Ethernet, it has a significantly different media access protocol. While Collision Detection works well on Ethernet, they cannot be used in wireless LAN.

The media access control of IEEE 802.11 is using carrier sense multiple access with collision avoidance (CSMA/CA) as the fundamental access. In 802.11 carrier sense (CS) is performed both at physical layer (physical carrier sensing) and at the MAC layer (virtual carrier sensing).

The IEEE 802.11 MAC protocol does not implement collision detection. There are a few reasons for this:

- Implementing a Collision Detection Mechanism would require the implementation of a Full Duplex radio, capable of transmitting and receiving at once. This approach would increase the price significantly.
- In radio systems received signal is weak compared to transmitted signal and therefore collision detection cannot be done by simple comparison.
- Even if one had collision detection and sensed no collision when sensing, a collision could still occur at the receiver. The reason for this is the two following properties of the wireless channel.

The 802.11 standard includes a basic Distributed Co-ordination Function (DCF). The DCF is the fundamental access method used to support asynchronous data transfer on the best effort basis. As specified in standards, the DCF must be supported by all the stations in a basic service set (BSS). The DCF is based on CSMA/CA.

There are two techniques used for packet transmitting in DCF:

- The default one is a two-way handshaking mechanism, also called basic access method. The destination station transmits a positive acknowledgement (ACK) message to signal a successful packet transmission.
- The other optional mechanism is a four-way handshaking access method, which uses the request-to-send/clear-to-send (RTS/CTS) technique to reserve the channel before data transmission.

Carrier Sensing Protocol with Collision Avoidance

The carrier sensing family of protocols is characterized by sensing the carrier and deciding according to it whether another transmission is ongoing. All the carrier sense multiple access (CSMA) protocols share the same philosophy: when a user generates a new packet the channel is sensed and if found idle the packet is transmitted immediately.

These kinds of algorithms are very effective when the medium is not heavily loaded, since it allows users to transmit with a minimum delay. However, there is always a chance of several users transmitting at the same time (i.e., collision), because the users sensed the medium free and decided to transmit at once. Because of the difficulties in detecting collisions at a wireless receiver, the IEEE 802.11 protocol tries to avoid collisions, rather than detect and recover from collisions.

The CSMA/CA protocol is designed to reduce the collision probability at the points where collisions would most likely occur. The highest probability of a collision exists when the medium has become idle after a busy state. This is because several users could have been waiting for the medium to be available again. This is the situation that necessitates a random back-off procedure to resolve medium contention conflicts. Also, the use of IFS (Inter Frame Space) helps to resolve the problem. CSMA/CA provides some carrier sense functions to avoid collisions.

11.9.1 IEEE 802.11 Architectures

In IEEE's proposed standard for wireless LANs (IEEE 802.11), there are two different ways to configure a network

- Ad-hoc.
- Infrastructure.

In the ad-hoc network, computers are brought together to form a network "on the fly". As shown in Figure 11.17, there is no structure to the network; there are no fixed points; and usually every node is able to communicate with every other node. A good example of this is the aforementioned meeting where employees bring laptop computers together to communicate and share design or financial information. Although it seems that order would be difficult to maintain in this type of network, algorithms such as the spokesman election algorithm (SEA) have been designed to "elect" one machine as the base station (master) of the network with the others being slaves. Another algorithm in ad-hoc network architectures uses a broadcast and flooding method to all other nodes to establish who's who.

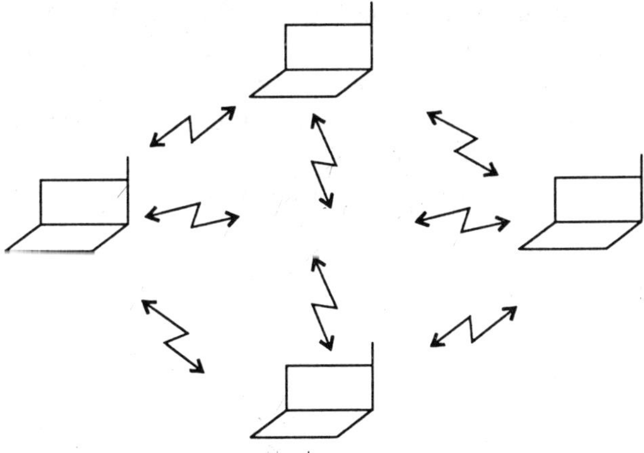

Fig. 11.17 Ad-hoc network

As shown in Figure 11.18, the second type of network structure used in wireless LAN's is **the infrastructure**. This architecture uses fixed network access points with which mobile nodes can communicate. These network access points are sometime connected to landlines to widen the LAN's capability by bridging wireless nodes to other wired nodes. If service areas overlap, handoffs can occur. This structure is very similar to the present day cellular networks around the world.

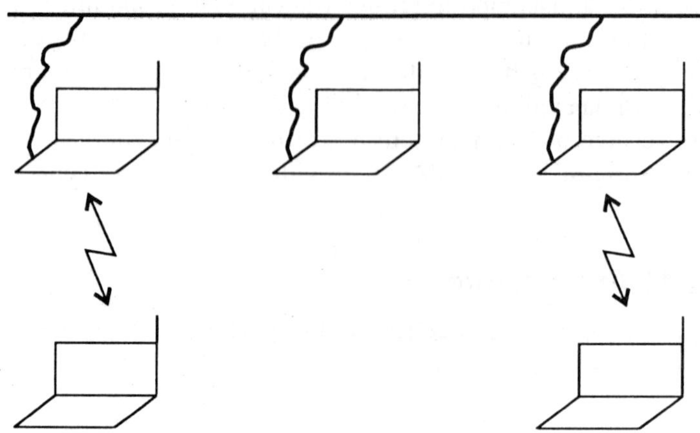

Fig. 11.18 Infrastructure network

11.10 Fiber Distributed Data Interface (FDDI)

Another high-speed token-passing network architecture is the Fiber Distributed Data Interface (FDDI). FDDI is a new standard for token ring using fiber for individual links. This network is much faster, extremely fault tolerant and can cover more distance than Token Ring. This technology uses fiber-optic cabling to reach speeds of 100-Mbps. Although FDDI lacks a Project 802 standard, it roughly maps to the IEEE 802.3 and 802.5. FDDI most represents the 802.5 token-passing model that represents the Token Ring topology as indicated earlier.

FDDI is frequently used as high-speed backbone technology because of its support for high bandwidth and greater distances than copper. It should be noted that relatively recently, a related copper specification, called Copper Distributed Data Interface (CDDI), has emerged to provide 100-Mbps service over copper. CDDI is the implementation of FDDI protocols over twisted-pair copper wire. (CDDI to be discussed later).

FDDI is an alternative to standard Ethernet for a number of reasons:

- Much faster.
- Greater maximum distance.
- Resistance to EMI.
- Improved fault tolerance.

The biggest difference between the Token Ring technology and FDDI is the use of fiber-optic cable, which increases the transmission speeds to 100-Mbps. A much greater maximum distance of two kilometers between workstations now exists within a FDDI network. This is due in part to the fiber-optic cabling used which also resists *electromagnetic interference* (*EMI*), which has always plagued copper-based cabling. These features have made FDDI an excellent choice for connecting LAN's or buildings together. In addition to high speed and resistance to EMI, fiber-optic cable cannot be tapped like copper-based cable can. However, the cost is still beyond reach of most networks to offer a FDDI solution for local area networks.

FDDI also introduces dual, counter-rotating rings. Workstations can connect to one ring or both, which still allows the workstation to communicate even if one of the rings fails. Although Token Ring has the ability to implement fault-tolerant techniques with redundant rings, many Token Ring networks use only one ring.

11.10.1 Features of FDDI

1. Supports data rates of 100-Mbps over 200 km.
2. Uses LED rather than lasers for safety reason.
3. Calls for less than 10-10 bit error rate. This means we worry much less about checksums etc.
4. In addition to data frames, FDDI also permits special synchronous frames for real-time data such as voice. The synchronous frames are generated every 125μ second to provide the 8000 samples per second PCM data.

11.10.2 FDDI Transmission Media

FDDI uses optical fiber as the primary transmission medium, but it also can run over copper cabling. As mentioned earlier, FDDI over copper is referred to as *Copper-Distributed Data Interface* (*CDDI*). Optical fiber has several advantages over copper media. In particular, security, reliability and performance all are enhanced with optical fiber media because fiber does not emit electrical signals. A physical medium that does emit electrical signals (copper) can be tapped and therefore would permit unauthorized access to the data that is transiting the medium. In addition, fiber is immune to electrical interference from radio frequency interference (RFI) and electromagnetic interference (EMI). Fiber historically has supported much higher bandwidth (throughput potential) than copper, although recent technological advances have made copper capable of transmitting at 100 Mbps. Finally, FDDI allows 2 km between stations using multimode fiber and even longer distances using a single mode.

FDDI defines two types of optical fiber: single-mode and multimode. A *mode* is a ray of light that enters the fiber at a particular angle. *Multimode* fiber uses LED as the light-generating device, while *single-mode* fiber generally uses lasers.

11.10.3 FDDI Frame Format

The FDDI frame format is similar to the format of a Token Ring frame. FDDI frames can be as large as 4,500 bytes. Figure 11.19 shows the frame format of an FDDI data frame and token.

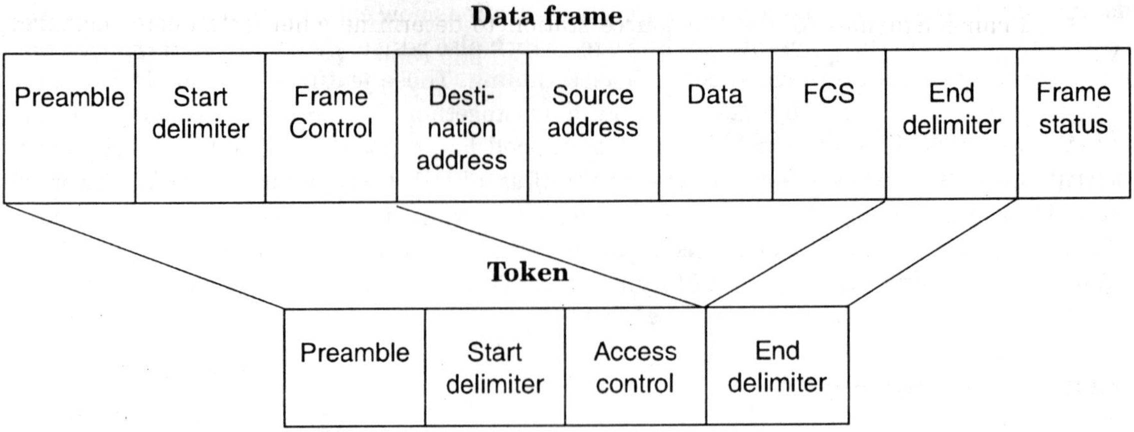

Fig. 11.19 The FDDI frame is similar to that of a token ring frame

FDDI Frame Fields

The following descriptions summarize the FDDI data frame and token fields illustrated in Figure 11.19.

- **Preamble (PA)**—16 (or more) IDLE symbols. Gives a unique sequence that prepares each station for an upcoming frame.
- **Start Delimiter (SD)**—Indicates the beginning of a frame by employing a signaling pattern that differentiates it from the rest of the frame. The 2 symbols *J* and *K* are used to show the start of the frame and also to allow interpretation of correct symbol boundaries.
- **Frame Control (FC)**—Indicates the size of the address fields and whether the frame contains asynchronous or synchronous data, among other control information. 2 symbols indicating whether or not this is an information frame or a MAC frame (e.g., the token), with some additional control information for the station identified by the DA.
- **Destination Address (DA)**—Contains a unicast (singular), multicast (group) or broadcast (every station) address. As with Ethernet and Token Ring addresses, FDDI destination addresses are 6 bytes long.
- **Source Address (SA)**—Identifies the single station that sent the frame. As with Ethernet and Token Ring addresses, FDDI source addresses are 6 bytes long.
- **Data**—Contains either information destined for an upper-layer protocol or control information.
- **Frame Check Sequence (FCS)**—Is filled by the source station with a calculated cyclic redundancy check value dependent on frame contents (as with Token Ring and Ethernet). The destination address recalculates the value to determine whether the frame was damaged in transit. If so, the frame is discarded.
- **End Delimiter**—Contains unique symbols; cannot be data symbols that indicate the end of the frame.

- **Frame Status**—Allows the source station to determine whether an error occurred; identifies whether the frame was recognized and copied by a receiving station.

11.10.4 Operation Of FDDI

FDDI's operation is similar to that of token ring. FDDI uses dual-ring architecture with traffic on each ring flowing in opposite directions (called counter-rotating). The primary purpose of the dual rings is to provide superior reliability and robustness. Figure 11.20 shows the counter-rotating primary and secondary FDDI rings.

The dual rings consist of a primary and a secondary ring. During normal operation, the primary ring is used for data transmission and the secondary ring remains idle. Stations attached to the FDDI may be connected to both rings, **dual attach stations (DASs)** or only to the primary ring, **single attach station (SASs)**. Although, the stations are logically attached in a ring, the physical connection is more conveniently realized in a hub-star fashion by using wiring concentrators.

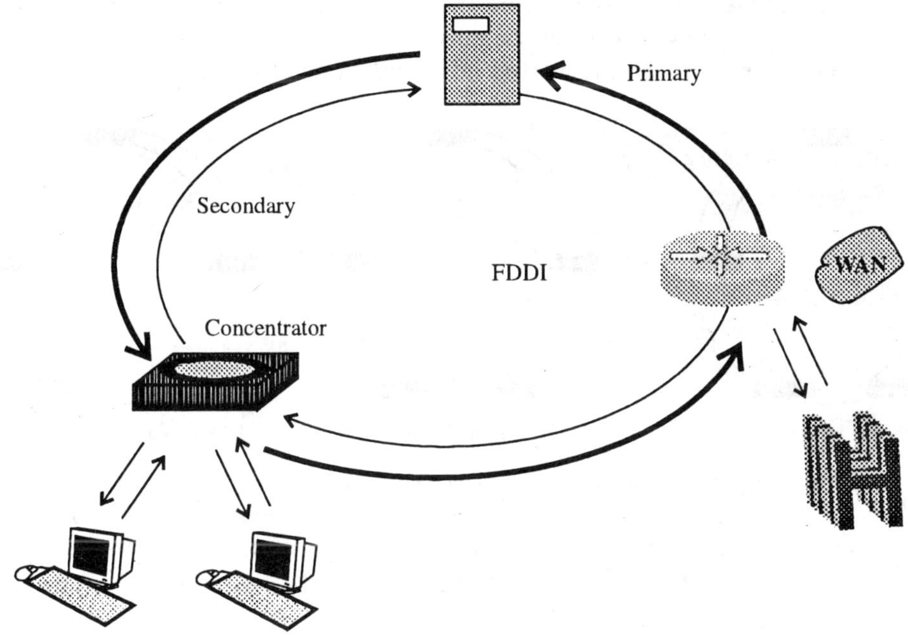

Fig. 11.20 FDDI uses counter-rotating primary and secondary rings

Access Method of FDDI—Token Passing

Token passing is the network access method for the FDDI architecture and still behaves as the original token-passing implementation. Of course, the fiber-optic cable has increased the speed at which the token travels around the network. Priorities can still be assigned to workstations and the active monitoring still remains. One reason FDDI can produce higher transmission rates than Token Ring is because a FDDI network can have several frames on the network at once. Once an FDDI station is done transmitting, the token is released. The

FDDI source does not have to wait for successful acknowledgements from the destination before the token is released. As with Token Ring, FDDI is well suited for high volumes of network traffic. This is due to the token-passing technology which eliminates collisions on the network.

SAS and DAS stations

A single-attached station (SAS) is a workstation or device that is attached to only one of the fiber-optic cable rings. This workstation can continue communicating with stations only on the same segment if the ring were to fail. A dual-attached station (DAS) is attached to both fiber-optic cable rings and can continue communicating with the remaining stations if one of the rings fails and can redirect traffic onto the secondary ring.

Beaconing and Wrapping

Beaconing still functions just as described in the section on Token Ring. However, a new technique known as *wrapping* has been introduced with the FDDI network. The dual, counter-rotating FDDI rings can benefit from improved fault tolerance when a cable fault on the network is detected. A single fault on the network can cause the primary ring to wrap the signal onto the secondary ring, as illustrated in Figure 11.21.

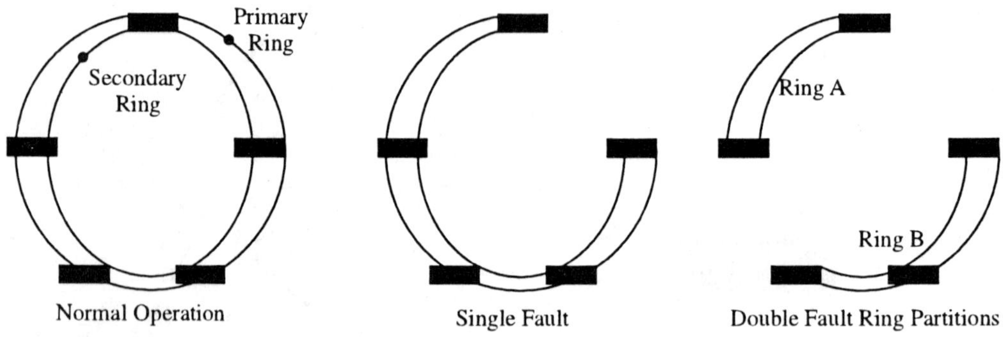

Fig. 11.21 Ring wrapping after a single fault and results of a double fault

Ring wrapping is the desired method of recovering from a broken link. Ring wrapping uses an optical bypass switch that bypasses the failed device rather than create a partitioned set of two networks.

FDDI Fault Tolerance

FDDI provides a number of fault-tolerant features. In particular, FDDI's dual-ring environment, the implementation of the optical bypass switch and dual-homing support make FDDI a resilient media technology.

Dual Ring

FDDI's primary fault-tolerant feature is the *dual ring*. If a station on the dual ring fails or is powered down or if the cable is damaged the dual ring is automatically wrapped (doubled back onto itself) into a single ring. When the ring is wrapped, the dual-ring topology becomes a single-ring topology. Data continues to be transmitted on the FDDI ring without performance impact during the wrap condition.

11.10.5 FDDI Specifications

FDDI specifies the physical and media-access portions of the OSI reference model. FDDI is not actually a single specification, but it is a collection of four separate specifications, each with a specific function. Combined, these specifications have the capability to provide high-speed connectivity between upper-layer protocols such as TCP/IP and IPX, and media such as fiber-optic cabling.

FDDI's four specifications are stated below:

- **Media Access Control (MAC)** : The MAC specification defines how the medium is accessed, including frame format, token handling, addressing, algorithms for calculating cyclic redundancy check (CRC) value and error-recovery mechanisms.
- **Physical Layer Protocol (PHY)** : The PHY specification defines data encoding/decoding procedures, clocking requirements, and framing, among other functions.
- **Physical-Medium Dependent (PMD)** : The PMD specification defines the characteristics of the transmission medium, including fiber-optic links, power levels, bit-error rates, optical components and connectors.
- **Station Management (SMT)** : The SMT specification defines FDDI station con-

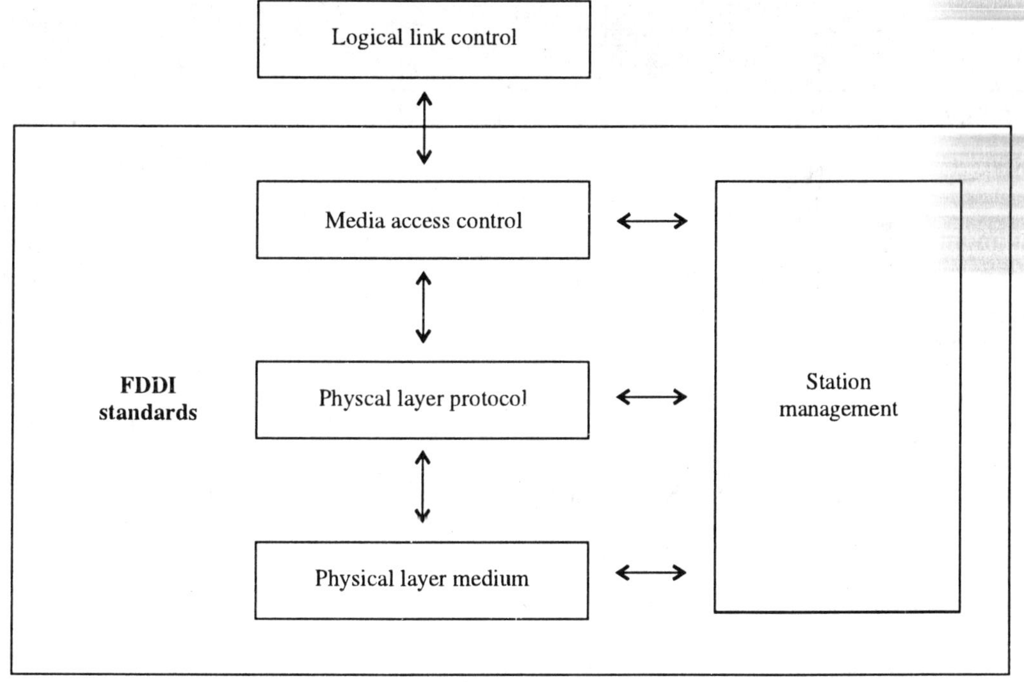

Fig. 11.22 FDDI Specifications map to the OSI hierarchical model

figuration, ring configuration and ring control features, including station insertion and removal, initialization, fault isolation and recovery, scheduling and statistics collection.

FDDI is similar to IEEE 802.3 Ethernet and IEEE 802.5 Token Ring in its relationship with the OSI model. Its primary purpose is to provide connectivity between upper OSI layers of common protocols and the media used to connect network devices. Figure 11.22 illustrates the four FDDI specifications and their relationship to each other and to the IEEE-defined Logical Link Control (LLC) sublayer. The LLC sublayer is a component of Layer 2, the MAC layer, of the OSI reference model.

11.11 Copper Distributed Data Interface (CDDI)

Copper Distributed Data Interface (CDDI) is a technology just like FDDI, except that copper-based media such as UTP or STP is used rather than fiber-optic cabling. However, the cost is greatly reduced, as well as the maximum cable lengths. The fiber-optic cable length used in FDDI is two kilometers, where a CDDI copper cable is limited to 100 meters.

Like FDDI, CDDI provides data rates of 100 Mbps and uses dual-ring architecture to provide redundancy. CDDI supports distances of about 100 meters from desktop to concentrator.

Table 11.1 Summarizes the topologies the media they employ and the hardware they require.

	Ethernet Thinnet (10Base2)	Ethernet Thicknet (10Base5)	Twisted-pair (10BaseT)	Token Ring	FDDI
Topology	Bus	Bus	Star	Ring/Star	Ring/Star
Media	Thin Coaxial	Thick Coaxial	Unshielded Twisted-pair	Shielded or Unshielded Twisted-pair	Fiber-optic
Maximum nodes	30 per segment	100 per segment	1024	STP = 260, UTP = 72 per MSAU	1000 per ring
Maximum connected segments	5	5	N/A	33 MSAUs	500
Maximum cable length	185m	500m	100m	45–100m, depends on cable	2000m

Table 11.1 : Topologies, Media and Hardware.

• • •

12

Network Layer

Introduction

The network layer is concerned with getting packets from the source all the way to the destination. This function contrasts with the goal of the data link layers whose purpose is to just transmit the bits from one end of a wire to the other end. The network layer design issues include the service provided to the transport layer, routing of packets through the subnet, congestion control and connection of multiple networks together.

12.1 Design Issues for the Network Layer

The network layer has been designed with the following goals:

1. The services provided should be independent of the underlying technology. Users of the service need not be aware of the physical implementation of the network. This design goal has great importance when we consider the great variety of networks in operation. In the area of Public networks, networks in underdeveloped countries are nowhere near the technological skill of those in the countries like the US or Ireland. The design of the layer must not disable us from connecting to networks of different technologies.
2. The transport layer (that is the host computer) should be shielded from the number, type and different topologies of the subnets it uses. That is, all the transport layer want is a communication link; it need not know how that link is made.
3. Finally, there is a need for some uniform addressing scheme for network addresses.

With these goals in mind, two different types of service emerged: Connection oriented and connectionless. A connection-oriented service is one in which the user is given a "reliable" end-to-end connection. To communicate, the user requests a connection, then uses the connection to his hearts content, and then closes the connection. A telephone call is the classic example of a connection-oriented service.

In a connection-less service, the user simply bundles his information together, puts an address on it and then sends it off, in the hope that it will reach its destination. There is no guarantee that the bundle will arrive. So a connection less service is one reminiscent of the postal system. A letter is sent, that is, put in the post box. It is then in the "postal network" where it gets bounced around and hopefully will leave the network in the correct place, that is, in the addressee's letter box. We can never be totally sure that the letter will arrive, but we know that there is a high probability that it will and so we place our trust in the postal network.

Overview of Other Network Layer Issues

The network layer is responsible for routing packets from the source to destination. The *routing algorithm* is the piece of software that decides where a packet goes next (e.g., which output line, or which node on a broadcast channel).

For connectionless networks, the routing decision is made for each datagram. For connection-oriented networks, the decision is made once, at circuit setup time.

1. Routing Issues

The routing algorithm must deal with the following issues:

- **Correctness and simplicity :** Networks are never taken down; individual parts (e.g., links, routers) may fail, but the whole network should not.
- **Stability :** If a link or router fails, how much time elapses before the remaining routers recognize the topology change? (Some never do..)
- **Fairness and optimality :** An inherently intractable problem. Definition of optimality usually doesn't consider fairness. Do we want to maximize channel usage? Minimize average delay?

When we look at routing in detail, we'll consider these routing issuses again.

2. Congestion

The network layer also must deal with congestion:

- When more packets enter an area than can be processed, delays increase and performance decreases. If the situation continues, the subnet may have no alternative but to discard packets.
- If the delay increases, the sender may (incorrectly) retransmit, making a bad situation even worse.
- Overall, performance degrades because the network is using (wasting) resources processing packets that eventually get discarded.

3. Internetworking

Finally, when we consider internetworking—connecting different network technologies together—one finds the same problems, only worse:

- Packets may travel through many different networks.
- Each network may have a different frame format.
- Some networks may be connectionless, other connection oriented.

12.2 The Internal Organization Of The Network Layer

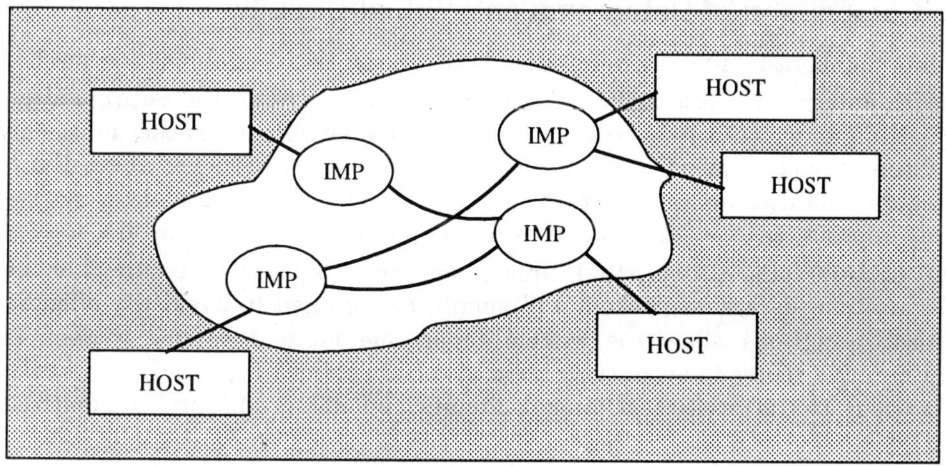

Fig. 12.1 General shape of a network

The above figure shows the general shape of a network. Your machine is called the host, and it is connected to the **IMP (Interface Message Processor)**. The terms *packet switch node, intermediate system* and *data switching exchange* are all synonyms for IMP. As you can see from the figure, you communicate with other hosts through a number of IMP's—these act as nodes which forward your messages to the correct destination.

We know of the two different classes of service offered by the network layer-connection oriented and connectionless. It is instructive now to see how these services are implemented within the network. The two mechanisms used are:

- Virtual Circuits.
- Datagrams.

Virtual Circuits

Virtual circuits are used to provide a connection-oriented service. This kind of service is ideal in situations where many packets of information are to be sent on the same route—rather than go through the effort of routing each packet separately, we set up a virtual path.

To do this, each IMP maintains a table of forwarding addresses for each virtual path. So, if the IMP receives a message, it can tell from the line on which it received that through which virtual circuit the message is on. The message can then be forwarded appropriately. On termination of the connection, each IMP removes the Virtual Circuit from its table, thus freeing it for further use.

Datagrams

For a connectionless service, datagrams are used. Each packet of information is bundled into a datagram with its destination address. Instead of each IMP having a table for virtual paths, it has a table of lines—which line to use for each IMP. In fact, these tables are used already for the Virtual Circuit service, for setting up the circuit in the first place.

12.2.1 Comparison of Datagrams and Virtual Circuits

Some points highlighting the key differences between the two communication mechanisms:

- With datagrams, each packet of information must contain the entire address of the machine to which it is to be sent. With a virtual circuit, the packet must only hold a virtual circuit number, a much smaller overhead. So in cases where the traffic is regular and involves small packets of data, the Virtual circuit is ideal. In cases where the information is in larger bundles and less frequent, datagrams are preferable.
- If an IMP fails, then virtual circuits are much harder to repair than datagram connections-datagram packets will simply be rerouted to avoid the offending node. Also, datagrams allow the system to become more dynamic, as they can take alternative routes to avoid congestion at certain IMPs.

The various characteristics of virtual circuits and datagrams are summarized in the following table:

	Virtual Circuit	Datagram
Connection Setup	Before Data Flow	Not required
Addressing	Network address mapped to Virtual Circuit Identifier	Source and destination network address included on each
State	Required for each Virtual Circuit	No state storage needed in routers
Routing	Selected at connection setup	Selected for each packet
Node Failure	Terminates all virtual circuits in the switch	Only packets in the router queue are lost
Complexity	Within the network switches	Within the host computers

12.3 Routing

Routing is moving information across a network from source to destination. Along the way, at least one intermediate node is typically encountered. Routing is often contrasted with bridging which seems to accomplish precisely the same thing. The primary difference between the two is that bridging occurs at Layer 2 (the link layer) of the OSI reference model, while routing occurs at Layer 3 (the network layer).

This distinction provides routing and bridging with different information to use in the process of moving information from source to destination. As a result, routing and bridging accomplish their tasks in different ways and, in fact, there are several different kinds of routing and bridging.

12.3.1 Routing Components

Routing involves two basic activities : determination of optimal routing paths and the transport of information groups (typically called *packets*) through a network. The latter of these is referred to as *switching*. Switching is relatively straightforward. Path determination, on the other hand, can be very complex.

Path Determination

A metric is a number assigned to a parameter and is used to quantify how "good" or "bad" that parameter is for a task. For example, path length is used by routing algorithms to determine the optimal path to a destination. To aid the process of path determination, routing algorithms initialize and maintain routing tables, which contain route information. Route information varies depending on the routing algorithm used.

Routing algorithms fill routing tables with a variety of information. Destination/next hop associations tell a router that a particular destination can be gained optimally by sending the packet to a particular router representing the "next hop" on the way to the final destination. Routing tables can also contain other information, such as information about the desirability of a path. Routers compare metrics to determine optimal routes. Metrics differ depending on the design of the routing algorithm being used. Routers communicate with one another (and maintain their routing tables) through the transmission of a variety of messages. The routing update message is one such message. Routing updates generally consist of all or a portion of a routing table. By analyzing routing updates from all routers, a router can build a detailed picture of network topology. A link-state advertisement is another example of a message sent between routers. Link-state advertisements inform other routers of the state of the sender's links. Link information can also be used to build a complete picture of network topology. Once the network topology is understood, routers can determine optimal routes to network destinations.

Metrics

Routing tables contain information used by switching software to select the best route. But how, specifically, are routing tables built? What is the specific nature of the information they contain? How do routing algorithms determine that one route is preferable to others?

Routing algorithms have used many different metrics to determine the best route. Sophisticated routing algorithms can base route selection on multiple metrics, combining them in a single (hybrid) metric. All of the following metrics have been used :

1. Path Length.

2. Reliability.
3. Delay.
4. Bandwidth.
5. Load.
6. Communication Cost.

Path Length

Path length is the most common routing metric. Some routing protocols allow network administrators to assign arbitrary costs to each network link. In this case, path length is the sum of the costs associated with each link traversed. Other routing protocols define hop count, a metric that specifies the number of passes through networking products (such as routers) that a packet must take to route from a source to a destination.

Reliability

Reliability, in the context of routing algorithms, refers to the reliability (usually described in terms of the bit-error rate) of each network link. Some network links may go down more often than others. Once down, some network links may be repaired more easily or more quickly than other links. Any reliability factors can be taken into account in the assignment of reliability ratings. Reliability ratings are usually assigned to network links by network administrators. They are typically arbitrary numeric values.

Delay

Routing delay refers to the length of time required to move a packet from source to destination through the network. Delay depends on many factors, including the bandwidth of intermediate network links, the port queues at each router along the way, network congestion on all intermediate network links and the physical distance to be traveled. Because it is a collection of several important variables, delay is a common and useful metric.

Bandwidth

Bandwidth refers to the available traffic capacity of a link. All other things being equal, a 10-Mbps Ethernet link would be preferable to a 64-kbps leased line. Although bandwidth is a rating of the maximum attainable throughput on a link, routes through links with greater bandwidth do not necessarily provide better routes than routes through slower links. If, for example, a faster link is much busier, the actual time required to send a packet to the destination may be greater through the fast link.

Load

Load refers to the degree to which a network resource (such as a router) is busy. Load can be calculated in a variety of ways, including CPU utilization and packets processed per second. Monitoring these parameters on a continual basis can itself be resource intensive.

Communication Cost

Communication cost is another important metric. Some companies may not care about performance as much as they care about operating expenditures. Even though line delay might be longer, they will send packets over their own lines rather than through public lines that will cost money for usage time.

12.3.2 Routing Protocols

A routing protocol communicates global topological information to each router, allowing it to make local decisions. Due to frequent changes and occasional failures of network elements, the routing protocol asynchronously updates routing tables at every router or switch controller. The updates are done through periodic exchange of routing table information between routers. This ensures that they have a consistent "view" of the network's topology.

The main requirements of any routing protocol are:

1. **Ensuring that tables at different routers are consistent** : Routing tables must be consistent so that routes can be found via a concatenation of local forwarding decisions.
2. **Minimizing the size of the routing table** : The size of the table affects the cost and efficiency of the routers. It is expected that the size of the routing tables will grow more slowly than the size of the network.
3. **Minimizing control messages** : Routing protocols require the use of control messages. Passing control messages is an overhead of routing operations and must be minimized (providing that their functionality is not reduced).
4. **Robustness** : Misrouting messages, so that they do not reach their destinations (entering a black hole) or causing loops and oscillations, must be kept to a minimum.

Routing protocols are broken into the Exterior Routing protocols that are used in the main part of the Internet and the Interior Routing protocols used within a trusted environment.

12.4 Routing Algorithms

Routing algorithms can be differentiated based on several key characteristics. First, the particular goals of the algorithm designer affect the operation of the resulting routing protocol. Second, there are various types of routing algorithms. Each algorithm has a different impact on network and router resources. Finally, routing algorithms use a variety of metrics that affect calculation of optimal routes.

Routing algorithms often have one or more of the following design goals:

- Optimality.
- Simplicity and low overhead.
- Robustness and stability.
- Rapid convergence.
- Flexibility.

Optimality

Optimality refers to the ability of the routing algorithm to select the "best" route. The best route depends on the metrics and metric weightings used to make the calculation. For example, one routing algorithm might use number of hops and delay, but might weight delay more heavily in the calculation. Naturally, routing protocols must strictly define their metric calculation algorithms.

Simplicity

Routing algorithms are also designed to be as simple as possible. In other words, the routing algorithm must offer its functionality efficiently, with a minimum of software and utilization overhead. Efficiency is particularly important when the software implementing the routing algorithm must run on a computer with limited physical resources.

Robustness

Routing algorithms must be robust. In other words, they should perform correctly in the face of unusual or unforeseen circumstances such as hardware failures, high load conditions and incorrect implementations. Because routers are located at network junction points, they can cause considerable problems when they fail. The best routing algorithms are often those that have withstood the test of time and proven stable under a variety of network conditions.

Rapid Convergence

Routing algorithms must converge rapidly. Convergence is the process of agreement, by all routers, on optimal routes. When a network event causes routes to either go down or become available, routers distribute routing update messages. Routing update messages permeate networks, stimulating recalculation of optimal routes and eventually causing all routers to agree on these routes. Routing algorithms that converge slowly can cause routing loops or network outages.

Figure 12.2 shows a routing loop. In this case, a packet arrives at Router 1 at time t1. Router 1 has already been updated and so knows that the optimal route to the destination calls for Router 2 to be the next stop. Router 1 therefore forwards the packet to Router 2. Router 2 has not yet been updated and so believes that the optimal next hop is Router 1. Router 2 therefore forwards the packet back to Router 1. The packet will continue to bounce back and forth between the two routers until Router 2 receives its routing update or until the packet has been switched the maximum number of times allowed.

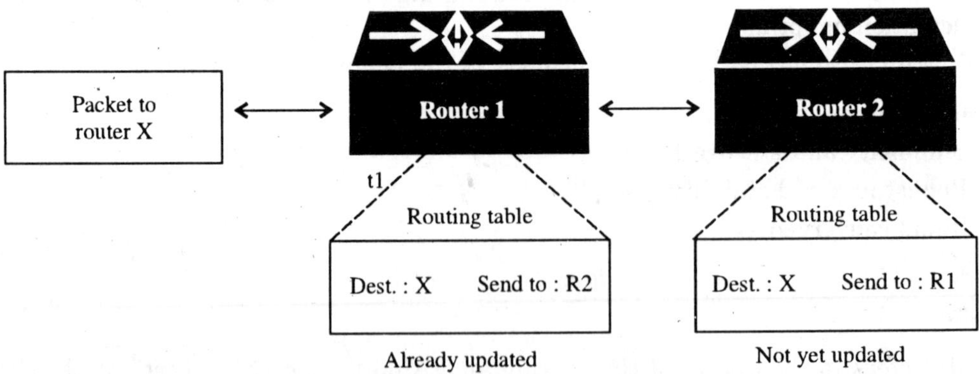

Fig. 12.2 Slow convergence and routing loops

Flexibility

Routing algorithms should also be flexible. In other words, routing algorithms should quickly and accurately adapt to a variety of network circumstances. For example, assume that a network segment has gone down. Many routing algorithms, on becoming aware of this problem, will quickly select the next-best path for all routes normally using that segment. Routing algorithms can be programmed to adapt to changes in network bandwidth, router queue size, network delay, and other variables.

Classes of Routing Algorithms

Routing algorithms can be classified as:

- Non-adaptive algorithms
- Adaptive algorithms

If a network is stable in its topology and traffic flow a **non-adaptive algorithm** is used. In this case all routes are computed initially and never change. This relieves the nodes from having to monitor changes and compute new routes. Alternately adaptive algorithms attempt to make routing decisions based on current traffic and topology.

Adaptive algorithms use such dynamic information as current topology, load, delay, etc. to select routes. Also known as dynamic routing. A dynamic algorithm can be run either periodically or in direct response to topology or link cost changes. While dynamic algorithms are more responsive to network changes, they are also more susceptible to problems such as routing loops and oscillation in routes. Adaptive algorithms can be further divided in the following types:

1. **Isolated** : Each router makes its routing decisions using only the local information it has on hand. Specifically, routers do not even exchange information with their neighbors.
2. **Centralized** : A centralized node makes all routing decisions. Specifically, the centralized node has access to global information.
3. **Distributed** : Algorithms that use a combination of local and global information.

In non-adaptive algorithms, routes never change once initial routes have been selected. Also called static routing. In static routing algorithms, routes change very slowly over time, often as a result of human intervention (for example, a human manually editing a router's forwarding table).

Obviously, adaptive algorithms are more interesting, as non-adaptive algorithms don't even make an attempt to handle failed links. Only two types of routing algorithms are typically used in the Internet: a dynamic global link state algorithm and a dynamic decentralized distance vector algorithm.

12.4.1 Shortest Path Algorithm

A path is the route taken by a data packet traveling between two network nodes. A network is typically highly complex so the correct path will not be obvious. Routing algorithms must overcome this complexity and make useful path choices. The notion of a *shortest path* is necessary when evaluating routing choices.

Dijkstra's algorithm (or variation) is used to find the shortest path. The basic idea of this algorithm is :

- Choose the source and put nodes connected to source in list to consider.
- From the list to consider choose the nearest node.

Distance Metrics

Shortest path routing requires that a cost metric be assigned to each link, so that that metric can be used to measure path lengths. Possible metrics: number of hops along a path, link capacities along a path, propagation delays along a path, per bit cost along a path or hybrids. In the following example we will consider two different metrics and find the path in each case.

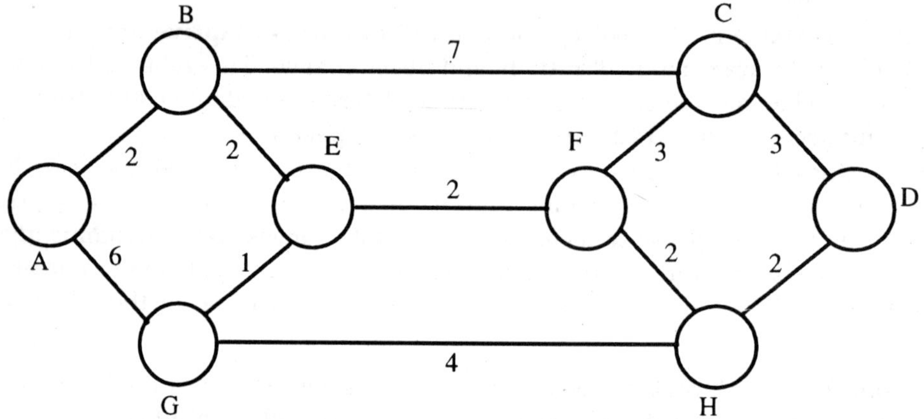

Fig. 12.3 Network with path lengths

An obvious metric of path length is number of hops. In the above example ABC is shorter than ABEF.

Many other metrics are commonly used; the ones chosen will greatly affect how optimal paths are found. The numbers on the links, on the network shown above, represent physical distance, it can be seen that ABEF is shorter than ABC. Other common metrics include mean queueing and transmission times, bandwidth, cost and average traffic. The labels in the above figure could be the result of a function of some or all of these metrics.

12.4.2 Flooding

Flooding is a form of isolated routing. It does not select a specific route. When a router receives a packet, it sends a copy of the packet out on each line (except the one on which it arrived):

- To prevent packets from looping forever, each router decrements a hop count contained in the packet header. Whenever the hop-count decrements to zero, the router discards the packet.

- To reduce looping even further:
  - ☐ add a sequence number to each packet's header.
  - ☐ each router maintains a private sequence number. When it sends a new packet, it copies the sequence number into the packet, and increments its private sequence number.
- For each source router S, a router:
  - ☐ keeps track of the highest sequence number seen from S.
  - ☐ whenever it receives a packet from S containing a sequence number lower than the one stored in its table, it discards the packet.
  - ☐ otherwise, it updates the entry for S and forwards the packet on.

Flooding wastes network resources by transmitting excessive numbers of packets.
Flooding is used mainly to transmit control information that must reach all nodes, but

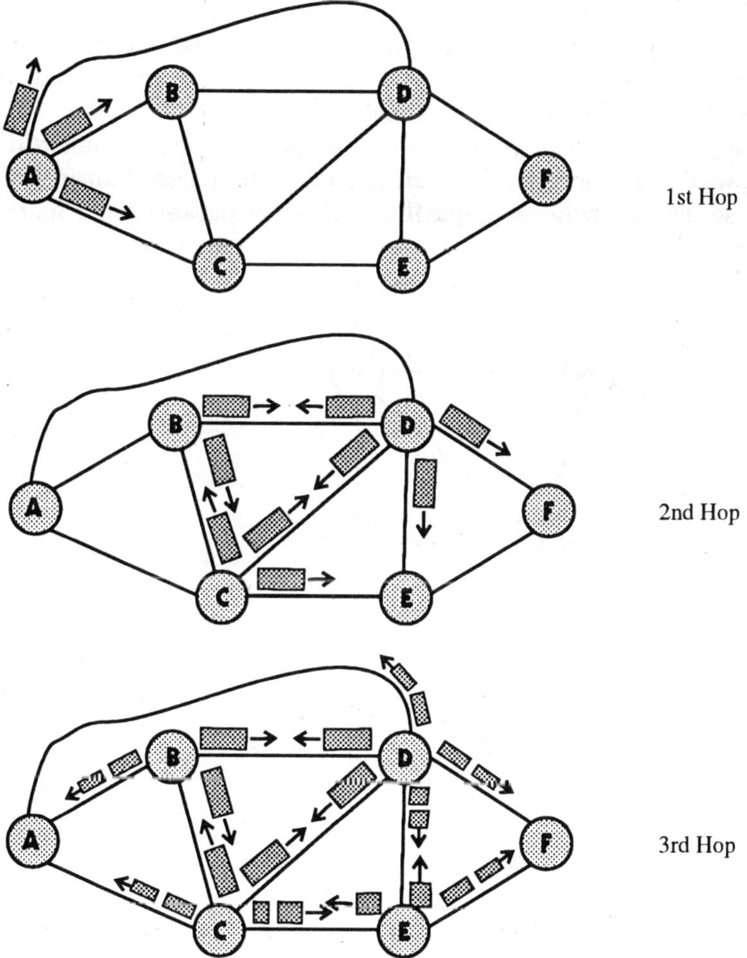

Fig. 12.4 An example illustrating flooding algorithm

when the network topology is not known. Figure 12.4 illustrates how packets are transmitted in flooding algorithm.

Flooding has several important uses:

- In military applications, the network must remain robust in the face of (extreme) hostility.
- Sending routing updates, because updates can't rely on the correctness of a router's routing table.
- Theoretical-chooses all possible paths, so it chooses the shortest one.

Another alternative of flooding is *selective flooding*, in which a router sends packets out only on those lines in the general direction of the destination. That is, don't send packets out on lines that clearly lead in the wrong direction.

12.4.3 Random Routing

In this algorithm, each node transmits a copy of each received packet on one outgoing link other than the one on which the packet was received. Random routing ensures good traffic distribution without knowledge of network topology.

Random routing is unlikely to provide least-cost paths; thus, routing will be sub-optimal and the network will carry more traffic than necessary (but less than in the flooding case). Delays will increase. The following example illustrates how packets are transmitted in random routing algorithm.

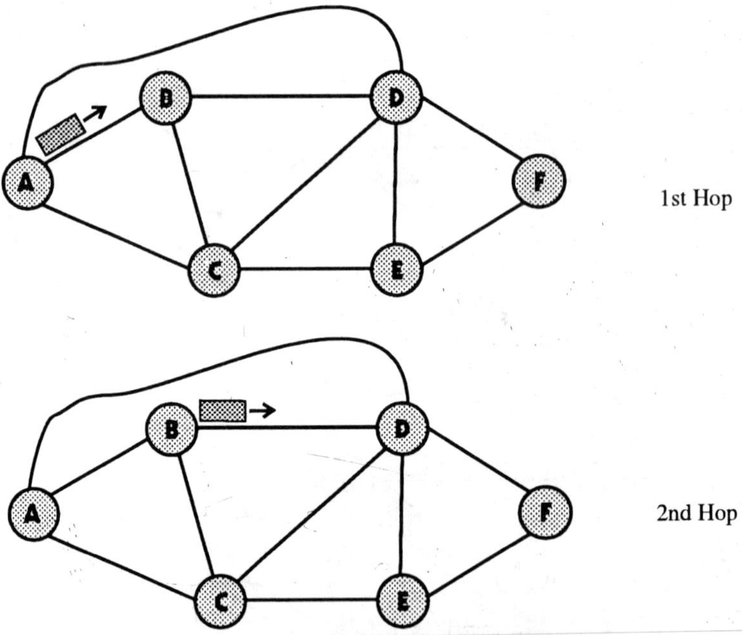

Fig. 12.5 (a)

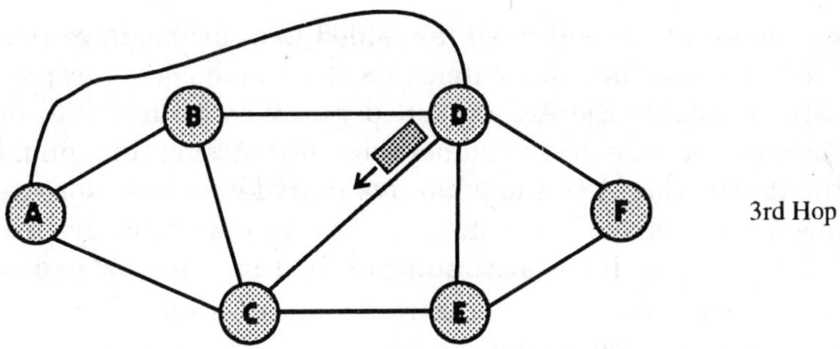

Fig. 12.5 (b) An example illustrating random routing

12.4.4 Flow Based Routing

The algorithms we've examined so far have been based on heuristics rather than on some sort of fundamental theory. Another approach is to develop a mathematical model of the network and define the routing problem as minimizing some objective function. The approach:

- Assume that traffic flows remain constant over time.
- Assume that we have an estimate of the traffic flowing between each router-router pair.
- Assume that we know the network's topology and the capacity of each link.

Our goal becomes: Find a set of routes that minimizes end-to-end delay. One possibility is to let cost be the sum across all links of the average delay multiplied by the amount of traffic carried by that link.

12.4.5 Hierarchical Routing

One of the fundamental issues regarding routing is scaling. As a network becomes larger, the amount of information that must be propagated increases and the routing calculation becomes increasingly expensive. Due to increase in the number of routers, the overhead involved in computing, storing and communicating the routing table information (e.g., least cost path changes) becomes prohibitive. Today's public Internet consists of millions of interconnected routers and more than 50 million hosts. Storing routing table entries to each of these hosts and routers would clearly require enormous amounts of memory. The overhead required to broadcast link state updates among millions of routers would leave no bandwidth left for sending the data packets! A solution is to have some routers do the routing for others: Hierarchical routing.

This problem can be solved by aggregating routers into "regions" or "autonomous systems" (ASs). Routers within the same AS all run the same routing algorithm (e.g., a LS or DV algorithm—described later on) and have full information about each other. The routing algorithm running within an autonomous system is called an **intra-autonomous system routing protocol**. It will be necessary, of course, to connect ASs to each other and thus one or more of the routers in an AS will have the added task for being responsible for routing packets to destinations outside the AS. Routers in an AS that have the responsibility of routing packets to destinations outside the AS are called **gateway routers**. In order for gateway routers to route packets from one AS to another (possibly passing through multiple other ASs before reaching the destination AS), the gateways must know how to route (i.e., determine routing paths) among themselves. The routing algorithm that gateways use to route among the various ASs is known as an **inter-autonomous system routing protocol**.

The problem of scale is solved since an intra-AS router need only to know about routers within its AS and the gateway router(s) in its AS.

Hierarchical routing is an approach that hides information from far-away nodes, reducing the amount of information a given router needs to perform routing. The following example explains hierarchical routing:

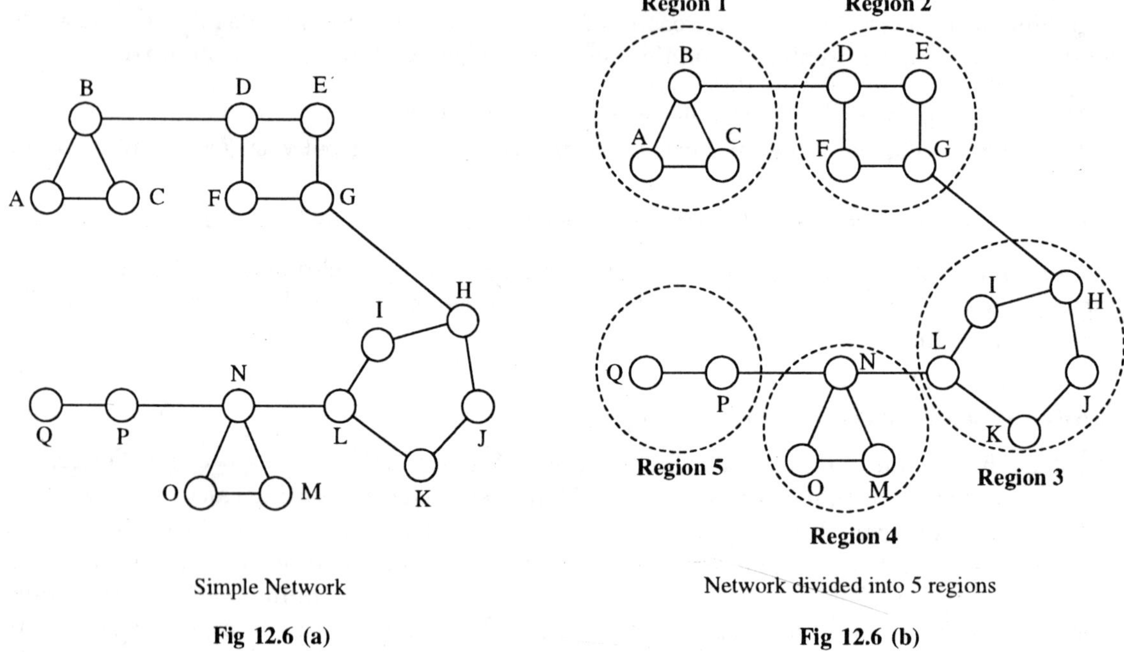

Simple Network

Fig 12.6 (a)

Network divided into 5 regions

Fig 12.6 (b)

The first table is A's routing table in case of simple network and second table shows hierarchical routing when network is divided into 5 regions.

In this type of routing, the tables can be summarized, so network efficiency improves. The above example shows two-level hierarchical routing. We can also use three- or four-level hierarchical routing.

In three-level hierarchical routing, the network is classified into a number of **clusters**. Each cluster is made up of a number of regions and each region contains a number or routers. Hierarchical routing is widely used in Internet routing and makes use of several routing protocols.

Destination	Line	Weight
A	—	—
B	B	1
C	C	1
D	B	2
E	B	3
F	B	3
G	B	4
H	B	5
I	C	5
J	C	6
K	C	5
L	C	4
M	C	4
N	C	3
O	C	4
P	C	2
Q	C	3

Destination	Line	Weight
A	—	—
B	B	1
C	C	1
Region 2	B	2
Region 3	C	2
Region 4	C	3
Region 5	C	4

Advantage : Scaling—Each router needs less information (table space) to perform routing.

Disadvantage : Sub optimal routes—The average path length increases because there may be a shorter path that bypasses the entry points, but we don't use it.

Hierarchical routing can be extended to multi-levels.

Example : Telephone system:

- Area code identifies a region.
- Area code plus the first three digits identify the central office within a specific region.

12.4.6 Broadcasting

Sending a packet to all destinations simultaneously is known as broadcasting. There are several ways to implement broadcasting:

1. **In broadcast networks, the implementation is trivial :** Designate a special address as the "all hosts address". Send a unicast packet to each destination. However, this approach makes poor use of resources.

2. **Flood packets to all nodes :** Flooding generates many packets and consumes too much bandwidth.
3. **Use multi-destination routing :** Each packet contains a list (or bitmap) of all destinations and when a router forwards a packet across two or more lines, it splits the packet and divides the destination addresses accordingly. This approach is similar to sending unicast packets, except that we don't send individual copies of each messages. However, the copy operations slow down the ability of a router to process many packets.
4. **Use a spanning tree :** If the network can be reduced to a tree (e.g., only one path between any two pairs of routers), copy a packet to each line of spanning tree except the one on which it arrived. It works only if each router uses the same spanning tree.
5. **Reverse Path Forwarding (RPF) :** Use a sink tree (assume sink/source trees are the same). When a packet arrives from router *X*, if the packet arrived on a line of the sink tree leading to *X*, the packet is traveling along the shortest path, so it must be the first copy we've seen. Copy the packet to all outgoing lines of the sink tree. If the packet arrives on another line, assume that the packet is a copy, it didn't arrive on the shortest path and discard it.

RPF is easy to implement and makes efficient use of bandwidth.

12.4.7 Dynamic Routing

The are two types of Dynamic Route Selection:

- Distance Vector Routing
- Link-State Routing

Basically, Distance Vector protocols determine best path on how far the destination is, while Link State protocols are capable of using more sophisticated methods taking into consideration link variables, such as bandwidth, delay, reliability and load. Distance Vector protocols judge best path on how far it is. Distance can be hops or a combination of metrics calculated to represent a distance value. Distance-vector routing protocols are simple and efficient in small networks and require little, if any management. However, they do not scale well and have poor convergence properties, which has led to the development of more complex but more scalable link-state routing protocols for use in large networks.

12.4.7.1 Distance vector routing

Distance-Vector is an algorithm that uses a direction to any link in the interconnection network to determine the best route. Distance Vector Routers advertise their presence to other routers on the network. Periodically, each router broadcasts their routing table information. Other Routers update their Routing Tables with this information. This process is effective but inefficient. Changes ripple through the network from router to router and take a while for all routers to become aware of the changes. Also, these broadcasts cause network traffic that can affect performance, more so on large networks with many routers.

The name distance vector is derived from the fact that routes are advertised as vectors of (distance, direction), where distance is defined in terms of a metric and direction is defined in terms of the next-hop router. For example, "Destination A is a distance of 5 hops away, in the direction of next-hop router *X*". As this statement implies, each router learns routes from its neighboring routers' perspectives and then advertises the routes from its own perspective. Because each router depends on its neighbors for information, which the neighbors in turn may have learned from their neighbors and so on, distance vector routing is sometimes facetiously referred to as "routing by rumor".

Distance-vector routing makes this assumption:

Each router knows the identity of every other router in the network.

The two popular Distance Vector routing protocols are the:

1. Routing Information Protocol (RIP)
2. Interior Gateway Routing Protocol (IGRP).

RIP : RIP is a relatively old but still commonly used interior gateway protocol created for use in small, homogeneous networks. It is a classical distance-vector routing protocol. With RIP, routers periodically exchange entire tables. Because this is inefficient, RIP is gradually being replaced by a newer protocol called Open Shortest Path First (OSPF).

RIP is a widely used protocol for managing router information within a self-contained network such as a corporate local area network or an interconnected group of such LANs. RIP uses broadcast User Datagram Protocol (UDP) data packets to exchange routing information. There are various metrics that Routing Protocols use to rate the value of different routes. The RIP uses the hop count that is the number of routers that can be traversed in a route.

IGRP : IGRP is a Cisco proprietary, distance-vector, routing protocol used by routers to exchange routing information. The goal of IGRP was to create a robust protocol for routing within an autonomous system (AS).

Working of distance-vector routing protocol

A very simple distance-vector routing protocol works as follows:

1. Initially, the router makes a list of which networks it can reach and how many hops it will cost. In the outset this will be the two or more networks to which this router is connected. This table is called a routing table. Example of routing table of a simple network is shown below:

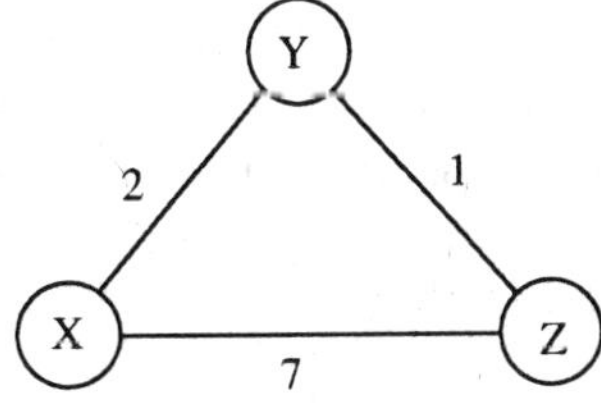

Fig. 12.7 A simple network

Routing table for X:

Destination	Cost	Next HOP
Y	2	Direct
Z	7	Direct

2. Periodically the routing table is shared with other routers on each of the connected networks via some specified inter-router protocol. This information is only shared in-between physically connected routers ("neighbors"), so routers on other networks are not reached by the new routing tables yet.
3. A new routing table is constructed based on the directly configured network interfaces, as before, with the addition of the new information received from other routers.
4. Bad routing paths are then purged from the new routing table. If two identical paths to the same network exist, only the one with the smallest hop-count is kept.
5. The new routing table is then communicated to all neighbors of this router. This way the routing information will spread and eventually all routers know the routing path to each network, which router it shall use to reach this network and to which router it shall route next.

Common Characteristics of Distance Vector Routing

A typical distance vector routing protocol uses a routing algorithm in which routers periodically send routing updates to all neighbors by broadcasting their entire route tables.

- **Periodic Updates**

Periodic updates means that at the end of a certain time period, updates will be transmitted. This period varies from protocol to protocol and usually in the range of 10 seconds to 90 seconds. At issue here is the fact that if updates are sent too frequently, congestion may occur; if updates are sent too infrequently, convergence time may be unacceptably high.

- **Neighbors**

In the context of routers, neighbors always mean routers sharing a common data link. A distance vector routing protocol sends its updates to neighboring routers and depends on them to pass the update information along to their neighbors. For this reason, distance vector routing is said to use hop-by-hop updates.

- **Broadcast Updates**

When a router first becomes active on a network, how does it find other routers and how does it announce its own presence? Several methods are available. The simplest is to send the updates to the broadcast address. Neighboring routers speaking the same routing protocol will hear the broadcasts and take appropriate action. Hosts and other devices uninterested in the routing updates will simply drop the packets.

- **Full Routing Table Updates**

Most distance vector routing protocols take the very simple approach of telling their neighbors everything they know by broadcasting their entire route table. Neighbors receiving these updates glean the information they need and discard everything else.

Example of distance vector algorithm

Figure 12.8 shows a distance vector algorithm in action and is explained in the following four steps. In this example, the metric is hop count.

Step - 1

At time t_0, routers A through D have just become active. Looking at the route tables across the top row, at t_0 the only information any of the four routers has is its own directly connected networks. The tables identify these networks and indicate that they are directly connected by having no next-hop router and by having a hop count of 0. Each of the four routers will broadcast this information on all links.

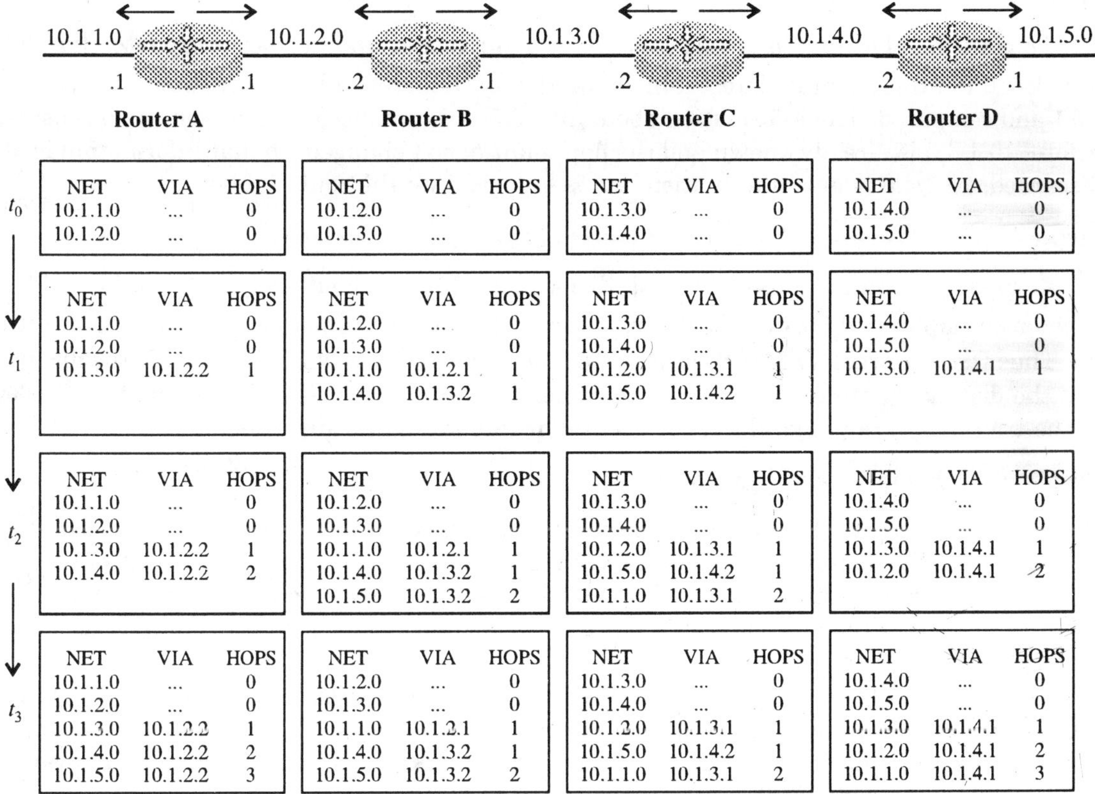

Router A:

Time	NET	VIA	HOPS
t_0	10.1.1.0	...	0
	10.1.2.0	...	0
t_1	10.1.1.0	...	0
	10.1.2.0	...	0
	10.1.3.0	10.1.2.2	1
t_2	10.1.1.0	...	0
	10.1.2.0	...	0
	10.1.3.0	10.1.2.2	1
	10.1.4.0	10.1.2.2	2
t_3	10.1.1.0	...	0
	10.1.2.0	...	0
	10.1.3.0	10.1.2.2	1
	10.1.4.0	10.1.2.2	2
	10.1.5.0	10.1.2.2	3

Router B:

Time	NET	VIA	HOPS
t_0	10.1.2.0	...	0
	10.1.3.0	...	0
t_1	10.1.2.0	...	0
	10.1.3.0	...	0
	10.1.1.0	10.1.2.1	1
	10.1.4.0	10.1.3.2	1
t_2	10.1.2.0	...	0
	10.1.3.0	...	0
	10.1.1.0	10.1.2.1	1
	10.1.4.0	10.1.3.2	1
	10.1.5.0	10.1.3.2	2
t_3	10.1.2.0	...	0
	10.1.3.0	...	0
	10.1.1.0	10.1.2.1	1
	10.1.4.0	10.1.3.2	1
	10.1.5.0	10.1.3.2	2

Router C:

Time	NET	VIA	HOPS
t_0	10.1.3.0	...	0
	10.1.4.0	...	0
t_1	10.1.3.0	...	0
	10.1.4.0	...	0
	10.1.2.0	10.1.3.1	1
	10.1.5.0	10.1.4.2	1
t_2	10.1.3.0	...	0
	10.1.4.0	...	0
	10.1.2.0	10.1.3.1	1
	10.1.5.0	10.1.4.2	1
	10.1.1.0	10.1.3.1	2
t_3	10.1.3.0	...	0
	10.1.4.0	...	0
	10.1.2.0	10.1.3.1	1
	10.1.5.0	10.1.4.2	1
	10.1.1.0	10.1.3.1	2

Router D:

Time	NET	VIA	HOPS
t_0	10.1.4.0	...	0
	10.1.5.0	...	0
t_1	10.1.4.0	...	0
	10.1.5.0	...	0
	10.1.3.0	10.1.4.1	1
t_2	10.1.4.0	...	0
	10.1.5.0	...	0
	10.1.3.0	10.1.4.1	1
	10.1.2.0	10.1.4.1	2
t_3	10.1.4.0	...	0
	10.1.5.0	...	0
	10.1.3.0	10.1.4.1	1
	10.1.2.0	10.1.4.1	2
	10.1.1.0	10.1.4.1	3

Fig. 12.8 Distance vector protocols converge hop-by-hop

Step - 2

At time t_1, the first updates have been received and processed by the routers. Look at router A's table at t_0. Router B's update to router *A* said that router *B* can reach networks 10.1.2.0 and 10.1.3.0, both 0 hops away. If the networks are 0 hops from *B*, they must be 1 hop from *A*. Router *A* incremented the hop count by 1 and then examined its route table. It already knew about 10.1.2.0 and the hop count (0) was less than the hop count *B* advertised, (1), so *A* disregarded that information.

Network 10.1.3.0 was new information, however, so *A* entered this in the route table. The source address of the update packet was router *B*'s interface (10.1.2.2) so that information is entered along with the calculated hop count.

Notice that the other routers performed similar operations at the same time t_1. Router *C*, for instance, disregarded the information about 10.1.3.0 from *B* and 10.1.4.0 from *C* but entered information about 10.1.2.0, reachable via *B*'s interface address 10.1.3.1 and 10.1.5.0, reachable via *C*'s interface 10.1.4.2. Both networks were calculated as 1 hop away.

Step - 3

At time t_2, the update period has again expired and another set of updates has been broadcast. Router *B* sent its latest table; router *A* again incremented *B*'s advertised hop counts by 1 and compared. The information about 10.1.2.0 is again discarded for the same reason as before. 10.1.3.0 is already known and the hop count hasn't changed, so that information is also discarded. 10.1.4.0 is new information and is entered into the route table.

Step - 4

At time t_3, the network is converged. Every router knows about every network, the address of the next-hop router for every network and the distance in hops to every network.

Thus Distance vector algorithms provide road signs to networks. They provide the direction and the distance, but no details about what lies along the route. And like the sign at the fork in the trail, they are vulnerable to accidental or intentional misdirection.

Problems of distance-vector protocols

Distance-vector protocols perform well in small internetworks fewer than 15 routers wide. Distance-vector protocols are preferred over link-state protocols in internetworks of this size due to their easy configuration. In addition, distance-vector protocols are easier to troubleshoot and understand. Problems do not arise until the internetwork becomes larger and more complex.

To understand the limitations of distance-vector protocols, you must first understand how they work. When a network change, such as a down link is detected, a distance-vector protocol updates its routing table and broadcasts the entire routing table to all other routers every 30 to 90 seconds when operating in a steady state. As the internetwork grows, you can expect to see the following problems when using distance-vector protocols:

- Convergence time increases.
- Routing loops occur.

- Networks become unreachable.
- Broadcast traffic increases.

Increased Convergence Time

Convergence takes so long because the routers now have to wait until another router volunteers a pathway to the down network. But before another router can volunteer a pathway, the routers must wait a set time limit to prevent routing loops. Convergence time increases as the network grows, because more routers need to be updated with route information. The more time it takes for the internetwork to converge, the slower the internetwork is perceived by end users. This is not a problem when there are only a few routers that need to be updated.

Routing Loops

Routing loops occur because routers on an internetwork are not updated at close to the same time. This causes routers to send outdated route information as though the information were new. Figure 12.9 shows a network before and after a link failure was detected. When Router 2 detects a link failure to network 10.1.5.0, it updates its routing table and sends its entire route table to the other routers on the internetwork. Router 3 receives the update from Router 2 and updates its routing table. At this point, any packets received on Router 3 destined for 10.1.5.0 will not be sent to Router 2.

Router 1 still has not received an update for network 10.1.5.0. Since Router 1 thinks 10.1.5.0 can still be reached via Router 4, this incorrect route information is sent in the route update to the other routers on the internetwork. Router 4 receives the update from Router 1 and updates its routing table. Before Router 1 receives an update that network 10.1.5.0 is down, it has already sent out updates letting other routers know that it has a live route to 10.1.5.0. The other routers send packets destined for 10.1.5.0 to Router 1, while Router 1 sends the same packets to Router 4. This creates a routing loop. This is not a problem on small internetworks with a few routers, because the routers are updated at close to the same time.

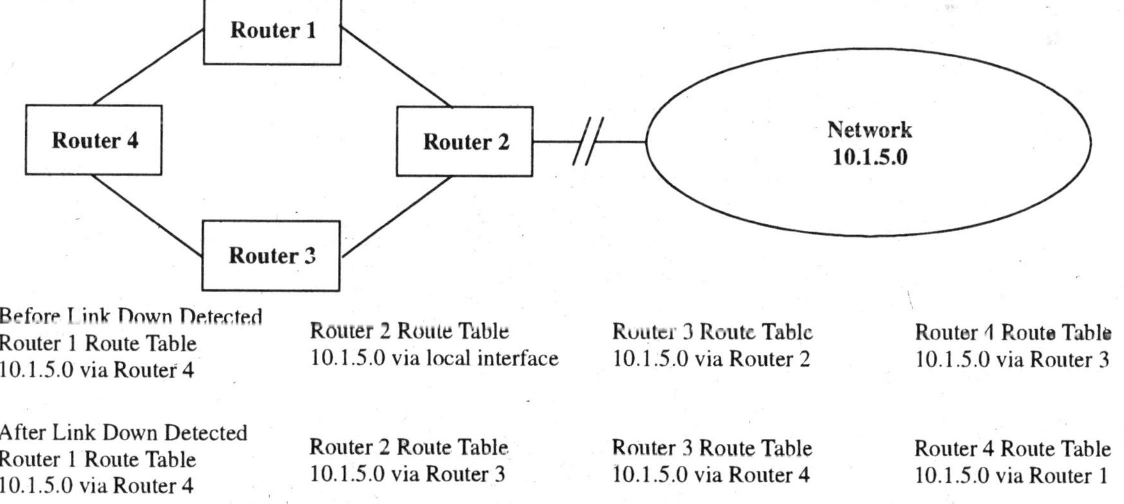

Fig. 12.9 Routing loop

Unreachable Networks

If distance-vector routing protocols are in use, internetwork growth can cause some networks to be unreachable. This is due to the hop-count limitation of distance-vector protocols. For example, RIP has a maximum hop count of 15. Any network more than 15 hops away is considered unreachable by RIP. Network growth should be monitored closely and a periodic re-evaluation of routing protocols should be done.

Increased Broadcasts

Distance-vector protocols are known for being "chatty". In other words, they put a constant flow of traffic on the internetwork. This traffic comes in the form of periodic broadcasts containing the entire route tables sent from routers running distance-vector protocols. The larger a network gets, the more routers there are to load the internetwork with broadcasts. Eventually, this process can cause varying degrees of slowness on the internetwork as network devices and end stations compete for bandwidth.

Organizations with large internetworks steer clear of protocols that operate using excessive broadcasts. The reason for this avoidance is that too many broadcasts can degrade network performance. When designing large internetworks, use routed protocols such as IP and routing protocols such as EIGRP or OSPF. This solution will allow your design to be more scalable and lacking in excessive broadcasts.

Possible solutions to the problems of distance vector protocols

Even though distance-vector protocols are plagued with routing issues as an internetwork grows, these protocols do have methods for functioning in these larger environments. These methods include the usage of timers and rules for preventing routing loops. Of course, if an internetwork grows too large and too complex, link-state routing protocols should be considered.

One method that distance-vector routing protocols use to manage routing loops is a **maximum hop count**. What this means for RIP is that a packet that has reached more than 15 hops in a routing loop will cause the router to mark the destination network as down in its routing table. This does not prevent a routing loop from occurring. It does, however, prevent a routing loop from continuing into infinity.

Split horizon is another method that distance-vector protocols use to solve the routing loop problem. Split horizon is basically a rule that states that route information cannot be sent back in the direction from which that information was received.

The last method that distance-vector protocols employ to defeat routing loops is **hold-downs**, which prevent periodic route updates from reinstating a route that has gone down. Hold-downs accomplish this using timers, allowing enough time for either the downed route to come back online or the network to stabilize before switching to the next best route. Hold-down timers are reset by triggered updates under the following circumstances:

- The hold-down timer expires.
- The router receives a processing task that is proportional to the number of links in the internetwork.
- The router receives another update indicating a change in the network's status.

Advantages of Distance Vector-Based Routing Protocols

- **Simpler :** Distance vector-based routing protocols are simple router advertisement processes that are easy to understand.
- **Easy to configure :** In its simplest incarnation, configuring a distance vector-based routing protocol is as easy as enabling it on the router interfaces.

Disadvantages of Distance Vector-Based Routing Protocols

- **Large routing tables :** Multiple routes to a given network ID can be reflected as multiple entries in the routing table. In a large internetwork with multiple paths, the routing table can have hundreds or thousands of entries.
- **High network traffic overhead :** Route advertising is done periodically even after the internetwork has converged.
- **Does not scale :** Between the size of the routing table and the high overhead, distance vector-based routing protocols do not scale well to large and very large internetworks.
- **High convergence time :** Due to the unsynchronized and unacknowledged way that distance vector information is exchanged; convergence of the internetwork can take several minutes. While converging, routing loops and black holes can occur.

12.4.7.2 Link-state routing

In distance-vector routing, the information about the topology of the network is distributed among the routers, which achieves efficiency but also creates problems. An alternate approach, used in link-state routing, is to give each router complete information about the graph of the network. Then, each router independently computes the optimal path to every destination.

The information available to a distance vector router has been compared to the information available from a road sign. Link state routing protocols are like a road map. A link state router cannot be fooled as easily into making bad routing decisions, because it has a complete picture of the network. The reason is that unlike the routing-by-rumor approach of distance vector, link state routers have first hand information from all their peer routers. Each router originates information about itself, its directly connected links, and the state of those links (hence the name). This information is passed around from router to router, each router making a copy of it, but never changing it. The ultimate objective is that every router has identical information about the internetwork and each router will independently calculate its own best paths.

Link State Routing protocols provide greater flexibility and sophistication than their Distance Vector counterparts. They reduce overall broadcast traffic and make better decisions about routing by taking characteristics such as bandwidth, delay, reliability, and load into consideration instead of basing their decisions solely on distance or hop count.

Link-State Routing reduces network traffic. Routers newly attached to network request information from nearby routers. Once information has been exchanged, routers only broadcast when something has changed. These messages contain information about the state of each link that the router has with other routers. They keep each other updated and therefore complete updates are seldom needed.

Link state protocols, sometimes called shortest path first or distributed database protocols, are built around a well-known algorithm from graph theory, E. W. Dijkstra's shortest path algorithm. Examples of link state routing protocols are:

- Open Shortest Path First (OSPF)
- The ISO's Intermediate System to Intermediate System (IS-IS)
- DEC's DNA Phase V
- Novell's NetWare Link Services Protocol (NLSP)

Although link state protocols are rightly considered more complex than distance vector protocols, the basic functionality is not complex at all:

1. Each router establishes a relationship—an adjacency—with each of its neighbors.
2. Each router sends *Link State Advertisements* (LSAs).
3. Each router stores a copy of all the LSAs it has seen in a database. If all works well, the databases in all routers should be identical.
4. The completed *topological database*, also called the *link state database*, describes a graph of the internetwork. Using the Dijkstra algorithm, each router calculates the shortest path to each network and enters this information into the route table.

General Link State Operation

Link State Routing protocols reduce broadcast traffic because they do not send out periodic broadcasts or send out their entire tables with each broadcast. Link state routing protocols exchange a complete copy of their route tables upon initialization. Thereafter route updates are multicast only when a change has occurred (triggered by a change in the topology), including only the change in the update not the entire table. Changes are flooded immediately and computed in parallel. If no changes occur, they do not generate an update.

Triggered updates improve convergence time by requiring routers to send an update message immediately upon learning of a route change. These updates are triggered by some event, such as a new link becoming available or an existing link failing.

All Link State protocols must build and maintain three separate tables (also referred to as databases):

- The neighbor table (also known as Adjacency database)
- Topology Map (also known as Link State database)
- Route Table (also known as Forwarding database)

Before traffic can be forwarded certain things must happen.

1. All routers attached to the same network must identify themselves and their neighbors, establishing a relationship with one another (referred to as adjacency). Adjacent routers form this relationship through the exchange of hello messages. From these hellos each local router builds its first table (the neighbor). Fig. 12.10(a)

shows the neighbor hello exchange and figure 12.10(b) shows a routers neighbor table. If this first stage fails, routing will never occur.

Note : Within hello messages routers announce themselves; identify the links they are directly attached to and the state of these links (up or down), among other things.).

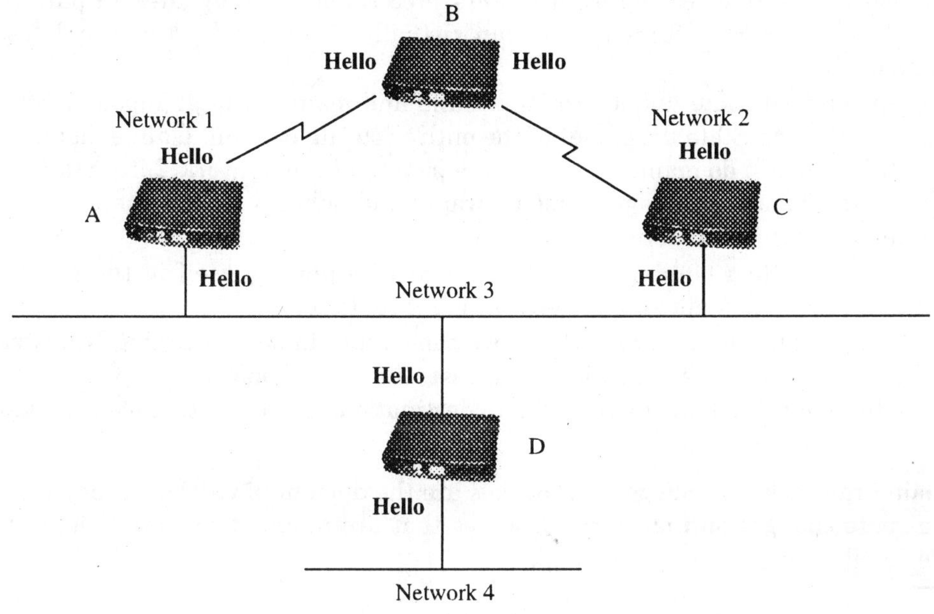

Fig. 12.10 (a) Link state routers exchange hello messages

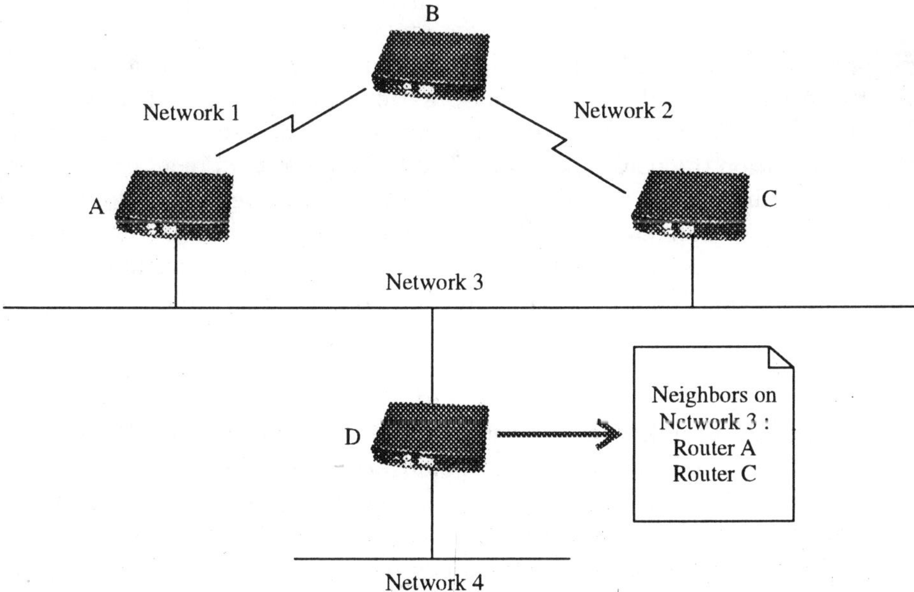

Fig. 12.10 (b) Router D has discovered two neighbors on network 3

2. Once the adjacency relationship is intact, route information may be exchanged by flooding updates throughout the routing domain. Unlike Distance Vector routing protocols, which must receive, process and wait for their periodic timer to expire before sending route updates on, any change in the network triggers Link State protocols to immediately flood route updates to all segments except the one from which it was received, with all routers processing these updates in parallel. This speeds up convergence as routers can virtually receive and process updates simultaneously.
3. From received route updates routers build and maintain local Topology Maps (also known as Link State database) of the entire routing domain. Unlike distance vector protocols, which do maintain a complete picture of the network, Link State protocols have first-hand knowledge of all networks and subnets within their area and the paths to reach these networks.
4. Each router then builds a logical tree structure placing itself in the root position, with all networks and subnets emanating from this root.
5. All Link State routing protocols derive their route table by running Dijikstra's SPF (Shortest Path First) algorithm against the tree (topology map or Link State database) placing lowest cost paths to destinations in the route table (also known as Forwarding Database).

The main drawbacks to Link State protocols are the amount of CPU overhead involved in calculating route changes and memory resources that are required to store neighbor tables, route tables, and a complete topology map.

Common Characteristics of Link State Routing

Neighbors

Neighbor discovery is the first step in getting a link state environment up and running. In keeping with the friendly neighbor terminology, a Hello protocol is used for this step. The protocol will define a Hello packet format and a procedure for exchanging the packets and processing the information the packets contain. The Hello packet will contain a router ID and the instance, an IP address from one of the router's interfaces. Beyond building adjacencies, Hello packets serve as keepalives to monitor the adjacency. If Hellos are not heard from an adjacent neighbor within a certain established time, the neighbor is considered unreachable and the adjacency is broken. A typical interval for the exchange of hello packets is 10 seconds, and a typical dead period is four times that.

Link State Flooding

After the adjacencies are established, the routers may begin sending out LSAs (Link State Advertisement). As the term flooding implies, the advertisements are sent to every neighbor. In turn, each received LSA is copied and forwarded to every neighbor except the one that sent the LSA. This process is the source of one of link state's advantages over distance vector. LSAs are forwarded almost immediately, whereas distance vector must run its algorithm and update its route table before routing updates, even the triggered ones, can be forwarded. As a result, link state protocols converge much faster than distance vector protocols converge when the topology changes.

The Link State Database

In addition to flooding LSAs and discovering neighbors, a third major task of the link state routing protocol is establishing the link state database. The link state or topological database stores the LSAs as a series of records. The important information for the shortest path determination process is the advertising router's ID, its attached networks and neighboring routers, and the cost associated with those networks or neighbors. So LSAs may include two types of generic information:

- *Router link information* advertises a router's adjacent neighbors with a triple of (Router ID, Neighbor ID, Cost), where cost is the cost of the link to the neighbor.
- *Stub network information* advertises a router's directly connected stub networks (networks with no neighbors) with a triple of (Router ID, Network ID, Cost).

Example of Link State Algorithm

In this algorithm, a router, based on information that has been collected from other routers, builds a graph of the network. This graph shows the location of routers in the network and their links to each other. Every link is labeled with a number called the **weight** or **cost**. This number is a function of delay time, average traffic, and sometimes simply the number of hops between nodes. For example, if there are two links between a node and a destination, the router chooses the link with the lowest weight.

The **Dijikstra algorithm** goes through these steps:

1. The router builds a graph of the network and identifies source and destination nodes, as V1 and V2 for example. Then it builds a matrix, called the "adjacency matrix". In this matrix, a coordinate indicates weight. For example, [i, j] is the weight of a link between V_i and V_j. If there is no direct link between V_i and V_j, this weight is identified as "infinity".
2. The router builds a status record set for every node on the network. The record contains three fields:
   - Predecessor field—The first field shows the previous node.
   - Length field—The second field shows the sum of the weights from the source to that node.
   - Label field —The last field shows the status of node. Each node can have one status mode: "permanent" or "tentative".
3. The router initializes the parameters of the status record set (for all nodes) and sets their length to "infinity" and their label to "tentative".
4. The router sets a T-node. For example, if V1 is to be the source T-node, the router changes V1's label to "permanent". When a label changes to "permanent", it never changes again. A T-node is an agent and nothing more.
5. The router updates the status record set for all tentative nodes that are directly linked to the source T-node.

6. The router looks at all of the tentative nodes and chooses the one whose weight to V_1 is lowest. That node is then the destination T-node.
7. If this node is not V2 (the intended destination), the router goes back to step 5.
8. If this node is V2, the router extracts its previous node from the status record set and does this until it arrives at V1. This list of nodes shows the best route from V1 to V2.

These steps are shown below as a flowchart.

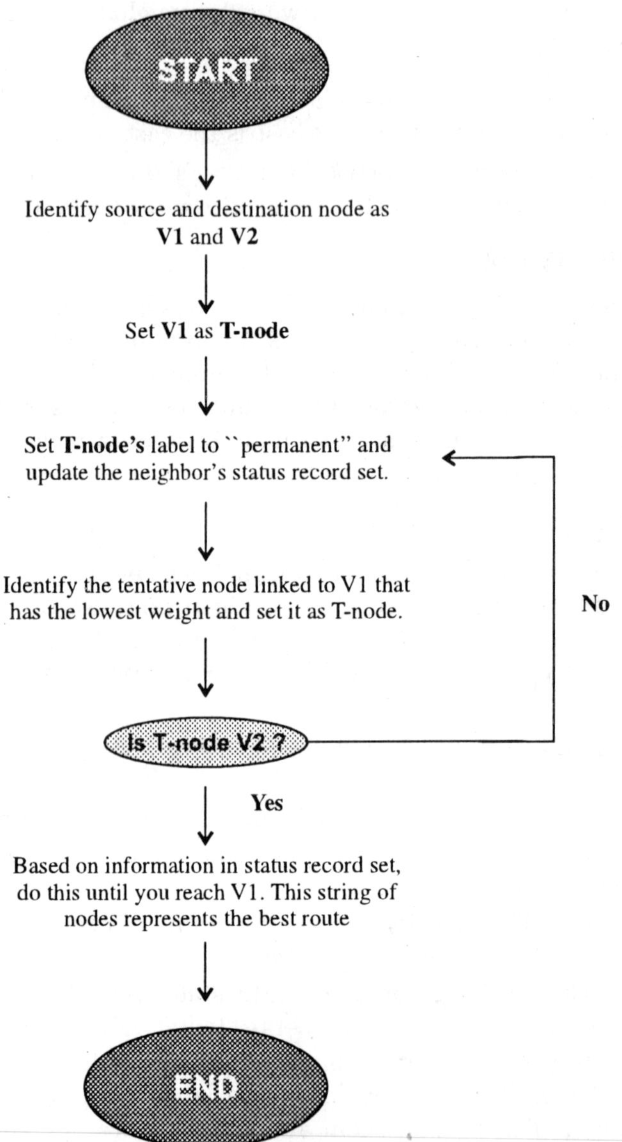

Fig. 12.11 Dijikstra algorithm

Example : Suppose we have a graph of network build according to link state algorithm as shown in figure 12.12 (a) and we are to find the best route between A and E. We can see that there are six possible routes between A and E (ABE, ACE, ABDE, ACDE, ABDCE, ACDBE). We have to use the above algorithm to find the best route.

1. The source node (A) has been chosen as T-node, and so its label is permanent.

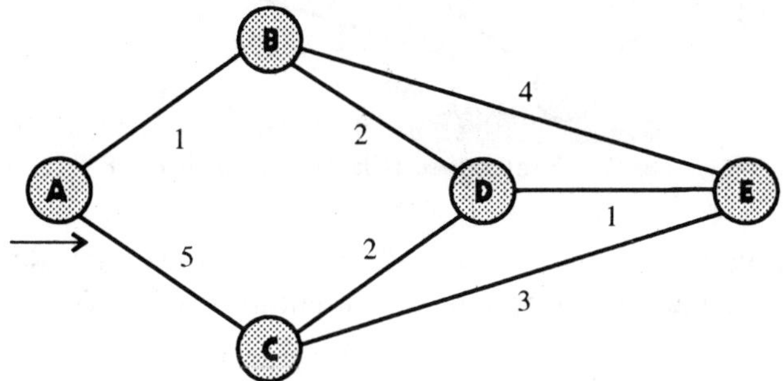

Fig. 12.12 (a) A network graph—Node A labelled as permanent

2. In this step, we see that the status record set of tentative nodes directly linked to T-node (B, C) has been changed. Also, since B has less weight, it has been chosen as T-node and its label has changed to permanent (see below).

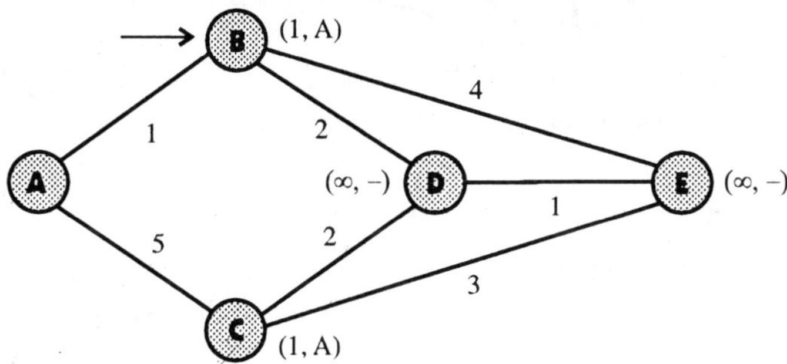

Fig. 12.12 (b) Node B labelled as permanent

3. In this step, like in step 2, the status record set of tentative nodes that have a direct link to T-node (D, E), has been changed. Also, since D has less weight, it has been chosen as T-node and its label has changed to permanent (see fig. 12.12 (c)).

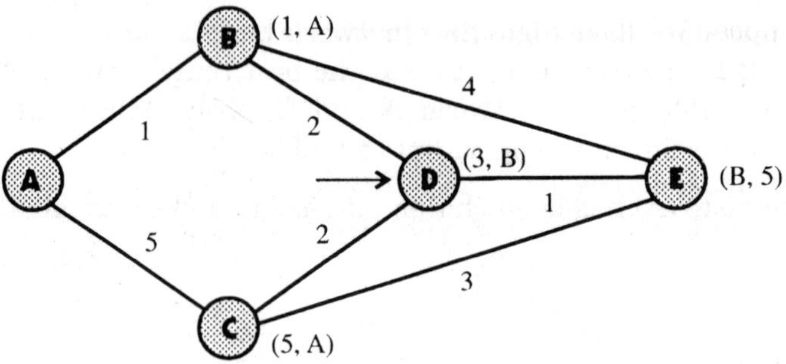

Fig. 12.12 (c) Node D labelled as permanent

4. In this step, we don't have any tentative nodes, so we just identify the next T-node. Since E has the least weight, it has been chosen as T-node.

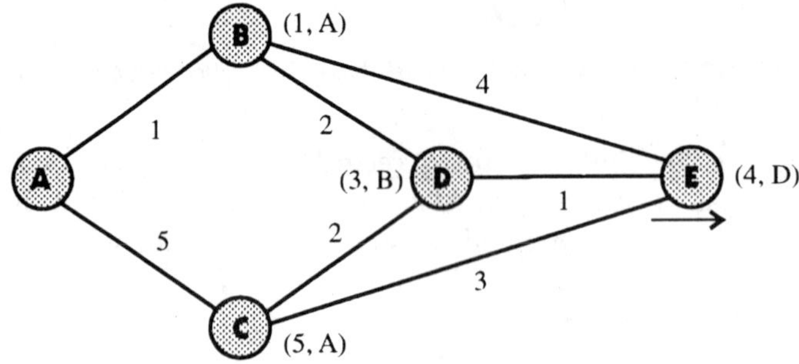

Fig. 12.12 (d) Node E labelled as permanent

5. E is the destination, so we stop here.

Now we have to identify the route. The previous node of E is D, and the previous node of D is B, and B's previous node is A. So the best route is ABDE. In this case, the total weigh is 4(1 + 2 + 1).

Although this algorithm works well, it's so complicated that it may take a long time for routers to process it, and the efficiency of the network fails. Also, if a router gives the wrong information to other routers, all routing decisions will be ineffective.

Advantages of Link State-Based Routing Protocols

- **Smaller routing tables :** Only a single optimal route for each network ID is stored in the routing table.
- **Low network overhead :** Link state based routers do not exchange any routing information when the internetwork has converged.
- **Ability to scale :** Between the smaller routing tables and low overhead, link state based routing protocols scale well to large and very large internetworks.
- **Lower convergence time :** Link state based routing protocols have a much lower convergence time and the internetwork is converged without routing loops.

Disadvantages of Link State-Based Routing Protocols

- **Complex :** Link state based routing protocols are much more complex and difficult to understand than distance vector based routing protocols.
- **More difficult to configure :** A link state based routing protocol implementation requires additional planning and configuration.
- **Resource intensive :** For very large internetworks, the database of link state advertisements and the calculation of routing table entries can be memory and processor intensive.

Potential Problems

- **Processing and memory required**—More memory is required due to the large amount of network information that needs to be managed. Recall that each router has a complete picture of the network.
- **Bandwidth consumed for initial link state "flood"**—A lot of bandwidth is consumed during initial link-state startup. This issue is called flooding. This is caused from all routers trying to converge the network and understand the network topology.
- **Unsynchronized updates and inconsistent path decisions**—This often happens when links become unavailable and the LSP has to be reconstructed. During the calculation other links go down as other come up. This creates problems.
- **Large network synchronization**—This adds to the problems due to the complete network topology that each router contains. Larger networks will run Hybrid protocols.

Implemented Solutions

- Reduce the need for resources.
- Coordinate link-state updates.

12.4.8 Comparing Distance-Vector Protocols to Link-State Routing Protocols

Both types have their place in internetworks. Distance-vector protocols were created when internetworks spanning hundreds of routers were uncommon. Link-state protocols, on the other hand, were specifically designed for these larger internetworks.

- **Distance-Vector**
  - ¤ Tell neighbors about distances to all destinations.
  - ¤ Node's computation depends on neighbors.
- **Link-State**
  - ¤ Tell all routers distance to each neighbor.
  - ¤ Each router computes its best paths.
- **Both are distributed algorithms**

The terms 'distance vector' and 'link state' are used to group routing protocols into two broad groups based on whether the protocol makes shortest path decisions based on a hop count metric or cost-based metrics. In distance-vector each node talks only to direct neighbors telling them all it knows. In link-state each node talks to all nodes telling them about direct neighbors.

Distance Vector

Distance vector protocols count the number of devices data must flow through to reach a destination. Each device is referred to as a 'hop', so the total number of hops between source and destination is the 'hop count'. Routes with lower hop counts are preferred.

Distance Vector algorithms require very little overhead in terms of processor power and memory, compared to Link State. Distance vector algorithms calculate only the hop count to destinations and choose best routes according to the hop count metric.

Link State

Link State protocols track the status and connection type (and therefore speed) of each link, and produce a calculated metric based on these and other factors, including some set by the network administrator. Distance Vector protocols differ from link state protocols because they see all hops as equal and only the number of hops matters. Link State protocols will take a path which has more hops, but that uses a faster medium over a path using a slower medium with fewer hops.

Because of their awareness of media types and other factors, link state protocols require more processing power (more circuit logic) and memory. Distance vector algorithms being simpler require simpler hardware.

When should distance-vector be used, and when should link-state routing be used?

There are arguments for and against each approach. The choice of strategy should be based on the properties of the given network, the main parameter being how frequently nodes are expected to go down or come up.

Stability

1. It is generally thought that link-state algorithms are more stable, because each router "knows" the entire network.
2. On the other hand, if the network is highly dynamic, it is possible for link-state algorithms to create routing loops while new topology information is being disseminated.

Running Time

1. Link-state algorithms converge more quickly than distance-vector algorithms.
2. In practice, the time for convergence depends on the network graph, the load on the routing protocol, and the exact sequence of link failure and recovery.

Overhead

1. Much of the overhead in link-state routing comes from the subroutine that prevents

corruption of the LSP database in case of node and/or link failure. The distance-vector algorithm does not have this overhead.

Memory

1. Typically, link-state implementations require more memory than distance-vector implementations.

The table below compares link-state protocols to distance-vector protocols:

Distance-Vector Protocol	Link-State Protocol
Must trust route tables of other routers; not always accurate.	Compiles an accurate topology map.
Calculates best path using hops.	Uses bandwidth analysis and other metrics for best-path calculation.
Updates only occur at preset intervals.	Updates occur whenever there is a link change.
Requires less memory.	Requires more memory.
Requires less processor utilization.	Requires more processor utilization.
Requires more bandwidth.	Requires less bandwidth.
Less complex configuration.	More complex configuration.
Sufficient for small internetworks.	Sufficient for large internetworks.

Now that you have a better idea of the pros and cons of the various routing protocols, here are some possible scenarios and their solutions.

Scenario and Solution

When routers have low memory but are connected to fast links.	Use a distance-vector routing protocol.
When routers have an abundance of memory but are connected to slow links.	Use link-state routing protocols.

12.5 Congestion Control

Congestion is said to occur in the network when the resource demands exceed the capacity and packets are lost due to too much queuing in the network. When routers are receiving packets faster than they can forward them, one of two things must happen:

- The subnet must prevent additional packets from entering the congested region until those already present can be processed.

- The congested routers can discard queued packets to make room for those that are arriving.

During congestion, the network throughput may drop to zero and the path delay may become very high. **A congestion control scheme** helps the network to recover from the congestion state. **A congestion avoidance scheme** allows a network to operate in the region of low delay and high throughput. Such schemes prevent a network from entering the congested state. Congestion avoidance is a prevention mechanism while congestion control is a recovery mechanism.

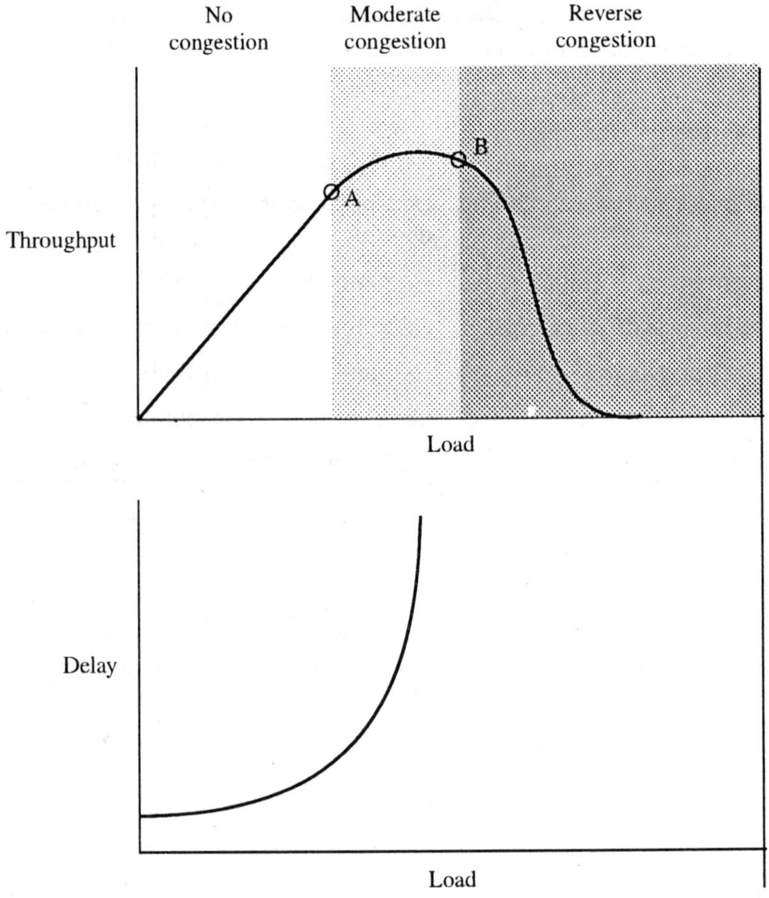

Fig. 12.13 Graph showing levels of congestion

12.5.1 Flow Control vs. Congestion Control

The terms flow control and congestion control are distinct. Flow control is an agreement between a source and a destination to limit the flow of packets without taking into account the load on the network. The purpose of flow control is to ensure that a packet arriving at a destination will find a buffer there. Congestion control is primarily concerned with controlling the traffic to reduce overload on the network. Flow control is a data link issue, and concerns only one sender outrunning a single receiver (e.g. a point-to-point link). Congestion control is a network layer issue, and is thus concerned with what happens when there is more data in the network than can be sent with reasonable packet delays, no lost packets, etc. Flow control is a local and congestion control is global. Flow control solves the problem of the destination resources being the bottleneck while congestion control solves the problem of the routers and links being the bottleneck. Different connections on a network can choose different flow control strategies, but nodes on the network should follow the same congestion control strategy, if it is to be useful. The two parties in flow control are generally interested in cooperating whereas the n parties (e.g., different users) in congestion control may be non-cooperative. Fairness is not an issue for the two cooperating parties whereas it is an important issue for n competing parties.

From the above discussion the main points of comparison are summarized in the following table:

• **Congestion control** is needed when buffers in packet switches overflow or congest.	• **Flow control** is needed when the buffers at the receiver are not depleted as fast as the data arrives.
• Congestion is end to end; it includes all hosts, links and routers.	• Flow is between one data sender and one receiver. It can be done on link-to-link or end-to-end basis.
• If viewed as a "congested buffer", then the switch tells the source of the data stream to slow down using congestion control notifications. When output buffers at a switch fill up and packets are dropped this leads to congestion control actions.	• If there is a queue on the input side of a switch, and link-by-link flow control is used, then as a "flow control" action the switch tells its immediate neighbor to slow down if the input queue fills up.

12.5.2 Causes of Congestion

The main causes of congestion are stated below:

1. Exhaustion of buffer space
2. Deadlock

1. Exhaustion of Buffer Space : Routers maintain packet queues (or buffers). Buffers fill up if either routers are too slow or combined input traffic rate exceeds the outgoing traffic rate. Insufficient buffer space leads to congestion.

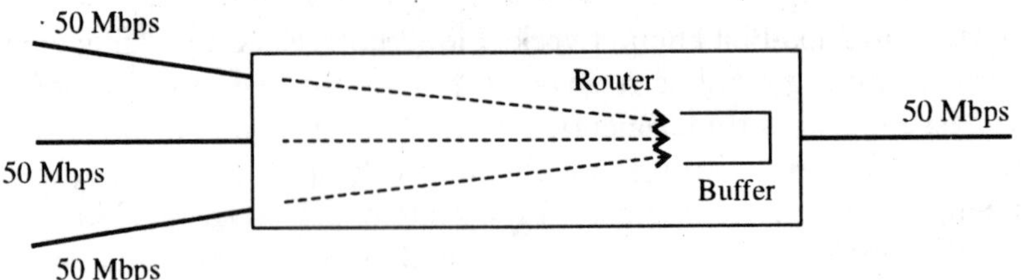

Fig. 12.14 Exhaustion of buffer space

2. **Deadlock** : It is a state in which the first router cannot proceed until the second router does something, and the second router cannot proceed until the first router does something. Both routers come to a completely halt and stay that way forever

Types of Deadlock

1. Store and Forward Lockup

- Direct Store and Forward Lockup
- Indirect Store and Forward Lockup

2. Reassembly Lockup

Direct Store and Forward Lockup

It is the simplest lockup between two routers.

Example :

- Suppose router A has five buffers, all of which are queued for output to router B.
- Similarly, router B has five buffers, all of which are queued for output to router A.
- If there is flow control on the link between routers A and B, then neither router can accept any incoming packets from the other. They are both stuck.

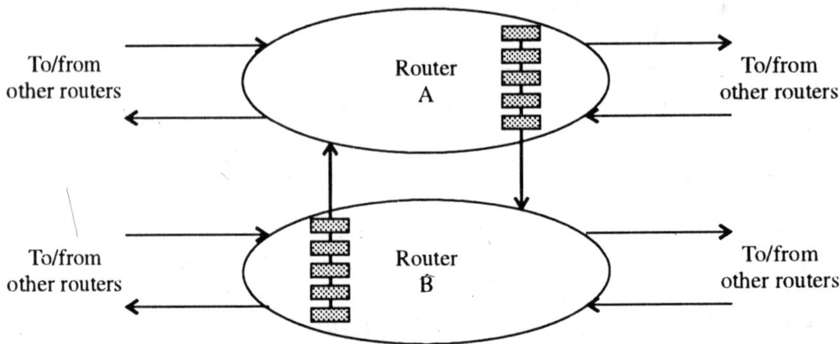

Fig. 12.15 (a) Direct store and forward lockup

Indirect Store and Forward Lockup

The same thing can happen on a larger scale.

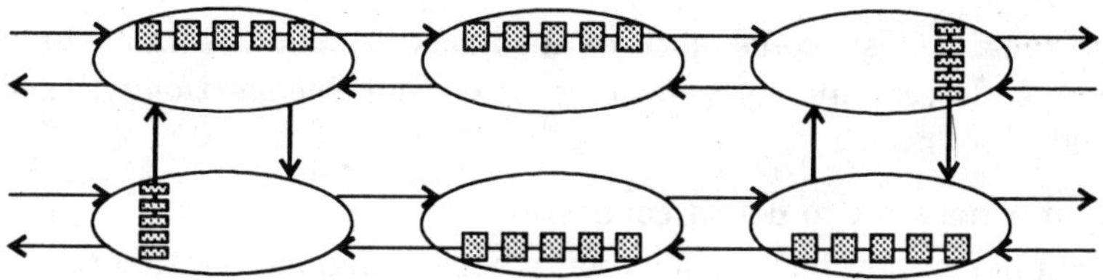

Fig. 12.15 (b) Indirect store and forward lockup

Reassembly Lockup

In some network layer implementations, the sending router must split messages into multiple network layer packets. The receiving routers reassemble split up packets into a single packet. If the receiving router's buffer fills up with incomplete packets, it cannot reassemble any more packets.

Congestion Control

We need congestion control so that the application can better achieve its goals of minimizing loss and delay, maximizing throughput. Congestion control algorithms are used to control the number of packets delivered in the network where the traffic is on the boundary of the network carrying capacity.

Desirable properties of congestion control

- Congestion control should result in many packets delivered at short delays.
- Protect network from congestive collapse but still transport as much data as possible.
- *Fairness* : Give all participating flows a "fair" share of available capacity.

Design options for congestion control mechanisms

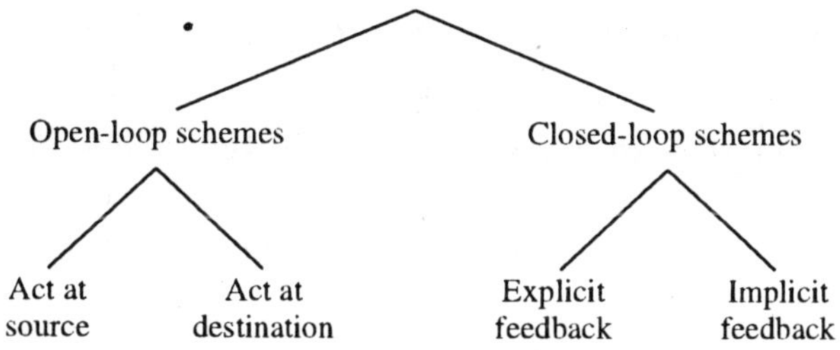

Fig. 12.16 Congestion control mechanisms

- **Open loop :** Design system up front so that it will work correct, no corrections at runtime necessary. It prevents congestion from every happening. It tends to be conservative and result in under utilization.
  - Request resources before using them.
  - Global (or regional) resource allocation.
  - Responds yes or no to each request for service.

- **Closed loop :** Use some sort of feedback to allow sender to adapt to current situation. It detects and corrects congestion. Some congestion will still occur until it is corrected.
  - □ Monitor network to detect congestion.
  - □ Pass information back to location where action can be taken.
  - □ Adjust system operation to correct the problem.
- **Explicit feedback :** Point where congestion occurs informs sender.
- **Implicit feedback :** No explicit action taken; congestion is deduced by sender from the network's behavior (e.g., missing acknowledgements)

12.5.3 Types of Congestion Control

There are two techniques for congestion control:

1. Preventive : The hosts and routers attempt to prevent congestion before it can occur.

2. Reactive : The hosts and routers respond to congestion after it occurs and then attempt to stop it.

Preventive Techniques:

- Resource reservation/Preallocation of resources
- Traffic shaping - Leaky/Token bucket
- Isarithmic control

Reactive Techniques:

- Load shedding
- Choke packets

12.5.3.1 Preallocation of Resources (Resource Reservation)

Preallocation schemes aim to prevent congestion from happening in the first place. For example, we can require that resources be preallocated before any packets can be sent, guaranteeing that resources will be available to process each packet.

In virtual circuit networks, for example, the sender opens a connection before sending data. During connection setup:

- Request resources (e.g., buffer space, connection bandwidth) from the network.
- If the network has enough available resources to support the new connection, the connection will be established.
- Otherwise, the connection will be rejected.

When the subnet is congested, it can refuse to open the connection, forcing the user to wait until sufficient resources become available.

Note: The ability of the subnet to reject requests to open connections is an important property of connection oriented networks

Resource Reservation: Example

Case 1 : Source attempts to connect to destination, and attempts to reserve 4 Mbps for the connection.

Result : Connection accepted. There is enough bandwidth available. Available link bandwidths updated.

Case 2 : Source attempts to connect to destination, and attempts to reserve 5 Mbps for the connection.

Result : Failure. There is not enough bandwidth available on one of the links.

12.5.3.2 Packet Discarding/Load Shedding

Packet discarding operates at the other end of the scale to preallocation of buffers.

If a packet arrives at one of the intermediate IMPs and there are no free buffers, then the packet will just be thrown away. Obviously it would be ridiculous to simply discard at will any packets for which there is no room, as they could potentially contain information which could lead to buffers becoming free. With this in mind, one buffer on each line can be permanently reserved to accept any incoming packet and look at its contents to see if it would be useful. Its contents can then be utilized or the packet discarded. Either a new buffer will become the 'customs' buffer or the old one will be cleared ready for the next packet to arrive and be checked. In this way, packets are not thrown away to the detriment of the network.

Intelligent Load Shedding

- Discarding packets does not need to be done randomly.
- Router should take other information into account. Possibilities:
  - Total packet dropping
  - Priority discarding
  - Age biased discarding

Total Packet Dropping

- When the buffer fills and a packet segment is dropped, drop all the rest of the segments from that packet, since they will be useless anyway.
- Only works with routers that segment and reassemble packets.

Priority Discarding

- Sources specify the priority of their packets.
- When a packet is discarded, the router chooses a low priority packet.
- Requires hosts to participate by labeling their packets with priority levels.

Age Biased Discarding

- When the router has to discard a packet, it chooses the oldest one in its buffer.
- This works well for multimedia traffic that requires short delays.

- This may not work so well for data traffic, since more packets will need to be retransmitted.

12.5.3.3 Isarithmic Congestion Control

Another approach to congestion avoidance is to limit the total number flow of packets in the subnet at any one time. This method attempts to tackle the fundamental reason for congestion within the subnet. Proposed by Davies in 1972, this method says that if congestion is caused by there being too many packets in the subnet, then it can be solved by setting an upper limit on the number allowed to be present at any given time.

The idea is similar to the token ring:

1. When a router accepts a packet from a host, it must obtain a permit before sending the packet into the subnet.
2. Obtaining a permit is analogous to "seizing the token", but there can be many permits in the subnet. When a router obtains a permit, it destroys it.
3. The destination router regenerates the permit when it passes the packet to the destination host.

The isarithmic congestion control method is however a long way from being ideal. Firstly the method does nothing about the fact that individual IMPs can become congested. Even though there are a limited number of packets allowed in the subnet, all of these could conceivably be going to the same IMP, causing congestion. Also, the procedure for dealing with the permits themselves is not very good. A fair way of distributing the permits throughout the subnet, and also allowing for a situation where a permit is accidentally destroyed, are both very difficult to do efficiently and effectively.

Thus, permit management and individual congestion problems at IMPs mean that the isarithmic congestion control method is not a suitable solution to the problem.

Isarithmic Control—Example

- Each host is initially allocated a pool of permits.

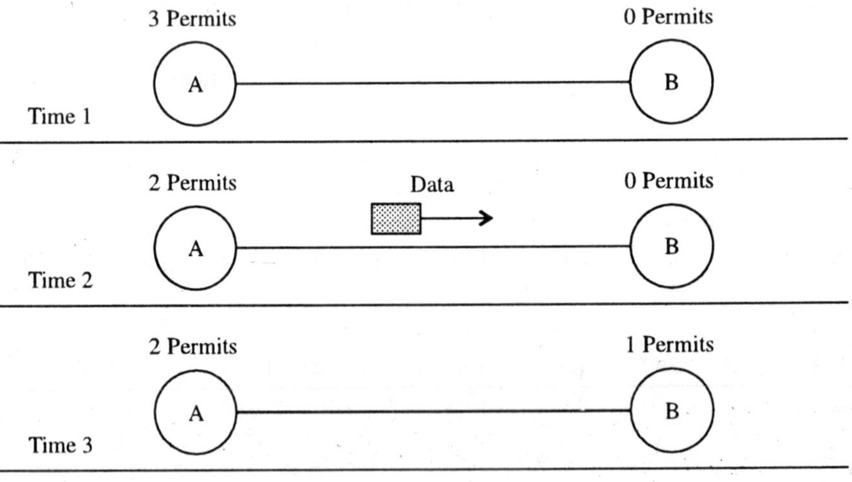

Fig. 12.17 Example showing isarithmic control

- Data packets carry "permits" between hosts.
- A host can't send a packet unless it has at least one permit.
- If no permit is available, the packet waits in the host until a permit becomes available.
- Isarithmic control is implemented at the hosts, not the routers
- Isarithmic control guarantees that the number of packets in the network will never exceed the number of permits initially present

■ Problem :

If a host doesn't send any packet, i.e. it just holds onto its permits, then the network will not be utilized fully.

Solution : Place a limit on the number of permits a host may keep. If the host has more than its allowed number of permits, it must transmit the excess permits to other hosts by piggybacking them onto other data packets or by using special permit-transport packets

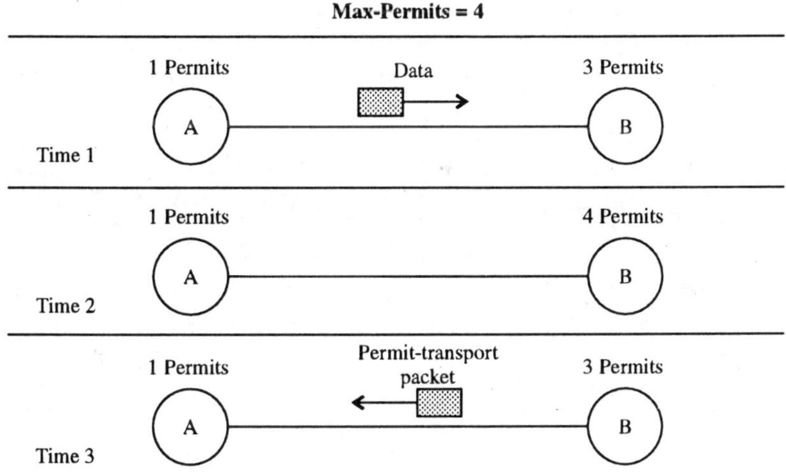

Fig. 12.18 A case of isarithmic control with max-permits = 4

Disadvantages of Isarithmic Congestion Control

1. Although we have limited the total number of packets in the subnet, we have no control over where in the subnet those packets will be. Thus, a router in one part of the subnet might be congested, while a router in another part remains idle, but unable to process packets for lack of permits.
2. Regenerating lost permits is difficult, because no single node knows how many permits are currently in the subnet.
3. How to distribute permits? Distribute among the routers or centralize for a known access point.

12.5.3.4 Choke Packets

A better method is to have each IMP monitor the level of traffic on its output lines. If this is below a certain level then everything is fine, but if the traffic goes above this level then the

IMP in question generates a choke packet containing the destination address of the offending packet. The source then retransmits that packet with a flag set so that no more choke packets will be generated because of it. It then slows down the rate at which it is currently sending. Any packets already on the move will be allowed to continue.

If the congestion clears, then the source can move back up to its normal speed.

How can a router measure congestion? A router might estimate the level of congestion by measuring the percentage of buffers in use, line utilizations, or average queue lengths.

The choke packet is sent from a router to all the sources of data associated with the congestion. The sources respond by reducing the flow by about a factor of two, which would mostly remove the congestion. However, this is not guaranteed as there can always be new hosts trying to transmit and these can have the effect of constantly bringing the congestion back above threshold. A source trying to complete a long transfer can be strongly hindered by lots of sources completing small transfers.

The reason for marking the packet as a choke packet is that we do not want routers sending out choke packets to other routers and having the generation of these packets spiral out of control by creating more congestion. Remember that when choke packets are first created they represent an increase in network demand and in the worst case this can lead to a reduction in throughput.

Choke Packets—Example

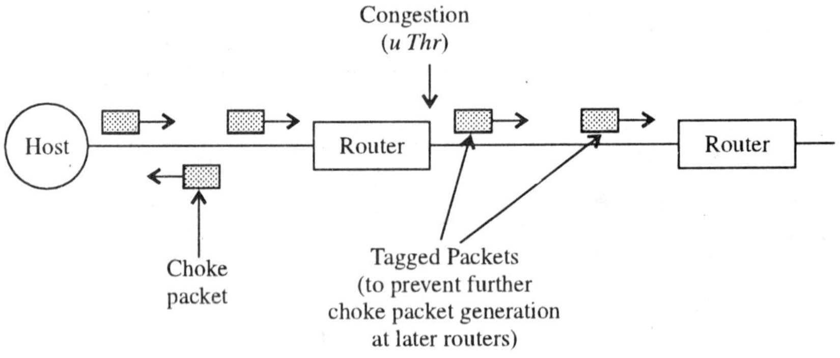

Fig. 12.19 Example of choke packets

- Each router monitors the utilization of each of its output lines.
- Associated with each line is a variable u, which reflects the utilization of that line.
- Whenever u moves above a given threshold value, the output line enters a "warning state".
- Each newly arriving packet checks if its output line is in the warning state.
- If so, the router sends a choke packet back to the source.
- The data packet is tagged (by setting a bit in its header) so that it will not generate any more choke packets at downstream routers.
- When the source host receives the choke packet, it is required to reduce its traffic generation rate to the specified destination by X%.

- Since other packets aimed at the same destination are probably already on their way to the congested location, the source host should ignore choke packets for that destination for a fixed time interval. After that, it resumes its response to choke packets.

Advantages:

Dynamic. Host sends as much data as it wants, the network informs it when it is sending too much.

Disadvantages:

1. Difficult to tune. By how much should a host slow down? The answer depends on how much traffic the host is sending, how much of the congestion it is responsible for, and the total capacity of the congested region. Such information is not readily available in practice.
2. After receiving a choke packet, the sending host should ignore additional choke packets for a short while because packets currently in transmission may generate additional choke packets. How long? Depends on such dynamic network conditions as delay.
3. Another problem stems from the global scale of networks. It can take a long time for a choke packet to reach the source. If the source is a fast machine it may have already sent a huge amount of data into the network.

12.5.3.5 Traffic Shaping

One of the causes of congestion is the inherent burstiness of computer network traffic. Traffic shaping means to smooth, or otherwise alter, the offered traffic as a function of time. Smooth traffic is easier to deal with the bursty traffic. A subnet may be able to handle on average 10 M packets in an hour, but it probably can't handle 10M packets in one minute and nothing for the next 59 minutes. Traffic shaping minimizes the occurrence of traffic bursts on the network. You can shape traffic by segmenting it, placing it into buffers, and delaying its propagation into the network. These actions ensure a more constant flow of network traffic.

Traffic shaping is performed at all packet interfaces (see the incoming packet traffic in Figure 12.20).

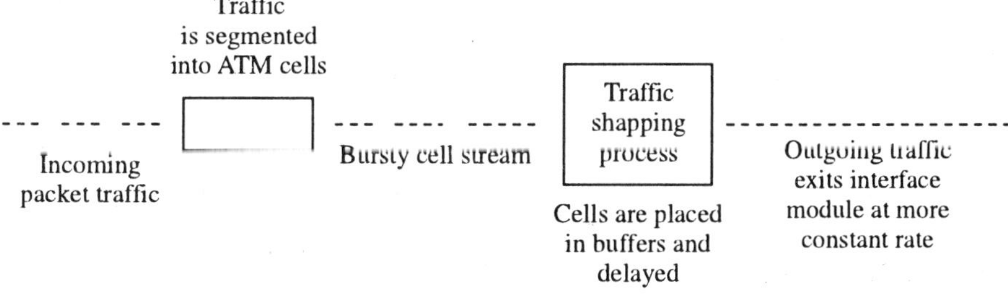

Fig. 12.20 Traffic Shaping

Related to traffic shaping is the whole idea of agreeing with a network service provider to a flow specification. A flow specification describes what sort of traffic you will put into the net, and what sort of quality if service you expect from it. Some of the qualities of service parameters are:

- Loss sensitivity (number of lost bytes per unit of time).
- Loss interval (the unit of time for calculating loss).
- Burst loss sensitivity (how long of a loss burst can be tolerated).
- Minimum delay (how large of a delay before the application notices).
- Maximum delay variation (the variance or jitter in the inter-packet delay).
- Quality of guarantee (how serious the spec is to the application).

The two algorithms for traffic shaping are:

- Leaky Bucket Algorithm.
- Token Bucket Algorithm.

Leaky Bucket Algorithm

It is basically a buffer that converts an unregulated, bursty traffic flow into a regulated, smooth, predictable flow. You put the buffer in between a traffic source and the subnet. The buffer acts like a single server queue with a finite queue length. Packets put in the buffer when it is full are thrown away. The buffer may drain onto the subnet either by some number of packets per unit time, or by some total number of bytes per unit time (helpful if packets vary greatly in size).

The leaky bucket algorithm behaves like a bucket with a hole in the bottom. Water can only leak from the bucket at a fixed rate. If data flows into the bucket faster than data flows out through the hole, the bucket eventually "overflows", causing data to be discarded until enough volume again exists in the bucket to accept new data. It provides a single server queueing model with a constant service time.

If packets are of fixed sizes (such as 53-byte ATM cells), one packet may be transmitted per unit time. If packets are of variable size, a fixed number of bytes (perhaps multiple packets) may be admitted. The leaky bucket algorithm enables an application to generate bursty traffic (high volume, for a short period) without saturating the network.

The leaky bucket algorithm uses two parameters to control traffic flow:

- **Average rate**—The average number of cells per second that "leak" from the hole in the bottom of the bucket and enter the network.
- **Burst rate**—The rate at which cells are allowed to accumulate in the bucket, expressed in cells per second. For example, if the average burst rate is 10 cells per second, a burst of 10 seconds allows 100 cells to accumulate in the bucket.

The leaky bucket algorithm also uses two state variables:

- **Current time**—The current wall clock time.

- **Virtual time**—A measure of how much data has accumulated in the bucket, expressed in seconds.

For example, if the average rate is 10 cells per second and 100 cells have accumulated in the bucket, then the virtual time is 10 seconds ahead of the current time.

Features of Leaky Bucket

It is a single-server queueing system with constant service time. Following are the main features of this system:

- Used in conjunction with resource reservation to police the host's reservation.
- The leaky bucket is a "traffic shaper": It changes the characteristics of packet stream.
- Each host is connected to the network by an interface containing leaky bucket.
- If a packet arrives at the queue when it is full, the packet is discarded, otherwise is appended to the end of the queue.
- The host is allowed to put one packet per clock tick from "leaky bucket" onto the network. (Enforced either by the interface card or by the operating system).
- Usually the network tells the leaky bucket the rate at which it may send packets when the connection begins.

Leaky Bucket: Analogy

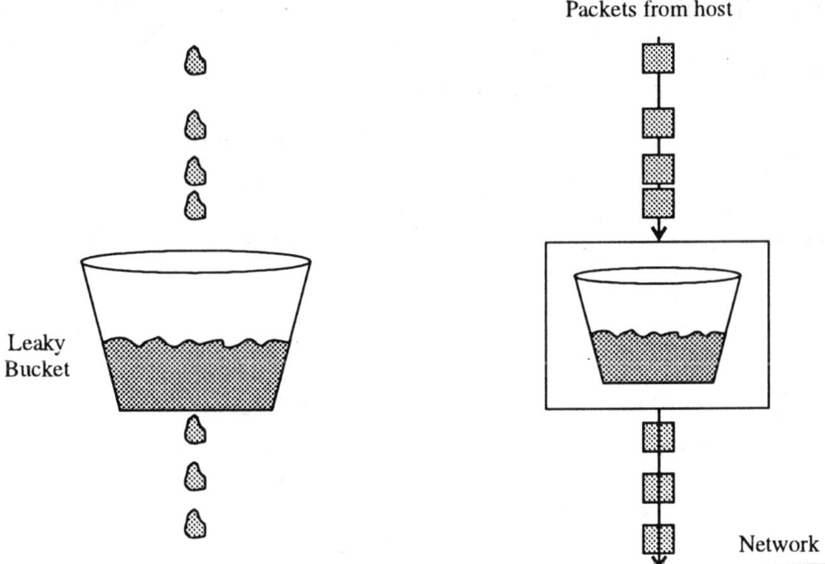

Fig. 12.21 Leaky bucket

Leaky Bucket doesn't allow bursty transmissions. In some cases, we may want to allow short bursts of packets to enter the network without smoothing them out. For this purpose we use a token bucket, which is a modified leaky bucket

Token Bucket Algorithm

The leaky bucket algorithm enforces a strict maximum traffic generation. It is often better to permit short bursts, but thereafter to constrain the traffic to some maximum. A variant on the leaky bucket is the token bucket. The bucket is filled with tokens at a certain rate. A packet must grab and destroy a token to leave the bucket. Packets are never lost; they just have to wait for an available token. Some bursts are allowed (up to the number tokens in the bucket) which is a good match for some applications (compromise with congestion and source needs).

Packets are placed in an "infinite" queue. Packets may enter the subnet whenever a token is available, else they must wait. The token bucket algorithm enables a host to transmit in short bursts, effectively "saving up" limited permission to generate a burst. The implementation of token bucket is just a counter (variable) that counts tokens: incremented by one every tick and decremented by one whenever packet is sent. When the counter hits 0, no packets can be sent.

Following are the main features of token bucket:

- The bucket holds tokens instead of packets.
- Tokens are generated and placed into the token bucket at a constant rate.
- When a packet arrives at the token bucket, it is transmitted if there is a token available. Otherwise it is buffered until a token becomes available.
- The token bucket has a fixed size, so when it becomes full, subsequently generated tokens are discarded.

Token Bucket: Analogy

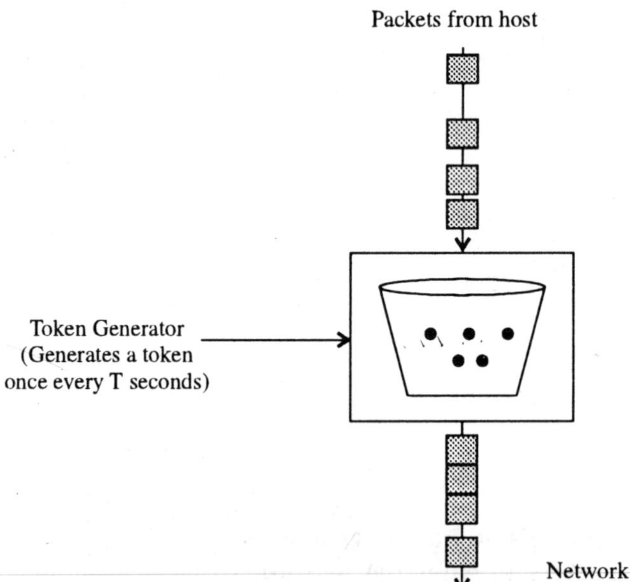

Fig. 12.22 Token bucket

Another way to illustrate token bucket:

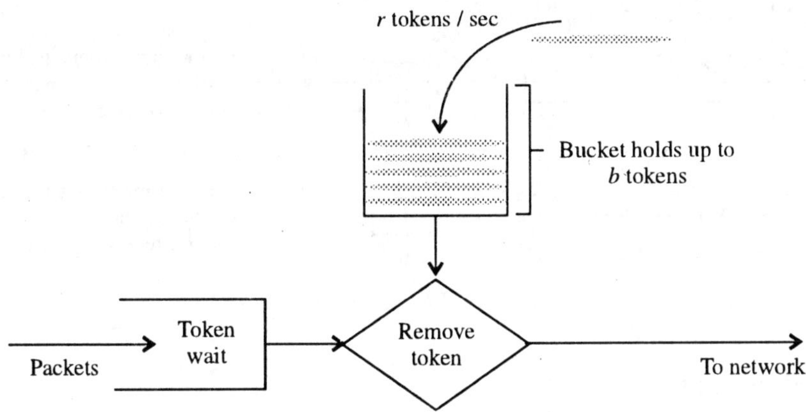

Fig. 12.23 Illustration of token bucket algorithm

Token Bucket vs. Leaky Bucket

Leaky bucket	Token bucket
• Leaky Bucket (LB) discards packets.	• Token Bucket (TB) discards tokens.
• With LB, a packet can be transmitted if the bucket is not full.	• With TB, a packet can only be transmitted if there are enough tokens to cover its length in bytes.
• LB sends the packets at an average rate.	• TB allows for large bursts to be sent faster by speeding up the output.
• LB does not allow saving, a constant rate is maintained.	• TB allows saving up tokens (permissions) to send large bursts.

0 1 2 3 4 5 6

Arrival time at bucket

0 1 2 3 4 5 6

Departure time from a leaky bucket
Leaky bucket rate = 1 packet / 2 time units
Leaky bucket size = 4 packets

0 1 2 3 4 5 6

Departure time from a token bucket
Token bucket rate = 1 tokens / 2 time units
Token bucket size = 2 tokens

Fig. 12.24(a) Case 1 : Short burst arrivals

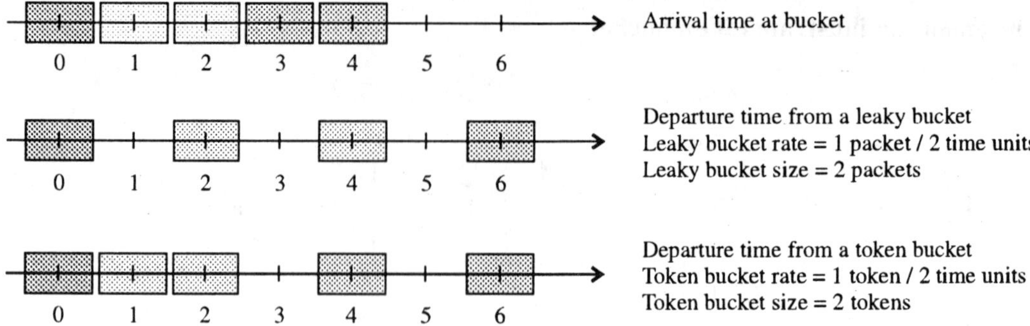

Fig. 12.24(b) Case 2 : Large burst arrivals

12.5.3.6 Flow Specification

It is also like traffic shaping open loop method applicable both to virtual circuits and datagrams. The sender, receiver, and subnet agree on flow specification:

- The maximum transmission rate.
- Maximum packet size.
- Token bucket rate and size.
- Minimum delay noticed.
- Maximum delay variation (jitter).
- Burst loss sensitivity (how many consecutive lost packets can be tolerated).

12.6 The IP Protocol

The Internet Protocol (IP) is a network-layer (Layer 3) protocol that contains addressing information and some control information that enables packets to be routed. IP represents the heart of the Internet protocols. IP has two primary responsibilities: providing connectionless, best-effort delivery of datagrams through an internetwork; and providing fragmentation and reassembly of datagrams to support data links with different maximum-transmission unit (MTU) sizes.

All transport protocol data packets such as UDP or TCP are encapsulated in IP data packets to be carried from one host to another. IP is a connection-less unreliable service meaning there is no guarantee that the data will reach the intended host. The datagrams may be damaged upon arrival, out of order, or not arrive at all. Therefore the layers above IP such as TCP are responsible for being sure correct data is delivered.

The Internet Protocol is the building block of the Internet. Its functions include:

- Defining the datagram, which is the basic unit of transmission in the Internet.
- Defining the Internet addressing scheme.
- Moving data between the Network Access Layer and the Host-to-Host Transport Layer.

- Routing datagrams to remote hosts.
- Performing fragmentation and re-assembly of datagrams.

12.6.1 Characteristics of IP

- First, IP is a **connectionless protocol**. This means that IP does not exchange control information (called a "handshake") to establish an end-to-end connection before transmitting data. In contrast, a connection-oriented protocol exchanges control information with the remote system to verify that it is ready to receive data before any data is sent. When the handshaking is successful, the systems are said to have established a connection. Internet Protocol relies on protocols in other layers to establish the connection if they require connection-oriented service.
- IP also relies on protocols in the other layers to provide error detection and error recovery. The Internet Protocol is sometimes called an **unreliable protocol** because it contains no error detection and recovery code. This is not to say that the protocol cannot be relied on - quite the contrary. IP can be relied upon to accurately deliver your data to the connected network, but it doesn't check whether that data was correctly received. Protocols in other layers of the TCP/IP architecture provide this checking when it is required.

12.6.2 IP Packet Format

The Internet Protocol (IP) uses a Datagram service to transfer packets of data between end systems using routers. An IP packet contains several types of information, as illustrated in figure 12.25.

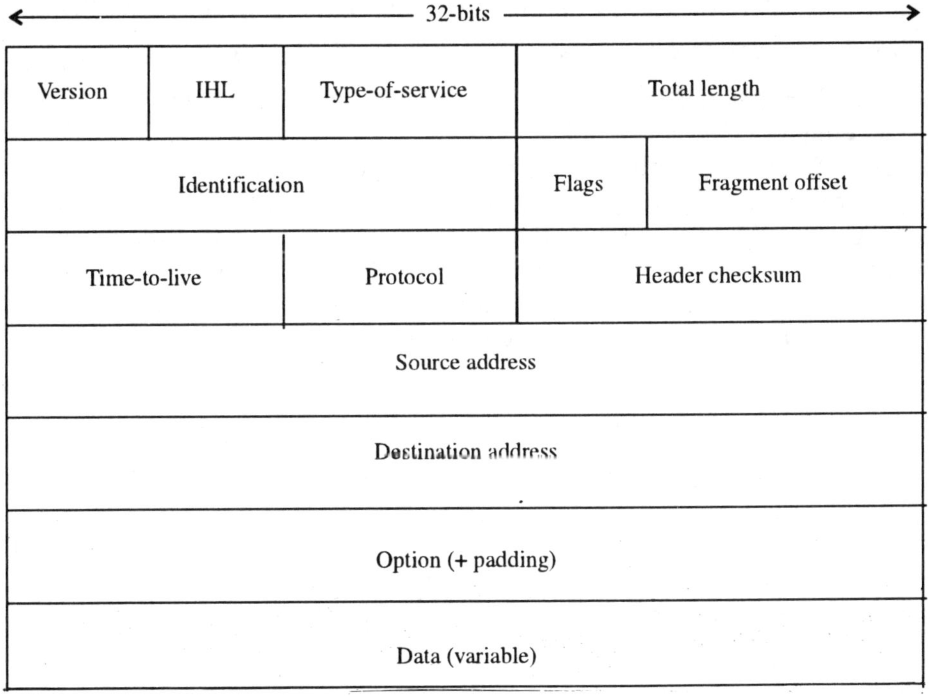

← 32-bits →

Version	IHL	Type-of-service	Total length	
Identification			Flags	Fragment offset
Time-to-live		Protocol	Header checksum	
Source address				
Destination address				
Option (+ padding)				
Data (variable)				

The various fields are described below:

1. **Version (4 bits)**—Indicates the IP protocol version, currently 4 or 6.
2. **IP Header Length (IHL) (4 bits)**—Indicates the datagram header length in 32-bit words.
3. **Type-of-Service (8 bits)**—Specifies how an upper-layer protocol would like a current datagram to be handled, and assigns datagrams various levels of importance. Only 4 bits are used which are minimize delay, maximize throughput, maximize reliability, and minimize monetary cost. Only one of these bits can be on. If all bits are off, the service is normal. Some networks allow a set precedence to control priority of messages; the bits are as follows:

- Bits 0-2: Precedence.
  - 111 - Network Control.
  - 110 - Internetwork Control.
  - 101 - CRITIC/ECP.
  - 100 - Flash Override.
  - 011 - Flash,
  - 010 - Immediate.
  - 001 - Priority.
  - 000 - Routine.
- Bit 3 : A value of 0 means normal delay. A value of 1 means low delay.
- Bit 4 : Sets throughput. A value of 0 means normal and a 1 means high throughput.
- Bit 5 : A value of 0 means normal reliability and a 1 means high reliability.
- Bit 6-7 are reserved for future use.

4. **Total Length (16-bits)**—Specifies the length, in bytes, of the entire IP packet, including the data and header.
5. **Identification (16-bits)**—Contains an integer that identifies the current datagram. This field is used to help piece together datagram fragments.
6. **Flags (3-bits)**—Consists of a 3-bit field of which the two low-order (least significant) bits control fragmentation. The low-order bit specifies whether the packet can be fragmented. The middle bit specifies whether the packet is the last fragment in a series of fragmented packets. The third or high-order bit is not used.

- Bit 0 - reserved.
- Bit 1 - The fragment bit. A value of 0 means the packet may be fragmented while a 1 means it cannot be fragmented. If this value is set and the packet needs further fragmentation, an ICMP error message is generated.
- Bit 2 - This value is set on all fragments except the last one since a value of 0 means this is the last fragment.

7. **Fragment Offset (13-bits)**—Indicates the position of the fragment's data relative

to the beginning of the data in the original datagram, which allows the destination IP process to properly reconstruct the original datagram.

8. **Time-to-Live (8-bits)**—Maintains a counter that gradually decrements down to zero, at which point the datagram is discarded. This keeps packets from looping endlessly.
9. **Protocol (8-bits)**—Indicates which upper-layer protocol receives incoming packets after IP processing is complete. This may be one or more of TCP, UDP, ICMP, IGMP or OSPF.
10. **Header Checksum (16-bits)**—Helps ensure IP header integrity.
11. **Source Address (32-bits)**—Specifies the sending node.
12. **Destination Address (32-bits)**—Specifies the receiving node.
13. **Options**—Allows IP to support various options, such as security. The various options are listed below:

Security and handling restrictions.

- Record route—Each router records its IP address.
- Time stamp—Each router records its IP address and time.
- Loose source routing—Specifies a set of IP addresses the datagram must go through.
- **Strict source routing**—The datagram can go through only the IP addresses specified.

14. **Data**—Contains upper-layer information.

Fragmentation is handled at the IP network layer and the messages are reassembled when they reach their final destination. If one fragment of a datagram is lost, the entire datagram must be retransmitted. This is why fragmentation is avoided by TCP. The data on the last line, item 14, is Ethernet data, or data depending on the type of physical network.

12.6.3 IP Addressing

As with any other network-layer protocol, the IP addressing scheme is integral to the process of routing IP datagrams through an internetwork. Each IP address has specific components and follows a basic format. These IP addresses can be subdivided and used to create addresses for subnetworks.

An address is a data structure understood by a network, which uniquely identifies the recipient within the network. Addresses in other places than computer networks: Addresses are used by the postal system to allow a postman to find a person's house; to allow a computer to uniquely identify a location in memory.

A unicast/broadcast IP address is a 32-bit value (i.e., four bytes), which is allocated to each system in the Internet. The 32-bit value uniquely identifies this system, and therefore no two systems may have the same IP address. Some systems have more than one IP address, in which case they may be reached by any of their IP addresses.

Each IP address consists of two parts, the network part (identifying the network number, or LAN collision domain, to which the computer is attached) and the host part (which identifies the host within the local network). IP addresses are normally written in a format known as "dotted decimal notation". In this format, each byte of the 4-byte address is expressed as a decimal (base 10) number (i.e., 0 to 255). The four decimal numbers are separated by "dots" or "periods" as shown below:

IP address "129.7.1.10" corresponds to a hexadecimal value of 0 × 8107010A.

IP Address Format

The 32-bit IP address is grouped eight bits at a time, separated by dots, and represented in decimal format (known as dotted decimal notation). Each bit in the octet has a binary weight (128, 64, 32, 16, 8, 4, 2, 1). The minimum value for an octet is 0, and the maximum value for an octet is 255. The figure 12.26 illustrates the basic format of an IP address.

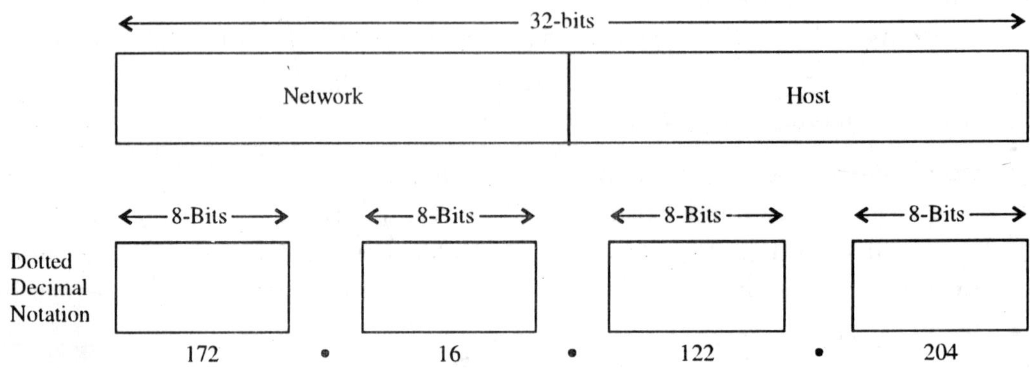

Fig. 12.26 An IP address consists of 32-bits, grouped into four octets

IP Subnet Addressing

IP networks can be divided into smaller networks called subnetworks (or subnets). Subnetting provides the network administrator with several benefits, including extra flexibility, more efficient use of network addresses and the capability to contain broadcast traffic (a broadcast will not cross a router).

Subnets are under local administration. As such, the outside world sees an organization as a single network and has no detailed knowledge of the organization's internal structure.

A given network address can be broken up into many subnetworks. For example, 172.16.1.0, 172.16.2.0, 172.16.3.0 and 172.16.4.0 are all subnets within network 171.16.0.0. (All 0s in the host portion of an address specifies the entire network.)

12.7 An Introduction To IPv6 : The New Internet Protocol

IPv6 is short for "Internet Protocol Version 6". IPv6 is designed by the IETF (Internet Engineering Task Force) to replace the current version Internet Protocol, IP Version 4 ("IPv4"). It is also referred to as the Next Generation Internet Protocol (IPng).

Most of today's Internet uses IPv4, which is now nearly twenty years old. IPv4 has been remarkably resilient in spite of its age, but it is beginning to have problems. Most importantly, there is a growing shortage of IPv4 addresses, which are needed by all new machines added to the Internet. The main issue surrounding IPv6 is addressing-or, the lack of addressing—because many experts believe that we are nearly out of the four billion addresses available in IPv4. Although this seems like a very large number of addresses, multiple large blocks are given to government agencies and large organizations. IPv6 could be the solution to many problems, but it is still not fully developed and is not a standard—yet!

IPv6 fixes a number of problems in IPv4, such as the limited number of available IPv4 addresses. It also adds many improvements to IPv4 in areas such as routing and network auto configuration. IPv6 is expected to gradually replace IPv4, with the two coexisting for a number of years during a transition period. At some point in the next three to seven years the Internet will require a deployed new version of the Internet protocol.

Two factors are driving this: routing and addressing. Global Internet routing based on the on 32-bit addresses of IPv4 is becoming increasingly strained. IPv4 addresses do not provide enough flexibility to construct efficient hierarchies that can be aggregated. Even if the IPv4 routing can be scaled to support a full IPv4 Internet, the Internet will eventually run out of network numbers. There is no question that an IPv6 is needed, but only a question of when.

12.7.1 Why IPv6?

There are a number of reasons why IPv6 is appropriate for the next generation of the Internet Protocol. It solves the Internet scaling problem, provides a flexible transition mechanism for the current Internet and was designed to meet the needs of new markets such as nomadic personal computing devices, networked entertainment and device control. It does this in an evolutionary way that reduces the risk of architectural problems.

IPv6 supports large hierarchical addresses that will allow the Internet to continue to grow and provide new routing capabilities not built into IPv4. It has anycast addresses that can be used for policy route selection and has scoped multicast addresses, which provide improved scalability over IPv4 multicast. It also has local use address mechanisms, which provide the ability for "plug and play" installation.

IPv6 provides a platform for new Internet functionality. This includes support for real-time flows, provider selection, host mobility, end-to-end security, auto-configuration, and auto-reconfiguration.

IPv6 is just a new version of IP. It can be installed as a normal software upgrade in Internet devices. It is interoperable with the current IPv4. IPv6 is designed to run well on high performance networks (e.g., ATM) and at the same time is still efficient for low bandwidth networks (e.g., wireless). In addition, it provides a platform for new Internet functionality that will be required in the near future.

Another positive outcome of IPv6 will be better Internet routing using QoS, Quality of Service, which routes packets based on priority. So for example, if one person is pinging a server and another is downloading a file, the one pinging will have less priority in their data transmission than the one downloading a file because the user who is downloading a file has created a data stream that will automatically gain more priority over the simple ICMP data packets.

Lastly, routing will be simplified because the IPv6 information header on each packet is far more flexible and can contain more detailed information than an IPv4 header thus allowing for faster routing of data across a network or the Internet.

IPv6 was designed to take an evolutionary step from IPv4. The changes from IPv4 to IPv6 fall primarily into the following categories:

- Expanded Routing and Addressing Capabilities : IPv6 increases the IP address size from 32-bits to 128-bits, to support more levels of addressing hierarchy and a much greater number of addressable nodes, and simpler auto-configuration of addresses. The scalability of multicast routing is improved by adding a "scope" field to multicast addresses.
- A new type of address called an "anycast address" is defined; to identify sets of nodes where a packet sent to an anycast address is delivered to one of the nodes. The use of anycast addresses in the IPv6 source route allows nodes to control the path, which their traffic flows.
- Header Format Simplification : Some IPv4 header fields have been dropped or made optional, to reduce the common-case processing cost of packet handling and to keep the bandwidth cost of the IPv6 header as low as possible despite the increased size of the addresses. Even though the IPv6 addresses are four times longer than the IPv4 addresses, the IPv6 header is only twice the size of the IPv4 header.
- Improved Support for Options : Changes in the way IP header options are encoded allows for more efficient forwarding, less stringent limits on the length of options, and greater flexibility for introducing new options in the future.
- Quality-of-Service Capabilities : A new capability is added to enable the labeling of packets belonging to particular traffic "flows" for which the sender requests special handling, such as non-default quality of service or "real-time" service.
- Authentication and Privacy Capabilities : IPv6 includes the definition of extensions that provide support for authentication, confidentiality and data integrity.

12.7.2 IPv6 Header Format

The IPv6 protocol consists of two parts, the basic IPv6 header and IPv6 extension headers.

IPv6 header:

Version	Traffic Class	Flow Label	
Payload Length		Next Header	Hop Limit
Source address			
Destination address			
Data			

Fig. 12.27 IPv6 header format

Version-(4-bits)—IPv6 version number.

Traffic Class-(8-bits)—Internet traffic priority delivery value.

Flow Label-(20-bits)—Used for specifying special router handling from source to destination(s) for a sequence of packets.

Payload Length-(16-bits unsigned)—Specifies the length of the data in the packet. When cleared to zero, the option is a hop-by-hop Jumbo payload.

Next Header-(8-bits)—Specifies the next encapsulated protocol. The values are compatible with those specified for the IPv4 protocol field.

Hop Limit-(8-bits unsigned)—For each router that forwards the packet, the hop limit is decremented by 1. When the hop limit field reaches zero, the packet is discarded.

Source address-(16-bytes)—The IPv6 address of the sending node.

Destination address-(16-bytes)—The IPv6 address of the destination node.

IPv6 Extensions

IPv6 includes an improved option mechanism over IPv4. IPv6 options are placed in separate extension headers that are located between the IPv6 header and the transport-layer header in a packet. Most IPv6 extension headers are not examined or processed by any router along a packet's delivery path until it arrives at its final destination. This facilitates a major improvement in router performance for packets containing options. In IPv4 the presence of any options requires the router to examine all options.

The other improvement is that unlike IPv4 options, IPv6 extension headers can be of arbitrary length and the total amount of options carried in a packet is not limited to 40 bytes. This feature plus the manner in which they are processed, permits IPv6 options to be used for functions that were not practical in IPv4. A good example of this is the IPv6 Authentication and Security Encapsulation options.

In order to improve the performance when handling subsequent option headers and the transport protocol which follows, IPv6 options are always an integer multiple of 8 octets long, in order to retain this alignment for subsequent headers.

The IPv6 extension headers that are currently defined are:

- Routing : Extended Routing.
- Fragmentation : Fragmentation and Reassembly.
- Authentication : Integrity and Authentication. Security
- Encapsulation : Confidentiality.
- Hop-by-Hop Option : Special options which require hop-by-hop processing.
- Destination Options : Optional information to be examined by the destination node.

12.7.3 IPv6 Addressing

To properly understand the addressing scheme of IPv6, we first have to understand the syntax of the actual address. With a standard IPv4 address, it consists of 32 bits broken into 8 bit segments separated by periods. For example:

11111111. 11111111. 11111111. 11111111 (binary)
255 . 255 . 255 . 255 (decimal)

With IPv6, you have a 128 bit address broken down into strings of 16 bits separated by colons. For example:

1111111111111111 : 1111111111111111 : 1111111111111111 : 1111111111111111 : 1111111111111111 : 1111111111111111 : 1111111111111111 : 1111111111111111 (binary)

FFFF : FFFF : FFFF : FFFF : FFFF : FFFF : FFFF : FFFF (Hexadecimal)

Let's look at an example of IPv6 address. The address is an eight-part hex address separated by colons (" : "). Each part n can equal a 16-bit number and is eight parts long, providing a 128-bit address length (16 * 8 = 128),

Addresses are n:n:n:n:n:n:n:n n = 4 digit hexadecimal integer,
16 * 8 = 128 address.

1080:0:0:0:8:800:200C:417A Unicast address
FF01:0:0:0:0:0:0:101 Multicast address

So for example, a 16-bit string such as "0010000111011010" would convert to 21DA in hexadecimal. Hexadecimal is a binary addressing system that takes 4-bits of data and converts it into an alphanumeric value from 0 to F. This chart should give you a little better idea of how the binary numbers, decimal numbers and hexadecimal values all compare to each other.

Binary	Hexadecimal	Decimal
0000	0	0
0001	1	1
0010	2	2
0011	3	3
0100	4	4
0101	5	5
0110	6	6
0111	7	7
1000	8	8
1001	9	9
1010	A	10
1011	B	11
1100	C	12
1101	D	13
1110	E	14
1111	F	15

As you notice, the binary digits are always 4 characters (4 bits). The hexadecimal numbers are all 1 character, and the decimal numbers range from 1-2 characters in size. Since a hexadecimal number can't take up more than 1 space, any number greater than 9 has to be represented with a letter ranging from A-F. The decimal column lists the decimal values of each binary number. Therefore, a 16-bit string of data would need to be represented by 4 characters of hexadecimal data, or as we listed before in our example, something like this: 21DA

Types of IPv6 Addresses

There are 3 types of addresses in IPv6: Unicast, Multicast, and Anycast.

Unicast

Unicast is a communication between a single host and a single receiver. Packets sent to a unicast address are delivered to the interface identified by that address, as seen in Figure 12.28.

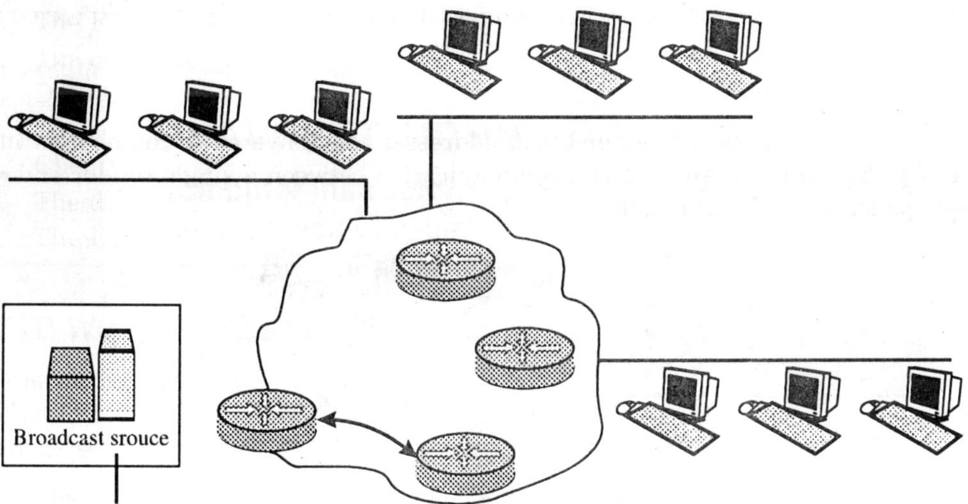

Fig. 12.28 Unicast sends packets to a specified interface

Multicast

Multicast is communication between a single host and multiple receivers. Packets are sent to all interfaces identified by that address, as seen in Figure 12.29.

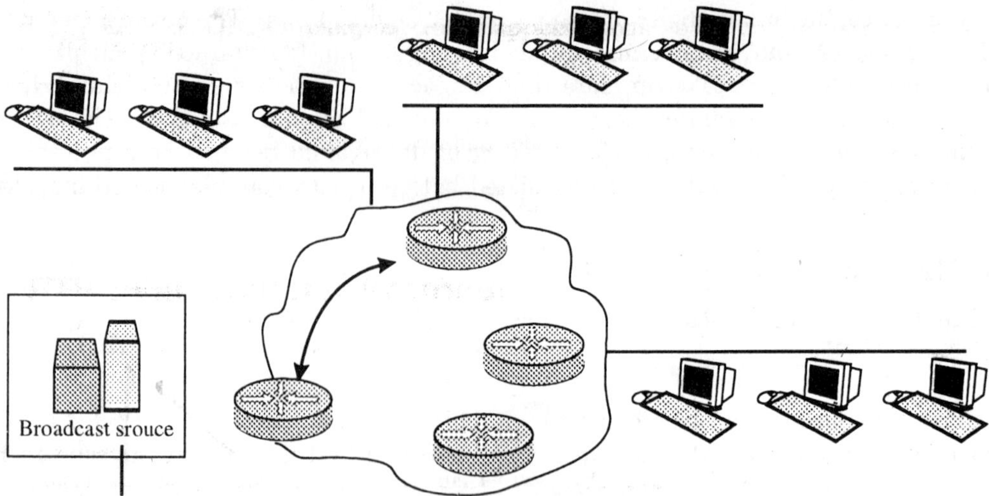

Fig. 12.29 Multicast sends packets to a subnet and defined devices listen for multicast packets

Anycast

Packets sent to an anycast address or list of addresses are delivered to the nearest interface identified by that address. Anycast is a communication between a single sender and a list of addresses, as shown in Figure 12.30.

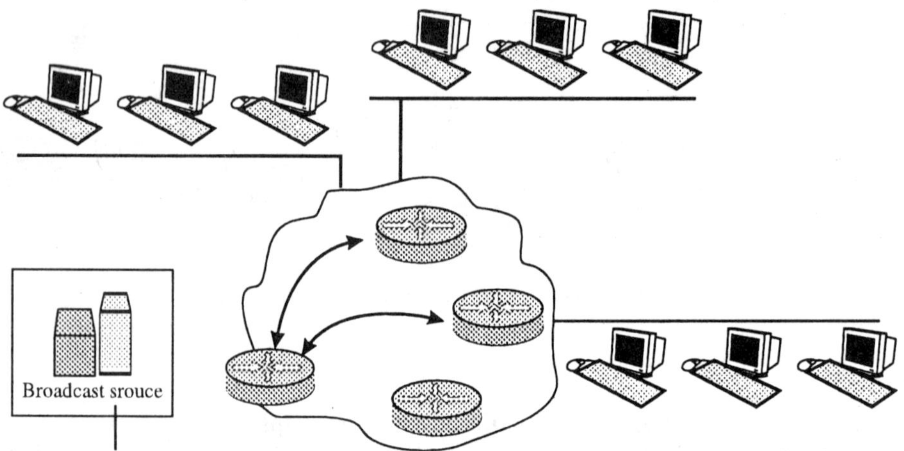

Fig. 12.30 Anycast sends packets to specified interface list and can contain end nodes and routers

Unicast addresses identify a single interface. Anycast addresses identify a set of interfaces such that a packet sent to an anycast address will be delivered to one member of the set. Multicast addresses identify a group of interfaces, such that a packet sent to a multicast address is delivered to all of the interfaces in the group. There are no broadcast addresses in IPv6, their function being superseded by multicast addresses.

Unicast is standard point A to point B data traffic. This would be nothing more than me sending data from my computer, across the Internet, to your computer and back again. That's the basic elements of Unicast addressing. So instead of needing to setup a special machine to dictate which server gets a given incoming connection first, IPv6 controls this automatically. Multicast is exactly how it sounds. Sending to one address on a subnet broadcasts to everyone on the subnet. This works the same as the broadcast address in IPv4.

Anycast identifies multiple network interfaces. In the simplest terms, the anycast address system is a "First man wins" system. Basically, if you have three network interfaces identified as part of a given anycast address and a request is sent to the anycast address, it is then forwarded to the first interface in the anycast group. Since that interface is not busy, the packet is then delivered to that interface. Say a second connection comes in and the first interface is busy. The connection is immediately routed over to the second interface. Then a third connection request comes in but now the first interface is not busy anymore so the data is routed to the first interface. This is a simple load balancing system built directly into IPv6.

Local use Addresses

While many things in IPv6 are new and unique, there are many things that are much the same as they are in IPv4, if not done in a slightly different way. One example of this is local use addresses. These consist of Link Local and Site Local addresses. Link local addresses are more or less the IPv6 equivalent to the MAC address already used on every network out there to identify individual pieces of networking hardware attached to the network. A link local address is automatically configured by the computer and is used for neighbor discovery and for querying of the DHCP server for an IP address and other information necessary on the network. These addresses are not world routable and are only used locally.

Site local addressing would be equivalent to the private network addresses used in Nat under IPv4. These addresses are not world routable and are used for data traffic within your local network itself. Compatibility is also a big factor with IPv6.

12.8 Address Resolution Protocol

The address resolution protocol (ARP) is a protocol used by the Internet Protocol (IP), specifically IPv4, to map IP network addresses to the hardware addresses used by a data link protocol. The protocol operates below the network layer as a part of the interface between the OSI network and OSI link layer. It is used when IPv4 is used over Ethernet.

For two machines on a given network to communicate, they must know the other machine's physical (or MAC) addresses. By broadcasting Address Resolution Protocols (ARPs), a host can dynamically discover the MAC-layer address corresponding to a particular IP network-layer address.

The term **address resolution** refers to the process of finding an address of a computer in a network. The address is "resolved" using a protocol in which a piece of information is sent by a client process executing on the local computer to a server process executing on a remote computer. The information received by the server allows the server to uniquely identify the network system for which the address was required and therefore to provide the required address. The address resolution procedure is completed when the client receives a response from the server containing the required address.

An Ethernet network uses two hardware addresses, which identify the source and destination of each frame, sent by the Ethernet. The destination address (all 1's) may also identify a broadcast packet (to be sent to all connected computers). The hardware address is also known as the Medium Access Control (MAC) address, in reference to the standards, which define Ethernet. Each computer network interface card is allocated a globally unique 6-byte link address when the factory manufactures the card (stored in a PROM). This is the normal link source address used by an interface. A computer sends all packets that it creates with its own hardware source link address, and receives all packets which match the same hardware address in the destination field or one (or more) pre-selected broadcast/multicast addresses.

The Ethernet address is a link layer address and is dependent on the interface card, which is used. IP operates at the network layer and is not concerned with the link addresses of individual nodes, which are to be used. The address resolution protocol (ARP) is therefore used to translate between the two types of address. The ARP client and server processes operate on all computers using IP over Ethernet. The processes are normally implemented as part of the software driver that drives the network interface card.

There are four types of ARP messages that may be sent by the ARP protocol. The types of message are:

1. ARP request.
2. ARP reply.
3. RARP request.
4. RARP reply.

To reduce the number of address resolution requests, a client normally caches resolved addresses for a (short) period of time. The ARP cache is of a finite size, and would become full of incomplete and obsolete entries for computers that are not in use if it was allowed to grow without check. The ARP cache is therefore periodically flushed of all entries. This deletes unused entries and frees space in the cache. It also removes any unsuccessful attempts to contact computers, which are not currently running.

12.9 Reverse Address Resolution Protocol (RARP)

RARP, which is the logical inverse of ARP, might be used by diskless workstations that do not know their IP addresses when they boot. RARP relies on the presence of a RARP server with table entries of MAC-layer-to-IP address mappings.

RARP allows a physical machine in a local area network to request its IP address from a gateway server's Address Resolution Protocol (ARP) table or cache. A network administrator creates a table in a local area network's gateway router that maps the physical machine (or Media Access Control—MAC address) addresses to corresponding Internet Protocol addresses (IP address). When a new machine is set up, its RARP client program requests from the RARP server on the router to be sent its IP address. Assuming that an entry has been set up in the router table, the RARP server will return the IP address to the machine, which can store it for future use.

RARP is available for Ethernet, Fiber Distributed-Data Interface and Token Ring LANs. ARP (Address Resolution Protocol) performs the opposite function as the RARP: mapping of an IP address to a physical machine address.

12.10 Internet Control Message Protocol (ICMP)

The Internet Control Message Protocol (ICMP) is a network-layer Internet protocol that provides message packets to report errors and other information regarding IP packet processing back to the source. This protocol is part of the Internet Layer and uses the IP datagram delivery facility to send its messages.

ICMP Messages

ICMPs generate several kinds of useful messages that are listed below:

- Destination Unreachable.
- Echo Request and Reply.
- Redirect.
- Time Exceeded.
- Router Advertisement.
- Router Solicitation.

If an ICMP message cannot be delivered, no second one is generated. This is to avoid an endless flood of ICMP messages.

When an ICMP **destination-unreachable message** is sent by a router, it means that the router is unable to send the package to its final destination. The router then discards the original packet. Two reasons exist for why a destination might be unreachable. Most commonly, the source host has specified a nonexistent address. Less frequently, the router does not have a route to the destination.

Destination-unreachable messages include four basic types:

- **Network unreachable** : Network-unreachable messages usually mean that a failure has occurred in the routing or addressing of a packet.
- **Host unreachable** : Host-unreachable messages usually indicate delivery failure, such as a wrong subnet mask.
- **Protocol unreachable** : Protocol-unreachable messages generally mean that the destination does not support the upper-layer protocol specified in the packet.
- **Port unreachable** : Port-unreachable messages imply that the TCP socket or port is not available.

An ICMP **echo-request message**, which is generated by the ping command, is sent by any host to test node reachability across an internetwork.

The ICMP **echo-reply message** indicates that the node can be successfully reached.

An ICMP **Redirect message** is sent by the router to the source host to stimulate more efficient routing. The router still forwards the original packet to the destination. ICMP redirects allow host routing tables to remain small because it is necessary to know the address of only one router, even if that router does not provide the best path. Even after receiving an ICMP Redirect message, some devices might continue using the less-efficient route.

An ICMP **Time-exceeded message** is sent by the router if an IP packet's Time-to-Live field (expressed in hops or seconds) reaches zero. The Time-to-Live field prevents packets from continuously circulating the internetwork if the internetwork contains a routing loop. The router then discards the original packet.

ICMP Router-Discovery Protocol (IDRP)

IDRP uses Router-Advertisement and Router-Solicitation messages to discover the addresses of routers on directly attached subnets. Each router periodically multicasts Router-Advertisement messages from each of its interfaces. Hosts then discover addresses of routers on directly attached subnets by listening for these messages. Hosts can use Router-Solicitation messages to request immediate advertisements rather than waiting for unsolicited messages.

IRDP offers several advantages over other methods of discovering addresses of neighboring routers. Primarily, it does not require hosts to recognize routing protocols, nor does it require manual configuration by an administrator.

Router-Advertisement messages enable hosts to discover the existence of neighboring routers, but not which router is best to reach a particular destination. If a host uses a poor first-hop router to reach a particular destination, it receives a Redirect message identifying a better choice.

• • •

13

Internetworking Devices

13.1 The Concept Of Internetworking

Once networks started becoming popular, it did not take long to realize that connecting many individual networks together would give even greater benefits. It was this realization, which helped the birth of the concept of internetworking that simply refers to the function of connecting individual networks together to form larger networks.

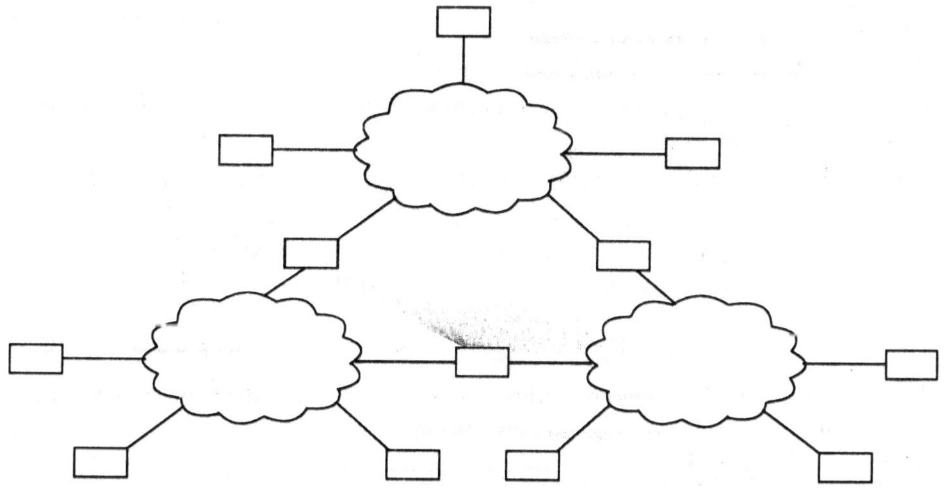

Fig. 13.1 A Simple internetwork

Definition

The art and science of connecting individual local-area networks (LANs) to create wide-area networks (WANs), and connecting WANs to form even larger WANs. Internetworking can be extremely complex because it generally involves connecting networks that use different protocols. Internetworking is accomplished with routers, bridges, and gateways.

The premise of internetworking is the connection of two or more networks into an integrated infrastructure capable of allowing communications to occur between the networks. More often, an internetwork is thought of as a network that provides services over the wide area. It should be noted that in all internetworking scenarios, the networks being connected maintain their individuality-they continue to operate as stand-alone networks. The internetworking capabilities are accessed only when the networks need to communicate.

Principal applications of internetworking are:

- Fast easy file sharing.
- News broadcast.
- E-Mail.
- Remote logon.
- Messaging gateways.
- Network management.
- Directory services.
- Knowledge discovery.

An Internet is a hierarchy of networks connected through gateways or bridges. An Internet may result from the merge of two homogeneous networks, or from the split of a homogeneous network into two connected homogeneous networks. A merge is interesting because it allows every node in the two networks to reach many more people and facilities. A split is interesting for the following reasons:

- **Geography** : The current network becomes too spread (for example, Ethernet has a maximum diameter of 2.5 km).
- **Overload** : The current network is overloaded. It is often more interesting to split than to install a more powerful network.
- **Reliability** : A split network allows progressive degradation of services if a network fails, whereas, a single network may disconnect all the computers if it fails.
- **Security** : It is much easier to enforce isolation of a class of users if these users are in a different network. For example, on our campus, the financial services are connected to a special Ethernet network, and special permission is required to access this network from the other networks on campus.

13.1.1 Why Internetworking?

There are many existing networks located at different places. It is desirable to connect them together for global communication and information exchange. In the future, there will still be multiple types of networks, because no single network technology can fulfill all the needs. It is necessary to connect them for communication.

From the user's point of view it is a set of application programs that use the underlying network to carry out useful communication tasks, e.g., World Wide Web, email, ftp and remote login.

The above applications can run on different types of computers. Different networks may not be compatible. Internetworking requires some additional hardware to interconnect the networks and some additional software on all the attached computers to execute a common set of internetworking protocols to ensure that these computers can communicate. Example: One vendor's email program may talk to another vendor's email program. Different networks may use different technology and methodology, different transmission media, addressing scheme, packet format and etc. No single network hardware can satisfy all constraints of different users/networks.

Internetworking is not simply a plug and play situation. Often there are incompatibility issues that must be dealt with before interoperability can be achieved. It is the consequence of interoperability that is central to internetworking technologies. Interoperability can be divided into two groups of concerns.

- The first is that of actual physical connectivity.
- The second is software-related—concerned with protocols, management and applications.

The two must come together to provide interconnectivity. Interconnectivity requires the use of some type of device to allow interoperability between LAN and WAN environments.

Features of Internetworks

Internetworking is more complex than networking, because internetworks must often combine different types of network architectures. Therefore, devices used to create internetworks typically must support:

- Different physical topologies.
- Several Network and Data Link Layer protocols.
- Different physical transmission media.

13.2 Introduction To Internetworking Devices

While the concept of Internetworking may seem simple, there is really a lot to be considered before attempting to interconnect a bunch of standalone networks together, assuming you really want the computers to talk to each other. For example, LANs were originally developed with no concept of communicating with other networks. As a result, some additional functionality and equipment need to be added to make this happen. These additional products which are generally referred to as hubs, repeaters, bridges, routers, switches and gateways - each having a specific task to perform in the overall internetworking scheme of thing.

Internetworking deals with the issues of interconnecting multiple, possibly heterogeneous networks. Physical networks can be connected at several levels. The main problems of internetworking come from the wide variety of types of networks that have to be connected together. Different devices have been built to handle different situations:

- **Repeaters and Hubs** : Repeaters and hubs receive a signal (bits) on a local area network (LAN) segment and regenerate the bit pattern to boost the signal and extend the physical length of the segment. These devices are transparent to the sending and receiving (end) devices. They are not technically internetworking devices, because they only extend the length of a cable, or transmit the same signal to several nodes; however, they are normally thought of as internetworking devices.
- **Bridges and Switches** : Bridges and switches usually connect networks of similar types, such as Ethernet or Token Ring, into a single logical internetwork. Translation bridges have been developed to connect dissimilar LAN types. Bridges and switches store and forward frames to other network segments, and are transparent to the end devices.
- **Routers** : Routers connect networks into internetworks that are physically unified, but in which each network retains its own independent identity. The primary purpose of a router is to find the best path from one network to another network, and forward packets between networks.
- **Gateways** : Gateways operate at higher layers of the protocol stack; some gateways operate on all layers. Gateways, also called protocol converters, connect different networking environments, such as Systems Network Architecture (SNA) and Transmission Control Protocol/Internet Protocol (TCP/IP) networks, by converting each header from the form of the sending environment to that of the receiving environment.
- **Brouters** : A brouter can work in either the second and third layers of the OSI model-the data link layer or the network layer. A brouter is a combination of a bridge and router combined. If it can't route a packet, it acts as a bridge.

Review of the Open Systems Interconnection Model

The Table 13.1 provides an overview of the primary functions of each layer of the OSI model, as well as the units of information and devices that correspond to each layer.

OSI Layer	Layer Function	Unit of Information	Address Type	Internetworking Devices
Application	Provide user functionality	Program/ Application Data		Gateways (Protocol Converters)
Presentation	Provide character representation, data compression, security	Characters and words		Gateways (Protocol Converters)

Session	Establish, conduct, and end sessions			Gateways (Protocol Converters)
Transport	Transfer messages between application	Message/Byte Stream	Application process address (port)	Gateways (Protocol Converters)
Network	Send individual packets across a network	Packet (datagram)	Network address	Routers, Layer 3 Switches
Data Link	Send frames to destination node	Frame	NIC address	Bridges, Switches
Physical	Send signals, representing bits, across physical media	Bit		Cables, Wireless Channels (Radio, Infrared, and Microwave), Connectors, Repeaters, and Hubs

Table 13.1

Now we will discuss each device in detail.

13.3 Repeaters

Repeaters, working at the Physical Layer, are the simplest type of internetworking device. They are used to amplify electrical signals carried by the network. The function of a repeater is to receive incoming signals (a packet of data), regenerate the signals to their original strength, and retransmit them. Repeaters are used to lengthen individual network segments to form a larger extended network. That is, repeaters allow a network to be constructed that exceeds the size limit of a single physical segment by allowing additional lengths of cable to be connected (see figure 13.2).

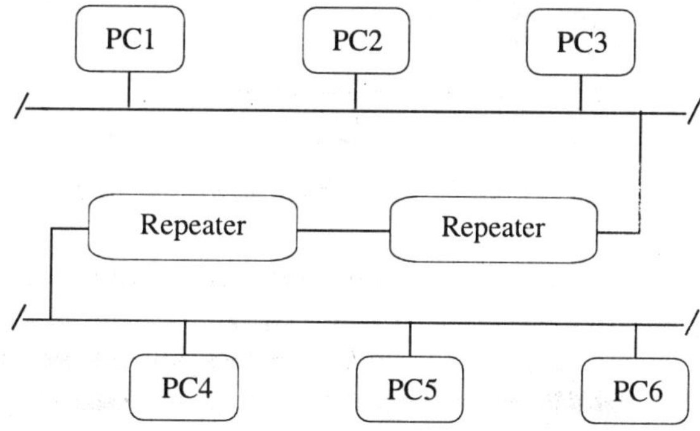

Fig. 13.2 Repeaters used to lengthen individual network segments

13.3.1 How Repeaters Work ?

As nodes are added to a LAN, the cable can be extended with electrically passive connectors that simply attach one segment to another. Eventually, the permissible length of the cable segment will be exceeded, or it will become necessary to connect different cable types. A repeater is used to address these needs.

Because a repeater operates at the Physical Layer of the OSI model, the job of a repeater is to repeat bits. If a "1" bit is received on the input port of a repeater, a "1" bit is regenerated, with a stronger signal, at the output of the repeater. If a "0" bit is received on the input port of a repeater, a "0" bit is regenerated at the output of the repeater. A repeater is considered a non-discriminating device, because all incoming signals are passed on to each connected segment. Because a repeater reproduces exactly what it receives, bit-by-bit, it can reproduce errors. However, repeaters are very fast (10 megabits per second [Mbps] for Ethernet) and cause very little delay.

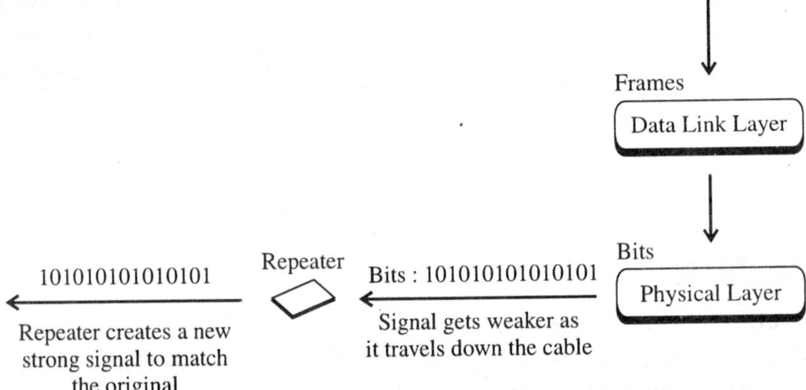

Fig. 13.3 Repeater and OSI model

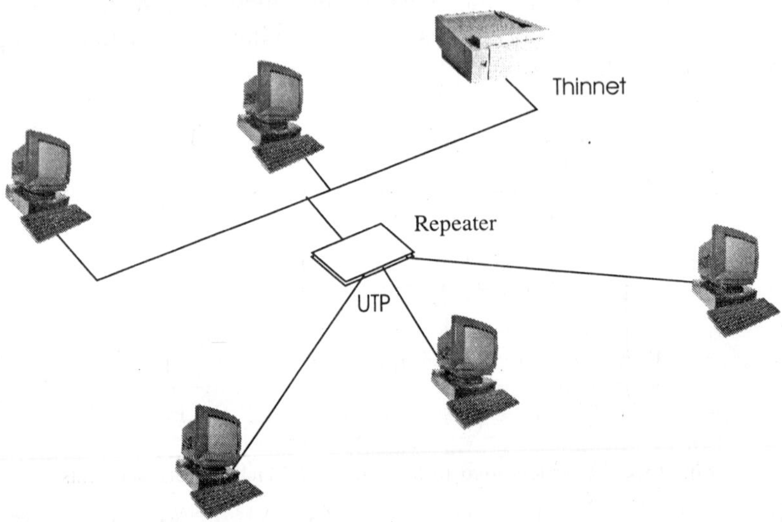

Fig. 13.4 Repeater and media types

A repeater can connect one segment of a LAN to another, possibly connecting different types of media. For example, a repeater can connect thin Ethernet cables to UTP Ethernet cables, as shown in figure 13.4.

Because it is only a signal-boosting device, a repeater cannot connect two different media access types (Data Link protocols) such as Token Ring and Ethernet. For a repeater to be used both network segments must be same network protocols for all layers, same media access control method, and the same physical transmission technique. This means we could connect two segments that use the CSMA/CD access methods, or connect two segments that are running under the token-passing access method. However, we cannot connect a CSMA/CD segment to a token-passing segment.

Keep in mind that a repeater is a Physical Layer device. It cannot recognize the contents or format of a frame, and it cannot convert one type of Data Link header to another.

As internetworking devices for Ethernet LANs, repeaters are feasible only for relatively small LANs (less than 100 nodes), confined to a small geographical area such as one or two floors of an office building. A repeater should not be used to connect heavily used LANs because it cannot isolate traffic between LAN segments. Because each bit is copied to the attached segments, all data passes through a repeater in both directions. Therefore, if we connect multiple LAN segments using a repeater, we may experience performance problems, because total network traffic will increase.

13.4 Hubs

Hubs are argued as not being real internetworking devices. The reason we are including them in the internetworking portion is that hubs are often incorporated into other internetworking devices in order to minimize the amount of equipment installed at customer sites.

A hub is a box with a number of connectors to which multiple nodes (PCs) are attached. It serves as a common termination point that can relay signals along the appropriate paths. All hubs provide connectivity, and some even provide management capabilities. A hub usually connects nodes that have a common architecture.

Like repeaters, hubs operate at the Physical Layer, and regenerate signals bit-by-bit as they travel down the physical medium. Both repeaters and hubs provide signals greater reach;

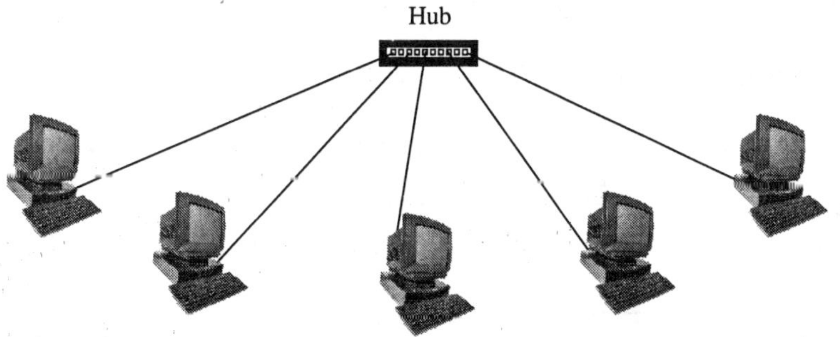

Fig. 13.5 Hub in a star topology

however, a hub also shares the same signals among a group of nodes. This clustering helps control the morass of cable and cable types found in many networks.

The Hub in figure 13.5 illustrates a simple hub configuration. It is important to realize that this structured wiring distinguishes between a network's physical and logical topologies. All hubs use a physical star topology; however, the logical topology of the network segment can be a ring, bus, tree or other structure, depending on the way a signal is passed from one node to the others.

13.5 Bridges

Bridges handle the first two layers of the OSI model-the physical layer and the data link layer. A hub is used to connect transmission medium of the same type and when the same MAC protocol is being used. To connect mediums of different types or to change between MAC protocols requires a bridge as shown in figure 13.6 and examples that follow.

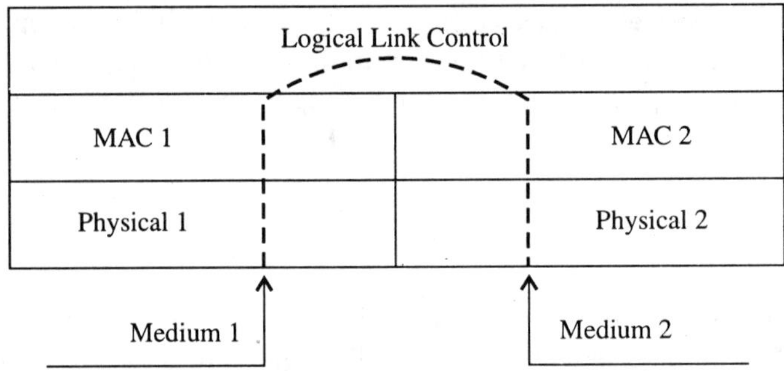

Fig. 13.6 Bridge used to connect mediums of different types

Example : A bridge may be used to convert from a copper wire (twisted pair) to an optical fiber medium.

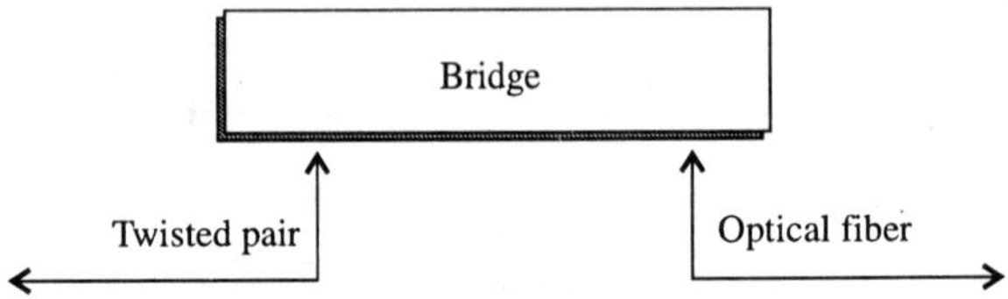

Example : A bridge may be used to convert from duplex to half-duplex.

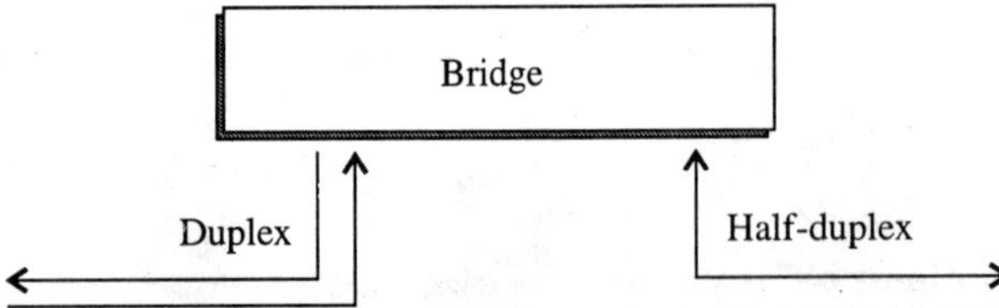

Also, bridges may consist of a number of interfaces or ports.

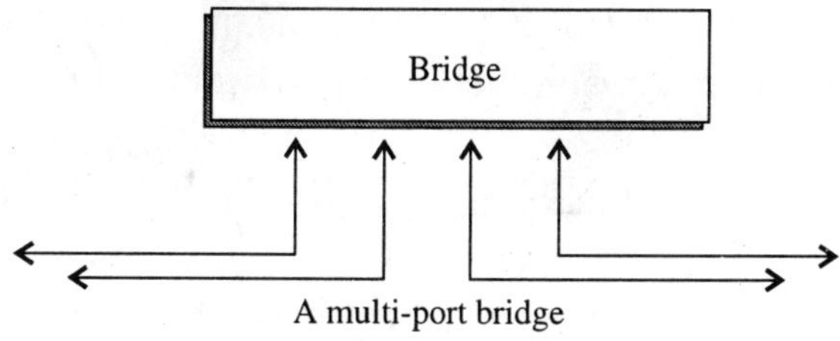

A multi-port bridge

Bridges are devices that pass packets between two LANs. The biggest benefit of a bridge is to create smaller networks, which can greatly increase the overall performance. In a LAN sharing a common wire, when one computer is talking all others must be listening. If a network of 100 computers is broken into two networks of 50 computers the overall bandwidth is doubled. The bridge connecting these two LAN segments allows a computer on one LAN to talk to a computer on the other LAN.

Like repeaters, bridges connect physically isolated networks to form a single logical network; however, a bridge has a little more intelligence and can provide some translation between dissimilar protocols.

For example, our token-passing segment wants to communicate with our CSMA/CD segment. The bridge will "repackage" the message from the token-passing segment into a format that the CSMA/CD segment will understand. Then, the bridge will act as a workstation on the CSMA/CD segment and contend for access. The same thing happens in reverse. A message is sent from the CSMA/CD segment to the token-passing segment. The bridge then "repackages" the message into a format the token-passing segment is expecting and waits for the token, just like any other workstation. An important point to remember is that a bridge will pass on any message it receives. Because the bridge is not smart enough to know that unlike LANs do not understand each other, it will go ahead and send the message. Because the two LANs speak a different "language", the message will be ignored.

13.5.1 How Bridges Work?

The most basic type of bridge attaches two or more LAN segments. The interface between a bridge and each LAN segment is known as a port. LANs attached to each port are called a network segment, as illustrated in the figure 13.7.

The bridge listens for every frame transmitted on each of its attached network segments, and compares each frame address to the bridge table maintained by its software. When a frame's destination is a device on a network segment other than the one on which it was transmitted, the bridge forwards the frame to the port connected to the destination segment. By forwarding only frames addressed to devices on other segments, bridges increase the effective throughput of the overall internetwork.

Bridges may be installed for any of the following reasons:

- To extend the distance or increase the number of devices that are part of the entire network.

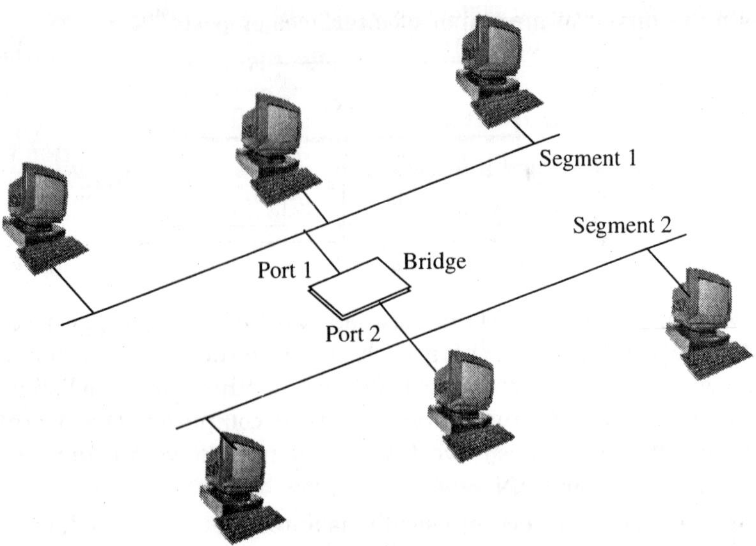

Fig. 13.7 Bridge ports and segments

- To improve the performance of the individual networks by reducing traffic. An excessive number of devices on a single network may affect network performance. It can be beneficial to split the network and connect the segments with a bridge.
- To link unlike networks such as Ethernet and Token-ring and forward packets between them.

13.5.2 Functions of Bridges

The various functions of bridges are discussed below:

1. **Frame forwarding and filtering :** When a data packet arrives at the bridge, the bridge reads the destination address and decides if the packet should be forwarded across the bridge or filtered and not sent. Without this function, all packets would be sent to all network segments. The purpose is to prevent locally addressed packets from crossing the bridge. A locally addressed packet is one where the network portion of the destination address is the same as the network portion of the source address-the packet is going to the same network from where it was sent.
2. **Loop resolution :** In an environment with many installed bridges, looping may occur. This is when a packet travels continuously over the network causing excess and unnecessary network traffic. Looping may be prevented or at least reduced by proper network design. Also, some bridges are able to detect looping packets and intercept them.
3. **Address tables :** Bridges need to know which packets to pass over the bridge and which packets to filter. Initially, with early bridges, address tables showing the locations of all attached devices had to be entered and updated by hand. Today, bridges are able to learn network addresses and build the address tables themselves.

They do so by examining packet flow-Transparent bridging-or by obtaining information through the use of explorer packets-Source Route bridging.

13.5.3 Classification of Bridges

Bridges can be broadly categorized into two groups-

- Local bridges
- Remote bridges

Local bridges provide a direct connection between multiple LAN segments in the same area. Remote bridges connect multiple LAN segments in different areas, usually over telecommunications lines. They provide connections over extended distances and have ports for connections to analog or digital telecommunications links. Remote bridges make use of MAN or WAN connectivity.

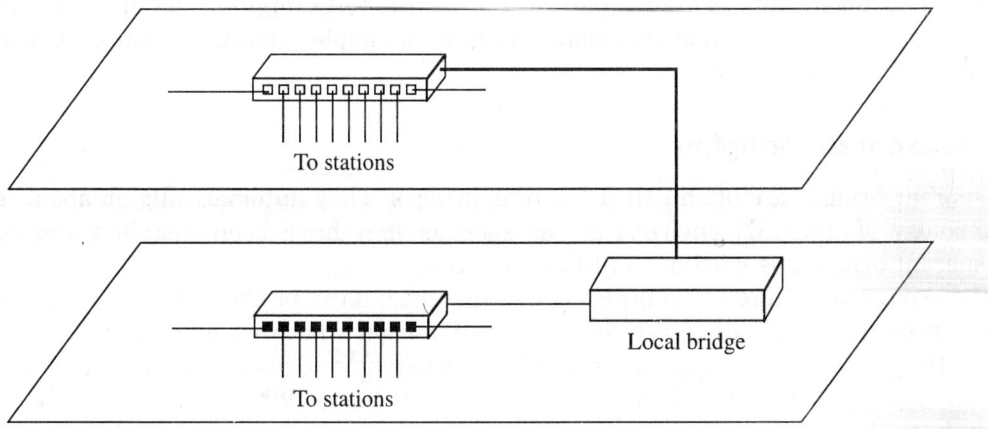

Fig. 13.8 Local bridging

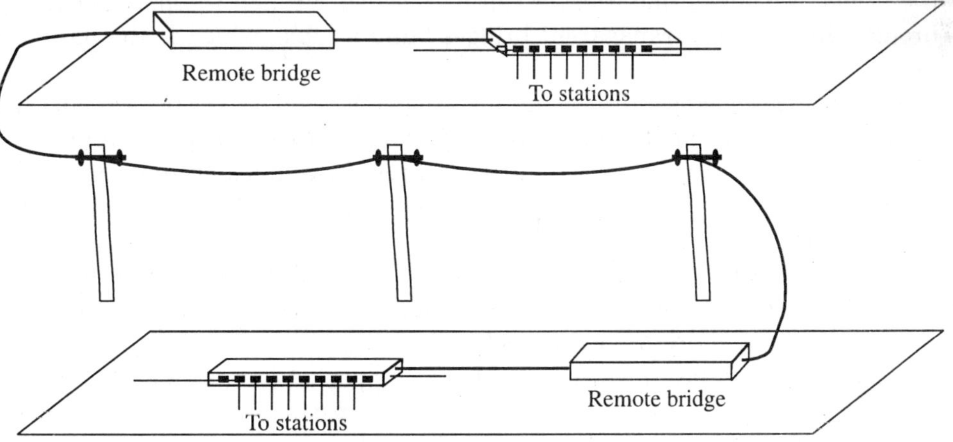

Fig. 13.9 Remote bridging

The critical part of a bridge is the software that builds and maintains its bridge table. Without this software, network administrators would have to manually create and maintain these tables. A bridge is categorized by the method or algorithm, that its software uses to build a bridge table. There are several types of bridging algorithms commonly used and each type has its own advantages and disadvantages. The basic types of bridging algorithms are stated below:

1. Transparent Bridging.
2. Spanning tree Bridging.
3. Source-routing Bridging.
4. Source-routing transparent Bridging.

Transparent bridging is found primarily in Ethernet environments, while *source-route bridging* occurs primarily in Token Ring environments. *Translational bridging* provides translation between the formats and transit principles of different media types (usually Ethernet and Token Ring). Finally, *source-route transparent bridging* combines the algorithms of transparent bridging and source-route bridging to enable communication in mixed Ethernet/Token Ring environments.

1. Transparent bridging

Transparent bridges are often called learning bridges. They automatically go about learning the topology of the LAN environment as soon as they have been installed and powered. Transparent bridging is used in the Ethernet environment.

Transparent bridges : A bridge is transparent if it can be connected to an existing LAN and not need to be explicitly given any information from a network administrator in order to work with the existing bridges on the LAN. Transparent bridges are so named because their presence and operation are transparent to network hosts. When transparent bridges are powered on, they learn the network's topology by analyzing the source address of incoming frames from all attached networks. If, for example, a bridge sees a frame arrive on line 1 from Host A, the bridge concludes that Host A can be reached through the network connected to line 1. Through this process, transparent bridges build a table, which is the basis for traffic forwarding.

Transparent bridges successfully isolate intrasegment traffic, thereby reducing the traffic seen on each individual segment. This usually improves network response times as seen by the user. The extent to which traffic is reduced and response times are improved depends on the volume of intersegment traffic relative to the total traffic as well as the volume of broadcast and multicast traffic.

As the packets arrive, the bridge looks at the source address and associates it with the network address. These are then noted in a bridge address table. This table is constantly being updated with new source addresses as the network changes.

A learning bridge examines the source field of every packet it sees on each port and builds up a picture of which addresses are connected to which ports. This means that it will NOT re-transmit a packet if it knows that the destination address is connected to the same port as the bridge saw the packet on. A special problem arises if a bridge sees a packet addressed to a destination that is not in its address table. In this case the packet is re-transmitted on every port except the one it was received on.

Bridges also age address table entries, if a given address has not been heard from in a specified period of time then the address is deleted from the address table. An Example of bridge address table is shown below:

Network address	Station address
345	98765
909	87654
345	12345
345	23456
909	23567

Table 13.2 Bridge Address Table

The bridge address table is used to forward arriving packets. If an address cannot be found in the table, a discovery process is initiated. A copy of the arriving packet is sent to all network segments except the one, which sent the packet. When the destination device recognizes the address on the packet it responds to the bridge. The bridge then makes a new entry in the table noting the network and station address of this formerly unknown device. Eventually the bridge can learn the address of every device on all attached networks.

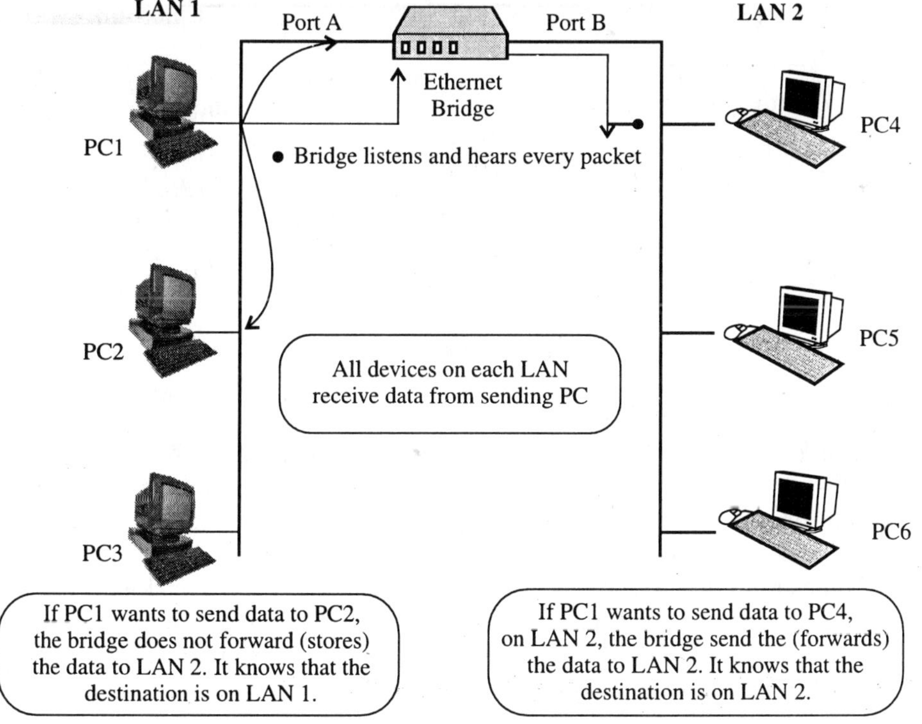

Fig. 13.10

Transparent Bridges operate according to the following rules:

1. Examine all packets on all active network ports for their source address.
2. Maintain a table that tracks, which port a source address has appeared on.
3. Look up the destination addresses in this table for all packets, and if a packet's matching port is different than the port it was received on, forward the packet to the matching port.
4. If no match is found, or if the destination address is the broadcast address, forward the packet out all active ports.

This scheme is acceptable on very simple network topologies. It will not work correctly if there are multiple paths to the same destination. In this case, packets will be forwarded in a "bridging loop" which will quickly use up the available network bandwidth on the segments in question.

Bridging Loops

Without a bridge-to-bridge protocol, the transparent bridge algorithm fails when there are multiple paths of bridges and local-area networks (LANs) between any two LANs in the internetwork. Figure 13.11 illustrates such a bridging loop.

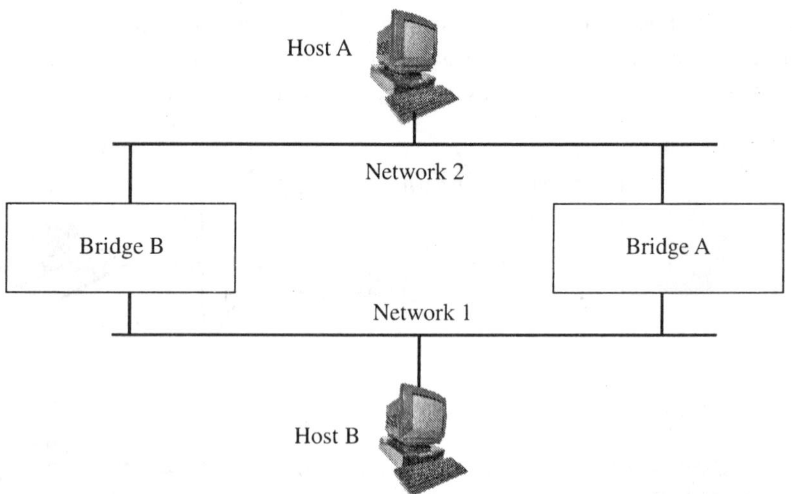

Fig. 13.11 Inaccurate forwarding and learning in transparent bridging environments

Suppose Host A sends a frame to Host B. Both bridges receive the frame and correctly conclude that Host A is on Network 2. Unfortunately, after Host B receives two copies of Host A's frame, both bridges will again receive the frame on their network 1 interfaces because all hosts receive all messages on broadcast LANs. In some cases, the bridges will then change their internal tables to indicate that Host A is on network 1. If so, when Host B replies to Host A's frame, both bridges will receive and subsequently drop the replies because their tables will indicate that the destination (Host A) is on the same network segment as the frame's source.

In addition to basic connectivity problems such as the one just described, the propagation of broadcast messages in networks with loops represents a potentially serious network problem. Referring again to Figure 13.11, assume that Host A's initial frame is a broadcast. Both bridges will forward the frames endlessly, using all available network bandwidth and blocking the transmission of other packets on both segments.

A topology with loops such as that shown in Figure 13.11 can be useful as well as potentially harmful. A loop implies the existence of multiple paths through the internetwork. A network with multiple paths from source to destination can increase overall network fault tolerance through improved topological flexibility.

2. Spanning Tree Bridges

To avoid bridging loops, an algorithm was developed which lets bridges shut off ports that provide duplicate paths to the same destination. The algorithm relies on the use of Bridge Protocol Data Units (BPDU packets), which provide information to all bridges about the "distance" in hops to each bridge port from a "root bridge". The root bridge is selected using settings entered into each bridge (with the Ethernet address acting as a tie-breaker).

Using BPDU information, a bridge can determine whether one of its ports provides an optimal path to the root bridge. If it does not, the port is shut down. If the path distance is optimal but is the same as another bridge's path, a simple protocol allows one of the ports to be shut down. In all other respects, spanning tree bridges operate in the same fashion as simple learning bridges.

Spanning tree bridges were also designed with transparency as a primary goal. A customer should be able to buy a bridge, insert it between two networks, and have everything work correctly with no hardware, software, or configuration changes on either hosts or existing bridges.

Spanning-Tree Algorithm (STA)

The spanning-tree algorithm (STA) was developed to preserve the benefits of loops while eliminating their problems. The STA designates a loop-free subset of the network's topology by placing those bridge ports that, if active, would create loops into a standby (blocking) condition. Blocking bridge ports can be activated in the event of primary link failure, providing a new path through the internetwork.

The spanning tree algorithm works by bridges interchanging special messages known as configuration bridge protocol data units. The configuration message contains enough information to enable the bridges to:

1. Elect a single bridge, from amongst all the connected bridges to be the "root" bridge.
2. Calculate the shortest path distance to the "root" bridge from each bridge.
3. For each LAN identify a "designated bridge" on that LAN that will be used for forwarding packets towards the root.
4. Choose a port on each bridge that gives the best path towards the root.
5. Select ports to be included in the spanning tree.

The effective topology after construction of the spanning tree is loop free, this is achieved by effectively choosing not to use certain links between bridges. The links are still there and may come into use if the network is re-configured.

Advantages

Easy to use. Just install the bridges. No software changes are needed.

Disadvantages

1. Does not support multi-path routing. By definition, only the bridges that belong to the spanning tree are used.
2. The path between any two hosts may not be the optimal path. An optimal path may traverse a bridge that is not part of the spanning tree and cannot be used.
3. Broadcast and multicast frames must be flooded in all cases.

Spanning tree bridges have become extremely popular in CSMA/CD networks. Vendors also offer bridges that connect LANs separated by fiber or phone links.

3. Source Routing Bridges

Source routing bridges take a completely opposite approach from spanning tree bridges:

1. They are not transparent. Hosts treat frames sent locally differently from those sent through bridges. Conceptually, the sending host specifies a road map saying which bridges the frame must go through to reach its destination.
2. Each LAN is assigned a 16-bit LAN number, and each bridge on a LAN is assigned a 4-bit bridge number. The numbers must be unique and are set by the network administrator.
3. Each frame carries a source route listing the path the frame is to take. The path consists of a sequence of {LAN number, bridge number} pairs.
4. Sending hosts (rather than bridges) chooses the source route. Host selects paths by broadcasting (flooding) special discovery frames. A discovery frame includes space for each bridge to add its number to the recorded path.
5. Eventually, a discovery frame reaches the destination host, which returns it to the sender. Each returned message contains a viable path, and the sending host chooses the shortest one.
6. Unfortunately, the discovery process leads to frame explosion. The destination may receive an exponential number of copies of the original frame.

SRB Algorithm

SRBs are so named because they assume that the complete source-to-destination route is placed in all inter-LAN frames sent by the source. SRBs store and forward the frames as indicated by the route appearing in the appropriate frame field. Figure 13.12 illustrates a sample SRB network.

Referring to Figure 13.12, assume that Host *X* wishes to send a frame to Host *Y*. Initially, Host *X* does not know whether Host *Y* resides on the same or a different LAN. To determine this, Host *X* sends out a test frame. If that frame returns to Host *X* without a positive indication that Host *Y* has seen it, Host *X* must assume that Host *Y* is on a remote segment.

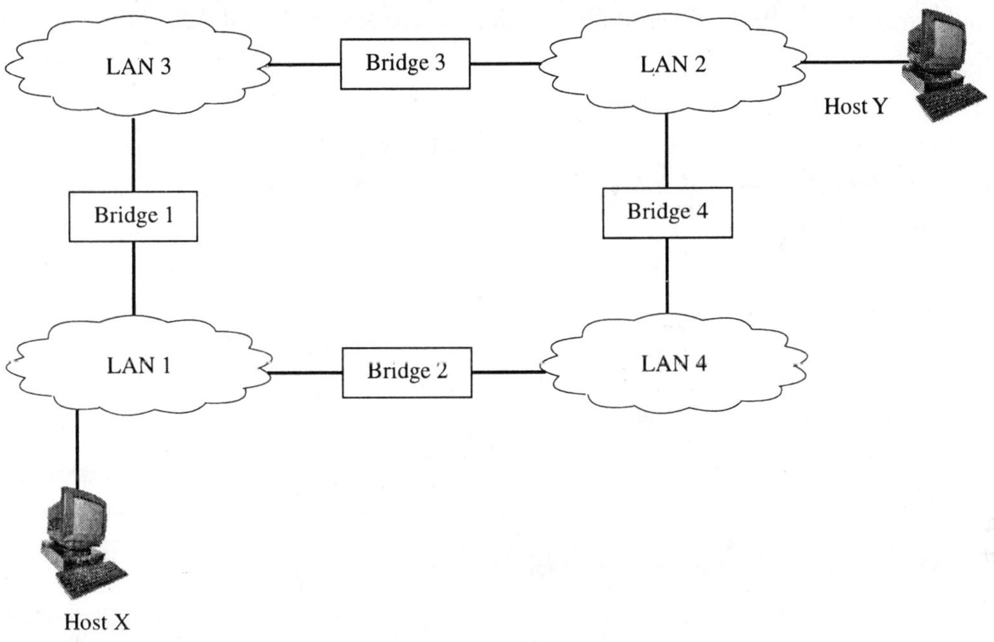

Fig. 13.12 SRB network diagram

To determine the exact remote location of Host *Y*, Host *X* sends an explorer frame. Each bridge receiving the explorer frame (Bridges 1 and 2 in this example) copies the frame onto all outbound ports. Route information is added to the explorer frames as they travel through the internetwork. When Host *X*'s explorer frames reach Host *Y*, Host *Y* replies to each individually using the accumulated route information. Upon receipt of all response frames, Host *X* chooses a path based on some predetermined criteria.

In the example in Figure 13.12, this process will yield two routes:

- LAN 1 to Bridge 1 to LAN 3 to Bridge 3 to LAN 2.
- LAN 1 to Bridge 2 to LAN 4 to Bridge 4 to LAN 2.

Host *X* must select one of these two routes. The IEEE 802.5 specification does not mandate the criteria Host *X* should use in choosing a route, but it does make several suggestions, including the following:

- First frame received.
- Response with the minimum number of hops.
- Response with the largest allowed frame size.
- Various combinations of the above criteria.

In most cases, the path contained in the first frame received will be used.

After a route is selected, it is inserted into frames destined for Host *Y* in the form of a routing information field (RIF). A RIF is included only in those frames destined for other LANs. The presence of routing information within the frame is indicated by the setting of the most significant bit within the source address field, called the routing information indicator (RII) bit.

Advantages :

Uses the optimal route. Also can make use of multiple paths to same destination. Because paths aren't required to always lie along the spanning tree, better use of resources.

Disadvantages :

1. Not transparent to hosts; hosts must participate in source routing. This is a significant disadvantage.
2. Installing new bridges non-trivial. Specifically, a system administrator must assign LAN numbers and bridge numbers. Improper configuration leads to disaster.
3. Each host must detect bridge failure on its own (e.g., using timeouts). With spanning tree bridges, the bridges hold that responsibility, and once they have reconfigured, all hosts start using the new path at the same time.

4. Source-Route Transparent Bridging

Source-Route Transparent (SRT) bridges combine implementations of the transparent bridging and the Source Routing bridging algorithms. SRT bridges use the Routing Information Indicator (RII) bit to distinguish between frames employing SRB and frames employing transparent bridging. If the RII bit is 1, a Routing Information Frame (RIF) is present in the frame, and the bridge uses the SRB algorithm. If the RII bit is 0, an RIF is not present, and the bridge uses transparent bridging.

SRT bridges are not perfect solutions to the problems of mixed media bridging. SRT bridges must still deal with the Ethernet/Token Ring incompatibilities described earlier. SRT bridging is likely to require hardware upgrades to SRBs to allow them to handle the increased burden of analyzing every packet. Software upgrades to SRBs may also be required. Further, in environments of mixed SRT bridges, transparent bridges, and SRBs, source routes chosen must traverse whatever SRT bridges and SRBs are available. The resulting paths can potentially be substantially inferior to spanning-tree paths created by transparent bridges. Finally, mixed SRB/SRT bridging networks lose the benefits of SRT bridging, so users will feel compelled to execute a complete cutover to SRT bridging at considerable expense. Still, SRT bridging permits the coexistence of two incompatible environments and allows communication between SRB and transparent bridging end nodes.

13.6 Switches

Switches are data communications devices that operate principally at Layer 2 of the OSI reference model. They are data link-layer devices that, like bridges, enable multiple physical LAN segments to be interconnected into a single larger network.

Switches are top of the line internetworking devices that employ ultra-fast memory transfer techniques to minimize segments to segments delay time. Most can operate as an ultra high-speed repeater, bridge, router or all three. Many switches even have the ability to dynamically configure what LAN segment a particular port or group of ports belongs to, regardless of the physical port to which it is attached.

Today, switching technology has emerged as the evolutionary heir to bridging-based internetworking solutions. Switching implementations now dominate applications in which bridging technologies were implemented in prior network designs. Superior throughput performance, higher port density, lower per-port cost, and greater flexibility have contributed to the emergence of switches as replacement technology for bridges and as complements to routing technology.

Upper-layer protocol transparency is a primary advantage of both bridging and switching. Because both device types operate at the link layer, they are not required to examine upper-layer information. This means that they can rapidly forward traffic representing any network layer protocol.

By dividing large networks into self-contained units, bridges and switches provide several advantages. Because only a certain percentage of traffic is forwarded, a bridge or switch diminishes the traffic experienced by devices on all connected segments. The bridge or switch will act as a firewall for some potentially damaging network errors and will accommodate communication between a larger number of devices than would be supported on any single LAN connected to the bridge. Bridges and switches extend the effective length of a LAN, permitting the attachment of distant stations that was not previously permitted.

Although bridges and switches share most relevant attributes, several distinctions differentiate these technologies. Bridges are generally used to segment a LAN into a couple of smaller segments. Switches are generally used to segment a large LAN into many smaller segments. Bridges generally have only a few ports for LAN connectivity, whereas switches generally have many. Small switches such as the Cisco Catalyst 2924XL have 24 ports capable of creating 24 different network segments for a LAN. Larger switches such as the Cisco Catalyst 6500 can have hundreds of ports. Switches can also be used to connect LANs with different media-for example, a 10-Mbps Ethernet LAN and a 100-Mbps Ethernet LAN can be connected using a switch. Some switches support cut-through switching, which reduces latency and delays in the network, while bridges support only store-and-forward traffic switching. Finally, switches reduce collisions on network segments because they provide dedicated bandwidth to each network segment.

13.6.1 Types of Switches

Switches are data link layer devices that, like bridges, enable multiple physical LAN segments to be interconnected into a single larger network. Similar to bridges, switches forward and flood traffic based on MAC addresses. Any network device will create some latency. Switches can use different forwarding techniques-two of these are stated below:

- Store-and-forward switching.
- Cut-through switching.

In *store-and-forward switching*, an entire frame must be received before it is forwarded. This means that the latency through the switch is relative to the frame size—the larger the frame size, the longer the delay through the switch.

Cut-through switching allows the switch to begin forwarding the frame when enough of the frame is received to make a forwarding decision. This reduces the latency through the switch. Store-and-forward switching gives the switch the opportunity to evaluate the frame for errors before forwarding it. This capability to not forward frames containing errors is one of the advantages of switches over hubs. Cut-through switching does not offer this advantage, so the switch might forward frames containing errors.

Many types of switches exist, including ATM switches, LAN switches, and various types of WAN switches.

ATM Switch

Asynchronous Transfer Mode (ATM) switches provide high-speed switching and scalable bandwidths in the workgroup, the enterprise network backbone, and the wide area. ATM switches support voice, video, and data applications, and are designed to switch fixed-size information units called cells, which are used in ATM communications. Figure 13.13 illustrates an enterprise network comprised of multiple LANs interconnected across an ATM backbone.

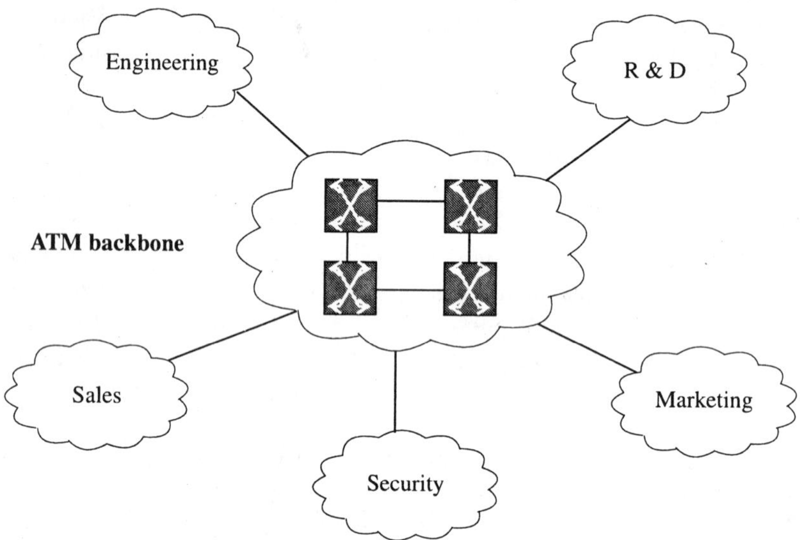

Fig. 13.13 Multi-LAN networks can use an ATM-based backbone when switching cells

LAN Switch

LAN switches are used to interconnect multiple LAN segments. LAN switching provides dedicated, collision-free communication between network devices, with support for multiple simultaneous conversations. LAN switches are designed to switch data frames at high speeds.

Figure 13.14 illustrates a simple network in which a LAN switch interconnects a 10-Mbps and a 100-Mbps Ethernet LAN.

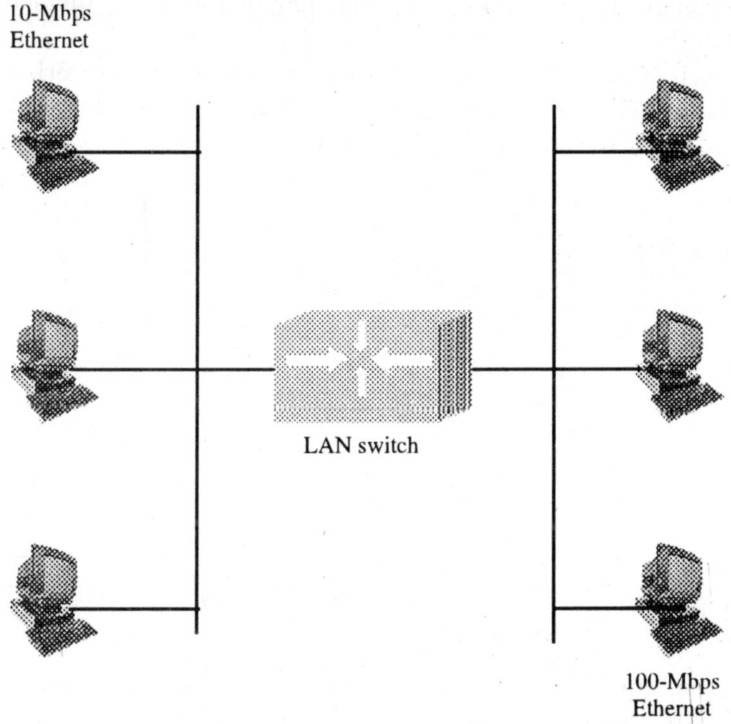

Fig. 13.14 A LAN switch can link 10-mbps and 100-mbps ethernet segments

13.7 Routers

Routers are internetworking devices that operate at the third layer of the OSI model—the Network layer. This makes their operation somewhat different from that of repeaters and MAC (Media Access Control) bridges. Both of these devices are used to connect networks that are identical with respect to the media access scheme used. Therefore, information was transferred based on MAC addresses. This also made these devices protocol independent-specifically, they are independent of the protocols working above the MAC layer.

Routers are able to provide connectivity for mixed MAC environments by working with a higher-layer protocol. This permits the connection of network segments that are different. However, it must be noted that the networks to be interconnected share that same protocol stack-routers are not capable of protocol translation. Most routers are multiprotocol routers and are capable of handling multiple Network layer protocols-the router must be equipped with appropriate software for each protocol to be supported.

Unlike bridges, routers can intelligently determine the most efficient path to any destination, based on predetermined delimiters.

In a heterogeneous environment, such as networks, a need of connection devices which would inter-connect two different technologies is essential. In this environment the router is that device. As it's name implies, the router also serves as a routing switch-board. Routers connect two or more networks and forward data packets between them. When data arrives from one of the segments, the router decides, according to it's routing table, to which segment to forward that data.

Even though each of the routers' connections is to one physical network, that one network could connect to other networks through the use of other routers. This way, many networks can interconnect. To understand how routing occurs in such networks, we'll refer to the following diagram:

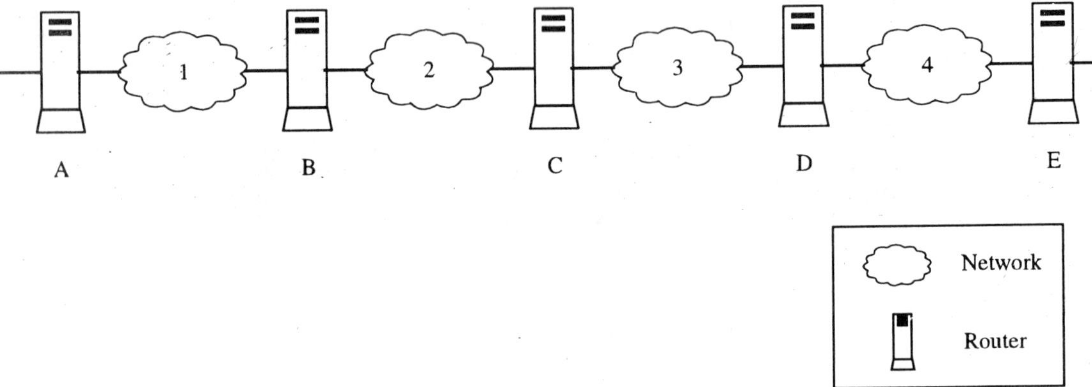

Fig. 13.15 A very simple network configuration

In the above configuration, router *B*'s table would say, for instance, that data going to network 4 should go to router *C*. Packets going from network 1 to network 4 would go through router B into network 2 and so on, till they reach their destination.

We would like to emphasize that routers know only about networks, and not about hosts. In IP networks, routers utilize the fact that each host's IP address contains two parts: the host's network address, and the host's number on that network. Routers examine the data destination address, extract, from it, the target network address, and decide, based on this network address, where to transfer the data.

A router is actually a special computer that is dedicated to the task of interconnecting networks. It moves information from its source to its destination regardless of the middleware. A router resembles a bridge (they both have conventional processor, memory and few different I/O interfaces, each for another network it connects), but while bridging occurs at the link layer, routing occurs at the network layer.

13.7.1 Router Responsibilities

The role of the router is to direct packets along the most efficient, economical route in mesh networks where there are many redundant paths from the source device to the destination device. Although some Network Operating Systems support routing by the file server, most routers are stand-alone devices. The routing function tends to slow the server performance. The throughput of a router is largely determined by its internal components and architecture.

Routers have two major responsibilities that are stated below:

1. **Optimizing the routing paths :** A router uses a routing algorithm to determine the optimal path to the destination. These algorithms maintain routing tables that contain route information such as destination/next hop association. Selecting a communications path through the network is a two-step process. The first step is to create and maintain a routing table and the second, to select the best path for the next step of the packet's journey. This second step is based on information found in the packet and in the routing table. Both routing tables and selection of pathways through the network form the basis of how routers function.
2. **Switching-transport of packets over networks :** When computer wants to send a packet over the net, it formats a packet with the router's physical address and the destination address (protocol address) of the target host. The router searches its routing tables for the destination host. If there is no entry for the destination host the router usually drops the packet, otherwise (there is an entry for the destination host) it replaces the physical address with the next hop's address and retransmits the packet. The next hop isn't necessarily the ultimate destination host; it may be another router that performs the same routing again. A packet may visit few routers/ hosts on its route, each time it's destination physical address changes.

13.7.2 Routers Versus Bridges

A problem commonly faced in internetworking concerns the choice between bridges and routers. The current trend is the development of devices providing the functionality of both bridges and routers. Until a single such unit is available, a choice will need to be made. The following table summarizes some characteristics of bridges and of routers.

Characteristic	MAC Bridge	Router
Network dependence	Links same-type LANs	Links all forms of LANs
Protocol dependence	Protocol independent at the LLC layer and above	Network layer protocols must be common
Bandwidth utilization	Fixed by the Spanning Tree Algorithm or Source Routing	Optimized for traffic loading across the entire network
Data flow control	Access limitation and filtering according to MAC address	Network address dependent; can exert flow control
WAN access	Usually single port	Possible to construct a complex mesh of point-to-point links
Management	Statistics about frames and bridge operations	Statistics about specific protocols
Performance	May suffer in heavy traffic environments	Similar to bridges but can limit traffic from sources by quenching

TABLE 13.3—Router/Bridge Comparison

Combined Bridge And Router Architectures

The distinction between bridges and routers is not as clear as it once was. Over time many intermediate devices have been introduced, including bridging routers, routing bridges, bridge routers, router bridges and brouters. What all of these devices have in common is that they perform some functions associated with bridges and some functions associated with routers.

Bridge routers and routing bridges are considered to be the same. They are essentially bridges that provide some routing functions. Router bridges and bridging routers are also considered to be the same. They are routers that perform some bridging functions. Brouters are considered to be true hybrid devices. Through the use of software, these devices can be reconfigured to function as a bridge, a router or to provide for a mix of the two functions.

Bridge/Router Systems

Bridge/router systems have their origins in the bridge environment. Often, this type of device is capable of supporting only one type of network technology—either all Ethernet or all Token-ring. Bridging-type functions dominate these devices but they are capable of routing specific Network layer protocols. Bridging performance is usually at full bridge speeds but routing tends to be done at lower speeds. Most can also be interconnected to standardized bridges and routers. Since these devices are bridge-based, most tend to be two-port devices with single processor architecture.

Router/Bridge Systems

Router/bridge systems have their origins in the router environment. These types of devices were of benefit in router-based networks where there were certain types of network traffic that could not be routed—they lacked a Network layer protocol. Using a router with some bridging capabilities allowed these unroutable protocols to be bridged instead. Routing-type functions predominate with bridging used most to transfer those protocols, which cannot be routed. The performance of these devices for both the routing and bridging functions is at full speed. Most can also be interconnected to standardized routers and bridges. These devices tend to be multiple port devices with each port supported by its own processor.

13.8 Brouters

A brouter can work in either the second and third layers of the OSI model—the data link layer or the network layer. Brouters combine the functions of a bridge and a router. If it can't route a packet, it acts as a bridge. Brouters are particularly useful if you have two or more different networks. Working as a bridge, a brouter is protocol independent and can be used to filter local area network traffic. Working as a router, a brouter is capable of routing packets across networks.

Brouters have an independent origin-they were not developed by either bridge or router manufacturers. Modern brouters are used primarily in new network installations where the functionality of both a bridge and a router is required. An advantage of brouters is that they can be readily adapted to new demands. Brouters are capable of functioning solely as bridges, solely as routers, or as true hybrid devices. However, they are usually proprietary devices that can be interconnected only to certain other devices. Full connectivity to standard bridges and routers is not always possible.

Bridging performance is usually at full bridging speeds while routing speeds tend to be slower. These devices tend to be software configurable and are supported by a single processor architecture.

13.9 Gateways

Gateways work at OSI model layer 7-the application layer. Gateways are special devices designed to overcome incompatibilities between networks. They are typically designed to perform a specific purpose (i.e., a system network architect (SNA) gateway) and are sometimes slow and expensive. However, they form an essential part of the internetworking system in situations where it is not practical or possible to use a single networking technology.

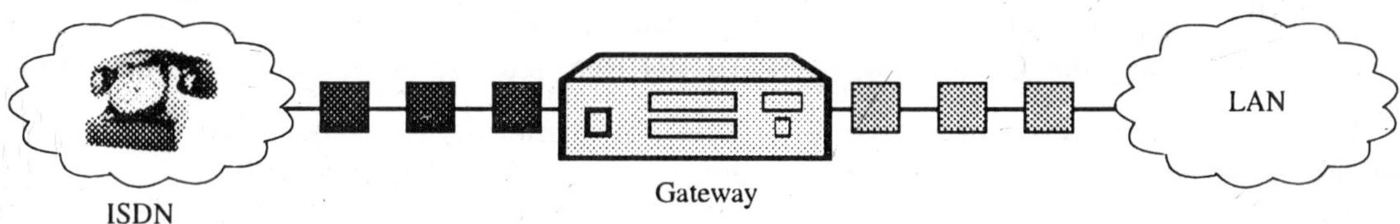

Fig. 13.16 Gateway connecting two dissimilar networks

Gateway is a term that once used to refer to a routing device. Today, in the TCP/IP world, the term router is used to describe such a device. The term gateway now refers to special-purpose devices that perform protocol conversions. Gateways implement application layer conversions of information received from various protocols.

A gateway functions to reconcile differences between two dissimilar networks. Messages are not only repackaged for transmission between different networks (CSMA/CD to token-passing), but the contents of the messages are converted into a format the destination can use and understand. A gateway is generally a dedicated computer with an interface card and at least some type of software for both of the environments being connected. The gateway then runs special software that provides the necessary conversion and translation services, which, in turn, allow the two environments to communicate.

The role of the gateway is to overcome problems associated with protocol incompatibility. Gateways are available as stand-alone devices or in the form of a network station functioning as a gateway server. In both cases, the gateway requires appropriate network adapters—LAN, WAN or both—and appropriate software. It is the software, which is responsible for translating the messages from the received format to the format understood by the destination system.

In the case of bridges and repeaters, their functionality was largely independent of the environments they interconnected. However, gateways are very dependent on the systems they are interconnecting. Each type of system requires a specific type of gateway. Therefore, an individual type of gateway has a limited range of capabilities.

Another major difference between gateways and other internetworking devices is the level of compatibility with respect to the OSI model. Repeaters, bridges and routers have little concern for the contents of the packets they transport. Gateways require compatibility at the uppermost layers of the OSI model. They are application-specific-gateways providing interconnection between electronic mail systems cannot be used for general file transfer purposes.

Examples of gateways found on todays markets are:

- **VocalTec Gateway :** A gateway that converts human speech traveling on analog phone lines into local area network protocol data, and vice-versa.
- **RadVision Gateway :** Converts video from digital phone lines into local area network protocol data, and vice-versa.

Gateways provide increased flexibility compared to bridges in terms of:

1. Translating addresses between dissimilar networks.
2. Fragmenting large packets for transmission across networks that carry only small maximum packet lengths.
3. Selecting an appropriate path through the subnet.
4. Enforcing policies (e.g., don't forward any local packets off of this network).

Because gateways do more work than bridges, they generally run slower than bridges. One important aspect of gateways is Gateway Ownership which is discussed below.

Gateway Ownership

One issue that arises with gateways is who owns them. Typically, bridges connect LANs of one organization, and the issue does not arise there. The ownership question is important because someone has to be responsible for the gateway's operation and dual ownership frequently leads to finger pointing when something goes wrong.

One solution is to use half gateways. If two countries are involved, for instance, each country owns its half of the gateway, with a wire separating the two. A special protocol operates over the wire, and each half of the gateway is responsible for implementing the protocol.

Responsibility Of Gateways

The primary functional responsibility of a gateway is to translate from one protocol stack to another. There are three ways in which a gateway may operate. These are as follows:

- **Remote protocol encapsulation :** In this case, the data from the remote system is encapsulated by the protocols used by the local system. The encapsulation is stripped away by the local system protocol stack as the data passes from the bottom layer to the upper layer. The application layer of the local protocol stack receives the data in its native format.
- **Local protocol encapsulation :** This is similar to remote protocol encapsulation, except the data from the local system is encapsulated by the protocols used by the remote system.
- **Protocol conversion :** In the case of protocol conversion, the gateway is responsible for reorganizing the data content. The reorganization places appropriate information in the correct position in the message. Protocol conversion is the process by which the data format used in one communications system is translated into the data format

used by another system. There are multiple levels at which protocol conversion may take place.

Some forms of encapsulation are supported by bridges and routers. However, gateways are the only devices capable of supporting both encapsulation and protocol conversion.

Selection of Gateways

Once the need for a gateway has been established, the next step is to decide the type of gateway that is needed. Some of the issues to consider when making a selection include the following:

- The types of network environments that need to be supported-LAN-to-LAN, LAN-to-WAN and/or WAN-to-WAN.
- The identification of the protocols being used and the protocols that will require translation.
- The number of network links that need to be supported.
- Whether or not routers will be part of the internetworking infrastructure.
- If any host computer systems need to be supported, and if so which one. Special interface boards may be required.
- The number of concurrent sessions that need to be supported by the gateways.
- The amount of buffer storage area needed to compensate for transmission speed mismatches.

• • •

14

Transport Layer

Introduction

The transport layer is the fourth layer of the OSI reference model. It provides transparent transfer of data between end systems using the services of the network layer (e.g., IP) below to move PDUs of data between the two communicating systems.

The basic function of the transport layer is to accept data from the session layer, split it up into smaller units if need be, pass these to the network layer, and ensure that the pieces all arrive correctly at the other end. Furthermore, all this must be done efficiently, and in a way that isolates the session layer from the inevitable changes in the hardware technology.

Under normal conditions, the transport layer creates a distinct network connection for each transport connection required by the session layer. If the transport connection requires a high throughput, however, the transport layer might create multiple network connections, dividing the data among the network connections to improve throughput. On the other hand, if creating or maintaining a network connection is expensive, the transport layer might multiplex several transport connections onto the same network connection to reduce the cost. In all cases, the transport layer is required to make the multiplexing transparent to the session layer.

The transport layer is a true source-to-destination or end-to-end layer. In other words, a program on the source machine carries on a conversation with a similar program on the destination machine, using the message headers and control messages. Many hosts are multi-programmed, which implies that multiple connections will be entering and leaving each host. There needs to be some way to tell which message belongs to which connection. The transport header is one place this information could be put.

In addition to multiplexing several message streams onto one channel, the transport layer must take care of establishing and deleting connections across the network. This requires some kind of naming mechanism, so that process on one machine has a way of describing with whom it wishes to converse. There must also be a mechanism to regulate the flow of information, so that a fast host cannot overrun a slow one. Flow control between hosts is distinct from flow control between switches, although similar principles apply to both.

The transport layer is important as it segments the data from the upper layers, and passes these onto the network layer, which adds the network address to the segments (these are then called packets). The network layer allows for delivery of these segments at the receiver. Once delivered the transport layer then takes over and reassembles the data segments back into a form that can be delivered to the layer above. These services are often known as end-to-end services, as the transport layer provides a logical connection between two end points on a network.

The transport service is said to perform "peer to peer" communication, with the remote (peer) transport entity. The data communicated by the transport layer is encapsulated in a transport layer PDU and sent in a network layer SDU. The network layer nodes (i.e., Intermediate Systems (IS)) transfer the transport PDU intact, without decoding or modifying the content of the PDU. In this way, only the peer transport entities actually communicate using the PDUs of the transport protocol.

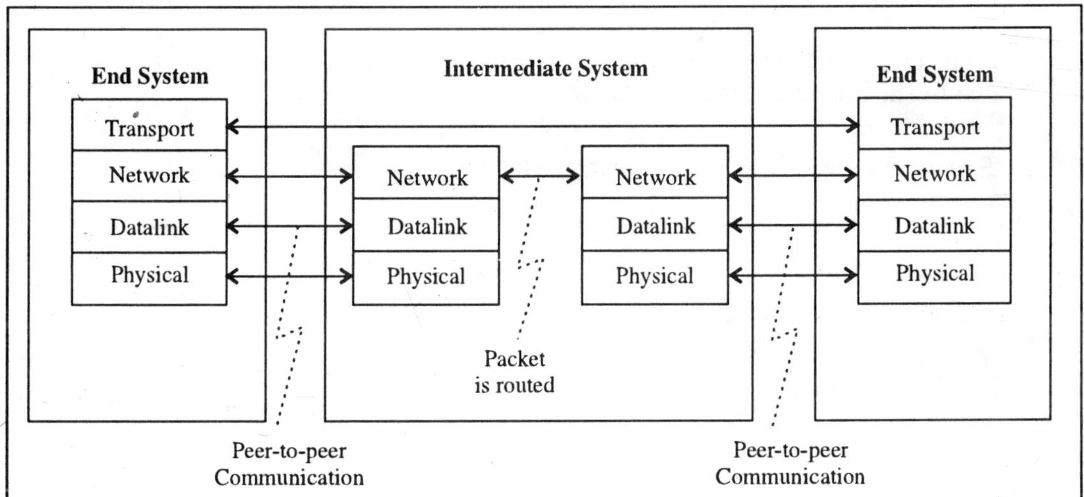

Fig. 14.1 Two end systems connected by an intermediate system (in this case a router)

14.1 Transport Layer Characteristics

- Transport Layer protocols reside in the source and destination nodes.
- Transport Layer provides a consistent service interface between applications and the network.
- Transport protocol normally included in operating system.
- Layers above transport are linked into user program.
- Transport Layer must provide reliable connection despite

- Packet loss due to best-effort connectionless network services or due to Virtual Circuit resets on "reliable" connection-oriented network Services
- Packet reordering that can occur with connectionless service or when a transport Connection is split across multiple Virtual Circuits

14.1.1 Transport Layer vs. DLL Layer

Transport Layer and Data Link Layer bear some resemblance: Both perform error control, resequencing, and flow control. Data Link layer operates on a link basis. Transport Layer operates end-to-end across a network.

Differences between datalink layer and transport layer protocols

1. **Addressing :** Datalink layer protocols don't need to deal with addresses. Transport layer protocols explicitly need addressing information.
2. **Connection establishment :** Datalink layer needs no such procedure. Initial connection establishment is elaborate in transport layer protocols.
3. **Subnet as storage :** Datalink layer protocols don't need to be concerned about a packet being (temporarily) stored at an intermediate router. Transport layer protocols need to be concerned about this possibility.
4. **Buffering and flow-control :** Much more complex in transport layer protocols due to the multitude of connections.

14.1.2 Services Provided by Transport Layer

The services provided by the transport layer are listed below:

- Addressing.
- Address/Name Resolution.
- Segment Development.
- Connection Services.

Addressing

Addressing at the Transport Layer deals with labeling a frame, identifying it as either a connection or a transaction.

Connection Identifiers—A connection identifier is also known as a port or socket. It labels each frame by conversation so the receiving device knows which process it has been transmitted from. This is for keeping track of multiple-message conversations.

Transaction Identifiers—They are used when frames sent are simple requests or responses. They are considered one-time events, and no multiple message conversations are tracked, even though there may be one going on.

Address/Name Resolution

Each network address is a binary number, often 32-bits. Keeping track of these addresses is near impossible for people wanting to transmit over a network. Therefore with some protocols, each address is assigned a name in recognizable words. A service on the network, (either at each device or by a central name server) translates the word addresses into numeric addresses. There are *two methods* of Address/Name Resolution:

Service-Requester-Initiated Address/Name Resolution—With this method, a device that wishes to request services broadcasts a packet requesting information for a name, address or service. The device corresponding to the name, address, or service sends back the required information needed to complete a transaction.

Service-Provider-Initiated Address/Name Resolution—This method consists of a central directory server (name server) that collects name, address and service information. The service providers broadcast this information periodically and devices requesting services request address information from the name server.

Segment Development

The Transport Layer is where incoming and outbound messages are broken down or recombined to fit the required size format. It also combines multiple small messages into a single segment to improve network efficiency when the messages are smaller than maximum allowable size. A connection identifier (CID) identifies each component. The CID enables the transport layer of the receiving device to deliver each message to the proper process.

Connection Services

The Transport Layer can also perform connection services such as:

- **Segment Sequencing**—When large messages are divided, the Transport Layer reorders them once received before reassembling them into a message.
- **Error Control**—To prevents errors from lost or duplicate segments, the Transport Layer enables the following strategies:
    - Unique segment sequence numbers.
    - Virtual circuits, permitting only one virtual circuit per session.
    - Timeouts removed from the network segments that have been misrouted and have remained on the network past a specified time.
    - Corruption is also detected by end-to-end error control by way of checksums.
- **End-to-End Flow Control**—Acknowledgements are used to manage end-to-end flow control. There are negative acknowledgements as well as go back *n* or selective repeat acknowledgements.

    Go back n—Request retransmission of packets starting at *n*.
    Selective Repeat—Request specific packets to be retransmitted.

14.1.3 Elements of Transport Protocols

- **Connection Management**—Establish, refuse and release connections. Manage mapping between transport and network connections or build a connection-oriented service from a connectionless network service.

- **Fragmentation and reassembly of application data**—Fragment data stream into packet sizes suitable for the network. Where multiple transport connections exist packets must be correctly associated with each connection. Receiver must reassemble packets and resequence the data stream.
- **Recovery from network failures**—Reassignment after network disconnects and resynchronization after network resets.
- **Error Control and Flow Control**—Especially for LANs.
- **Multiplexing**—Mapping multiple Transport Connections to one Network Connection.
- **Splitting and Recombining**—Mapping one Transport Connection to multiple Network Connections.

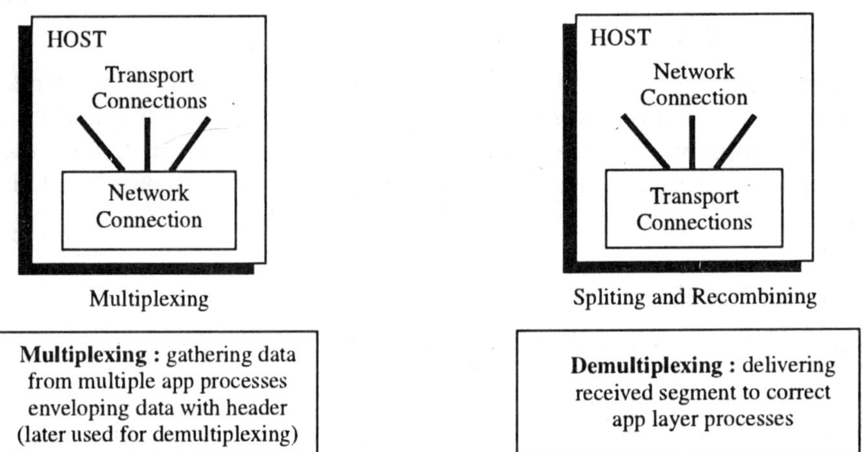

Fig. 14.2 Multiplexing and demultiplexing

14.1.4 Functions of the Transport Layer

The great trick of the transport level is to allow multiple applications to communicate over a network, at the same time. This is achieved by identifying each connection with a unique value (a socket number) and adding sequence numbers on each of the segments. Segments can also be sent to many different destinations (using the network layer to identify the destination).

- **Process-Level Addressing** : Addressing at layer two deals with hardware devices on a local network and layer three addressing identifies devices on a logical internetwork. Addressing is also performed at the transport layer, where it is used to differentiate between software programs. This is part of what enables many different software programs to use a network layer protocol simultaneously. The best example of transport-layer process-level addressing is the TCP and UDP port mechanism used in TCP/IP, which allows applications to be individually referenced on any TCP/IP device.

- **Multiplexing and Demultiplexing :** Transport layer protocols on a sending device multiplex the data received from many application programs for transport, combining them into a single stream of data to be sent. The same protocols receive data and then demultiplex it from the incoming stream of datagrams and direct each package of data to the appropriate recipient application processes.
- **Segmentation, Packaging and Reassembly :** The transport layer segments the large amounts of data it sends over the network into smaller pieces on the source machine and then reassemble them on the destination machine. This function is similar conceptually to the fragmentation function of the network layer; just as the network layer fragments messages to fit the limits of the data link layer, the transport layer segments messages to suit the requirements of the underlying network layer.
- **Connection Establishment, Management and Termination :** Transport layer connection-oriented protocols are responsible for the series of communications required to establish a connection, maintain it as data is sent over it and then terminate the connection when it is no longer required.
- **Acknowledgments and Retransmissions :** As mentioned above, the transport layer is where many protocols are implemented that guarantee reliable delivery of data. This is done using a variety of techniques, most commonly the combination of acknowledgments and retransmission timers. Each time data is sent a timer is started; if it is received, the recipient sends back an acknowledgment to the transmitter to indicate successful transmission. If no acknowledgment comes back before the timer expires, the data is retransmitted. Other algorithms and techniques are usually required to support this basic process.
- **Flow Control :** Transport layer protocols that offer reliable delivery also often implement *flow control* features. These features allow one device in a communication to specify to another that it must "throttle back" the rate at which it is sending data, to avoid bogging down the receiver with data. These allow mismatches in speed between sender and receiver to be detected and dealt with.

Transport Protocol Data Units

Data is exchanged between Transport peers in TPDU's. TPDU's are of course encapsulated within packets for transmission over the network. The protocols that are used by the Transport layer are essentially the same as underlying layers, e.g., TPDU's require sequence numbers for flow and error control.

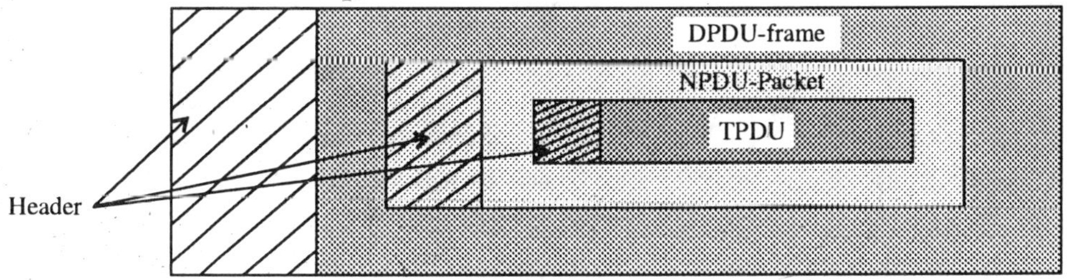

Fig. 14.3 TPDU's encapsulated within packets for transmission

TPDU's may be given the common name, *messages*. They may well be fragmented by the Network layer but this will be transparent to the Transport layer.

14.1.5 Transport Layer Protocols

At any time, a host may be using several network connections to various services on other hosts. IP allows packets to be routed between hosts on an Internet, but once a packet reaches its destination host, a mechanism is needed whereby it can be routed to the appropriate application. IP addresses themselves do not provide sufficient information to do this.

A solution to the problem is to use a higher-level protocol for this task, while still using IP as the underlying delivery mechanism. The simplest such higher-level protocol is the User Datagram Protocol (UDP). UDP datagrams consists of a header and zero or more bytes of actual data. The header has four fields: the source and destination ports, a data integrity checksum whose use is optional and the length of the datagram. The 'ports' are 16-bit numbers used to identify the connection end points on either side. A particular network connection is then identified by a four-tuple (source address, source port, destination address, destination port).

UDP is still connectionless and unreliable. To support connection-oriented applications which require reliable, in-sequence data streams, the Transport Control Protocol or TCP is used. Like UDP, TCP also uses ports to identify connection endpoints. Checksum usage in TCP is mandatory to ensure reliability. TCP headers include sequence numbers representing a byte offset in the data stream; these sequence numbers are used on the receiving end to arrange data received in TCP packets in the correct order. TCP makes use of acknowledgments to inform the sender that data has arrived correctly at the recipient (an acknowledgment consists of the sequence number of the next expected packet).

The most important transport protocol is TCP, which typically uses IP as an addressing scheme. TCP and IP (TCP/IP) are the standard protocols that are used on the Internet and

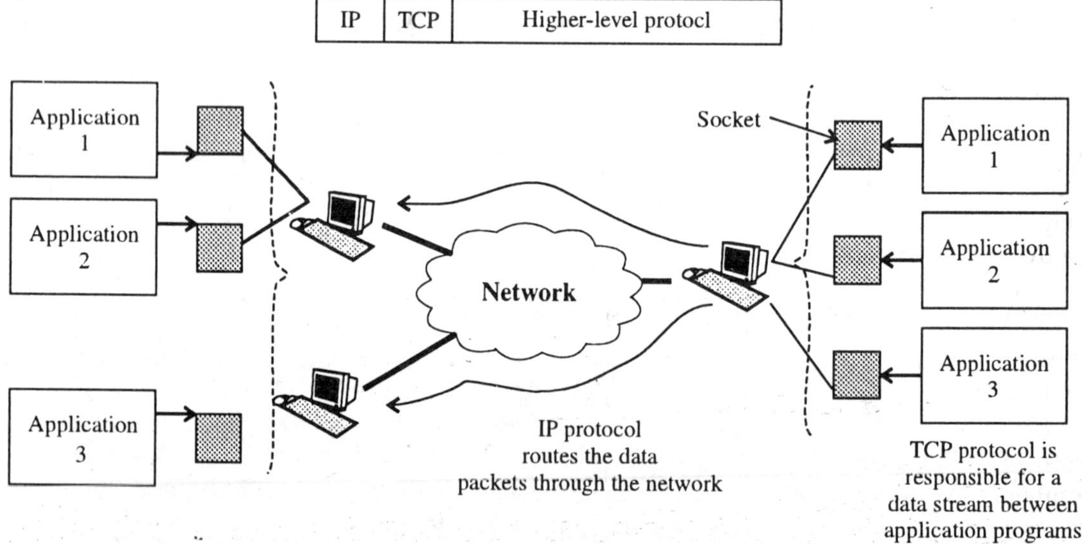

Fig. 14.4 TCP supporting multiple simultaneous connections of applications over a network

also on UNIX networks. TCP works well because it is simple, but reliable and it is an open system where no single vendor has control over its specification and its development. An important concept of TCP/IP communications is the usage of ports and sockets. A port identifies a process type (such as FTP, TELNET and so on) and the socket identifies a unique connection number. In this way, TCP/IP can support multiple simultaneous connections of applications over a network as shown in fig 14.4.

Before discussing the protocols in detail let us understand what are ports.

14.2 Ports

There are two meanings in common use for the term "port", one having to do with hardware and the other related to software ports. On computer and telecommunication devices (hardware) a port is generally a specific physical location for connecting to some other device. Usually this involves a socket and plug. Generally, there are one or more serial ports and one parallel port on a personal computer. The serial port supports sequential, bit-by-bit transmission to peripheral devices such as scanners. A parallel port supports multiple bit transmission to devices like printers. Newer computers may also employ USB (universal serial bus) ports. USB connections move data at up to 12 mbps, about 100 times faster than a typical serial port and more than four times faster than a parallel port.

This article is concerned with the second or software, type of port used in Internet communications. In software usage, a port is a logical, rather than physical, connection. When using the Internet communications protocol, transmission control protocol/Internet protocol (TCP/IP), designating a port is the way a client program specifies a particular server program on a computer in a network. Basically, a port number is a way to identify the specific process to which an Internet or other network message is to be forwarded when it arrives at a server.

Both TCP and UDP use ports to exchange information with applications. A *port* is an extension of an address, similar to adding an apartment or room number to a street address. A letter with a street address will arrive at the correct apartment building, but without the apartment number, it will not be delivered to the correct recipient. Ports work in much the same way. A packet can be delivered to the correct IP address, but without the associated port, there is no way to determine which application should act on the packet. Once the ports have been defined, it is possible for the different types of information that are sent to one IP address to then be sent to the appropriate applications. By using ports, a service running on a remote computer can determine what type of information a local client is requesting, can determine the protocol needed to send that information, and maintain simultaneous communication with a number of different clients.

For example, if a local computer attempts to connect to the website www.gnduonline.org, whose IP address is 92.70.122.203, with a web server running on port 70, the local computer would connect to the remote computer using the socket address : 92.70.122.203 : 70.

Higher-level applications that use TCP/IP such as the web protocol and hypertext transfer protocol (HTTP) use ports with pre-assigned numbers. These are well-known ports, to which numbers have been assigned by the Internet Assigned Numbers Authority. Some application processes are given port numbers dynamically when each connection is made.

When a server program is started via a port connection, it is said to bind to its designated port number. When another client program wants to use that server, it also must send a request to bind to the designated port number. Ports are used in TCP to name the ends of logical connections that carry long-term conversations. To the extent possible, these same port assignments are used with UDP.

Port numbers can be changed via software settings or can be remapped internally using routers that can change header information. Headers provide the basis for synchronizing communications sessions, control of errors, routing and firewall management. The following table provides a description of a typical header.

Data Link/ Physical Header	IP Address/Header	Port Address	Data
Locates the correct device on the local area network (network interface-hardware layer of TCP/IP)	Locates the correct device in a network using TCP/IP (internetworking layer of TCP/IP)	Locates the correct application/service (transport layer of TCP/IP)	Data

Table 14.1: Internet Addressing–TCP/IP

When sending information, each layer in the protocol stack adds a header to the data. Conversely, at the receiving end, each layer removes a header. A connection in TCP/IP might look like this (see explanation of numbering below the example):

185.15.4.1,	1160,	185.15.4.3,	23,	TCP
(1)	(2)	(3)	(4)	(5)

1. Source or client IP address. The final segment is the host identifier.
2. Source or client port that would be randomly assigned.
3. Destination or server IP address (here, because the first three segments are the same as the source address, this is the same network; different host).
4. Destination or server port. In this case, port 23 for a Telnet application/request.
5. TCP protocol.

Any address scheme can be used for an isolated network with some restrictions depending on the type of network.

14.2.1 Classification of Ports

Port numbers are divided into three ranges: the well-known ports, the registered ports and the dynamic and/or private ports.

The well-known ports—0 through 1023 : The well-known ports are assigned by the Internet Assigned Numbers Authority (IANA) and are typically used by system-level or root processes. Well-known applications running as servers and passively listening for connections typically use these ports. Some examples include: FTP (21), TELNET (23), SMTP (25) and HTTP (80).

The registered ports—1024 through 49151 : Listed by the IANA and on most systems can be used by ordinary user processes or programs executed by ordinary users. Registered ports are typically used by end user applications as ephemeral source ports when contacting servers, but they can also identify named services that have been registered by a third party.

The dynamic and/or private ports—49152 through 65535 : Not listed by IANA because of their dynamic nature. Dynamic/private ports can also be used by end user applications, but are less commonly so. Dynamic/private ports do not contain any meaning outside of any particular TCP connection. There are 65535 possible ports officially recognized.

Socket

A socket is a network communications endpoint. The analogy is to a wire (the network data connection) being plugged into a socket. Sockets come in two primary types:

- An active socket is connected to a remote active socket via an open data connection. Closing the connection destroys the active sockets at each endpoint.
- A passive socket is not connected, but rather awaits an incoming connection, which will spawn a new active socket.

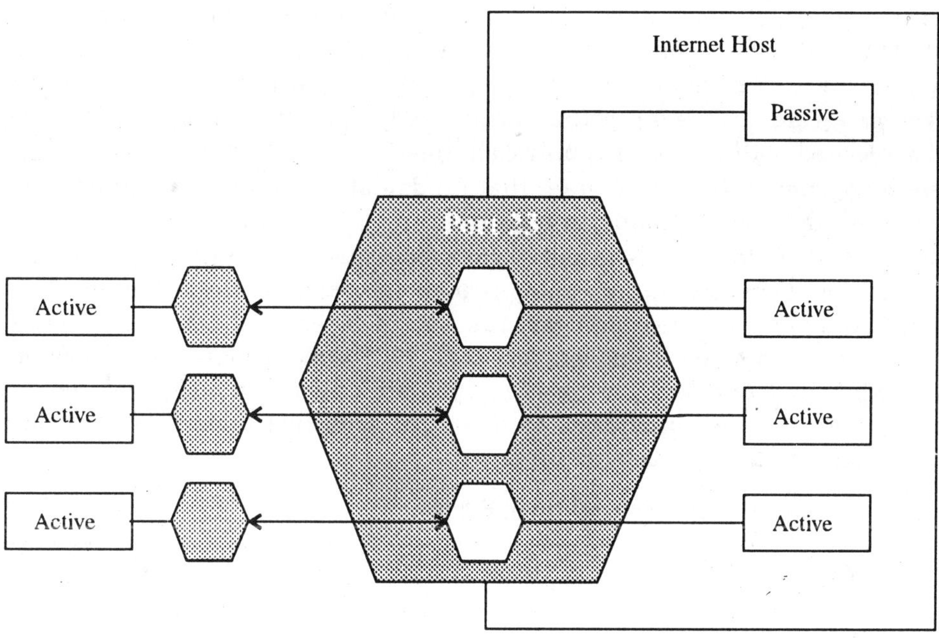

Fig. 14.5 A port having single passive socket and multiple active sockets

A socket is not a port, though there is a close relationship between them. A socket is associated with a port, though this is a many-to-one relationship. Each port can have a single passive socket, awaiting incoming connections, and multiple active sockets, each corresponding to an open connection on the port as is illustrated in figure 14.5.

14.3 Client Server Model

We have covered the underlying network transport mechanism and can now consider how distributed applications are built on top of this. Almost all network-based applications are based on a client-server model of interaction. A server is a program that offers a service to other programs on the same or other hosts on the network. A client is a program that requests service from a server. Servers usually run continuously and can typically service multiple requests from multiple clients, often concurrently. Clients, on the other hand, usually have a limited lifetime.

For Transport layer connection to be established a process must be listening to a Transport address and a second process must make a connection request. Typically processes don't listen to Transport addresses. A process must register with the operating system to "bind" to a Transport address. The process that is listening is called a server. The process that is making the connection request is called a *client*. For example the telnet program is a client program. It can be used to connect to a given process by specifying the host address and transport address.

The processes (application programs) are associated (dynamically or statically) with port numbers. The destination port is used for presenting data to the corresponding program (= demultiplexing at destination). The source port is stored by destination for responses.

Server program : It is a program that is ready to receive data at any time on a given port and associated with a process running all time.

Client program : It is a program that sends data to a server program and does not expect to receive data before taking an initiative.

In the TCP/IP world, servers usually listen for requests on well-known ports that have been reserved for their service (for example, mail servers typically listen on TCP port 25). Clients, on the other hand, use arbitrary, unused, non-reserved ports for their connection endpoints. By convention, port numbers less than 1024 are considered privileged and for use by servers, while port numbers greater than 1023 are considered non-privileged and for use by clients (there are a few exceptions to this). The following table lists some of the most common services and their associated ports.

Common TCP and UDP Services and their Ports

Service	Protocol	Port	Description
FTP	TCP	20, 21	File Transfer Service
telnet	TCP	23	Virtual terminal service
SMTP	TCP	25	Electronic mail transfer
DNS	TCP/UDP	53	Domain name service
TFTP	UDP	69	Trivial file transfer
HTTP	TCP	80	World wide web hyper text transfer
POPS	TCP	110	Electronic mail retrieval
SNMP	UDP	161, 162	Network management service

Generic Network Server Algorithm

```
start listening for requests on the well known port
loop forever
begin
        if a request is received from some client
        then create a slave process to handle that
                                    client's request
end
```

Servers usually operate according to this general algorithm. By running a slave process to handle each client request, the server can deal with multiple concurrent requests.

Process Server

To prevent a large number of sleeping servers, a process server can bind to a number of different Transport addresses and hand-over an incoming connection request to an actual server of the requested type. An example is illustrated in the figure 14.6.

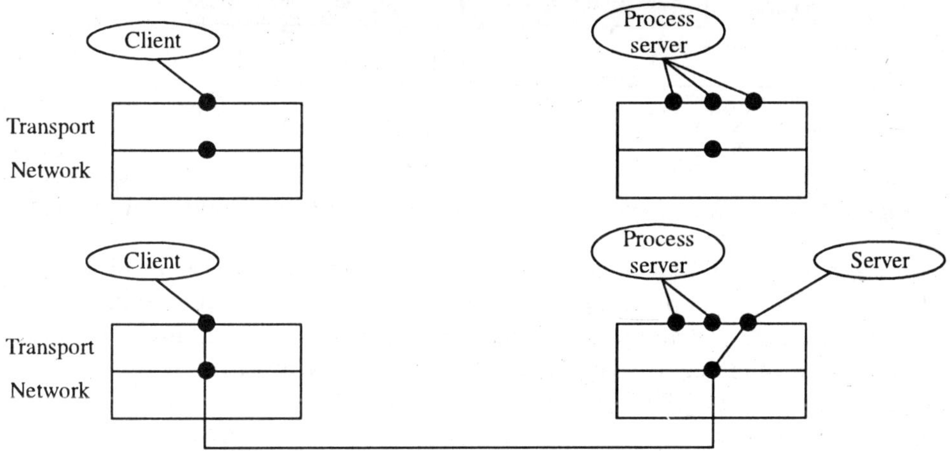

Fig. 14.6 A process server that hands over a connection request to the actual server

14.4 Transmission Control ProtocoL (TCP)

The **Transmission Control Protocol (TCP)** is one of the core protocols of the Internet protocol suite. Using TCP, programs on networked computers can create connections to one another, over which they can send data. The protocol guarantees that data sent by one endpoint will be received in the same order by the other, and without any pieces missing. It also distinguishes data for different applications (such as a Web server and an email server) on the same computer.

TCP supports many of the Internet's most popular applications, including HTTP and SMTP.

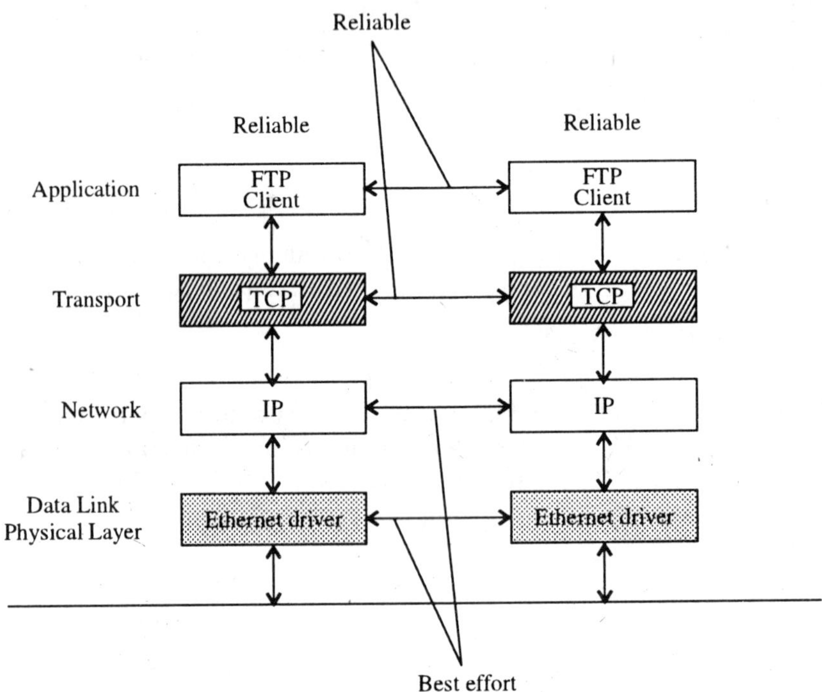

Fig. 14.7 TCP providing reliable data transfer to FTP over an IP network using ethernet

TCP is stream oriented, that is TCP protocol entities exchange streams of data. Individual bytes of data (e.g., from an application or session layer protocol) are placed in memory buffers and transmitted by TCP in transport Protocol Data Units (for TCP these are usually known as "segments"). The reliable, flow-controlled TCP service is much more complex than UDP, which only provides a Best Effort service. To implement the service, TCP uses a number of protocol timers that ensure reliable and synchronized communication between the two End Systems.

TCP provides reliability with a mechanism called *Positive Acknowledgment with Re-transmission* (PAR). Simply stated, a system using PAR sends the data again, unless it hears from the remote system that the data arrived okay. The unit of data exchanged between cooperating TCP modules is called a segment. Each segment contains a checksum that the recipient uses to verify that the data is undamaged. If the data segment is received undamaged, the receiver sends a positive acknowledgment back to the sender. If the data segment is damaged, the receiver discards it. After an appropriate time-out period, the sending TCP module re-transmits any segment for which no positive acknowledgment has been received.

14.4.1 Aspects of TCP

The main aspects of TCP are:

- **Data transfer**—Data is transmitted between two applications by packaging the data within TCP segments. This data is buffered and forwarded whenever necessary. A push function can be used when the data is required to be sent immediately.
- **Reliability**—TCP uses sequence numbers and positive acknowledgements (ACK) to keep track of transmitted segments. Thus, it can recover from data that is damaged, lost, duplicated, or delivered out of order, such as:
  - *Time-outs*—The transmitter waits for a given time (the timeout interval), and if it does not receive an ACK, the data is retransmitted.
  - *Sequence numbers*—The sequence numbers are used at the receiver to correctly order the packets and to delete duplicates.
  - *Error detection and recovery*—Each packet has a checksum, which is checked by the receiver. If it is incorrect the receiver discards it, and can use the acknowledgements to indicate the retransmission of the packets.
- **Flow control**—TCP returns a window with every ACK. This window indicates a range of acceptable sequence numbers beyond the last segment successfully received. It also indicates the number of bytes that the sender can transmit before receiving further acknowledgements.
- **Multiplexing**—To support multiple connections to a single host, TCP provides a set of ports within each host. This, along with the IP addresses of the source and destination, makes a socket, and a pair of sockets uniquely identifies each connection. Ports are normally associated with various services and allow server programs to listen for defined port numbers.
- **Connections**—A connection is defined by the sockets, sequence numbers and window sizes. Each host must maintain this information for the length of the connection. When the connection is closed, all associated resources are freed. As TCP connections can be made with unreliable hosts and over unreliable communication channels, TCP uses a handshake mechanism with clock-based sequence numbers to avoid inaccurate connection initialization.
- **Precedence and security**—TCP allows for different security and precedence levels. TCP information contains simple acknowledgement messages and a set of sequential numbers. It also supports multiple simultaneous connections using destination and source port numbers, and manages them for both transmission and reception. As with IP, it supports data fragmentation and reassembly and data multiplexing/ demultiplexing.

The set-up and operation of TCP is as follows:

- When a host wishes to make a connection, TCP sends out a request message to the destination machine that contains unique numbers called a socket number, and a port number. The port number has a value that is associated with the application (for example a TELNET connection has the port number 23 and an FTP connection has the port number 21). The message is then passed to the IP layer, which assembles a datagram for transmission to the destination.

- When the destination host receives the connection request, it returns a message containing its own unique socket number and a port number. The socket number and port number thus identify the virtual connection between the two hosts.
- After the connection has been made, the data can flow between the two hosts (called a Data stream).

After TCP receives the stream of data, it assembles the data into packets, called TCP segments. After the segment has been constructed, TCP adds a header (called the protocol data unit) to the front of the segment. This header contains information such as a checksum, the port number, the destination and source socket numbers, the socket number of both machines and segment sequence numbers. The TCP layer then sends the packaged segment down to the IP layer, which encapsulates it and sends it over the network as a datagram.

Ports and Sockets

As previously mentioned, TCP adds a port number and socket number for each host. The port number identifies the required service, whereas the socket number is a unique number for that connection. Thus, a node can have several TELNET connections with the same port number but each connection will have a different socket number. A port number can be any value but there is a standard convention that most systems adopt.

14.4.2 TCP Header Format

The sender's TCP layer communicates with the receiver's TCP layer using the TCP protocol data unit. It defines parameters such as the source port, destination port, and so on as illustrated in figure 14.8.

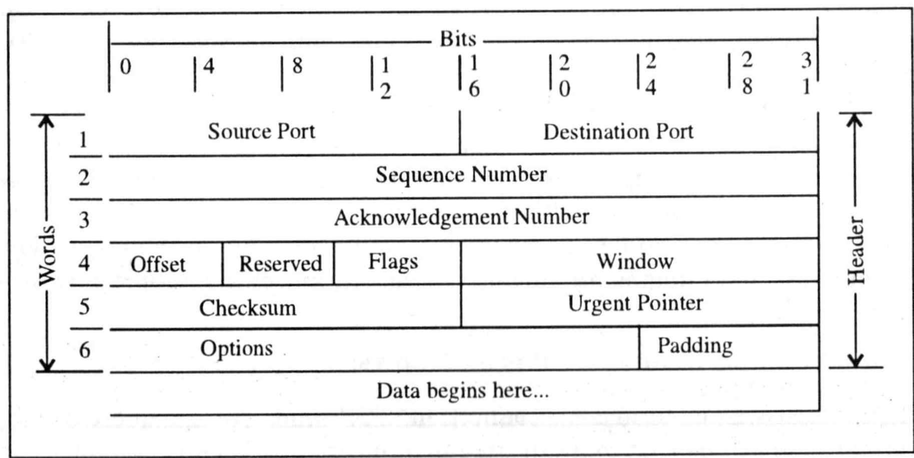

Fig. 14.8 TCP header format

The fields in TCP header format are explained below:

- **Source and destination port number**—These are 16-bit values that identify the local port number (source number and destination port number).
- **Sequence number**—This identifies the current sequence number of the data segment. This allows the receiver to keep track of the data segments received. Any segments that are missing can be easily identified. The sequence number is the first data byte of the DATA segment (except when SYN is present). If SYN is present the sequence number is the initial sequence number (ISN) and the first data octet is ISN + 1.
- **Acknowledgement number**—When the ACK bit is set, it contains the value of the next sequence number the sender of the packet is expecting to receive. This is always set after the connection is made.
- **Data offset**—This is a 32-bit value that identifies the start of the data. It is defined as the number of 32-bit words in the header (as the TCP header always has a multiple number of 32-bit words).
- **Flags**—The flag field is defined as UAPRSF, where U is the urgent flag (URG), A the acknowledgement flag (ACK), P the push function (PSH), R the reset flag (RST), S the sequence synchronize flag (SYN) and F the end-of-transmission flag (FIN). These fields are defined below:
    1. URG (1-bit)—The urgent pointer is valid.
    2. ACK (1-bit)—Makes the acknowledgement number valid.
    3. PSH (1-bit)—High priority data for the application.
    4. RST (1-bit)—Reset the connection.
    5. SYN (1-bit)—Turned on when a connection is being established and the sequence number field will contain the initial sequence number chosen by this host for this connection.
    6. FIN (1-bit)—The sender is done sending data.
- **Window**—This is a 16-bit value and gives the number of data bytes that the receiving host can accept at a time, beginning with the one indicated in the acknowledgement field of this segment.
- **Checksum**—This is a 16-bit checksum for the data and header. It is the 1's complement of the 1's complement sum of all the 16-bit words in the TCP header and data. The checksum is assumed to be a zero when calculating the checksum.
- **UrgPtr**—This is the urgent pointer and is used to identify an important area of data (most systems do not support this facility). It is only used when the URG bit is set. This field communicates the current value of the urgent pointer as a positive offset from the sequence number in this segment.
- **Padding (variable)**—The TCP header padding is used to ensure that the TCP header ends and data begins on a 32-bit boundary. The padding is composed of zeros.
- **Options**—This is possibly added to segment header.

In TCP, a packet is termed as the complete TCP unit; that is, the header and the data. A segment is a logical unit of data, which is transferred between two TCP hosts. Thus a packet is made up of a header and a segment.

14.4.3 Protocol Operation in Detail

TCP connections contain three phases:

- Connection establishment.
- Data transfer.
- Connection termination.

A 3-way handshake is used to establish a connection. A four-way handshake is used to tear-down a connection. During connection establishment, parameters such as sequence numbers are initialized to help ensure ordered delivery and robustness.

Connection Establishment (3-Way Handshake)

While it is possible for a pair of end hosts to initiate a connection between them simultaneously, typically one end opens a socket and listens passively for a connection from the other. This is commonly referred to as a passive open, and it designates the server-side of a connection. The client-side of a connection initiates an active open by sending an initial SYN segment to the server as part of the 3-way handshake. The server -side should respond to a valid SYN request with a SYN/ACK. Finally, the client-side should respond to the server with an ACK, completing the 3-way handshake and connection establishment phase.

The type of handshake used by TCP is called a three-way handshake because three segments are exchanged. Figure 14.9 shows the simplest form of the three-way handshake. Host *A* begins the connection by sending host *B* a segment with the "Synchronize sequence numbers" (SYN) bit set. This segment tells host *B* that *A* wishes to set up a connection, and it tells *B* what sequence number host *A* will use as a starting number for its segments. (Sequence numbers are used to keep data in the proper order.) Host *B* responds to *A* with a segment that has the "Acknowledgment" (ACK) and SYN bits set. *B*'s segment acknowledges the receipt of *A*'s segment, and informs *A* which Sequence Number host *B* will start with. Finally, host *A* sends a segment that acknowledges receipt of B's segment, and transfers the first actual data.

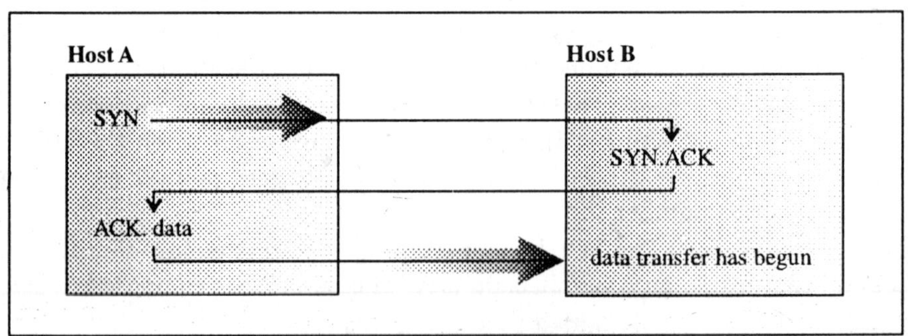

Fig. 14.9 Three-way handshake

Data Transfer

During the data transfer phase, a number of key mechanisms determine TCP's reliability and robustness. These include using sequence numbers for ordering received TCP segments and detecting duplicate data, checksums for segment error detection, and acknowledgements and timers for detecting and adjusting to loss or delay.

During the TCP connection establishment phase, initial sequence numbers (ISNs) are exchanged between the two TCP speakers. These sequence numbers are used to identify data in the byte stream, and are numbers that identify (and count) application data bytes. There is always pair of sequence numbers included in every TCP segment, which is referred to as the sequence number and the acknowledgement number. A TCP sender refers to its own sequence number simply as the sequence number, while the TCP sender refers to receiver's sequence number as the acknowledgement number. To maintain reliability, a receiver acknowledges TCP segment data by indicating it has received up to some location of contiguous bytes in the stream. An enhancement to TCP, called selective acknowledgement (SACK), allows a TCP receiver to acknowledge out of order blocks.

Through the use of sequence and acknowledgement numbers, TCP can properly deliver received segments in the correct byte stream order to a receiving application. Sequence numbers are 32-bit, unsigned numbers, which wrap to zero on the next byte in the stream after 2^{32}-1. One key to maintaining robustness and security for TCP connections is in the selection of the ISN.

A 16-bit checksum, consisting of the one's complement of the one's complement sum of the contents of the TCP segment header and data, is computed by a sender, and included in a segment transmission. (The one's complement sum is used because the end-around carry of that method means that it can be computed in *any* multiple of that length—16-bit, 32-bit, 64-bit, etc. and the result, once *folded*, will be the same.) The TCP receiver recomputes the checksum on the received TCP header and data. The complement was used (above) so that the receiver does not have to zero the checksum field, after saving the checksum value elsewhere; instead, the receiver simply computes the one's complement sum with the checksum in setup, and the result should be –0. If so, the segment is assumed to have arrived intact and without error.

Note that the TCP checksum also covers a 96-bit pseudo header containing the Source Address, the Destination Address, the Protocol, and TCP length. This provides protection against misrouted segments.

The TCP checksum is a quite weak check by modern standards. Data Link Layers with a high probability of bit error rates may require additional link error correction/detection capabilities. If TCP were to be redesigned today, it would most probably have a 32-bit cyclic redundancy check specified as an error check instead of the current checksum. The weak checksum is partially compensated for by the common use of a CRC or better integrity check at layer 2, below both TCP and IP, such as is used in PPP or the Ethernet frame. However, this does not mean that the 16-bit TCP checksum is redundant: remarkably, surveys of Internet traffic have shown that software and hardware errors that introduce errors in packets between CRC-protected hops are common, and that the end-to-end 16-bit TCP checksum catches most of these simple errors. This is the end-to-end principle at work.

Acknowledgements for data sent, or lack of acknowledgements, are used by senders to implicitly interpret network conditions between the TCP sender and receiver. Coupled with timers, TCP senders and receivers can alter the behavior of the flow of data. This is more generally referred to as flow control, congestion control and/or congestion avoidance. TCP uses a number of mechanisms to achieve high performance and avoid congesting the network (i.e., send data faster than either the network or the host on the other end, can utilize it). These mechanisms include the use of a sliding window, the slow-start algorithm, the congestion avoidance algorithm, the fast retransmit and fast recovery algorithms and more. Enhancing TCP to reliably handle loss, minimize errors, manage congestion and go fast in very high-speed environments are ongoing areas of research and standards development.

TCP window size

The TCP receive window size is the amount of received data (in bytes) that can be buffered during a connection. The sending host can send only that amount of data before it must wait for an acknowledgment and window update from the receiving host. The Windows TCP/IP stack is designed to self-tune itself in most environments and uses larger default window sizes than earlier versions.

Windows scaling

For more efficient use of high bandwidth networks, a larger TCP window size may be used. The TCP window size field controls the flow of data and is limited to 2-bytes or a window size of 65,535 bytes. Since the size field cannot be expanded, a scaling factor is used. TCP window scale is an option used to increase the maximum window size from 65,535 bytes to 1 Gigabyte. The window scale option is used only during the TCP 3-way handshake. The window scale value represents the number of bits to left-shift the 16-bit window size field. The window scale value can be set from 0 (no shift) to 14.

Connection termination

The connection termination phase uses a four-way handshake, with each side of the connection terminating independently. Therefore, a typical teardown requires a pair of FIN and ACK segments from each TCP endpoint.

Alternatives to TCP

However, TCP is not appropriate for many applications, and newer transport layer protocols are being designed and deployed to address some of the inherent weaknesses. For example, real-time applications often do not need and will suffer from TCP's reliable delivery mechanisms. In those types of applications it is often better to deal with some loss, errors or congestion than to try to adjust for them. Example applications that do not typically use TCP include real-time streaming multimedia (such as Internet radio), real-time multiplayer games and voice over IP (VoIP). Any application that does not require reliability or that wants to minimize functionality, may choose to avoid using TCP. In many cases, the User Datagram Protocol (UDP) may be used in place of TCP when just application multiplexing services are required.

14.5 User Datagram Protocol (UDP)

TCP allows for a reliable connection-based transfer of data. The User Datagram Protocol (UDP) is an unreliable connection-less approach, where datagrams are sent into the network without any acknowledgements or connections (and thus relies on high-level protocols to provide for these). The User Datagram Protocol gives application programs direct access to a datagram delivery service, like the delivery service that IP provides. This allows applications to exchange messages over the network with a minimum of protocol overhead.

The **User Datagram Protocol (UDP)** is one of the core protocols of the Internet protocol suite. Using UDP, programs on networked computers can send short messages known as datagrams to one another. UDP does not provide the reliability and ordering guarantees that TCP does; datagrams may arrive out of order or go missing without notice. However, as a result, UDP is faster and more efficient for many lightweight or time-sensitive purposes. Common network applications that use UDP includes the Domain Name System (DNS), streaming media applications, Voice over IP, and online games. UDP is widely used for streaming audio and video, voice over IP (VoIP) and videoconferencing, because there is no time to retransmit erroneous or dropped packets.

The service provided by UDP is an unreliable service that provides no guarantees for delivery and no protection from duplication (e.g., if this arises due to software errors within an Intermediate System (IS)). "Unreliable" merely means that there are no techniques in the protocol for verifying that the data reached the other end of the network correctly. Within your computer, UDP will deliver data correctly. The simplicity of UDP reduces the overhead from using the protocol and the services may be adequate in many cases.

It is a protocol within the TCP/IP protocol suite that is used in place of TCP when a reliable delivery is not required. There is less processing of UDP packets than there is for TCP. If UDP is used and a reliable delivery is required, packet sequence checking and error notification must be written into the applications. UDP is "connectionless" and does not use a handshake to start a session. It just sends out packets.

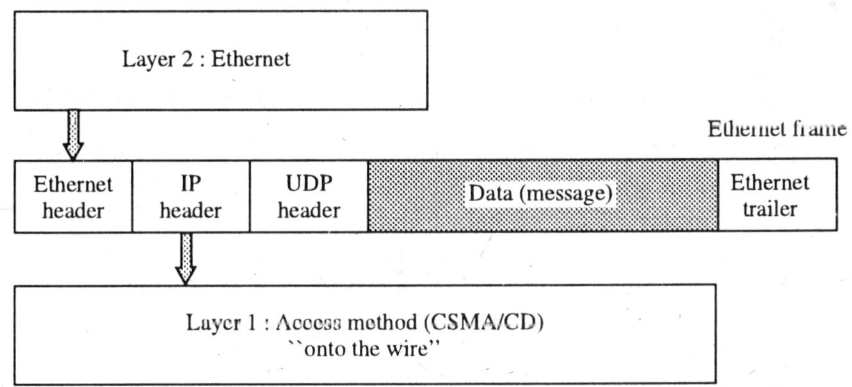

UDP within an ethernet frame

Fig. 14.10 A UDP packet is framed just like a TCP packet.
This shows a UDP packet in an Ethernet frame ready for transmission over the network.

Lacking reliability, UDP applications must generally be willing to accept some loss, errors or duplication. Some applications such as TFTP may add rudimentary reliability mechanisms into the application layer as needed. Most often, UDP applications do not require reliability mechanisms and may even be hindered by them. If an application requires a high degree of reliability, a protocol such as the Transmission Control Protocol may be used instead.

Lacking any congestion avoidance and control mechanisms, network-based mechanisms are required to minimize potential congestion collapse effects of uncontrolled, high rate UDP traffic loads. In other words, since UDP senders cannot detect congestion, network-based elements such as routers using packet queueing and dropping techniques will often be the only tool available to slow down excessive UDP traffic. The Datagram Congestion Control Protocol (DCCP) is being designed as a partial solution to this potential problem by adding end host congestion control behavior to high-rate UDP streams such as streaming media.

14.5.1 UDP Header Format

A computer may send UDP packets without first establishing a connection to the recipient. The computer completes the appropriate fields in the UDP header (PCI) and forwards the data together with the header for transmission by the IP network layer. The UDP header consists of only 4 header fields of which two are optional. The source and destination port fields are 16-bit fields that identify the sending and receiving process.

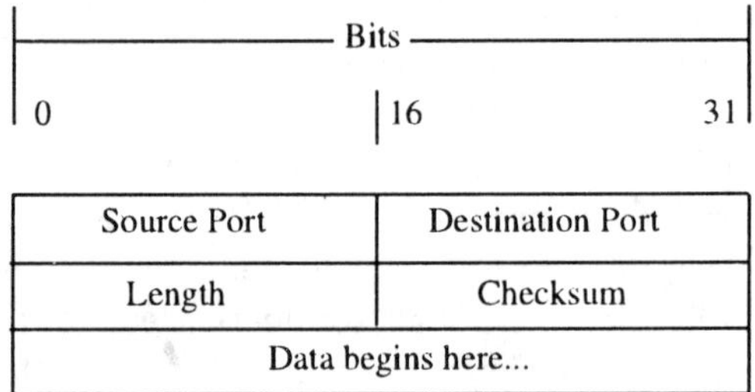

Fig. 14.11 UDP header format

The UDP header consists of four fields each of 2-bytes in length. The fields are:

- **Source Port :** This is an optional field and is set to a zero if not used. It identifies the local port number, which should be used when the destination host requires to contact the originator. (UDP packets from a client use this as a service access point (SAP) to indicate the session on the local client that originated the packet. UDP packets from a server carry the server SAP in this field) Since UDP is stateless and a UDP sender may not solicit replies, the source port is optional. If not used, the source port should be set to zero.
- **Destination Port :** Port to connect to on the destination. (UDP packets from a client use this as a service access point (SAP) to indicate the service required from the remote server. UDP packets from a server carry the client SAP in this field).
- **UDP length :** Number of bytes in the datagram, including the UDP header and the

data. (The number of bytes comprising the combined UDP header information and payload data) The port fields are followed by a mandatory length field specified as bytes of the UDP datagram including the data. The minimum value of the length field is 8 (octets).

- **UDP Checksum :** The 16-bit 1's complement of the 1's complement sum of the IP header, the UDP header, the data (which, if necessary, is padded with zero bytes at the end, to make an even number of bytes). (A checksum to verify that the end-to-end data has not been corrupted by routers or bridges in the network or by the processing in an end system. The algorithm to compute the checksum is the Standard Internet Checksum algorithm. If this check is not required, the value of 0×0000 is placed in this field, in which case the data is not checked by the receiver.) The remaining header field is a 16-bit checksum field covering the header and data. The checksum is also optional, but almost always used in practice.

Like for other transport protocols, the UDP header and data are not processed by Intermediate Systems (IS) in the network, and are delivered to the final destination in the same form as originally transmitted.

At the final destination, the UDP protocol layer receives packets from the IP network layer. These are checked using the checksum (when > 0, this checks correct end-to-end operation of the network service) and all invalid PDUs are discarded. UDP does not make any provision for error reporting if the packets are not delivered. Valid data are passed to the appropriate session layer protocol identified by the source and destination port numbers (i.e., the session service access points).

Generally, clients set the source port number to a unique number that they choose themselves—usually based on the program that started the connection. Since this number is returned by the server in responses, this lets the sender know which "conversation" incoming packets are to be sent to. The destination port of packets sent by the client is usually set to one of a number of well-known ports. These usually correspond to one of a number of different applications, e.g., port 23 is used for telnet, and port 80 is used for web servers.

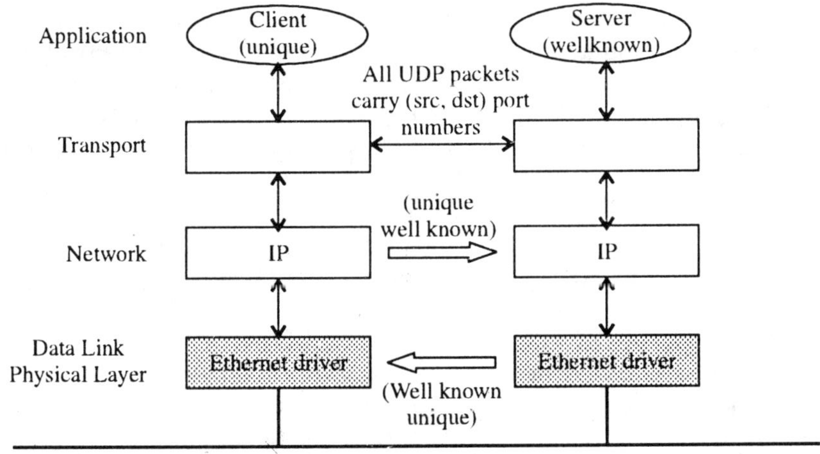

Fig. 14.12 UDP transmitting packets over an IP network using ethernet

A server process (program), listens for UDP packets received with a particular well-known port number and tells its local UDP layer to send packets matching this destination port number to the server program. It determines which client these packets come from by examining the received IP source address and the received unique UDP source port number. Any responses which the server needs to send to back to a client are sent with the source port number of the server (the well-known port number) and the destination port selected by the client.

14.5.2 Applications

UDP is used when hosts do not require making a connection with the other side, and where reliability is built into a high-layer protocol. It is also used when there is no segmentation of data (as there are no segment values). Some applications are solely TCP or solely UDP, whereas the rest can use either. For example:

- **TCP applications** : FTP, TELNET, SMTP, FINGER, DNS and LOGIN.
- **UDP applications** : RIP, TFTP, NFS and SNMP.
- **TCP or UDP applications** : HTTP, POP-3 and ECHO.

Applications of UDP include:

- **DNS** : Supports domain name mapping to IP addresses.
- **NFS** : Supports a distributed file system.
- **SNMP** : Supports network management for network devices.
- **TFTP (Trivial FTP)** : A simplified version of FTP (typically used to update computers/routers with firmware updates).

Applications programmers choose UDP as a data transport service for a number of reasons. If the amount of data being transmitted is small, the overhead of creating connections and ensuring reliable delivery may be greater than the work of re-transmitting the entire data set. In this case, UDP is the most efficient choice for a Transport Layer protocol. Applications that fit a query-response model are also excellent candidates for using UDP. The response can be used as a positive acknowledgment to the query. If a response isn't received within a certain time period, the application just sends another query. Still other applications provide their own techniques for reliable data delivery, and don't require that service from the transport layer protocol. Imposing another layer of acknowledgment on any of these types of applications is inefficient.

14.6 The Stream Control Transmission Protocol (SCTP)

It is a transport layer protocol defined in 2000 by the IETF (Internet Engineering Task Force—Founded in 1986, the IETF is a non-membership, open, voluntary standards organization dedicated to identifying problems and opportunities in IP data networks and proposing technical solutions to the Internet community). As a transport protocol, SCTP is equivalent in a sense to TCP or UDP. Indeed it provides some similar services as TCP, ensuring reliable, in-sequence transport of messages with congestion control. While TCP is byte-oriented, SCTP deals with framed messages.

SCTP is a reliable transport protocol operating on top of a potentially unreliable connectionless packet service such as IP. It offers acknowledged error-free non-duplicated transfer of datagrams (messages). Detection of data corruption, loss of data and duplication of data is achieved by using checksums and sequence numbers. A selective retransmission mechanism is applied to correct loss or corruption of data.

SCTP can be used as the transport protocol for applications where monitoring and detection of loss of session is required. For such applications, the SCTP path/session failure detection mechanisms, especially the heartbeat, will actively monitor the connectivity of the session.

A major contribution of SCTP is multi-homing support, where one (or both) endpoints of a connection can consist of more than one IP address, enabling transparent fail-over between hosts or network cards.

It offers the following services to its users:

- Acknowledged error-free non-duplicated transfer of user data.
- Data fragmentation to conform to discovered path MTU size.
- Sequenced delivery of user messages within multiple streams, with an option for order-of-arrival delivery of individual user messages.
- Optional bundling of multiple user messages into a single SCTP packet.
- Network-level fault tolerance through supporting of multi-homing at either or both ends of an association.

The design of SCTP includes appropriate congestion avoidance behavior and resistance to flooding and masquerade attacks.

14.7 The Datagram Congestion Control Protocol (DCCP)

It is a message-oriented transport layer protocol that is currently under development in the IETF. Applications that might make use of DCCP include those with timing constraints on the delivery of data such that reliable in-order delivery, when combined with congestion control, is likely to result in some information arriving at the receiver after it is no longer of use. Such applications might include streaming media and Internet telephony. Congestion control is the way that a network protocol discovers the available network capacity on a particular path. The primary motivation for the development of DCCP is to provide a way for such applications to gain access to standard congestion control mechanisms without having to implement them at the application layer.

DCCP is intended for applications that require the flow-based semantics of TCP, but which do not want TCP's in-order delivery and reliability semantics, or which would like different congestion control dynamics than TCP. Similarly, DCCP is intended for applications that do not require features of SCTP such as sequenced delivery within multiple streams.

To date most such applications have used either TCP, with the problems described above, or used UDP and implemented their own congestion control mechanisms (or no congestion control at all). The purpose of DCCP is to provide a standard way to implement congestion control and congestion control negotiation for such applications. One of the motivations for DCCP is to enable the use of ECN (Explicit Congestion Notification—explained below), along with conformant end-to-end congestion control, for applications that would otherwise be using UDP. In addition, DCCP implements reliable connection setup, teardown, and feature negotiation.

A DCCP connection contains acknowledgement traffic as well as data traffic. Acknowledgements inform a sender whether its packets arrived, and whether they were ECN marked. Acks are transmitted as reliably as the congestion control mechanism in use requires, possibly completely reliably.

IP ECN (Explicit Congestion Notification)

ECN is only used when the two hosts signal that they want to use it. With this method, an ECN bit is used to signal that there is explicit congestion. This is better in some ways than the indirect packet delete congestion notification but it requires explicit support by both hosts to be effective. Some outdated or buggy network equipment drops packets with the ECN bit set, rather than ignoring the bit.

• • •

15

Session And Presentation Layer

Introduction to the Session Layer

The fifth layer in the OSI Reference Model is the session layer. It is the lowest of the three upper layers, which collectively are concerned mainly with software application issues and not with the details of network and Internet implementation.

The name of this layer tells you much about what it is designed to do : to allow devices to establish and manage sessions. In general terms, a session is a persistent logical linking of two software application processes, to allow them to exchange data over a prolonged period of time. In some discussions, these sessions are called dialogs; they are roughly analogous to a telephone call made between two people.

The term "session" is somewhat vague, and this means that there is sometimes disagreement on the specific functions that belong at the session layer or even whether certain protocols belong at the session layer or not. To understand the meaning of session let us first differentiate between a "connection" and a "session". Connections are normally the province of layer four and layer three, yet a Transmission Control Protocol (TCP) connection, for example, can persist for a long time. The longevity of TCP connections makes them hard to distinguish from "sessions".

So we can say that a connection between two presentation layer processes is called a session. A presentation entity (PE) can only communicate with another PE through initiating or accepting a session connection. There may be a number of concurrent or consecutive session connections between the two PEs.

A session is a series of related connection-oriented transmissions between network nodes.

Another way to look at it is that a session is the interrelated communications between two or more presentation entities, which emphasizes that the Session layer provides services to the Presentation layer.

The session layer resides above the transport layer, and provides "value added" services to the underlying transport layer services. The session layer (along with the presentation layer) add services to the transport layer that are likely to be of use to applications, so that each application doesn't have to provide its own implementation.

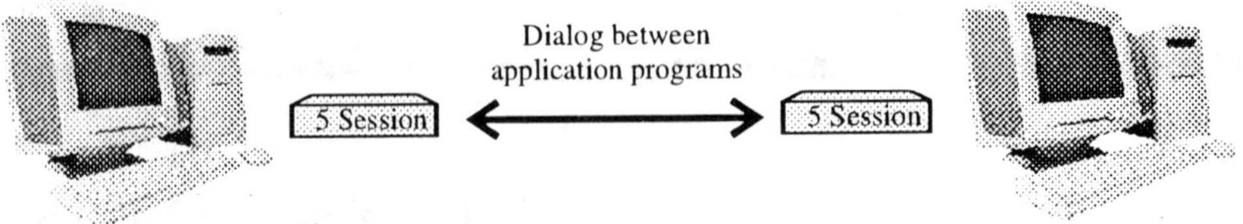

Fig. 15.1 Layer 5-Session Layer

Administration of Session in Session Layer

A session is a formal dialog between a service requester and a service provider. Sessions have at least three phases:

- **Connection establishment** : In this phase, a service requester requests initiation of a service. During the setup process, communication is established and rules are agreed upon. The connection establishment phase establishes the parameters for the communication session. Actually, the connection establishment phase is comprised of several tasks, including the following:
  - Specification of required services.
  - User login authentication and other security procedures.
  - Negotiation of protocols and protocol parameters.
  - Notification of connection Ids.
  - Establishment of dialog control, as well as acknowledgment of numbering and retransmission procedures.
- **Data transfer** : After the connection is established, the devices involved can initiate a dialog (data transfer phase). Besides exchanging data, these devices exchange acknowledgments and other control data that manage the dialog. Because of the rules agreed upon during setup, each party to the dialog knows what to expect. Communication is therefore efficient, and errors are easy to detect. The Session layer also can incorporate protocols to resume dialogs that have been interrupted. After a formal dialog has been established, devices recognize a lost connection whenever the connection has not been formally released. Therefore, a device realizes that a connection has been lost when the device fails to receive an expected acknowledgment or data transmission.

  Data transfer is provided in four forms : normal, expedited, capability and typed.

Normal data transfer is the ordinary data delivery method. **Expedited data** has some priority and is able to bypass some restrictions that might impede the transfer of normal data. Expedited data is restricted to small packets, whereas normal data has no such restriction. **Typed** and **capability data** types are specific to the Session Layer. They are used principally to permit overrides of dialog control mechanisms that may be in effect.

- **Connection release** : When the session is completed, the dialog is terminated in an orderly fashion. Within a certain time period, two devices can reenter the session that was interrupted but not released. The connection release phase is an orderly process that shuts down communication and releases resources on the service provider.

In connectionless mode the only purpose of the session layer is to provide a one-to-one mapping of transport to session addresses.

15.1 Design Issues Of Session Layer

The session layer provides the following services:

1. Dialog Management

A dialog is defined to be the series of sessions used for a complex process or transfer of a large quantity of data. Dialog management is basically deciding whose turn it is to talk. Some applications operate in half-duplex mode, whereby the two sides alternate between sending and receiving messages and never send data simultaneously.

In the ISO protocols, dialog management is implemented through the use of a data token. The token is sent back and forth and a user may transmit only when it possesses the token. The Session layer manages dialogs between two computers by establishing, managing, and terminating communications. As illustrated in Figure 15.2, dialogs can take three forms:

- **Simplex dialogs** : These dialogs are responsible for only one-way data transfers. An example is a fire alarm, which sends an alarm message to the fire station but cannot (and does not need to) receive messages from the fire station.
- **Half-duplex dialogs** : These dialogs handle two-way data transfers in which the data flows in only one direction at a time. When one device completes a transmission, this device must "turn over" the medium to the other device so that this second device has a turn to transmit. For example, CB radio operators, converse on the same communication channel. When one operator is finished transmitting, he must release his transmit key so that the other operator can send a response.
- **Full-duplex dialogs** : This third type of dialog permits two-way simultaneous data transfers by providing each device with a separate communication channel. Voice telephones are full-duplex devices, and either party to a conversation can talk at any time. Most computer modems can operate in full-duplex mode.

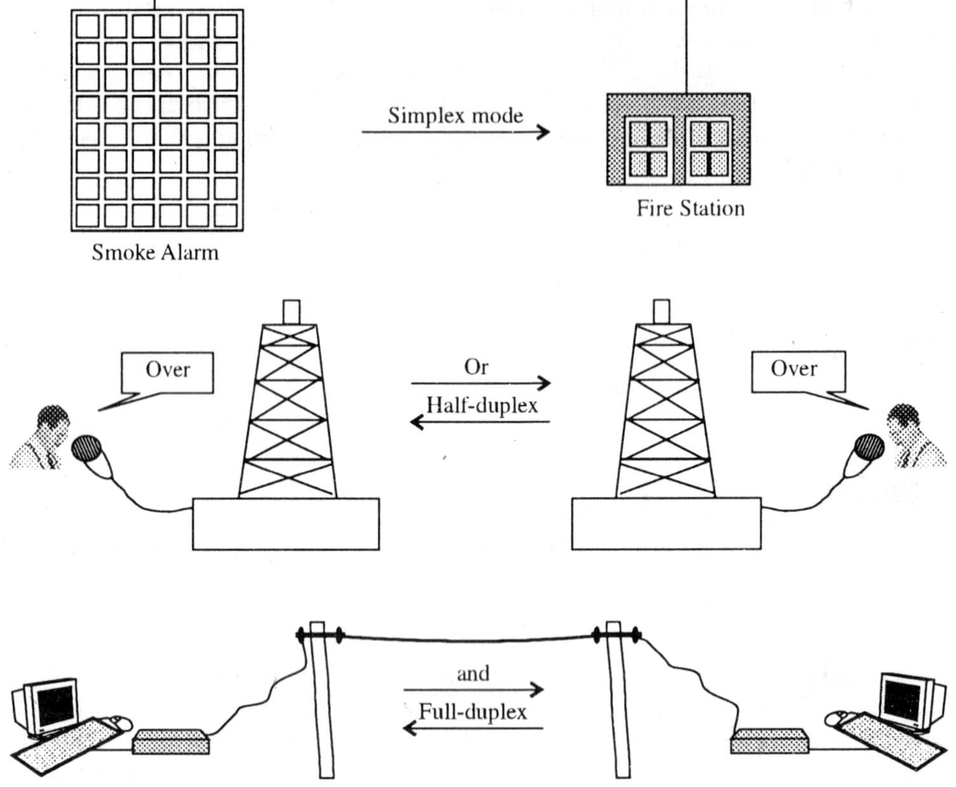

Fig. 15.2 Simplex and duplex communication modes

The Session layer also marks the data stream with checkpoints and monitors the receipt of those checkpoints. In the event of a failure, the sending PC can retransmit starting with the data sent after the last checkpoint, rather than resending the whole message.

2. Synchronization

It is basically moving the two session entities into a known state. The transport layer handles only communication errors, synchronization deals with upper layer errors. In a file transfer, for instance, the transport layer might deliver data correctly, but the application layer might be unable to write the file because the file system is full.

Users can split the data stream into pages, inserting synchronization points between each page. When an error occurs, the receiver can resynchronize the state of the session to a previous synchronization point. This requires that the sender hold data as long as may be needed.

Synchronization is achieved through the use of sequence numbers. The ISO protocols provide both major and minor synchronization points. When resynchronizing, one can only go back as far as the previous major synchronization point. In addition, major synchronization points are acknowledged through explicit messages (making their use expensive). In contrast, minor synchronization points are just markers. So following synchronization methods can be defined:

- **Initial synchronization** : Occurs when the session ID and start sequence numbers are generated.
- **Major synchronization** : During reset of session, it reestablishes ID and sequence numbers.
- **Minor synchronization** : Fine tunes in existing sessions, assumes prior data is okay.
- **Resynchronization**
  - Restart but use checkpoints in prior data.
  - Abandon—drop session and reinitiate, discarding data.

3. Activity Management

It allows the user to delimit data into logical units called activities. Each activity is independent of activities that come before and after it, and an activity can be processed on its own. Activities might be used to delimit files of a multi-file transfer.

Activities are also used for quarantining, collecting all the messages of a multi-message exchange together before processing them. The receiving application would begin processing messages only after all the messages had arrived. This provides a way of helping to insure that all or none of a set of operations are performed.

For example, a bank transaction may consist of locking a record, updating a value, and then unlocking the record. If an application processed the first operation, but never received the remaining operations (due to client or network failures), the record would remain locked forever. Quarantining addresses this problem.

Quarantine service allows for a sending PE (Presentation Entity) to request that an integral number of SSDUs should not be made available to the receiving PE until explicitly released by the sending PE. This is transparent to the receiving PE and some or all data may be discarded by the sending PE without it knowing.

4. Exception Handling

A general purpose mechanism for reporting errors. It allows for PEs to be notified of unrecoverable session malfunctions and other problems not covered by other services.

The collection of services available on a particular connection is subject to selection by the Presentation entity that establishes the connection. Specific Session-Layer services are grouped together into functional units. Functional units define a number of frequently chosen operational styles and their selection is a matter of negotiation at the time of connection establishment.

World-Wide Web applications often require large files to travel across the network. Session Layer services could be employed to assist in recovery of interrupted transfers. The synchronization issue is dealt with by the client/server mode of operation. The client requests a file from the server and the server sends it if possible. The client then goes on with other processing. Synchronization between the client and server is not an issue in this model.

15.2 Session Layer Protocols

The session layer implementation of the OSI protocol suite consists of a session protocol and a session service. The session protocol allows session-service users (SS-users) to communicate with the session service. An SS-user is an entity that requests the services of the session layer. Such requests are made at session-service access points (SSAPs), and SS-users are uniquely identified by using an SSAP address.

Session service provides four basic services to SS-users.

1. It establishes and terminates connections between SS-users and synchronizes the data exchange between them.
2. It performs various negotiations for the use of session layer tokens, which the SS-user must possess to begin communicating.
3. It inserts synchronization points in transmitted data that allow the session to be recovered in the event of errors or interruptions.
4. Finally, it enables SS-users to interrupt a session and resume it later at a specific point.

The following services and protocols are defined on the Sessions layer:

- RPC (Remote Procedure Call).
- ASP (AppleTalk Session Protocol).
- SQL (Structured Query Language).
- NFS (Network File Services).
- SCP (Serial Communications Protocol).
- ZIP (AppleTalk Zone Information Protocol).

From the above list of protocols we will discuss RPC in detail.

15.2.1 Remote Procedure Call (RPC)

RPC is a powerful technique for constructing distributed, client-server based applications. It is based on extending the notion of conventional, or local procedure calling, so that the called procedure need not exist in the same address space as the calling procedure. The two processes may be on the same system, or they may be on different systems with a network connecting them. By using RPC, programmers of distributed applications avoid the details of the interface with the network. The transport independence of RPC isolates the application from the physical and logical elements of the data communications mechanism and allows the application to use a variety of transports.

RPC makes the client/server model of computing more powerful and easier to program. RPC was developed by Sun Microsystems, and is a collection of tools and library functions.

Important applications built on top of RPC are NFS, the Network Filesystem, and NIS, the Network Information System.

Remote Procedure Call provides a different paradigm for accessing network services. Instead of accessing remote services by sending and receiving messages, a client invokes services by making a local procedure call. The local procedure hides the details of the network communication.

Purpose of RPC

Remote Procedure Call (RPC) is a client/server infrastructure that increases the interoperability, portability and flexibility of an application by allowing the application to be distributed over multiple heterogeneous platforms. It reduces the complexity of developing applications that span multiple operating systems and network protocols by insulating the application developer from the details of the various operating system and network interfaces.

Characteristics of RPC

The main characteristics of RPC are listed below:

- No reliability is implemented with RPC and reliability is left to the application.
- RPC does not rely on a specific transport protocol.
- RPC can run on any operating system.
- Fields for client and server identification and authorization are provided.

The main goal of RPC is to hide the existence of the network from a program. As a result, RPC doesn't quite fit into the OSI model:

1. The message-passing nature of network communication is hidden from the user. The user doesn't first open a connection, read and write data and then close the connection. Indeed, a client often does not even know they are using the network.
2. RPC often omits many of the protocol layers to improve performance. Even a small performance improvement is important because a program may invoke RPCs often.

RPC is especially well suited for client-server (e.g., query-response) interaction in which the flow of control alternates between the caller and callee. Conceptually, the client and server do not both execute at the same time. Instead, the thread of execution jumps from the caller to the callee and then back again. When making a remote procedure call:

1. The calling environment is suspended, procedure parameters are transferred across the network to the environment where the procedure is to execute and the procedure is executed there.
2. When the procedure finishes and produces its results, its results are transferred back to the calling environment, where execution resumes as if returning from a regular procedure call.

How RPC Works ?

An RPC is analogous to a function call. Like a function call, when an RPC is made, the calling arguments are passed to the remote procedure and the caller waits for a response to be returned from the remote procedure. The client makes a procedure call that sends a request to the server and waits. The thread is blocked from processing until either a reply is received, or it times out. When the request arrives, the server calls a dispatch routine that performs the requested service and sends the reply to the client. After the RPC call is completed, the client program continues. RPC specifically supports network applications.

A remote procedure is uniquely identified by the triple: (program number, version number, procedure number). The program number identifies a group of related remote procedures, each of which has a unique procedure number. A program may consist of one or more versions. Each version consists of a collection of procedures that are available to be called remotely. Version numbers enable multiple versions of an RPC protocol to be available simultaneously. Each version contains a number of procedures that can be called remotely. Each procedure has a procedure number.

The following steps take place during an RPC:

1. A client invokes a client stub procedure, passing parameters in the usual way. The client stub resides within the client's own address space.
2. The client stub marshalls the parameters into a message. Marshalling includes converting the representation of the parameters into a standard format and copying each parameter into the message.
3. The client stub passes the message to the transport layer, which sends it to the remote server machine.
4. On the server, the transport layer passes the message to a server stub, which demarshalls the parameters and calls the desired server routine using the regular procedure call mechanism.
5. When the server procedure completes, it returns to the server stub (e.g., via a normal procedure call return), which marshalls the return values into a message. The server stub then hands the message to the transport layer.
6. The transport layer sends the result message back to the client transport layer, which hands the message back to the client stub.
7. The client stub demarshalls the return parameters and execution returns to the caller.

The Remote Procedure Call (RPC) message protocol consists of two distinct structures: the call message and the reply message. The message flows are displayed as follows:

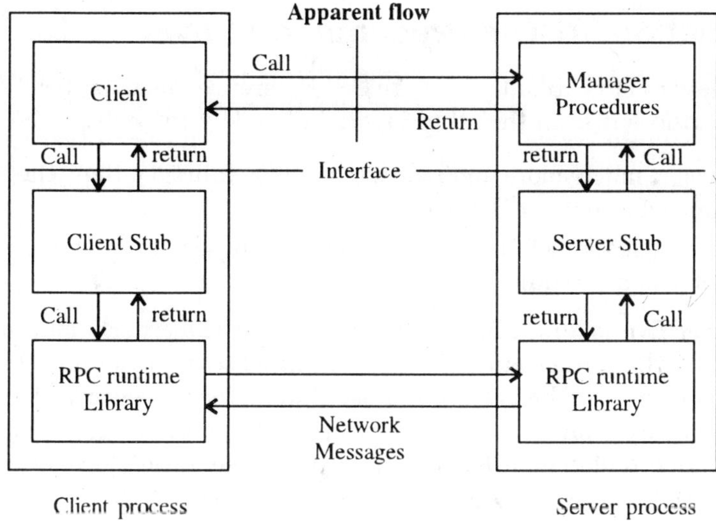

Fig. 15.3 Remote procedure call flow

RPC Issues

Some of the issues that must be addressed by RPC are listed below:

- **Marshalling :** Parameters must be marshalled into a standard representation. Parameters consist of simple types (e.g., integers) and compound types (e.g., C structures or Pascal records). Moreover, because each type has its own representation, the types of the various parameters must be known to the modules that actually do the conversion. For example, 4 bytes of characters would be uninterpreted, while a 4-byte integer may need to the order of its bytes reversed.
- **Semantics :** Call-by-reference not possible: the client and server don't share an address space. That is, addresses referenced by the server correspond to data residing in the client's address space. One approach is to simulate call-by-reference using copy-restore. In copy-restore, call-by-reference parameters are handled by sending a copy of the referenced data structure to the server, and on return replacing the client's copy with that modified by the server.
  However, copy-restore doesn't work in all cases. For instance, if the same argument is passed twice, two copies will be made and references through one parameter only changes one of the copies.
- **Binding :** How does the client know who to call, and where the service resides? The most flexible solution is to use dynamic binding and find the server at run time when the RPC is first made. The first time the client stub is invoked, it contacts a name server to determine the transport address at which the server resides.

15.3 Introduction To The Presentation Layer

The presentation layer is the sixth layer of the OSI Reference Model protocol stack, and second from the top. It is different from the other layers in two key respects.

- First, it has a much more limited and specific function than the other layers; it's actually somewhat easy to describe.
- Second, it is used much less often than the other layers and in many types of connections it is not required.

Unlike the lower five layers, which merely deal with the orderly movement of bits from source to destination, the presentation layer is concerned with preserving the 'meaning' of the information transported. It is the job of the presentation layer to encode structured data from the internal format used on the sending machine to a bit stream format suitable for transmission, and then to decode it to the required representation at the destination.

The name of this layer suggests its main function as well: it deals with the presentation of data. More specifically, the presentation layer is charged with taking care of any issues that might arise where data sent from one system needs to be viewed in a different way by the other system. It also takes care of any special processing that must be done to data from the time an application tries to send it until the time it is sent over the network.

The name "Presentation layer" has caused considerable confusion in the industry because some people mistakenly believe that this layer presents data to the user. However, the name has nothing to do with displaying data. Instead, this function is performed by applications running above the Application layer. The Presentation layer is so named because it presents a uniform data format to the Application layer. As a matter of fact, this layer is not commonly implemented because applications typically perform most Presentation layer functions.

The presentation layer serves as the data translator for the network. This layer on the sending computer translates the data sent by the application layer into a common format. At the receiving computer, the presentation layer translates the common format to a format known to the application layer.

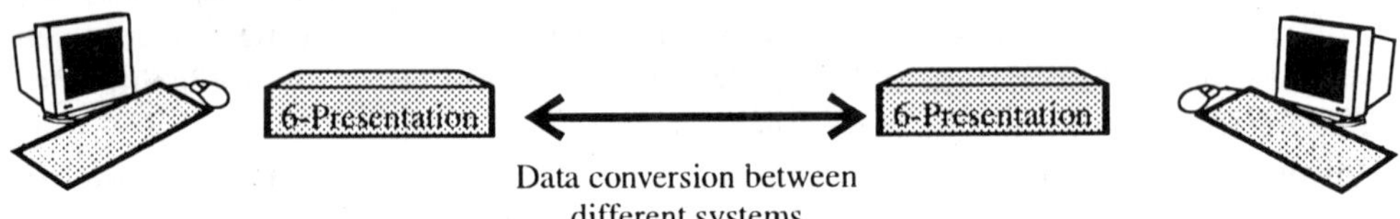

Fig. 15.4 Layer 6-Presentation Layer

15.4 Design Issues of Presentation Layer

The presentation layer is responsible for presenting data in a form that the receiving device can understand. The presentation layer serves as the translator for devices that need to communicate over a network. Layer 6 provides three main functions that are explained below:

- **Translation :** Networks can connect very different types of computers together : PCs, Macintoshes, UNIX systems, AS/400 servers and mainframes can all exist on the same network. These systems have many distinct characteristics and represent data in different ways; they may use different character sets for example. The presentation layer handles the job of hiding these differences between machines.
- **Compression :** Compression (and decompression) may be done at the presentation layer to improve the throughput of data. (More explanation in next section)
- **Encryption :** Some types of encryption (and decryption) are performed at the presentation layer. This ensures the security of the data as it travels down the protocol stack. For example, one of the most popular encryption schemes that is usually associated with the presentation layer is the Secure Sockets Layer (SSL) protocol. Not all encryption is done at layer 6, however; some encryption is often done at lower layers in the protocol stack.

After receiving data from the application layer, the presentation layer performs one, or all, of its functions on the data before it sends it to the session layer. At the receiving station, the presentation layer takes the data from the session layer and performs the required functions before passing it to the application layer.

On the receiving end, the Presentation layer converts the machine-independent data from the network into the format required for the local system. This conversion could include the following:

- **Bit-order translation :** When binary numbers are transmitted through a network, they are sent one bit at a time. The transmitting computer can start at either end of the number. Some computers start at the most-significant digit (MSD); others start at the least-significant digit (LSD).
- **Byte-order translation :** Complex values generally must be represented with more than one byte, but different computers use different conventions to determine which byte should be transmitted first. Intel microprocessors, for example, start with the least-significant byte and are called *little endian.* Motorola microprocessors, on the other hand, start with the most-significant byte and are called *big endian.* Byte-order translation might be needed to reconcile these differences when transferring data between a PC and a Macintosh.
- **Character code translation :** Different computers use different binary schemes for representing character sets. For instance: *ASCII*, the American Standard Code for Information Interchange, is used to represent English characters on all microcomputers and most minicomputers; *EBCDIC*, the Extended Binary Coded Decimal Interchange Code, is used to represent English characters on IBM mainframes; and *Shift JIS* is used to represent Japanese characters.
- **File Syntax Translation :** File formats differ between computers. For instance, Macintosh files actually consist of two related files called a data fork and a resource fork. PC files, on the other hand, consist of a single file.

Presentation Layer Role in the OSI Model

The reason that the presentation layer is not always used in network communications is that the jobs mentioned above are simply not always needed. Compression and encryption are usually considered "optional" and translation features are also only needed in certain circumstances. Another reason why the presentation layer is sometimes not mentioned is that its functions may be performed as part of the application layer.

The fact that the translation job done by the presentation layer isn't always needed means that it is common for it to be "skipped" by actual protocol stack implementations. This means that protocols at layer seven may talk directly with those at layer five.

Now let us discuss the main functions of presentation layer in detail in next sections.

15.4.1 Data Formatting

To understand how data formatting works, imagine two dissimilar systems. The first system uses Extended Binary Coded Decimal Interchange Code (EBCDIC) to represent characters onscreen. The second system uses American Standard Code for Information Interchange (ASCII) for the same function. Layer 6 provides the translation between these two different types of codes.

Layer 6 standards also determine how graphic images are presented. Three of these standards are as follows:

- **PICT**—is a picture format used to transfer QuickDraw graphics between programs on the MAC operating system.
- **TIFF** (Tagged Image File Format)—a format for high-resolution, bit-mapped images.
- **JPEG** (Joint Photographic Experts Group)—graphic format used most often to compress still images of complex pictures and photographs.

Other Layer 6 standards guide the presentation of sound and movies. Included in these standards are the following:

- **MIDI** (Musical Instrument Digital Interface)—for digitized music.
- **MPEG** (Motion Picture Experts Group) is a standard for the compression and coding of motion video for CDs and digital storage.
- QuickTime is a standard that handles audio and video for programs on both MAC and PC operating system.

Conversions standards defined on the Presentation Layer for data conversion and formatting:

Category	Standards
Data Conversion	ASCII, EBCDIC, encryption
Audio/video conversion	MIDI, MPEG, QuickTime, AVI
Graphics conversion	GIF, JPEG, PICT, TIFF

15.4.2 Data Encryption

Encryption is scrambling the data so that only authorized participants can unscramble the messages of a conversation. Recall, that it's easy to "wiretap" transmission media such as Ethernets.

Layer 6 is also responsible for data encryption. Data encryption protects information during its transmission. Financial transactions (e.g., credit card information) use encryption to protect sensitive information as it traverses the Internet. An encryption key is used to encrypt the data at its source and then to decrypt the data at its destination.

The location of encryption in the OSI model has been so controversial that all mention of the subject was omitted from the initial standard. In theory, encryption can be done in any layer, but in practice three layers seem the most suitable: physical, transport, and presentation.

When encryption is done on the physical layer, an encryption unit is inserted between each computer and the physical medium. Every bit leaving the computer is encrypted and every bit entering a computer is decrypted. This scheme is called link encryption. It is simple, but relatively inflexible.

When encryption is done in the transport layer, the entire session is encrypted. A more sophisticated approach is to put it in the presentation layer, so that only those data structures or fields requiring encryption must suffer the overhead of it.

The messages to be encrypted, known as **plaintext** are transformed by a function that is parameterized by a key. The output of this is known as **ciphertext.** There are three main ways to achieve this in increasing complexity.

- **Substitution ciphers** use a direct mapping function and are open to cracking. For example if we are dealing with straight alphabetical characters we might employ the following substitution.
  - ☐ plaintext : abcdefghijklmnopqrstuvwxyz.
  - ☐ ciphertext : QWERTYUIOPASDFDFGHJKLZXCVBNM.

This general system is called a monoalphabetical substitution with the key being the 26-letter string corresponding to the full alphabet.

This type of encipherment is easily attacked by using the statistical properties of natural languages. i.e., we might note that *e* is the most common letter and decipher the ciphertext on this statistical basis.

- **Transposition ciphers** reorder the letters but do not disguise them. You use a key to reorder the original plaintext. However like a substitution cipher it is open to attack.
- The **Data Encryption Standard** is recognized as an industry standard currently. It is based on both substitution and transposition techniques. Operating on a 64-bit stream of plaintext a series of substitutions and permutations are performed using a 56-bit key. To make it even more effective the key may be changed over time by EX-ORing with the plaintext at either end. This leads to the key being dependent on the history of all previous transmissions of that session.

Despite all its complexity, DES is basically a monoalphabetic substitution cipher using a 64-bit alphabet. (More about encryption in chapter 17)

15.4.3 Data Compression

The presentation layer is also responsible for the compression of files. Data compression squeezes data so it requires less disk space for storage and less bandwidth on a data transmission channel. Communications equipment like modems, bridges and routers use compression schemes to improve throughput over standard phone lines or leased lines. Compression is also used to compress voice telephone calls transmitted over leased lines so that more calls can be placed on those lines. In addition, compression is essential for videoconferencing applications that run over data networks. Compression works by using algorithms (complex mathematical formulas) to shrink the size of the files. The algorithm searches each file for repeating bit patterns and then replaces them with a token. A token is a much shorter bit pattern that represents the long pattern.

The aim of data compression is to reduce redundancy in stored or communicated data, thus increasing effective data density. Data compression has important application in the areas of file storage and distributed systems. Most compression schemes take advantage of the fact that data contains a lot of repetition. For example, alphanumeric characters are normally represented by a 7-bit ASCII code, but a compression scheme can use a 3-bit code to represent the eight most common letters.

In addition, long stretches of "nothing" can be replaced by a value that indicates how much "nothing" there is. For example, silence in a compressed audio recording can be replaced by a value that indicates how long that silence is. White space in a compressed graphic image can be replaced by a value that indicates the amount of white space.

A simple characterization of data compression is that it involves transforming a string of characters in some representation (such as ASCII) into a new string (of bits, for example) which contains the same information but whose length is as small as possible. Data compression has important application in the areas of data transmission and data storage. Many data processing applications require storage of large volumes of data and the number of such applications is constantly increasing as the use of computers extends to new disciplines. At the same time, the proliferation of computer communication networks is resulting in massive transfer of data over communication links.

Compressing data to be stored or transmitted reduces storage and/or communication costs. When the amount of data to be transmitted is reduced, the effect is that of increasing the capacity of the communication channel. Similarly, compressing a file to half of its original size is equivalent to doubling the capacity of the storage medium. It may then become feasible to store the data at a higher, thus faster, level of the storage hierarchy and reduce the load on the input/output channels of the computer system.

Two important compression concepts are lossy and lossless compression:

- **Lossy compression :** With lossy compression, it is assumed that some loss of information is acceptable. The best example is a videoconference where there is an acceptable amount of frame loss in order to deliver the image in real time. People may appear jerky in their movements, but you still have a grasp for what is happening on the other end of the conference. In the case of graphics files, some resolution may be lost in order to create a smaller file. The loss may be in the form of color depth or graphic detail. For example, high-resolution details can be lost if a picture is going to be displayed on a low-resolution device. Loss is also acceptable in voice and audio compression, depending on the desired quality. The techniques that we will discuss under this category are listed below:

- JPEG.
- MPEG.

- **Lossless compression :** With lossless compression, data is compressed without any loss of data. It assumes you want to get everything back that you put in. Critical financial data files are examples where lossless compression is required. The techniques that we will discuss under this category are listed below:

  - Run-Length Encoding
  - Huffman Encoding
  - Lempel-Ziv-Welch Encoding

The removal of information in the lossy technique is acceptable for images, because the loss of information is usually imperceptible to the human eye. While this trick works on humans, you may not be able to use lossy images in some situations, such as when scanners are used to locate details in images.

Lossy compression can provide compression ratios of 100 : 1 to 200 : 1, depending on the type of information being compressed. Lossless compression ratios usually only achieve a 2 : 1 compression ratio. Lossy compression techniques are often "tunable" in that you can turn the compression up to improve throughput, but at a loss in quality. Compression can also be turned downed to the point at which there is little loss of image, but throughput will be affected.

15.4.3.1 Basic compression techniques

Data compression is often referred to as coding, where coding is a very general term encompassing any special representation of data that satisfies a given need. Information theory is defined to be the study of efficient coding and its consequences, in the form of speed of transmission and probability of error. Data compression may be viewed as a branch of information theory in which the primary objective is to minimize the amount of data to be transmitted.

Because compression algorithms are software-based, overhead exists that can cause problems in real-time environments. Compression is processor intensive, so for real-time data transmissions like network links, you will need a system on both ends of the link that can compress and decompress data without causing appreciable delays. Some applications may not tolerate any delays, in which case you may need to tune the compression levels and/or boost the processing power to remove those delays.

Another consideration is that compression affects the portability of files. You will need to make sure that all recipients have the software needed to decompress files. Note that some files are already compressed to begin with and don't benefit from any further external compression techniques. Some graphics file formats, such as TIFF (Tagged Image File Format), are automatically compressed when they are stored.

File compression is handled in several ways. Various utilities are available that let you compress files one at a time or as a group. Groups of files can be compressed into a single file that is much easier to send to another user. A decompression utility unpacks the files. Nearly universal file compression utilities are PKZip and WINZip from Niko Mak Computing. A file or a group of files can be compressed into a zip file (called an archive if multiple files are compressed into it) that can be decompressed by anybody else that has the utility, or you can create self-extracting files that can be opened by anyone who does not have the utility. Most operating systems, including DOS, NetWare, Windows NT, and others, now include disk compression software. Some file encryption utilities also include compression routines so you can make files private and compress files in the same steps.

There are three general approaches to data compression that are listed below:

- Finite Set of Symbols.
- Huffman Encoding.
- Context Dependent Encoding.

Each approach assumes that the data stream can be transformed into a more compact representation, which the receiver reconstructs back into the original data.

1. Finite Set of Symbols

Consider a library with many branch offices in which the previous days transactions are sent to every other branch after closing. Transactions consist of checked out and returned books. We could exchange information in the following ways:

1. We could send the name of the book, its author, the copy number etc. together with the type of transaction.
2. Alternatively, the library could maintain a sitewide table assigning a unique ID number to every book in every branch. Transactions could then refer to the book's ID number, rather than its title. Because book IDs are small (e.g., a few bytes), less data will be transmitted.

The above technique is used throughout programming. We frequently exchange pointers and array subscripts to avoid the cost of transferring large amounts of data between subroutines.

The previous approach assumes that all objects occur with equal frequency and that the set of objects (e.g., books) is finite. If we examine text, however, we immediately notice that some words appear more often than others. We could reduce the number of bits needed to represent a document by using a coding scheme that employs small code words to represent common words and longer code words to represent words the appear infrequently.

2. Adaptive Huffman Coding and Lempel-Ziv-Welch Algorithms

These compression techniques use a symbol dictionary to represent recurring patterns. The dictionary is dynamically updated during compression as new patterns occur. For data transmissions, the dictionary is passed to a receiving system so it knows how to decode the characters. For file storage, the dictionary is stored with the compressed file.

Huffman encoding is a technique used to encode symbols according to the frequency of their use. The algorithm is as follows:

1. Create a set of nodes, one node per symbol, with a node's value given by the probability of its occurrence in the data.
2. Find the two nodes having the smallest value, remove them from the set and create a new node having the two removed nodes as children and assign the new node a value that is the sum of its children's values. Add the new node back to the set of nodes.
3. Repeat step 2 until only one node remains. We now have a tree, whose probability value is one.
4. The encoding for each symbol is the path from the root to the symbol. Using a code of 0 for a left child, 1 for a right child, the length of each symbol's encoding is proportional to the relative probability of its occurrence.

One drawback with Huffman encoding, however, is that symbols have differing lengths, making it relatively expensive (computationally) to decode. Also, A single-bit error can wipe out the entire message.

In the **Lempel-Ziv data-compression algorithm**, all single character strings occupy the table. As new strings appear, a tree structure is created, similar to Figure 15.5, which shows the "*T*" branch of the tree. Note that a three-character word can be deduced by following any branch of the tree. Each branch of the tree is identified by a codeword and the codeword is sent in any transmissions. If a new string appears, nodes are added to an appropriate branch of the tree and a new codeword is generated to represent it.

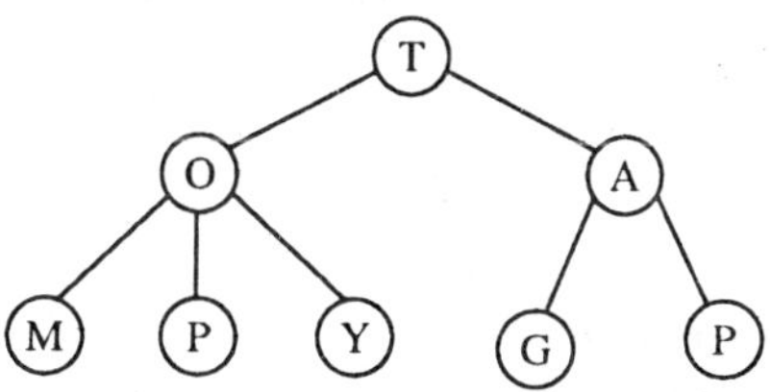

Fig. 15.5 Lempel-Ziv data compression

3. Context Dependent Encoding

The last technique, context dependent encoding, recognizes that the probability of a particular symbol occurring next depends on the previous symbol. For instance, the probability that a "T" directly follows a "*Q*" is about 4 times less than the probability of a "*U*" following a "*Q*".

The main disadvantage of conditional probability methods is the increase in table space.

Each symbol has its own table that gives the codes for those symbols immediately following it. For K symbols, the tables will contain K^2 entries. All K symbols have K entries for the symbols that follow them.

One variation to this technique is as follows:

1. Use 5-bit code to represent symbols.
2. Have four different "modes", where the current mode determines the meaning of symbols. Four symbols are reserved to denote a switch to another mode. For instance, different modes could represent upper-case characters, lower-case characters, numeric and special characters, and control characters.
3. The underlying assumption is that lower-case letters are likely to follow lower-case letters, numbers are likely to occur in groups, etc.
4. The occurrence of a mode symbol signifies a mode change.
5. Our 5-bit code now represents $4 \times 28 = 112$ different values.

One advantage that the above technique has over Huffman encoding is that symbols are all fixed length, making encoding and decoding using table lookups very efficient. In addition, it is more immune to transmission errors.

Run Length Encoding

Another alternative, run length encoding, is used to encode data containing repetitive symbols. Consider binary strings of 0s and 1s. One way to handle long runs of 0 is to use a k-bit symbol that tells how many 0 bits occurred between consecutive 1's. A code word of all 1's means that the true distance is $2^K - 1$ plus the value of the following symbol(s). For example:

00010000101001100000000000000000000000000100000001 (47-bits)
consists of runs of length 3, 4, 1, 2, 0, 23 and 7.

Using 4-bit symbols, it would be encoded as:

0011 0100 0001 0010 0000 1111 0100 0111, for 32-bits

and a savings of 15/47 = 30%.

Using 3-bit symbols, it would be encoded as:

011 100 001 010 000 111 111 111 010 111 000 for 33-bits.

15.4.3.2 Graphics/video compression

There are number of compression techniques designed to store graphic images in a much smaller space. Image compression also improves throughput when images files are transmitted from one place to another. Several compression techniques are discussed below:

- **DCT (discrete cosine transform) :** DCT is a common compression technique in which data is represented as a series of cosine waves. In the case of video, this technique replaces continuous sampling with an equation that represents the data. In the case of a still image, 8×8 blocks of information are converted into a wave that describes the number of color shifts and the extent of change in those color shifts.

- **Fractal compression :** The basic idea is to break an image down into smaller and smaller tiles. The compression engine (a dedicated board) searches for matching patterns in the image using a mathematical transformation that manipulates tiles in various ways. Repetitive patterns are saved to reconstruct the original, and unmatched data that is considered unimportant is discarded.
- **Wavelet transform :** When using a wavelet transform to describe an image, an average of the coefficients-in this case, pixels-is taken. Then the detail coefficients are calculated. Another average is taken, and more detail coefficients are calculated. This process continues until the image is completely described or the level of detail necessary to represent the image is achieved. As more detail coefficients are described, the image becomes clearer and less blocky. Once the wavelet transform is complete, a picture can be displayed at any resolution by recursively adding and subtracting the detail coefficients from a lower-resolution version. This technique is used by Iterated Systems.

JPEG (Joint Photographic Experts Group) Compression

It is an ITU and ISO standardized method for compressing still images using DCT, which converts three-dimensional color and coordinate image information into a format that is more responsive to compression. Color information is also encoded and some is discarded, depending on the desired end-results resolution. Compression can be lossless or lossy. The resulting information is then compressed using RLE, a special technique that compresses similar regions.

MPEG (Motion Picture Experts Group)

MPEG is developing several video compression standards that define formatting, data rates and compression techniques for international use. MPEG uses compression methods like DCT. Note that JPEG and MPEG are not related, although they are developed by the same organization. JPEG is for still images while MPEG is specifically designed for motion video.

• • •

16

Application Layer

Introduction

In the Open Systems Interconnection (OSI) communications model, the Application layer provides services for an application program to ensure that effective communication with another application program in a network is possible. This layer provides the interface to the communications environment, which is used by the application process. It is responsible for communicating application process parameters.

The application layer contains a variety of protocols that are commonly needed. For example, there are hundreds of incompatible terminal types in the world. Consider the plight of a full screen editor that is supposed to work over a network with many different terminal types, each with different screen layouts, escape sequences for inserting and deleting text, moving the cursor, etc.

One way to solve this problem is to define an abstract network virtual terminal for which editors and other programs can be written to deal with. To handle each terminal type, a piece of software must be written to map the functions of the network virtual terminal onto the real terminal. For example, when the editor moves the virtual terminal's cursor to the upper left-hand corner of the screen, this software must issue the proper command sequence to the real terminal to get its cursor there too. All the virtual terminal software is in the application layer.

Another application layer function is file transfer. Different file systems have different file naming conventions, different ways of representing text lines, and so on. Transferring a file between two different systems requires handling these and other incompatibilities. This work, too, belongs to the application layer, as do electronic mail, remote job entry, directory lookup, and various other general-purpose and special-purpose facilities.

The Applications distributed over networks share common needs. They are:

1. Establish a context for communication between separated processes.
2. Execute instructions on a remote system.
3. Reliable transfer of larger data volumes.
4. Coordinate components of a distributed application to avoid inconsistencies of state in shared data.

The Application layer is NOT the application itself that is doing the communication. It is a service layer that provides these services:

- Information transfer.
- Identification of intended communication partner, by name, address or some other description.
- Establishment of the authority of the application process to use the communication services.
- Determination of the availability of intended communication partner.
- Agreement of privacy mechanisms required for communication.
- Authentication of intended communication partners.
- Resource costing.
- Determination of the adequacy of the resources available for intended communication.
- Determination of service quality.
- Synchronization between applications.
- Selection of dialogue discipline. Including initiation and release procedures.
- Agreement on who has responsibility for error recovery.
- Agreement on procedures ensuring data integrity.

It may be convenient to think of the Application layer as the high-level set-up services for the application program or an interactive user.

Application Requirements

- **Bandwidth** : How many bits/sec required? Smooth or bursty traffic stream?
- **Holding time** : How long does application run?
- **Data-level reliability** : Reliable (in-order, no loss) delivery needed?
- **Performance** : Constraints on maximum application-to-application delay, tail of delay distribution?
- **QoS** : Quality of service guarantees required?
- **Communication structure** : 1-1, 1-many, many-many?
- **Security** : Authentication, encryption required?

Internet applications

Concerning the Internet application layer, it consists of a set of protocols providing different services. Among these, the most popular are:

- SMTP, IMAP, POP3 for electronic mail applications;
- HTTP, FTP for data transfer;
- TELNET for terminal emulation;
- RTP, RTCP, SIP for multimedia applications.

Now we will discuss all these protocols in detail.

16.1 FTP : File Transfer Protocol

FTP (File Transfer Protocol) is the simplest and most secure way to exchange files over the Internet. The most common use for FTP is to download files from the Internet. In addition, the ability to transfer files back-and-forth makes FTP almost essential for anyone creating a Web page, amateurs and professionals alike.

When downloading a file from the Internet you're actually transferring the file to your computer from another computer over the Internet. This is why the T (transfer) is in FTP. You may not know where the computer is that the file is coming from but you most likely know it's URL or Internet address.

Most often, a computer with the FTP address is dedicated to receive FTP connection. Just as a computer that is setup to host Web pages is referred to as a Web server or Website, a computer dedicated to receiving an FTP connection is referred to as an FTP server or FTP site. An FTP site is like a large filing cabinet. With a traditional filing cabinet, the person who does the filing has the option to label and organize the files however they see fit. They also decide which files to keep locked and which remain public. It is the same with an FTP site.

FTP Basics

FTP exists primarily for the transfer of data between two end points. The two objectives of the protocol are to:

- Promote the sharing of files.
- Transfer data reliably and efficiently.

FTP differs from HTTP fundamentally as it is an application made up of two distinct TCP connections:

- **Control connection** : This TCP-based connection is used to provide a communications channel for the delivery of commands and replies. This is effectively the mechanism that enables the user to tell the server which file is being requested, which directory it is in, and so forth.
- **Data connection** : The second TCP-based connection is used for the actual transfer of user data. Once the Control connection has been used to exchange information on which file is required, the Data connection is used to transfer the file between the client and server.

Using these two communication connections, two distinct modes of operation determine in which direction the connections are established: Active mode and Passive mode.

How FTP Works in Active Mode ?

FTP creates both a control and a data connection in order to transfer files. Within an Active FTP session, the Control connection is established from the client to the server, with the Data connection established back from the server to the client.

The control connection is based on telnet and is used to negotiate the parameters for the data transfer. This is called an active FTP connection.

1. The client FTP application opens a control connection to the server on destination port 21, and specifies a source port as the source to which the FTP server should respond (using TCP).
2. The FTP server responds on port 21.
3. The FTP server and client negotiate the data transfer parameters.
4. The FTP server opens a second connection for data on port 20 to the original client.
5. The client responds on the data port, completing a TCP connection.
6. Data transfer begins.
7. The server indicates the end of the data transfer
8. Client closes the connection once the data is received.
9. The data connection is closed.
10. The FTP connection is closed.

How FTP Works in Passive Mode ?

Passive mode FTP works similarly to Active mode FTP with one major exception: both the Control and Data connections within a Passive mode FTP session are established from the client to the server. The passive mode behavior of an FTP server:

1. The client opens a connection to the server on TCP port 21 (command channel).
2. The server accepts the connection.
3. The server initiates a connection to the client using port 20 as the source port (for the data channel).
4. The client accepts the connection and acknowledges all data transfers on port 20.

The objectives of FTP are :

1. To promote sharing of files (computer programs and/or data).
2. To encourage indirect or implicit use of remote computers.
3. To shield a user from variations in file storage systems among different hosts.
4. To transfer data reliably and efficiently.

Disadvantages are :

1. Passwords and file contents are sent in clear text, which can be intercepted by eavesdroppers.
2. Multiple TCP/IP connections are used, one for the control connection, and one for each download, upload or directory listing. Firewall software needs additional logic to account for these connections.
3. It is hard to filter active mode FTP traffic on the client side by using a firewall, since the client must open an arbitrary port in order to receive the connection. This problem is largely resolved by using passive mode FTP.
4. It is possible to abuse the protocol's built-in proxy features to tell a server to send data to an arbitrary port of a third computer.

16.2 HTTP : Hyper Text Transfer Protocol

The Hyper Text Transfer Protocol, or HTTP, must be the most widely used Application layer protocol in the world today. It forms the basis of what most people understand the Internet to be-the World Wide Web. Its purpose is to provide a lightweight protocol for the retrieval of Hyper Text Markup Language (HTML) and other documents from Web sites throughout the Internet. Each time you open a Web browser to surf the Internet, you are using HTTP over TCP/IP.

It's the network protocol used to deliver virtually all files and other data (collectively called resources) on the World Wide Web, whether they're HTML files, image files, query results, or anything else. Usually, HTTP takes place through TCP/IP sockets.

A browser is an HTTP client because it sends requests to an HTTP server (Web server), which then sends responses back to the client. The standard (and default) port for HTTP servers to listen on is 80, though they can use any port.

HTTP is used to transmit resources, not just files. A resource is some chunk of information that can be identified by a URL (it's the R in URL). The most common kind of resource is a file, but a resource may also be a dynamically generated query result, the output of a CGI script, a document that is available in several languages, or something else.

Basic HTTP Page Retrieval

In this section we will see how a basic browser retrieves a Web page from a Web server. The first important point to note is that a Web page is typically made up of many dozens of objects, ranging from the HTML base through to the images that are present on the page. The HTML can be thought of as the template for the page overall, instructing the browser on the layout of the text, font sizes and colors, background color of the page, and which other images need to be retrieved to make up the page.

The processes take place in the following order:

1. Client sends a request for the required page to the Web server.
2. The server analyzes the request and sends back an acknowledgment to the client along with the HTML code required to make the page.
3. The client will begin interpreting the HTML and building the page.
4. The client, in subsequent requests, will retrieve any embedded objects, such as images or other multimedia sources.

Once all elements of the page have been retrieved, the client browser will display the completed Web page.

The HTTP URL (Uniform Resource Locator)

The URL is the most important piece of information that the client browser includes. The URL is defined as being a combination of the host where the site is located, the scheme used to retrieve the page, and the full path and filename. Optionally, the URL may include information such as the TCP port number to be used or a unique reference point within a larger page.

Cookies—The HTTP State Management Mechanism

The biggest challenges in HTTP environments, whether content switched or not, is maintaining some form of client-side state that enables Web servers and intermediary devices to recognize the client session and understand the current status of the user session. In HTTP, cookies take the form of a small piece of text information that is implanted into the user's browser either permanently or temporarily. The term **cookie** is commonly used in computing to describe an opaque piece of information held during a session and, unfortunately, seems to have no more interesting origin than that. Once the backend server has implanted the cookie into the user's browser, the information can be used for a number of different applications ranging from content personalization, user session persistence for online shopping, and the collection of demographic and statistical information on Web site usage.

16.3 DNS : Domain Name System

Domain naming, and its most visible component, the Domain Name System (DNS), is critical to the operation of the Internet. The average phone number, with area code, is 10 digits in length and encodes 10^10, or 10,000,000,000 possibilities. The Internet IP address, at 32 bits, encodes 2^32 or 4,294,967,296 possibilities. For human engineering purposes, how can we build an effective directory of these difficult large numbers?

The telephone company solves this problem with lots of large paper directories, and operators you call and ask about numbers not in your directory. Internet solves this problem with a hierarchy of simple, mnemonic names, called domain names. Instead of remembering 205.216.138.22, all I need to know is the host's domain name—quick.com. Some people think the dots in a domain name correspond to the dots in the numeric address. This is not the case.

There are always three periods in an IP address, separating its four constituent bytes. There are a variable number of periods in a domain name.

Domain Name Service is the service used to convert human readable names of hosts to IP addresses. Host names are not case sensitive and can contain alphabetic or numeric letters or the hyphen. Avoid the underscore. A fully qualified domain name (FQDN) consists of the host name plus domain name as in the following example:

computername.domain.com

Three main components of DNS are listed below:

1. Resolver
2. Name server
3. Database of resource records (RRs)

The part of the system sending the queries is called the **resolver** and is the client side of the configuration. The **name server** answers the queries. The main function of DNS is the mapping of IP addresses to human readable names.

The Domain Name System (DNS) is basically a large database that resides on various computers and it contains the names and IP addresses of various hosts on the Internet and various domains. The Domain Name System is used to provide information to the Domain Name Service to use when queries are made. The service is the act of querying the database, and the system is the data structure and data itself. The Domain Name System is similar to a file system in Unix or DOS starting with a root. Branches attach to the root to create a huge set of paths. Each branch in the DNS is called a label. Each label can be 63 characters long, but most are less. Each text word between the dots can be 63 characters in length, with the total domain name (all the labels) limited to 255 bytes in overall length. The domain name system database is divided into sections called **zones**.

DNS names are assigned through the Internet Registries by the Internet Assigned Number Authority (IANA). The domain name is a name assigned to an Internet domain. For example, mycollege.edu represents the domain name of an educational institution. The names microsoft.com and 3Com.com represent the domain names of those commercial companies. Naming hosts within the domain is up to individuals who administer their domain.

Access to the Domain name database is through a resolver that may be a program or part of an operating system that resides on users workstations. The resolver will send requests to the name servers to return information requested by the user. The requesting computer tries to connect to the name server using its IP address rather than the name.

DNS servers and their databases

For any group of computers partaking of the DNS naming scheme there is likely to be a single definitive list of DNS names and associated IP addresses. The group of computers included in this list is called a **zone**. A zone could be a top-level national domain or a university department. Within a zone DNS service for subsidiary zones may be **delegated** along with a subsidiary domain. The computer that maintains the master list for a zone is said to have **authority** for that zone and will be the primary name server for that zone, there will also be secondaries for that zone. When any process needs to determine an IP address given a DNS address it calls upon the local host to resolve the address.

Name Servers

A name server is an Internet host running software capable of processing DNS requests. There are three types of name servers:

1. The primary master builds its database from files that were preconfigured on its hosts, called zone or database files. The name server reads these files and builds a database for the zone it is authoritative for.
2. Secondary masters can provide information to resolvers just like the primary masters, but they get their information from the primary. Any updates to the database are provided by the primary.
3. Caching name server—It gets all its answers to queries from other name servers and saves (caches) the answers. It is a non-authoritative server.

The caching name server generates no zone transfer traffic. A DNS Server that can communicate outside of the private network to resolve a DNS name query is referred to as forwarder.

Primary and Secondary Name Servers

Typically, a single name server will be configured as the primary name server for a domain. For backup purposes, a number of other name servers may be configured as secondary name servers. From the standpoint of DNS, there is no difference between primary and secondary name servers, since the resolving algorithm simply uses a domain's NS records in the order provided. Typically, the primary name server is listed first, followed by the secondaries, but this is not a requirement. In fact, if a group of domains is served by a set of name servers, the ordering of the name servers may be mixed among the domains, to facilitate load balancing.

DNS can refer either to the entire system, or to the protocol that makes it work.

Structure and message format

DNS is hierarchical in structure. A domain is a subtree of the domain name space.

- **3 letter codes**

The DNS was originally introduced in the United States of America and the final component of an address was intended to indicate the type of organization hosting the computer. Some of the three letter final labels (edu, gov, mil) are still only used by organizations based in the USA, others can be used anywhere in the world.

The three letter codes are:

Code	Meaning
com	Commercial. Now international.
edu	Educational.
gov	Government.
int	International Organization.
mil	Military.
net	Network related.
org	Miscellaneous Organization.

- **Two letter codes**

The final two letter codes indicate the country of origin, e.g., the two letter code us is used by some sites in the United States of America. In some countries there are sub-domains indicating the type of organization such as ac.uk, co.uk, sch.uk in the United Kingdom and edu.au and com.au in Australia. Most European countries have not adopted this useful practice.

The figure 16.1 shows a partial DNS hierarchy. At the top is what is called the root and it is the start of all other branches in the DNS tree. It is designated with a period. Each branch moves down from level to level. When referring to DNS addresses, they are referred to from the bottom up with the root designator (period) at the far right.

Example : "myhost.mygrp.mycorp.com".

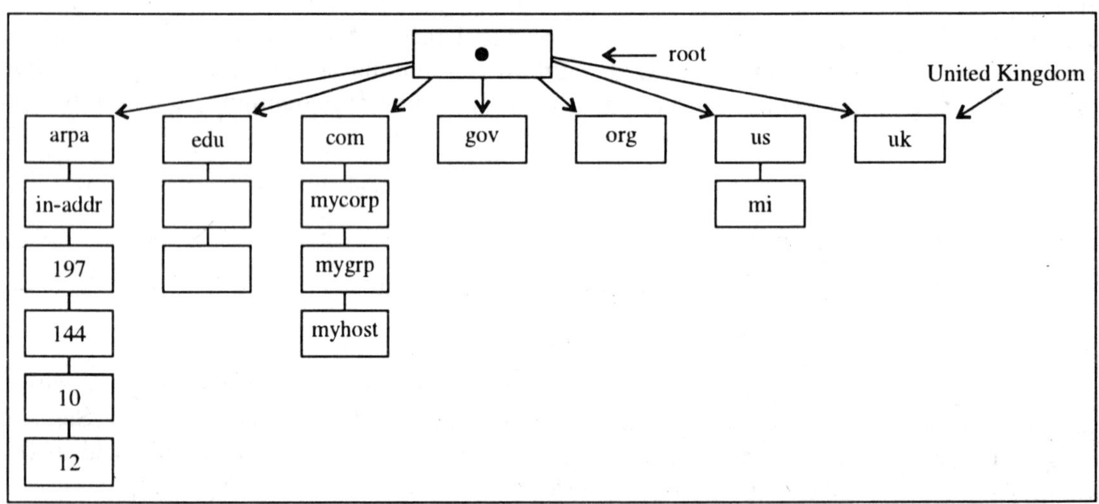

Fig. 16.1 Partial DNS hierarchy

Partial DNS hierarchy

To obtain a domain address it is necessary to identify the administrator of the required domain and then all that is basically necessary is to send the administrator the required code and the associated IP address and they will, if they accept the request, include the details in their databases.

DNS Query Types

There are following types of queries issued:

1. **Recursive** queries received by a server forces that server to find the information requested or post a message back to the querier that the information cannot be found.
2. **Iterative** queries allow the server to search for the information and pass back the best information it knows about. This is the type that is used between servers. Clients used the recursive query.
3. **Reverse**—The client provides the IP address and asks for the name. In other queries the name is provided, and the IP address is returned to the client.

Generally (but not always), a server-to-server query is iterative and a client-resolver-to-server query is recursive. You should also note that a server can be queried or it can be the person placing a query. Therefore, a server contains both the server and client functions. A server can transmit either type of query. If it is handed a recursive query from a remote source, it must transmit other queries to find the specified name, or send a message back to the originator of the query that the name could not be found.

16.4 RTSP : Real Time Streaming Protocol

In the modern Internet, applications are required to deliver value. Application layer protocols such as RTSP enables the delivery of real-time video and audio in variable qualities. The other Application layer protocols we've looked at so far in this chapter work in a request/response manner, whereby the client asks for some piece of content, the content is delivered using TCP or UDP, and then the client application can display the content to the user. While these mechanisms are suitable for a large number of applications in the Internet, there also exists a requirement to deliver content, be it images, audio, video, or a combination of all three, in real time. Imagine if a user were to try to watch a full-screen video file of a one-hour movie using HTTP or FTP as the Application layer protocol. The movie file might be several hundred megabytes, if not several gigabytes, in size. Even with modern broadband services deliverable to the home, this type of large file size does not fit well in the "download then play" model we saw previously.

RTSP uses a combination of reliable transmission over TCP (used for control) and best-efforts delivery over UDP (used for content) to stream content to users. By this, we mean that the file delivery can start and the client-side application can begin displaying the audio and video content before the complete file has arrived. In terms of our one-hour movie example, this means that the client can request a movie file and watch a "live" feed similar to how one would watch a TV. Along with this "on demand" type service, RTSP also enables the delivery of live broadcast content that would not be possible with traditional download and play type mechanisms.

The Components of RTSP Delivery

RTSP is the control protocol for the delivery of multimedia content across IP networks. It is based typically on TCP for reliable delivery and has a very similar operation and syntax to HTTP. RTSP is used by the client application to communicate to the server information such as the media file being requested, the type of application the client is using, the mechanism of delivery of the file (unicast or multicast, UDP or TCP), and other important control information commands such as DESCRIBE, SETUP, and PLAY. The actual multimedia content is not typically delivered over the RTSP connection(s), although it can be interleaved if required. RTSP is analogous to the remote control of the streaming protocols.

16.4.1 Real Time Transport Protocol (RTP)

RTP is the Internet-standard protocol for the transport of real-time data, including audio and video. It can be used for media-on-demand as well as interactive services such as Internet telephony. RTP consists of a data and a control part. The latter is called RTCP.

The data part of RTP is a thin protocol providing support for applications with real-time properties such as continuous media (e.g., audio and video), including timing reconstruction, loss detection, security and content identification.

RTP is the protocol used for the actual transport and delivery of the real-time audio and video data. As the delivery of the actual data for audio and video is typically delay sensitive, the lighter weight UDP protocol is used as the Layer 4 delivery mechanism, although TCP might also be used in environments that suffer higher packet loss. The RTP flow when delivering the content is unidirectional from the server to the client. One interesting part of the RTP operation is that the source port used by the server when sending the UDP data is always even-although it is dynamically assigned. The destination port (i.e., the UDP port on which the client is listening) is chosen by the client and communicated over the RTSP control connection.

16.4.2 Real Time Control Protocol (RTCP)

RTCP is a complimentary protocol to RTP and is a bidirectional UDP-based mechanism to allow the client to communicate stream-quality information back to the object server. The RTCP UDP communication always uses the next UDP source port up from that used by the RTP stream, and consequently is always odd.

RTCP provides support for real-time conferencing of groups of any size within an internet. This support includes source identification and support for gateways like audio and video bridges as well as multicast-to-unicast translators. It offers quality-of-service feedback from receivers to the multicast group as well as support for the synchronization of different media streams.

16.5 SSL : Secure Sockets Layer

This protocol is neither a Layer 4 transport protocol nor an Application layer protocol, but one that sits between these layers to provide security services to many modern Internet applications. Secure Sockets Layer, or SSL, has been one of the major forces in Internet security technology since its inception by Netscape Communications, and continues to be included in all major browsers. This has enabled Web application developers to deliver secure content and services using traditional HTTP servers with few changes required in terms of the setup of the basic server or restructuring of the HTML content. The other major advantage of the integration of SSL into all major browsers is its transparency to the user. SSL typically gets used without the knowledge of the client, other than the appearance of a small padlock in the corner of the browser window, thus meaning that no additional level of expertise is required to use Internet applications with this security.

The Need for Application Security

The need for security within Internet applications is clear—the Internet is still a public network with little or no security infrastructure designed to protect all users. Imagine using the online services of your favorite bank. Passing important data such as your bank account number, password, and balance across the Internet using only HTTP represents a huge personal security risk, as the data is potentially visible to any device sitting between your browser and the bank's Web site. SSL can be used very effectively to hide all of all the application data as it traverses the Internet to prevent anybody snooping the connection from reading personal data—a process referred to as encryption.

The second important feature provided by *SSL* for Internet application is authentication; in other words, the ability for the client to be able to distinguish the Web site as valid. Imagine in our previous bank example if another rogue site were to masquerade as the bank's Web site. This might allow the rogue site to intercept the personal and banking details of thousands of customers, not a welcome situation. SSL provides mechanisms to implement authentication as a way for each side to identify itself to the other.

The final security element that is provided by SSL is tamper detection. Imagine finally that someone were to sit between the client and the bank's Web site and change certain pieces of data as they pass back and forth. This would give the opportunity to alter key personal and banking data and potentially set up fraudulent transactions. SSL provides mechanisms for each side to ensure that the Application layer data being sent and received has not changed in any way as it traverses the Internet.

For the Internet to continue to grow, not only in size, but also as a credible medium for business and commerce, it must be able to provide mechanisms such as SSL as a way to guarantee security.

16.6 SIP : Session Initiation Protocol

The Session Initiation Protocol (SIP) is a signalling protocol used for establishing sessions in an IP network. A session could be a simple two-way telephone call or it could be a collaborative multi-media conference session. The ability to establish these sessions means that a host of innovative services become possible, such as voice-enriched e-commerce, web page click-to-dial, Instant Messaging with buddy lists, and IP Centrex services.

SIP is a request-response protocol that closely resembles two other Internet protocols, HTTP and SMTP (the protocols that power the world wide web and email); consequently, SIP sits comfortably alongside Internet applications. Using SIP, telephony becomes another web application and integrates easily into other Internet services. SIP is a simple toolkit that service providers can use to build converged voice and multimedia services.

16.7 Internet e-mail Protocols

In this section first we will discuss meanings of Internet and E-mail and then we will discuss Internet E-mail protocols.

16.7.1 Introduction to Internet

The Internet is a computer network made up of thousands of networks worldwide. No one knows exactly how many computers are connected to the Internet. It is certain, however, that these number in the millions and are growing. No one is in charge of the Internet. There are organizations that develop technical aspects of this network and set standards for creating applications on it, but no governing body is in control. The Internet backbone, through which Internet traffic flows, is owned by private companies.

The Internet enables the individual user to reach other people and institutions all over the world and exchange or obtain information. Companies can provide via the Internet information about them, or obtain information about other companies, and offer their own products and services.

The Internet was created by the Advanced Research Projects Agency (ARPA) of the U.S. government in 1960's, and was first known as the ARPANet. At that stage the Internet's first computers were at academic and government institutions. They were mainly used for accessing files and to send email. Since 1983 the Internet has accommodated a lot of changes and continues to keep developing. The last two decades has seen the Internet accommodate such things as network LANs and ATM and frame switched services. The Internet continues to evolve with it becoming available on mobile phones and pagers and possibly on televisions in the future.

"Internet" refers to the global information system that,

- Is logically linked together by a globally unique address space based on the Internet Protocol (IP) or its subsequent extensions.
- Is able to support communications using the Transmission Control Protocol/Internet Protocol (TCP/IP) suite or its subsequent extensions, and/or other IP-compatible protocols.
- Provides, uses or makes accessible, either publicly or privately, high level services layered on the communications and related infrastructure.

Internet offers many opportunities for information and communication. Everyone who has access to the Internet can make use of the following services:

- Electronic mail (e-mail) : To send and receive post (mail).
- SMS (Short Message Service) : To send messages from GSM to GSM, or from PC to GSM.
- Telnet, or remote login : To log in to another computer from a distance.
- FTP (File Transfer Protocol) : To receive files from a computer at a distance and to examine and store them on your own computer.
- Gopher : A text-only, non-graphic method to receive Internet documents.
- Video-conferencing.
- World Wide Web.

All computers on the Internet communicate with one another using the Transmission Control Protocol/Internet Protocol suite, abbreviated to TCP/IP. Computers on the Internet use client/server architecture. This means that the remote server machine provides files and services to the user's local client machine. Software can be installed on a client computer to take advantage of the latest access technology.

Components of the Internet

- **World Wide Web**

The World Wide Web (Web or WWW) is a system of Internet servers that supports hypertext to access several Internet protocols on a single interface. Almost every protocol type available on the Internet is accessible on the Web. This includes e-mail, FTP, Telnet, and Usenet News. In addition to these, the World Wide Web has its own protocol: HyperText Transfer Protocol, or HTTP.

The World Wide Web provides a single interface for accessing all these protocols. This creates a convenient and user-friendly environment. It is not necessary to be conversant in these protocols within separate, command-level environments, as was typical in the early days. The Web gathers together these protocols into a single system. Because of this feature, and because of the Web's ability to work with multimedia and advanced programming languages, the Web is the fastest-growing component of the Internet.

The World Wide Web consists of files, called pages or home pages, containing links to documents and resources throughout the Internet.

- **e-Mail**

Electronic mail or e-mail allows computer users locally and worldwide to exchange messages. Each user of e-mail has a mailbox address to which messages are sent. Messages sent through e-mail can arrive within a matter of seconds. (Discussed in next section).

- **Telnet**

Telnet is a program that allows you to log into computers on the Internet and use online databases, library catalogs, chat services, and more. (Discussed later on)

- **FTP**

FTP stands for File Transfer Protocol. This is both a program and the method used to transfer files between computers.

- **Usenet News**

Usenet News is a global electronic bulletin board system in which millions of computer users exchange information on a vast range of topics. The major difference between Usenet News and e-mail discussion groups is the fact that Usenet messages are stored on central computers, and users must connect to these computers to read or download the messages posted to these groups. This is distinct from e-mail distribution, in which messages arrive in the electronic mailboxes of each list member.

Usenet itself is a set of machines that exchanges messages, or articles, from Usenet discussion forums, called newsgroups. Usenet administrators control their own sites, and decide which (if any) newsgroups to sponsor and which remote newsgroups to allow into the system.

- **Chat And Instant Messaging**

Chat programs allow users on the Internet to communicate with each other by typing in real time. They are sometimes included as a feature of a Web site, where users can log into the "chat room" to exchange comments and information about the topics addressed on the site. Chat may take other, more wide-ranging forms. For example, America Online is well known for sponsoring a number of topical chat rooms.

Internet Relay Chat (IRC) is a service through which participants can communicate to each other on hundreds of channels. These channels are usually based on specific topics. To access IRC, you must use an IRC software program.

16.7.2 Introduction to e-mail

Electronic mail (or e-mail) can be defined as "the exchange of computer-stored messages by telecommunications". These messages, usually in text form, are sent from one computer via telephone lines. When you send a message, it usually is stored on a remote computer until the receiver goes online and checks his or her mail. Electronic mail, or e-mail, is the most widely used Internet service. E-mail makes it possible for you to:

- Communicate with students.
- Send or post student assignments.
- Receive student papers and projects.
- Establish class discussions online.
- Communicate with friends who have e-mail accounts.
- Meet and interact with people all over the world.
- Participate in electronic conferences and discussions on an unlimited range of topics.
- Subscribe to electronic services.

- Get answers to technical questions.
- Take online workshops or classes.
- Mail any electronic text and graphics to anyone with an e-mail address.

Advantages of E-mail over other forms of Communication

There are three main advantages : it's cheap, fast and convenient.

Compared with the cost of a phone call, a fax or regular mail (snail mail), you will save money. Some e-mail software programs are even free, and you can even sign up with free e-mail service online. Next, you can't beat the speed of e-mail. Why wait days or weeks for your mail to arrive when you can send a message in seconds? Finally, you can write and send messages easily to one person or a hundred at one time. In addition, you can send graphics, pictures, files, and even movies via e-mail.

The parts of an e-mail address

e-mail addresses often have three parts: (1) the user name, (2) the host or domain name, and (3) the type of domain. Look at this example: **john@yahoo.com**

The first part, **john**, is the username which identifies the recipient. The next part, **yahoo**, is the host or domain name of the mail server where the recipient's mailbox is located. The final part, **.com**, identifies the type of domain (e.g., **.com** for commercial sites, **.edu** for educational institutions, **.org** for non-profit groups, etc.). In some cases, instead of the extension .com, you might see a two-letter country extension like .in for India, .jp for Japan, .fr for France, or .ru for Russia.

e-mail Program Classifications

In general, all email applications fall into at least one of three classifications. Each classification plays a specific role in the process of moving and managing email messages. While most users are only aware of the specific email program they use to receive and send messages, each one is important for ensuring that email arrives at the correct destination. The different types of Email programs are listed below:

- Mail Transfer Agent.
- Mail Delivery Agent.
- Mail User Agent.

Mail Transfer Agent

A Mail Transfer Agent (MTA) transfers email messages between hosts using SMTP. A message may involve several MTAs as it moves to its intended destination. Most users are totally unaware of the presence of MTAs, even though every email message is sent through at least one MTA.

While the delivery of messages between machines may seem rather straightforward, the entire process of deciding if a particular MTA can or should accept a message for delivery is quite complicated. In addition, due to problems from spam, use of a particular MTA is usually restricted by the MTA's configuration or by the lack of access to the MTA's network.

Many modern email client programs can act as an MUA when sending email. However, this action should not be confused with the role of a true MTA. The sole reason email client programs are capable of sending out email (like an MTA) is because the host running the application does not have its own MTA. This is particularly true for email client programs on non-Unix-based operating systems. However, these client programs only send outbound messages to an MTA they are authorized to use and do not directly deliver the message to the intended recipient's email server.

Mail Delivery Agent

A Mail Delivery Agent (MDA) is utilized by the MTA to deliver email to a particular user's mailbox. In many cases, an MDA is actually a Local Delivery Agent (LDA), such as /bin/mail or Procmail. However, Sendmail can also play the role of an MDA, such as when it accepts a message for a local user and appends it to their email spool file. Any program that actually handles a message for delivery to the point where it can be read by an MUA can be considered an MDA. Note that MDAs do not transport messages between systems or interface with the end user.

Many users do not directly utilize MDAs, because only MTAs and MUAs are necessary to send and receive email. However, some MDAs may be used to sort messages before they are read by a user, which is a big help if you receive a lot of email.

Mail User Agent

A Mail User Agent (MUA) is synonymous with an email client application. An MUA is a program that, at the very least, allows a user to read and compose email messages. Many MUAs are capable of retrieving messages via the POP or IMAP protocols, setting up mailboxes to store messages, and sending outbound messages to an MTA.

Protocols

Email, like other network services, uses a variety of protocols. These protocols allow different machines, often running different operating systems and utilizing different email programs, to communicate with one another and transfer mail so it arrives in the proper place. The following protocols are those most commonly used to transfer email from system to system:

- SMTP : Simple Mail Transfer Protocol.
- POP : Post Office Protocol.
- IMAP : Internet Message Access Protocol.
- MIME : Multipurpose Internet Mail Extensions.

Today, email is delivered using client/server architecture. An email message is created using mail client program. This program then sends the message to a server. The server then forwards the massage to the recipient's email server, where the message is then supplied to the recipient's email client.

Unlike the majority of Internet applications, the electronic mail use two different protocols, one for sending and another for getting messages.

For sending mails, SMTP is used. For retrieving messages from the server, POP3 or IMAP are used. The following protocols discussed are the most commonly used in the transfer of e-mail.

16.7.3 SMTP : Simple Mail Transfer Protocol

The SMTP protocol is used for the transmission of e-mails. SMTP takes care of sending your email to another computer. Normally your email is sent to an email server (SMTP server), and then to another server or servers, and finally to its destination. SMTP can only transmit pure text. It cannot transmit binary data like pictures, sounds or movies. SMTP uses the MIME protocol to send binary data across TCP/IP networks. The MIME protocol converts binary data to pure text.

The Simple Mail Transfer Protocol is the most widely used protocol to send messages by Message Transfer Agents (MTA) on the Internet. SMTP defines the message format and the message transfer agent (MTA) stores and forwards the mail. SMTP was originally designed for only plain text (ASCII text), but MIME and other encoding methods enable executable programs and multimedia files to be attached to and transported with the e-mail message.

MTAs are client or server programs that perform email services, such as sending or receiving mail for a host computer. The protocol is designed to transfer mail independently of any specific transmission subsystem.

Sender and receiver MTAs send commands and replies in a structured, lock-step process. The sender MTA initiates the transaction steps by sending SMTP commands to the receiver. The receiver MTA replies to the sender with numeric reply codes, followed by a text string with additional information about the reply code.

One important point to make about the SMTP protocol is that it does not require authentication. This allows anyone on the Internet to send email to anyone else or even to large groups of people. It is this characteristic of SMTP that makes junk email or spam possible. Modern SMTP servers attempt to minimize this behavior by allowing only known hosts access to the SMTP server. Those servers that do not impose such restrictions are called open relay servers.

The Mail Transaction

The sender MTA initiates a two-way TCP communication channel between it and the receiver MTA, generally on port 25. Once the connection is open, the receiver MTA sends reply code 220 indicating that it is ready. The sender MTA then sends the HELO command with the client host as an argument. The HELO command identifies the sender MTA to the receiver MTA, and the receiver MTA will respond with a reply code 250. This tells the sender MTA that the connection is open and ready to go. This step in the transaction identifies and confirms host addresses for both the sender and receiver MTAs.

The reverse-path is the full reverse source route list, starting with the current client host and ending with the user mailbox. The reverse-path is modified by each MTA as the message travels toward its destination. Before transferring a message to the next relay host, the current host will remove its name from the beginning of the forward-path and adds its name to the beginning of the reverse path.

If the mailbox address is acceptable to the receiver MTA, it transmits a reply code 250 to the sender MTA. If it cannot fulfill the request, it transmits a reply code of 550. One reason it may not be able to fulfill the request is because the mailbox is incorrect or non-existent.

The next step is for the sender MTA to issue the DATA command. There are no arguments to this command; it simply tells the receiver that the sender is ready to start sending the message. The receiver MTA will transmit a reply code 354 indicating that it is ready to receive the message. Once the sender MTA receives the correct reply code, it sends the mail data to the receiver.

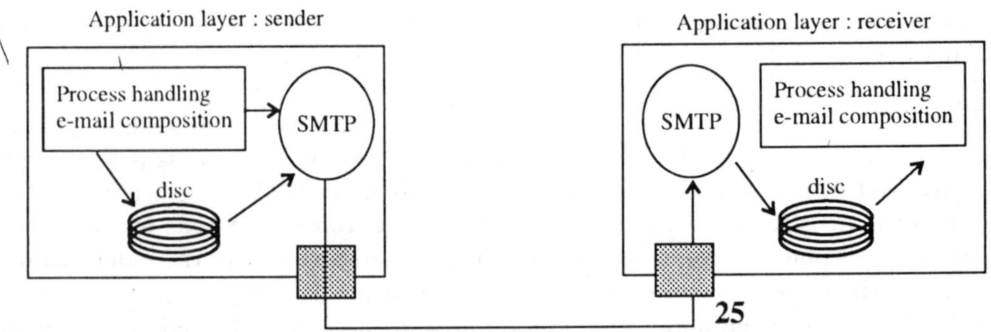

Fig. 16.2 Pictorial view of SMTP

16.7.4 POP : Post Office Protocol

There are two primary protocols used by email client applications to retrieve email from mail servers: the **Post Office Protocol (POP)** and the **Internet Message Access Protocol (IMAP)**. Unlike SMTP, both of these protocols require connecting clients to authenticate using a username and password. By default, passwords for both protocols are passed over the network unencrypted.

The Post Office Protocol (POP) allows email clients to pull off email from remote servers and save those messages on their local machine. Most POP email clients are automatically configured to delete the message on the email server after it has been successfully transferred to the client's system, though this can usually be changed.

The Post Office Protocol, version 3 (POP3) is the most commonly used protocol used for retrieving email messages on the Internet. It is designed for user-to-mailbox access. Facilities are provided for user authentication and mailbox manipulation. Authentication takes the form of a password transmitted as clear text, so POP3 should be used carefully if security is of concern.

POP is fully compatible with important Internet messaging standards, such as Multipurpose Internet Mail Extensions (MIME), which allow for email attachments.

POP works best for users who have one system on which to read email. It also works well for users who do not have a persistent connection to the Internet or the network containing the mail server. Unfortunately for those with slow network connections, POP requires client programs upon authentication to download the entire content of each message. This can take a long time if any messages have large attachments.

The POP protocol has been around for quite a few years and is supported by a large number of e-mail clients. POP was designed to be used as an "offline" protocol in which users connect to a server and download messages in their inbox to their local PC or MAC system. The user has the option of removing messages from the server or leaving them on the server (not recommended.) Leaving messages in the inbox on the server can create a great deal of extra load on the server system, since each time the user reconnects, the POP server must once again scan all of the messages in the inbox to determine which ones are new. Once the messages are downloaded, the user then processes them in offline mode; responding to messages, filing messages to various local folders, etc. The POP protocol does not allow you to create, manage, or manipulate folders or messages on the mail server.

Operation of POP

To connect to a POP server, the email client opens a TCP connection to port 110 on the server. At the time the connection is made, the POP server sends the POP client a greeting, after which the two machines send each other commands and responses specified in the protocol. As part of this communication, the POP client is asked to authenticate itself in what is called the **Authentication State**, where the user's username and password are sent to the POP server. If authentication is successful, then the POP client moves on to the **Transaction State**, where commands like LIST, RETR, and DELE can be used to list, download, and delete the messages from the server, respectively. Messages set to be deleted are not actually removed from the server until the POP client sends the QUIT command to end the session. At this point, the POP server enters the Update State, where it deletes the flagged messages and cleans up any resources remaining from this session.

POP is a much simpler protocol than IMAP, due to the fact that fewer commands can be sent between the client and the server. POP is also somewhat more popular, although most major email clients can use either protocol quite well.

Most POP users only have one system that they use to read email, and they download their messages to that machine for storage. POP also works well if you do not have a constant connection to the Internet or network containing your mail server, although IMAP can now be configured to store messages locally so that you can view them when disconnected from the network.

16.7.5 IMAP : Internet Message Access Protocol

Although the POP3 protocol is the most widely used mail retrieval protocol used today, there is an alternative that overcomes some of its limitations. The Internet Message Access Protocol (IMAP) was designed as a superset of POP3 and enhances both message retrieval and management.

The IMAP protocol is used by email programs (like Microsoft Outlook) just like the POP protocol. The main difference between the IMAP protocol and the POP protocol is that the IMAP protocol will not automatically download all your emails each time your email program connects to your email server. The IMAP protocol allows you to see through your email messages at the email server before you download them. With IMAP you can choose to download your messages or just delete them. This way IMAP is perfect if you need to connect to your email server from different locations, but only want to download your messages when you are back in your office.

When using an IMAP mail server, email messages remain on the server where users can read or delete them. IMAP also allows client applications to create, rename or delete mail directories on the server to organize and store email.

IMAP is particularly useful for those who access their email using multiple machines. The protocol is also convenient for users connecting to the mail server via a slow connection, because only the email header information is downloaded for messages until opened, saving bandwidth. The user also has the ability to delete messages without viewing or downloading them.

For convenience, IMAP client applications are capable of caching copies of messages locally, so the user can browse previously read messages when not directly connected to the IMAP server. IMAP, like POP, is fully compatible with important Internet messaging standards, such as MIME, which allow for email attachments.

The IMAP protocol provides a superset of the features provided by POP, but also has much more advanced capabilities with regard to message and mailbox management on the mail server. For instance, you can delete messages, search for text in messages, store messages in different folders, or even create and delete folders on the server system. On most systems you have the option of leaving your messages on the server or moving to your local system. The advantage to leaving the messages on the server is that you can then access them from any PC with Internet access and which has an IMAP client loaded. Of course, it is assumed that you will actively manage the messages in your mailbox; move messages out of the inbox, delete what you don't need, etc.

16.7.6 MIME : Multipurpose Internet Mail Extensions

The Multipurpose Internet Mail Extension (MIME) protocol was developed to define a method of moving multimedia files through existing email gateways. Multipurpose Internet Mail Extensions (MIME), a standards-track Internet format defined by an Internet Engineering Task Force Working Group, offers a simple standardized way to represent and encode a wide variety of media types, including textual data in non-ASCII character sets, for transmission via Internet mail.

MIME (Multipurpose Internet Mail Extensions) is one of the Internet protocol standards defined by the Internet Engineering Task Force (IETF). Once associated primarily with electronic mail, MIME has evolved to become an important element supporting multimedia applications on the Net. In order to understand MIME and how it operates, it's helpful to step back and see how it got to where it is today.

MIME defines extensions to SMTP to support binary attachments of arbitrary format. The designers of MIME have learned a lot from the old SMTP protocol and its mailers

Two Main Functions of MIME

- MIME encodes binary data so that it can be passed over the Internet.

- Remember that the Internet is a 7-bit ASCII word.
- Even the 8-bit extensions don't work, because there are issues of line length and file formatting.

- MIME labels encoded data so that the "content" can be properly understood at the other end.
    - For example, "this is a Word document".

The original Internet mail message protocol was designed with text mail messages in mind. A mail message was defined as a block of plain text preceded by specially defined headers specifying routing or other information about the message (e.g., where the message was from, who it was to, whom copies were sent to, etc.). This specification said little about the format of the message *content.* At the time (which was not that long ago!), electronic mail messages were plain text files, so that concerns about the format of content were unwarranted.

Today there is enormous demand for electronic mail that can deliver messages containing components such as HTML text documents, image files, sound, and even video data, in addition to regular text. However, such messages can be widely communicated only if all mail-handling programs share a standard for constructing, encoding and transporting such complex, *multipurpose*, messages.

The MIME protocol provides this common standard. MIME provides an extensible format for including multimedia components within a mail message. MIME defines several document headers, placed inside the document, that specify such things as the nature of a message (multipart or single part), how the message parts are separated, the data content of each part, and the encoding scheme used to encode each part.

16.8 Telnet

The Internet implements the TCP/IP protocol to allow computers to converse with each other over networks. Telnet is an example of a program that makes use of this protocol. This program allows a person to log into and use a distant computer supporting TCP/IP protocols almost as if sitting physically at that computer. It is an application designed for reliable communication between two hosts to support user interaction with a remote system. It is one of the oldest IP protocols and from it several other protocols were developed.

It is best understood in the context of a user with a simple terminal using the local telnet program (known as the client program) to run a login session on a remote computer where his communications needs are handled by a telnet server program. It should be emphasized that the telnet server can pass on the data it has received from the client to many other types of process including a remote login server.

The purpose of the TELNET Protocol is to provide a fairly general, bi-directional, eight-bit byte oriented communications facility. Its primary goal is to allow a standard method of interfacing terminal devices and terminal-oriented processes to each other. It is envisioned that the protocol may also be used for terminal-terminal communication ("linking") and process-process communication (distributed computation).

A telnet server listens for connections on TCP port 23. When a connection is opened from a telnet client to a server, the client attempts to connect to the remote machine using TCP on port 23 and uses a local port above 1023. The remote server will then provide services over that TCP connection. The client sends in ASCII text data and the server responds according to it's design. Telnet is the most basic of all TCP based protocols. When the client receives input from the user, it forwards that information to the telnet server.

Characteristics of Telnet

A TELNET connection is a Transmission Control Protocol (TCP) connection used to transmit data with interspersed TELNET control information. The TELNET Protocol is built upon three main ideas:

- First, the concept of a "Network Virtual Terminal".
- Second, the principle of negotiated options
- Third, a symmetric view of terminals and processes.

1. When a TELNET connection is first established, each end is assumed to originate and terminate at a "Network Virtual Terminal" or NVT. An NVT is an imaginary device that provides a standard, network-wide, intermediate representation of a canonical terminal. This eliminates the need for "server" and "user" hosts to keep information about the characteristics of each other's terminals and terminal handling conventions. All hosts, both user and server, map their local device characteristics and conventions so as to appear to be dealing with NVT over the network, and each can assume a similar mapping by the other party. The NVT is intended to strike a balance between being overly restricted (not providing hosts a rich enough vocabulary for mapping into their local character sets), and being overly inclusive (penalizing users with modest terminals). The "user" host is the host to which the physical terminal is normally attached, and the "server" host is the host that is normally providing some service.
2. The principle of negotiated options takes cognizance of the fact that many hosts will wish to provide additional services over and above those available within an NVT, and many users will have sophisticated terminals and would like to have elegant, rather than minimal, services. Independent of, but structured within the TELNET Protocol are various "options" that will be sanctioned and may be used with the "DO, DON'T, WILL, WON'T" structure to allow a user and server to agree to use a more elaborate (or perhaps just different) set of conventions for their TELNET connection. Such options could include changing the character set, the echo mode, etc. The basic strategy for setting up the use of options is to have either party (or both) initiate a request that some option take effect. The other party may then either accept or reject the request. If the request is accepted the option immediately takes effect; if it is rejected the associated aspect of the connection remains as specified for an NVT. Clearly, a party may always refuse a request to enable, and must never refuse a request to disable some option since all parties must be prepared to support the NVT.
3. The symmetry of the negotiation syntax can potentially lead to non-terminating acknowledgment loops—each party seeing the incoming commands not as acknow-

ledgments but as new requests which must be acknowledged. To prevent such loops, the following rules prevail:

- Parties may only request a change in option status; i.e., a party may not send out a "request" merely to announce what mode it is in.
- If a party receives what appears to be a request to enter some mode it is already in, the request should not be acknowledged. This non-response is essential to prevent endless loops in the negotiation. It is required that a response be sent to requests for a change of mode—even if the mode is not changed.
- Whenever one party sends an option command to a second party, whether as a request or an acknowledgment, and use of the option will have any effect on the processing of the data being sent from the first party to the second, then the command must be inserted in the data stream at the point where it is desired that it take effect.

For the average web user telnet is not so important as it was a few years ago, since many of the features it once made available are now otherwise accessible via browsers. People who have accounts on multi-user computers (particularly those using unix/linux operating systems), however, still find telnet to be an indispensable tool for accessing their work, from home, from the road or from around the world.

16.9 SNMP : Simple Network Management Protocol

The Simple Network Management Protocol (SNMP) is an application-layer protocol designed to facilitate the exchange of management information between network devices. By using SNMP-transported data (such as packets per second and network error rates), network administrators can more easily manage network performance, find and solve network problems, and plan for network growth.

Simple Network Management Protocol (**SNMP**) is a widely used protocol for monitoring the health and welfare of network equipment (e.g., routers), computer equipment and even devices like UPSs.

SNMP is based on the manager/agent model. SNMP is referred to as "simple" because the agent requires minimal software. Most of the processing power and the data storage resides on the management system, while a complementary subset of those functions resides in the

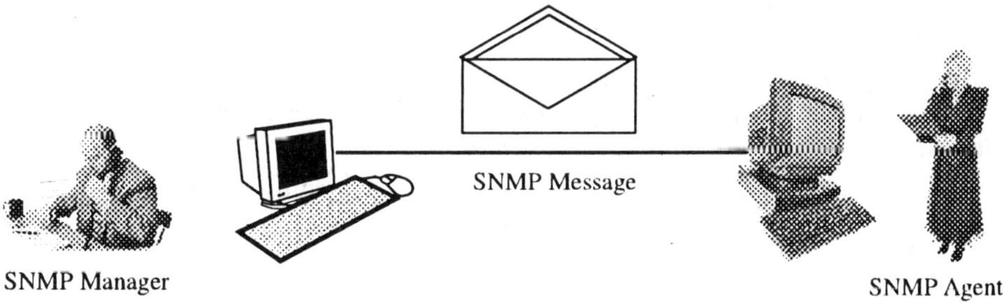

Fig. 16.3 Pictorial view of SNMP

managed system. SNMP is an asymmetric protocol, operating between a management station (smart) and an agent (dumb).

Like the Transmission Control Protocol (TCP), SNMP is an Internet protocol. Internet protocols are created by the Internet community, a group of individuals and organizations that developed and/or regularly use a large, diverse international network called the Internet. The Internet derived from the Advanced Research Projects Agency network (ARPANET), which was created by packet switching researchers in the early 1970s.

There are two versions of SNMP: Version 1 and Version 2. Most of the changes introduced in Version 2 increase SNMP's security capabilities. Other changes increase interoperability by more rigorously defining the specifications for SNMP implementation. SNMP's creators believe that after a relatively brief period of coexistence, SNMP Version 2 (SNMPv2) will largely replace SNMP Version 1 (SNMPv1). SNMP is part of a larger architecture called the Internet Network Management Framework (NMF).

Today, SNMP is the most popular protocol for managing diverse commercial internetworks as well as those used in universities and research organizations. SNMP-related standardization activity continues even as vendors develop and release state-of the-art, SNMP-based management applications. SNMP is a relatively simple protocol, yet its feature set is sufficiently powerful to handle the difficult problems presented in trying to manage today's heterogeneous networks.

SNMP Basic Components

An SNMP-managed network consists of three key components:

- Managed devices.
- Agents.
- Network-management systems (NMSs).

A **managed device** is a network node that contains an SNMP agent and that resides on a managed network. Managed devices collect and store management information and make this information available to NMSs using SNMP. Managed devices, sometimes called network elements, can be routers and access servers, switches and bridges, hubs, computer hosts, or printers.

An **agent** is a network-management software module that resides in a managed device. An agent has local knowledge of management information and translates that information into a form compatible with SNMP.

An **NMS** executes applications that monitor and control managed devices. NMSs provide the bulk of the processing and memory resources required for network management. One or more NMSs must exist on any managed network.

Figure 16.4 illustrates the relationships of these three components.

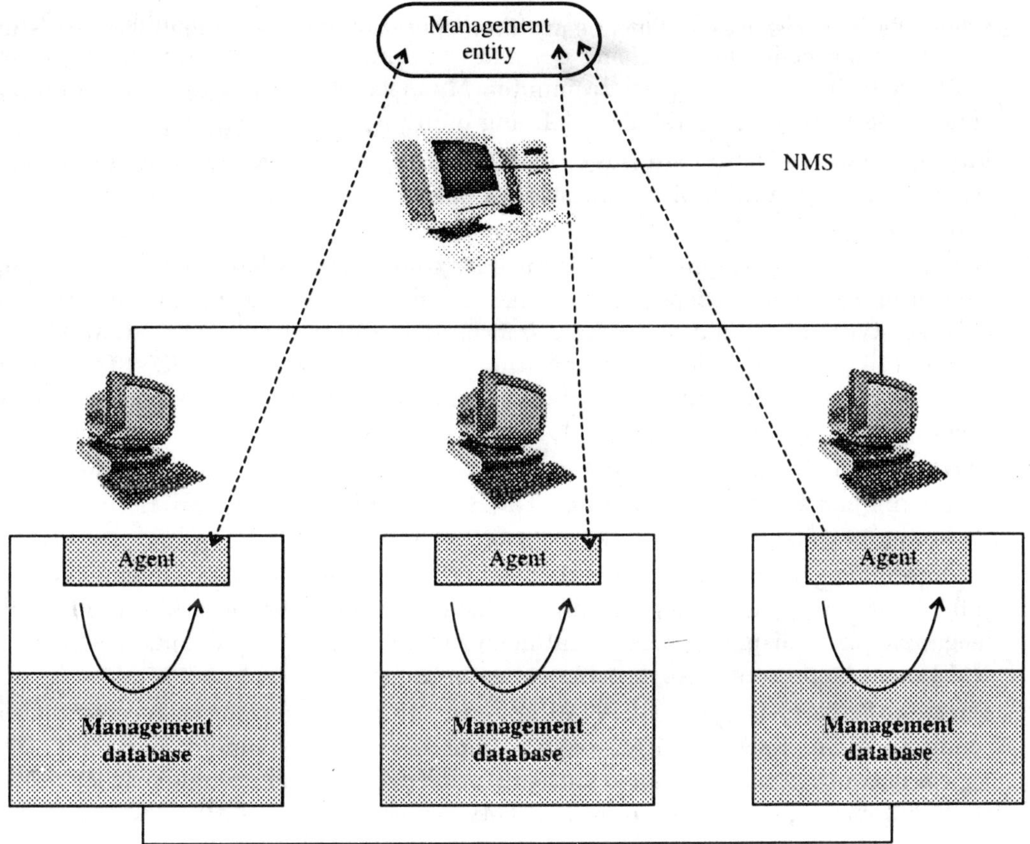

Fig. 16.4 SNMP-managed network consists of managed devices, agents, and NMSs

SNMP Technology

SNMP is part of the Internet network management architecture. This architecture is based on the interaction of many entities that are described in the following section.

The Internet Management Model

A network management system comprises:

- **Network elements**—Sometimes called managed devices, network elements are hardware devices such as computers, routers, and terminal servers that are connected to networks.
- **Agents**—Agents are software modules that reside in network elements. They collect and store management information such as the number of error packets received by a network element.
- **Managed object**—A managed object is a characteristic of something that can be managed. For example, a list of currently active TCP circuits in a particular host

computer is a managed object. Managed objects differ from variables, which are particular object instances. Using our example, an object instance is a single active TCP circuit in a particular host computer. Managed objects can be scalar (defining a single object instance) or tabular (defining multiple, related instances).

- **Management information base (MIB)**—A MIB is a collection of managed objects residing in a virtual information store. Collections of related managed objects are defined in specific MIB modules.
- **Syntax notation**—A syntax notation is a language used to describe a MIB's managed objects in a machine-independent format. Consistent use of a syntax notation allows different types of computers to share information. Internet management systems use a subset of the International Organization for Standardization's (ISO's) *Open System Interconnection* (OSI) *Abstract Syntax Notation* 1 (ASN.1) to define both the packets exchanged by the management protocol and the objects that are to be managed.
- **Structure of Management Information (SMI)**—The SMI defines the rules for describing management information. The SMI is defined using ASN.1.
- **Network management stations (NMSs)**—Sometimes called consoles, these devices execute management applications that monitor and control network elements. Physically, NMSs are usually engineering workstation-caliber computers with fast CPUs, megapixel color displays, substantial memory and abundant disk space. At least one NMS must be present in each managed environment.
- **Parties**—A party is a logical SNMPv2 entity that can initiate or receive SNMPv2 communication. Each SNMPv2 party comprises a single, unique party identity, a logical network location, a single authentication protocol and a single privacy protocol. SNMPv2 messages are communicated between two parties. An SNMPv2 entity can define multiple parties, each with different parameters. For example, different parties can use different authentication and/or privacy protocols.
- **Management protocol**—A management protocol is used to convey management information between agents and NMSs. SNMP is the Internet community's de facto standard management protocol.

SNMP Basic Commands

Managed devices are monitored and controlled using four basic SNMP commands: read, write, trap and traversal operations.

The **read** command is used by an NMS to monitor managed devices. The NMS examines different variables that are maintained by managed devices.

The **write** command is used by an NMS to control managed devices. The NMS changes the values of variables stored within managed devices.

The **trap** command is used by managed devices to asynchronously report events to the NMS. When certain types of events occur, a managed device sends a trap to the NMS.

Traversal operations are used by the NMS to determine which variables a managed device supports and to sequentially gather information in variable tables, such as a routing table.

The SNMPv2 specifications discuss two primary security protocols: one for authentication and one for privacy. These are the **Digest Authentication Protocol** and the **Symmetric Privacy Protocol**. The authentication protocol is designed to reliably identify the integrity of the originating SNMPv2 party. It consists of authentication information required to support the authentication protocol used. The privacy protocol is designed to protect information within the SNMPv2 message from disclosure. Only authenticated messages can be protected from disclosure. In other words, authentication is required for privacy.

The Digest Authentication Protocol verifies that the message received is the same one that was sent. Data integrity is protected using a 128-bit message digest calculated according to the Message Digest 5 (MD5) algorithm. The digest is calculated at the sender and enclosed with the SNMPv2 message. The receiver verifies the digest. A secret value, known only to the sender and the receiver, is prefixed to the message. After the digest is used to verify message integrity, the secret value is used to verify the message's origin.

To help ensure message privacy, the Symmetric Privacy Protocol uses a secret encryption key known only to the sender and the receiver. Before the message is authenticated, this protocol uses the Data Encryption Standard (DES) algorithm to effect privacy. DES is a documented National Institute of Standards and Technology (NIST) and American National Standards Institute (ANSI) standard. (DES discussed in chapter 17)

• • •

17

Network Security

Introduction To Network Security

Network security is a complicated subject, historically only tackled by well-trained and experienced experts. However, as more and more people become "wired", an increasing number of people need to understand the basics of security in a networked world.

Network security involves any and all countermeasures taken to protect a network from threats to its integrity. As modern networks have continued to grow and as more and more networks have been connected to the public Internet, the threats to the integrity and privacy of a company's networks have also grown. The attacks that are made on a network are increasingly more complex and pervasive, and the tools used for such purposes are easy to acquire. For example, anyone can log on to an Internet search engine and perform a search on hacking and be presented with an immense amount of sites that offer information and tools on hacking. Therefore, the need for network security is obvious. But what exactly is involved in a good network security policy?

A network security plan should be as comprehensive as possible. This not only includes physical aspects, such as locating your servers in a secure room, use of fault tolerance and power protection, but also includes all the steps taken to protect the data on your network. This would include setting up user accounts and passwords, setting permissions and access rights, the use of encryption for sensitive data, virus monitoring, and intrusion detection, to name just a few of the critical elements involved. And if your network is connected to any other networks, such as the Internet, then your network security plan should also include the implementation of a firewall. An effective network security strategy requires identifying threats and then choosing the most effective set of tools to combat them.

Definition

- *Security is a state of well-being of information and infrastructures in which the possibility of successful yet undetected theft, tampering, and disruption of information and services is kept low or tolerable.*
- *Security rests on confidentiality, authenticity, integrity, and availability.*

17.1 Need of Network Security

Information is a strategic resource. A significant portion of organizational budget is spent on managing information. There are many types of information and it has several security related objectives like:

- Confidentiality (secrecy)—protect information value.
- Integrity—protect information accuracy.
- Availability—ensure information delivery.

Network Security Goals

The various goals of network security are listed below:

- **Confidentiality :** Confidentiality is the concealment of information or resources. Information should not be disclosed or revealed to unauthorized persons; the same as privacy—keeping private documents private.
- **Integrity :** Integrity refers to the trustworthiness of data or resources in terms of preventing improper and unauthorized changes. Information should be safe from modification without the sender's or owner's consent.
- **Authentication :** Authenticity is the identification and assurance of the origin of information. The sender of the information really is who he/she claims to be.
- **Non-repudiation :** Principally, the sender cannot deny that he/she actually sent the message (non-repudiation of origin). In some cases also, the sender can prove the information was available to the recipient (non-repudiation of delivery) and the receiver cannot deny receipt of the message (non-repudiation of receipt).
- **Accessibility :** The information should be available to authorized users when required; and not available to unauthorized users.

These goals and their possible solutions are listed in the table below:

Security goal	Non-electronic Solutions	Electronic Solutions
Confidentiality	Sealed letter, opaque envelope	Encryption
Integrity	Hologram on credit card, indelible ink	Message digest
Authentication	Photo ID card, knowing personal details	Digital signature
Non-repudiation	Notarized signature, registered post	Digital signature
Accessibility	Locks, guards	Password, firewall

Network Security Tradeoffs

In network security, as in any form of information security, sometimes compromises have to be made between opposing forces.

Security versus Access : Protection of information involves a trade-off between security and accessibility. At one extreme information could be completely secure by storing it on a computer that no one ever uses. However this totally defeats the purpose for which the information was created. A more realistic approach to network security is to assess the possible threats to the data and then minimize the threat as much as possible without making it difficult for legitimate users to access the information.

Cost versus Benefits : Security economics requires that cost of security measures to protect information—both financial costs and user inconvenience—should not exceed the value of the information. Network managers must justify the cost of controls and safeguards in light of the expected frequency of attacks and the anticipated loss resulting from a successful attack. For example, an expensive firewall can be justified to protect a vital and vulnerable asset such as a company's Web site. However, the company's office equipment database would not require any projection other than normal back-up procedures.

17.1.1 Security Threats and Attacks

A **threat** is a potential violation of security. These are flaws in design, implementation, and operation. It is a circumstance, condition or event with the potential to cause harm to personnel and/or network resources in the form of destruction, disclosure, modification of data, denial of service, and/or fraud, waste, and abuse. Network security threats include impersonation, denial of service, packet replay, and packet modification.

An **attack** is any action that violates security. There are generally two types of attacks:

- Active attack.
- Passive attack.

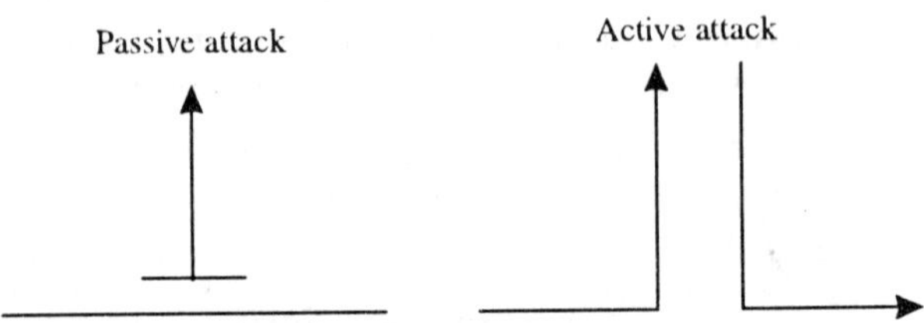

Fig. 17.1 Types of Attacks

Active attack : It is an attack on a computer network with the intent to insert, destroy, modify or divert data. Active attacks are difficult to prevent because preventive security reduces accessibility. Instead the primary goal is to detect active attacks and quickly recover from any disruption or delays caused by the attack. Active attack can actively modify communications or data.

Passive Attacks : It is an attack on a computer network with the intent to monitor network data transmission to read messages or analyze traffic. Passive attacks are difficult to detect because they do not involve alteration of the data. The emphasis is on prevention, rather than detection. Passive attack can only observe communications or data.

Types and Sources of Network Threats

1. Denial-of-Service

DoS (Denial-of-Service) attacks are probably the worst, and most difficult to address. These are the worst, because they're very easy to launch, difficult (sometimes impossible) to track, and it isn't easy to refuse the requests of the attacker, without also refusing legitimate requests for service.

Multi-user, multi-tasking operating systems are subject to denial of service attacks where one user can render the system unusable for legitimate users by hogging a resource or damaging or destroying resources so that they cannot be used. Denial of service attacks may be caused deliberately or accidentally. Taking precautions to prevent a system against unintentional denial of service attacks will help to prevent intentional denial of service attacks.

Three common forms of network denial of service attacks are service overloading, message flooding, and signal grounding. The premise of a DoS attack is simple: send more requests to the machine than it can handle. There are toolkits available in the underground community that make this a simple matter of running a program and telling it which host to blast with requests. The attacker's program simply makes a connection on some service port, perhaps forging the packet's header information that says where the packet came from, and then dropping the connection. If the host is able to answer 15 requests per second, and the attacker is sending 45 per second, obviously the host will be unable to service all of the attacker's requests, much less then any legitimate requests.

It is important for system administrators to protect against denial of service threats without denying access to legitimate users. In general, denial of service attacks are hard to prevent. Many denial of service attacks can be hindered by restricting access to critical accounts, resources, and files, and protecting them from unauthorized users. Some things that can be done to reduce the risk of being stung by a denial of service attack include:

- Not running your visible-to-the-world servers at a level too close to capacity.
- Using packet filtering to prevent obviously forged packets from entering into your network address space.
- Keeping up-to-date on security-related patches for your hosts' operating systems.

2. Eavesdropping

Eavesdropping allows a cracker to make a complete transcript of network activity. As a result, a cracker can obtain sensitive information, such as, passwords, data and procedures for performing functions. It is possible for a cracker to eavesdrop using wiretapping, eavesdropping by radio and eavesdropping via auxiliary ports on terminals. It is also possible to eavesdrop using software that monitors packets sent over the network. In most cases, it is difficult to detect that a cracker is eavesdropping.

Many network programs, such as telnet and ftp are vulnerable to eavesdroppers obtaining passwords that are often sent across the network unencrypted. Network programs that involve file transfer are susceptible to eavesdroppers obtaining the contents of files. Encryption can be used to prevent eavesdroppers from obtaining data traveling over unsecured networks.

3. Unauthorized Access

Unauthorized access is a very high-level term that can refer to a number of different sorts of attacks. The goal of these attacks is to access some resource that your machine should not provide the attacker. For example, a host might be a web server, and should provide anyone with requested web pages. However, that host should not provide command shell access without being sure that the person making such a request is someone who should get it, such as a local administrator.

4. Executing Commands Illicitly

It's obviously undesirable for an unknown and untrusted person to be able to execute commands on your server machines. There are two main classifications of the severity of this problem:

- Normal user access
- Administrator access

A normal user can do a number of things on a system (such as read files, mail them to other people, etc.) that an attacker should not be able to do. This might, then, be all the access that an attacker needs. On the other hand, an attacker might wish to make configuration changes to a host (perhaps changing its IP address, putting a start-up script in place to cause the machine to shut down every time it's started, or something similar). In this case, the attacker will need to gain administrator privileges on the host.

5. Confidentiality Breaches

There is certain information that could be quite damaging if it fell into the hands of a competitor, an enemy, or the public. In these cases, it's possible that compromise of a normal user's account on the machine can be enough to cause damage (Like obtaining information that can be used against the company, etc.)

While many of the executors of these sorts of break-ins are merely thrill-seekers interested in nothing more than to see a shell prompt for your computer on their screen, there are those who are more malicious. It can also be possible that someone who is normally interested in nothing more than the thrill could be persuaded to do more: perhaps a dishonest competitor is willing to hire such a person to hurt you.

6. Packet Replay

Packet replay refers to the recording and re-transmission of message packets in the network. Packet replay is a significant threat for programs that require authentication sequences, because an intruder could replay legitimate authentication sequence messages to gain access to a system. Packet replay is frequently undetectable, but can be prevented by using packet time-stamping and packet sequence counting.

7. Packet Modification

Packet modification is a significant integrity threat that involves one system intercepting and modifying a packet destined for another system. In many cases, packet information may not only be modified, but it may also be destroyed.

8. Destructive Behavior

Among the destructive sorts of break-ins and attacks, there are two major categories.

- **Data Diddling**
  The data diddler is likely the worst sort, since the fact of a break-in might not be immediately obvious. Perhaps he's toying with the numbers in your spreadsheets, or changing the dates in your projections and plans. Maybe he's changing the account numbers for the auto-deposit of certain paychecks. In any case, rare is the case when you'll come in to work one day, and simply know that something is wrong. An accounting procedure might turn up a discrepancy in the books three or four months after the fact. Trying to track the problem down will certainly be difficult, and once that problem is discovered, how can any of your numbers from that time period be trusted? How far back do you have to go before you think that your data is safe?
- **Data Destruction**
  Some of those perpetrate attacks are simply twisted jerks who like to delete things. In these cases, the impact on your computing capability—and consequently your business—can be nothing less than if a fire or other disaster caused your computing equipment to be completely destroyed.

Where do these threats come from?

An attacker can gain access to your equipment through any connection that you have to the outside world. This includes Internet connections, dial-up modems and even physical access. In order to be able to adequately address security, all possible avenues of entry must be identified and evaluated. The security of that entry point must be consistent with your stated policy on acceptable risk levels.

17.1.2 Security Management Techniques

Security management is the glue that holds together the other building blocks of a strong security solution. It involves facilities for coordinating users' service requirements and mechanism implementations throughout the enterprise network and across the Internet.

Security Policy and Mechanism

- **Policy :** A statement of what is, and is not allowed.
- **Mechanism :** A procedure, tool, or method of enforcing a policy.

Security mechanisms implement functions that help prevent, detect, and respond to recovery from security attacks. Security functions are typically made available to users as a set of security services through APIs or integrated interfaces.

Three basic building blocks are used:

- Encryption is used to provide confidentiality. It can provide authentication and integrity protection.
- Digital signatures are used to provide authentication, integrity protection, and non-repudiation.
- Checksums/hash algorithms are used to provide integrity protection and provide authentication.

One or more security mechanisms are combined to provide a security service. We will be discussing these security mechanisms in detail in next sections.

A typical security protocol provides one or more services. Services are built from mechanisms. Mechanisms are implemented using algorithms.

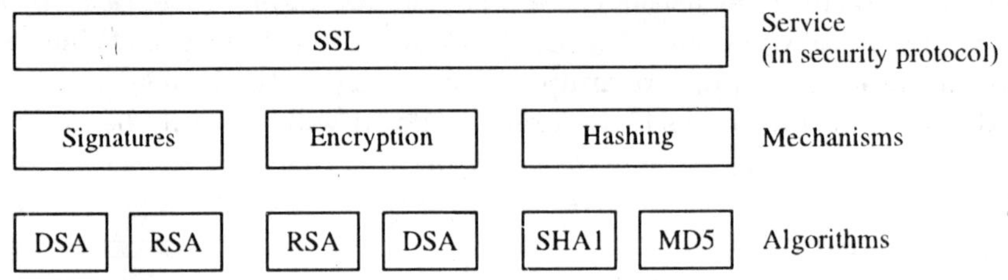

Fig. 17.2 Security Levels

Network Security Tools

The various network security tools are listed below:

Antivirus software packages : These packages counter most virus threats if regularly updated and correctly maintained.

Secure network infrastructure : Switches and routers have hardware and software features that support secure connectivity, perimeter security, intrusion protection, identity services, and security management. Dedicated network security hardware and software-tools such as firewalls and intrusion detection systems provide protection for all areas of the network and enable secure connections.

Virtual private networks : These networks provide access control and data encryption between two different computers on a network. This allows remote workers to connect to the network without the risk of a hacker or thief intercepting data.

Identity services : These services help to identify users and control their activities and transactions on the network. Services include passwords, digital certificates, and digital authentication keys.

Encryption : Encryption ensures that messages cannot be intercepted or read by anyone other than the authorized recipient.

None of these approaches alone will be sufficient to protect a network, but when they are layered together, they can be highly effective in keeping a network safe from attacks and other threats to security.

17.2 Cryptography

Cryptography is the study of secret (crypto-) writing (-graphy). It is concerned with developing algorithms that may be used to :

- Conceal the context of some message from all except the sender and recipient (privacy or secrecy), and/or
- Verify the correctness of a message to the recipient **(authentication)**.

It forms the basis of many technological solutions to computer and communications security problems.

Cryptography, the encoding of messages to render them unreadable by anyone other than their intended recipient(s), is centuries old. Caesar cipher is one of the traditional cryptography techniques. The "Caesar Cipher" is so named because it was used by Julius Caesar. With the advent of modern computer technology, many of these older ciphers became trivially crackable using brute-force attacks. Modern cryptography, essential to the security of computer networks, is done with complex algorithms implemented on high-speed computer systems.

There are two kinds of cryptosystems: **symmetric** and **asymmetric**. Symmetric cryptosystems use the same key (the secret key) to encrypt and decrypt a message and asymmetric cryptosystems use one key (the public key) to encrypt a message and a different key (the private key) to decrypt it. Asymmetric cryptosystems are also called public key cryptosystems.

Symmetric cryptosystems have a problem: how do you transport the secret key from the sender to the recipient securely and in a tamperproof fashion? If you could send the secret key securely, then, in theory, you wouldn't need the symmetric cryptosystem in the first place—because you would simply use that secure channel to send your message. Frequently, trusted couriers are used as a solution to this problem. Another, more efficient and reliable solution is a public key cryptosystem. A public-key cryptosystem has public encryption and private decryption.

17.2.1 Classical Cryptographic Techniques

Classical Cryptographic Techniques have two basic components of classical ciphers:

- **Substitution :** In substitution ciphers letters are replaced by other letters.
- **Transposition :** In transposition ciphers the letters are arranged in a different order. These ciphers may be:
    - ¤ *Monoalphabetic*—Only one substitution/ transposition is used.
    - ¤ *Polyalphabetic*—Where several substitutions/ transpositions are used.

Several such ciphers may be concatenated together to form a **product cipher**.

Caesar Cipher - A Monoalphabetic Cipher

Replace each letter of message by a letter a fixed distance away. E.g., use the 3rd letter on. It was reputedly used by Julius Caesar.

e.g., L FDPH L VDZ L FRQTXHUHG
I CAME I SAW I CONQUERED

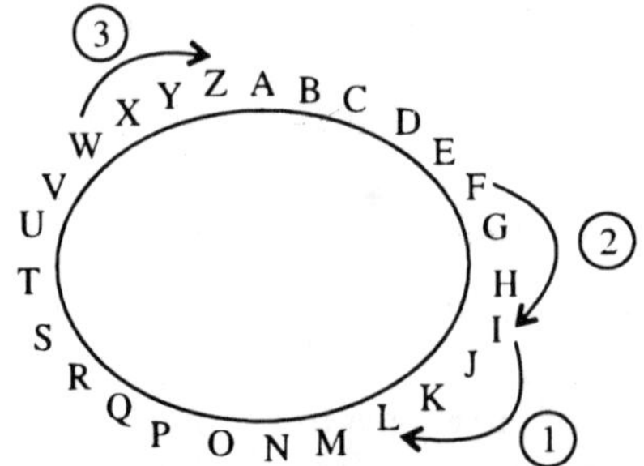

i.e., mapping is
ABCDEFGHIJKLMNOPQRSTUVWXYZ
DEFGHIJKLMNOPQRSTUVWXYZABC

Fig. 17.3 A monoalphabetic cipher

Decryption consists of :

- Writing the message out in columns.
- Reading off the message by reordering columns.
- Uses read out keys.

Generally speaking, computer cryptographic tasks can be broken into two general categories:

- Encryption
- Authentication

17.2.2 Encryption

Encryption refers to the scrambling of information so that the original message cannot be determined by unauthorized recipients. An encryption algorithm is applied to the message, referred to as the plaintext, and a key to produce ciphertext, which ideally appears to be random bits. A decryption algorithm converts the ciphertext back into plaintext, but only if given the correct key. Conventional, or symmetric, algorithms use the same key for both encryption and decryption. Public key algorithms use paired keys, one for encryption and another for decryption.

Important terms to be used in this section are listed below:

Plaintext : The original intelligible message.
Ciphertext : The transformed message.

Cipher : An algorithm for transforming an intelligible message into one that is unintelligible by transposition and/or substitution methods.

Key : Some critical information used by the cipher, known only to the sender and receiver.

Encipher (encode) : The process of converting plaintext to ciphertext using a cipher and a key.

Decipher (decode) : The process of converting ciphertext back into plaintext using a cipher and a key.

Cryptanalysis : The study of principles and methods of transforming an unintelligible message back into an intelligible message without knowledge of the key. Also called codebreaking.

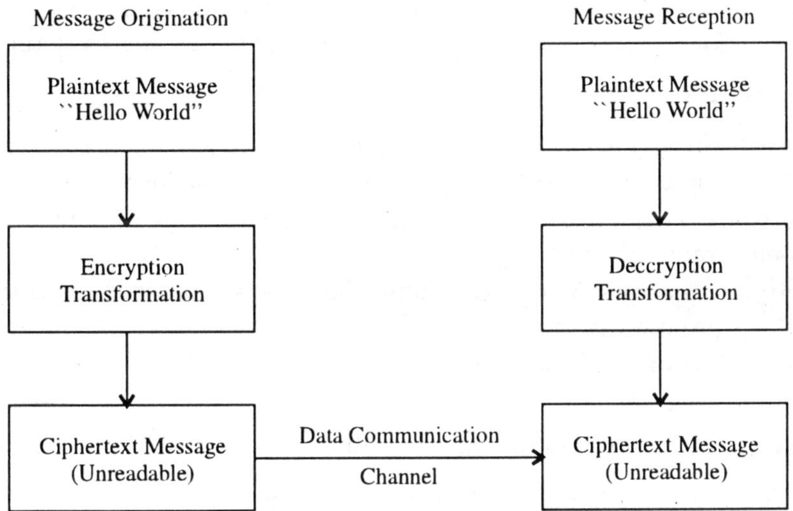

Fig. 17.4 Message encryption and decryption

Encryption to Insure Data and Transaction Security

Data security : It ensures the privacy and confidentiality of data in electronic messages. The goal is to defeat any attempt to read or change the data in the message. Data security is insured with encryption.

Transaction security : It ensures the authentication of remote users in network transactions. The goal is to defeat any attempt to assume another identity while involved with electronic mail or other forms of data communication.

Encryption : The transformation of information into a representation unreadable by anyone without a decryption key. Encryption requires:

- **Encryption algorithm :** A mathematical procedure for scrambling, or unscrambling, data. Different encryption products differ principally in the algorithm or algorithmic procedures used to encrypt the data.

- **Key** : A unique code for use with the algorithm (two keys are required in public key cryptography)
- **Information** : Target of the encryption process.

For example, a simple encryption procedure from a typical decoder ring might be:

- **Algorithm** : Shift each letter of the alphabet a certain number of spaces to the left.
- **Key** : The number of places to shift the letter. (e.g., 3 spaces)
- **Information** : Institute of Chartered Accountants of Scotland

Applying algorithm + key (information) = Institute of Chartered Accountants of Scotland
fkpqfqrqb lc zexoqboba xzzlrkqxkqp lc pzlqixka

In order to decrypt the message the algorithm must be known as well as the key. Note that the decryption key for this message is 23 spaces (e.g., I is 23 spaces to the left of F).

Encryption is used to insure:

- **Confidentiality** : A message intended for an individual can only be read by that person. Non-electronic example: sealed envelope marked "private and confidential".
- **Authenticity** : The message is genuine; it really did come from the person who sent it. Non-electronic example : signature.
- **Integrity** : The message is complete and was not altered in transport –either accidentally or on purpose.
- **Non-repudiation** : A person cannot later deny that they sent the message or that the message was altered.

The various encryption algorithms that we will discuss are listed below :

- Conventional Encryption or Secret-key cryptography
- Public-key Encryption or Public-key cryptography

17.2.2.1 Conventional encryption

It is also known as Secret-key cryptography. In this algorithm a shared key is used by the sender and the receiver. While simple to implement, distribution of the key represents a major problem. Anyone who intercepts the key in transit can read all encrypted messages using that key. In electronic commerce where one must deal with a large number of individuals it is impractical to assume that key management will be flawless. Thus secret-key cryptography is unlikely to be a major part of electronic commerce.

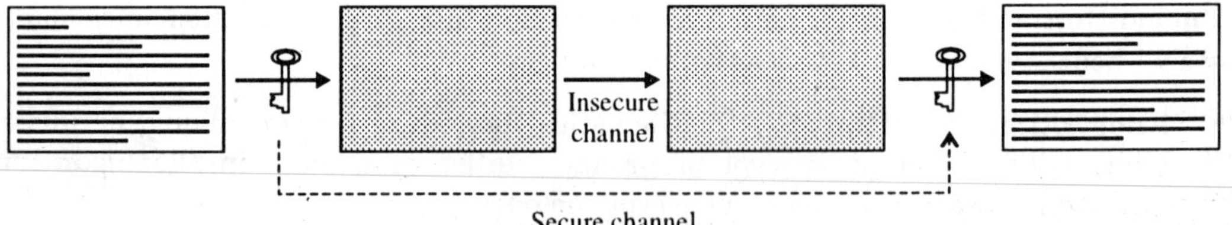

Fig. 17.5 Conventional encryption

In this scheme the problem of communicating a large message in secret reduced to communicating a small key in secret.

17.2.2.2 Public-key encryption

It is also known as **Public-key cryptography**. This scheme involves the creation of a key pair—a private key that is kept secret and a public key that is published, perhaps on a personal home page or in an e-mail signature file. The two keys work together in a matched set so what one key locks the other key can unlock. The keys must be used in pairs; obviously a public key cannot both lock and unlock the same message.

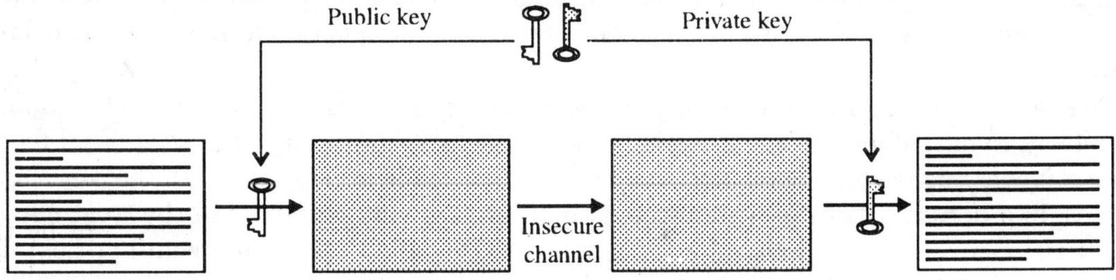

Fig. 17.6 Public-key encryption

In this scheme anyone can encrypt with the public key, only one person can decrypt with the private key.

17.2.3 Authentication

Authentication is the verification of a message's sender. Authentication requires protecting a message so it cannot be altered, usually by attaching to it a digital signature. Typically, the signature is formed by computing a hash of the message, which is encrypted using a public key cryptosystem, insuring that nobody without the proper key can generate a valid signature. Note that authentication is different from encryption, since the actual message may be completely unencrypted, and cryptography used only to validate the identify of the creator.

Often, much attention is given to the algorithm and little paid to the key. In fact, just as with login passwords, cryptographic systems are only as secure as their keys, making key management a critical and often neglected concern. Certificates have emerged as a clever way of managing large-scale key distribution. The following techniques will be discussed under this section:

1. Digital signature.
2. Hash Functions.

17.2.3.1 Digital signature

A digital signature is approximately the reverse of the public cryptography process outlined above. Some public-key algorithms can be used to generate digital signatures. A digital signature is a small amount of data that was created using some secret key, and there is a public key that can be used to verify that the signature was really generated using the corresponding private key. The algorithm used to generate the signature must be such that without knowing the secret key it is not possible to create a signature that would verify as valid.

Digital signatures are used to verify that a message really comes from the claimed sender (assuming only the sender knows the secret key corresponding to his/her public key). They can also be used to **timestamp** documents: a trusted party **signs** the document and its timestamp with his/her secret key, thus testifying that the document existed at the stated time.

Digital signatures can also be used to testify (or certify) that a public key belongs to a particular person. This is done by signing the combination of the key and the information about its owner by a trusted key. The digital signature by a third party (owner of the trusted key), the public key and information about the owner of the public key are often called certificates.

The reason for trusting that third party key may again be that it was signed by another trusted key. Eventually some key must be a root of the trust hierarchy (that is, it is not trusted because it was signed by somebody, but because you believe a priori that the key can be trusted). In a **centralized key infrastructure** there are very few roots in the trust network (e.g., trusted government agencies; such roots are also called certification authorities). In a **distributed infrastructure** there need not be any universally accepted roots, and each party may have different trusted roots (such of the party's own key and any keys signed by it).

A digital signature of an arbitrary document is typically created by computing a **message digest** from the document, and concatenating it with information about the signer, a timestamp, etc. The resulting string is then encrypted using the private key of the signer using a suitable algorithm. The resulting encrypted block of bits is the signature. It is often distributed together with information about the public key that was used to sign it. To verify a signature, the recipient first determines whether it trusts that the key belongs to the person it is supposed to belong to (using the web of trust or a priori knowledge), and then decrypts the signature using the public key of the person. If the signature decrypts properly and the information matches that of the message (proper message digest etc.), the signature is accepted as valid. Several methods for making and verifying digital signatures are freely available.

Digital Certificate : An important aspect of public key cryptography and digital signatures is distribution of the public keys. Digital Certificate is a data structure, digitally signed by a certification authority that binds a public-key value to the identity of the entity holding the corresponding private key. These digital certificates will be placed in our e-mail programs and Web browsers.

SET : Secure Electronic Transactions

To reduce the incidence of credit card fraud over the Internet, VISA and MasterCard are developing SET—a single technical standard for safeguarding payment card purchases made on the Internet.

The five business objectives of SET are:

- Provide confidentiality of payment and ordering information.
- Ensure integrity for all transmitted data.
- Provide authentication that a cardholder is a legitimate user of an account.

- Provide authentication that a merchant can accept bank card payments through its relationship with a financial institution. (called the acquirer)
- Facilitate and encourage interoperability across software and network providers.

The major advantage of SET over existing security systems is the use of digital certificates that provide an easy and convenient way to ensure that the participants in an electronic commerce transaction can trust each other. The card company (VISA or MasterCard) will provide digital certificates to the card-issuing financial institution and the institution will provide a digital certificate to the cardholder. A similar process takes place for the merchant. At the time of the transaction, each party's SET-compliant software checks the digital certificates and validates both merchant and cardholder before any information is exchanged.

A number of parties are involved:

- Software on the cardholder's computer. (e.g., Netscape, Microsoft)
- Software on the merchant's network computer (e.g., Netscape, Sun, Microsoft). The merchant benefits by having a better way of identifying the purchaser, leading to lower fraud losses and fewer chargebacks.
- Technology residing at the acquirer's (the merchant's bank) location to decrypt the financial information.
- The certificate authorities, to issue digital certificates.

SET will probably work like this:

- VISA/MasterCard will certify banks to be certification authorities.
- Banks will issue digital certificates to merchants and cardholders.
- Your public key will be made available through your browser, e-mail, etc.
- Your private key will be password-protected on your hard disk.
- When purchasing a product or service, the public and private keys of the purchaser and the seller will be used to authenticate the transaction and encrypt it for privacy.

17.2.3.2 Hash functions

Hash Functions take a block of data as input, and produce a **hash** or **message digest** as output. The usual intent is that the hash can act as a signature for the original data, without revealing its contents. Therefore, it's important that the hash function be irreversible—not only should it be nearly impossible to retrieve the original data, it must also be unfeasible to construct a data block that matches some given hash value. Given the exact same input twice, the hash function should always produce the same output. Even a single bit changed in the input, though, should produce a different hash value. The hash value should be small enough to be manageable in further manipulations, yet large enough to prevent an attacker from randomly finding a block of data that produces the same hash.

Hash Functions creates a unique "fingerprint" for a message.

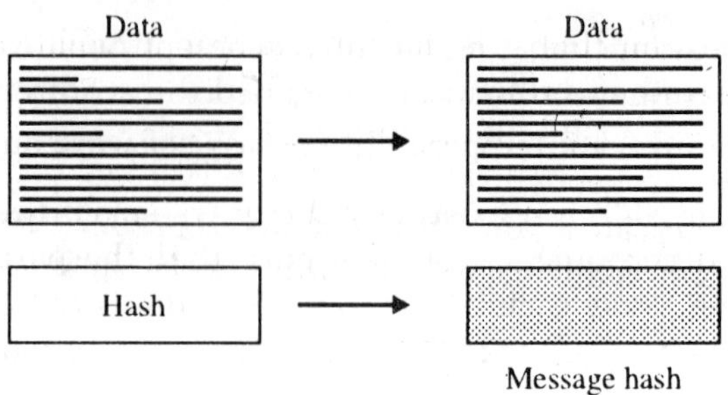

Fig. 17.7 Conversion of data to message hash

Anyone can alter the data and calculate a new hash value. Hash has to be protected in some way.

MAC (Message Authentication Code)

Message Authentication Code, adds a password/key to a Hash. Only the password holder(s) can generate the MAC.

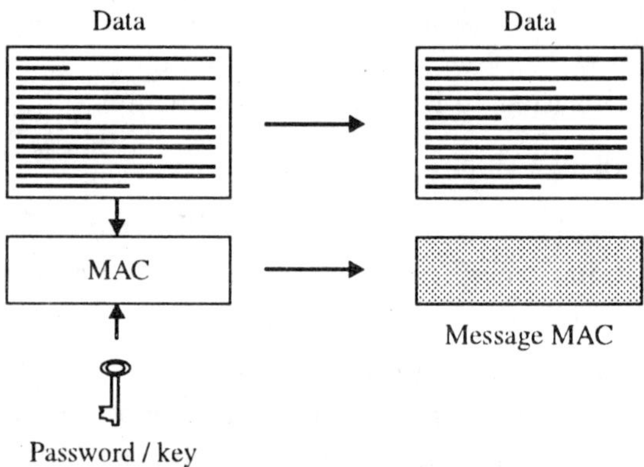

Fig. 17.8 Key added to hash

MD5 is perhaps the most widely used hash function at this time. It takes an arbitrarily sized block of data as input and produces a 128-bit (16-byte) hash. It uses bitwise operations, addition, and a table of values based on the sine function to process the data in 64-byte blocks.

Hash functions can't be used directly for encryption, but are very useful for authentication. One of the simplest uses of a hash function is to protect passwords. UNIX systems, in particular, will apply a hash function to a user's password and store the hash value, not the password itself. To authenticate the user, a password is requested, and the response runs through the hash function. If the resulting hash value is the same as the one stored, then the user must have supplied the correct password, and is authenticated. Since the hash function is irreversible, obtaining the hash values doesn't reveal the passwords to an attacker. In practice, though, people will often use guessable passwords, so obtaining the hashes might reveal passwords to an attacker who, for example, hashes all the words in the dictionary and compares the results to the password hashes.

Another use of hash functions is for interactive authentication over the network. Transmitting a hash instead of an actual password has the advantage of not revealing the password to anyone sniffing on the network traffic. If the password is combined with some changing value, then the hashes will be different every time, preventing an attacker from using an old hash to authenticate again. This approach is used in PPP's authentication scheme. The server sends a random challenge to the client, which combines the challenge with the password, computes the hash value, and sends it back to the server. The server, possessing both the stored secret password and the random challenge, performs the same hash computation, and checks its result against the reply from the client. If they match, then the client must know the password to have correctly computed the hash value. Since the next authentication would involve a different random challenge, the expected hash value would be different, preventing an attacker from using a replay attack.

A slight variant of this scheme can be used to generate data signatures. Assume that both the sender and recipient of some data message share a secret value. Then, by combining the data message with the secret, and running it through a hash function, a signature is generated in the form of the hash value. The data message is transmitted along with the signature. The recipient combines the received message with the secret, generates a hash value, and checks to make sure it's identical to the signature. The message's authenticity is thus verified.

Thus, hash functions, though not encryption algorithms in their own right can be used to provide significant security services, mainly identity authentication.

17.3 RSA Algorithm

Cryptographic algorithms are the basic building blocks of cryptographic applications and protocols. In cryptography, **RSA** is an algorithm for public key encryption. The RSA algorithm can be used for both public key encryption and digital signatures. Its security is based on the difficulty of factoring large integers.

The algorithm was described in 1977 by Ron Rivest, Adi Shamir and Len Adleman and the letters **RSA** are the initials of their surnames. RSA is widely used in electronic commerce protocols, and is believed to be secure given sufficiently long keys.

How the RSA System Works ?

The algorithm involves multiplying two large prime numbers (a prime number is a number divisible only by that number and 1) and through additional operations deriving a set of two numbers that constitutes the public key and another set that is the private key. Once the keys have been developed, the original prime numbers are no longer important and can be discarded. Both the public and the private keys are needed for encryption /decryption but only the owner of a private key ever needs to know it. Using the RSA system, the private key never needs to be sent across the Internet. The private key is used to decrypt text that has been encrypted with the public key.

Operation of RSA

The RSA algorithm works as follows:

1. Take two large primes, p and q.
2. Compute their product $n = p.q$; n is called the modulus.
3. Choose a number, e, less than n and relatively prime to $(p-1)(q-1)$, which means e and $(p-1)(q-1)$ have no common factors except 1.
4. Find another number d such that $(ed-1)$ is divisible by $(p-1)(q-1)$.
5. The values e and d are called the public and private exponents, respectively.
6. The public key is the pair (n, e).
7. The private key is (n, d).
8. The factors p and q may be destroyed or kept with the private key.

It is currently difficult to obtain the private key d from the public key(n, e). However if one could factor n into p and q, then one could obtain the private key d. Thus the security of the RSA system is based on the assumption that factoring is difficult. The discovery of an easy method of factoring would "break" RSA.

The **keys generated** by the above algorithm are listed below:

The **public key** consists of

- n, the modulus, and
- e, the public exponent (sometimes known as *encryption exponent*).

The **private key** consists of

- n, the modulus, which is public and appears in the public key, and
- d, the private exponent (sometimes known as *decryption exponent*), which must be kept secret.

Next we will discuss how the RSA system can be used for encryption and digital signatures.

Encrypting Messages

Suppose ***A*** wants to send a message m to ***B***. ***A*** creates the ciphertext c by exponentiating:

$$c = m^e \bmod n$$

where e and n are ***B's*** public key; m is the plaintext and c is the ciphertext.

A sends c to ***B***.

Decrypting Messages

To decrypt, ***B*** also exponentiates:

$$m = c^d \bmod n;$$

The relationship between e and d ensures that ***B*** correctly recovers m. Since only ***B*** knows d, only ***B*** can decrypt this message.

A working example

Here is an example of RSA encryption and decryption. The parameters used here are artificially small. We let

$p = 61$	First prime number (to be kept secret or deleted securely)
$q = 53$	Second prime number (to be kept secret or deleted securely)
$n = pq = 3233$	Modulus (to be made public)
$e = 17$	Public exponent (to be made public)
$d = 2753$	Private exponent (to be kept secret)

The public key is (e, n). The private key is d.

The encryption function is:

$$\text{encrypt}(m) = c = m^e \bmod n = m^{17} \bmod 3233$$

The decryption function is:

$$\text{decrypt}(c) = m = c^d \bmod n = c^{2753} \bmod 3233$$

To encrypt the plaintext value 123, we calculate

$$\text{encrypt}(123) = 123^{17} \bmod 3233 = 855$$

To decrypt the ciphertext value 855, we calculate

$$\text{decrypt}(855) = 855^{2753} \bmod 3233 = 123$$

Digital Signature

RSA can also be used to sign a message. The procedure is described below:

- Suppose ***A*** wants to send a message m to ***B*** in such a way that ***B*** is assured the message is both authentic, has not been tampered with, and from ***A***.
- ***A*** creates a digital signature s by exponentiating:

  $$s = m^d \bmod n, \text{ (as done when decrypting a message),}$$

  where d and n are ***A's*** private key.
- ***A*** sends m and s to ***B***.
- To verify the signature, ***B*** exponentiates and checks that the message m is recovered:

  $$m = s^e \bmod n, \text{ (as done when encrypting a message),}$$

  where e and n are ***A's*** public key.
- ***B*** compares the resulting value with the message's actual value. If the two agree, he knows that the author of the message was in possession of ***A's*** secret key, and that the message has not been tampered with since.

Thus encryption and authentication take place without any sharing of private keys: each person uses only another's public key or their own private key. Anyone can send an encrypted message or verify a signed message, but only someone in possession of the correct private key can decrypt or sign a message.

There are a few possible interpretations of "breaking" the RSA system. The most damaging would be for an attacker to discover the private key corresponding to a given public key; this would enable the attacker both to read all messages encrypted with the public key and to forge signatures.

The following table might help us to remember what kind of key is to be used for encryption and for digital signatures:

To do this	Use whose	Kind of key
Send an encrypted message	Use the receiver's	Public key
Send an encrypted signature	Use the sender's	Private key
Decrypt an encrypted message	Use the receiver's	Private key
Decrypt an encrypted signature (and authenticate the sender)	Use the sender's	Public key

17.4 DES (Data Encryption Standard)

Data Encryption Standard is the name of the Federal Information Processing Standard (FIPS), which describes the data encryption algorithm (DEA). The DEA is also defined in the ANSI standard X3.92. DES is sometimes referred to as the DEA (the Data **Encryption Algorithm**). DES provides a description of the mathematical algorithms for encrypting (enciphering) and decrypting (deciphering) binary coded information.

DES describes an algorithm that takes a fixed-length string of plaintext bits and transforms it through a series of complicated operations into another ciphertext bit string of the same length. In the case of DES, the block size is 64-bits. DES also uses a key to customise the transformation, so that decryption can only be performed by those who know the particular key used to encrypt. The key consists of 64-bits; however, only 56 of these are actually used by the algorithm. Eight bits are used solely for checking parity, and are thereafter discarded. Hence the effective key length is 56-bits.

Authorized users of encrypted computer data must have the key that was used to encipher the data in order to decrypt it. Unauthorized recipients of the cipher who know the algorithm but do not have the correct key cannot derive the original data algorithmically. Anyone who does have the key and the algorithm can easily decipher the cipher and obtain the original data. A standard algorithm based on a secure key thus provides a basis for exchanging encrypted computer data by issuing the key used to encipher it to those authorized to have the data.

Operation of DES

The algorithm's overall structure is shown in Figure 17.9 : there are 16 identical stages of processing, termed rounds. There is also an initial and final permutation, termed IP and FP, which are inverses (IP "undoes" the action of FP, and vice versa). Before the main rounds, the block is divided into two 32-bit halves and processed alternately; this criss-crossing is known as the Feistel scheme.

[**Note** : (A **permutation** is simply an ordered sequence with no two elements the same, drawn from a fixed set of symbols, and of maximum length.)
(**Feistel cipher**—In cryptography, a **Feistel cipher** is a block cipher with a particular structure, named after IBM cryptographer Horst Feistel; it is also commonly known as a **Feistel network**. The Feistel structure has the advantage that encryption and decryption operations are very similar, even identical in some cases, requiring only a reversal of the key schedule. Therefore the size of the code or circuitry required to implement such a cipher is nearly halved.)]

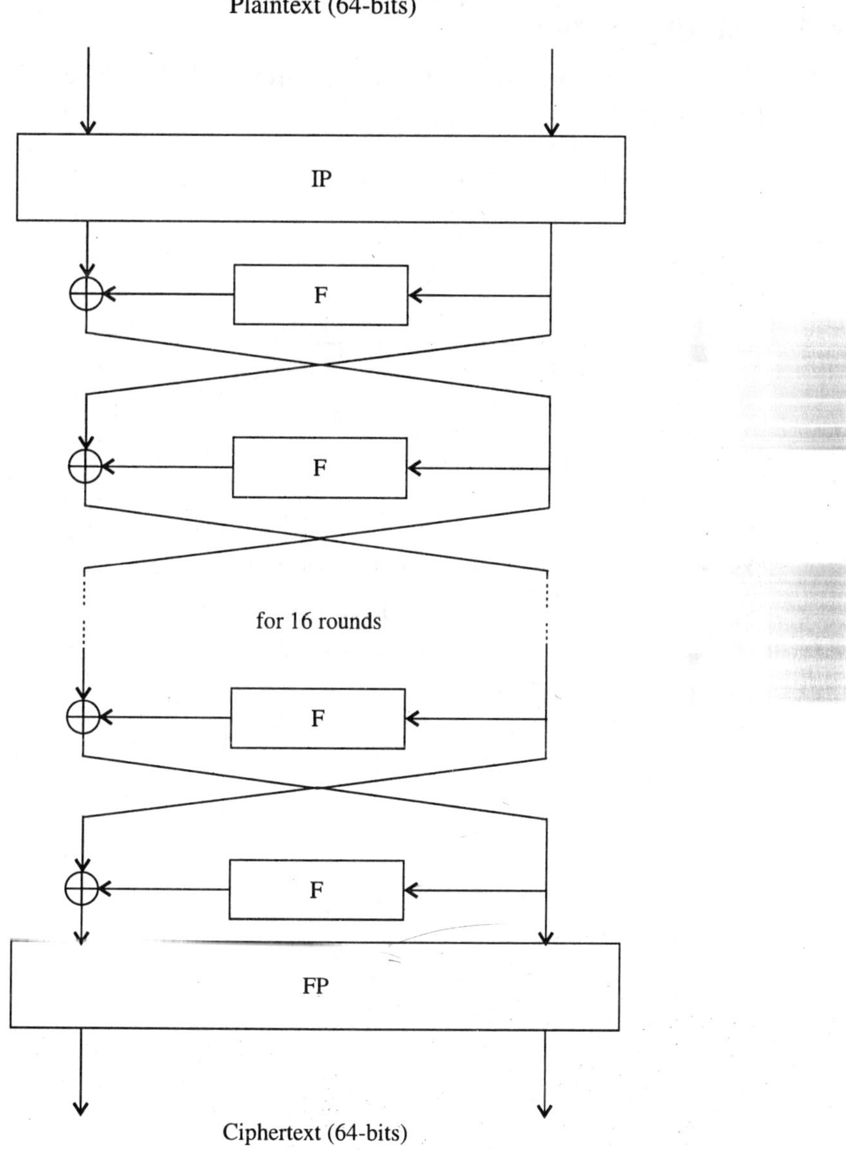

Fig. 17.9 The overall feistel structure of DES

The Feistel structure ensures that decryption and encryption are very similar processes - the only difference is that the subkeys are applied in the reverse order when decrypting. The rest of the algorithm is identical. This greatly simplifies implementation, particularly in hardware, as there is no need for separate encryption and decryption algorithms.

The ⊕ symbol denotes the exclusive-OR (XOR) operation. The *F-function* scrambles half a block together with some of the key. The output from the F-function is then combined with the other half of the block, and the halves are swapped before the next round. After the final round, the halves are not swapped; this is a feature of the Feistel structure which makes encryption and decryption similar processes.

The Feistel (F) Function

The F-function, depicted in Figure 17.10, operates on half a block (32-bits) at a time and consists of four stages:

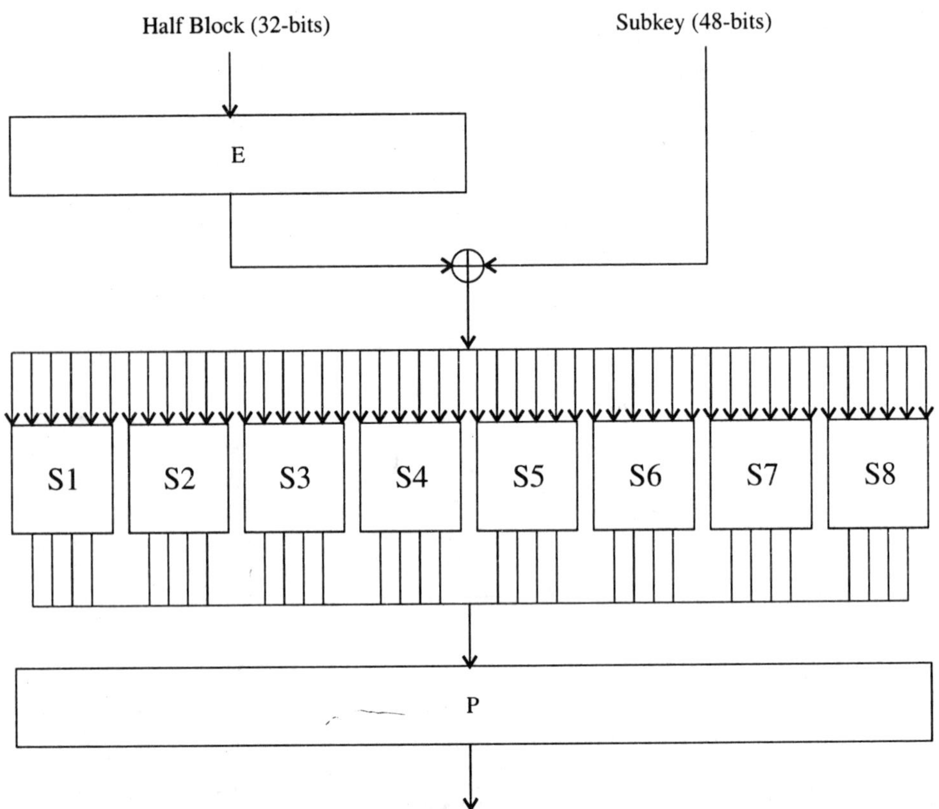

Fig. 17.10 The Feistel function (F-function) of DES

1. **Expansion**—The 32-bit half-block is expanded to 48-bits using the expansion permutation, denoted E in the diagram, by duplicating some of the bits.
2. **Key mixing**—The result is combined with a subkey using an XOR operation. Sixteen

48-bit subkeys—one for each round—are derived from the main key using the key schedule (described below).

3. **Substitution**—After mixing in the subkey, the block is divided into eight 6-bit pieces before processing by the *S-boxes*, or *substitution boxes*. Each of the eight S-boxes replaces its six input bits with four output bits according to a non-linear transformation, provided in the form of a lookup table. The S-boxes provide the core of the security of DES—without them, the cipher would be linear, and trivially breakable.
4. **Permutation**—Finally, the 32 outputs from the S-boxes are rearranged according to a fixed permutation, the P-box.

Key Schedule

In cryptography, the algorithm for computing the subkeys for each round in a product cipher from the encryption (or decryption) key is called the **key schedule**.

Figurc 17.11 illustrates the key schedule for encryption—the algorithm which generates the subkeys. Initially, 56-bits of the key are selected from the initial 64 by Permuted Choice 1 (PC-1)—the remaining eight bits are either discarded or used as parity check bits. The 56-bits are then divided into two 28-bit halves; each half is thereafter treated separately. In successive rounds, both halves are rotated left by one or two bits (specified for each round), and then 48

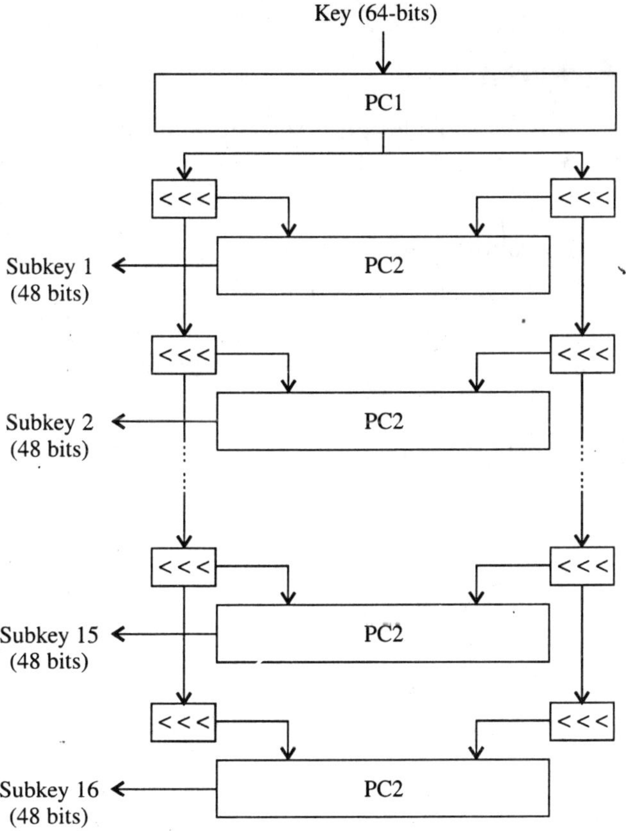

Fig. 17.11 The key-schedule of DES ("< < <" in the diagram denotes the rotations)

subkey bits are selected by *Permuted Choice* 2 (*PC*-2)—24-bits from the left half, and 24 from the right. The rotations (denoted by "<" in the diagram) mean that a different set of bits is used in each subkey; each bit is used in approximately 14 out of the 16 subkeys.

The key schedule for decryption is similar—it must generate the keys in the reverse order. Hence the rotations are to the right, rather than the left.

Applications

Data encryption (cryptography) is utilized in various applications and environments. In general, cryptography is used to protect data while it is being communicated between two points or while it is stored in a medium vulnerable to physical theft. Communication security provides protection to data by enciphering it at the transmitting point and deciphering it at the receiving point.

File security provides protection to data by enciphering it when it is recorded on a storage medium and deciphering it when it is read back from the storage medium. In the first case, the key must be available at the transmitter and receiver simultaneously during communication. In the second case, the key must be maintained and accessible for the duration of the storage period.

DES is now considered to be insecure for many applications. This is chiefly due to the 56-bit key size being too small; DES keys have been broken in less than 24 hours.

17.5 Network Firewall

In building construction, a firewall is designed to keep a fire from spreading from one part of the building to another. A network firewall, however, can be better compared to a moat of a medieval castle:

- It restricts people to entering at one carefully controlled point.
- It prevents attackers from getting close to other defenses.
- It restricts people to leaving at one carefully controlled point.
- Usually, a network firewall is installed at a point where the protected subnetwork is connected to a less trusted network.

Example : Connection of a corporate local area network to the Internet.

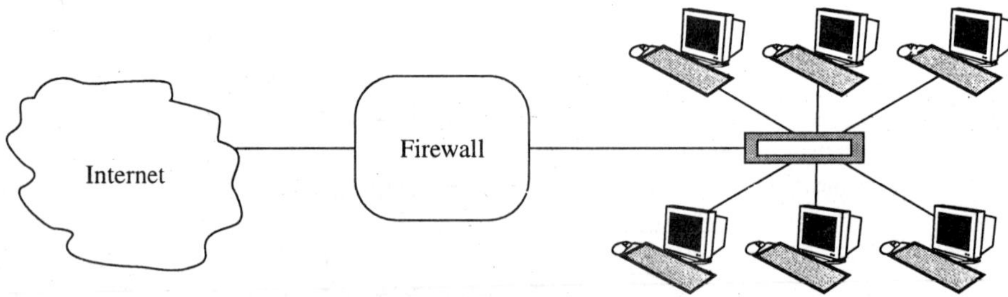

Fig. 17.12 Network firewall

The term firewall is used to refer to any hardware or software that acts as a barrier between connected networks. It can be a router, gateway or special purpose computer that monitors and controls the flow of data between networks. A firewall functions as a gatekeeper, monitoring and controlling what information enters and leaves a network.

A firewall filters the traffic flowing between an internal private network (trusted) and an external public network (untrusted) in order to protect the internal network. It is interesting to note that a firewall not only protects the internal network from attacks from the outside, but it also filters what data can leave the network as well.

The firewall can be thought of as a pair of mechanisms: one that exists to block traffic, and the other that exists to permit traffic. Some firewalls place a greater emphasis on blocking traffic, while others emphasize permitting traffic. Probably the most important thing to recognize about a firewall is that it implements an access control policy. If you don't have a good idea of what kind of access you want to allow or to deny, a firewall really won't help you. Administrators for firewalls managing the connectivity for a large number of hosts therefore have a heavy responsibility.

Trusted and Untrusted Networks

Trusted networks are defined as "the networks inside your security perimeter, and are usually the networks you are trying to protect". Untrusted networks are defined as "the networks outside your security perimeter. They are untrusted because they are often beyond your control". In other words, untrusted networks are those that may offer services or information that you need to access, but because you are not in control of administering these networks, they are untrusted in the sense that you limit the communications between them and your network. An example of this might be a client network you connect to gain access to certain information. There are also "unknown" networks, which would include any network not specifically defined in your firewall's configuration, which would include the majority of the networks you visit on the Internet.

Two Fundamental Approaches Regarding Firewall Policy

- Default deny strategy:
  - "Everything that is not explicitly permitted is denied"
  - Examine the services the users of the protected network need.
  - Consider the security implications of these services and how the services can be safely provided.
  - Allow only those services that can be safely provided and for which there is a legitimate need.
  - Deny any other service.
- Default permit strategy:
  - "Everything that is not explicitly forbidden is denied"
  - Permit every service that is not considered dangerous. Example: Network file system (NFS) and X-Windows is not permitted across the firewall.

- Incoming telnet connections are only allowed to one specific host.

After studying the above two policies we can say that the firewall can be configured in one of two ways:

A **closed firewall** is one in which access is denied unless specifically permitted. The firewall manager essentially starts with a blank permit list and adds only those functions that are explicitly allowed. This configuration appeals to network managers because it increases security. However, users consider it too restrictive since it may deny them access to useful network services.

An **open firewall** is one in which access is permitted unless specifically denied. This configuration increases access but decreases security because it is impossible to know all the possible threats to be guarded against.

17.5.1 Need of Firewall

The Internet, like any other society, is plagued with the kind of jerks who enjoy the electronic equivalent of writing on other people's walls with spray paint, tearing their mailboxes off, or just sitting in the street blowing their car horns. Some people try to get real work done over the Internet, and others have sensitive or proprietary data they must protect. Usually, a firewall's purpose is to keep the jerks out of your network while still letting you get your job done.

Many traditional-style corporations and data centers have computing security policies and practices that must be adhered to. In a case where a company's policies dictate how data must be protected, a firewall is very important, since it is the embodiment of the corporate policy. Frequently, the hardest part of hooking to the Internet, if you're a large company, is not justifying the expense or effort, but convincing management that it's safe to do so. A firewall provides not only real security—it often plays an important role as a security blanket for management.

Lastly, a firewall can act as your corporate "ambassador" to the Internet. Many corporations use their firewall systems as a place to store public information about corporate products and services, files to download, bug-fixes, and so forth. Several of these systems have become important parts of the Internet service structure (e.g., UUnet.uu.net) and have reflected well on their organizational sponsors.

Uses of a Firewall

- The principal responsibility of the firewall is to prevent unwanted and potentially damaging intrusion into a private network. To do so all traffic between the inside network and outside networks must pass through the firewall. Then only authorized traffic based on the security policy is allowed through.
- Firewalls can also be used for network management and monitoring purposes (e.g., corporate policies that prohibit employees accessing non-business Web sites during working hours can be enforced by a firewall that records this information).
- Firewalls are also capable of scanning incoming files for viruses, encrypting and decrypting incoming and outgoing traffic and performing a host of other security and network

management functions. However, as network managers ask the firewall to do more, processing network traffic slows down. Accordingly, these processing-intensive functions are usually carried out elsewhere.

What can a firewall protect against?

Some firewalls permit only email traffic through them, thereby protecting the network against any attacks other than attacks against the email service. Other firewalls provide less strict protections, and block services that are known to be problems.

Generally, firewalls are configured to protect against unauthenticated interactive logins from the "outside world". This, more than anything, helps prevent vandals from logging into machines on your network. More elaborate firewalls block traffic from the outside to the inside, but permit users on the inside to communicate freely with the outside. The firewall can protect you against any type of network-borne attack if you unplug it.

Firewalls are also important since they can provide a single "choke point" where security and audit can be imposed. Unlike in a situation where a computer system is being attacked by someone dialing in with a modem, the firewall can act as an effective "phone tap" and tracing tool. Firewalls provide an important logging and auditing function; often they provide summaries to the administrator about what kinds and amount of traffic passed through it, how many attempts there were to break into it, etc. Providing this choke point can serve the same purpose on your network as a guarded gate can for your site's physical premises. That means anytime you have a change in zones or levels of sensitivity, such a checkpoint is appropriate. A company rarely has only an outside gate and no receptionist or security staff to check badges on the way in. If there are layers of security on your site, it's reasonable to expect layers of security on your network.

Summary of what firewalls can do

- A firewall is a focus for security decisions.
- A firewall can enforce a security policy, i.e. concerning access control.
- A firewall can log Internet activity efficiently.
- A firewall can limit exposure to security problems in one part of a network.

What can't a firewall protect against?

Firewalls can't protect against attacks that don't go through the firewall. Many corporations that connect to the Internet are very concerned about proprietary data leaking out of the company through that route. Unfortunately for those concerned, a magnetic tape can just as effectively be used to export data. Many organizations that are terrified (at a management level) of Internet connections have no coherent policy about how dial-in access via modems should be protected. It's silly to build a 6-foot thick steel door when you live in a wooden house, but there are a lot of organizations out there buying expensive firewalls and neglecting the numerous other back-doors into their network. For a firewall to work, it must be a part of a consistent overall organizational security architecture.

Firewall policies must be realistic and reflect the level of security in the entire network.

For example, a site with top secret or classified data doesn't need a firewall at all: they shouldn't be hooking up to the Internet in the first place, or the systems with the really secret data should be isolated from the rest of the corporate network.

Another thing a firewall can't really protect you against is traitors or idiots inside your network. While an industrial spy might export information through your firewall, he's just as likely to export it through a telephone, FAX machine, or floppy disk. Floppy disks are a far more likely means for information to leak from your organization than a firewall! Firewalls also cannot protect you against stupidity. Users who reveal sensitive information over the telephone are good targets for social engineering; an attacker may be able to break into your network by completely bypassing your firewall, if he can find a "helpful" employee inside who can be fooled into giving access to a modem pool. Before deciding this isn't a problem in your organization, ask yourself how much trouble a contractor has getting logged into the network or how much difficulty a user who forgot his password has getting it reset. If the people on the help desk believe that every call is internal, you have a problem. Lastly, firewalls can't protect against tunneling over most application protocols to trojaned or poorly written clients. (**Trojan horse programs :** Delivery vehicles for destructive code, which appear to be harmless or useful software programs such as games.) There are no magic bullets and a firewall is not an excuse to not implement software controls on internal networks or ignores host security on servers. Tunneling bad things over HTTP, SMTP, and other protocols is quite simple and trivially demonstrated.

Viruses

Firewalls can't protect very well against things like viruses. There are too many ways of encoding binary files for transfer over networks, and too many different architectures and viruses to try to search for them all. In other words, a firewall cannot replace security-consciousness on the part of your users. In general, a firewall cannot protect against a data-driven attack—attacks in which something is mailed or copied to an internal host where it is then executed. This form of attack has occurred in the past against various versions of sendmail, ghostscript and scripting mail user agents like Outlook.

Organizations that are deeply concerned about viruses should implement organization-wide virus control measures. Rather than trying to screen viruses out at the firewall, make sure that every vulnerable desktop has virus-scanning software that is run when the machine is rebooted. Blanketing your network with virus scanning software will protect against viruses that come in via floppy disks, modems, and Internet. Trying to block viruses at the firewall will only protect against viruses from the Internet and the vast majority of viruses are caught via floppy disks.

Nevertheless, an increasing number of firewall vendors are offering virus-detecting firewalls. They're probably only useful for naive users exchanging Windows-on-Intel executable programs and malicious-macro-capable application documents. There are many firewall-based approaches for dealing with problems like the "I LOVE YOU" worm and related attacks, but these are really oversimplified approaches that try to limit the damage of something that is so stupid it never should have occurred in the first place. Do not count on any protection from attackers with this feature.

Summary of what firewalls cannot do

- A firewall can't protect against malicious insiders.
- A firewall can't protect against connections that don't go through it. If, for example, there is a modem pool behind a firewall that provides PPP service to access a subnetwork, the firewall cannot provide any protection against malicious traffic from dial-in users.
- A firewall can't protect against completely new threats.
- A firewall can't fully protect against viruses.
- A firewall can't set itself up correctly. (Cost of operation)

17.5.2 Basic Types of Firewalls

There are three basic types of firewalls that are explained below:

1. Application Gateways

The first firewalls were application gateways, and are sometimes known as proxy gateways. These are made up of bastion hosts that run special software to act as a proxy server. (**Bastion Host** : A computer that must be highly secured because it is more vulnerable to attacks than other hosts on a subnetwork. A bastion host in a firewall is usually the main point of contact for user processes of hosts of internal networks with processes of external hosts). This software runs at the Application Layer of the ISO/OSI Reference Model, hence the name. Clients behind the firewall must be proxitized (that is, must know how to use the proxy, and be configured to do so) in order to use Internet services. Traditionally, these have been the most secure, because they don't allow anything to pass by default, but need to have the programs written and turned on in order to begin passing traffic. These are also typically the slowest, because more processes need to be started in order to have a request serviced.

2. Packet Filtering

It is the action a device takes to selectively control the flow of data to and from a network. Packet filtering is an important technique to implement access control on the subnetwork-level for packet-oriented networks, e.g., the Internet. A synonym for packet filtering is screening

It is a technique whereby routers have ACLs (Access Control Lists) turned on. By default, a router will pass all traffic sent in and will do so without any sort of restrictions. Employing ACLs is a method for enforcing your security policy with regard to what sorts of access you allow the outside world to have to your internal network, and vice versa.

There is less overhead in packet filtering than with an application gateway, because the feature of access control is performed at a lower ISO/OSI layer (typically, the transport or session layer). Due to the lower overhead and the fact that packet filtering is done with routers, which are specialized computers optimized for tasks related to networking, a packet filtering gateway is often much faster than its application layer cousins.

There are problems with this method, though. Remember, TCP/IP has absolutely no means of guaranteeing that the source address is really what it claims to be. As a result, we have to use layers of packet filters in order to localize the traffic. We can't get all the way down to the actual host, but with two layers of packet filters, we can differentiate between a packet that came from the Internet and one that came from our internal network. We can identify which network the packet came from with certainty, but we can't get more specific than that.

3. Hybrid Systems

In an attempt to marry the security of the application layer gateways with the flexibility and speed of packet filtering, some vendors have created systems that use the principles of both.

In some of these systems, new connections must be authenticated and approved at the application layer. Once this has been done, the remainder of the connection is passed down to the session layer, where packet filters watch the connection to ensure that only packets that are part of an ongoing (already authenticated and approved) conversation are being passed.

Other possibilities include using both packet filtering and application layer proxies. (**Proxy** : It is a program that deals with external servers on behalf of internal clients. Proxies relay approved client requests to real servers and also relay the servers' answers back to the clients.) The benefits here include providing a measure of protection against your machines that provide services to the Internet (such as a public web server), as well as provide the security of an application layer gateway to the internal network. Additionally, using this method, an attacker, in order to get to services on the internal network, will have to break through the access router, the bastion host, and the choke router.

17.5.3 Firewall Architectures

A firewall generally has at least two interfaces in order to connect your internal network to external networks, the "inside" interface, which connects to your internal LAN, and the "outside" interface, which connects to your router or Internet connection. Most high-end firewalls include support for multiple interfaces, which is often necessary for today's large enterprise networks.

The Simple Packet Filter Architecture

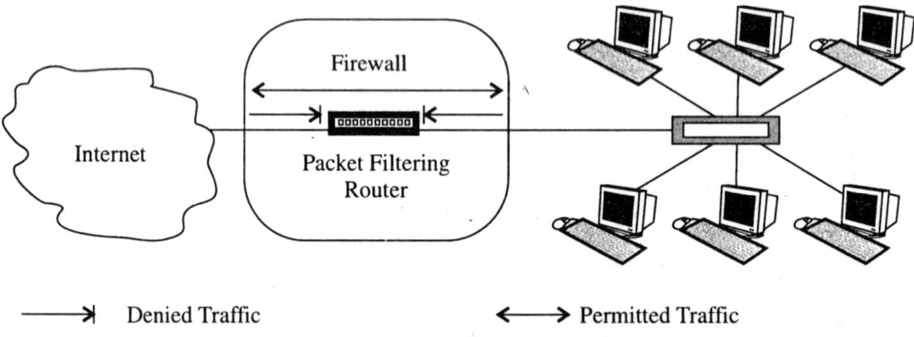

Fig. 17.13 Simple packet filter architecture

The simplest architecture just consists of a packet filtering router. It can be either realized with:

- A standard workstation (e.g., Linux PC) with at least two network interfaces plus routing and filtering software.
- A dedicated router device, which usually also offers filtering capabilities.

The Dual-Homed Host Architecture

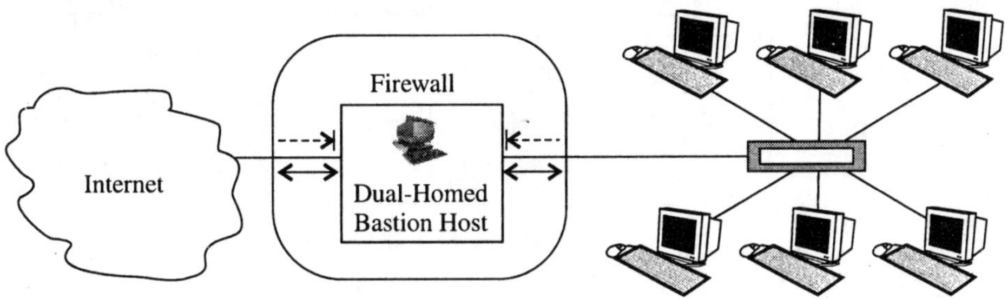

Fig. 17.14 Dual-homed host architecture

The important property of the dual-homed host is that it has at least two network interfaces. The dual homed host provides:

- Proxy services to internal and / or external clients.
- Eventually packet filtering capabilities if it is also acting as a router.

Drawback : As all permitted traffic passes through the bastion host, this might introduce a performance bottleneck

The Screened Host Architecture

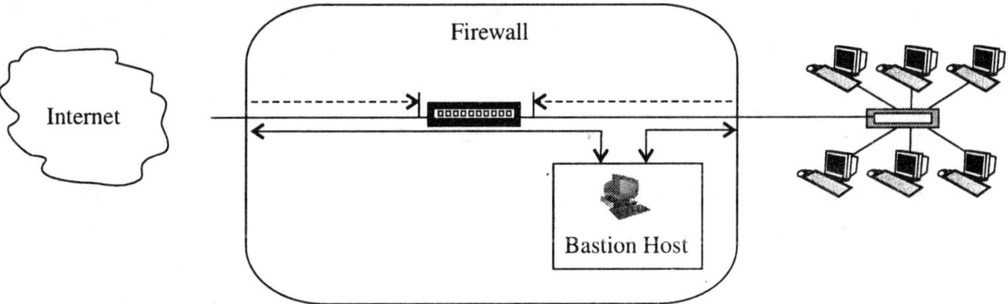

Fig. 17.15 Screened host architecture

The packet filter:

- Allows permitted IP traffic to flow between the screened host and the Internet.
- Blocks all direct traffic between other internal hosts and the Internet.

The screened host provides proxy services:

- Despite partial protection by the packet filter the screened host acts as a bastion host.

The Screened Subnet Architecture

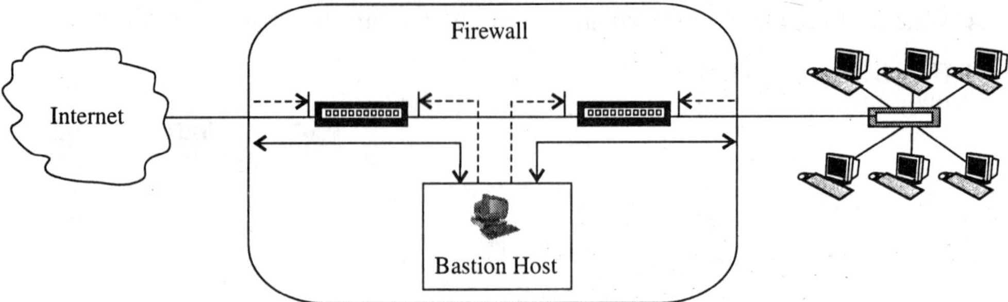

Fig. 17.16 Screened subnet architecture

A perimeter network is created between two packet filters. The inner packet filter serves for additional protection in case the bastion host is ever compromised. For example, this avoids a compromised bastion host to sniff on internal traffic.

The perimeter network is also a good place to host a publicly accessible information server, e.g., a www-server.

The Split Screened Subnet Architecture

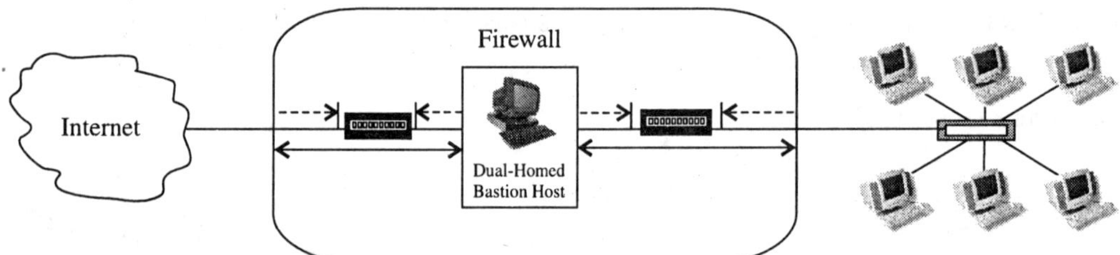

Fig. 17.17 Split screened subnet architecture

A dual-homed bastion host splits the perimeter network in two distinct networks. This provides defense in depth, as: The dual-homed bastion host provides finer control on the connections, as his proxy services are able to interpret application protocols. The bastion host is protected from external hosts by an outer packet filter. The internal hosts are protected from the bastion host by an inner packet filter

Disadvantages and drawbacks of firewalls

- In the interest of maximizing security, firewalls can cut users off from useful network services. Especially, a closed or "deny unless specifically permitted" policy may restrict access and create frustration among potential customers.
- Firewalls may give administrators a false sense of security so other aspects of host-based security become inappropriately relaxed. A technical approach to security may overlook the human factor.

- The complexities of firewalls make it easy to make mistakes and leaves holes in the security implementation.
- Because they represent a checkpoint for all network traffic, they may create a traffic bottleneck.
- Firewalls cannot protect against insider attacks, still the greatest security threat to host-based information.

A final word about firewalls: Selecting and installing firewalls is not a straightforward task. The critical nature of the security requirements and the complexity of the task (e.g., bastion hosts, network segmentation and dual-homed gateways) means construction and maintenance of firewalls are best left to experts.

• • •

18

Some Network Standards

Introduction To Standards

A standard is a set of rules used to implement or accomplish a task. Standards are the things that make the Internet work. Almost always they take the form of protocols that everyone has agreed on.

Role of Standards

Standardized protocols provide a common meeting ground for software designers. Without standards, it is unlikely that an IBM computer could transfer files from a Macintosh, or print to a NetWare server, or login to a Sun. The technical literature of the Internet consists primarily of standard protocols that define how software and hardware from wildly divergent sources can interact on the net.

Sources of Standards

Standards can be classified in two ways:

- De facto.
- De jure.

De facto standards are common practices; **de jure standards** have been blessed by some official standards body. In the Internet, many different organizations try to play the standards game. IETF, the Internet Engineering Task Force, is chief among them. IETF issues the RFCs (Requests For Comments) that define Internet Standards and it is IETF's working groups that do the real work of developing new and enhanced Internet standards. ISO, the International Standards Organization, issues the OSI standards. IEEE, the Institute of

Electrical and Electronic Engineers, issues key LAN standards such as Ethernet and Token-Ring. ANSI, the American National Standards Institute, issues FDDI.

Requests For Comments (RFCs)

IETF's standards deserve special mention, since it is these standards, more than any other, that make the Internet work. IETF issues its standards as Requests For Comments (RFCs), but not all RFCs are standards. The Internet Society (ISOC), IETF's parent organization, has a long-standing commitment to open standards.

In this chapter we will focus on **International Standards bodies : ITU-T** that is discussed next. In the end of chapter we will discuss some OSI application tools like FTAM and VTAM.

18.1 International Standards Bodies : ITU-T (formerly CCITT)

The ITU (International Telecommunications Union), headquartered in Geneva, Switzerland is an international organization within which governments and the private sector coordinate global telecom networks and services. ITU activities include:

- The coordination, development, regulation and standardization of telecommunications.
- Organization of regional and world TELECOM events.

Standards Documents and Series: ITU-T : X series

The main standards that we will discuss in this chapter under ITU-T are listed below:

- **X.25**—Interface between data terminal equipment (DTE) and data circuit-terminating equipment (DCE) for terminals operating in the packet mode and connected to public data networks by dedicated circuit.
- **Message Handling Systems : –X.400**—Message handling services : Message handling system and service overview.
- **Directory Services : –X.500**—Information technology—OSI—The directory : Overview of concepts, models and services

OSI Applications Tools

OSI Applications tools are used to perform communication tasks, such as exchanging files, and logging on to remote systems. We can transfer files with FTAM, and access remote systems with Virtual Terminal.

18.2 Introduction to X.25

X.25 is an International Telecommunication Union-Telecommunication Standardization Sector (ITU-T) protocol standard for WAN communications. X.25 is basically a protocol for packet-switched networks. It defines how connections between user devices and network devices are established and maintained. The protocol supports connection-oriented (conventional) and connectionless (datagram) communication. X.25 is designed to operate effectively regardless of the type of systems connected to the network. It is used in both private and public data networks.

It is typically used in the **packet-switched networks (PSNs)** of common carriers, such as the telephone companies. Subscribers are charged based on their use of the network. The development of the X.25 standard was initiated by the common carriers in the 1970s.

An X.25 network transfers data via packet switching. With this method, information is taken from many different users and combined into discrete data packets. These data packets are then forwarded to the Packet Data Network (PDN). Each data packet is quickly routed through the network cloud to its destination using self-contained routing information.

A primary advantage of the X.25 network is that packet switching offers a significant cost savings compared to circuit switching. It is similar to dial-up for data but your business will only have to pay for the time that the caller is talking.

18.2.1 X.25 Devices and Protocol Operation

X.25 network devices fall into three general categories:

- Data terminal equipment (DTE)
- Data circuit-terminating equipment (DCE)
- Packet-switching exchange (PSE)

Data terminal equipment devices are end systems that communicate across the X.25 network. They are usually terminals, personal computers, or network hosts, and are located on the premises of individual subscribers.

Data circuit-terminating equipment devices are communications devices, such as modems and packet switches that provide the interface between DTE devices and a PSE, and are generally located in the carrier's facilities.

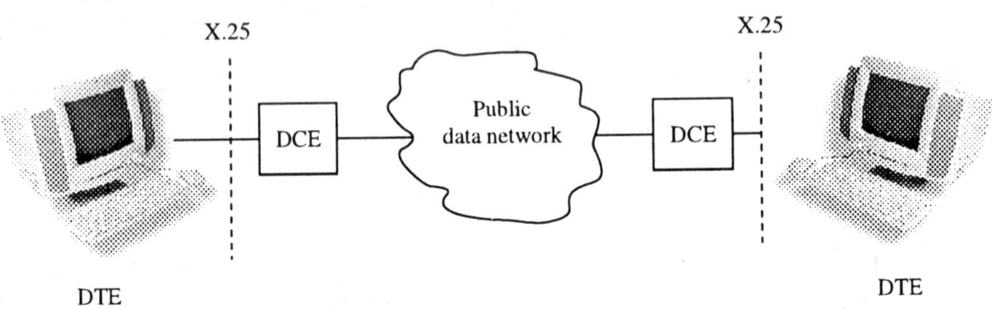

Fig. 18.1 X.25 seen as an interface protocol between DTE and DCE

PSEs (Packet-switching exchange) are switches that compose the bulk of the carrier's network. They transfer data from one DTE device to another through the X.25 PSN. Figure 18.2 illustrates the relationships among the three types of X.25 network devices.

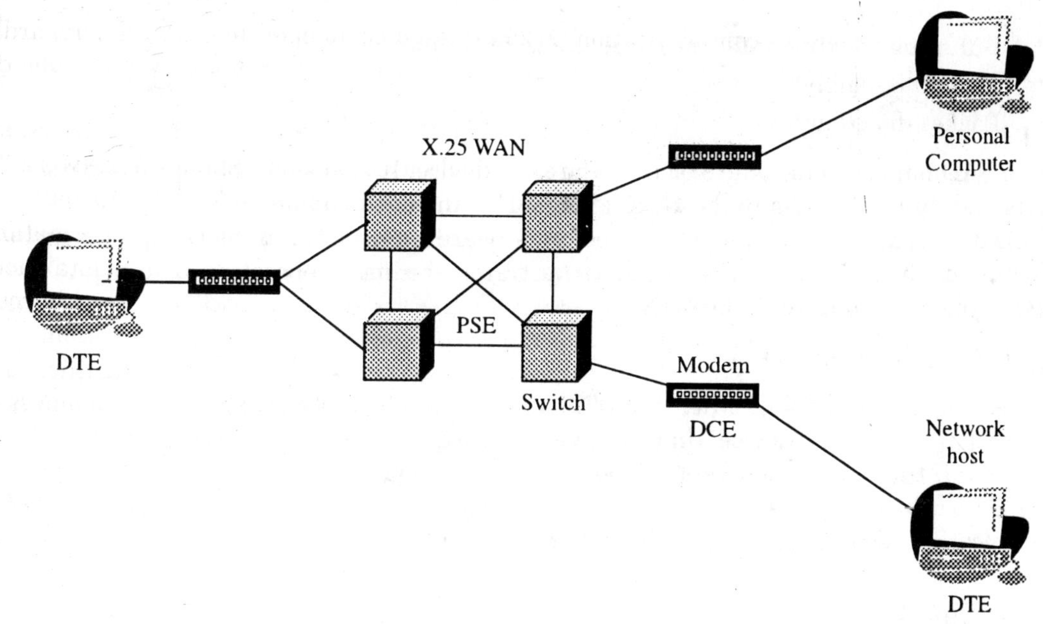

Fig. 18.2 DTE's, DCE's and PSEs make up an X.25 network

Packet Assembler/Disassembler

The packet assembler/disassembler (PAD) is a device commonly found in X.25 networks. PADs are used when a DTE device, such as a character-mode terminal, is too simple to implement the full X.25 functionality. The PAD is located between a DTE device and a DCE device, and it performs **three primary functions**:

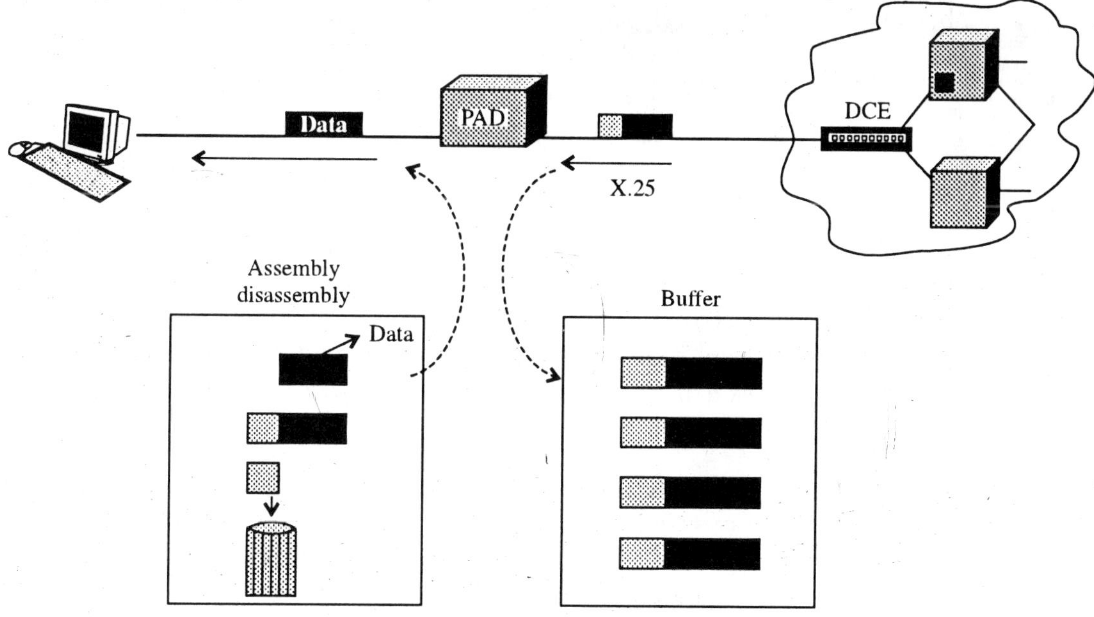

Fig. 18.3 The PAD buffers, assembles and disassembles data packets

- Buffering (storing data until a device is ready to process it)
- Packet assembly
- Packet disassembly

The PAD buffers data sent to or from the DTE device. It also assembles outgoing data into packets and forwards them to the DCE device. (This includes adding an X.25 header.) Finally, the PAD disassembles incoming packets before forwarding the data to the DTE. (This includes removing the X.25 header.) Figure 18.3 illustrates the basic operation of the PAD when receiving packets from the X.25 WAN.

X.25 Session Establishment

X.25 sessions are established when one DTE device contacts another to request a communication session. The DTE device that receives the request can either accept or refuse the connection. If the request is accepted, the two systems begin full-duplex information transfer. Either DTE device can terminate the connection. After the session is terminated, any further communication requires the establishment of a new session.

18.2.2 Levels of X.25

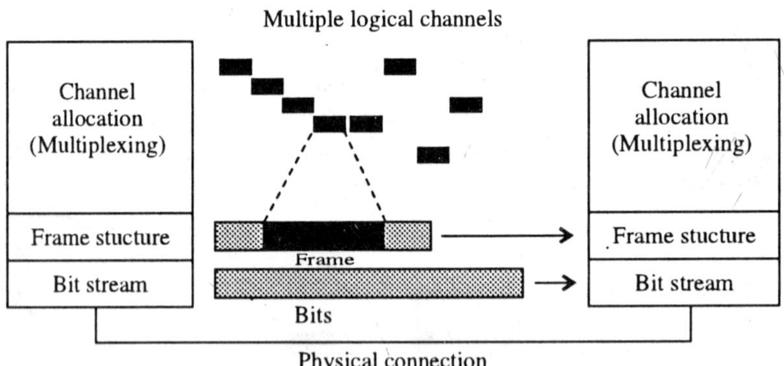

Fig. 18.4 Logical channels in X.25

X.25 comes with three levels based on the first three layers of the Open Systems Interconnection (OSI) seven layers architecture as defined by the International Standard Organization (ISO). . Level 1 gives a basic bit stream on the physical circuit; level 2 divides the bit stream into manageable frames; and level 3 allocates this physical circuit to a number of logical channels ("dynamic multiplexing").

The levels are:

- **The Physical Level** describes the interface with the physical environment. It is similar to the Physical Layer in the OSI model.
- **The Link Level** responsible for the reliable communication between the DTE and the DCE. It is similar to the Data Link Layer in the OSI model.

- **The Packet Level** describes the data transfer protocol in the packet switched network. It is similar to the Network Layer in the OSI model.

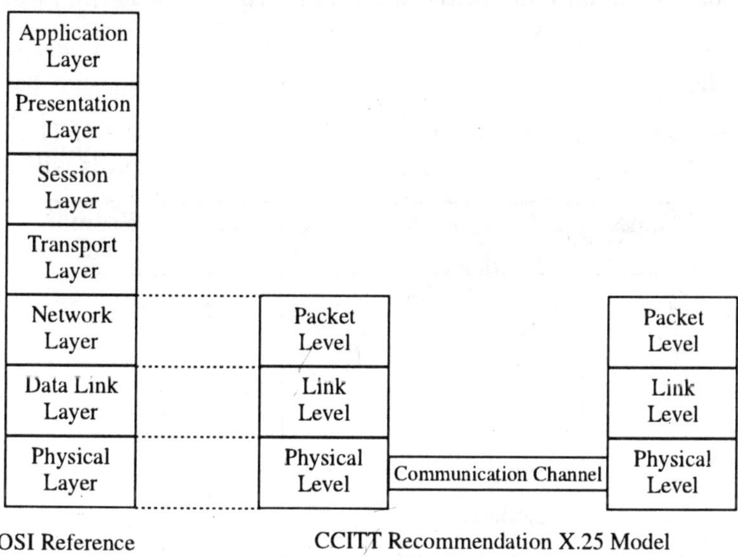

Fig. 18.5 Correspondence between OSI and X.25 levels

Now we will discuss these levels in detail.

The Physical Level

The physical level (level 1) deals with the electrical, mechanical, procedural and functional interface between the DTE and the DCE. The physical level is specified by the X.21, X.21-bis and the V.24 recommendation for modems and interchange circuits.

- **X.21** is a CCITT recommendation for operation of digital circuits. The X.21 interface operates over eight interchange circuits (i.e., signal ground, DTE common return, transmit, receive, control, indication, signal element timing and byte timing).
- **X.21-bis** is a CCITT recommendation that defines the analogue interface to allow access to the digital circuit switched network using an analogue circuit. X.21-bis provides procedures for sending and receiving addressing information, which enable a DTE to establish switched circuits with other DTEs that have access to the digital network. X.21bis is a physical layer protocol used in X.25 that defines the electrical and mechanical procedures for using the physical medium. X.21bis handles the activation and deactivation of the physical medium connecting DTE and DCE devices. It supports point-to-point connections, speeds up to 19.2 kbps and synchronous, full-duplex transmission over four-wire media.
- **V.24** is also a CCITT recommendation; it provides procedures that enable the DTE to

operate over a leased analogue circuit connecting it to a packet switching node or concentrator.

Now we will discuss in more detail the X.21 interface since it is the most commonly used one.

X.21 Digital Interface

In 1976 CCITT recommended a digital signaling interface called X.21. The recommendation specifies how the DTE can setup and clear calls by exchanging signals with the DCE.

Line	Name	From DTE	From DCE
G	Signal ground		
Ga	DTE common return	X	
T	Transmit	X	
R	Receive		X
C	Control	X	
I	Indication		X
S	Signal element timing		X
B	Byte timing		X

Fig. 18.6 X.21 Interchange circuit

The physical connector has 15 pins, but not all of them are used. The DTE uses the ***T*** and ***C*** circuits to transmit data and control information. The DCE uses the ***R*** and ***I*** circuits for data and control. The ***S*** circuit contains a signal stream emitted by the DCE to provide timing information so the DTE knows when each bit interval starts and stops. The ***B*** circuit may also provide to group the bits into byte frames.

The Link Level

The link level (also called level 2, or frame level) ensures reliable transfer of data between the DTE and the DCE, by transmitting the data as a sequence of frames (a frame is an individual data unit which contains address, control, information field etc.).

The functions performed by the link level include:

- Transfer of data in an efficient and timely fashion.
- Synchronization of the link to ensure that the receiver is in step with the transmitter.
- Detection of transmission errors and recovery from such errors.
- Identification and reporting of procedural errors to higher levels, for recovery.

The link level uses data link control procedures that are compatible with the High Level Data Link (HDLC) standardized by ISO, and with the Advanced Data Communications Control

Procedures (ADCCP) standardized by the U.S. American National Standards Institute (ANSI).

There are several protocols that can be used in the link level:

- **Link Access Protocol, Balanced (LAPB)** is derived from HDLC and is the most commonly used. It enables to form a logical link connection besides all the other characteristics of HDLC.
- **Link Access Protocol (LAP)** is an earlier version of LAPB and is seldom used today.
- **Link Access Procedure, D Channel (LAPD)** is derived from LAPB and it is used for Integrated Services Digital Networks (ISDN) i.e., it enables data transmission between DTEs through D channel, especially between a DTE and an ISDN node.
- **Logical Link Control (LLC)** is an IEEE 802 Local Area Network (LAN) protocol that enables X.25 packets to be transmitted through a LAN channel.

We now discuss LAPB in more detail since, as we mentioned before, it is the most commonly used.

LAPB-Link Access Protocol, Balanced

The LAPB protocol uses the following frame structure:

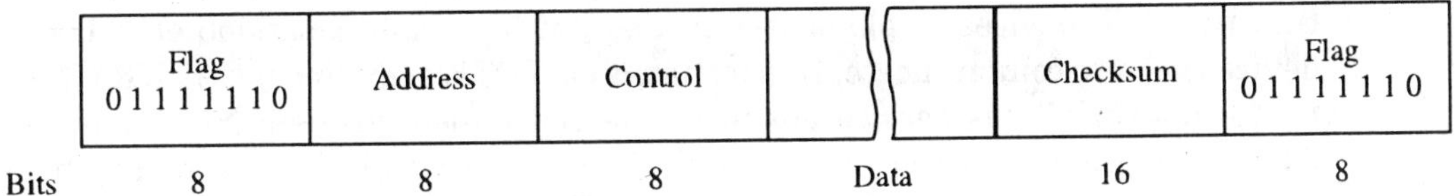

Fig. 18.7 Frame structure of LAPB

- The **Flag** fields indicate the start and end of the frame.
- The **Address** field contain the address of the DTE/DCE, it is most important in multidrop lines, where it is used to identify one of the terminals.
- The **Control** field contains sequence numbers, commands and responses for controlling the data flow between the DTE and the DCE. It indicates whether the frame is an I-frame, an S-frame or a U-frame.
- The **Checksum** field indicates whether or not errors occur in the transmission. It is a variation of the Cyclic Redundancy Code (CRC).

There are three kinds of frames:

1. **Information** : This kind of frame contains the actual information being transferred. The control field in these frames contains the frame sequence number.
2. **Supervisory** : There are various types of supervisory frames:
   - ¤ RECEIVE READY—Acknowledgment frame indicating the next frame expected.
   - ¤ REJECT—Negative acknowledgment frame used to indicate transmission error detection.

- RECEIVE NOT READY (RNR)—Just as RECEIVE READY but tells the sender to stop sending due to temporary problems.

3. **Unnumbered :** This kind of frames is used only for control purposes.
LAPB also provides the following commands:

- DISC (DISConnect)—Allows the machine to announce that it is going down.
- SNRT (Set Normal Response Time)—Allows a machine that has just come back on line to announce its presence.
- FRMR (FRaMe Reject)—Used to indicate that a frame with correct checksum but impossible semantics arrived.

The Packet Level

The packet level (also called level 3 or network level) creates network data units called packets that contain control information and user data. The packet level provides procedures for handling the following services:

- **Switched Virtual Circuit (SVC)—often called virtual circuit (VC) :** Two types of X.25 virtual circuits exist: switched and permanent. Switched virtual circuits are temporary connections used for sporadic data transfers. They require that two DTE devices establish, maintain, and terminate a session each time the devices need to communicate. It is initiated by a DTE signaling a CALL REQUEST to the network. This service ensures orderly (sequenced) delivery of packets in either direction between two DTEs. Switched virtual Circuit is established whenever two DTEs want to communicate. This service is the most frequently used by the X.25 protocol.
- **Permanent Virtual Circuit (PVC)** is a permanent association existing between two DTEs, which do not require call setup (connect) or call clearing (disconnect) action by the DTE. Therefore, DTEs can begin transferring data whenever necessary because the session is always active.
- **Datagrams (DG)** is a self-contained user data unit, containing sufficient information to be routed to the destination DTE (independently of all other data units) without a need of a call to be established. The data units are transmitted one at a time with no guarantee of final delivery, and no guarantee of orderly delivery. Each datagram must contain complete address and control information to enable it to be delivered to the proper destination DTE.
- **Fast Select** is a service that enables the control packet that sets up the VC to carry data as well.
- **Other Services :** The packet level also provides the **call setup** and call clearing procedures required for the VC service. The packet level deals with flow control to ensure that a user (DTE) does not overwhelm the other user with packets, and to maintain timely and efficient delivery of packets. The packet level also handles errors at packet level to abort or restart VCs if necessary.

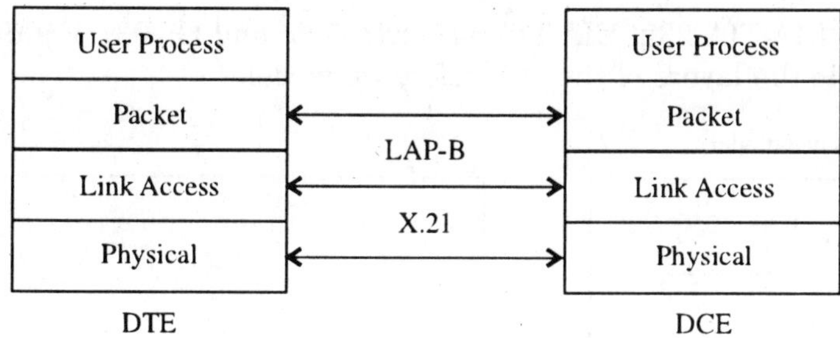

Fig. 18.8 X.25 Protocol layers

Call Setup

When DTE A wants to communicate with DTE B, it must set up a connection by building a CALL REQUEST packet, and passing it to it's DCE. DTE B gets the packet through the subnet and it's DCE. If DTE B wishes to accept the call, it sends a CALL ACCEPTED packet back. When DTE A receives the CALL ACCEPTED packet the Virtual Circuit is established.

At this point the two DTEs may use a full-duplex connection to exchange data packets. When either side wants to finish the call, it sends a CLEAR REQUEST packet to the other side, which then sends a CLEAR CONFIRMATION packet back as an acknowledgment.

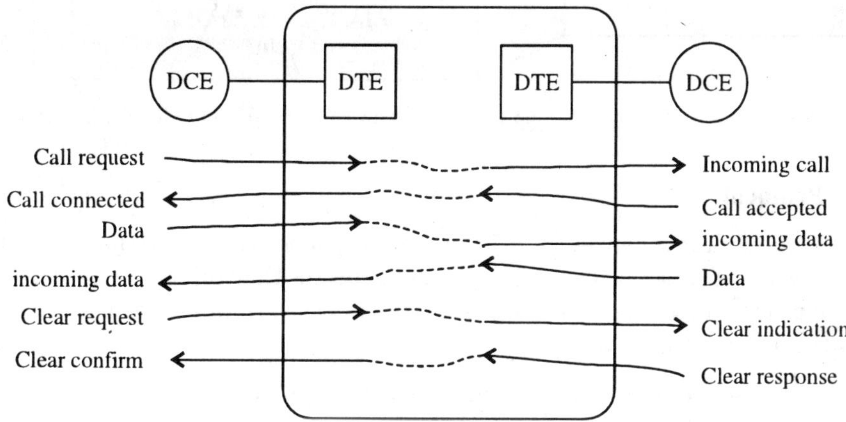

Fig. 18.9 Pictorial view of call setup

The DTE determines the circuit number on outgoing calls and the DCE determines the circuit number on incoming calls. If both simultaneously choose the same number then Call Collision occurs. X.25 specifies that in this case, the outgoing call is put through and the incoming one is cancelled.

18.2.3 The X.25 Protocol Suite

The X.25 protocol suite maps to the lowest three layers of the OSI reference model. The following protocols are typically used in X.25 implementations: Packet-Layer Protocol (PLP), Link Access Procedure, Balanced (LAPB), and those among other physical-layer serial interfaces (such as EIA/TIA-232, EIA/TIA-449, EIA-530, and G.703). Figure 18.10 maps the key X.25 protocols to the layers of the OSI reference model.

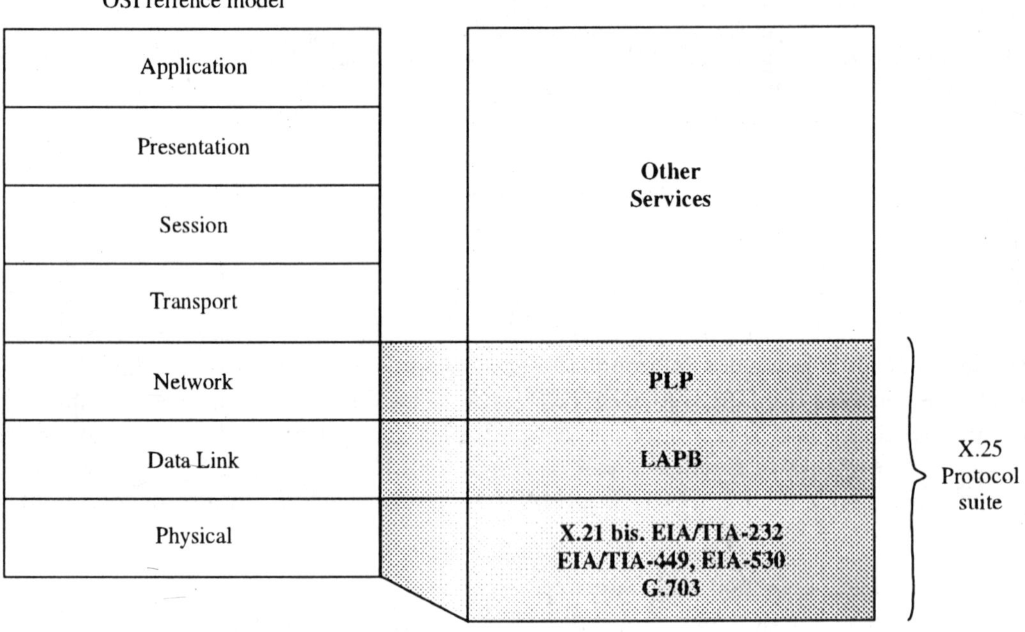

Fig. 18.10 Key X.25 protocols map to the three lower layers of the OSI reference model

Packet-Layer Protocol

PLP is the X.25 network layer protocol. PLP manages packet exchanges between DTE devices across virtual circuits. PLPs also can run over Logical Link Control 2 (LLC2) implementations on LANs and over Integrated Services Digital Network (ISDN) interfaces running Link Access Procedure on the D channel (LAPD).

The PLP operates in five distinct modes that are listed below:

- **Call setup mode** is used to establish SVCs (Switched Virtual Circuits) between DTE devices.
- **Data transfer mode** is used for transferring data between two DTE devices across a virtual circuit.
- **Idle mode** is used when a virtual circuit is established but data transfer is not occurring.
- **Call clearing mode** is used to end communication sessions between DTE devices and to terminate SVCs.
- **Restarting mode** is used to synchronize transmission between a DTE device and a locally connected DCE device.

18.2.4 User Services

An X.25 network may be used in a variety of environments. For instance, X.25 is well suited in applications where:

1. Communications are primarily asynchronous (though frequent synchronous applications are now being used).
2. Line quality may not be good (X.25's error correction capabilities overcome poor line quality).
3. Data volume is relatively small and bursty.
4. A company wants to use packet switching to decrease transmission expenses.

X.25 is used primarily by companies and institutions. X.25 networks are used in a large number of applications, such as:

- Information retrieval in national and international databases
- Traffic from terminals to a mainframe (transaction processing)
- File transfer
- Electronic mail
- Automatic teller machines and card-operated petrol pumps

Terminals and network connection elements

A number of more or less complex types of terminal can be connected to an X.25 network. Each connection is represented by an addressable port in the data network. Examples of terminals or network connection elements include:

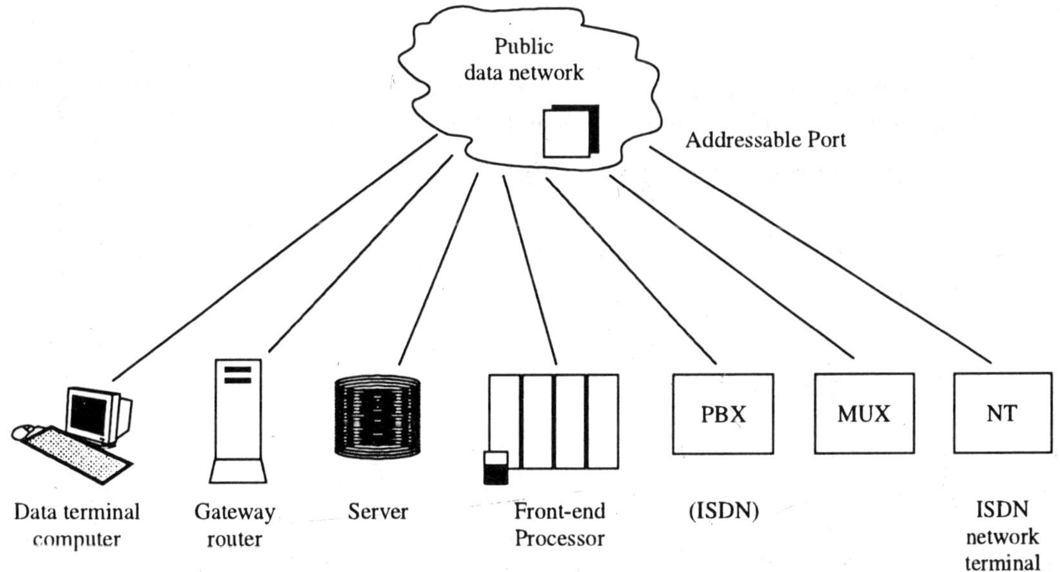

Fig. 18.11 Examples of X.25 data terminal equipment (DTE) points

- Computer
- Server
- Front-end processor
- PBX
- Gateway to another network
- Subscriber multiplexer
- Cluster with dumb terminals
- Protocol converter; for example, packet assembler/disassembler (PAD) or black boxes.

18.3 Introduction To X.400

X.400 is the short name for the set of standards from the International Organization for Standardization (ISO) and the International Telecommunication Union (ITU) that describe a mail service. Originally published in 1984 by CCITT in 1988 and later re-written jointly by ISO and CCITT, X.400 is a standard that conforms to layer 7 of the OSI and is a standard used for transporting e-mail messages. X.400 is an alternative standard to the commonly used SMTP. It is the only non-proprietary standard for interchange of electronic mail that has the sanction of an official standards body. SMTP, however, is the unofficial and prevalent mail standard.

Example of SMTP e-mail address:

support@computerhope.com

Example of a X.400 e-mail address:

G=support; O=computerhope.com

X.400 has been defined to run over various network transports including Ethernet, X.25, TCP/IP and dial-up lines. Following is the format of an X.400 address:

/c= /admd= /prmd= /o= /s= /g=

where, /c = country
/admd = administrative management domain (public e-mail service)
/prmd = private management domain (in-house e-mail)
/o = organization
/s = surname
/g = given name

Need of X.400

Electronic mail has now been established as an important service in many areas. This has been achieved through a number of different (and hence incompatible) message protocols, leading to a situation where there are islands of electronic mail connectivity.

With the introduction of the CCITT X.400 recommendations on message handling systems, the aim was to supply a single international standard for the electronic interchange of messages.

With the massive and continuing growth in the internet and its associated protocols, one might think that, for better or worse, it is unlikely that another protocol will displace it (in the near future in any case) as the primary means for exchanging electronic mail messages. This may be the case—but the fact remains that there are several other substantial networks out there and the Internet mail protocols were not designed with generality and connectivity with other systems in mind.

There is a clear need to have a common international standard which can be used as a mechanism to glue together the disjoint services in order to provide a single coherent global electronic mail service.

18.3.1 X.400 Components

In this section we discuss the main components of the X.400 model for the interchange of electronic mail messages—their purpose and the services they provide.

The main components of the model are:

- Message Transfer Agents (MTA's)
- Message Stores (MS's)
- User Agents (UA's)
- Access Units (AU's)

From the users, point of view, immediate interaction with the system is carried out through a User Agent. **The user agent** allows the user to compose, submit, and receive mail messages. The User Agent is the interface between the user and the MTS. A user uses a UA to send and receive messages via the MTS. The actual transmission of messages is done via a **Message Transfer Agent** (MTA). These perform all the routing and delivery functions needed.

The **message store** is available to the MTA at all times (often co-located) and supplies a store and forward service to the User Agent. This is particularly useful in the more distributed modern environment where the User Agent may be running on a users personal machine and hence might not be available for long periods of time.

The MTA delivers the message to the Message store, which may well store the message for a considerable period of time, an option not available to the high-traffic MTA, and which is outside the scope of the service the MTA is supposed to provide. The user may then connect to the message store at any time and fetch the messages stored for him/her by the Message Store. When this system is used, the user typically conducts all his business through the message store, including message submission.

Access Units define how interpersonnel-messaging users can communicate with users of pre-X.400 technologies, such as telex, teletex and even postal delivery services. An AU is a device that interfaces with the MTS on one side and with a pre-X.400 service on the other side. It converts formats, service elements, and protocols. An AU can provide non-X.400 services bidirectional flow of messages.

18.3.2 X.400 Protocols

The Protocols defined by the standard are:

- P1—MTA to MTA.
- P3—MTA to UA.
- P7—UA to MS.
- P2/P22—Interpersonal Messaging protocol (P2-1984, P22-1988).

The **P1 protocol** is an end-to-end message transfer service. The P1 protocol handles the layout of a message sent from one Message Transfer Agent (MTA) to another Message Transfer Agent. This protocol is the equivalent of a letter and an envelope. The 'envelope' is known as the P1 header and the 'letter' is the P2 Message. Addresses of the recipient must be globally unique for the P1 Protocol.

The **P3 protocol** is a protocol for communication between User Agents and MTA's. The User Agent (UA) prepares a message and transmits it to the Message Transfer Agent (MTA). This protocol is also used to deliver a message directly to the User Agent (UA) from the Message Transfer Agent (MTA) because the User Agent is not always available.

The **P7 protocol** is an increasingly widely used protocol for communication between the User Agent and the Message Store. P7 provides facilities to select messages selectively from the Message Store (MS). Typical P7 operations are:

- Bind to Message Store.
- Unbind from Message Store.
- List Messages held in Message store.
- Fetch Messages/Notifications/Reports.
- Submit Messages/Notifications/Reports.
- Delete message from Message store.

The **P2/P22 protocol** defines the format of a highly structured memo-like document. The two main components are the heading and the body part(s). The heading specifies things like the originator and recipient of the message, copy and blind copy recipients of the message, whether the originator wishes to receive a notification for the message and in what circumstances etc.

The body part may be one of many forms of data—those specified by the standard include Ia5 text, G3Fax, Images, Audio data etc. Messages may also be encapsulated within messages, providing a very clean and structured forwarding mechanism.

18.3.3 Advantages of X.400

The main feature of X.400 that is fairly immediately apparent from the standard is it's generality and extensibility. The standard was designed to last through changes in the capabilities of technology—as happened with the advent of personal computers with support for multiple media. The way that other protocols (such as X.435) can be added to the X.400

family of standards is a significant advantage that may allow X.400 to benefit from new communications applications, which may arise in the future.

One of the advantages that X.400 has at the moment is that including support for multimedia messages. Thus, the handling of multimedia mail messages is handled gracefully in X.400, since it is an integral part of the standard, rather than something that was added later.

18.3.4 Disadvantages of X.400

One of the main problems with the OSI standards is that too much influence has been exerted by PTT's (Post Telephone Telegraph) to define a standard that will increase their profits. More concrete and less subjective complaints would be such things as the standards documents themselves - in terms of readability, organization, notation and language, they are exceedingly poorly written.

Some people might claim that they are meant to be a formal definition of the standards and are not meant to satisfy the above criteria, but this arguement breaks down when non-conformant or incompatible software is written because developers could not understand, or failed to understand correctly, obtuse or poorly expressed definitions.

In addition, other standards bodies (and not just 'informal' ones such as the Internet Engineering Task Force (IETF)) can produce documents that, if not exactly aesthetically pleasing, are nonetheless significantly more readable and helpful to the developer. (The American National Standards Institute for example).

Cumbersome and over-complicated solutions—again, this is a matter of ones point of view. From the point of view of the Internet "camp", the OSI protocol family is too inefficient and cumbersome to be successful in the real world. From the point of view of the OSI camp, they are merely paying the price for safety and reliability.

Not enough emphasis on implementability and simplicity. Again we see a difference in philosophy between the two camps—according to the Internet camp, a standard is useless unless it can be implemented straight away. The OSI camp tends to aim for "ideal" systems, which may not be suited for current technology. (In terms of speed of system necessary, resources consumed etc.).

18.3.5 X.400 vs. SMTP

X.400 offers the following:

- Acceptance in the standards communities.
- Commercial vendors of service.
- Defined ways to transfer things other than ASCII text (but only a few systems have implemented them).
- Standard notification of delivery to a user's mailbox and notification of a message being read by the user (these are often implemented).

SMTP offers the following:

- Simplicity.
- Wide acceptance.
- Public domain implementations.
- Public domain user interfaces.

18.4 Introduction To X.500

It is an OSI protocol for managing online directories of users and resources. X.500 can be used to support X.400 and other messaging systems, but it is not restricted to e-mail usage. X.500 is a standard for distributed directory services. The standard encompasses both the structure of the X.500 database and also the protocol used in querying the database. X.500 can be used for different types of directories. Its most notable implementation is a global White Pages service containing in excess of a million names contributed to by X.500 servers in dozens of countries.

X.500 provides a hierarchical database structure (for example, country/organization/organizational unit/person). The database consists of entries (one per object) that may describe persons, network resources, organizations, and so on, each with its own set of attributes.

The X.500 directory service is a global directory service. Its components cooperate to manage information about objects such as countries, organizations, people, machines, and so on in a worldwide scope. It provides the capability to look up information by name (a **white-pages** service) and to browse and search for information (a *yellow-pages* service).

The information is held in a **directory information base (DIB)**. Entries in the DIB are arranged in a tree structure called the **directory information tree (DIT)**. Each entry is a named object and consists of a set of attributes. Each attribute has a defined attribute type and one or more values. The directory schema defines the mandatory and optional attributes for each class of object (called the object class). Each named object may have one or more object classes associated with it.

The X.500 namespace is hierarchical. An entry is unambiguously identified by a **distinguished name (DN)**. A distinguished name is the concatenation of selected attributes from each entry, called the **relative distinguished name (RDN)**, in the tree along a path leading from the root down to the named entry.

Users of the X.500 directory may (subject to access control) interrogate and modify the entries and attributes in the DIB.

The DIB, DSA and DCA : An X.500 directory is called a "Directory Information Base" (DIB) or white pages. The program that maintains the DIBs is called a "Directory Server Agent" (DSA). A Directory Client Agent (DCA) is used to search DSA sites for names and addresses.

Replication and Access Control : X.500 was published in 1988 but the 1993 edition of X.500 added replication and access control. Using the Directory Information Shadowing Protocol (DISP), replication allows a portion of the Directory Information Tree (DIT) to be copied between nodes. Access control allows or denies access to a particular attribute of a directory entry based on the identity of the requesting user.

18.4.1 Protocols

The X.500 standard defines a protocol (among others) for a client application to access the X.500 directory. Called the **Directory Access Protocol (DAP)**, it is layered on top of the **Open Systems Interconnection (OSI)** protocol stack.

Application Programming Interfaces

The X.500 standard itself does not define an API for accessing the directory. Again, the X.500 standard is mainly concerned with interoperability between directory clients and directory servers and between different directory servers.

One standard API that has been defined for the X.500 is the X/Open Specifications API to Directory Services (XDS), a C language-based API that client programs use for accessing X.500 directories.

Access

X.500 is based on the client-server model. The user with an X.500 client (known in the X.500 world as a Directory User Agent or DUA) can query an X.500 server (Directory System Agent or DSA). The server maintains the local X.500 database, but it can also communicate with other X.500 servers. If a query cannot be answered locally it may be passed on automatically to other X.500 servers and the response passed back to the user. To the user, it appears that the entire directory is accessible from the local server. As well as queries, X.500 also supports data management functions (addition, modification and deletion of entries).

X.500 : Directory Access Protocol (DAP)

X.500, the directory Access Protocol (DAP) by ITU-T (X.500) and also ISO is a standard way to develop an electronic directory of people in an organization so that it can be part of a global directory available to anyone in the world with Internet access.

In the X.500 directory architecture, the client queries and receives responses from one or more servers in the server Directory Service with the Directory Access Protocol (DAP) controlling the communication between the client and the server

A Directory System Agent (DSA) is the database in which the directory information is stored. This database is hierarchical in form, designed to provide fast and efficient search and retrieval. The DSAs are interconnected from the Directory Information Tree (DIT). The user interface program for access to one or more DSAs is a Directory User Agent (DUA). DUAs include whois, finger, and programs that offer a graphical user interface.

The Directory System Protocol (DSP) controls the interaction between two or more Directory System Agents and between a Directory User Agent and a Directory System Agent. This is done in such a way that an end user can access information in the Directory without needing to know the exact location of that specific piece of information.

18.4.2 Key features of X.500

- **Decentralized Maintenance :** Each site running X.500 is responsible ONLY for its local part of the Directory, so updates and maintenance can be done instantly.

- **Powerful Searching Capabilities :** X.500 provides powerful searching facilities that allow users to construct arbitrarily complex queries.
- **Single Global Namespac :** Much like the DNS, X.500 provides a single homogeneous namespace to users. The X.500 namespace is more flexible and expandable than the DNS.
- **Structured Information Framework :** X.500 defines the information framework used in the Directory, allowing local extensions.
- **Standards-Based Directory Services :** As X.500 can be used to build a standards-based directory, applications which require directory information (e-mail, automated resources locators, special-purpose directory tools) can access a planet's worth of information in a uniform manner.

X.500 is criticized to be too complex for most implementations. To address the issue, the University of Michigan developed a simpler TCP/IP-based version of DAP, the Lightweight Directory Access Protocol (LDAP), for use on the Internet. LDAP offers much of the same basic functionality as DAP and can be used to query data from proprietary directories as well as from an open X.500 service. Within the past year, most major suppliers of e-mail and directory-services software have expressed interest in LDAP, which is fast becoming a de facto directory protocol for the Internet.

18.5 FTAM : File Transfer Access And Management Protocol

FTAM is an OSI Application layer protocol for File Transfer Access and Management. FTAM attempted to combine into a single protocol both file transfer, similar in concept to the Internet FTP, as well as remote access to open files, similar to NFS.

The File Transfer Access and Management protocol (FTAM), an ISO application protocol, offers file transfer services between client (initiator) and server (responder) systems in an open environment. FTAM also provides access to files and management of files on diverse systems. Similar to FTP (File Transfer Protocol) and NFS (Network File System) in the TCP/IP environment, FTAM is designed to help users access files on diverse systems that use compatible FTAM implementations.

Definition

An application service element that enables user application processes to move files between end open systems and to manage and access a remote set of files, which may be distributed. Also called: Electronic File Transfer Access Method, File Transfer Access Method, File Transfer Access and Management, and EFTAM.

In FTAM system, connection-oriented information about the user and the session is maintained by a server until the session is taken down. Files are transferred between systems by first establishing a connection-oriented session. The FTAM client contacts the FTAM server and requests a session. Once the session is established, file transfer can take place. FTAM uses the concept of a virtual filestore, which provides a common view of files. The FTAM file system hides the differences between different vendor systems. FTAM specifies document types as files with straight binary information or text files in which each line is terminated with a carriage return. Data is interpreted as records and FTAM provides the virtual filestore capabilities that store record-oriented structured files.

FTAM stores files according to record indices so that FTAM users can manipulate files down to the record level. In this respect, FTAM has some relational database features. For example, users can lock files or lock individual records.

The FTAM facilities (appending, copying, deleting, listing, and renaming) operate on files stored on both local FTAM systems (**local files**) and remote FTAM systems (**remote files**). Using FTAM, you can copy, append, delete, rename, and inspect the file attributes of local files, remote files, or both.

FTAM provides the following **service classes** :

- The **transfer service class** allows the exchange of files or parts of files. These are generally the simple basic file transfer tasks, allowing single operations with a minimum number of interactions.
- The **access service class** allows the initiating system to perform several operations on individual FADUs or on the whole file.
- The **management service class** allows the user control over the virtual filestore in order to create or delete files, read and modify attributes etc.
- The **transfer-and-management service class** combines the capabilities of the transfer service class with those of the limited file management functional unit to support directory navigation and simple functions.

FTAM has the following key user facilities to operate files locally and remotely:

- **FTAM appending facility** (APPEND/APPLICATION_PROTOCOL=FTAM)—This facility allows you to append one or more input files to the end of a single output file, within local or between local and remote FTAM applications.
- **FTAM copying facility** (COPY/APPLICATION_PROTOCOL=FTAM)—This facility allows you to copy one or more input files to a single output file, within local or between local and remote FTAM applications.
- **FTAM deletion facility** (DELETE/APPLICATION_PROTOCOL=FTAM)—This facility allows you to delete remote files.
- **FTAM directory facility** (DIRECTORY/APPLICATION_PROTOCOL=FTAM)—It enables user to display file attributes for one or more files.
- **FTAM renaming facility** (RENAME/APPLICATION_PROTOCOL=FTAM)—It enables user to rename files.

Each FTAM system contains an FTAM application that implements the FTAM standard on the system. A distinct FTAM application name identifies a specific FTAM application. To access a remote file, you must identify both the remote file and the FTAM application on the remote FTAM system. An FTAM command causes FTAM to communicate with the FTAM applications you specify.

When you issue an FTAM command involving at least one remote file, the following series of events take place:

1. FTAM uses your process to perform the operation that you specify in your command.
2. From your process, FTAM initiates an association for each FTAM application that you specify in the command. (An association is a cooperative link between two OSI application processes.) The software that initiates an association for a user process is called the initiator.
3. The software that receives an initiator's request for an association is called a responder. If a responder accepts a request for an association, the responder's system may start up an application process to support the responder's side of the association.
4. The responder's process handles the requested file operation.
5. When the file operation completes, the FTAM initiator ends the association and returns the control of your process to your local system.

18.6 VTAM : Virtual Telecommunications Access Method

To take advantage of today's networking technology, terminals need access to applications on a variety of local and remote systems. In the single-vendor environment, this is rarely a problem. The difficulty arises in the multivendor environment when diverse systems need to communicate. The OSI solution to this problem is the **Virtual Terminal (VT)**, an abstract representation of a real terminal, complete with terminal operations (reads text from the keyboard, writes text to the screen, moves the cursor, and so on). Using this model, any terminal connected to a system running VT can access any other system running VT, regardless of type.

The Virtual Terminal standard is made up of the service definition (ISO 9040) and the protocol (ISO 9041). The VT software adheres to these standards, and enables applications and systems supporting different types of terminals to interact with each other.

VTAM (Virtual Telecommunications Access Method) is an IBM application program interface (API) for communicating with telecommunication devices and their users. VTAM was the first IBM program to allow programmers to deal with devices as "logical units" without having to understand the details of line protocol and device operation. Prior to VTAM, programmers used IBM's Basic Telecommunications Access Method (BTAM) to communicate with devices that used the binary synchronous (BSC) and start-stop line protocols.

VTAM became part of IBM's strategic Systems Network Architecture (SNA), which in turn became part of the more comprehensive Systems Application Architecture (SAA). As the computer industry turned to open standard architectures, IBM began to de-emphasize its proprietary architectures in favour of becoming a participant and leader in developing open standard architectures. However, most of its customer base retains a large investment in legacy applications and system skills based on VTAM, SNA, and SAA.

VTAM's interface consists of "macro instructions" that set up connection control blocks and then do SENDs to devices and either synchronous or asynchronous READs from them. Typically, legacy programs written in COBOL, PL/1 and assembler language use VTAM to communicate with interactive devices and their users. Programs that use VTAM macro instructions are generally exchanging text strings (for example, online forms and the user's form input) and the most common interactive device used with VTAM programs was the 3270 Information Display System.

VTAM controls communications in Systems Network Architecture (SNA) networks. VTAM supports several network protocols, including SDLC and Token Ring. VTAM is now known as the SNA Services feature of Communications Server for OS/390.

Virtual Terminal Interactions

VT interactions involve two systems : the system that initiates the interaction and the system that responds. These two systems are often referred to as **the terminal implementation** and **the host implementation**.

With some VT software, terminal and host implementations can both initiate an interaction or respond to one. With the DECnet/OSI VT software, the terminal implementation can only initiate an interaction and the host implementation can

only respond. Therefore, the documentation refers to these systems as the initiator and the responder.

When an initiator requests a connection to a responder, and the responder accepts the request, this is referred to as negotiating an association. Both systems must then agree on the context in which the virtual terminal will exist. This context, the **virtual terminal environment (VTE)**, is a set of pre-defined values both sides use to translate information (by means of local mapping) that the virtual terminal transfers to both systems. These pre-defined values describe the capabilities of the Virtual Terminal, such as cursor addressing, forms processing and color capabilities.

In a virtual terminal association, the initiator and responder communicate by sharing information about changes to a data store called the **conceptual communications area**. This data store contains different types of data structures called objects, including:

- **Display objects**—to model a terminal's display and keyboard operations.
- **Control objects**—to model a terminal's control sequences (such as one that rings the bell on a terminal).
- **Device objects**—to model characteristics of real devices and help map display objects.

The systems only communicate changes to the conceptual communications area; both sides of the virtual terminal association assume that the rest of the data store's contents

remain unchanged. A virtual terminal protocol machine on each side of the virtual terminal association maintains a separate copy of the conceptual communications area.

Virtual Terminal Operation in a Network

The following process occurs during a virtual terminal association between two systems:

1. The initiator requests an association with a remote responder. Both systems must agree on the VTE for the virtual terminal.
2. After the association takes place, the initiator maps the keyboard operations that a user can enter to specific virtual terminal representations as defined by the VTE.
3. The initiator then transfers this information across the network to the responder.
4. The responder then maps the virtual terminal information to local commands that its software understands.
5. The responder performs the operation requested by the initiator. If the request generates a response, this information is mapped to the appropriate VT operation. The responder then sends this information across the network to the initiator.
6. The initiator receives the virtual terminal information from the responder and maps this information to commands that the terminal understands.

The user sees no difference between the behavior of VT and that of a terminal directly connected to a responder.

● ● ●

EXERCISES

Chapter 1

1. Explain different tasks to be accomplished in the communications model.
2. Define computer networks. Discuss various uses and abuses of computer networks.
3. Explain the need of computer networking. Discuss its applications also.
4. What are the various network types and what are the factors that differentiate these types?
5. What is LAN, WAN and Internet? Briefly explain various services of Internet.
6. Discuss the components required to design a network.
7. Explain with examples the difference between LAN, MAN and WAN.
8. What are the features of client-server networks? How do they differ from peer-to-peer networks?
9. Explain different types of servers. How servers are different to desktop computers?
10. Explain networking hardware.

Chapter 2

1. What do your mean by network topology? Discuss different network topologies alongwith their relative merits and demerits.
2. Differentiate between star and ring topologies.
3. Compare and contrast bus and star topology.
4. Discuss advantages and disadvantages of mesh topology and hierarchical topology.
5. What are the various ways of connecting nodes in a network? Compare these in terms of costs, expandability and speed.
6. Which network topology is most suitable for computer lab of your institute and why?

Chapter 3

1. What do you mean by network protocol? Discuss the various elements and functions of protocols.
2. List the points of differences between simplex, half-duplex and full-duplex mode of transmission.

3. Differentiate between:
   (a) Interfaces and services
   (b) CO and CL services
   (c) Protocol hierarchy and layers.
4. What do you mean by layered protocols? How do they work? Discuss with examples.
5. What is OSI reference model? Why layered approach is followed in this model? Explain.
6. Sketch and explain ISO-OSI reference model in detail.
7. Compare and contrast the delivery of data units in TL, DLL and NL.
8. Explain the major functions performed by session and presentation layer.
9. Explain the layers of OSI model where the following functions are performed:
   (a) Routing of packets
   (b) Framing
   (c) Data compression and serurity.
10. What is TCP/IP reference model ? What function does it play in the working of Internet? Explain its working.
11. Discuss various points of comparison between OSI and TCP/IP.
12. Discuss services provided by application layer in the TCP/IP model.
13. Discuss the critiques of OSI and TCP/IP model.

Chapter 4

1. What are the various physical media used for transmission of information from one end to other? Explain each of these with diagrams. Compare their relative features.
2. Explain briefly the merits and demerits of various transmission media.
3. Explain different types of twisted pair cable discussing advantages and disadvantages of each.
4. Differentiate between twisted pair cable and co-axial cable.
5. Discuss merits and demerits of using co-axial cable.
6. Discuss in detail the working principle of fiber optics as a communications media. Compare fiber optics with other transmission media.
7. Write in detail about any two types of transmission media that do not make use of physical wires to transfer data.
8. Discuss limitations of wireless technology.
9. How does satellite networks work? Discussss.

10. Explain line of sight transmission.
11. Compare Infrared technology to radio waves.

Chapter 5

1. What is electromagnetic spectrum? How various parts of it are used for data transmission?
2. What are the different types of signals used for communication of information?
3. Differentiate between analog and digital transmission. Explain with examples.
4. Discuss advantages of digital communication over analog communication.
5. Define modulation and describe following with suitable diagrams:
   (a) Amplitude modulation
   (b) Frequency modulation
   (c) Phase modulation
6. Explain the basic difference between frequency and phase modulation.
7. What are the commonly used digital modulation techniques? Explain the principle of FSK in detail.
8. Explain pulse code modulation.
9. What is a modem? Explain different categories of modems.
10. Explain difference between:
    (a) Synchronous and asynchronous data transfer.
    (b) bps and band rate.
11. Explain the purpose of codec.

Chapter 6

1. What do you mean by switching? Explain its various types, giving merits and demerits of each.
2. Discuss the key elements and applications of circuit and pocket switching.
3. What is packet switching? Briefly discuss two popular approaches to packet switching.
4. Compare and contrast:
   (a) Message and packet switching.
   (b) Circuit and message switching.
   (c) Packet and circuit switching.

Chapter 7

1. Illustrate different types of multiplexing techniques possible for signals.
2. Explain the use of multiplexing in networks.
3. Explain difference between TDM and STDM.
4. Explain the multiplexing technique for optical communications.
5. Explain theory of FDM. Also discuss its applications.
6. Compare various multiplexing techniques.

Chapter 8

1. Explain various features of PSTN. Also discuss PSTN signaling methods.
2. Although PSTN does a good job but why many business drivers are striving to change it a new network?
3. Explain the following in brief:
   (a) Evolution of ISDN.
   (b) ISDN system architecture.
4. Explain different services provided by ISDN. How narrowband ISDN is different from broadband ISDN?
5. Why do we need on ATM? Explain the ATM cell format.
6. Discuss important design issues of ATM.
7. Discuss ATM is B-ISDN reference model.

Chapter 9

1. Discuss services offered by data link layer to network layer.
2. Discuss various framing methods used by data link layer to break the bit stream into discrete frames.
3. How the following is achieved at data link layer?
   (a) Error control
   (b) Flow control
4. Discuss in brief various error detection and correction techniques.
5. Explain principle of error detection. Also discuss LRC method for detection of error.
6. Discuss classification of data link protocols.
7. Explain utopia and PAR.

8. What are the general assumptions made for sliding window protocols?
9. Discuss in brief the following SWPs:
   (a) Go back n.
   (b) A protocol using selective repeat.
10. Explain the structure of HDLC and PPP.

Chapter 10

1. Compare and contrast static and dynamic channel allocation.
2. Compare and contrast pure ALOHA and slotted ALOHA. Show mathematically efficiency of both in relation to performance.
3. What are CSMA protocols? Write algorithms for persistent and non-persistent CSMA.
4. Explain CSMA with collision detection.
5. Discuss different categories of collision free protocols with examples.

Chapter 11

1. Write short note on IEEE standards.
2. Discuss frame format of IEEE 802.2.
3. Explain the following in context with 802.3:
   (a) Frame format.
   (b) Cabling.
   (c) MAC sub layer protocol.
   (d) Binary exponential alogarithm.
4. Compare main features of IEEE standard 802.4 and 802.5.
5. What is medium access control? How is it implemented in aken ring LAN?
6. How medium access is controlled in token bus?
7. Discuss the performance of token based protocols.
8. Discuss architecture of DQDB.
9. How does FDDI work? Also discuss its applications. How it is different from CDDI?

Chapter 12

1. Discuss design issues for the network layer. Also explain its internal organization.
2. Compare datagrams and virtual circuits.

3. What are routing algorithms? Discuss their significance and suitability.
4. Explain the various classes routing algorithms. What are the properties desirable in a routing algorithm?
5. Explain shortest path routing by taking suitable example.
6. What is adaptive routing? Discuss one such algorithm.
7. Briefly discuss various ways of broadcast routing.
8. Compare distance vector and link state routing algorithms.
9. What is congestion control? Differentiate between open loop and closed loop congestion.
10. Define congestion. What are various techniques for congestion control? Explain any two.
11. Discuss the main causes of congestion. What are the effects of congestion?
12. How congestion takes place in networks? Explain packet discarding algorithm for congestion control.
13. Differentiate between leaky bucket and token bucket algorithms.
14. Why IPv6 is appropriate for the next generation of the Internet protocol?
15. Explain different types of messages generated by ICMP.

Chapter 13

1. List various types of internetworking devices.
2. Explain the working of repeaters.
3. Define and compare hub and switch.
4. Discuss the functions, uses and the comparison of bridge, gateway, router and repeater.
5. What do you mean by a switch? What functions does it perform in networking?
6. Differentiate between transparent and source routing bridges.
7. Define router. Discuss how router based networking is carried out.
8. What is the difference between?
   (a) A router and a bridge.
   (b) A bridge and gateway.

Chapter 14

1. Discuss the comparison between transport layer and data link layer.
2. Discuss the services and elements of transport protocols.
3. Name a few transport layer protocols.
4. What is a port? Briefly discuss various types of ports.
5. Define socket with its types.
6. Discuss 3-way handshaking used in TCP protocol.
7. Discuss the usage of ports. List down few well-known ports.
8. Discuss UDP header format. Why sometimes application programmers choose UDP as a data transport service?
9. Compare applications of TCP and UDP.
10. For what applications SCTP and DCCP are used as the transprot protocols?

Chapter 15

1. How session is administered in session layer?
2. Discuss various design issues for session layer and presentation layer.
3. Discuss the working of Token management and synchronization of session layer.
4. Explain the purpose and working of RPC. Also list the main issues to be addressed by RPC.
5. What is data compression? Discuss one lossless compression technique with example.
6. Why is data compression important in networks? Discuss various techniques of compressing the data in networks.

Chapter 16

1. Define FTP. How connection is established to an anonymous FTP site?
2. Explain the working of various modes of FTP.
3. Explain how a browser retrieves web page from web server using HTTP.
4. Explain components of DNS. Also discuss various kinds of name servers.
5. Explain purpose of RTSP, SSL and SIP.
6. Define internet. What is role and responsibility of ISP? Discuss internet addressing.
7. List and briefly explain the applications of internet.

8. What is e-mail? Explain how e-mail transfers a message from a user's computer in India to a user's computer in Europe.
9. Write briefly about working of e-mail. Also explain its advantages over conventional mail system.
10. Discuss the role of user agent and message transfer agent in e-mail system.
11. Explain the various protocols used for sending and retrieving e-mails.
12. Explain the characteristics of TELNET.
13. What is remote login? How does it work.
14. Discuss various components of SNMP.
15. What is internet commerce? How is it going to affect business world?

Chapter 17

1. How can security be enforced in networks?
2. What are the main security threats to a network? Explain different sources of network threats.
3. What are the issues involved in answering the network security? Explain by taking examples.
4. What is cryptography? How does it provide network security?
5. What do you understand by data encryption? Give different methods used for it.
6. Why digital signatures are used?
7. Explain working of RSA algorithm with example.
8. Explain operation of DES.
9. What do you mean by network firewall? Also explain its purpose and types.

Chapter 18

1. Explain the role of X.25 protocol.
2. Explain need of X.400. Also discuss its various components.
3. Discuss characteristics of X.500.
4. Explain te purpose of FTAM and VTAM.

INDEX

A

B

C

D

E

J

K

L

M

N

O

P

Q

R

S

T

U

V

W

X